Justin Huntly McCarthy, Richard Franc Burton, Isabel Burton

**Lady Burton's Edition of her Husband's Arabian Nights**

Vol. 6

Justin Huntly McCarthy, Richard Franc Burton, Isabel Burton

**Lady Burton's Edition of her Husband's Arabian Nights**
*Vol. 6*

ISBN/EAN: 9783744761956

Printed in Europe, USA, Canada, Australia, Japan

Cover: Foto ©Thomas Meinert / pixelio.de

More available books at **www.hansebooks.com**

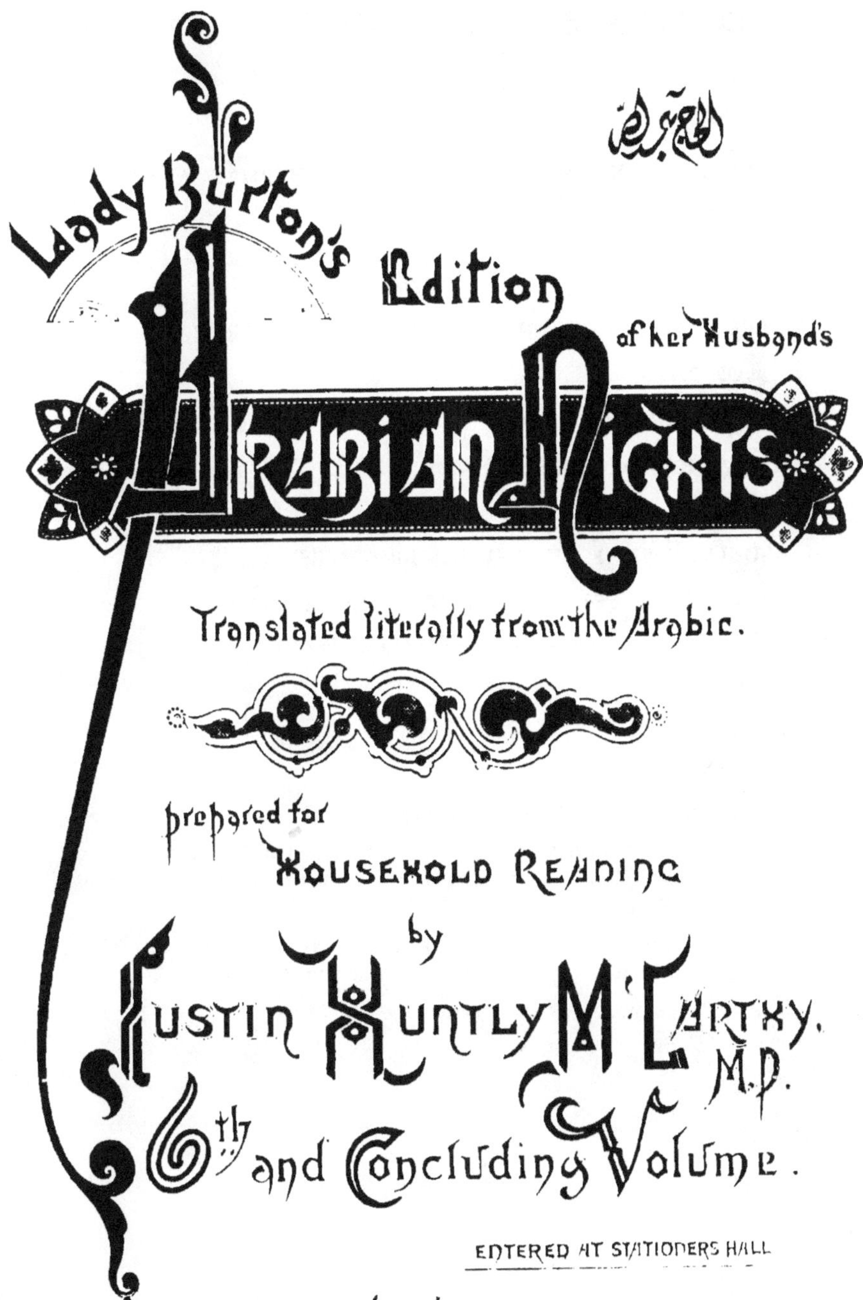
Lady Burton's Edition
of her Husband's
Arabian Nights
Translated literally from the Arabic.
prepared for
Household Reading
by
Justin Huntly McCarthy, M.P.
6th and Concluding Volume.
ENTERED AT STATIONERS HALL

London.
Waterlow & Sons Limited, London Wall
1886.

# CONTENTS OF THE SIXTH VOLUME.

## Now when it was the Nine Hundred and Forty-fifth Night.

She pursued, It hath reached me, O auspicious King, that Abdullah of the Sea said to Abdullah of the Land, "And if a thousand or more of this kind hear an Adamite cry a single cry, forthright all die, nor hath one of them power to remove from his place; so, whenever a son of Adam falleth into the sea, we take him and anoint him with this fat and go round about the depths with him, and whenever we see a Dandan or two or three or more, we bid him cry out and they all die forthright for his once crying." Quoth the fisherman, "I put my trust in Allah;" and doffing his clothes, buried them in a hole which he dug in the beach; after which he rubbed his body from head to heels with that ointment. Then he descended into the water and diving, opened his eyes and the brine did him no hurt: so he walked right and left, and if he would, he rose to the sea-face, and if he would, he sank to the base. And he beheld the water as it were a tent over his head, yet it wrought him no hurt. Then said the Merman to him, "What seest thou, O my brother?" and said he, "O my brother, I see naught save weal[1]; and indeed thou spakest truth in that which thou saidst to me; for the water doth me no hurt." Quoth the Merman, "Follow me." So he followed him and they ceased not faring on from place to place whilst Abdullah discovered before him and on his right and left mountains of water and solaced himself by gazing thereon and on the various sorts of fish, some great and some small, which disported themselves in the main. Some of them favoured buffaloes,[2] others oxen and others dogs and yet others human beings; but all to which they drew near fled, whenas they saw the fisherman, who said to the Merman, "O my brother, how is it that I see all the fish to which we draw near flee from us afar?" Said the other, "Because they fear thee, for all things that Allah hath made fear the son of Adam.[3]" The fisherman ceased not to

---

[1] An euphemistic answer, *unberüfen* as the Germans say.

[2] It is a temptation to derive this word (the classical "Bubalis") from *bœuf à l'eau*, but I fear that the theory will not hold water. The "buffaloes" of Alexandria laughed it to scorn.

[3] Here the writer's zoological knowledge is at fault. Animals, which never or very rarely see man, have no fear of him whatever. This is well-known to those who visit the Gull-fairs at Ascension Island, Santos and many other isolated rocks; the hen birds will peck at the intruder's ankles but they do not rise from off their eggs. For details concerning the "Gull-fair" of the Summer Islands consult p. 4 "The History of the Bermudas," edited by Sir J. H. Lefroy for the Hakluyt Society, 1882. I have seen birds on Fernando Po peak quietly await

divert himself with the marvels of the deep, till they came to a high mountain and fared on beside it. Suddenly, he heard a mighty loud cry and turning, saw some black thing, the bigness of a camel or bigger, coming down upon him from the liquid mountain and crying out. So he asked his friend, "What is this, O my brother?" and the Merman answered, "This is the Dandan. He cometh in search of me, seeking to devour me; so cry out at him, O my brother, ere he reach us; else he will snatch me up and devour me." Accordingly Abdullah cried out at the beast and behold, it fell down dead; which when he saw, he said, "Glorified be the perfection of God and His praise! I smote it not with sword nor knife; how cometh it that, for all the vastness of the creature's bulk, it could not bear my cry, but died?" Replied the Merman, "Marvel not, for, by Allah, O my brother, were there a thousand or two thousand of these creatures, yet could they not endure the cry of a son of Adam." Then they walked on till they made a city, whose inhabitants the fisherman saw to be all women, there being no male among them; so he said to his companion, "O my brother, what city is this and what are these women?" "This is the city of women; for its inhabitants are of the women of the sea." "Are there any males among them?" "No! The King of the Sea banisheth them hither, and all the women of the sea, with whom he is wroth, he sendeth to this city, and they cannot leave it; for, should one of them come forth therefrom, any of the beasts of the sea that saw her would eat her. But in other cities of the main there are both males and females." Thereupon asked the fisherman, "Are there then other cities than this in the sea?" and the Merman answered, "There are many." Quoth the fisherman, "And is there a Sultan over you in the sea?" "Yes," quoth the Merman. Then said Abdullah, "O my brother, I have indeed seen many marvels in the main!" But the Merman said, "And what hast thou seen of its marvels?[1] Hast thou not heard the saying:—The marvels of the sea are more manifold than the marvels of the land?" "True," rejoined the fisherman, and fell to gazing upon those women, whom he saw with faces like moons and hair like women's hair, but their hands and feet were in their middle and they had tails like fishes' tails. Now when the

---

a second shot; and herds of antelopes, the most timid of animals, in the plains of Somali-land, only stared but were not startled by the report of the gun. But Arabs are not the only moralists who write zoological nonsense; witness the notable verse,

Birds in their little nests agree,

when the feathered tribes are the most pugnacious of breathing beings.

[1] Meaning, "Thou hast as yet seen little or nothing." In most Eastern tongues a question often expresses an emphatic assertion.

Merman had shown him the people of the city, he carried him forth therefrom and forewalked him to another city, which he found full of folk, both males and females, formed like the women aforesaid and having tails; but there was neither selling nor buying amongst them, as with the people of the land, nor were they clothed. Said Abdullah, "O my brother, I see folk all unclothed;" and the other said, "This is because the folk of the sea have no clothes." Quoth Abdullah, "This is unlawful!" and quoth the other, "We are not all of one religion: some of us are Moslems, believers in the Unity, others Nazarenes and what not else; and each marrieth in accordance with the ordinances of his creed; but those of us who marry are mostly Moslems." The fisherman continued, "Ye are naked and have neither buying nor selling among you: of what then is your wives' dowry? Do ye give them jewels and precious stones?" The Merman rejoined, "Gems with us are only stones without worth; but upon the Moslem who is minded to marry they impose a dowry of a certain number of fishes of various kinds that he must catch, a thousand or two thousand, more or less, according to the agreement between himself and the bride's father. As soon as he bringeth the amount required, the families of the bride and bridegroom assemble and eat the marriage-banquet; after which they bring him in to his bride, and he catcheth fish and feedeth her; or, if he be unable, she catcheth fish and feedeth him." Abdullah marvelled at this, and the Merman carried him to another city and thence to another and yet another, till he had diverted him with the sight of eighty cities, and he saw the people of each city unlike those of every other. Then said he to the Merman, "O my brother, are there yet other cities in the main?" whereto said the other, "And what hast thou seen of the cities of the sea and its wondrous spectacles? By the virtue of the noble Prophet, the benign, the compassionate, were I to show thee every day a thousand cities for a thousand years, and in each city a thousand marvels, I should not have shown thee one carat of the four-and-twenty carats of the cities of the sea and its miracles! I have but shown thee our own province and country, nothing more." The fisherman thus resumed, "O my brother, since this is the case, what I have seen sufficeth me, for I am a-weary of eating fish, and these fourscore days I have been in thy company, thou hast fed me, morning and night, upon nothing but raw fish, neither broiled nor boiled." "And what is broiled and boiled?" "We broil fish with fire and boil it in water and dress it in various ways and make many dishes of it." "And how should we come by fire in the sea? We know not broiled nor boiled nor aught else of the kind." "We also fry it in olive-oil and oil of sesame[1]." "How should we come by olive-oil and oil of sesame in the sea? Verily we know nothing of that thou namest." "True, but O my brother, thou hast shown me many cities; yet hast thou not shown me thine own city." "As for mine own city, we passed it a long way, for it is near the land whence we came, and I left it and came with thee hither, thinking only to divert thee with the sight of the greater cities of the sea." "That which I have seen of them sufficeth me; and now I would have thee show me thine own city." "So be it," answered Abdullah of the Sea; and, returning on his traces, carried him back thither and said to him, "This is my city." Abdullah of the Land looked and saw a city small by comparison with those he had seen; then he entered with his comrade of the deep and they fared on till they came to a cave. Quoth the Merman, "This is my house and all the houses in the city are like this, caverns great and small in the mountains; as are also those of every other city of the sea. For whoso is minded to make him a house must repair to the King and say to him, I wish to make me a house in such a place. Whereupon the King sends with him a band of the fish called 'Peckers,'[2] which have beaks that crumble the hardest rock, appointing for their wage a certain quantum of fish. They betake themselves to the mountain chosen by the intended owner and therein pierce the house, whilst the owner catcheth fish for them and feedeth them, till the cave is finished, when they wend their ways and the house-owner taketh up his abode therein. On such wise do all the people of the sea; they traffic not one with other nor serve each other save by means of fish; and their food is fish and they themselves are a kind of fish."[3] Then he said to him, "Enter!" So Abdullah entered and the Merman cried out, saying, "Ho, daughter mine!" when behold, there came to him a damsel with a face like the rondure of the moon and hair long, hips heavy, eyes black-edged and waist slender; but she was unclothed and had a tail. When she saw Abdullah of the Land, she said to her sire, "O my father, what is this No-tail[4] thou hast brought with thee?" He

---

[1] Arab. "Shiraj" = oil extracted from rape-seed but especially from sesame. The Persians pronounce it "Síraj" apparently unaware that it is their own word "Shírah" (= juice, in Arabic garb) and have coined a participle "Musayrij," *e.g.* Bú-i-musayrij, taint of sesame-oil applied especially to the Jews who very wisely prefer, in Persia and elsewhere, oil which is wholesome to butter which is not. The Moslems, however, declare that its immoderate use in cooking taints the exudations of the skin.

[2] Arab. "Nakkárún," probably congeners of the redoubtable "Dandán."

[3] Bresl. Edit. xi. 78. The Mac. says "They are all fish" (Kullu-hum) and the Bul. "Their food (aklu-hum) is fish."

[4] Arab. "Az'ar," usually = having thin hair. The general term for tailless is "abtar." See Koran cviii. 3, where it means childless.

replied, "O my daughter, this is my friend of the land, from whom I used to bring thee the fruits of the ground. Come hither and salute him with the salam." So she came forward and saluted the fisherman with loquent tongue and eloquent speech: and her father said to her, "Bring meat for our guest, by whose visit a blessing hath betided us:"[1] whereupon she brought him two great fishes, each the bigness of a lamb, and the Merman said to him, "Eat." So he ate for stress of hunger, despite himself; because he was tired of eating fish and they had naught else save fish. Before long, in came the Merman's wife, who was beautiful of form and favour and with her two children, each having in his hand a young fish, which he craunched as a man would craunch a cucumber. When she saw the fisherman with her husband, she said, "What is this No-Tail?" And she and her sons and their sister came up to him and fell to saying, "Yea, by Allah, he is tailless!" and they laughed at him. So he said to the Merman, "O my brother, hast thou brought me hither to make me a butt and a laughing-stock for thy children and thy consort?"——And Shahrazad perceived the dawn of day and ceased to say her permitted say.

## Now when it was the Nine Hundred and Forty-sixth Night,

She resumed, It hath reached me, O auspicious King, that Abdullah of the Land said to Abdullah of the Sea, "O my brother, hast thou brought me hither to make me a butt and a laughing-stock for thy children and thy consort?" Cried the Merman, "Pardon, O my brother! Those who have no tails are rare among us, and whenever one such is found, the Sultan taketh him, to make fun of him, and he abideth a marvel amongst us, and all who see him laugh at him. But, O my brother, excuse these young children and this woman, for they lack wits." Then he cried out to his family, saying, "Silence!" so they were afraid and held their peace; whilst he went on to soothe Abdullah's mind. Presently, as they were talking, behold, in came some ten Mermen, tall and strong and stout, and said to him, "O Abdullah, it hath reached the King that thou hast with thee a No-tail of the No-tails of the earth." Answered the Merman, "Yes; and this is he; but he is not of us nor of the children of the sea. He is my friend of the land and hath come to me as a guest and I purpose to carry him back to the land." Quoth

---

[1] A common formula of politeness.

they, "We cannot depart but with him; so, an thou have aught to say, arise and come with him before the King; and whatso thou wouldst say to us, say thou that same to the King." Then quoth the Merman to the fisherman, "O my brother, my excuse is manifest, and we may not disobey the King: but go thou with me to him and I will do my best to deliver thee from him, Inshallah! Fear not, for he deemeth thee of the children of the sea; but, when he seeth thee, he will know thee to be of the children of the land, and he will surely entreat thee honourably and restore thee to the earth." And Abdullah of the Land replied, "'Tis thine to decide, I will trust in Allah and wend with thee." So he took him and carried him to the King who, when he saw him, laughed at him and said, "Welcome to the No-tail!" And all who were about the King began to laugh at him and say, "Yea, by Allah, he is tailless!" Then Abdullah of the Sea came forward and acquainted the King with the fisherman's case, saying, "This man is of the children of the earth and he is my comrade and cannot live amongst us, for that he loveth not the eating of fish, except it be fried or boiled; wherefore I desire that thou give me leave to restore him to the land." Whereto the King replied, "Since the case is so, and he cannot live among us, I give thee leave to restore him to his place, after due entertainment," presently adding, "Bring him the guest-meal." So they brought him fish of various kinds and colours, and he ate, in obedience to the royal behest; after which the King said to him, "Ask a boon of me." Quoth he, "I ask of thee that thou give me jewels;" and the King said, "Carry him to the jewel-house and let him choose that whereof he hath need." So his friend carried him to the jewel-house and he picked out whatso he would, after which the Merman brought him back to his own city and pulling out a purse, said to him, "Take this deposit and lay it on the tomb of the Prophet, whom Allah save and assain!" And he took it, knowing not what was therein. Then the Merman went forth with him, to bring him back to land, and by the way he heard singing and merrymaking and saw a table spread with fish and folk eating and singing and holding mighty high festival. So Abdullah of the Land said to his friend, "What aileth these people to rejoice thus? Is there a wedding among them?" Replied Abdullah of the Sea, "Nay; one of them is dead." Asked the fisherman, "Then do ye, when one dieth amongst you, rejoice for him and sing and feast?" and the Merman answered, "Yes: and ye of the earth, what do ye?" Quoth Abdullah of the Land, "When one dieth amongst us, we weep and keen for him and the women beat their faces and rend the bosoms of their raiment, in token of mourning for the dead." But Abdullah the Merman stared at him with wide eyes and said to him, "Give me the deposit!" So he gave it to him. Then he set him ashore and said to him, "I have broken off our companionship and our amity; wherefore from this day forward thou shalt no more see me, nor I see thee." Cried the fisherman, "Why sayst thou this?" and the other said, "Are ye not, O folk of the land, a deposit of Allah?" "Yes." "Why then," asked the Merman, "is it grievous to you that Allah should take back His deposit and wherefore weep ye over it? How can I entrust thee with a deposit for the Prophet (whom Allah save and assain!) seeing that when a child is born to you, ye rejoice in it, albeit the Almighty setteth the soul therein as a deposit; and yet, when he taketh it again, it is grievous to you and ye weep and mourn? Since it is hard for thee to give up the deposit of Allah, how shall it be easy to thee to give up the deposit of the Prophet?[1] Wherefore we need not your companionship." Saying thus he left him and disappeared in the sea. Thereupon Abdullah of the Land donned his dress and taking the jewels, went up to the King, who met him lovingly and rejoiced at his return, saying, "How dost thou, O my son-in-law, and what is the cause of thine absence from me this while?" So he told him his tale and acquainted him with that which he had seen of marvels in the sea, whereat the King wondered. Then he told him what Abdullah the Merman had said;[2] and the King replied, "Indeed 'twas thou wast at fault to tell him this." Nevertheless, he continued for some time to go down to the shore and call upon Abdullah of the Sea, but he answered him not nor came to him; so, at last, he gave up all hope of him and abode, he and the King his father-in-law and the families of them both in the happiest of ease and the practice of righteous ways, till there came to them the Destroyer of delights and the Severer of societies and they died all. Wherefore glory be to the Living, who dieth not, whose is the empire of the Seen and the Unseen, who over all things is Omnipotent and is gracious to His servants and knoweth their every intent! And amongst the tales they tell is one anent

---

[1] Bresl. Edit. xi. 82; meaning, "You will probably keep it for yourself." Abdullah of the Sea is perfectly logical; but grief is not. We weep over the deaths of friends mostly for our own sake: theoretically we should rejoice that they are at rest; but practically we are afflicted by the thought that we shall never again see their pleasant faces.

[2] *i.e.* about rejoicing over the newborns and mourning over the dead.

## *TALE OF HARUN AL-RASHID AND ABU HASAN, THE MERCHANT OF OMAN.*

THE Caliph Harun Al-Rashid was one night wakeful exceedingly; so he called Masrur and said to him as soon as he came, "Fetch me Ja'afar in haste." Accordingly, he went out and returned with the Wazir, to whom said the Caliph, "O Ja'afar, wakefulness hath mastered me this night and forbiddeth sleep from me, nor wot I what shall drive it away from me." Replied Ja'afar, "O Commander of the Faithful, the wise say:—Looking on a mirror, entering the Hammam-bath and hearkening unto song banish care and chagrin." He rejoined, "O Ja'afar I have done all this, but it hath brought me naught of relief, and I swear by my pious forbears unless thou contrive that which shall abate from me this insomny, I will smite thy neck." Quoth Ja'afar, "O Commander of the Faithful, wilt thou do that which I shall counsel thee?" whereupon quoth the Caliph, "And what is that thou counsellest?" He replied, "It is that thou take boat with us and drop down Tigris River with the tide to a place called Karn al-Sirát, so haply we may hear what we never heard or see what we never saw, for 'tis said:—The solace of care is in one of three things; that a man see what he never before saw or hear what he never yet heard or tread an earth he erst hath never trodden. It may be this shall be the means of remedying thy restlessness, O Commander of the Faithful, Inshallah! There, on either side of the river, are windows and balconies, one facing other, and it may be we shall hear or see from one of these somewhat wherewith our hearts may be heartened." Ja'afar's counsel pleased the Caliph, so he rose from his place and taking with him the Wazir and his brother Al-Fazl and Isaac[1] the boon-companion and Abu Nowas and Abu Dalaf[2] and Masrur the Sworder——And Shahrazad was surprised by the dawn of day and ceased saying her permitted say.

---

[1] *i.e.* Ishak of Mosul, for whom see Night cclxxix. The Bresl. Edit. has Fazil for Fazl.

[2] Abu Dalaf al-Ijili, a well-known soldier, equally famed for liberality and culture.

## Now when it was the Nine Hundred and Forty-seventh Night,

She said, It hath reached me, O auspicious King, that when the Caliph arose from his seat with Ja'afar and the rest of the party, all entered the wardrobe, where they donned merchant's gear. Then they went down to the Tigris and embarking in a gilded boat, dropped down with the stream till they came to the place they sought, when they heard the voice of a damsel singing to the lute and chanting these couplets:—

To him when the wine cup is near I declare, * While in coppice loud shrilleth and trilleth Hazár,
"How long this repining from joys and delight? * Wake up, for this life is a borrowèd ware!"
Take the cup from the hand of the friend who is dear * With languishing eyelids and languorous air.
I sowed on his cheek a fresh rose, which amid * His side-locks the fruit of granado-tree bare.
Thou wouldst deem that the place where he tare his fair cheek[1] * Were ashes, while cheeks hue incendiary wear.
Quoth the blamer, "Forget him! But where's my excuse * When his side-face is growing the downiest hair?"[2]

When the Caliph heard this, he said, "O Ja'afar, how goodly is that voice!" and the Wazir replied, "O our lord, never smote my hearing aught sweeter or goodlier than this singing! But, fair my lord, hearing from behind a wall is only half hearing; how would it be an we heard it from behind a curtain?" Quoth the Caliph, "Come, O Ja'afar, let us play the parasites with the master of this house; and haply we shall look upon the songstress, face to face;" and quoth Ja'afar, "I hear and I obey." So they landed and sought admittance; when behold, there came out to them a young man, fair of favour, sweet of speech and fluent of tongue, who said to them, "Well come and welcome, O lords that honour me with your presence! Enter in all comfort and convenience!" So they went in (and he with them) to a saloon with four faces, whose ceiling was decorated with gold and its walls adorned with ultramarine.[3] At its upper end was a daïs, whereon stood a goodly row of seats[4] and thereon sat an hundred damsels like moons. The house-master

---

[1] Arab. "Takhmísh," alluding to the familiar practice of tearing face and hair in grief for a loss, a death, etc.

[2] *i.e.* when he is in the very prime of life.

[3] Arab. "Lázuward": see Night cxxxiv.

[4] Arab. "Sidillah." The Bresl. Edit. (v. 99), has, "a couch of ivory and ebony, whereon was that which befitted it of mattresses and cushions * * * * and on it five damsels."

cried out to them, and they came down from their seats. Then he turned to Ja'afar and said to him, "O my lord, I know not the honourable of you from the more honourable: Bismillah! deign he that is highest in rank among you favour me by taking the head of the room, and let his brethren sit each in his several stead." So they sat down, each according to his degree, whilst Masrur abode standing before them in their service; and the host asked them, "O my guests, with your leave, shall I set somewhat of food before you?" and they answered, "Yes." Hearing this he bade his handmaids bring food, whereupon four damsels with girded waists placed in front of them a table, whereon were rare meats of that which flieth and walketh earth and swimmeth seas, sand-grouse and quails and chickens and pigeons; and written on the raised edge of the tray were verses such as sorted with the entertainment. So they ate till they had enough and washed their hands, after which said the young man, "O my lords, if you have any want let us know it, that we may have the honour of satisfying it." They replied, "'Tis well: we came not to thy dwelling save for the sake of a voice we heard from behind the wall of thy house, and we would fain hear it again and know her to whom it belongeth. So, an thou deem right to vouchsafe us this favour, it will be of the generosity of thy nature, and after we will return whence we came." Quoth the host, "Ye are welcome;" and, turning to a black slave-girl, said to her, "Fetch me thy mistress Such-an-one." So she went away and returning with a chair of chinaware, cushioned with brocade, set it down: then withdrew again and presently reappeared with a damsel, as she were the moon on the night of its full, who sat down on the chair. Then the black girl gave her a bag of satin wherefrom she brought out a lute, inlaid with gems and jacinths and furnished with pegs of gold.——And Shahrazad perceived the dawn of day and ceased to say her permitted say.

## Now when it was the Nine Hundred and Forty-eighth Night,

She continued, It hath reached me, O auspicious King, that when the damsel came forward, she took her seat upon the chair and brought out from its case a lute, and behold, it was inlaid with gems and jacinths and furnished with pegs of gold. Then she tuned its strings, even as saith the poet of her and her lute in these lines:—

She sits it in lap like a mother fond * And she strikes the strings that can make it speak:

And ne'er smiteth her right an injurious touch * But her left repairs of her right
the wreak.[1]

Then she strained the lute to her bosom, bending over it as mother bendeth over babe, and swept the strings which complained as child to mother complaineth; after which she played upon it and began improvising these couplets :—

An Time my lover restore me I'll blame him fain, * Saying, "Pass, O my dear,
the bowl and in passing drain
The wine, which hath never mixed with the heart of man * But he passes to joy
from annoy and to pleasure from pain."
Then Zephyr arose to his task of sustaining the cup: * Didst e'er see full Moon
that in hand the star hath ta'en?[2]
How oft I talked thro' the night, when its rounded Lune * Shed on darkness of
Tigris' bank a beamy rain!
And when Luna sank in the West 'twas as though she'd wave * O'er the length
of the watery waste a gilded glaive.

When she had made an end of her verse, she wept with sore weeping and all who were in the place wept aloud till they were well-nigh dead; nor was there one of them but took leave of his wits and rent his raiment and beat his face for the goodliness of her singing. Then said Al-Rashid, "This damsel's song verily denoteth that she is a lover departed from her beloved." Quoth her master, "She hath lost father and mother;" but quoth the Caliph, "This is not the weeping of one who hath lost mother and father, but the yearning of one who hath lost him she loveth." And he was delighted with her singing and said to Isaac, "By Allah, never saw I her like!" and Isaac said, "O my lord, indeed I marvel at her with utterest marvel and am beside myself for delight." Now Al-Rashid with all this stinted not to look upon the house-master and note his charms and the daintiness of his fashion; but he saw on his face a pallor as he would die; so he turned to him and said, "Ho, youth!" and the other said, "Adsum—at thy service, O my lord." The Caliph asked, "Knowest thou who we are?" and he answered, "No." Quoth Ja'afar, "Wilt thou that I tell thee the names of each of us?" and quoth the young man, "Yes;" when the Wazir said, "This is the Commander of the Faithful, descendant of the uncle of the Prince of the Apostles," and named to him the others of the company; after which quoth Al-Rashid, "I wish that thou acquaint

---

[1] *i.e.* As she untunes the lute by "pinching" the strings over-excitedly with her right, her other hand retunes it by turning the pegs.

[2] *i.e.* The slim cupbearer (Zephyr) and fair-faced girl (Moon) handed round the bubbling bowl (star).

me with the cause of the paleness of thy face, whether it be acquired or natural from thy birth-tide." Quoth he, "O Prince of True Believers, my case is wondrous and my affair marvellous; were it graven with gravers on the eye-corners it were a warner to whoso will be warned." Said the Caliph, "Tell it to me: haply thy healing may be at my hand." Said the young man, "O Commander of the Faithful, lend me thine ears and give me thy whole mind." And he, "Come; tell it me, for thou makest me long to hear it." So the young man began:—Know then, O Prince of True Believers, that I am a merchant of the merchants of the sea and come from Oman city, where my sire was a trader and a very wealthy trader, having thirty ships trafficking upon the main, whose yearly hire was thirty thousand dinars; and he was a generous man and had taught me writing and all whereof a wight hath need. When his last hour drew near, he called me to him and gave me the customary charge; then Almighty Allah took him and admitted him to His mercy and may He continue the Commander of the Faithful on life! Now my late father had partners trading with his coin and voyaging on the ocean. So one day, as I sat in my house with a company of merchants, a certain of my servants came in to me and said, "O my lord, there is at the door a man who craveth admittance to thee!" I gave leave and he came in, bearing on his head a something covered. He set it down and uncovered it, and behold it was a box wherein were fruits out of season and herbs conserved in salt and fresh, such as are not found in our land. I thanked him and gifted him with an hundred dinars, and he went away grateful. Then I divided these things amongst my friends and guests who were present and asked them whence they came. Quoth they, "They come from Bassorah," and praised them and went on to portray the beauties of Bassorah and all agreed that there was naught in the world goodlier than Baghdad and its people. Then they fell to describing Baghdad and the fine manners of its folk and the excellence of its air and the beauty of its ordinance, till my soul longed for it and all my hopes clave to looking upon it. So I arose and selling my houses and lands, ships and slaves, negroes and handmaids, I got together my good, to wit, a thousand thousand dinars, besides gems and jewels, wherewith I freighted a vessel and setting out therein with the whole of the property, voyaged awhile. Then I hired a barque and embarking with all my monies sailed up the river for some days till we arrived at Baghdad. I enquired where the merchants abode and what part was pleasantest for domicile and was answered, "The Karkh quarter." So I went thither and hiring a house in a thoroughfare called the Street of Saffron, transported all my goods to it and took up my lodging therein for some time. At last one day which was a Friday, I sallied forth to solace myself carrying with me somewhat of coin. I went first to a cathedral-mosque, called the Mosque of Mansur, where the Friday service was held, and when we had made an end of congregational prayers, I fared forth with the folk to a place hight Karn al-Sirat, where I saw a tall and goodly mansion, with a balcony overlooking the river-bank and pierced with a lattice-window. So I betook myself thither with a company of folk and sighted there an old man sitting, handsomely clad and exhaling perfumes. His beard forked upon his breast in two waves like silver-wire, and about him were four damsels and five pages. So I said to one of the folk, "What is the name of this old man and what is his business?" and the man said, "His name is Táhir ibn al-Aláa, and he is a keeper of open house: all who go in to him eat and drink and look upon fair faces." Quoth I, "By Allah, this long while have I wandered about in search of something like this!"——And Shahrazad was surprised by the dawn of day and ceased saying her permitted say.

## Now when it was the Nine Hundred and Forty-ninth Night,

She pursued, It hath reached me, O auspicious King, that the young merchant cried, "By Allah this long while I have gone about in search of something like this! So I went up to the Shaykh, O Commander of the Faithful, and saluting him said to him, "O my lord, I need somewhat of thee!" He replied, "What is thy need?" and I rejoined, "'Tis my desire to be thy guest to-night." He said, "With all my heart;" whereupon he committed me to a page, who carried me to a Hammam within the house and served me with goodly service. When I came out of the Bath he brought me to a chamber and knocked at the door, whereupon out came a handmaid, to whom said he, "Take thy guest!" She met me with welcome and cordiality, laughing and rejoicing, and brought me into a mighty fine room decorated with gold. I considered her and saw her like the moon on the night of its fulness having in attendance on her two damsels as they were constellations. She made me sit and seating herself by my side, signed to her slave-girls who set before us a tray covered with dishes of various kinds of meats, pullets and quails and sand-grouse and pigeons. So we ate our sufficiency, and never in my life ate I aught more delicious than this food. When we had eaten she bade remove the tray and set on the service of wine and flowers, sweetmeats and fruits. When I had made an end of eating and the tray had been removed, she took the lute and sang thereto these couplets:—

O waftings of musk from the Babel-land! * Bear a message from me which my longings have planned:
My troth is pledged to that place of yours, * And to friends there 'biding—a noble band;
And wherein dwells she whom all lovers love * And would hend, but she cometh to no man's hand.

After this I went to the Shaykh and heard a great noise and loud voices; so I asked him, "What is to do?" and he answered, saying, "This is the night of our remarkablest nights, when all souls embark on the river and divert themselves by gazing one upon other. Hast thou a mind to go up to the roof and solace thyself by looking at the folk?" "Yes," answered I, and went up to the terrace-roof[1] whence I could see a gathering of people with flambeaux and cressets, and great mirth and merriment. Then I went up to the end of the roof and beheld there, behind a goodly curtain, a little chamber in whose midst stood a couch of juniper[2]-wood plated with shimmering gold and covered with a handsome carpet. On this sat a lovely young lady, confounding all beholders with her beauty and comeliness and symmetry and perfect grace. When I saw her, O Prince of True Believers, I could not contain myself nor knew where I was, so dazed and dazzled was I by her beauty: but, when I came down, I questioned the damsel with whom I was and described the young lady to her. "What wilt thou with her?" asked she; and I, "She hath taken my wit." "O Abu al-Hasan, hast thou a mind to her?" "Ay, by Allah! for she hath captivated my heart and soul." "This is the daughter of Tahir ibn al-Alaa; she is our mistress and we are all her handmaids; and she is a regret to the heart of Kings!"[3] "By Allah, I will spend all I have on this damsel!" So saying, I lay, heartsore for desire, through the livelong night till the morning, when I repaired to the Hammam and presently donned a suit of the richest royal raiment

[1] Arab. "Al-Sath," whence the Span. Azotea. The lines that follow are from the Bresl. Edit. v. 110.

[2] This "'Ar'ar" is probably the Callitris quadrivalvis whose resin ("Sandarac") is imported as varnish from African Mogador to England. Also called Thuja, it is of cypress shape, slow growing and finely veined in the lower part of the base. Most travellers are agreed that it is the Citrus-tree of Roman Mauritania, concerning which Pliny (xiii. 29) gives curious details, a single table costing from a million sesterces (£900) to 1,400,000. For other details see p. 95, "Morocco and the Moors," by my late friend Dr. Leared (London: Sampson Low, 1876).

[3] *i.e.* Kings might sigh for her in vain.

and betaking myself to Ibn al-Alaa, told him of my love. Accordingly he took me and carried me to an apartment than which my eyes never saw a goodlier on the earth's face and there I found the young lady seated. When I saw her, O Commander of the Faithful, my reason was confounded with her beauty, for she was like the full moon on its fourteenth night,——And Shahrazad perceived the dawn of day and ceased to say her permitted say.

## Now when it was the Nine Hundred and Fiftieth Night,

She resumed, It hath reached me, O auspicious King, that the young man continued to describe before the Prince of True Believers the young lady's characteristics, saying :—She was like the full moon on her fourteenth night, a model of grace and symmetry and loveliness. Her speech shamed the tones of the lute, and it was as it were she whom the poet meant in these verses[1] :—

A fair one, to idolaters if she her face should show, They'd leave their idols and her face for only Lord would know.
If in the Eastward she appeared unto a monk, for sure, He'd cease from turning to the West and to the East bend low ;
And if into the briny sea one day she chanced to spit, Assuredly the salt sea's floods straight fresh and sweet would grow.

And that of another :—

I looked at her one look and that dazed me * Such rarest gifts of mind and form to see,
When doubt inspired her that I loved her, and * Upon her cheeks the doubt showed showily.

I saluted her and she said to me, "Well come and welcome and fair welcome !" and taking me by the hand, O Prince of True Believers, made me sit down by her side ; whereupon, of the excess of my desire, I fell a-weeping for fear of severance and pouring forth the tears of the eye, recited these two couplets :—

I love the nights of parting though I joy not in the same * Time haply may exchange them for the boons of Union day :
And the days that bring Union I unlove for single thought, * Seeing everything in life lacking steadfastness of stay.

Then she strave to solace me with soft sweet speech, but I was drowned in the deeps of passion, fearing even in union the pangs of disunion, for excess of longing and ecstasy of passion ; and I be-

---

[1] These lines occur before. I quote Mr. Payne.

thought me of the lowe of absence and estrangement and repeated these two couplets :—

I thought of estrangement in her embrace * And my eyes rained tears red as 'Andam-wood.
So I wiped the drops on that long white neck ; * For camphor[1] is wont to stay flow of blood.

Then she bade bring food and there came four damsels, who set before us food and fruits and confections and flowers and wine, such as befit none save kings. So, O Commander of the Faithful, we ate, and sat over our wine, compassed about with blooms and herbs of sweet savour, in a chamber suitable only for kings. Presently, one of her maids brought her a silken bag, which she opened and taking thereout a lute, laid it in her lap and smote its strings, whereat it complained as child complaineth to mother, and she sang these two couplets :—

Drink not pure wine except from hand of slender youth * Like wine for daintiness and like him eke the wine :
For wine no joyance brings to him who drains the cup * Save bring the cup-boy cheek as fair and fain and fine.

So I abode with her, O Commander of the Faithful, month after month in similar guise, till all my money was spent ; wherefore I began to bethink me of separation as I sat with her one day and my tears railed down upon my cheeks like rills, and I became not knowing night from light. Quoth she, "Why dost thou weep?" and quoth I, "O light of mine eyes, I weep because of our parting." She asked, "And what shall part me and thee, O my lord?" and I answered, "By Allah, O my lady, from the day I came to thee, thy father hath taken of me, for every day, five hundred dinars, and now I have nothing left. Right soothfast is the saw :—Penury maketh strangerhood at home and money maketh a home in strangerhood ; and indeed the poet speaks truth when he saith :—

Lack of good is exile to man at home ; * And money shall house him where'er he roam."

She replied, "Know that it is my father's custom, whenever a merchant abideth with him and hath spent all his capital, to entertain him three days ; then doth he put him out and he may return to us nevermore. But keep thou thy secret and conceal thy case and I will so contrive that thou shalt abide with me till such time as Allah

---

[1] A most unsavoury comparison to a Persian, who always connects camphor with the idea of a corpse.

will ;[1] for, indeed, there is in my heart a great love for thee. Thou must know that all my father's money is under my hand and he wotteth not its full tale ; so, every morning, I will give thee a purse of five hundred dinars which do thou offer to my sire, saying:—Henceforth, I will pay thee only day by day. He will hand the sum to me, and I will give it to thee again, and we will abide thus till such time as may please Allah."[1] Thereupon I thanked her and kissed her hand ; and on this wise, O Prince of True Believers, I abode with her a whole year, till it chanced on a certain day that she beat one of her handmaids grievously and the slave-girl said, "By Allah, I will assuredly torture thy heart even as thou hast tortured me!" So she went to the girl's father and exposed to him all that had passed, first and last, which when Tahir ibn Alaa heard he arose forthright and coming in to me, as I sat with his daughter, said, "Ho, Such-an-one!" and I said, "At thy service." Quoth he, "'Tis our wont, when a merchant grow poor with us, to give him hospitality three days ; but thou hast had a year with us, eating and drinking and doing what thou wouldst." Then he turned to his pages and cried to them, "Pull off his clothes." They did as he bade them and gave me ten dirhams and an old suit worth five silvers ; after which he said to me, "Go forth ; I will not beat thee nor abuse thee ; but wend thy ways and if thou tarry in this town, thy blood be upon thine own head." So I went forth, O Commander of the Faithful, in my own despite, knowing not whither to hie, for had fallen on my heart all the trouble in the world and I was occupied with sad thought and doubt. Then I bethought me of the wealth which I had brought from Oman and said in myself, "I came hither with a thousand thousand dinars, part price of thirty ships, and have made away with it all in the house of yonder ill-omened man, and now I go forth from him, bare and broken-hearted! But there is no Majesty and there is no Might save in Allah, the Glorious, the Great!" Then I abode three days in Baghdad, without tasting meat or drink, and on the fourth day seeing a ship bound for Bassorah, I took passage in her of the owner, and when we reached our port, I landed and went into the bazar, being sore anhungered. Presently, a man saw me, a grocer, whom I had known aforetime, and coming up to me, embraced me, for he had been my friend and my father's friend before me. Then he questioned me of my case, seeing me clad in those tattered clothes ; so I told him all that had befallen me, and he said, "By Allah, this is not the act of a sensible man!

[1] Arab. "Ilà má sháa' lláh," *i.e.* as long as you like.

But after this that hath befallen thee what dost thou purpose to do?" Quoth I, "I know not what I shall do," and quoth he, "Wilt thou abide with me and write my outgo and income and thou shalt have two dirhams a day, over and above thy food and drink?" I agreed to this and abode with him, O Prince of True Believers, selling and buying, till I had gotten an hundred dinars; when I hired me an upper chamber by the river-side, so haply a ship should come up with merchandise, that I might buy goods with the dinars and go back with them to Baghdad. Now it fortuned that one day, there came ships with merchandise, and all the merchants resorted to them to buy, and I went with them on board, when behold, there came two men out of the hold and setting themselves chairs on the deck, sat down thereon. The merchants addressed themselves to the twain with intent to buy, and the man said to one of the crew, "Bring the carpet." Accordingly he brought the carpet and spread it, and another came with a pair of saddle-bags, whence he took a budget and emptied it on the carpet; and our sights were dazzled with that which issued therefrom of pearls and corals and jacinths and carnelians and other jewels of all sorts and colours.——And Shahrazad was surprised by the dawn of day and ceased saying her permitted say.

## Now when it was the Nine Hundred and Fifty-first Night,

She said, It hath reached me, O auspicious King, that the young merchant, after recounting to the Caliph the matter of the bag and its containing jewels of all sorts, continued:—Presently, O Commander of the Faithful, said one of the men on the chairs, "O company of merchants, we will sell but this to-day, by way of spending money, for that we are weary." So the merchants fell to bidding one against other for the jewels, and bid till the price reached four hundred dinars. Then said to me the owner of the bag (for he was an old acquaintance of mine, and when he saw me, he came down to me and saluted me), "Why dost thou not speak and bid like the rest of the merchants?" I said, "O my lord, by Allah, the shifts of fortune have run against me and I have lost my wealth and have only an hundred dinars left in the world." Quoth he, "O Ománi, after this vast wealth, can only an hundred dinars remain to thee?" And I was abashed before him, and my eyes filled with tears; whereupon he looked at me, and indeed my case was grievous to him. So he said to the merchants, "Bear witness against me that I have sold all that is in this bag of various gems and precious stones to this man for an hundred gold pieces, albeit I know them to be worth so many thousand dinars, and this is a present from me to him." Then he gave me the saddle-bag and the carpet, with all the jewels that were thereon, for which I thanked him, and each and every of the merchants present praised him. Presently I carried all this to the jewel-market and sat there to sell and buy. Now among the precious stones was a round amulet of the handiwork of the masters,[1] weighing half a pound: it was red of the brightest, a carnelian on both whose sides were graven characts and characters, like the tracks of ants; but I knew not its worth. I sold and bought a whole year, at the end of which I took the amulet[2] and said, "This hath been with me some while, and I know not what it is nor what may be its value." So I gave it to the broker, who took it and went round with it and returned, saying, "None of the merchants will give me more than ten dirhams for it." Quoth I, "I will not sell it at that price;" and he threw it in my face and went away. Another day I again offered it for sale, and its price reached fifteen dirhams; whereupon I took it from the broker in anger and threw it back into the tray. But a few days after, as I sat in my shop, there came up to me a man, who bore the traces of travel, and saluting me, said, "By thy leave, I will turn over what thou hast of wares." Said I, "'Tis well," and indeed, O Commander of the Faithful, I was still wroth by reason of the lack of demand for the talisman. So the man fell to turning over my wares, but took naught thereof save the amulet, which when he saw, he kissed his hand and cried, "Praised be Allah!" Then said he to me, "O my lord, wilt thou sell this?" and I replied, "Yes," being still angry. Quoth he, "What is its price?" And I asked, "How much wilt thou give?" He answered, "Twenty dinars;" so I thought he was making mock of me and exclaimed, "Wend thy ways." But he resumed, "I will give thee fifty dinars for it." I made him no answer, and he continued, "A thousand dinars." But I was silent, declining to reply, whilst he laughed at my silence and said, "Why dost thou not return me an answer?" "Hie thee home," repeated I, and was like to quarrel with him. But he bid thousands after thousands, and I still made him no reply, till he said, "Wilt thou sell it for twenty thousand dinars?" I still thought he was mocking me; but the people gathered about me and all of them said, "Sell to him, and if

---

[1] *i.e.* of gramarye.

[2] Arab. "Ta'wiz" = the Arab Tilasm, our Talisman, a charm, an amulet; and in India mostly a magic square. The subject is complicated and occupies in Herklots some sixty pages, 222-284.

he buy not, we will all up and at him and drub him and thrust him forth the city." So quoth I to him, "Wilt thou buy or dost thou jest?" and quoth he, "Wilt thou sell or dost thou joke?" I said, "I will sell if thou wilt buy;" then he said, "I will buy it for thirty thousand dinars; take them and make the bargain; so I cried to the bystanders, "Bear witness against him," adding to him, "But on condition that thou acquaint me with the virtues and profit of this amulet for which thou payest all this money." He answered, "Close the bargain, and I will tell thee this;" I rejoined, "I sell it to thee;" and he retorted, "Allah be witness of that which thou sayst and testimony!" Then he brought out the gold and giving it to me, took the amulet, and set it in his bosom; after which he turned to me and asked, "Art thou content?" Answered I, "Yes," and he said to the people, "Bear witness against him that he hath closed the bargain and touched the price, thirty thousand dinars." Then he turned to me and said, "Harkye, my poor fellow, hadst thou held back from selling, by Allah I would have bidden thee up to an hundred thousand dinars, nay, even to a thousand thousand!" When I heard these words, O Commander of the Faithful, the blood fled my face, and from that day there overcame it this pallor thou seest. Then said I to him, "Tell me the reason of this and what is the use of this amulet." And he answered, saying:—Know that the King of Hind hath a daughter, never was seen a thing fairer than she, and she is possessed with a falling sickness.[1] So the King summoned the Scribes and men of science and Divines, but none of them could relieve her of this. Now, I was present in the assembly; so I said to him, "O King, I know a man called Sa'adu'lláh the Babylonian, than whom there is not on the face of the earth one more masterly in these matters, and if thou see fit to send me to him, do so." Said he, "Go to him;" and quoth I, "Bring me a piece of carnelian." Accordingly he gave me a great piece of carnelian and an hundred thousand dinars and a present, which I took, and with which I betook myself to the land of Babel. Then I sought out the Shaykh and, when he was shown to me, I delivered to him the money and the present, which he accepted and, sending for a lapidary, bade him fashion the carnelian into this amulet. Then he abode seven months in observation of the stars, till he chose out an auspicious time for engraving it, when

---

[1] The Bul. and Mac. Edits. give the Princess's malady, in error, as Dáa al-Sudá' (megrims), instead of Dáa al-Sar' (epilepsy), as in the Bresl. Edit. The latter would mean that she is possessed by a demon, again the old Scriptural theory.

he carved upon it these talismanic characters which thou seest, and I took it and returned with it to the King.——And Shahrazad perceived the dawn of day and ceased to say her permitted say.

## Now when it was the Nine Hundred and Fifty-second Night,

She continued, It hath reached me, O auspicious King, that the young man said to the Commander of the Faithful:—So after the Shaykh had spoken, I took this talisman and returned with it to the King. Now the Princess was bound with four chains, and every night a slave-girl lay with her and was found in the morning with her throat cut. The King took the amulet and laid it upon his daughter who was straightway made whole. At this he rejoiced with exceeding joy and invested me with a vest of honour and gave alms of much money; and he caused set the amulet in the Princess's necklace. It chanced, one day, that she embarked with her women in a ship and went for a sail on the sea. Presently one of her maids put out her hand to her, to sport with her, and the necklace brake asunder and fell into the waves. From that hour the Possessor[1] of the Princess returned to her, wherefore great grief betided the King and he gave me much money, saying, "Go thou to Shaykh Sa'adu'llah and let him make her another amulet, in lieu of that which is lost." I journeyed to Babel, but found the old man dead; whereupon I returned and told the King, who sent me and ten others to go round about in all countries, so haply we might find a remedy for her: and now Allah hath caused me happen on it with thee." Saying these words, he took from me the amulet, O Commander of the Faithful, and went his ways. Such, then, is the cause of the wanness of my complexion. As for me, I repaired to Baghdad, carrying all my wealth with me, and took up my abode in the lodgings where I lived whilome. On the morrow, as soon as it was light, I donned my dress and betook myself to the house of Tahir ibn al-Alaa, that haply I might see her whom I loved, for the love of her had never ceased to increase upon my heart. But when I came to his home, I saw the balcony broken down and the lattice builded up; so I stood awhile, pondering my case and the shifts of Time, till there came to me a serving man, and I questioned him, saying, "What hath God done with Tahir ibn al-Alaa?" He answered, "O my brother, he hath repented to Almighty Allah." Quoth I, "What was the cause of his

[1] Arab. "'Al-'Áriz" = the demon who possessed her.

repentance?" and quoth he, "O my brother, in such a year there came to him a merchant, by name Abu al-Hasan the Omani, who abode with his daughter awhile, till his wealth was all spent, when the old man turned him out, broken-hearted. Now the girl loved him with exceeding love and, when she was parted from him, she sickened of a sore sickness and became nigh upon death. As soon as her father knew how it was with her, he sent after and sought for Abu al-Hasan through the lands, pledging himself to bestow upon whoso should produce him an hundred thousand dinars; but none could find him nor come on any trace of him; and she is now hard upon death." Quoth I, "And how is it with her sire?" and quoth the servant, "He hath sold all his girls, for grief of that which hath befallen him, and hath repented to Almighty Allah." Then asked I, "What wouldst thou say to him who should direct thee to Abu al-Hasan the Omani?" and he answered, "Allah upon thee, O my brother, that thou do this and quicken my poverty and the poverty of my parents[1]!" I rejoined, "Go to her father and say to him, Thou owest me the reward for good news, for that Abu al-Hasan the Omani standeth at the door." With this he set off trotting, as he were a mule loosed from the mill, and presently came back, accompanied by Shaykh Tahir himself, who no sooner saw me than he returned to his house and gave the man an hundred thousand dinars which he took and went away blessing me. Then the old man came up and embraced me and wept, saying, "O my lord, where hast thou been absent all this while? Indeed, my daughter hath been killed by reason of her separation from thee; but come with me into the house." So we entered and he prostrated himself in gratitude to the Almighty, saying, "Praised be Allah who hath reunited us with thee!" Then he went in to his daughter and said to her, "The Lord hath healed thee of this sickness;" and said she, "O my papa, I shall never be whole of my sickness, save I look upon the face of Abu al-Hasan." Quoth he, "An thou wilt eat a morsel and go to the Hammam, I will bring thee in company with him." Asked she, "Is it true that thou sayest?" and he answered, "By the Great God, 'tis true!" She rejoined, "By Allah, if I look upon his face, I shall have no need of eating!" Then said he to his page, "Bring in thy lord." Thereupon I entered, and when she saw me, O Prince of True Believers, she fell down in a swoon, and presently coming to herself, recited this couplet:—

Yea, Allah hath joinèd the parted twain, * When no thought they thought e'er to meet again.

---

[1] Alluding to the favourite Eastern saying, "The poor man hath no life."

Then she sat upright and said, "By Allah, O my lord, I had not deemed to see thy face ever more, save it were in a dream!" So she embraced me and wept, and said, "O Abu al-Hasan, now will I eat and drink." The old man her sire rejoiced to hear these words and they brought her meat and drink and we ate and drank, O Commander of the Faithful. After this, I abode with them awhile, till she was restored to her former beauty, when her father sent for the Kazi and the witnesses and bade write out the marriage-contract between her and me and made a mighty great bride-feast; and she is my wife to this day and this is my son by her." So saying he went away and returned with a boy of rare beauty and symmetry of form and favour to whom said he, "Kiss the ground before the Commander of the Faithful." He kissed ground before the Caliph, who marvelled at his beauty and glorified his Creator; after which Al-Rashid departed, he and his company, saying, "O Ja'afar, verily, this is none other than a marvellous thing, never saw I nor heard I aught more wondrous." When he was seated in the palace of the Caliphate, he cried, "O Masrur!" who replied, "Here am I, O my lord!" Then said he, "Bring the year's tribute of Bassorah and Baghdad and Khorasan, and set it in this recess.[1]" Accordingly he laid the three tributes together and they were a vast sum of money, whose tale none might tell save Allah. Then the Caliph bade draw a curtain before the recess and said to Ja'afar, "Fetch me Abu al-Hasan." Replied Ja'afar, "I hear and obey," and going forth, returned presently with the Omani, who kissed ground before the Caliph, fearing lest he had sent for him because of some fault that he had committed when he was with him in his house. Then said Al-Rashid, "Harkye, O Omani!" and he replied, "Adsum, O Prince of True Believers! May Allah ever bestow his favours upon thee!" Quoth the Caliph, "Draw back yonder curtain." Thereupon Abu al-Hasan drew back the curtain from the recess and was confounded and perplexed at the mass of money he saw there. Said Al-Rashid, "O Abu al-Hasan, whether is the more, this money or that thou didst lose by the amulet?"[2] and he answered, "This is many times the greater, O Commander of the Faithful!" Quoth the Caliph, "Bear witness, all ye who are present, that I give this money to this young man." So Abu al-Hasan kissed ground and was abashed and wept before the Caliph for excess of joy. Now

---

[1] In this and the following lines some change is necessary for the Bresl. and Mac. texts are very defective. The Arabic word here translated "recess" is "Aywán," prop. a hall, an open saloon.

[2] *i.e.* by selling it for thirty thousand gold pieces, when he might have got a million for it.

when he wept, the tears ran down from his eyelids upon his cheeks and the blood returned to its place and his face became like the moon on the night of its fulness. Whereupon quoth the Caliph, "There is no god but *the* God! Glory be to Him who decreeth change upon change and is Himself the Everlasting who changeth not." Saying these words, he bade fetch a mirror and showed Abu al-Hasan his face therein, which when he saw, he prostrated himself, in gratitude to the Most High Lord. Then the Caliph bade transport the money to Abu al-Hasan's house and charged the young man not to absent himself from him, so he might enjoy his company as a cup-companion. Accordingly he paid him frequent visits, till Al-Rashid departed to the mercy of Almighty Allah; and glory be to Him who dieth not, the Lord of the Seen and the Unseen! And among tales they tell is one touching

## *IBRAHIM AND JAMILAH.*[1]

AL-KHASÍB,[2] Wazir of Egypt, had a son named Ibrahím, than whom there was none goodlier, and of his fear for him, he suffered him not to go forth, save to the Friday prayers. One day, as the youth was returning from the mosque, he came upon an old man, with whom were many books; so he lighted down from his horse and, seating himself beside him, began to turn over the tomes and examine them. In one of them he espied the semblance of a woman which all but spoke, never was seen on the earth's face one more beautiful; and as this captivated his reason and confounded his wit, he said to the old man, "O Shaykh, sell me this picture." The bookseller kissed ground between his hands and said, "O my lord, 'tis thine without price.[3]" Ibrahim gave him an hundred dinars and, taking

---

[1] The tale is not in the Bresl. Edit.

[2] Al-Khasíb (= the fruitful) was the son of 'Abd al-Hamíd and intendant of the tribute of Egypt under Harun Al-Rashid, but neither Lord nor Sultan. Lane (iii. 669) quotes three couplets in his honour by Abu Nowás from p. 119 of "Elmacini (Al-Makín) Historia Saracenica."

If our camel visit not the land of Al-Khasib, what man after Al-Khasib shall they visit?
For generosity is not his neighbour; nor hath it sojourned near him; but generosity goeth wherever he goeth:
He is a man who purchaseth praise with his wealth, and who knoweth that the periods of Fortune revolve.

[3] The old story "Alà júdi-k" = upon thy generosity, which means at least ten times the proper price.

the book in which was the picture, fell to gazing upon it and weeping night and day, abstaining from meat and drink and sleep. Then said he in his mind, "An I ask the bookseller of the painter of this picture, haply he will tell me; and if the original be living, I will seek access to her; but, if it be only a picture, I will leave doting upon it and plague myself no more for a thing which hath no real existence."——And Shahrazad was surprised by the dawn of day and ceased saying her permitted say.

## Now when it was the Nine Hundred and Fifty-third Night,

She pursued, It hath reached me, O auspicious King, that the youth Ibrahim said in his mind, "An I ask the bookseller of the painter of this picture, haply he will tell me; and, if it be only a picture, I will leave doting upon it and plague myself no more for a thing which hath no real existence." So on the next Friday he betook himself to the bookseller, who sprang up to receive him, and said to him, "O uncle, tell me who painted this picture." He replied, "O my lord, a man of the people of Baghdad painted it, by name Abu al-Kásim al-Sandaláni, who dwelleth in a quarter called Al-Karkh; but I know not of whom it is the portraiture." So Ibrahim left him without acquainting any of his household with his case, and returned to the palace, after praying the Friday prayers. Then he took a bag and filling it with gold and gems to the value of thirty thousand dinars, waited till the morning, when he went out, without telling any, and presently overtook a caravan. Here he saw a Badawi and asked him, "O uncle, what is the distance between me and Baghdad;" and the other answered, "O my son, where art thou and where is Baghdad?[1] Verily, between thee and it is two months' journey." Quoth Ibrahim, "O nuncle, an thou wilt guide me to Baghdad, I will give thee an hundred dinars and this mare under me that is worth other thousand gold pieces;" and quoth the Badawi, "Allah be witness of what we say! Thou shalt not lodge this night but with me." So Ibrahim agreed to this and passed the night with him. At break of dawn, the Badawi took him and fared on with him in haste by a near road, for his greed to the mare and the promised good: nor did they leave wayfaring till they came to the walls of Baghdad, when said the wildling, "Praised be Allah for safety! O my lord, this is Baghdad." Whereat Ibrahim rejoiced with exceeding joy and alighting from the mare, gave her to the

[1] *i.e.* The distance is enormous.

Desert-man, together with the hundred dinars. Then he took the bag and entering the city walked on, enquiring for the quarter Al-Karkh and the station of the merchants, till Destiny drave him to a by-way, wherein were ten houses, five fronting five, and at the farther end was a two-leaved door with a silver ring. By the gate stood two benches of marble, spread with the finest carpets, and on one of them sat a man of handsome aspect and reverend, clad in sumptuous clothing and attended by five Mamelukes like moons. When the young Ibrahim saw the street, he knew it by the description the bookseller had given him; so he salamed to the man, who returned his salutation and bidding him welcome, made him sit down and asked him of his case. Quoth Ibrahim, "I am a stranger man and desire of thy favour that thou look me out a house in this street where I may take up my abode." With this the other cried out, saying, "Ho, Ghazálah!"[1] and there came forth to him a slave-girl, who said, "At thy service, O my lord!" Said her master, "Take some servants and fare ye all and every to such a house and clean it and furnish it with whatso is needful for this handsome youth." So she went forth and did his bidding; whilst the old man took the youth and showed him the house; and he said, "O my lord, how much may be the rent of this house?" The other answered, "O bright of face, I will take no rent of thee whilst thou abidest therein." Ibrahim thanked him for this and the old man called another slave-girl, whereupon there came forth to him a damsel like the sun, to whom said he, "Bring the chess." So she brought it and one of the servants set the cloth;[2] whereupon said the Shaykh to Ibrahim, "Wilt thou play with me?" and he answered, "Yes." So they played several games and Ibrahim beat him, when his adversary exclaimed, "Well done, O youth! Thou art indeed perfect in qualities. By Allah, there is not one in Baghdad can beat me, and yet thou hast beaten me!" Now when they had made ready the house and furnished it with all that was needful, the old man delivered the keys to Ibrahim and said to him, "O my lord, wilt thou not enter my place and eat of my bread?" He assented and walking in with him, found it a handsome house and a goodly, decorated with gold and full of all manner pictures and furniture galore and other things, such as tongue faileth to set out. The old man welcomed him and called for food, whereupon they brought a table of the

---

[1] A gazelle; here the slave-girl's name.

[2] Herklots (Pl. vii. fig. 2) illustrates the cloth used in playing the Indian game, Pachísí. The "board" is rather European than Oriental, but it has of late years spread far and wide, especially the backgammon board.

make of Sana'a of Al-Yaman and spread it with all manner rare viands, than which there was naught costlier nor more delicious. So Ibrahim ate his sufficiency, after which he washed his hands and proceeded to inspect the house and furniture. Presently, he turned to look for the leather bag, but found it not and said in himself, "There is no Majesty and there is no Might save in Allah, the Glorious, the Great! I have eaten a morsel worth a dirham or two and have lost a bag wherein is thirty thousand dinars' worth: but I seek aid of Allah!" And he was silent and could not speak—— And Shahrazad perceived the dawn of day and ceased to say her permitted say.

## Now when it was the Nine Hundred and Fifty-fourth Night

She resumed, It hath reached me, O auspicious King, that when the youth Ibrahim saw that his bag was lost, he was silent and could not speak for the greatness of his trouble. Presently his host brought the chess and said to him, "Wilt thou play with me?" and he said, "Yes." So they played and the old man beat him. Ibrahim cried, "Well done!" and left playing and rose: upon which his host asked him, "What aileth thee, O youth?" whereto he answered, "I want the bag." Thereat the Shaykh rose and brought it out to him, saying, "Here it is, O my lord. Wilt thou now return to playing with me?" "Yes," replied Ibrahim. Accordingly they played and, as the young man beat him, quoth the Shaykh, "When thy thought was occupied with the bag, I beat thee: but, now I have brought it back to thee, thou beatest me. But, tell me, O my son, what countryman art thou?" Quoth Ibrahim, "I am from Egypt," and quoth the oldster, "And what is the cause of thy coming to Baghdad?" whereupon Ibrahim brought out the portrait and said to him, "Know, O uncle, that I am the son of Al-Khasib, Wazir of Egypt, and I saw with a bookseller this picture, which bewildered my wit. I asked him who painted it and he said, "He who wrought it is a man, Abu al-Kasim al-Sandalani hight, who dwelleth in a street called the Street of Saffron in the Karkh quarter of Baghdad." Accordingly I took with me somewhat of money and came hither alone, none knowing of my case; and I desire of the fulness of thy favour that thou direct me to Abu al-Kasim, so I may ask him of the cause of his painting this picture and whose portrait it is. And whatsoever he desireth of me, I will give him that same." Said his host, "By Allah, O my son, I am Abu al-Kasim al-Sandalani, and this is a prodigious thing how Fate hath thus driven thee to me!" Now when Ibrahim heard these words, he rose to him and embraced him and kissed his head and hands, saying, "Allah upon thee, tell me whose portrait it is!" The other replied, "I hear and I obey," and rising, opened a closet and brought out a number of books, wherein he had painted the same picture. Then said he, "Know, O my son, that the original of this portrait is my cousin, the daughter of my father's brother, whose name is Abú al-Lays.[1] She dwelleth in Bassorah of which city her father is governor, and her name is Jamílah—the beautiful. There is not on the face of the earth a fairer than she; but she is averse from men and cannot hear the word 'man' pronounced in her presence. Now I once repaired to my uncle, to the intent that he should marry me to her, and was lavish of wealth to him; but he would not consent thereto: and when his daughter knew of this she was indignant and sent to me to say, amongst other things:—An thou have wit, tarry not in this town; else wilt thou perish and thy sin shall be on thine own neck.[2] For she is a virago of viragoes. Accordingly I left Bassorah, brokenhearted, and limned this likeness of her in books and scattered them abroad in various lands, so haply they might fall into the hands of a comely youth like thyself and he contrive access to her and peradventure she might fall in love with him, purposing to take a promise of him that, when he should have wedded her, he would show her to me, though I look but for a moment from afar off." When Ibrahim son of Al-Khasib heard these words, he bowed his head awhile in thought and Al-Sandalani said to him, "O my son, I have not seen in Baghdad a fairer than thou, and meseems that, when she seeth thee, she will love thee. Art thou willing, therefore, in case thou be united with her, to show her to me, if I look but for a moment from afar?" Ibrahim replied, "Yes;" and the painter rejoined, "This being so, tarry with me till thou set out." But the youth retorted, "I cannot tarry longer; for my heart with love of her is all afire." "Have patience three days," said the Shaykh, "till I fit thee out a ship, wherein thou mayst fare to Bassorah." Accordingly he waited whilst the old man equipped him a craft and stored therein all that he needed of meat and drink and so forth. When the three days were past, he said to Ibrahim, "Make thee ready for the voyage; for I have prepared thee a packet-boat furnished with all thou requirest. The craft is my property and the seamen are of my servants. In the vessel is what will suffice thee till thy return, and I have charged the crew to serve

---

[1] *i.e.* "Father of the Lion."
[2] Or as we should say, "Thy blood will be on thine own head."

thee till thou come back in safety." Thereupon Ibrahim farewelled his host and embarking, sailed down the river till he came to Bassorah, where he pulled out an hundred dinars for the sailors; but they said, "We have gotten our hire of our lord." However he replied, "Take this by way of largesse; and I will not acquaint him therewith." So they took it and blessed him. Then the youth landed and entering the town asked, "Where do the merchants lodge?" and was answered, "In a Khan called the Khan of Hamadán."[1] So he walked to the market wherein stood the Khan, and all eyes were fixed upon him and men's sight was attracted to him by reason of his exceeding beauty and loveliness. He entered the caravanserai, with one of the sailors in his company; and, asking for the porter, was directed to an aged man of reverend aspect. He saluted him and the doorkeeper returned his greeting; after which Ibrahim said to him, "O uncle, hast thou a nice chamber?" He replied, "Yes," and taking him and the sailor, opened to them a handsome room decorated with gold, and said, "O youth, this chamber befitteth thee." Ibrahim pulled out two dinars and gave them to him, saying, "Take these to key-money."[2] And the porter took them and blessed him. Then the youth Ibrahim sent the sailor back to the ship and entered the room, where the doorkeeper abode with him and served him, saying, "O my lord, thy coming hath brought us joy!" Ibrahim gave him a dinar, and said, "Buy us herewith bread and meat and sweetmeats and wine." Accordingly the doorkeeper went to the market; and buying ten dirhams' worth of victual, brought it back to Ibrahim and gave him the other ten dirhams. But he cried to him, "Spend them on thyself;" whereat the porter rejoiced with passing joy. Then he ate a scone with a little kitchin[3] and gave the rest to the concierge, adding, "Carry this to the people of thy household." The porter carried it to his family and said to them, "Methinketh there is not on the face of the earth a more generous than the young man who has come to lodge with us this day, nor yet a pleasanter than he. An he abide with us, we shall grow rich." Then he returned to Ibrahim and found him weeping; so he sat down and began to rub[4] his feet and kiss them, saying, "O my lord, wherefore weepest

---

[1] Called after the famous town in Persian Mesopotamia, which however is spelt with the lesser aspirate, in the geographical work of Sádik-i-Ispaháni, London: Oriental Transl. Fund, 1882.

[2] Arab. "Hulwán al-miftáh." Mr. Payne compares it with the French denier à Dieu, given to the concierge on like occasions.

[3] Arab. "'Udm," a relish, the Scotch "kitchen," Lat. Opsonium, Ital. Companatico and our "by-meat." See Night 284.

[4] Arab. "Kabasa" = he shampoo'd.

thou? May Allah not make thee weep!" Said Ibrahim, "O uncle, I have a mind to drink with thee this night;" and the porter replied, "Hearing and obeying!" So he gave him five dinars and said, "Buy us fresh fruit and wine;" and presently added other five, saying, "With these buy also for us dessert [1] and flowers and five fat fowls and bring me a lute." The doorkeeper went out and, buying what he had ordered, said to his wife, "Strain this wine and cook us this food and look thou dress it daintily, for this young man overwhelmeth us with his bounties." She did as he bade her, to the utmost of desire; and he took the victuals and carried them to Ibrahim son of the Sultan.——And Shahrazad was surprised by the dawn of day and ceased saying her permitted say.

## Now when it was the Nine Hundred and Fifty-fifth Night,

She said, It hath reached me, O auspicious King, that then they ate and drank and made merry, and Ibrahim wept and repeated the following verses:—

O my friend! an I rendered my life, my sprite, * My wealth and whatever the world can unite;
Nay, th' Eternal Garden and Paradise [2] * For an hour of Union my heart would buy't!

Then he sobbed a great sob and fell down a-swoon. The porter sighed, and when he came to himself, he said to him, "O my lord, what is it makes thee weep and who is she to whom thou alludest in these verses? Indeed, she cannot be but as dust to thy feet." But Ibrahim arose and for all reply brought out a parcel of the richest raiment that women wear and said to him, "Take this to thy Harim." So he carried it to his wife and she returned with him to the young man's lodging, and behold, she found him weeping. Quoth the doorkeeper to him, "Verily, thou breakest our hearts! Tell us what fair one thou desirest, and she shall be naught save thy handmaid." Quoth he, "O uncle, know that I am the son of Al-Khasib, Wazir of Egypt, and I am enamoured of Jamilah, daughter of Abu al-Lays the Governor." Exclaimed the porter's wife, "Allah! Allah! O my brother, leave this talk, lest any hear of us and we perish. Verily there is not on earth's face a more

---

[1] Arab. "Nukl." See supra, Night 944.

[2] Arab. "Jannat al-Khuld" and "Firdaus," two of the Heavens repeatedly noticed.

masterful than she, nor may any name to her the word 'man,' for she is averse from men. Wherefore, O my son, turn from her to other than her." Now when Ibrahim heard this, he wept with sore weeping, and the doorkeeper said to him, "I have nothing save my life; but that I will risk for thy love and find thee a means of winning thy will." Then the twain went out from him, and on the morrow he betook himself to the Hammam and donned a suit of royal raiment, after which he returned to his lodging, when behold, the porter and his wife came in to him and said, "Know, O my lord, that there is a humpbacked tailor here who seweth for the lady Jamilah. Go thou to him and acquaint him with thy case; haply he will show thee the way of attaining thine aim." So the youth Ibrahim arose and betaking himself to the shop of the humpbacked tailor, went in to him and found with him ten Mamelukes as they were moons. He saluted them with the salam, and they returned his greeting and bade him welcome and made him sit down; and indeed they rejoiced in him and were amazed at his charms and loveliness, especially the hunchback, who was confounded at his beauty of form and favour. Presently he said to the Gobbo, "I desire that thou sew me up my pocket;" and the tailor took a needleful of silk and sewed up his pocket which he had torn purposely; whereupon Ibrahim gave him five dinars and returned to his lodging. Quoth the tailor, "What thing have I done for this youth, that he should give me five gold pieces?" And he passed the night pondering his beauty and generosity. And when morning morrowed Ibrahim repaired to the shop and saluted the tailor, who returned his salam and welcomed him and made much of him. Then he sat down and said to the Hunchback, "O uncle, sew up my pocket, for I have rent it again." Replied the tailor, "On my head and eyes, O my son," and sewed it up; whereupon Ibrahim gave him ten ducats and he took them, amazed at his beauty and generosity. Then said he, "By Allah, O youth, for this conduct of thine needs must be a cause, this is no matter of sewing up a pocket. But tell me the truth of thy case. If thou wish for one of my slaves, by Allah, they are each and every as the dust at thy feet! and behold, they are all thy slaves and at thy command. Or if it be other than this, tell me." Replied Ibrahim, "O uncle, this is no place for talk, for my case is wondrous and my affair marvellous." Rejoined the tailor, "An it be so, come with me to a place apart." So saying, he rose up in haste and took the youth by the hand and, carrying him into a chamber behind the shop, said, "Now tell me thy tale, O youth." Accordingly Ibrahim related his story first and last to the tailor, who was amazed at his speech and cried, "O youth, fear Allah for thyself:[1] indeed she of whom thou speakest is a virago and averse from men. Wherefore, O my brother, do thou guard thy tongue, else thou wilt destroy thyself." When Ibrahim heard the hunchback's words, he wept with sore weeping and, clinging to the tailor's skirts, said, "Help me, O my uncle, or I am a dead man; for I have left my kingdom and the kingdom of my father and grandfather and am become a stranger in the lands and lonely; nor can I endure without her." When the tailor saw how it was with him, he pitied him and said, "O my son, I have but my life and that I will venture for thy love, for thou makest my heart ache. But by to-morrow I will contrive thee somewhat whereby thy soul shall be solaced." Ibrahim blessed him and, returning to the Khan, told the doorkeeper what the hunchback had said, and he answered, "Indeed, he hath dealt kindly with thee." Next morning the youth donned his richest dress and, taking a purse of gold, repaired to the Gobbo and saluted him. Then he sat down and said, "O uncle, keep thy word with me." Quoth the hunchback, "Arise forthright and take thee three fat fowls and three ounces[2] of sugar-candy and two small jugs, which do thou fill with wine; also a cup. Lay all these in a budget[3] and to-morrow, after the morning-prayers, take boat with them, saying to the boatman:—I would have thee row me down the river below Bassorah. An he say to thee:—I cannot go farther than a parasang, do thou answer:—As thou wilt; but, when he shall have come so far, lure him on with money to carry thee farther; and the first flower-garden thou wilt descry after this will be that of the lady Jamilah. Go up to the gate as soon as thou espiest it and there thou wilt see two high steps, carpeted with brocade, and seated thereon a Quasimodo like me. Do thou complain to him of thy case and crave his favour: belike he will have compassion on thy condition and bring thee to the sight of her, though but for a moment from afar. This is all I can do for thee; and unless he be moved to pity for thee, we be dead men, I and thou. This then is my rede and the matter rests with the Almighty." Quoth Ibrahim, "I seek aid of Allah; whatso He willeth becometh; and there is no Majesty

[1] *i.e.* "Have some regard for thy life."

[2] Arab. "Awák," plur. of Úkiyyah, a word known throughout the Moslem East. As an ounce it weighs differently in every country and in Barbary (Mauritania), which we call Marocco, it is a nominal coin containing twelve Flús (fulús), now about = a penny. It is a direct descendant from the "Uk" or "Wuk" (ounce) of the hieroglyphs (see Sharpe's Egypt or any other Manual) and first appeared in Europe as the Greek οὐγκία.

[3] Arab. "Kárah," usually a large bag.

and there is no Might save in Allah!" Then he left the hunchback tailor and returned to his lodging, where, taking the things his adviser had named, he laid them in a bag. On the morrow, as soon as it was day, he went down to Tigris bank, where he found a boatman asleep; so he awoke him and, giving him ten sequins, bade him row him down the river below Bassorah. Quoth the man, "O my lord, it must be on condition that I go no farther than a parasang; for if I pass that distance by a span, I am a lost man, and thou too." And quoth Ibrahim, "Be it as thou wilt." Thereupon he took him and dropped down the river with him till he drew near the flower-garden, when he said to him, "O my son, I can go no farther; for, if I pass this limit, we are both dead men." Hereat Ibrahim pulled out other ten dinars and gave them to him, saying, "Take this spending money and better thy case therewithal." The boatman was ashamed to refuse him and fared on with him, crying, "I commit the affair to Allah the Almighty!"——And Shahrazad perceived the dawn of day and ceased to say her permitted say.

## Now when it was the Nine Hundred and Fifty-sixth Night,

She continued, It hath reached me, O auspicious King, that when the youth Ibrahim gave the boatman other ten dinars, the man took them, saying, "I commit the affair to Allah the Almighty!" and fared on with him down stream. When they came to the flower-garden, the youth sprang out of the boat, in his joy, a spring of a spear's throw from the land, and cast himself down, whilst the boatman turned and fled. Then Ibrahim fared forward and found all as it had been described by the Gobbo: he also saw the garden-gate open, and in the porch a couch of ivory, whereon sat a hump-backed man of pleasant presence, clad in gold-laced clothes and hending in hand a silvern mace plated with gold. So he hastened up to him and seizing his hand kissed it; whereupon asked the hunchback, "Who art thou and whence comest thou and who brought thee hither, O my son?" And indeed, when the man saw Ibrahim Khasib-son, he was amazed at his beauty. He answered, "O uncle, I am an ignorant lad and a stranger;" and he wept. The hunchback had pity on him and taking him up on the couch, wiped away his tears and said to him, "No harm shall come to thee. An thou be in debt, may Allah settle thy debt: and if thou be in fear, may Allah appease thy fear!" Replied Ibrahim, "O uncle, I am neither in fear nor am I in debt, but have money in plenty, thanks to Allah." Rejoined the other, "Then, O my son, what is thy need that thou venturest thyself and thy loveliness to a place wherein is destruction?" So he told him his story and disclosed to him his case, whereupon the man bowed his head earthwards awhile, then said to him, "Was he who directed thee to me the humpbacked tailor?" "Yes," answered Ibrahim, and the keeper said, "This is my brother, and he is a blessed man!" presently adding, "But, O my son, had not affection for thee sunk into my heart, and had I not taken compassion on thee, verily thou wert lost, thou and my brother and the doorkeeper of the Khan and his wife. For know that this flower-garden hath not its like on the face of the earth and that it is called the Garden of the Wild Heifer,[1] nor hath any entered it in all my life long, save the Sultan and myself and its mistress Jamilah; and I have dwelt here twenty years and never yet saw any else attain to this stead. Every forty days the Lady Jamilah cometh hither in a bark and landeth in the midst of her women, under a canopy of satin, whose skirts ten damsels hold up with hooks of gold, whilst she entereth, and I see nothing of her. Natheless, I have but my life and I will risk it for the sake of thee." Then he took him by the hand and carried him into the flower-garden which, when he saw, he deemed it Eden, for therein were trees intertwining and palms high towering and waters welling and birds with various voices carolling. Presently, the keeper brought him to a domed pavilion and said to him, "This is where the Lady Jamilah sitteth." So he examined it and found it of the rarest of pleasances, full of all manner paintings in gold and lapis lazuli. It had four doors, whereto man mounted by five steps, and in its centre was a cistern of water, to which led down steps of gold all set with precious stones. In the middle of the basin was a fountain of gold, with figures, large and small, and water jetting in jets from their mouths; and when, by reason of the issuing forth of the water, they attuned themselves to various tones, it seemed to the hearer as though he were in Eden. Round the pavilion ran a channel of water, turning a Persian wheel[2] whose buckets[3] were silvern covered with brocade. To the left of the pavilion[4] was a lattice of

---

[1] Arab. "Lúlúah," which may mean the Union-pearl; but here used in the sense of "wild cow," the bubalus antelope, alluding to the *farouche* nature of Mistress Jamilah. We are also told infrà that the park was full of "Wuhúsh" = wild cattle.

[2] Arab. "Sákiyah," the venerable old Persian wheel, for whose music see Pilgrimage ii. 198. But "Sákiyah" is also applied, as here, to the water-channel which turns the wheel.

[3] Arab. "Kawádís," plur. of "Kádús," the pots round the rim of the Persian wheel: usually they are of coarse pottery.

[4] In the text "Sákiyah," a manifest error for "Kubbah."

silver, giving upon a green park, wherein were all manner wild cattle and gazelles and hares, and on the right hand was another lattice, overlooking a meadow full of birds of all sorts, warbling in various voices and bewildering the hearers' wits. Seeing all this the youth was delighted and sat down in the doorway by the gardener, who said to him, "How seemeth to thee my garden?" Quoth Ibrahim, "'Tis the Paradise of the world!" Whereat the gardener laughed. Then he rose and was absent awhile, and presently returned with a tray full of fowls and quails and other dainties including sweetmeats of sugar, which he set before Ibrahim, saying, "Eat thy sufficiency." So he ate his fill, whereat the keeper rejoiced and cried, "By Allah, this is the fashion of Kings and sons of Kings!"[1] Then said he, "O Ibrahim, what hast thou in yonder bag?" Accordingly he opened it before him and the keeper said, "Carry it with thee; 'twill serve thee when the Lady Jamilah cometh; for when once she is come, I shall not be able to bring thee food." Then he rose and taking the youth by the hand, brought him to a place fronting the pavilion, where he made him an arbour[2] among the trees and said to him, "Get thee up here, and when she cometh thou wilt see her and she will not see thee. This is the best I can do for thee, and on Allah be our dependence! Whenas she singeth, drink thou to her singing, and whenas she departeth, thou shalt return in safety whence thou camest, Inshallah!" Ibrahim thanked him and would have kissed his hand, but he forbade him. Then the youth laid the bag in the arbour and the keeper said to him, "O Ibrahim, walk about and take thy pleasure in the garth and eat of its fruits, for thy mistress's coming is appointed to be to-morrow." So he solaced himself in the garden and ate of its fruits; after which he nighted with the keeper. And when morning morrowed and showed its sheen and shone, he prayed the dawn-prayer and presently the keeper came to him with a pale face, and said to him, "Rise, O my son, and go up into the arbour: for the slave-girls are come to order the place, and she cometh after them;"——And Shahrazad was surprised by the dawn of day and ceased saying her permitted say.

---

[1] Easterns greatly respect a *belle fourchette*, especially when the eater is a lover.

[2] Arab. "'Arishah," a word of many meanings, tent, nest, vine-trellis, etc.

## Now when it was the Nine Hundred and Fifty-seventh Night,

She pursued, It hath reached me, O auspicious King, that when the keeper came to Ibrahim Khasib-son in the Garden he said to him, "Rise, O my son, and go up into the arbour; for the slave-girls are come to order the place and she cometh after them. So beware lest thou spit or sneeze or blow thy nose,[1] else we are dead men, I and thou." Hereupon Ibrahim rose and went up into his nest, whilst the keeper fared forth, saying, "Allah grant thee safety, O my son!" Presently, behold, up came four slave-girls, whose like none ever saw, and entering the pavilion, doffed their outer dresses and washed it. Then they sprinkled it with rose-water and incensed it with ambergris and aloes-wood and spread it with brocade. After these came fifty other damsels, with instruments of music, and amongst them Jamilah, within a canopy of red brocade, whose skirts the handmaidens bore up with hooks of gold, till she had entered the pavilion, so that Ibrahim saw naught of her or of her raiment. Accordingly he said to himself, "By Allah, all my travail is lost! But needs must I wait to see how the case will be." Then the damsels brought meat and drink and they ate and drank and washed their hands, after which they set her a royal chair and she sat down; and all played on instruments of music and with ravishing voices incomparably sang. Presently, out ran an old woman, a duenna, and clapped hands and danced, whilst the girls pulled her about, till the curtain was lifted and forth came Jamilah laughing. Ibrahim gazed at her and saw that she was clad in costly robes and ornaments, and on her head was a crown set with pearls and gems. About her long

---

[1] To spit or blow the nose in good society is "vulgar." Sneezing (Al-'Atsah) is a complicated affair. For Talmudic traditions of death by sneezing see Lane (M. E. chapt viii). Amongst Hindus sneezing and yawning are caused by evil spirits whom they drive away by snapping thumb and forefinger as loudly as possible. The pagan Arabs held sneezing a bad omen, which often stopped their journeys. Moslems believed that when Allah placed the Soul (life?) in Adam, the dry clay became flesh and bone, and the First Man, waking to life, sneezed and ejaculated "Alhamdolillah;" whereto Gabriel replied, "Allah have mercy upon thee, O Adam!" Mohammed, who liked sneezing because accompanied by lightness of body and openness of pores, said of it, "If a man sneeze and say 'Alhamdolillah' he averts seventy diseases of which the least is leprosy" (Juzám); also, "If one of you sneeze, let him exclaim, 'Alhamdolillah,' and let those around salute him in return with, 'Allah have mercy upon thee!' and lastly let him say, 'Allah direct you and strengthen your condition.'" Moderns prefer, Allah avert what may joy thy foe! (= our God bless you!) to which the answer is "Alhamdolillah!" Mohammed disliked yawning (Suabá or Thuabá), because not beneficial as a sneeze, and said, "If one of you gape and cover not his mouth, a devil leaps into it." This is still a popular superstition from Baghdad to Marocco.

fair neck she wore a necklace of unions and her waist was clasped with a girdle of chrysolite bugles, with tassels of rubies and pearls. The damsels kissed ground before her, and, "When I considered her" (quoth Ibrahim), "I took leave of my senses and wit and I was dazed and my thought was confounded for amazement at the sight of loveliness whose like is not on the face of the earth. So I fell into a swoon and coming to myself, weeping-eyed, recited these two couplets :—

I see thee and close not mine eyes for fear, * Lest their lids prevent me beholding thee :
An I gazed with mine every glance, these eyne * Ne'er could sight all the loveliness moulding thee."

Then said the old Kahramánah[1] to the girls, "Let ten of you arise and dance and sing." And Ibrahim when looking at them said in himself, "I wish the lady Jamilah would dance." When the handmaidens had made an end of their pavane, they gathered round the Princess and said to her, "O my lady, we long for thee to dance amongst us, so the measure of our joy may be fulfilled, for never saw we a more delicious day than this." Quoth Ibrahim to himself, "Doubtless the gates of Heaven are open[2] and Allah hath granted my prayer." Then the damsels kissed her feet and said to her, "By Allah, we never saw thee broadened of breast as to-day!" Nor did they cease exciting her, till she doffed her outer dress and stood in a gown of cloth of gold,[3] broidered with various jewels, unveiling a face as it were the moon on the night of fulness. Then she began to dance, and Ibrahim beheld motions he had never in his life seen their like, for she showed such wondrous skill and marvellous invention, that she made men forget the dancing of bubbles in wine-cups and called to mind the inclining of the turbands from head-tops;[4] even as saith of her the poet[5] :—

A dancer whose form is like branch of Bán! * Flies my soul well nigh as his steps I greet :
While he dances no foot stands still and meseems * That the fire of my heart is beneath his feet.

---

[1] A duenna, nursery governess, etc.

[2] For this belief see the tale called "The Night of Power."

[3] The Anglo-Indian "Kincob" (Kimkh'áb); brocade, silk flowered with gold or silver.

[4] Lane finds a needless difficulty in this sentence, which is far-fetched only because Kuus (cups) requires Ruus (head-tops) by way of jingle. It means only "'Twas merry in hall when beards wag all."

[5] The Mac. Edit. gives two couplets which have already occurred from the Bul. Edit.

And as quoth another[1]:—

A dancer whose figure is like a willow-branch : my soul almost quitteth me at the sight of her movements.
No foot can remain stationary at her dancing, she is as though the fire of my heart were beneath her feet.

Quoth Ibrahim :—As I gazed upon her, she chanced to look up and caught sight of me, whereupon her face changed and she said to her women, "Sing ye till I come back to you." Then, taking up a knife half a cubit long, she made towards me, crying, "There is no Majesty and there is no Might save in Allah, the Glorious, the Great!" Now when I saw this, I well-nigh lost my wits; but, whenas she drew near me and face met face, the knife dropped from her hand, and she exclaimed, "Glory to him who changeth men's hearts!" Then said she to me, "O youth, be of good cheer, for thou art safe from what thou dost fear!" Whereupon I fell to weeping, and she to wiping away my tears with her hand and saying, "O youth, tell me who thou art, and what brought thee hither." I kissed the ground before her and seized her skirt; and she said, "No harm shall come to thee; for, by Allah, no male hath ever filled mine eyes[2] but thyself! Tell me, then, who thou art." So I recited to her my story from first to last, whereat she marvelled and said to me, "O my lord, I conjure thee by Allah, tell me if thou be Ibrahim bin al-Khasib?" I replied, "Yes!" and she threw herself upon me, saying, "O my lord, 'twas thou madest me averse from men; for, when I heard that there was in the land of Egypt a youth than whom there was none more beautiful on earth's face, I fell in love with thee by report, and my heart became enamoured of thee, for that which reached me of thy passing comeliness, so that I was, in respect of thee, even as saith the poet:—

Mine ear forewent mine eye in loving him; * For ear shall love before the eye at times.

So praised be Allah who hath shown thy face! But, by the Almighty, had it been other than thou, I had crucified the keeper of the garden and the porter of the Khan and the tailor and him who had recourse to them!" And presently she added, "But how shall I contrive for somewhat thou mayst eat, without the knowledge of my women?" Quoth I, "With me is somewhat we may

---

[1] The lines are half of four couplets cited before, so I quote Lane.
[2] *i.e.* none hath pleased me. I have quoted the popular saying, "The son of the quarter filleth not the eye;" *i.e.* women prefer stranger faces.

eat and drink;" and I opened the bag before her. She took a fowl and began to morsel me and I to morsel her; which when I saw, it seemed to me that this was a dream. Then I brought out wine and we drank, what while the damsels sang on; nor did they leave to do thus from morn to noon, when she rose and said, "Go now and get thee a boat and await me in such a place, till I come to thee: for I have no patience left to brook severance." I replied, "O my lady, I have with me a ship of my own, whose crew are in my hire, and they await me." Rejoined she, "This is as we would have it" and returning to her women,——And Shahrazad perceived the dawn of day and ceased saying her permitted say.

## Now when it was the Nine Hundred and Fifty-eighth Night,

She resumed, It hath reached me, O auspicious King, that when the Lady Jamilah returned to her women, she said to them, "Come, let us go back to our palace." They replied, "Why should we return now, seeing that we use to abide here three days?" Quoth she, "I feel an exceeding oppression in myself, as though I were sick, and I fear lest this increase upon me."[1] So they answered, "We hear and obey," and donning their walking-dresses went down to the river-bank and embarked in a boat; whereupon behold, the keeper of the garden came up to Ibrahim and said to him, knowing not what had happened, "O Ibrahim, thou hast not had the luck to enjoy the sight of her, and I fear lest she have seen thee, for 'tis her wont to tarry here three days." Replied Ibrahim, "She saw me not nor I her; for she came not forth of the pavilion."[2] Rejoined the keeper, "True, O my son, for, had she seen thee, we were both dead men: but abide with me till she come again next week, and thou shalt see her and take thy fill of looking at her." Replied the Prince, "O my lord, I have with me money and fear for it: I also left men behind me and I dread lest they take advantage of my absence."[3] He retorted, "O my son 'tis grievous to me to part with thee;" and he embraced and farewelled him. Then Ibrahim

---

[1] Here after the favourite Oriental fashion, she tells the truth but so enigmatically that it is more deceptive than an untruth; a good Eastern quibble infinitely more dangerous than an honest downright lie. The consciousness that the falsehood is part fact applies a salve to conscience and supplies a force lacking in the mere fib. When an Egyptian lies to you look straight in his eyes and he will most often betray himself either by boggling or by a look of injured innocence.

[2] Another true lie.

[3] Arab. "Yastaghíbúní," lit. = they deem my absence too long.

returned to the Khan where he lodged, and foregathering with the doorkeeper, took of him all his property, and the porter said, "Good news, Inshallah!"[1] But Ibrahim said, "I have found no way to my want, and now I am minded to return to my people." Whereupon the porter wept; then taking up his baggage, he carried them to the ship and bade him adieu. Ibrahim repaired to the place which Jamilah had appointed him and awaited her there till it grew dark, when, behold, she came up, disguised as a bully-boy with rounded beard and waist bound with a girdle. In one hand she held a bow and arrows and in the other a bared blade, and she asked him, "Art thou Ibrahim, son of Al-Khasib, lord of Egypt?" "He I am," answered the Prince; and she said, "What ne'er-do-well art thou, who comest to debauch the daughters of Kings? Come: speak with the Sultan."[2] Therewith (quoth Ibrahim) I fell down in a swoon and the sailors died[3] in their skins for fear; but, when she saw what had betided me, she pulled off her beard and throwing down her sword, ungirdled her waist, whereupon I knew her for the Lady Jamilah and said to her, "By Allah, thou hast rent my heart in sunder!"[4] adding to the boatmen, "Hasten the vessel's speed." So they shook out the sail and putting off, fared on with all diligence; nor was it many days ere we made Baghdad, where suddenly we saw a ship lying by the river-bank. When her sailors saw us, they cried out to our crew, saying, "Ho, Such-an-one and Such-an-one, we give you joy of your safety!" Then they drave their ship against our craft and I looked and in the other boat beheld Abu al-Kasim al-Sandalani, who when he saw us exclaimed, "This is what I sought: go ye in God's keeping; as for me, I have a need to be satisfied!" Then he turned to me and said, "Praised be Allah for safety! Hast thou accomplished thine errand?" I replied, "Yes!" Now Abu al-Kasim had a flambeau before him; so he brought it near our boat,[5] and when Jamilah saw him, she was troubled and her colour changed: but when he saw her, he said, "Fare ye in Allah's safety. I am bound to Bassorah, on business for the Sultan; but the gift is for him who

[1] An euphemistic form of questioning after absence: "Is all right with thee?"

[2] Arab. "Kallim al-Sultan!" the formula of summoning which has often occurred in The Nights.

[3] Lane translates "almost died;" Payne "well-nigh died;" but the text says "died." I would suggest to translators

Be bould, be bould and everywhere be bould!

[4] He is the usual poltroon contrasted with the manly and masterful girl, a conjunction of the lioness and the lamb sometimes seen in real life.

[5] That he might see Jamilah as Ibrahim had promised.

is present."[1] Then he brought out a box of sweetmeats, wherein was Bhang and threw it into our boat; whereupon quoth I to Jamilah, "O coolth of mine eyes, eat of this." But she wept and said, "O Ibrahim, wottest thou who that is?" and said I, "Yes, 'tis Such-an-one." Replied she, "He is my first cousin, son of my father's brother,[2] who sought me aforetime in marriage of my sire; but I would not accept of him. And now he is gone to Bassorah and most like he will tell my father of us." I rejoined, "O my lady, he will not reach Bassorah till we are at Mosul." But we knew not what lurked for us in the Secret Purpose. Then (continued Ibrahim) I ate of the sweetmeat, but hardly had it reached my stomach when I smote the ground with my head; and lay there till near dawn, when I sneezed and the Bhang issued from my nostrils. With this, I opened my eyes and found myself naked and cast out among ruins; so I buffeted my face and said in myself, "Doubtless this is a trick Al-Sandalani hath played me." But I knew not whither I should wend, for I had upon me naught save my bag-trousers.[3] However, I rose and walked on a little, till I suddenly espied the Chief of Police coming towards me, with a posse of men with swords and targes;[4] whereat I took fright and seeing a ruined Hammam hid myself there. Presently, my foot stumbled upon something; so I put my hand to it, and it became befouled with blood. I wiped my hand upon my bag-trousers, unknowing what had befouled it, and put it out a second time, when it fell upon a corpse whose head came up in my hand. I threw it down, saying, "There is no Majesty and there is no Might save in Allah, the Glorious, the Great!" and I took refuge in one of the corner-cabinets of the Hammam. Presently the Wali stopped at the bath-door and said, "Enter this place and search." So ten of them entered with cressets, and I of my fear retired behind a wall and looking upon the corpse, saw it to be that of a young lady[5]

---

[1] A popular saying, *i.e.* les absents ont toujours tort.

[2] Who had a prior right to marry her, but not against her consent after she was of age.

[3] Arab. "Sirwál." In Al-Hariri it is a singular form (see No. ii. of the twelve riddles in Ass. xxiv.); but Mohammed said to his followers, "Tuakhkhizú" (adopt ye) "Saráwílát." The latter is regularly declinable but the broken form Saráwíl is imperfectly declinable on account of its "heaviness," as are all plurals whose third letter is an Alif followed by i or í in the next syllable.

[4] Arab. "Matárik" from mitrak or mitrakah a small wooden shield coated with hide. This even in the present day is the policeman's equipment in the outer parts of the East.

[5] Arab. "Sabíyah," for which I prefer Mr. Payne's "young lady" to Lane's "damsel"; the latter should be confined to Járiyah as both bear the double sense of girl and slave (or servant) girl. "Bint" again is daughter, maid or simply girl.

with a face like the full moon; and her head lay on one side and her body clad in costly raiment on the other. When I saw this my heart fluttered with affright. Then the Chief of Police entered and said, "Search the corners of the bath." So they entered the place wherein I was, and one of them seeing me, came up hending in hand a knife half a cubit long. When he drew near me, he cried, "Glory be to God, the Creator of this fair face! O youth, whence art thou?" Then he took me by the hand and said, "O youth, why slewest thou this woman?" Said I, "By Allah, I slew her not, nor wot I who slew her, and I entered not this place but in fear of you!" And I told him my case, adding, "Allah upon thee, do me no wrong, for I am in concern for myself!" Then he took me and carried me to the Wali who, seeing the marks of blood on my hand said, "This needeth no proof: strike off his head!"——And Shahrazad was surprised by the dawn of day and ceased saying her permitted say.

## Now when it was the Nine Hundred and Fifty-ninth Night,

She said, It hath reached me, O auspicious King, that Ibrahim continued:—Then they carried me before the Wali and he, seeing the blood-stains on my hand, cried, "This needeth no proof: strike off his head!" Now hearing these words, I wept with sore weeping, the tears streaming from my eyes, and recited these two couplets[1]:—

We trod the steps that for us were writ, * And whose steps are written he needs must tread;
And whose death is decreed in one land to be * He ne'er shall perish in other stead.

Then I sobbed a single sob and fell a-swoon; and the headsman's heart was moved to ruth for me and he exclaimed, "By Allah, this is no murtherer's face!" But the Chief said, "Smite his neck." So they seated me on the rug of blood and bound my eyes; after which the Sworder drew his sword and asking leave of the Wali, was about to strike off my head, whilst I cried out, "Alas my strangerhood!" when lo and behold! I heard a noise of horse coming up and a voice calling aloud, "Leave him! Stay thy hand, O Sworder!" Now there was for this a wondrous reason and a marvellous cause; and 'twas thus. Al-Khasib, Wazir of Egypt, had

[1] The sense of them is found in Night xxxviii.

sent his Head Chamberlain to the Caliph Harun al-Rashid with presents and a letter, saying, "My son hath been missing this year past, and I hear that he is in Baghdad; wherefore I crave of the bounty of the Viceregent of Allah that he make search for tidings of him and do his endeavour to find him and send him back to me with the Chamberlain." When the Caliph read the missive, he commanded the Chief of Police to search out the truth of the matter, and he ceased not to enquire after Ibrahim, till it was told that he was at Bassorah, whereupon he informed the Caliph, who wrote a letter to the viceroy and giving it to the Chamberlain of Egypt, bade him repair to Bassorah and take with him a company of the Wazir's followers. So, of his eagerness to find the son of his lord, the Chamberlain set out forthright and happened by the way upon Ibrahim, as he stood on the rug of blood. When the Wali saw the Chamberlain, he recognised him and alighted to him; and he asked, "What young man is that and what is his case?" The Chief told him how the matter was and the Chamberlain said (and indeed he knew him not for the son of the Sultan[1]), "Verily this young man hath not the face of one who murthereth." And he bade loose his bonds; so they loosed him and the Chamberlain said, "Bring him to me!" and they brought him, but the officer knew him not, his beauty being all gone for the horrors he had endured. Then the Chamberlain said to him, "O youth, tell me thy case and how cometh this slain woman with thee." Ibrahim looked at him and knowing him, said to him, "Woe to thee! Dost thou not know me? Am I not Ibrahim, son of thy lord? Haply thou art come in quest of me." With this the Chamberlain considered him straitly and knowing him right well, threw himself at his feet; which when the Wali saw, his colour changed; and the Chamberlain cried to him "Fie upon thee, O tyrant! Was it thine intent to slay the son of my master Al-Khasib, Wazir of Egypt?" The Chief of Police kissed his skirt, saying, "O my lord,[2] how should I know him? We found him in this plight and saw the girl lying slain by his side." Rejoined the Chamberlain, "Out on

---

[1] Here the text is defective, but I hardly like to supply the omission. Mr. Payne introduces from below, "for that his charms were wasted and his favour changed by reason of the much terror and affliction he had suffered." The next lines also are very abrupt and unconnected.

[2] Arab. "Yá Mauláya!" the term is still used throughout Moslem lands; but in Barbary, where it is pronounced "Mooláee," Europeans have converted it to "Muley" as if it had some connected with the mule. Even in Robinson Crusoe we find "Muly" or "Moly Ismael" (chap ii.); and we hear the high-sounding name Maulá-i-Idrís, the patron saint of the Sunset Land, debased to "Muley Drís."

thee! Thou art not fit for the office. This is a lad of fifteen and he hath not slain a sparrow; so how should he be a murtherer? Why didst thou not have patience with him and question him of his case?" Then the Chamberlain and the Wali cried to the men, "Make search for the young lady's murtherer." So they re-entered the bath and finding him, brought him to the Chief of Police, who carried him to the Caliph and acquainted him with that which had occurred. Al-Rashid bade slay the slayer and sending for Ibrahim, smiled in his face and said to him, "Tell me thy tale and that which hath betided thee." So he recounted to him his story from first to last, and it was grievous to the Caliph, who called Masrur his Sworder, and said to him, "Go straightway and fall upon the house of Abu al-Kasim al-Sandalani and bring me him and the young lady." The eunuch went forth at once and breaking into the house, found Jamilah bound with her own hair and nigh upon death; so he loosed her and taking the painter, carried them both to the Caliph, who marvelled at Jamilah's beauty. Then he turned to Al-Sandalani and said, "Take him and cut off his hands, wherewith he beat this young lady; then crucify him and deliver his monies and possessions to Ibrahim." They did his bidding, and as they were thus, behold, in came Abu al-Lays, Governor of Bassorah, the Lady Jamilah's father, seeking aid of the Caliph against Ibrahim bin al-Khasib, Wazir of Egypt, and complaining to him that the youth had taken his daughter. Quoth Al-Rashid, "He hath been the means of delivering her from torture and slaughter." Then he sent for Ibrahim, and when he came, he said to Abu al-Lays, "Wilt thou not accept of this young man, son of the Sultan of Egypt, as husband to thy daughter?" Replied Abu al-Lays, "I hear and I obey Allah and thee, O Commander of the Faithful;" whereupon the Caliph summoned the Kazi and the witnesses and married the young lady to Ibrahim. Furthermore, he gave him all Al-Sandalani's wealth and equipped him for his return to his own country, where he abode with Jamilah in the utmost of bliss and the most perfect of happiness, till there came to them the Destroyer of delights and the Sunderer of societies; and glory be to the Living who dieth not! They also relate, O auspicious King, a tale anent

## *ABU AL-HASAN OF KHORASAN.*[1]

The Caliph Al-Mu'tazid Bi 'llah[2] was a high-spirited Prince and a noble-minded lord; he had in Baghdad six hundred Wazirs and of the affairs of the folk naught was hidden from him. He went forth one day, he and Ibn Hamdún,[3] to divert himself with observing his lieges and hearing the latest news of the people; and, being overtaken with the heats of noonday, they turned aside from the main thoroughfare into a little by-street, at the upper end whereof they saw a handsome and high-builded mansion, discoursing of its owner with the tongue of praise. They sat down at the gate to take rest, and presently out came two eunuchs as they were moons on their fourteenth night. Quoth one of them to his fellow, "Would Heaven some guest would seek admission this day! My master will not eat but with guests and we are come to this hour and I have not yet seen a soul." The Caliph marvelled at their speech and said, "This is a proof of the house-master's liberality; there is no help but that we go in to him and note his generosity, and this shall be a means of favour betiding him from us." So he said to the eunuch, "Ask leave of thy lord for the admission of a company[4] of strangers." For in those days it was the Caliph's wont, whenas he was minded to observe his subjects, to disguise himself in merchant's garb. The eunuch went in and told his master, who rejoiced, and rising, came out to them in person. He was fair of favour and fine of form, and he appeared clad in a tunic of Níshápúr[5] silk and a

---

[1] Lane omits this tale because "it is very similar, but inferior in interest, to the Story told by the Sultan's Steward."

[2] Sixteenth Abbaside, A.H. 279–289 (= A.D. 891-902). "He was comely, intrepid, of grave exterior, majestic in presence, of considerable intellectual power and the fiercest of the Caliphs of the House of Abbas. He once had the courage to attack a lion" (Al-Siyuti). I may add that he was a good soldier and an excellent administrator, who was called Saffáh the Second because he refounded the House of Abbas. He was exceedingly fanatic and died of excess, having first kicked his doctor to death, and he spent his last moments in versifying.

[3] Hamdún bin Ismá'íl, called the Kátib or Scribe, was the first of his family who followed the profession of a Nadím or cup-companion. His son Ahmad (who is in the text) was an oral transmitter of poetry and history. Al-Siyúti (p. 390) and De Slane Ibn Khall. (ii. 304) notice him.

[4] Probably the Caliph had attendants, but the text afterwards speaks of them as two. Mac. Edit. iv. p. 558, line 2; and a few lines below, "the Caliph and the man with him."

[5] Arab. "Naysábúr," the famous town in Khorasan where Omar-i-Khayyán (whom our people will call Omar Khayyám) was buried and where his tomb is

gold laced mantle; and he dripped with scented waters and wore on his hand a signet-ring of rubies. When he saw them, he said to them, "Well come and welcome to the lords who favour us with the utmost of favour by their coming!" So they entered the house and found it such as would make a man forget family and fatherland, for it was like a piece of Paradise.——And Shahrazad perceived the dawn of day and ceased to say her permitted say.

## Now when it was the Nine Hundred and Sixtieth Night,

She continued, It hath reached me, O auspicious King, that when the Caliph entered the mansion, he and the man with him, they saw it to be such that would make one forget family and fatherland, for it was like a piece of Paradise. Within it was a flower-garden, full of all kinds of trees, confounding sight, and its dwelling-places were furnished with costly furniture. They sat down and the Caliph fell to gazing at the house and the household gear. (Quoth Ibn Hamdun) I looked at the Caliph and saw his countenance change, and being wont to know from his face whether he was amused or anangered, said to myself, "I wonder what hath vexed him." Then they brought a golden basin and we washed our hands, after which they spread a silken cloth and set thereon a table of rattan. When the covers were taken off the dishes, we saw therein meats rare as the blooms of Prime in the season of their utmost scarcity, twofold and single, and the host said, "Bismillah, O my lords! By Allah, hunger pricketh me; so favour me by eating of this food, as is the fashion of the noble." Thereupon he began tearing fowls apart and laying them before us, laughing the while and repeating verses and telling stories and talking gaily with pleasant sayings such as sorted with the entertainment. We ate and drank, then removed to another room, which confounded beholders with its beauty and which reeked with exquisite perfumes. Here they brought us a tray of fruits freshly-gathered and sweetmeats the finest flavoured, whereat our joys increased and our cares ceased. But withal the Caliph (continued Ibn Hamdun) ceased not to wear a frowning face and smiled not at that which gladdened all souls, albeit it was his

---

still a place of pious visitation. A sketch of it has lately appeared in the illustrated papers. For an affecting tale concerning the astronomer-poet's tomb, borrowed from the Nigáristán, see the Preface by the late Mr. Fitzgerald, whose admirable excerpts from the Rubaiyat (101 out of 820 quatrains) have made the poem popular among all the English-speaking races.

wont to love mirth and merriment and the putting away of cares, and I wot that he was no envious wight and oppressor. So I said to myself, "Would Heaven I knew what is the cause of his moroseness and why we cannot dissipate his ill-humour!" Presently they brought the tray of wine which friends doth conjoin and clarified draughts in flagons of gold and crystal and silver, and the host smote with a rattan-wand on the door of an inner chamber, whereupon behold, it opened and out came three damsels, high bosomed virginity, with faces like the sun at the fourth hour of the day, one a lutist, another a harpist and the third a dancer-artiste. Then he set before us dried fruits and confections and drew between us and the damsels a curtain of brocade, with tassels of silk and rings of gold. The Caliph paid no heed to all this, but said to the host, who knew not who was in his company, "Art thou noble?"[1] Said he, "No, my lord; I am but a man of the sons of the merchants and am known among the folk as Abú al-Hasan Ali, son of Ahmad of Khorasan." Quoth the Caliph, "Dost thou know me, O man?" and quoth he, "By Allah, O my lord, I have no knowledge of either of your honours!" Then said I to him, "O man, this is the Commander of the Faithful, Al-Mu'tazid Bi'llah, grandson of Al-Mutawakkil alà 'llah."[2] Whereupon he rose and kissed the ground before the Caliph, trembling for fear of him, and said, "O Prince of True Believers, I conjure thee, by the virtue of thy pious forbears, an thou have seen in me any shortcomings or lack of good manners in thy presence, do thou forgive me!" Replied the Caliph, "As for that which thou hast done with us of honouring and hospitality nothing could have exceeded it; and as for that wherewith I have to reproach thee here, an thou tell me the truth respecting it and it commend itself to my sense, thou shalt be saved from me; but, an thou tell me not the truth, I will take thee with manifest proof and punish thee with such punishment as never yet punished any." Quoth the man, "Allah forbid that I tell thee a lie! But what is it that thou reproachest to me, O Commander of the Faithful?" Quoth the Caliph "Since I entered thy mansion and looked upon its grandeur, I have noted the furniture and vessels therein, nay, even to thy clothes, and behold, on all of them is the name of my grandfather Al-Mutawakkil

---

[1] Arab. "A-Sharíf anta?" (with the Hamzah-sign of interrogation) = Art thou a Sharíf (or descendant of the Apostle)?

[2] Tenth Abbaside (A.H. 234–247 = 848-861), grandson of Al-Rashid and born of a slave concubine. He was famous for his hatred of the Alides (he destroyed the tomb of Al-Husayn) and claimed the pardon of Allah for having revived orthodox traditionary doctrines. He compelled the Christians to wear collars of wood or leather and was assassinated by five Turks.

ala 'llah."[1] Answered Abu al-Hasan, "Yes, O Commander of the Faithful (the Almighty protect thee), truth is thine inner garb and sincerity is thine outer garment, and none may speak otherwise than truly in thy presence." The Caliph bade him be seated and said, "Tell us." So he began, "Know, O Commander of the Faithful, that my father belonged to the markets of the money-changers and druggists and linendrapers and had in each bazar a store and an agent and all kinds of goods. Moreover, behind the money-changer's shop he had an apartment, where he might be private, appointing the shop for buying and selling. His wealth was beyond count and to his riches there was none amount; but he had no child other than myself, and he loved me and was tenderly fain of me. When his last hour was at hand, he called me to him and commended my mother to my care and charged me to fear Almighty Allah. Then he died, may Allah have mercy upon him and continue the Prince of True Believers on life! And I gave myself up to pleasure and eating and drinking and took to myself comrades and intimates. My mother used to forbid me from this, and to blame me therefor, but I would not hear a word from her, till my money was all gone, when I sold my lands and houses and naught was left me save the mansion wherein I now dwell, and it was a goodly stead, O Commander of the Faithful. So I said to my mother, "I wish to sell the house;" but she said, "O my son, an thou sell it, thou wilt be dishonoured and wilt have no place wherein to take shelter." Quoth I, "'Tis worth five thousand dinars, and with one thousand of its price I will buy me another house and trade with the rest." Quoth she, "Wilt thou sell it to me at that price?" and I replied, "Yes." Whereupon she went to a coffer and opening it, took out a porcelain vessel, wherein were five thousand dinars. When I saw this meseemed the house was all of gold, and she said to me, "O my son, think not that this is of thy sire's good. By Allah, O my son, it was of my own father's money, and I have treasured it up against a time of need; for in thy father's day I was a wealthy woman and had no need of it." I took the money from her, O Prince of True Believers, and fell again to feasting and

---

[1] His father was Al-Mu' tasim bi 'llah (A.H. 218-227 = 833-842) the son of Al-Rashid by Máridah, a slave-concubine of foreign origin—Al-Mu'tasim was brave and of high spirit, but destitute of education; and his personal strength was such that he could break a man's elbow between his fingers. He imitated the apparatus of Persian kings; and he was called the "Octonary" because he was the 8th Abbaside; the 8th in descent from Abbas; the 8th son of Al-Rashid; he began his reign in A.H. 218; lived 48 years; was born under Scorpio (8th Zodiacal sign); was victorious in 8 expeditions; slew 8 important foes and left 8 male and 8 female children.

carousing and merrymaking with my friends, unheeding my mother's words and admonitions, till the five thousand dinars came to an end, when I said to her, "I wish to sell the house." Said she, "O my son, I forbade thee from selling it before, of my knowledge that thou hadst need of it; so how wilt thou sell it a second time?" Quoth I, "Be not longsome of speech with me, for I must and will sell it;" and quoth she, "Then sell it to me for fifteen thousand dinars, on condition that I take charge of thine affairs." So I sold her the house at that price and gave up my affairs into her charge, whereupon she sought out the agents of my father and gave each of them a thousand dinars, keeping the rest in her own hands and ordering the outgo and the income. Moreover she gave me money to trade withal, and said to me, "Sit thou in thy father's shop." So I did her bidding, O Commander of the Faithful, and took up my abode in the chamber behind the shop in the market of the money-changers, and my friends came and bought of me and I sold to them: whereby I made good cheape and my wealth increased. When my mother saw me in this fair way, she discovered to me that which she had treasured up of jewels and precious stones, pearls, and gold, and I bought back my houses and lands that I had squandered and my wealth became great as before. I abode thus for some time, and the factors of my father came to me and I gave them stock-in-trade, and I built me a second chamber behind the shop. One day, as I sat there, according to my custom, O Prince of True Believers, there came up to me a damsel, never saw eyes a fairer than she of favour, and said, "Is this the private shop of Abu al-Hasan Ali ibn Ahmad al-Khorasani?" Answered I, "Yes," and she asked, "Where is he?" "He am I," said I, and indeed my wit was dazed at the excess of her loveliness. She sat down and said to me, "Bid thy page weigh me out three hundred dinars." Accordingly I bade him give her that sum and he weighed it out to her, and she took it and went away, leaving me stupefied. Quoth my man to me, "Dost thou know her?" and quoth I, "No, by Allah!" He asked, "Then why didst thou bid me give her the money?" and I answered, "By Allah, I knew not what I said, of my amazement at her beauty and loveliness!" Then he rose and followed her, without my knowledge, but presently returned, weeping and with the mark of a blow on his face. I enquired of him what ailed him, and he replied, "I followed the damsel, to see whither she went; but, when she was aware of me, she turned and dealt me this blow and all but knocked out my eye." After this, a month passed without her coming, O Commander of the Faithful, and I abode bewildered for love of her; but, at the end of this time, she suddenly appeared again and saluted me, whereat I was like to fly for joy. She asked me how I did and said to me, "Haply thou saidst to thyself, What manner of trickstress is this, who hath taken my money and made off?" Answered I, "By Allah, O my lady, my money and my life are all thy very own!" With this she unveiled herself and sat down to rest, with the trinkets and ornaments playing over her face and bosom. Presently, she said to me, "Weigh me out three hundred dinars." "Hearkening and obedience," answered I, and weighed out to her the money. She took it and went away, and I said to my servant, "Follow her." So he followed her, but returned dumbstruck, and some time passed without my seeing her. But, as I was sitting one day, behold, she came up to me and after talking awhile, said to me, "Weigh me out five hundred dinars, for I have need of them." I would have said to her, "Why should I give thee my money?" but my love immense hindered me from utterance; for, O Prince of True Believers, whenever I saw her, I trembled in every joint and my colour paled and I forgot what I would have said and became even as singeth the poet:—

"'Tis naught but this! When a-sudden I see her, • Mumchance I bide nor a word can say her."

So I weighed out for her the five hundred ducats, and she took them and went away; whereupon I arose and followed her myself, till she came to the jewel-bazar, where she stopped at a man's shop and took of him a necklace. Then she turned and seeing me, said, "Pay him five hundred dinars for me." When the jeweller saw me, he rose to me and made much of me, and I said to him, "Give her the necklace and set down the price to me." He replied, "I hear and obey," and she took it and went away; ——And Shahrazad was surprised by the dawn of day and ceased saying her permitted say.

## Now when it was the Nine Hundred and Sixty-first Night,

She pursued, It hath reached me, O auspicious King, that Abu Hasan the Khorasani thus pursued his tale:—So I said to the jeweller, "Give her the necklace and set down the price to me." Then she took it and went away; but I followed her, till she came to the Tigris and boarded a boat there, whereupon I signed with my hand to the ground, as who should say, "I kiss it before thee." She went off laughing, and I stood watching her, till I saw her land and enter a palace, which when I considered, I knew it for the palace of the Caliph Al-Mutawakkil. So I turned back, O Commander of the Faithful, with all the cares in the world fallen on my heart, for she had of me three thousand dinars, and I said to myself, "She hath taken my wealth and ravished my wit, and peradventure I shall lose my life for her love." Then I returned home and told my mother all that had befallen me, and she said, "O my son, beware how thou have to do with her after this, or thou art lost." When I went to my shop, my factor in the drug-market, who was a very old man, came to me and said, "O my lord, how is it that I see thee changed in case and showing marks of chagrin? Tell me what aileth thee." So I told him all that had befallen me with her and he said, "O my son, this is indeed one of the handmaidens of the palace of the Commander of the Faithful and haply she is the Caliph's favourite : so do thou reckon the money as spent for the sake of Almighty Allah[1] and occupy thyself no more with her. An she come again, beware lest she have to do with thee, and tell me of this, that I may devise thee some device lest perdition betide thee." Then he fared forth and left me with a flame of fire in my heart. At the end of the month behold, she came again and I rejoiced in her with exceeding joy. Quoth she, "What ailed thee to follow me?" and quoth I, "Excess of passion that is in my heart urged me to this," and I wept before her. She wept for ruth of me and said, "By Allah, there is not in thy heart aught of love-longing but in my heart is more! Yet how shall I do? By Allah, I have no resource save to see thee thus once a month." Then she gave me a bill saying, "Carry this to Such-an-one of such a trade, who is my agent, and take of him what is named therein." But I replied, "I have no need of money; be my wealth and my life thy sacrifice!" Quoth she, "I will right soon contrive thee a means of access to me, whatever trouble it cost me." Then she farewelled me and fared forth, whilst I repaired to the old druggist and told him what had passed. He went with me to the palace of Al-Mutawakkil which I knew for that which the damsel had entered; but the Shaykh was at a loss for a device. Presently he espied a tailor sitting with his prentices at work in his shop, opposite the lattice giving upon the river bank, and said to me, "Yonder is one by whom thou shalt win thy wish; but first tear thy pocket and go to him and bid him sew it up. When he hath done this, give him ten dinars." "I hear and obey," answered I, and taking with

---

[1] *i.e.* as it were given away in charity.

me two pieces[1] of Greek brocade, I went to the tailor and bade him make of them four suits, two with long-sleeved coats and two without. When he had finished cutting them out and sewing them, I gave him to his hire much more than of wont, and he put out his hand to me with the clothes; but I said, "Take them for thyself and for those who are with thee." And I fell to sitting with him and sitting long: I also bespoke of him other clothes and said to him, "Hang them out in front of thy shop, so the folk may see them and buy them." He did as I bade him, and whoso came forth of the Caliph's palace and aught of the clothes pleased him, I made him a present thereof, even to the doorkeeper. One day of the days the tailor said to me, "O my son, I would have thee tell me the truth of thy case; for thou hast bespoken of me an hundred costly suits, each worth a mint of money, and hast given the most of them to the folk. This is no merchant's fashion, for a merchant calleth an account for every dirham, and what can be the sum of thy capital that thou givest these gifts and what thy gain every year? Tell me the truth of thy case, that I may assist thee to thy desire;" presently adding, "I conjure thee by Allah, tell me, art thou not in love?" "Yes," replied I; and he said, "With whom?" Quoth I, "With one of the handmaids of the Caliph's palace;" and quoth he, "Allah put them to shame! How long shall they seduce the folk? Knowest thou her name?" Said I, "No;" and said he, "Describe her to me." So I described her to him and he cried, "Out on it! This is the lutanist of the Caliph Al-Mutawakkil and his pet concubine. But she hath a Mameluke,[2] and do thou make friends with him; it may be he shall become the means of thy having access to her." Now as we were talking, behold, out walked the servant in question from the palace, as he were a moon on the fourteenth night; and, seeing that I had before me the clothes which the tailor had made me, and they were of brocade of all colours, he began to look at them and examine them. Then he came up to me and I rose and saluted him. He asked, "Who art thou?" and I answered, "I am a man of the merchants." Quoth he, "Wilt thou sell these clothes?" and quoth I, "Yes." So he chose out five of them and said to me, "How much these five?" Said I, "They are a present to thee from me in earnest of friendship between me and thee." At this he rejoiced and I went home,

---

[1] Arab. "Shukkah," a word much used in the Zanzibar trade, where it means a piece of long-cloth one fathom long. See my "Lake Regions of Central Africa," vol. i. 147, etc.

[2] He is afterwards called in two places "Khâdim" = eunuch.

and fetching a suit embroidered with jewels and jacinths, worth three thousand dinars, returned therewith and gave it to him. He accepted it and carrying me into a room within the palace, said to me, "What is thy name among the merchants?" Said I, "I am a man of them.[1]" He continued, "Verily I misdoubt me of thine affair." I asked, "Why so?" and he answered, "Because thou hast bestowed on me a costly gift and won my heart therewith, and I make certain that thou art Abu al-Hasan of Khorasan the Shroff." With this I fell a-weeping, O Prince of True Believers; and he said to me, "Why dost thou weep? By Allah, she for whom thou weepest is yet more longingly in love with thee than thou with her! And indeed her case with thee is notorious among all the palace women. But what wouldst thou have?" Quoth I, "I would have thee succour me in my calamity." So he appointed me for the morrow and I returned home. As soon as I rose next morning, I betook myself to him and waited in his chamber till he came in and said to me, "Know that yesternight when, after having made an end of her service by the Caliph, she returned to her apartment, I related to her all that had passed between me and thee and she is minded to meet with thee. So stay with me till the end of the day." Accordingly I stayed with him till dark, when the Mameluke brought me a shirt of gold-inwoven stuff and a suit of the Caliph's apparel, and clothing me therein, incensed me[2] and I became like the Commander of the Faithful. Then he brought me to a gallery with rows of rooms on either side and said to me, "These are the lodgings of the chief of the slave-girls; and when thou passest along the gallery, do thou lay at each door a bean, for 'tis the custom of the Caliph to do this every night.——And Shahrazad perceived the dawn of day and ceased to say her permitted say.

## Now when it was the Nine Hundred and Sixty-second Night,

She resumed, It hath reached me, O auspicious King, that the Mameluke said to Abu Hasan, "When thou passest along the gallery set down at each door a bean, for 'tis the custom of the Caliph so to do, till thou come to the second passage on thy right

---

[1] A courteous way of saying, "Never mind my name: I wish to keep it hidden." The formula is still popular.

[2] Arab. "Bakhkhara-ní," *i.e.* fumigated me with burning aloes-wood, Calumba or similar material.

hand, when thou wilt see a door with a marble threshold.[1] Touch it with thy hand or, an thou wilt, count the doors, which are so many, and enter the one whose marks are thus and thus. There thy mistress will see thee and take thee in with her. As for thy coming forth, verily Allah will make it easy to me, though I carry thee out in a chest." Then he left me and returned, whilst I went on, counting the doors and laying at each a bean. When I had reached the middle of the gallery, I heard a great clatter and saw the light of flambeaux coming towards me. As the light drew near me, I looked at it and behold, the Caliph himself came, surrounded by the slave-girls carrying waxen lights, and I heard one of the women[2] say to another, "O my sister, have we two Caliphs? Verily, the Caliph whose perfumes and essences I smelt, hath already passed by my room and he hath laid the bean at my door, as is his wont; and now I see the light of his flambeaux, and here he cometh with them." Replied the other, "Indeed this is a wondrous thing, for disguise himself in the Caliph's habit none would dare." Then the light drew near me, whilst I trembled in every limb; and up came an eunuch, crying out to the slaves and saying, "Hither!" Whereupon they turned aside to one of the chambers and entered. Then they came out again and walked on till they came to the chamber of my mistress and I heard the Caliph say, "Whose chamber is this?" They answered, "This is the chamber of Shajarat al-Durr." And he said, "Call her." So they called her and she came out and kissed the feet of the Caliph, who said to her, "Wilt thou drink to-night?" Quoth she, "But for thy presence and the looking on thine auspicious countenance, I would not drink, for I incline not to wine this night." Then quoth the Commander of the Faithful to the eunuch, "Bid the treasurer give her such necklace;" and he commanded to enter her chamber. So the waxen lights entered before him and he followed them into the apartment. At the same moment, behold, there came up a damsel, the lustre of whose face outshone that of the flambeau in her hand, and drawing near she said, "Who is this?" Then she laid hold of me and carrying me into one of the chambers, said to me, "Who art thou?" I kissed the ground before her, saying, "I implore thee by Allah, O my lady, spare my blood and have ruth on me and commend thyself unto Allah by saving my life!" and I wept for fear of death. Quoth she, "Doubtless thou art a robber;" and quoth I, "No. by Allah, I am no

---

[1] In sign of honour. The threshold is important amongst Moslems: in one of the Mameluke Soldans' sepulchres near Cairo I found a granite slab bearing the "cartouche" (shield) of Khufu (Cheops) with the four hieroglyphs hardly effaced.

[2] *i.e.* one of the women by whose door he had passed.

robber. Seest thou on me the signs of thieves?" Said she, "Tell me the truth of thy case and I will put thee in safety." So I said, "I am a silly lover and an ignorant, whom passion and my folly have moved to do as thou seest, so that I am fallen into this slough of despond." Thereat cried she, "Abide here till I come back to thee;" and going forth she presently returned with some of her handmaid's clothes wherein she clad me and bade me follow her; so I followed her till she came to her apartment and commanded me to enter. I went in and she led me to a couch, whereon was a mighty fine carpet, and said, "Sit down here: no harm shall befal thee. Art thou not Abu al-Hasan Ali the Khorasani, the Shroff?" I answered, "Yes," and she rejoined, "Allah spare thy blood, given thou speak truth! An thou be a robber, thou art lost, more by token that thou art dressed in the Caliph's habit and incensed with his scents. But, an thou be indeed Abu al-Hasan, thou art safe and no hurt shall happen to thee, for that thou art the friend of Shajarat al-Durr, who is my sister and ceaseth never to name thee and to tell us how she took of thee money, yet wast thou not chagrined, and how thou didst follow her to the river bank and madest sign as thou wouldst kiss the earth in her honour; and her heart is yet more aflame for thee than is thine for her. But how camest thou hither? Was it by her order or without it? She hath indeed imperilled thy life.[1] But what seekest thou in this assignation with her?" I replied, "By Allah, O my lady, 'tis I who have imperilled my own life, and my aim in foregathering with her is but to look on her and hear her pretty speech." She said, "Thou hast spoken well;" and I added, "O my lady, Allah is my witness when I declare that my soul prompteth me to no offence against her honour." Cried she, "In this intent may Allah deliver thee! Indeed compassion for thee hath gotten hold upon my heart." Then she called her handmaid and said to her, "Go to Shajarat al-Durr and say to her:—Thy sister saluteth thee and biddeth thee to her; so favour her by coming to her this night, according to thy custom, for her breast is straitened. "The slave-girl went out and presently returning, told her mistress that Shajarat al-Durr said, "May Allah bless me with thy long life and make me thy ransom! By Allah, hadst thou bidden me to other than this, I had not hesitated: but the Caliph's migraine constraineth me and thou knowest my rank with him." But the other said to her damsel, "Return to her and say:—Needs must thou come to my mistress upon a private matter between thee and her!"

---

[1] Epistasis without the prostasis, "An she ordered thee so to do:" the situation justifies the rhetorical figure.

So the girl went out again and presently returned with the damsel, whose face shone like the full moon. Her sister met her and embraced her; then said she, "Ho, Abu al-Hasan, come forth to her and kiss her hands!" Now I was in a closet within the apartment; so I walked out, O Commander of the Faithful, and when my mistress saw me, she threw herself upon me and strained me to her bosom, saying, "How camest thou in the Caliph's clothes and his ornaments and perfumes? Tell me what hath befallen thee." So I related to her all that had befallen me and what I had suffered for affright and so forth; and she said, "Grievous to me is what thou hast endured for my sake and praised be Allah who hath caused the issue to be safety, and the fulfilment of safety is thy entering my lodging and that of my sister." Then she carried me to her own apartment, saying to her sister, "I have covenanted with him that I will not be united to him unlawfully; but, as he hath risked himself and incurred these perils, I will be earth to his treading and dust to his sandals!"——And Shahrazad was surprised by the dawn of day and ceased saying her permitted say.

## Now when it was the Nine Hundred and Sixty-third Night,

She said, It hath reached me, O auspicious King, that quoth the damsel to her sister, "I have covenanted with him that I will not be united to him unlawfully; but, as he hath risked himself and incurred these perils, I will be earth for his treading and dust to his sandals!" Replied her sister, "In this intent may Allah deliver him!" and my mistress rejoined, "Soon shalt thou see how I will do, so I may lawfully foregather with him and there is no help but that I lavish my heart's blood to devise this." Now as we were in talk, behold, we heard a great noise and, turning, saw the Caliph making for her chamber, so engrossed was he by the thought of her; whereupon she took me, O Prince of True Believers, and hid me in a souterrain[1] and shut down the trap-door upon me. Then she went out to meet the Caliph, who entered and sat down, whilst she stood between his hands to serve him, and commanded to bring wine. Now the Caliph loved a damsel by name Banjah, who was the mother of Al-Mu'tazz bi 'llah;[2] but they had fallen out and

---

[1] Arab. "Sardáb," = an underground room.

[2] Thirteenth Abbaside, A.H. 252-255 (= 866-869). His mother was a Greek slave called Kabíhah (Al-Mas'udi and Al-Siyuti); for which "Banjah" is probably a clerical error. He was exceedingly beautiful and was the first to ride out

parted; and in the pride of her beauty and loveliness she would not make peace with him, nor would Al-Mutawakkil, for the dignity of the Caliphate and the kingship, make peace with her neither humble himself to her, albeit his heart was aflame with passion for her, but sought to solace his mind from her with her mates among the slave-girls. Now he loved Shajarat al-Durr's singing; so he bade her sing, when she took the lute and, tuning the strings, sang these verses :—

The world-tricks I admire betwixt me and her; * How, us parted, the World would to me incline:
I shunned thee till said they, "He knows not Love;" * I sought thee till said they, "No patience is mine!"
Then, O Love of her, add to my longing each night * And, O Solace, thy comforts for Doomsday assign!
Soft as silk is her touch and her low sweet voice * 'Twixt o'er much and o'er little aye draweth the line:
And eyne whereof Allah "Be ye!" said and they * Became to man's wit as the working of wine.

When the Caliph heard these verses, he was pleasured with exceeding pleasure, and I also, O Commander of the Faithful, was pleasured in my hiding-place, and but for the bounty of Almighty Allah, I had cried out and we had been disgraced. Then she sang also these couplets:

I embrace him, yet after him yearns my soul * For his love, but can aught than embrace be nigher?
I kiss his lips to assuage my lowe; * But each kiss gars it glow with a fiercer fire.

The Caliph was delighted and said, "O Shajarat al-Durr, ask a boon of me." She replied, "O Commander of the Faithful, I ask of thee my freedom, for the sake of the reward thou wilt obtain therein."[1] Quoth he, "Thou art free for the love of Allah;" whereupon she kissed ground before him. He resumed, "Take the lute and sing me somewhat on the subject of my slave-girl, of whom I am enamoured with warmest love: the folk seek my pleasure and I seek hers." So she took the lute and sang these two couplets :—

My charmer, who spellest my piety,[2] * On all accounts I'll woo thee, woo *thee*,
Or by humble suit which besitteth Love * Or by force more fitting my sovranty.

---

with ornaments of gold. But he was impotent in the hands of the Turks, who caused the mob to depose him and kill him—his death being related in various ways.

[1] *i.e.* The reward from Allah for thy good deed.

[2] Arab. "Nusk," a part of the Zahid's asceticism.

The Caliph admired these verses and said, "Now, take up thy lute and sing me a song setting out my case with three damsels who hold the reins of my heart and make rest depart; and they are thyself and that wilful one and another I will not name, who hath not her like.[1] So she took the lute and playing a lively measure, sang these couplets :—

Three lovely girls hold my bridle-rein * And in highest stead my heart over-reign.
I have none to obey amid all mankind * But obeying them I but win disdain :
This is done through the Kingship of Love, whereby * The best of my kingship they made their gain.

The Caliph marvelled with exceeding marvel at the aptness of these verses to his case, and his delight inclined him to reconciliation with the recalcitrant damsel. So he went forth and made for her chamber whither a slave-girl preceded him and announced to her the coming of the Caliph. She advanced to meet him and kissed the ground before him; then she kissed his feet and he was reconciled to her and she was reconciled to him. Such was the case with the Caliph; but as regards Shajarat al-Durr, she came to me rejoicing and said, "I am become a free woman by thy blessed coming! Surely Allah will help me in that which I shall contrive, so I may foregather with thee in lawful way." And I said, "Alhamdolillah!" Now as we were talking, behold her Mameluke-eunuch entered and we related to him that which had passed, when he said, "Praised be Allah who hath made the affair to end well, and we implore the Almighty to crown His favours with thy safe faring forth the palace!" Presently appeared my mistress's sister, whose name was Fátir, and Shajarat al-Durr said to her, "O my sister, how shall we do to bring him out of the palace in safety; for indeed Allah hath vouchsafed me manumission and, by the blessing of his coming, I am become a free woman." Quoth Fatir, "I see nothing for it but to dress him in woman's gear." So she brought me a suit of women's clothes and clad me therein; and I went out forthwith, O Commander of the Faithful; but, when I came to the midst of the palace, behold, I found the Caliph seated there, with the eunuchs in attendance upon him. When he saw me, he misdoubted of me with exceeding doubt, and said to his suite, "Hasten and bring me yonder handmaiden who is faring forth." So they brought me back to him and raised the veil from my face, which when he saw, he

[1] Arab. "Munázirah," the verbal noun of which, "Munázarah," may also mean "dispute." The student will distinguish between "Munazarah" and "Munafarah" = a contention for precedence in presence of an umpire.

knew me and questioned me of my case. I told him the whole truth, hiding naught, and when he heard my story, he pondered my case awhile, and going without stay or delay into Shajarat al-Durr's chamber, said to her, "How couldst thou prefer before me one of the sons of the merchants?" She kissed ground between his hands and told him her tale from first to last, in accordance with the truth; and he hearing it had compassion upon her and his heart relented to her and he excused her by reason of love and its circumstance. Then he went away and her eunuch came in to her and said, "Be of good cheer; for, when thy lover was set before the Caliph, he questioned him and he told him that which thou toldest him, word by word." Presently the Caliph returned and calling me before him, said to me, "What made thee dare to violate the palace of the Caliphate?" I replied, "O Commander of the Faithful, 'twas my ignorance and passion and my confidence in thy clemency and generosity that drave me to this." And I wept and kissed the ground before him. Then said he, "I pardon you both," and bade me be seated. So I sat down and he sent for the Kazi Ahmad ibn Abi Duwád[1] and married me to her. Then he commanded to make over all that was hers to me, and they displayed her to me[2] in her lodging. After three days I went forth and transported all her goods and gear to my own house; so everything thou hast seen, O Commander of the Faithful, in my house and whereof thou misdoubtest, is of her marriage-equipage. After this, she said to me one day, "Know that Al-Mutawakkil is a generous man and I fear lest he remember us with ill mind, or that some one of the envious remind him of us; wherefore I purpose to do somewhat that may ensure us against this." Quoth I, "And what is that?" and quoth she, "I mean to ask his leave to go the pilgrimage and repent[3] of singing." I replied, "Right is this rede thou redest;" but, as we were talking, behold, in came a messenger from the Caliph to seek her, for that Al-Mutawakkil loved her singing. So she went with the officer and did her service to the Caliph, who said to her, "Sever not thyself from us;"[4] and she

---

[1] The Mac. Edit. gives by mistake "Abú Dáúd": the Bul. correctly "Abú Duwád." He was Kázi al-Kuzát (High Chancellor) under Al-Mu'tasim, Al-Wasik bi 'llah (Vathek) and Al-Mutawakkil.

[2] Arab. "Zaffú" = they led the bride to the bridegroom's house; but here used in the sense of displaying her as both were in the palace.

[3] *i.e.* renounce the craft which though not sinful (Harám) is "Makrúh" or religiously unpraiseworthy; Mohammed having objected to music, and indeed to the arts in general.

[4] Arab. "Lá tankati'í;" do not be too often absent from us. I have noticed the whimsical resemblance of "Kat'" and our "cut;" and here the metaphorical sense is almost identical.

answered, "I hear and I obey." Now it chanced one day, after this, she went to him, he having sent for her, as was his wont; but, before I knew, she came back, with her raiment rent and her eyes full of tears. At this I was alarmed, misdoubting me that he had commanded to seize upon us, and said, "Verily we are Allah's and unto Him shall we return! Is Al-Mutawakkil wroth with us?" She replied, "Where is Al-Mutawakkil? Indeed Al-Mutawakkil's rule is ended and his trace is blotted out!" Cried I, "Tell me what hath happened;" and she, "He was seated behind the curtain, drinking, with Al-Fath bin Khákán[1] and Sadakah bin Sadakah, when his son Al-Muntasir fell upon him, with a company of the Turks,[2] and slew him; and merriment was turned to misery and joy to weeping and wailing for annoy. So I fled, I and the slave-girl, and Allah saved us." When I heard this, O Commander of the Faithful, I arose forthright and went down stream to Bassorah, where the news reached me of the falling out of war between Al-Muntasir and Al-Musta'ín bi 'llah;[3] wherefore I was affrighted and transported my wife and all my wealth to Bassorah. This, then, is my tale, O Prince of True Believers, nor have I added to or taken from it a single syllable. So all that thou seest in my house, bearing the name of thy grandfather, Al-Mutawakkil, is of his bounty to us, and the fount of our fortune is from thy noble sources;[4] for indeed ye are people of munificence and a mine of beneficence.—The Caliph marvelled at his story and rejoiced therein with joy exceeding: and Abu al-Hasan brought forth to him the lady and the children she had borne him, and they kissed ground before the Caliph, who wondered at their beauty. Then he called for inkcase and paper and wrote Abu al-Hasan a patent of exemption from taxes on his lands and houses for twenty years. Moreover, he rejoiced in him and made him his cup-companion, till the world parted them and they took up their abode in the tombs after having dwelt under palace-domes; and glory be to Allah, the King Merciful of doom. And they also tell a tale concerning

---

[1] See Ibn Khallikan, ii. 455.

[2] The Turkish body-guard.

[3] Twelfth Abbaside (A.H. 248—252 = 862—866) the son of a slave-girl Mukhárik. He was virtuous and accomplished, comely, fair-skinned, pock-marked and famed for defective pronunciation; and he first set the fashion of shortening men's capes and widening the sleeves. After many troubles with the Turks, who were now the Prætorian guard of Baghdad, he was murdered at the instigation of Al-Mu'tazz, who succeeded him, by his Chamberlain Sa'id bin Salih.

[4] Arab. "Usúl," his forbears, his ancestors.

## *KAMAR AL-ZAMAN AND THE JEWELLER'S WIFE.*[1]

THERE was once, in time of old, a merchant hight Abd al-Rahmán, whom Allah had blessed with a son and daughter, and for their much beauty and loveliness, he named the girl Kaukab al-Sabáh and the boy Kamar al-Zamán.[2] When he saw what Allah had vouchsafed the twain of beauty and loveliness, brilliancy and symmetry, he feared for them the evil eyes[3] of the espiers and the jibing tongues of the jealous and the craft of the crafty and the wiles of the wicked and shut them up from the folk in a mansion for the space of fourteen years, during which time none saw them save their parents and a slave-girl who served them. Now their father could recite the Koran, even as Allah sent it down, as also did his wife, wherefore the mother taught her daughter to read and recite it and the father his son, till both had gotten it by heart. Moreover, the twain learned from their parents writing and reckoning and all manner of knowledge and polite letters, and needed no master. When Kamar al-Zaman came to years of manhood, the wife said to her husband, "How long wilt thou keep thy son Kamar al-Zaman sequestered from the eyes of the folk? Is he a girl or a boy?" He answered, "A boy." Rejoined she, "An he be a boy, why dost thou not bear him to the bazar and seat him in thy shop, that he may know the folk and they know him, to the intent that it may become notorious among men that he is thy son, and do thou teach him to sell and to buy. Peradventure somewhat may befal thee; so shall the folk know him for thy son and he shall lay his hand on thy leavings. But, an thou die, as the case now is, and he say to the folk:—I am the son of the merchant Abd al-Rahman, verily they will not believe him, but will cry:—We have never seen thee and we knew not that he had

[1] Lane rejects this tale; but he quotes the following marginal note by his Shaykh:—"Many persons (women) reckon marrying a second time amongst the most disgraceful of actions. This opinion is commonest in the country towns and villages; and my mother's relations are thus distinguished; so that a woman of them, when her husband dieth or divorceth her while she is young, passeth in widowhood her life, however long it may be, and disdaineth to marry a second time." I fear that this state of things belongs to the good old days now utterly gone by; and the loose rule of the stranger, especially the English, in Egypt, will renew the scenes which characterised Sind when Sir Charles Napier hanged every husband who cut down an erring wife. I have elsewhere noticed the ignorant idea that Moslems deny to women souls and seats in Paradise, whilst Mohammed canonised two women in his own family.

[2] "Moon of the age," a name which has before occurred.

[3] The Malocchio or gettatura, so often noticed.

a son, wherefore the Government will seize thy goods, and thy child will be despoiled. In like manner the girl; I mean to make her known among the folk, so may be some one of her condition may ask her in marriage, and we will wed her to him and rejoice in her." Quoth he, "I did thus of my fear for them from the eyes of the folk," ——And Shahrazad perceived the dawn of day and ceased to say her permitted say.

## Now when it was the Nine Hundred and Sixty-fourth Night

She continued, It hath reached me, O auspicious King, that when the Merchant's wife spake to him in such wise, he replied, "I did thus of my fear for them from the eyes of the folk, and because I love them both, and love is jealous exceedingly, and well saith he who spoke these verses:—

Of my sight I am jealous for thee, of me, * Of thyself, of thy stead, of thy destiny:
Though I shrined thee in eyes by the craze of me * In such nearness irk I should never see:
Though wert thou by my side all the days of me * Till Doomsday I ne'er had enough of thee.

Said his wife, "Put thy trust in Allah, for no harm betideth him whom He protecteth, and carry him with thee this very day to the shop." Then she clad the boy in the costliest clothes and he became a seduction to all who on him cast sight and an affliction to the heart of every wight. His father took him and carried him to the market, whilst all who saw him were ravished with him and accosted him, kissing his hand and saluting him with the salam. Quoth one, "Indeed the sun hath risen in such a place and blazeth in the bazar;" and another, "The rising-place of the full moon is in such a quarter;" and a third, "The new moon of the Festival[1] hath appeared to the creatures of Allah." And they went on to allude to the boy in talk and call down blessings upon him. But his father scolded the folk for following his son to gaze upon him, because he was abashed at their talk, but he could not hinder one of them from talking; so he fell to abusing the boy's mother and cursing her because she had been the cause of his bringing him out. And as he gazed about he still saw the people crowding upon

---

[1] The crescent of the month Zu 'l-Ka'dah, when the Ramazan-fast is broken. This allusion is common.

him behind and before. Then he walked on till he reached his shop and opening it, sat down and seated his son before him: after which he again looked out and found the thoroughfare blocked with a press, for all the passers-by, going and coming, stopped before the shop to stare at that beautiful face and could not leave him, and all the men and women crowded in knots about him, applying to themselves the words of him who said:—

Thou madest Beauty to spoil man's sprite * And saidst, "O my servants, fear My reprove:"
But lovely Thou lovest all loveliness * How, then, shall Thy servants refrain from Love?

When the merchant Abd al-Rahman saw the folk thus gathering about him and standing in rows, both women and men, to fix eyes upon his son, he was sore ashamed and confounded and knew not what to do; but presently there came up from the end of the bazar a man of the wandering Dervishes, clad in haircloth, the garb of the pious servants of Allah, and seeing Kamar al-Zaman sitting there as he were a branch of Bán springing from a mound of saffron, poured forth copious tears and recited these two couplets:—

A wand uprising from a sandy knoll, * Like full moon shining brightest sheen, I saw;
And said, "What is thy name?" Replied he "Lúlú" * "What (asked I) Lily?" and he answered "Lá, lá?"[1]

Then the Dervish fell to walking, now drawing near and now moving away,[2] and wiping his gray hairs with his right hand, whilst the heart of the crowd was cloven asunder for awe of him. When he looked upon the boy, his eyes were dazzled and his wit confounded. Then he came up to the boy and gave him a root[3] of sweet basil, whereupon his father put forth his hand to his pouch and brought out for him some small matter of silver, saying, "Take thy portion, O Dervish, and wend thy ways." He took the dirhams, but sat down on the masonry-bench alongside the shop and opposite the boy, and fell to gazing upon him and heaving sigh upon sigh, whilst his tears flowed like springs founting. The folk began to look at him and remark upon him, saying, "All Dervishes

---

[1] This line contains one of the Yes, Yes and No, No trifles alluded to before. Captain Lockett (M. A. 103) renders it, "I saw a fawn upon a hillock whose beauty eclipsed the full moon. I said, What is thy name? she answered *Deer*. What my *Dear*, said I, but she replied, *No*, no!" To preserve the sound I have sacrificed sense: Lúlú is a pearl, Li? lí? (=for me, for me?), and Lá! Lá != no! no!

[2] Arab. "Al-huwayná," a rare term.

[3] Arab. "'Irk" = a root, which must here mean a sprig, a twig. The basil grows to a comparatively large size in the East.

are bad fellows." Now when Abd al-Rahman saw this case, he arose and said to the boy, "Come, O my son, let us lock up the shop and hie us home, for it booteth not to sell and buy this day: and may Almighty Allah requite thy mother that which she hath done with us, for she was the cause of all this!" Then said he, "O Dervish, rise, that I may shut my shop." So the Dervish rose and the merchant shut his shop, and taking his son, walked away. The Dervish and the folk followed them till they reached their place, when the boy went in, and his father, turning to the mendicant, said to him, "What wouldst thou, O Dervish, and why do I see thee weep?" He replied, "O my lord, I would fain be thy guest this night, for the guest is the guest of Almighty Allah." Quoth the merchant, "Welcome to the guest of God: enter, O Dervish!" ——And Shahrazad was surprised by the dawn of day and ceased saying her permitted say.

## Now when it was the Nine Hundred and Sixty-fifth Night,

She pursued, It hath reached me, O auspicious King, that when the merchant, the father of Kamar al-Zaman, heard the saying of the Dervish, "I am Allah's guest," he replied, "Welcome to the guest of God: enter, O Dervish!" But he said to himself, "An the beggar be thinking to cast the evil eye upon the boy, needs must I slay him this very night and bury him secretly; but, an there be no craft in him, the guest shall eat his portion." Then he brought him into a saloon, where he left him with Kamar al-Zaman, after he had said privily to the lad, "O my son, sit thou beside the Dervish when I am gone out, but if he seek to hurt thee, I, who will be watching you from the window overlooking the saloon, will come down to him and kill him." So, as soon as Kamar al-Zaman was alone in the room with the Dervish, he sat down by his side and the old man began to look upon him and sigh and weep. Whenever the lad bespake him, he answered him kindly, trembling the while and would turn to him groaning and crying, and thus he did till supper was brought in, when he fell to eating, with his eyes on the boy, but refrained not from shedding tears. When a fourth part of the night was past and talk was ended and sleep-tide came, Abd al-Rahman came and said to the Dervish, "O my brother, since thou art in such case, why dost thou weep and sigh when thou seest my son? Say me, is there a reason for this?" He replied, "There is;" and Abd al-Rahman pursued, "When I saw thee weep at his sight, I deemed evil of thee, thinking thou wouldst bewitch the lad. But now I know thee for one of those who are virtuous to the end. Now Allah upon thee, tell me the cause of thy weeping!" The Dervish sighed and said, "O my lord, chafe not a closed wound."[1] But the merchant said, "There is no help but thou tell me;" and the other began:—Know thou that I am a Dervish who wander in the lands and the countries, and take warning by the display[2] of the Creator of Night and Day. It chanced that one Friday I entered the city of Bassorah in the undurn——And Shahrazad perceived the dawn of day and ceased to say her permitted say.

## Now when it was the Nine Hundred and Sixty-sixth Night,

She resumed, It hath reached me, O auspicious King, that the Dervish said to the merchant:—Know, then, that I a wandering mendicant chanced one Friday to enter the city of Bassorah in the undurn and saw the shops open and full of all manner wares and meat and drink; but the place was deserted and therein was neither man nor woman nor girl nor boy: nor in the markets and the main streets was there dog or cat nor sounded sound nor friend was found. I marvelled at this and said to myself, "I wonder whither the people of the city be gone with their cats and dogs and what hath Allah done with them?" Now I was anhungered so I took hot bread from a baker's oven and going into the shop of an oilman, spread the bread with clarified butter and honey and ate. Then I entered the shop of a sherbet-seller and drank what I would; after which, seeing a coffee-shop open, I went in and found the pots on the fire, full of coffee;[3] but there was no one there. So I drank my fill and said, "Verily, this is a wondrous thing! It seemeth as though Death had stricken the people of this city and they had all died this very hour, or as if they had taken fright at something which befel them and fled, without having time to shut their shops." Now whilst pondering this matter, lo! I heard a sound of a band of drums beating; whereat I was afraid and hid myself for a while: then, looking out through a crevice, I saw damsels, like moons, come walking through the market, two by two, with uncovered heads and faces displayed. They were in forty pairs, thus numbering fourscore, and in their midst a young lady, riding on a horse that could hardly

---

[1] Arab. "Sákin" = quiescent, Let a sleeping hound lie.

[2] Arab. "Ásár," lit. traces, *i.e.* the works, the mighty signs and marvels.

[3] The mention of coffee now frequently occurs in this tale and in that which follows: the familiar use of it showing a comparatively late date, and not suggesting the editor's or the copyist's hand.

move his legs for that which was upon it of silvern trappings and golden and jewelled housings. Her face was wholly unveiled, and she was adorned with the costliest ornaments and clad in the richest of raiment and about her neck she wore a collar of gems and on her bosom were necklaces of gold; her wrists were clasped with bracelets which sparkled like stars, and her ankles with bangles of gold set with precious stones. The slave-girls walked before her and behind and on her right and left, and in front of her was a damsel bearing in baldric a great sword, with grip of emerald and tassels of jewel-encrusted gold. When that young lady came to where I lay hid, she pulled up her horse and said, "O damsels, I hear a noise of somewhat within yonder shop: so do ye search it, lest haply there be one hidden there, with intent to enjoy a look at us whilst we have our faces unveiled." So they searched the shop opposite the coffee-house[1] wherein I lay hid, whilst I abode in terror; and presently I saw them come forth with a man and they said to her, "O our lady, we found a man there and here he is before thee." Quoth she to the damsel with the sword, "Smite his neck." So she went up to him and struck off his head; then, leaving the dead man lying on the ground, they passed on. When I saw this, I was affrighted; but my heart was taken with love of the young lady. After an hour or so, the people reappeared and everyone who had a shop entered it; whilst the folk began to come and go about the bazars and gathered around the slain man, staring at him as a curiosity. Then I crept forth from my hiding place by stealth, and none took note of me, but love of that lady had gotten possession of my heart, and I began to enquire of her privily. None, however, gave me news of her; so I left Bassorah, with vitals yearning for her love; and when I came upon this thy son, I saw him to be the likest of all creatures to the young lady; wherefore he reminded me of her and his sight revived the fire of passion in me and kindled anew in my heart the flames of love-longing and distraction. And such is the cause of my shedding tears!" Then he wept with sore weeping till he could no more, and said, "O my lord, I conjure thee by Allah, open the door to me, so I may gang my gait!" Accordingly Abd al-Rahman opened the door and he went forth. Thus fared it with him; but as regards Kamar al-Zaman, when he heard the Dervish's story, his heart was taken with love of the lady and passion gat the mastery of him, and raged in him longing and distraction; so, on the morrow, he said to his

[1] Arab. "Al-Kahwah," the place being called from its produce. See Pilgrimage i. 317-18.

sire, "All the sons of the merchants wander about the world to attain their desire, nor is there one of them but his father provideth for him a stock-in-trade wherewithal he may travel and traffic for gain. Why, then, O my father, dost thou not outfit me with merchandise, so I may fare with it and find my luck?" He replied, "O my son, such merchants lack money; so they send their sons to foreign parts for the sake of profit and pecuniary gain and provision of the goods of the world. But I have monies in plenty, nor do I covet more: why then should I exile thee? Indeed, I cannot brook to be parted from thee an hour, more especially as thou art unique in beauty and loveliness and perfect grace and I fear for thee." But Kamar al-Zaman said, "O my father, nothing will serve but thou must furnish me with merchandise wherewithal to travel; else will I fly from thee at unawares though without money or merchandise. So, an thou wish to solace my heart, make ready for me a stock-in-trade, that I may travel and amuse myself by viewing the countries of men." Abd al-Rahman, seeing his son enamoured of travel, acquainted his wife with this, saying, "Verily, thy son would have me provide him with goods, so he may fare therewith to far regions, albeit Travel is Travail.[1]" Quoth she, "What is there to displease thee in this? Such is the wont of the sons of the merchants and they all vie one with other in glorifying globe-trotting and gain." Quoth he, "Most of the merchants are poor and seek growth of good; but I have wealth galore." She replied, "More of a good thing hurteth not; and, if thou comply not with his wish, I will furnish him with goods of my own monies. Quoth Abd al-Rahman, "I fear strangerhood for him, inasmuch as wayfare is the worst of woefare;" but she said, "There is no harm in strangerhood for him when it leadeth to gaining good; and, if we consent not, our son will go away and we shall seek him and not find him and be dishonoured among the folk." The merchant accepted his wife's counsel and provided his son with merchandise to the value of ninety thousand gold pieces, whilst his mother gave him a purse containing forty bezel-stones, jewels of price, the least of the value of one thereof being five hundred ducats, saying, "O my son, be careful of this jewellery for 'twill be of service to thee." Thereupon Kamar al-Zaman took the jewels and set out for Bassorah,——And Shahrazad was surprised by the dawn of day and ceased saying her permitted say.

---

[1] Arab. "Al-Ghurbah Kurbah:" the translation in the text is taken from my late friend Edward Eastwick, translator of the Gulistan and author of a host of works which show him to have been a ripe Oriental scholar.

## Now when it was the Nine Hundred and Sixty-seventh Night,

She said, It hath reached me, O auspicious King, that Kamar al-Zaman took the jewels and set out for Bassorah after he had laid them in a belt, which he buckled about his waist; and he stayed not till there remained naught but a day's journey between that city and himself; when the Arabs came out upon him and stripped him naked and slew his men and servants; but he lay himself down among the slain and wallowed in their blood, so that the wildlings took him for dead and left him without even turning him over and made off with their booty. When the Arabs had gone their ways, Kamar al-Zaman arose, having naught left but the jewels in his girdle, and fared on nor ceased faring till he came to Bassorah. It chanced that his entry was on a Friday and the town was void of folk, even as the Dervish had informed him. He found the market-streets deserted and the shops wide open and full of goods; so he ate and drank and looked about him. Presently, he heard a band of drums beating and hid himself in a shop, till the slave-girls came up, when he looked at them; and, seeing the young lady riding amongst them, love and longing overcame him and desire and distraction overpowered him, so that he had no force to stand. After a while, the people re-appeared and the bazars filled. Whereupon he went to the market and, repairing to a jeweller and pulling out one of his forty gems, sold it for a thousand dinars, wherewith he returned to his place and passed the night there; and when morning morrowed he changed his clothes and going to the Hammam came forth as he were the full moon. Then he sold other four stones for four thousand dinars and sauntered solacing himself about the main streets of Bassorah, clad in the costliest of clothes; till he came to a market, where he saw a barber's shop. So he went in to the barber, who shaved his head; and, picking up an acquaintance with him, the youth said to him, "O my father, I am a stranger in these parts and yesterday I entered this city and found it void of folk, nor was there in it any living soul, man nor Jinni. Then I saw a troop of slave-girls and amongst them a young lady riding in state:" and he went on to tell him all he had seen. Said the barber, "O my son, hast thou told any but me of this?" and he said, "No." The other rejoined, "Then, O my son, beware thou mention this before any but myself; for all folk cannot keep a secret, and thou art but a little lad, and I fear lest the talk travel from man to man till it reach those whom it concerneth and they slay thee. For know, O my son, that this thou hast seen, none ever kenned nor knew in any other than our city. As for the people of Bassorah they are dying of this annoy; for every Friday forenoon they shut up the dogs and cats to hinder them from going about the market-streets, and all the people of the city enter the cathedral-mosques, where they lock the doors on them,[1] and not one of them can pass about the bazar nor even look out of casement; nor wotteth any the cause of this calamity. But, O my son, to-night I will question my wife concerning the reason thereof, for she is a midwife and entereth the houses of the notables and knoweth all the city news. So Inshallah, do thou come to me to-morrow and I will tell thee what she shall have told me." With this Kamar al-Zaman pulled out a handful of gold and said to him, "O my father, take this gold and give it to thy spouse, for she is become my mother." Then he gave him a second handful, saying, "Take this for thyself." Whereupon quoth the barber, "O my son, sit thou in thy place, till I go to my wife and ask her and bring thee news of the true state of the case." So saying, he left him in the shop, and going home, acquainted his wife with the young man's case, saying, "I would have thee tell me the truth of this city-business, so I may report it to this young merchant, for he hath set his heart on weeting the reason why men and beasts are forbidden the market-streets every Friday forenoon; and methinks he is a lover, for he is open-handed and liberal, and if we tell him what he would trow, we shall get great good of him." Quoth she, "Go back and say to him:—Come, speak with thy mother, my wife, who sendeth her salam to thee and saith to thee, Thy wish is won." Accordingly he returned to the shop, where he found Kamar al-Zaman sitting awaiting him and repeated him the very words spoken by his spouse. Then he carried him in to her and she welcomed him and bade him sit down: whereupon he pulled out an hundred ducats and gave them to her, saying, "O my mother, tell me who this young lady may be." Said she:—Know, O my son, that there came a gem to the Sultan of Bassorah from the King of Hind, and he was minded to have it pierced. So he summoned all the jewellers in a body and said to them, "I wish you to drill me this jewel. Whoso pierceth it, I will give him whatsoever he shall ask; but if he break it, I will cut off his head." At this they were afraid and said, "O King of

---

[1] The fiction may have been suggested by the fact that in all Moslem cities from India to Barbary the inner and outer gates are carefully shut during the noontide devotions, *not* "because Friday is the day on which creation was finished and Mohammed entered Al-Medinah;" but because there is a popular idea that in times now approaching, the Christians will rise up against the Moslems during prayers and will repeat the "Sicilian Vespers."

the age, a jewel is soon spoilt and there are few who can pierce gems without injury, for most of them have a flaw. So do not thou impose upon us a task to which we are unable; for our hands cannot avail to drill this jewel. However, our Shaykh[1] is more experienced than we." Asked the King, "And who is your Shaykh?" and they answered, "Master Obayd: he is more versed than we in this art and hath wealth galore and of skill great store. Therefore do thou send for him to the presence and bid him pierce thee this jewel." Accordingly the King sent for Obayd and bade him pierce the jewel, imposing on him the condition aforesaid. He took it and pierced it to the liking of the King, who said to him, "Ask a boon of me, O master!" and said he, "O King of the age, allow me delay till to-morrow." Now the reason of this was that he wished to take counsel with his wife, who is the young lady thou sawest riding in procession; for he loveth her with exceeding love, and of the greatness of his affection for her, he doth naught without consulting her; wherefore he put off asking till the morrow. When he went home he said to her, "I have pierced the King a jewel and he hath granted me a boon which I deferred asking till to-morrow, that I might consult thee. Now what dost thou wish, that I may ask it?" Quoth she, "We have riches such as fires may not consume; but, an thou love me, ask of the King to make proclamation in the streets of Bassorah that all the townsfolk shall every Friday enter the mosques two hours before the hour of prayer, so none may abide in the town at all, great or small, except they be in the mosques or in the houses and the doors be locked upon them, and that every shop of the town be left open. Then will I ride with my slave-women through the heart of the city and none shall look on me from window or lattice; and everyone whom I find abroad I will kill."[2] So he went in to the King and begged of him this boon, which he granted him and caused proclamation to be made amongst the Bassorites——And Shahrazad perceived the dawn of day and ceased to say her permitted say.

## Now when it was the Nine Hundred and Sixty-eighth Night,

She continued, It hath reached me, O auspicious King, that when the Jeweller begged his boon, the King bade proclamation be made amongst the Bassorites to the effect aforesaid, but the people objected

---

[1] *i.e.* the Syndic of the Guild of Jewellers.

[2] This is an Arab Lady Godiva of the wrong sort.

that they feared for their goods from the cats and dogs; wherefore he commanded to shut the animals up till the folk should come forth from the Friday prayers. So the jeweller's wife fell to sallying forth every Friday, two hours before the time of congregational prayer, and riding in state through the city with her women; during which time none dareth pass through the market-place nor look out of casement or lattice. This, then, is what thou wouldest know and I have told thee who she is; but, O my son, was it thy desire, only to have news of her or hast thou a mind to meet her? Answered he, "O my mother, 'tis my wish to foregather with her." Quoth she, "Tell me what valuables thou hast with thee;" and quoth he, "O my mother, I have with me precious stones of four sorts, the first worth five hundred dinars each, the second seven hundred, the third eight hundred and the fourth a thousand ducats." She asked, "Art thou willing to spend four of these?" and he answered, "I am ready to spend all of them." She rejoined:—Then, arise, O my son, and go straight to thy lodging and take a bezel-gem of those worth five hundred sequins, with which do thou repair to the jewel market and ask for the shop of Master Obayd, the Shaykh of the Jewellers. Go thither and thou wilt find him seated in his shop, clad in rich clothes, with workmen under his hand. Salute him and sit down on the front shelf of his shop;[1] then pull out the jewel and give it to him, saying, "O master, take this stone and fashion it into a seal-ring for me with gold. Make it not large, a Miskál[2] in weight and no more; but let the fashion of it be thy fairest." Then give him twenty dinars and to each of his prentices a dinar. Sit with him awhile and talk with him, and if a beggar approach thee, show thy generosity by giving him a dinar, to the intent that he may affect thee, and after this, leave him and return to thy place. Pass the night there, and next morning take an hundred dinars and bring them and give them to thy father the barber, for he is poor. Quoth Kamar al-Zaman, "Be it so," and returning to his caravanserai, took a jewel worth five hundred gold pieces and went with it to the jewel-bazar. There he enquired for the shop of Master Obayd, Shaykh of the Jewellers, and they directed him thereto. So he went thither and saw the Shaykh, a man of austere aspect and robed in sumptuous raiment, with four journeymen under his hand. He addressed him with "Peace be upon you!" and the jeweller returned his greeting, and welcoming him made him sit down. Then he brought out

---

[1] This is explained in my Pilgrimage, i. 99 et seq.

[2] About three pennyweights. It varies, however, everywhere, and in Marocco the "Mezkal" as they call it is an imaginary value, no such coin existing.

the jewel and said, "O master, I wish thee to make me this jewel into a seal-ring with gold. Let it be the weight of a Miskal and no more, but fashion it excellently." Then he pulled out twenty dinars and gave them to him, saying, "This is the fee for chasing and the price of the ring shall remain."[1] and he gave each of the apprentices a gold piece, wherefore they loved him, and so did Master Obayd. Then he sat talking with the jeweller and whenever a beggar came up to him he gave him a gold piece and they all marvelled at his generosity. Now Master Obayd had tools at home, like those he had in the shop, and whenever he was minded to do any unusual piece of work, it was his custom to carry it home and do it there, that his journeymen might not learn the secrets of his wonderful workmanship.[2] His wife used to sit before him, and when she was sitting thus and he looking at her,[3] he would fashion all manner of marvellously wroughten trinkets, such as were fit for none but Kings. So he went home and sat down to mould the ring with admirable workmanship. When his wife saw him thus engaged, she asked him, "What wilt thou do with this bezel-gem?" and he answered, "I mean to make it into a ring with gold, for 'tis worth five hundred dinars." She enquired, "For whom?" and he answered, "For a young merchant, who is fair of face, with eyes that wound with desire and cheeks that strike fire and mouth like the seal of Sulaymán and cheeks like the bloom of Nuu'mán and lips red as coralline and neck like the antelope's, long and fine. His complexion is white, dashed with red, and he is well-bred, pleasant and generous, and doth thus and thus." And he went on to describe to her now his beauty and loveliness, and then his perfection and bounty, and ceased not to vaunt his charms and the generosity of his disposition, till he had made her in love with him. So she said to him, "Is aught of my charms found in him?" Said he, "He hath all thy beauties; and he is thy counterpart in qualities. Meseemeth his age is even as thine, and but that I fear to hurt thy feelings, I would say that he is a thousand times handsomer than thou art." She was silent, yet the fire of fondness was kindled in her heart. And the jeweller ceased not to talk

---

[1] *i.e.* over and above the value of the gold, etc.

[2] This was the custom of contemporary Europe, and more than one master cutler has put to death an apprentice playing Peeping Tom to detect the secret of sword-making.

[3] Among Moslems husbands are divided into three species; (1) of "Bahr," who is married for love: (2) of "Dahr," for defence against the world, and (3) of "Mahr," for marriage-settlements (money). Master Obayd was an unhappy compound of the two latter, but he did not cease to be a man of honour.

with her and to set out Kamar al-Zaman's charms before her till he had made an end of moulding the ring; when he gave it to her and she put it on her finger, which it fitted exactly. Quoth she, "O my lord, my heart loveth this ring and I long for it to be mine and will not take it from my finger." Quoth he, "Have patience! The owner of it is generous, and I will seek to buy it of him, and if he will sell it, I will bring it to thee. Or if he have another such stone, I will buy it and fashion it for thee into a ring like this."—— And Shahrazad was surprised by the dawn of day and ceased saying her permitted say.

## Now when it was the Nine Hundred and Sixty-ninth Night,

She pursued, It hath reached me, O auspicious King, that the jeweller said to his wife, "Have patience! The owner of it is generous and I will seek to buy it of him; and, if he will sell it, I will bring it to thee; or, if he have another such stone I will buy it and fashion it for thee into a ring like this." On this wise it fared with the jeweller and his wife; but as regards Kamar al-Zaman, he passed the night in his lodging and on the morrow he took an hundred dinars and carried them to the old woman, the barber's wife, saying to her, "Accept these gold pieces," and she replied, "Give them to thy father." So he gave them to the barber and she asked, "Hast thou done as I bade thee?" He answered, "Yes," and she said, "Go now to the Shaykh, the jeweller, and if he give thee the ring, put it on the tip of thy finger and pull it off in haste and say to him, O master, thou hast made a mistake; the ring is too tight. He will say, O merchant, shall I break it and mould it again larger? And do thou say, It booteth not to break it and fashion it anew. Take it and give it to one of thy slave-women. Then pull out another stone worth seven hundred dinars and say to him, Take this stone and set it for me, for 'tis handsomer than the other. Give him thirty dinars and to each of the prentices two, saying, These gold pieces are for the chasing, and the price of the ring shall remain. Then return to thy lodging for the night and on the morrow bring me two hundred ducats, and I will complete thee the rest of the device." So the youth went to the jeweller, who welcomed him and made him sit down in his shop; and he asked him, "Hast thou done my need?" "Yes," answered Obayd and brought out to him the seal-ring; whereupon he set it on his finger-tip and pulling it off in haste, cried, "Thou hast made a mistake, O master;" and threw it to him, saying, "'Tis too strait for my finger." Asked the jeweller, "O merchant, shall I make it larger?" But he answered, "Not so; take it as a gift and give it to one of thy slave-girls. Its worth is trifling, some five hundred dinars; so it booteth not to fashion it over again." Then he brought out to him another stone worth seven hundred sequins and said to him, "Set this for me: 'tis a finer gem." Moreover he gave him thirty dinars and to each of his workmen two. Quoth Obayd, "O my lord, we will take the price of the ring when we have made it."[1] But Kamar al-Zaman said, "This is for the chasing, and the price of the ring remains over." So saying, he went away home, leaving the jeweller and his men amazed at the excess of his generosity. Presently the jeweller returned to his wife and said:—O Halímah,[2] never did I set eyes on a more generous than this young man, and as for thee, thy luck is good, for he hath given me the ring without price, saying, "Give it to one of thy slave-women." And he told her what had passed, adding, "Methinks this youth is none of the sons of the merchants, but that he is of the sons of the Kings and Sultans." Now the more he praised him, the more she waxed in distraction for him. So she took the ring and put it on her finger, whilst the jeweller made another one, a little larger than the first. When he had finished moulding it, she put it on her finger, under the first, and said, "Look, O my lord, how well the two rings show on my finger! I wish they were both mine." Said he, "Patience! It may be I shall buy thee this second one." Then he lay that night and on the morrow he took the ring and went to his shop. As for Kamar al-Zaman, as soon as it was day he repaired to the barber's wife and gave her two hundred dinars. Quoth she, "Go to the jeweller and when he giveth thee the ring, put it on thy finger and pull it off again in haste, saying:—Thou hast made a mistake, O master! This ring is too large. A master like thyself, when the like of me cometh to him with a piece of work, it behoveth him to take right measure; and if thou hadst measured my finger, thou hadst not erred. Then pull out another stone worth a thousand dinars and say to him:—Take this and set it, and bestow this ring upon one of thy slave-women. Give him forty ducats and to each of his journeymen three, saying, This is for the chasing, and for the cost of the ring, that shall remain. And see what he will say. Then bring three hundred dinars and give them to thy

[1] The Mac. Edit. here is a mass of blunders and misprints.

[2] The Mac. Edit. everywhere calls her "Sabiyah" = the young lady, and does not mention her name Halimah = the Mild, the Gentle till the cmlxxivth Night. I follow Mr. Payne's example by introducing it earlier into the story, as it avoids vagueness and repetition of the indefinite.

father the barber, that he may mend his fortune withal, for he is a poor man." Answered Kamar al-Zaman, "I hear and obey," and betook himself to the jeweller, who welcomed him, and making him sit down, gave him the ring. He took it and put it on his finger; then pulled it off in haste and said, "It behoveth a master like thyself, when the like of me bringeth him a piece of work, to take his measure. Hadst thou measured my finger, thou hadst not erred; but take it and give it to one of thy slave-women." Then he brought out to him a stone worth a thousand sequins and said to him, "Take this and set it in a signet-ring for me after the measure of my finger." Quoth Obayd, "Thou hast spoken sooth and art in the right;" and took his measure, whereupon he pulled out forty gold pieces and gave them to him, saying, "Take these for the chasing and the price of the ring shall remain." Cried the jeweller, "O my lord, how much hire have we taken of thee: verily, thy bounty to us is great!" "No harm," replied Kamar al-Zaman and sat talking with him awhile and giving a dinar to every beggar who passed by the shop. Then he left him and went away, whilst the jeweller returned home and said to his wife, "How generous is this young merchant! Never did I set eyes on a more open-handed or a comelier than he; no, nor a sweeter of speech." And he went on to recount to her his charms and generosity and was loud in his praise. Cried she, "O thou lack-tact,[1] since thou notest these qualities in him, and indeed he hath given thee two seal-rings of price, it behoveth thee to invite him and make him an entertainment and entreat him lovingly. When he seeth that thou affectest him and cometh to our place, we shall surely get great good of him; and if thou grudge him the banquet do thou bid him and I will entertain him of my moneys." Quoth he, "Dost thou know me to be niggardly, that thou sayest this say?" and quoth she, "Thou art no niggard, but thou lackest tact. Invite him this very night and come not without him. An he refuse, conjure him by the divorce oath and be persistent with him." "On my head and eyes," answered he and moulded the ring till he had finished it, after which he passed the night and went forth on the morrow to his shop and sat there. On this wise it was with him; but as for Kamar al-Zaman, he took three hundred dinars and carrying them to the old wife, gave them to her for the barber, her husband. Said she, "Most like he will invite thee to his house this day; and if he do this and thou pass the night there,

[1] Arab. "Adím al-Zauk," = without savour, applied to an insipid mannerless man as "bárid" (cold) is to a fool. "Ahl Zauk" is a man of pleasure, a voluptuary, a hedonist.

tell me in the morning what befalleth thee and bring with thee four hundred dinars and give them to thy father." Answered he, "Hearing and obeying." And as often as he ran out of money, he would sell some of his stones. So he repaired to the jeweller, who rose to him and received him with open arms, greeted him heartily and sought companionship with him. Then he gave him the ring, and he found it after the measure of his finger and said to the jeweller, "Allah bless thee, O prince of artists! The setting is conformable, but the stone is not to my liking."——And Shahrazad perceived the dawn of day and ceased to say her permitted say.

## Now when it was the Nine Hundred and Seventieth Night,

She resumed, It hath reached me, O auspicious King, that Kamar al-Zaman said to the jeweller, "The setting is conformable to my wishes, but the stone is not to my liking. I have a handsomer than this: so take the seal-ring and give it to one of thy slave-women." Then he handed to him a fourth stone and an hundred dinars, saying, "Take thy hire and excuse the trouble we have given thee." Obayd replied, "O merchant, all the trouble thou hast given us thou hast requited us and hast overwhelmed us with thy great bounties: and indeed my heart is taken with love of thee and I cannot brook parting from thee. So, Allah upon thee, be thou my guest this night and heal my heart." He rejoined, "So be it; but needs must I go to my Khan, that I may give a charge to my domestics and tell them that I shall sleep abroad to-night, so they may not expect me." "Where dost thou lodge?" asked the jeweller; and he answered, "In such a Khan." Quoth Obayd, "I will come for thee there;" and quoth the other, "'Tis well." So the jeweller repaired to the Khan before sundown, fearing lest his wife should be anangered with him, if he returned home without his guest; and, carrying Kamar al-Zaman to his house, seated him in a saloon that had not its match. Halimah saw him, as he entered and was ravished with him. They talked till supper was served when they ate and drank; after which appeared coffee and sherbets, and the jeweller ceased not to entertain him with talk till eventide, when they prayed the obligatory prayers. Then entered a handmaid with two cups[1] of night drink, which when they had drunk, drowsiness overcame them and they slept. Presently in came the jeweller's

[1] Arab. "Finján," the egg-shell cups from which the Easterns still drink coffee.

wife and seeing them asleep, looked upon Kamar al-Zaman's face, and her wit was confounded at his beauty. Presently she rained down kisses on his cheeks, till the forebrow of Morn grew white and the dawn broke forth in light; when she put in his pocket four cockals[1] and went away. Then she sent her maid with something like snuff, which she applied to their nostrils and they sneezed and awoke, when the slave-girl said, "O my lords, devotion is a duty; so rise ye and pray the dawn-prayer." And she brought them basin and ewer.[2] Quoth Kaman al-Zamar, "O master, 'tis late and we have overslept overselves;" and quoth the jeweller, "O my friend, verily the air of this room is heavy; for, whenever I sleep in it, this happeneth to me." Rejoined Kamar al-Zaman, "True," and proceeded to make the Wuzu-ablution; but, when he put the water to his face, his cheeks burned. Cried he, "Prodigious! If the air of the room be heavy and we have been drowned in sleep, what aileth my cheeks that they burn me?" And he said to the jeweller, "O master, my cheeks burn me." The other replied, "I guess this cometh of the mosquito-bites." "Strange!" said Kamar al-Zaman. "Hath this thing happened to thee?" Replied Obayd, "No! But whenever I have by me a guest like thee, he complaineth in the morning of the mosquito-bites, and this happeneth only when he is like thee beardless. If he be bearded the mosquitoes sting him not, and naught hindereth them from me but my beard: it seems mosquitoes love not bearded men."[3] Rejoined Kamar al-Zaman, "True." Then the maid brought them early breakfast and they broke their fast and went out. Kamar al-Zaman betook himself to the old woman, who exclaimed, when she saw him, "Tell me what thou hast seen." Said he, "I have seen nothing. Only I supped with the house-master in a saloon and prayed the night prayer, after which we fell asleep and woke not till morning." She laughed and said, "What be those marks on thy cheeks?" He answered, "'Twas the mosquitoes of

---

[1] Arab. "Awáshik," a rare word, which Dozy translates "osselet" (or osselle) and Mr. Payne, "hucklebones," concerning which he has obliged me with this note. Chambaud renders osselet by "petit os avec lequel les enfants jouent." Hucklebone is the hip-bone, but in the plural it applies to our cockals or cockles: Latham gives "hucklebone," (or cockal), one of the small vertebræ of the os coccygis. and Littleton translates "Talus," a hucklebone, a bone to play with like a dye, a play call cockal. (So also in Rider). Hucklebones and knucklebones are syn.; but the latter is modern and liable to give a false idea, besides being tautological. It has nothing to do with the knuckles and derives from the German "Knöchel" (dialetically Knöchelein) a bonelet.

[2] For ablution after sleep and before prayer. The address of the slave-girl is perfectly natural: in a Moslem house we should hear it this day; nor does it show the least sign of forwardness."

[3] The perfect stupidity of the old fool is told with the driest Arab humour.

the saloon that did this with me;" and she rejoined, "'Tis well. But did the same thing betide the house master?" He retorted, "Nay; but he told me that the mosquitoes of that saloon molest not bearded men, but sting those only who have no hair on face, and that whenever he hath for guest one who is beardless, the stranger awaketh complaining of the mosquito-bites; whereas an he have a beard, there befalleth him naught of this." Said she, "Sooth thou speakest: but say me, sawest thou aught save this?" And he answered, "I found four cockals in my pocket." Quoth she, "Show them to me." So he gave them to her and she laughed and said, "Thy mistress laid these in thy pocket." He asked, "How so?" And she answered, "'Tis as if she said to thee, in the language of signs:[1]—An thou wert in love, thou wouldst not sleep, for a lover sleepeth not: but thou hast not ceased to be a child and fit for nothing but to play with these cockals. So what drave thee to fall in love with the fair? Now she came to thee by night and finding thee asleep, scored thy cheeks with her kisses and left thee this sign. But she will certainly send her husband to invite thee again to-night; so, when thou goest home with him, hasten not to fall asleep, and on the morrow bring me five hundred dinars and come and acquaint me with what hath passed, and I will perfect for thee the device." Answered he, "I hear and obey," and went back to the Khan. Thus it befel him; but as regards the jeweller's wife, she said to her husband, "Is the guest gone?" Answered he, "Yes: but, O Halimah,[2] the mosquitoes plagued him last night and scarified his cheeks, and indeed I was abashed before him." She rejoined, "This is the wont of the mosquitoes of our saloon; for they love none save the beardless. But do thou invite him again to-night." So he repaired to the Khan where the youth abode, and, bidding him, carried him to his house, where they ate and drank and prayed the night-prayer in the saloon, after which the slave-girl entered and gave each of them a cup of night-drink,——And Shahrazad was surprised by the dawn of day and ceased saying her permitted say.

## Now when it was the Nine Hundred and Seventy-first Night,

she said, It hath reached me, O auspicious King, that the slave-girl went in to the twain and gave each of them a cup of night-

---

[1] This is a rechauffé of the language of signs in "Aziz and Azizah."
[2] In the Mac. Edit. "Yá Fulánah" = O certain person.

drink, and they drank and fell asleep. Presently, in came Halimah and said, "O good-for-nothing, how canst thou sleep and call thyself a lover? A lover sleepeth not!" Then she kissed his cheeks, till the morning, when she put in his pocket a knife and sent her handmaid to arouse them. And when the youth awoke, his cheeks were on fire, for excess of redness. Quoth the jeweller, "Did the mosquitoes plague thee last night?" and quoth the other, "Nay!" for he now knew the deceit and left complaining. Then he felt the knife in his pocket and was silent; but when he had broken his fast and drunk coffee, he left the jeweller, and going to the Khan, took five hundred dinars of gold and carried them to the old woman, to whom he related what had passed, saying, "I slept despite myself, and when I woke at dawn I found nothing but a knife in my pocket." Exclaimed the old trot, "May Allah protect thee from her this next night! For she saith to thee by this sign, An thou sleep again, I will cut thy throat. Thou wilt once more be bidden to the jeweller's house to-night,[1] and if thou sleep, she will slay thee." Said he, "What is to be done?" and said she, "Tell me what thou atest and drankest before sleeping." Quoth he, "We supped as was our wont and prayed the night-prayer, after which there came in to us a maid, who gave each of us a cup of night-drink, which when I had drunk, I fell asleep and awoke not till the morning." Quoth the old woman, "The mischief is in the cup; so, when the maid giveth it to thee, take it from her, but drink not and wait till the master of the house have drunken and fallen asleep; then say to her, Give me a draught of water, and she will go to fetch thee the gugglet. Thereat do thou empty the cup behind the pillow and lie down and feign sleep. So when she cometh back with the gugglet, she will deem that thou hast fallen asleep after having drunk off the cup, and will leave thee; and presently the case will appear to thee; but beware of disobeying my bidding." Answered he, "I hear and I obey," and returned to the Khan. Meanwhile the jeweller's wife said to her husband, "A guest's due honour is three nights' entertainment: so do thou invite him a third time;" whereupon he betook himself to the youth, and inviting him, carried him home and sat down with him in the saloon. When they had supped and prayed the night-prayer, behold, in came the handmaid and gave each of them a cup. Her master drank and fell asleep; but Kamar al-Zaman forbore to drink, whereupon quoth the maid, "Wilt thou not drink, O my lord?" Answered he, "I am athirst, bring me the gugglet."

---

[1] Arab. "Laylat al-kábilah," lit. = the coming night; our to-night.

Accordingly she went to fetch it, and he emptied the cup behind the pillow and lay down. When the slave-girl returned, she saw him lying down and going to her mistress said, "He hath drunk off the cup and fallen asleep;" whereupon quoth Halimah to herself, "Verily, his death is better than his life." Then, taking a sharp knife, she went in to him, saying, "Three times, and thou notedst not the sign, O fool.[1] So now I will rip up thy maw." When he saw her making for him knife in hand, he opened his eyes and rose, laughing; whereupon said she, "'Twas not of thine own wit, that thou camest at the meaning of the sign, but by the help of some wily cheat; so tell me whence thou hadst this knowledge." "From an old woman," replied he, "between whom and me befel such and such;" and he told her all that had passed. Quoth she, "If thou have a mind to my company, take me a house beside thine own and we will abide thus, now I sitting with thee till the time of sleep, and now with me thou. Then I will go to my place and thou to thy Harim, and this will be a better rede than that I hinder thee from thy Harim every night. Then will my husband come to me and take counsel with me, and I will advise him to turn out our neighbour, for the house wherein he liveth is our house and he renteth it of us: and once thou art in the house, Allah will make easy to us the rest of our scheme." And presently she added, "Go now and do as I bid thee." Answered he, "I hear and obey;" whereupon she left him and went away, whilst he lay down and feigned to be asleep. Presently, the handmaid came and aroused them; and when the jeweller awoke, he said to his guest, "O merchant, have the mosquitoes worried thee?" He replied, "No," and Obayd said, "Belike thou art grown used to them." Then they broke their fast and drank coffee, after which they fared forth to their affairs, and Kamar al-Zaman betook himself to the old crone, and related to her what had passed.——And Shahrazad perceived the dawn of day and ceased to say her permitted say.

## Now when it was the Nine Hundred and Seventy-second Night,

She continued, It hath reached me, O auspicious King, that when Kamar al-Zaman betook himself to the old crone, he related to her what had passed. Quoth she, "O my son, here endeth my contrivance, and now I am at the term of my devices." Upon this he

---

[1] Arab. "Ya Ahmak," which in Marocco means a madman, a maniac, a Santon.

left her and returned to the Khan where, as eventide evened, the jeweller came to him and invited him. He said, "I cannot go with thee." Asked the merchant, "Why so? I love thee and cannot brook separation from thee: Allah upon thee, come with me!" The other replied, "An it be thy wish to continue our comradeship and keep up the friendship betwixt thee and me, take me a house by the side of thine own, and when thou wilt, thou shalt pass the evening with me and I with thee; but, as soon as the time of sleep cometh, each of us shall hie him to his own home and lie there." Quoth Obayd, "I have a house adjoining mine, which is my own property: so go thou with me to-night, and to-morrow I will have the house untenanted for thee." Accordingly he went with him and they supped and prayed the night-prayer, after which the jeweller drank the cup of drugged[1] liquor and fell asleep: but in Kamar al-Zaman's cup there was no trick; so he drank it and slept not. Then came the jeweller's wife and sat chatting with him through the dark hours, whilst her husband lay like a corpse. When he awoke in the morning as of wont, he sent for his tenant and said to him, "O man, quit me the house, for I have need of it." "On my head and eyes," answered the other, and voided the house to him, whereupon Kamar al-Zaman took up his abode therein and transported thither all his baggage. The jeweller passed that evening with him, then went to his own house. On the next day his wife sent for a cunning builder and bribed him with money to make her an underground-way[2] from her chamber to Kamar al-Zaman's house, with a trap-door under the earth. So, before the youth was ware, she came in to him with two bags of money, and he said to her, "Whence comest thou?" She showed him the tunnel and said to him, "Take these two bags of his money." Then she sat with him, when she said, "Wait for me, till I go to him and wake him, so he may fare to his shop, and I return to thee." He sat expecting her, whilst she went away and awoke her husband, who made the Wuzu-ablution and prayed and went to his shop. As soon as he was gone, she took four bags and, carrying them through the souterrain to Kamar al-Zaman, said to him, "Store these up;" then she

---

[1] Arab. "'Amal" = action, operation. In Hindostani it is used (often with an Alif for an Ayn) as intoxication, *e.g.* Amal páni (strong waters), and applied to Sharáb (wine), Bozah (beer), Tádi (toddy or the fermented juice of the Tád, *Borassus flabelliformis*), Naryáli (juice of the cocoa-nut tree), Sayndi (of the wild date, *Elate Sylvestris*), Afyún (opium and its preparations, as post = poppy seeds), and various forms of *Cannabis Sativa*, as Ganja, Charas, Madad, Sabzi, etc., for which see Herklots' Glossary.

[2] Arab. "Sardáb," mostly an underground room, but here a tunnel.

sat with him awhile, after which she retired to her home and he betook himself to the bazar. When he returned at sundown, he found in his house ten purses and jewels and much besides. Presently the jeweller came to him and carried him to his own house, where they passed the evening in the saloon, till the handmaid came in according to custom, and brought them the drink. Her master drank and fell asleep, whilst naught betided Kamar al-Zaman for that his cup was wholesome and there was no trick therein. Then came Halimah, who sat down with him, whilst the slave-girl transported the jeweller's goods to Kamar al-Zaman's house by the secret passage. Thus they did till morning, when the handmaid awoke her lord and gave them to drink coffee, after which they went each his own way. On the third day the wife brought out to him a knife of her husband's, which he had chased and wrought with his own hand, and which he priced at five hundred dinars. But there was no knife like it, and because of the eagerness with which folk sought it of him, he had laid it up in a chest and could not bring himself to sell it to anyone in creation. Quoth she, "Take this knife and set it in thy waist-shawl and go to my husband and sit with him. Then pull out the knife and say to him, O master, look at this knife I bought to-day and tell me if I have the worst or the best of the bargain. He will know it, but will be ashamed to say to thee, This is my knife; so he will ask thee, Whence didst thou buy it and for how much? and do thou make answer:—I saw two Levantines[1] disputing, and one said to the other, Where hast thou been? Quoth his companion, I have been with my love, and whenever I foregather with her, she giveth me ten dirhams; but this day she said to me, My hand is empty of silver for thee to-day, but take this knife of my husband's. So I took it and intend to sell it. The knife pleased me, and hearing his tale I said to him, Wilt thou sell it to me? when he replied, Buy. So I got it of him for three hundred gold pieces and I wonder whether it was cheap or dear. And note what my husband will say to thee. Then talk with him awhile and rise and come back to me in haste. Thou wilt find me awaiting thee at the tunnel-mouth, and do thou give me the knife." Replied Kamar al-Zaman, "I hear and I obey," and taking the knife set it in his waist-shawl. Then he went to the shop of the jeweller, who saluted him with the salam and welcomed him and made him sit down. He spied the knife in his waist-shawl, at which he wondered and said to himself, "That is my knife: who

---

[1] Arab. "Al-Láwandiyah": this and the frequent mention of coffee and presently of a watch (sá'ah) show that the tale in its present state cannot be older than the end of the sixteenth century.

can have conveyed it to this merchant?" And he fell a-musing and saying in his mind, "I wonder an it be my knife or a knife like it!" Presently Kamar al-Zaman pulled it out and said to him, "Harkye, master; take this knife and look at it." Obayd took it and knew it right well, but was ashamed to say, "This is my knife." ——And Shahrazad was surprised by the dawn of day and ceased saying her permitted say.

## Now when it was the Nine Hundred and Seventy-third Night

She pursued, It hath reached me, O auspicious King, that when the jeweller took the knife from Kamar al-Zaman, he knew it, but was ashamed to say, "This is my knife." So he asked, "Where didst thou buy it?" Kamar al-Zaman answered as Halimah had charged him, and the jeweller said, "The knife was cheap at that price, for it is worth five hundred dinars." But fire flamed in his heart and his hands were tied from working at his craft. Kamar al-Zaman continued to talk with him, whilst he was drowned in the sea of solicitude, and for fifty words wherewith the youth bespoke him, he answered him but one; for his heart ached and his frame was racked and his thoughts were troubled, and he was even as saith the poet:—

I have no words though folk would have me talk * And who bespeak me find me thought-waylaid:
Plunged in the Care-sea's undiscovered depths, * Nor aught of difference see 'twixt man and maid!

When Kamar al-Zaman saw his case thus changed, he said to him, "Belike thou art busy at this present," and leaving him, returned in hottest haste to his own house, where he found Halimah standing at the passage-door awaiting him. Quoth she, "Hast thou done as I bade thee?" and quoth he, "Yes." She asked, "What said he to thee?" and he answered, "He told me that the knife was cheap at that price, for that it was worth five hundred dinars: but I could see that he was troubled; so I left him and know not what befel him after that." Cried she, "Give me the knife and reck thou not of him." Then she took the knife and restoring it to its place, sat down. Now after Kamar al-Zaman's departure fire flamed in the jeweller's heart and suspicion was sore upon him and he said to himself, "Needs must I get up and go look for the knife and cut down doubt with certainty." So he rose and repaired to his house and went in to his wife, snorting like a dragon;[1] and she said to him, "What mattereth thee, O my lord?" He asked, "Where is my knife?" and she answered, "In the chest," and smote hand upon breast, saying, "O my grief! Belike thou hast fallen out with some one and art come to fetch the knife to smite him withal." Said he, "Give me the knife. Let me see it." But said she, "Not till thou swear to me that thou wilt not smite anyone therewith." So he swore this to her and she opened the chest and brought out to him the knife and he fell to turning it over, saying, "Verily, this is a wondrous thing!" Then quoth he to her, "Take it and lay it back in its place;" and she, "Tell me the meaning of all this." He answered, "I saw with our friend a knife like this," and told her all that had passed between himself and the youth, adding, "But, when I found it in the chest, my suspicion ended in certainty." Said she, "Haply thou misdoubtedst of me and deemedst that I was the Levantine's friend and had given him the knife." He replied, "Yes; I had my doubts of this; but, when I saw the knife, suspicion was lifted from my heart." Rejoined she, "O man, there is now no good in thee!" And he fell to excusing himself to her, till he appeased her; after which he fared forth and returned to his shop. Next day, she gave Kamar al-Zaman her husband's watch, which he had made with his own hand and whereof none had the like, saying, "Go to his shop and sit by his side and say to him:—I saw again to-day him whom I saw yesterday. He had a horologe in his hand and said to me, Wilt thou buy this watch? Quoth I, Whence hadst thou it? and quoth he, I was with my friend and she gave me this watch. So I bought it of him for eight-and-fifty gold pieces. Look at it: is it cheap at the price or dear? Note what my husband shall say to thee; then return to me in haste and give me the watch." So Kamar al-Zaman repaired to the jeweller and did with him as she had charged him. When Obayd saw the watch, he said, "This is worth seven hundred ducats;" and suspicion entered into him. Then the youth left him and returning to the wife, gave her back the watch. Presently, her husband suddenly came in snorting, and said to her, "Where is my watch?" Said she, "Here it is;" and he cried, "Give it to me." So she brought it to him and he exclaimed, "There is no Majesty and there is no Might save in Allah, the Glorious, the Great!" and she too exclaimed, "O man, there is something the matter with thee. Tell me what it is." He replied,

---

[1] Arab. "Su'bán."

"What shall I say? Verily, I am bewildered by these chances!" And he recited these couplets[1]:—

Although the Merciful be doubtless with me,
Yet am I sore bewildered, for new griefs
Have compassed me about, or ere I knew it,
I have endured till Patience self became
Impatient of my patience.—I have endured
Waiting till Heaven fulfil my destiny.—
I have endured till e'en endurance owned
How I bore up with her; (a thing more bitter
Than bitter aloes) yet though a bitterer thing
Is not, than is that drug, it were more bitter
To me should Patience leave me unsustained.

Then said he to his wife, "O woman, I saw with the merchant our friend, first my knife, which I knew, for that its fashion was a device of my own wit, nor doth its like exist; and he told me of it a story that troubled the heart: so I came back and found it at home. Again to-day I see him with the watch, whose fashion also is of my own device, nor is there the fellow of it in Bassorah, and of this also he told me a story that saddened my heart. Wherefore I am bewildered in my wit and know not what is to come to me." Quoth she, "The purport of thy speech is that thou suspectedst me of being the friend of that merchant, and eke of giving him thy good; so thou camest to question me and make proof of my perfidy; and, had I not shown thee the knife and the watch, thou hadst been certified of my treason. But since, O man, thou deemest me this ill deme, henceforth I will never again break with thee bread nor drain with thee drink, for I loathe thee with the loathing of prohibition."[2] So he gentled her and excused himself till he had appeased her, and returned, repenting him of having bespoken her thus, to his shop, where he sat——And Shahrazad perceived the dawn of day and ceased to say her permitted say.

---

[1] The lines have occurred before; when I have noted the punning "Sabr" = patience or aloes. I quote Torrens: the Templar, however, utterly abolishes the pun in the last couplet:—

The case is not at my command; but in fair Patience hand * I'm set by Him who order'th all and doth such case command.

"Amr" here = case (circumstance) or command (order) with a suspicion of reference to Murr = myrrh, bitterness. The reader will note the resignation to Fate's decrees which here and in a host of places elevates the tone of the book.

[2] *i.e.* as one loathes that which is prohibited, and with a loathing which makes it unlawful for me to dwell with thee as thy wife.

## Now when it was the Nine Hundred and Seventy-fourth Night,

She resumed, It hath reached me, O auspicious King, that when the jeweller quitted his wife, he repented having bespoken her thus, and, returning to his shop, he sat there in disquiet sore and anxiety galore, between belief and unbelief About eventide he went home alone, not bringing Kamar al-Zaman with him: whereupon quoth his wife, "Where is the merchant?" and quoth he, "In his lodgings." She asked, "Is the friendship between thee and him grown cold?" and he answered, "By Allah, I have taken a dislike to him, because of that which hath betided me from him."[1] Quoth she, "Go fetch him, to please me." So he arose and went in to Kamar al-Zaman in his house; where he saw his own goods strewn about and knew them. At this sight, fire was kindled in his heart and he fell a-sighing. Quoth the youth, "How is it that I see thee melancholy?" Obayd was ashamed to say, "Here are my goods in thy house: who brought them hither?" so he replied only, "A vexation hath betided me; but come thou with me to my house, that we may solace ourselves there." The other rejoined, "Let me be in my place: I will not go with thee." But the jeweller conjured him to come and took him to his house, where they supped and passed the evening together, Kamar al-Zaman talking with the jeweller, who was drowned in the sea of solicitude, and for a hundred words wherewith the guest bespoke him, answered him only one word. Presently, the handmaid brought them two cups of drink, as usual, and they drank; whereupon the jeweller fell asleep, but the youth abode on wake, because his cup was not drugged. Then came Halimah and said to her lover, "How deemest thou of yonder fool, who is drunken in his heedlessness and weeteth not the wiles of women? There is no help for it but that I cozen him into divorcing me. To-morrow I will disguise myself as a slave-girl and walk after thee to his shop, where do thou say to him, O master, I went to-day into the Khan of Al Yasinjíyah, where I saw this damsel and bought her for a thousand dinars. Look at her for me and tell me whether she was cheap at that price or dear. Then uncover to him my face and show me to him; after which do thou carry me back to thy house, whence I will go to my chamber by the secret passage, so I may see the issue of our affair with him." Then the twain passed the night in mirth and merriment, converse and good cheer, dalliance and delight, till dawn, when

---

[1] This is quite natural to the sensitive Eastern.

she returned to her own place and sent the handmaid to arouse her lawful lord and her lover. Accordingly they arose and prayed the dawn-prayer and brake their fast and drank coffee, after which Obayd repaired to his shop and Kamar al-Zaman betook himself to his own house. Presently, in came Halimah to him by the tunnel, in the guise of a slave-girl, and indeed she was by birth a slave-girl.[1] Then he went out and she walked behind him, till he came to the jeweller's shop and, saluting him, sat down and said, "O master, I went into the Khan of Al-Yasirjiyah to-day, to look about me, and saw this damsel in the broker's hands. She pleased me; so I bought her for a thousand dinars and I would have thee look upon her and see if she be cheap at that price or no." So saying, he uncovered her face and the jeweller saw her to be his own wife, clad in her costliest clothes, tricked out in her finest trinkets and kohl'd and henna'd, even as she was wont to adorn herself before him in the house. He knew with full knowledge her face and dress and trinkets, for those he had wrought with his own hand, and he saw on her fingers the seal-rings he had newly made for Kamar al-Zaman, whereby he was certified with entire assurance that she was indeed his very wife. So he asked her, "What is thy name, O slave-girl?" and she answered, "Halimah," naming to him her own name; whereat he was amazed and said to the youth, "For how much didst thou buy her?" He replied, "For a thousand dinars;" and the jeweller rejoined, "Thou hast gotten her gratis: for her rings and clothes and trinkets are worth more than that." Said Kamar al-Zaman, "May Allah rejoice thee with good news! Since she pleaseth thee, I will carry her to my house;" and Obayd said, "Do thy will." So he took her off to his house, whence she passed through the secret passage to her own apartment and sat there. Meanwhile, fire flamed in the jeweller's heart and he said to himself, "I will go see my wife. If she be at home, this slave-girl must be her counterpart, and glory be to Him who alone hath no counterpart! But, if she be not at home, 'tis she herself without a doubt." Then he set off running, and coming to his house, found his wife sitting in the same clothes and ornaments he had seen upon her in the shop; whereupon he beat hand upon hand, saying, "There is no Majesty and there is no Might save in Allah, the Glorious, the Great!" "O man," asked she, "art thou mad or what aileth thee? 'Tis not thy wont to do thus, and needs must it be that something hath befallen thee." Answered he, "If thou wilt have me tell thee, be not vexed." Quoth

[1] Hence, according to Moslem and Eastern theory generally, her treasonable conduct.

she, "Say on"; so he said, "Our friend the merchant hath bought a slave-girl, whose shape is as thy shape and her height as thy height; moreover, her name is even as thy name and her apparel is the like of thine apparel. Brief, she resembleth thee in all her attributes, and on her fingers are seal-rings like thy seal-rings and her trinkets are as thy trinkets. So, when he displayed her to me, methought it was thyself and I was perplexed concerning my case. Would we had never seen this merchant nor companied with him; and would he had never left his own country and we had not known him, for he hath troubled my life which before was serene, causing ill-feeling to succeed good faith and making doubt to enter into my heart." Said she, "Look in my face: belike I am she who was with him and he is my lover, and I disguised myself as a slave-girl and agreed with him that he should display me to thee, so he might lay a snare for thee." He replied, "What words are these? Indeed, I never suspected that thou wouldst do the like of this deed. Now that jeweller was unversed in the wiles of women and knew not how they deal with men, nor had he heard the saying of him who said:—

A heart bore thee off in chase of the fair, * As fled Youth and came Age wi' his hoary hair:
Laylà troubles me and love-joys are far; * And rival and risk bring us cark and care.
An would'st ask me of woman, behold I am * In physic of womankind wise and ware:
When grizzleth man's head and his moneys fail, * His lot in their love is a poor affair.

Nor that of another:[1]—

Gainsay women; he obeyeth Allah best, who saith them nay And he prospers not who giveth them his bridle-rein to sway:
For they'll hinder him from winning to perfection in his gifts, Though a thousand years he study, seeking after wisdom's way.

And a third:—

Women Satans are, made for woe of man: * To Allah I fly from such Satanesses!
Whom they lure by their love he to grief shall come * And lose worldly bliss and the Faith that blesses.

Said she, "Here am I sitting in my chamber; so go thou to him forthright and knock at the door and contrive to go into him quickly.

---

[1] These lines have occurred before: I quote Mr. Payne.

An thou see the damsel with him 'tis a slave-girl of his who resembleth me (and Glory be to Him who hath no resemblance ! [1]) But, an thou see no slave-girl with him, then am I myself she whom thou sawest with him in the shop, and thine ill thought of me will be stablished." "True," answered Obayd, and went out leaving her, whereupon she passed through the hidden passage, and seating herself by Kamar al-Zaman, told him what had passed, saying, "Open the door quickly and show me to him." Now, as they were talking, behold, there came a knocking at the door. Quoth Kamar al-Zaman, "Who is at the door?" and quoth the jeweller, "I, thy friend: thou displayedst to me thy slave-girl in the bazar, and I rejoiced for thee in her, but my joy in her was not completed; so open the door and let me look at her again." Rejoined he, "So be it," and opened the door to him, whereupon he saw his wife sitting by him. She rose and kissed their hands; and he looked at her; then she talked with him awhile and he saw her not to be distinguished from his wife in aught and said, "Allah createth whatso He will!" Then he went away more disheartened than before and returned to his own house where he saw his wife sitting, for she had foregone him thither by the souterrain.——And Shahrazad was surprised by the dawn of day and ceased saying her permitted say.

## Now when it was the Nine Hundred and Seventy-fifth Night

She said, It hath reached me, O auspicious King, that the young lady forewent her spouse by the souterrain as he fared through the door and sat down in her upper chamber; [2] so as soon as he entered she asked him, "What hast thou seen?" and he answered, "I found her with her master; and she resembleth thee." Then said she, "Off to thy shop and let this suffice thee of ignoble suspicion and never again deem ill of me." Said he, "So be it: accord me pardon for what is past." And she, "Allah grant thee grace!" [3] whereupon he kissed her right and left and went back to his shop. Then she again betook herself to Kamar al-Zaman through the underground passage, with four bags of money, and said to him, "Equip thyself at once for the road and be ready to carry off the

---

[1] This ejaculation, as the waw shows, is parenthetic; spoken either by Halimah, by Shahrazad, or by the writer.

[2] Arab. "Kasr," here meaning an upper room.

[3] To avoid saying, I pardon thee.

money without delay, against I devise for thee the device I have in mind." So he went out and purchased mules and loaded them and made ready a travelling litter; he also bought Mamelukes and eunuchs, and sending, without let or hindrance, the whole without the city, returned to Halimah and said to her, "I have made an end of my affairs." Quoth she, "And I on my side am ready; for I have transported to thy house all the rest of his moneys and treasures and have left him nor little nor much, whereof he may avail himself. All this is of my love for thee, O dearling of my heart, for I would sacrifice my husband to thee a thousand times. But now it behoveth thou go to him and farewell him saying:— I purpose to depart after three days and am come to bid thee adieu: so do thou reckon what I owe thee for the hire of the house, that I may send it to thee and acquit my conscience. Note his reply and return to me and tell me; for I can no more: I have done my best, by cozening him, to anger him with me and cause him to put me away, but I find him none the less infatuated with me. So nothing will serve us but to depart to thine own country." And quoth he, "O rare! an but dreams prove true!"[1] Then he went to the jeweller's shop and sitting down by him, said to him, "O master, I set out for home in three days' time, and am come to farewell thee. So I would have thee reckon what I owe thee for the hire of the house, that I may pay it to thee and acquit my conscience." Answered Obayd, "What talk is this? Verily, 'tis I who am indebted to thee. By Allah, I will take nothing from thee for the rent of the house, for thou hast brought down blessings upon us! However, thou desolatest me by thy departure, and but that it is forbidden to me, I would certainly oppose thee and hinder thee from returning to thy country and kinsfolk." Then he took leave of him, whilst they both wept with sore weeping, and the jeweller went with him, and when they entered Kamar al-Zaman's house, there they found Halimah who stood before them and served them: but when Obayd returned home, he found her sitting there; nor did he cease to see her thus in each house by turns, for the space of three days, when she said to Kamar al-Zaman, "Now have I transported to thee all that he hath of moneys and hoards and carpets and things of price, and there remaineth with him naught save the slave-girl, who used to come into you with the night drink; but I cannot part with her, for that she is my kinswoman and she is dear to me as a confidante. So I will beat her and be wroth with her, and

[1] A proverbial saying which here means I could only dream of such good luck.

when my spouse cometh home, I will say to him :—I can no longer put up with this slave-girl nor stay in the house with her ; so take her and sell her. Accordingly he will sell her and do thou buy her, that we may carry her with us." Answered he, "No harm in that." So she beat the girl, and when the jeweller came in he found her weeping and asked her why she wept. Quoth she, "My mistress hath beaten me." He then went in to his wife and said to her, "What hath that accursed girl done, that thou hast beaten her?" She replied, "O man, I have but one word to say to thee, and 'tis that I can no longer bear the sight of this girl ; so take her and sell her, or else divorce me." Quoth he, "I will sell her, that I may not cross thee in aught;" and when he went out to go to the shop he took her and passed with her by Kamar al-Zaman. No sooner had he gone out than his wife slipped through the underground passage to Kamar al-Zaman, who placed her in the litter, before the Shaykh her husband reached him. When the jeweller came up and the lover saw the slave-girl with him, he asked him, "What girl is this?" and the other answered, "'Tis my slave-girl who used to serve us with the night-drink ; she hath disobeyed her mistress, who is wroth with her and hath bidden me sell her." Quoth the youth, "An her mistress have taken an aversion to her, there is for her no abiding with her ; but sell her to me, that I may smell your scent in her, and I will make her handmaid to my slave Halimah." "Good," answered Obayd ; "take her." Asked Kamar al-Zaman, "What is her price?" but the jeweller said, "I will take nothing from thee, for thou hast been bountiful to us." So he accepted her from him and said to Halimah, "Kiss thy lord's hand." Accordingly she came out from the litter, and kissing Obayd's hand, remounted, whilst he looked hard at her. Then said Kamar al-Zaman, "I commend thee to Allah, O Master Obayd! Acquit my conscience of responsibility."[1] Answered the jeweller, "Allah acquit thee! and carry thee safe to thy family!" Then he bade him farewell and went to his shop weeping, and indeed it was grievous to him to part from Kamar al-Zaman, for that he had been his friend, and friendship hath its debtorship ; yet he rejoiced in the dispelling of the doubts which had befallen him anent his wife, since the young man was now gone and his suspicions had not been stablished. Such was his case ; but as regards Kamar al-Zaman, the young lady said to him, "An thou wish for safety, travel with me by other than

[1] A good old custom amongst Moslems who have had business transactions with each other: such acquittance of all possible claims will be quoted on "Judgment-Day," when debts will be severely enquired into.

the wonted way."——And Shahrazad perceived the dawn of day and ceased to say her permitted say.

## Now when it was the Nine Hundred and Seventy-sixth Night,

She continued, It hath reached me, O auspicious King, that when Halimah said to Kamar al-Zaman, "An thou wish for safety, travel with me by other than the wonted way," he replied, "Hearing and obeying;" and, taking a road other than that used by folk, fared on without ceasing from region to region till he reached the confines of Egypt-land [1] and sent his sire a letter by a runner. Now his father the merchant Abd al-Rahman was sitting in the market among the merchants, with a heart on fire for separation from his son, because no news of the youth had reached him since the day of his departure; and while he was in such case the runner came up and cried, "O my lords, which of you is called the merchant Abd al-Rahman?" They said, "What wouldst thou of him?" and he said, "I have a letter for him from his son Kamar al-Zaman, whom I left at Al-Arísh.[2]" At this Abd al-Rahman rejoiced and his breast was broadened, and the merchants rejoiced for him and gave him joy of his son's safety. Then he opened the letter and read as follows:— "From Kamar al-Zaman to the merchant Abd al-Rahman. And after. Peace be upon thee and upon all the merchants. An ye ask concerning us, to Allah be the praise and the thanks. Indeed we have sold and bought and gained and are come back in health, wealth and weal." Whereupon Abd al-Rahman opened the door [3] of rejoicing and made banquets and gave feasts and entertainments

---

[1] Arab. "Kutr (tract or quarter) Misr," vulgarly pronounced "Masr." I may remind the reader that the Assyrians called the Nile-valley "Musur," whence probably the Heb. "Misraim," a dual form denoting Upper and Lower Egypt, which are still distinguished by the Arabs into Sa'id and Misr. The hieroglyphic term is Ta-mera = Land of the Flood; and the Greek Aigyptos is probably derived from Kahi-Ptah (region of the great God Ptah) or Ma Ka Ptah (House of the soul of Ptah). The word "Copt" or "Kopt," in Egyptian "Kubti" and pronounced "Gubti," contains the same consonants.

[2] Now an unimportant frontier fort and village dividing Syria-Palestine from Egypt and famed for the French battle with the Mamelukes (Feb. 19, 1799) and the convention for evacuating Egypt. In the old times it was an important site built upon the "River of Egypt," now a dried up Wady; and it was the chief port of the then populous Najab or South Country. According to Abulfeda it derived its name (the "boothy," the nest) from a hut built there by the brothers of Joseph when stopped at the frontier by the guards of Pharaoh. But this is usual Jewish infection of history.

[3] Arab. "Báb." which may also = "chapter" or category. In Egypt "Báb" sometimes means a sepulchral cave hewn in a rock (plur. "Bibán) from the Coptic "Bib."

galore, sending for instruments of music and addressing himself to festivities after rarest fashion. When Kamar al-Zaman came to Al-Sálihiyah,[1] his father and all the merchants went forth to meet him, and Abd al-Rahman embraced him and strained him to his bosom and sobbed till he swooned away. When he came to himself he said, "Oh 'tis a boon day, O my son, whereon the Omnipotent Protector hath reunited us with thee!" ..d he repeated the words of the bard:—

The return of the friend is the best of all boons, * And the joy-cup circles o' morns and noons:
So well come, welcome, fair welcome to thee * The light of the time and the moon o' full moons.

Then, for excess of joy, he poured forth a flood of tears rom his eyes and he recited also these two couplets:—

The Moon o' the Time,[2] shows unveilèd light; * And his journey done, at our door doth alight:
His locks as the nights of his absence are black * And the sun upstands from his collar's[3] white.

Then the merchants came up to him and saluting him, saw with him many loads and servants and a travelling litter enclosed in a spacious circle.[4] So they took him and carried him home; and when Halimah came forth from the litter, his father held her a seduction to all who beheld her. Presently they opened her an upper chamber, as it were a treasure from which the talismans had been loosed:[5] and when his mother saw her, she was ravished with her and deemed her a queen of the wives of the Kings. So she rejoiced in her and questioned her; and she answered, "I am wife to thy son;" and the mother rejoined, "Since he is wedded to thee we must make thee a splendid marriage-feast, that we may rejoice in thee and in my son." On this wise it befel her; but as regards

---

[1] *i.e.* "The Holy," a town some three marches (60 miles) N. East of Cairo; thus showing the honour done to our unheroic hero. There is also a Sálihiyah quarter or suburb of Damascus famous for its cemetery of holy men; but the facetious Cits change the name to Zálliniyah = causing to stray; in allusion to its Kurdish population. Baron von Hammer reads "le faubourg Adelieh" built by Al-Malik Al-Adil and founds a chronological argument on a clerical error.

[2] Kamar al-Zaman; the normal pun on the name; a practice as popular in the East as in the West, and worthy only of a pickpocket in either place.

[3] Arab. "Azrár," plur. of "Zirr," and lit. = "buttons," *i.e.* of his robe collar, from which his white neck and face appear shining as the sun.

[4] Arab. "Dáirah": the usual enclosure of Kanáts or tent-flaps pitched for privacy during the halt.

[5] *i.e.* it was so richly ornamented that it resembled an enchanted hoard whose spells, hiding it from sight, had been broken by some happy treasure seeker.

the merchant Abd al-Rahman, when the folk had dispersed and each had wended his way, he foregathered with his son and said to him, "O my son, what is this slave-girl thou hast brought with thee and for how much didst thou buy her?"[1] Kamar al-Zaman said, "O my father, she is no slave-girl; but 'tis she who was the cause of my going abroad." Asked his sire, "How so?" and he answered, "'Tis she whom the Dervish described to us the night he lay with us; for indeed my hopes clave to her from that moment and I sought not to travel save on account of her. The Arabs came out upon me by the way and stripped me and took my money and goods, so that I entered Bassorah alone, and there befel me there such and such things;" and he went on to relate to his parent all that had befallen him from commencement to conclusion. Now when he had made an end of his history, his father said to him, "O my son, and after all this didst thou marry her?" "No; but I have promised her marriage." "Is it thine intent to marry her?" "An thou bid me marry her, I will do so; otherwise I will not marry her." Thereupon quoth his father, "An thou marry her, I am quit of thee in this world and in the next, and I shall be incensed against thee with sore indignation. How canst thou wed her, seeing that she hath dealt thus with her husband? For, even as she did with her spouse for thy sake, so will she do the like with thee for another's sake, because she is a traitress and in a traitor there is no trusting. Wherefore an thou disobey me, I shall be wroth with thee; but, an thou give ear to my word, I will seek thee out a girl handsomer than she, who shall be pure and pious, and marry thee to her, though I spend all my substance upon her; and I will make thee a wedding without equal and will glory in thee and in her: for 'tis better that folk should say, Such-an-one hath married Such-an-one's daughter, than that they say, He hath wedded a slave-girl sans birth or worth." And he went on to persuade his son to give up marrying her, by citing in support of his say, proofs, stories, examples, verses and moral instances, till Kamar al-Zaman exclaimed, "O my father, since the case is thus, 'tis not right and proper that I marry her." And when his father heard him speak on such wise, he kissed him between the eyes saying, "Thou art my very son, and as I live, O my son, I will assuredly marry thee to a girl who hath not her equal!" Then the merchant set Obayd's wife and her handmaid in a chamber high up

[1] The merchant, who is a "stern parient" and exceedingly ticklish on the Pundonor, saw at first sight her servile origin, which had escaped the mother. Usually it is the other way.

in the house, and before locking the door upon the twain, he appointed a black slave-girl to carry them their meat and drink, and he said to Halimah, "Ye shall abide imprisoned in this chamber, thou and thy maid, till I find one who will buy you, when I will sell you to him. An ye resist, I will slay you both, for thou art a traitress, and there is no good in thee." Answered she, "Do thy will: I deserve all thou canst do with me." Then he locked the door upon them and gave his Harim a charge respecting them, saying, "Let none go up to them nor speak to them, save the black slave-girl who shall give them their meat and drink through the casement of the upper chamber." So she abode with her maid, weeping and repenting her of that which she had done with her spouse. Meanwhile Abd al-Rahman sent out the marriage-brokers to look out a maid of birth and worth for his son, and the women ceased not to make search, and as often as they saw one girl, they heard of a fairer than she, till they came to the house of the Shaykh al-Islam [1] and saw his daughter. In her they found a virgin whose equal was not in Cairo for beauty and loveliness, symmetry and perfect grace, and she was a thousand-fold handsomer than the wife of Obayd. So they told Abd al-Rahman of her, and he and the notables repaired to her father and sought her in wedlock of him. Then they wrote out the marriage contract and made her a splendid wedding; after which Abd al-Rahman gave bride-feasts and held open house forty days. On the first day he invited the doctors of the law, and they held a splendid nativity;[2] and on the morrow he invited all the merchants, and so on during the rest of the forty days, making a banquet every day to one or other class of folk, till he had bidden all the Olema and Emirs and Antients [3] and Magistrates, whilst the kettle-drums were drummed and the pipes were piped and the merchant sat to greet the guests, with his son by his side, that he might solace himself by gazing on the folk, as they ate from the

---

[1] Not the head of the Church, or Chief Pontiff, but the Chief of the Olema and Fukahá (Fákihs or D.D.'s), men learned in the Law (divinity). The order is peculiarly Moslem and the title shows the modern date of the tale.

[2] Arab. "Maulid," prop. applied to the Birth-feast of Mohammed, which begins on the 3rd day of Rabí al-Awwal (third Moslem month) and lasts a week or ten days (according to local custom), usually ending on the 12th and celebrated with salutes of cannon, circumcision-feasts, marriage-banquets, Zikr-litanies, perlections of the Koran and all manner of solemn festivities, including the "powder-play" (Láb al-Bárút) in the wilder corners of Al-Islam. It is also applied to the birth-festivals of great Santons (as Ahmad al-Badawi), for which see Lane M. E. chapt. xxiv. In the text it is used like the Span. "Funcion" or the Hind "Tamáshá," any great occasion of merry-making.

[3] Arab. "Sanájik," plur. of Sanjak (Turk.) = a banner, also applied to the bearer (ensign or cornet) and to a military rank mostly corresponding with Bey or Colonel.

trays. Each night Abd al-Rahman illuminated the streets and the quarter with lamps, and there came every one of the mimes and jugglers and mountebanks and played all manner play; and indeed it was a peerless wedding. On the last day he invited the Fakirs, the poor and the needy, far and near, and they flocked in troops and ate, whilst the merchant sat, with his son by his side.[1] And among the paupers, behold, entered Shaykh Obayd the jeweller, and he was naked and weary and bare on his face the marks of wayfare. When Kamar al-Zaman saw him, he knew him and said to his sire, "Look, O my father, at yonder poor man who is but now come in by the door." So he looked and saw him clad in worn clothes and on him a patched gown[2] worth two dirhams: his face was yellow and he was covered with dust and was as he were an offcast of the pilgrims.[3] He was groaning as groaneth a sick man in need, walking with a tottering gait and swaying now to the right and then to the left, and in him was realized his saying who said[4]:—

Lack-gold abaseth man and doth his worth away, Even as the setting sun that pales with ended day.
He passeth 'mongst the folk and fain would hide his head; And when alone, he weeps with tears that never stay.
Absent, none taketh heed to him or his concerns; Present, he hath no part in life or pleasance aye.
By Allah, whenas men with poverty are cursed, But strangers midst their kin and countrymen are they!

And the saying of another:—

The poor man fares by everything opposed: * On him to shut the door Earth ne'er shall fail:
Thou seest men abhor him sans a sin, * And foes he finds albe no cause avail:
The very dogs, when sighting wealthy man, * Fawn at his feet and wag the flattering tail;
Yet, an some day a pauper loon they sight, * All at him bark and, gnashing fangs, assail.

——And Shahrazad was surprised by the dawn of day and ceased saying her permitted say.

---

[1] I have followed Mr. Payne's ordering of the text, which, both in the Mac. and Bul. Edits., is wholly inconsequent and has not the excuse of rhyme.

[2] Arab. "Jilbáb," a long coarse veil or gown which in Barbary becomes a "Jallábiyah," a striped and hooded cloak of woollen stuff.

[3] *i.e.* a broken down pilgrim left to die on the road.

[4] These lines have occurred before. I quote Mr. Payne.

## Now when it was the Nine Hundred and Seventy-seventh Night

She pursued, It hath reached me, O auspicious King, that when his son said to Abd al-Rahman, "Look at yonder pauper!" he asked, "O my son, who is this?" And Kamar al-Zaman answered, "This is Master Obayd the jeweller, husband to the woman who is imprisoned with us." Quoth Abd al-Rahman, "Is this he of whom thou toldest me?" and quoth his son, "Yes; and indeed I wot him right well." Now the manner of Obayd's coming thither was on this wise. When he had farewelled Kamar al-Zaman he went to his shop, and thence going home laid his hand on the door, whereupon it opened and he entered and found neither his wife nor the slave-girl, but saw the house in sorriest plight, quoting in mute speech his saying who said:[1]—

The chambers were like a bee-hive well stocked: when their bees quitted it, they became empty.

When he saw the house void, he turned right and left and presently went round about the place, like a madman, but came upon no one. Then he opened the door of his treasure-closet, but found therein naught of his money nor his hoards; whereupon he recovered from the intoxication of fancy and shook off his infatuation and knew that it was his wife herself who had turned the tables upon him and outwitted him with her wiles. He wept for that which had befallen him, but kept his affairs secret, so none of his foes might crow over him nor any of his friends be concerned, knowing that, if he disclosed his secret, it would bring him naught but dishonour and contumely from the folk; wherefore he said in himself, "O Obayd, hide that which hath betided thee of affliction and ruination; it behoveth thee to do in accordance with his saying who said:—

If a man's breast with bane he hides be straitenèd, * The breast that tells its hidden bale is straiter still.

Then he locked up his house and, making for his shop, gave it in charge of one of his apprentices, to whom said he, "My friend the young merchant hath invited me to accompany him to Cairo, for solacing ourselves with the sight of the city, and sweareth that he will not march except he carry us with him, me and my wife. So, O my son, I make thee my steward in the shop, and if the King ask for me, say thou to him:—He is gone with his Harim

[1] These lines have occurred in Night dcxix, where the pun on Khaliyah is explained. I quote Lane.

to the Holy House of Allah."[1] Then he sold some of his effects and bought camels and mules and Mamelukes, together with a slave-girl,[2] and placing her in a litter, set out from Bassorah after ten days. His friends farewelled him and none doubted but that he had taken his wife and gone on the Pilgrimage, and the folk rejoiced in this, for that Allah had delivered them from being shut up in the mosques and houses every Friday. Quoth some of them, "Allah grant he may never return to Bassorah, so we may no more be boxed up in the mosques and houses every Friday, for that this usage had caused the people of Bassorah exceeding vexation!" Quoth another, "Methinks he will not return from his journey, by reason of the much-praying of the people of Bassorah against him."[3] And yet another, "An he return, 'twill not be but in reversed case."[4] So the folk rejoiced with exceeding joy in the jeweller's departure, after they had been in mighty great chagrin, and even their cats and dogs were comforted. When Friday came round, however, the crier proclaimed as usual that the people should repair to the mosques two hours before prayer-time or else hide themselves in their houses, together with their cats and dogs; whereat their breasts were straitened and they assembled in general assembly and, betaking themselves to the royal divan, stood between his hands and said, "O King of the age, the jeweller hath taken his Harim and departed on the pilgrimage to the Holy House of Allah: so the cause of our restraint hath ceased to be, and why therefore are we now shut up?" Quoth the King, "How came this traitor to depart without telling me? But, when he cometh back from his journey, all will not be save well;[5] so go ye to your shops and sell and buy, for this vexation is removed from you." Thus far concerning the King and the Bassorites; but as for the jeweller, he fared on ten days' journey, and, as he drew near Baghdad, there befel him that which had befallen Kamar al-Zaman, before his entering Bassorah; for the Arabs[6] came out upon

---

[1] The usual pretext of "God-bizness," as the Comoro men call it. For the title of the Ka'abah see my Pilgrimage vol. iii. 149.

[2] This was in order to travel as a respectable man; he could also send the girl as a spy into the different Harims to learn news of the lady who had eloped.

[3] A polite form of alluding to their cursing him.

[4] *i.e.* on account of the King taking offence at his unceremonious departure.

[5] *i.e.* It will be the worse for him.

[6] I would here remind the reader that "'Arabiyyun," pl. 'Urb, is a man of pure Arab race, whether of the Ahl al-Madar (= people of mortar, *i.e.* citizens) or Ahl al-Wabar (= tents of goat or camel's hair); whereas "A'rábiyyun," pl. A'ráb, is one who dwells in the desert, whether Arab or not. Hence the verse:—

They name us Al-A'ráb, but Al-'Urb is our name.

him and stripped him and took all he had, and he escaped only by feigning himself dead. As soon as they were gone, he rose and fared on, naked as he was, till he came to a village, where Allah inclined to him the hearts of certain kindly folk, who covered his body with some old clothes; and he asked his way, begging from town to town, till he reached the city of Cairo the God-guarded. There, burning with hunger, he went about alms-seeking in the market-streets, till one of the townsfolk said to him, "O poor man, off with thee to the house of the wedding-festival and eat and drink; for to-day there is open table for paupers and strangers." Quoth he, "I know not the way thither;" and quoth the other, "Follow me and I will show it to thee." He followed him till he brought him to the house of Abd al-Rahman, and said to him, "This is the house of the wedding; enter and fear not, for there is no door-keeper at the door of the festival." Accordingly he entered and Kamar al-Zaman knew him and told his sire, who said, "O my son, leave him at this present: belike he is anhungered; so let him eat his sufficiency and recover himself and after we will send for him." Accordingly they waited till Obayd had eaten his fill and washed his hands and drunk coffee and sherbets of sugar flavoured with musk and ambergris and was about to go out, when Abd al-Rahman sent after him a page, who said to him, "Come, O stranger, and speak with the merchant Abd al-Rahman." "Who is he?" asked Obayd; and the man answered, "He is the master of the feast." Thereupon the jeweller turned back, thinking that he meant to give him a gift, and coming up to Abd al-Rahman, saw his friend Kamar al-Zaman and went nigh to lose his senses for shame before him. But Kamar al-Zaman rose to him and, embracing him, saluted him with the salam, and they both wept with sore weeping. Then he seated him by his side, and Abd al-Rahman said to his son, "O destitute of good taste, this is no way to receive friends! Send him first to the Hammam and despatch after him a suit of clothes of the choicest, worth a thousand dinars."[1] Accordingly they carried

---

[1] I would remind the reader that the Dinár is the golden denarius (or solidus) of Eastern Rome, while the Dirham is the silver denarius, whence denier, danaro, dinheiro, etc., etc. The oldest dinars date from A.H. 91-92 (= 714-15), and we find the following description of one struck in A.H. 96 by Al-Walid the Sixth Ommiade:—

Obverse.
- Area. "There is no iláh but Allah: He is one: He hath no partner."
- Circle. "Mohammed is the Messenger of Allah, who hath sent him with the true Guidance and Religion that he manifest it above all other Creeds."

Reverse.
- Area. "Allah is one: Allah is Eternal: He begetteth not, nor is He begot."
- Circle. "Bismillah: This dinar was struck anno Heg. 96.

him to the bath, where they washed his body and clad him in a costly suit, and he became as he were Consul of the Merchants. Meanwhile the bystanders questioned Kamar al-Zaman of him, saying, "Who is this and whence knowest thou him?" Quoth he, "This is my friend, who lodged me in his house and to whom I am indebted for favours without number, for that he entreated me with exceeding kindness. He is a man of competence and condition and by trade a jeweller, in which craft he hath no equal. The King of Bassorah loveth him dearly and holdeth him in high honour and his word is law with him." And he went on to enlarge before them on his praises, saying, "Verily, he did with me thus and thus and I have shame of him and know not how to requite him his generous dealing with me." Nor did he leave to extol him, till his worth was magnified to the bystanders and he became venerable in their eyes; so they said, "We will all do him his due and honour him for thy sake. But we would fain know the reason why he hath departed his native land and the cause of his coming hither, and what Allah hath done with him that he is reduced to this plight?" Replied Kamar al-Zaman, "O folk, marvel not, for a son of Adam is still subject to Fate and Fortune, and what while he abideth in this world, he is not safe from calamities. Indeed he spake truly who said these couplets:—

The world tears man to shreds, so be thou not * Of those whom lure of rank and title draws :
Nay ; 'ware of slips and turn from sin aside * And ken that bane and bale are worldly laws :
How oft high Fortune falls by least mishap * And all things bear inbred of Change a cause !

Know that I entered Bassorah in yet iller case and worse distress than this man, for that he entered Cairo with his shame hidden by rags; but I indeed came into his town with my nakedness uncovered, one hand behind and another before; and none availed me but Allah and this dear man. Now the reason of this was that the Arabs stripped me and took my camels and mules and loads and slaughtered my pages and serving-men; but I lay down among the slain and they thought that I was dead, so they went away and left me. Then I arose and walked on, mother-naked, till

---

See "'Ilâm-en-Nas" (Warnings for Folk), a pleasant little volume by Mrs. Godfrey Clarke (London, King and Co., 1873), mostly consisting of the minor tales from The Nights, especially this group between Nights ccxlvii. and cdlxi.; but rendered valuable by the annotations of my old friend, the late Frederick Ayrton.

I came to Bassorah where this man met me and clothed me and lodged me in his house; he also furnished me with money, and all I have brought back with me I owe to none save to Allah's goodness and his goodness. When I departed, he gave me great store of wealth and I returned to the city of my birth with a heart at ease. I left him in competence and condition, and haply there hath befallen him some bale of the banes of Time, that hath forced him to quit his kinsfolk and country, and there happened to him by the way the like of what happened to me. There is nothing strange in this; but now it behoveth me to requite him his noble dealing with me and do according to the saying of him who saith :—

O who praisest Time with the fairest appraise, * Knowest thou what Time hath made and unmade?
What thou dost at least be it kindly done,[1] * For with pay he pays shall man be repaid.

As they were talking and telling the tale, behold, up came Obayd as he were Consul[2] of the Merchants; whereupon they all rose to salute him and seated him in the place of honour. Then said Kamar al-Zaman to him, "O my friend, verily, thy day[3] is blessed and fortunate! There is no need to relate to me a thing that befel me before thee. If the Arabs have stripped thee and robbed thee of thy wealth, verily our money is the ransom of our bodies, so let not thy soul be troubled; for I entered thy city naked and thou clothedst me and entreatedst me generously, and I owe thee many a kindness. But I will requite thee——And Shahrazad perceived the dawn of day and ceased to say her permitted say.

## Now when it was the Nine Hundred and Seventy-eighth Night,

She resumed, It hath reached me, O auspicious King, that Kamar al-Zaman said to Master Obayd the jeweller, "Verily I entered thy city naked and thou clothedst me and I owe thee many a kindness. But I will requite thee and do with thee even as thou didst with me; nay, more: so be of good cheer and eyes clear of tear." And he went on to soothe him and hinder him from speech, lest he should name his wife and what she had done with him; nor did he

---

[1] The reader will note the persistency with which the duty of universal benevolence is preached.
[2] Arab. from Pers. "Shah-bandar."
[3] *i.e.* of thy coming, a popular compliment.

cease to ply him with saws and moral instances and verses and conceits and stories and legends and console him, till the jeweller saw his drift and took the hint and kept silence concerning the past, diverting himself with the tales and rare anecdotes he heard and repeating in himself these lines:—

On the brow of the World is a writ; an thereon thou look, * Its contents will compel thine eyes tears of blood to rain:
For the World never handed to humans a cup with right, * But with left it compelled them a beaker of ruin to drain.

Then Kamar al-Zaman and his father took Obayd and carrying him into the saloon of the Harim, shut themselves up with him; and Abd al-Rahman said to him, "We did not hinder thee from speaking before the folk, but for fear of dishonour to thee and to us: but now we are private; so tell me all that hath passed between thee and thy wife and my son." So he told him all, from beginning to end, and when he had made an end of his story, Abd al-Rahman asked him, "Was the fault with my son or with thy wife?" He answered, "By Allah, thy son was not to blame, and the fault lieth with my wife." Then Abd al-Rahman arose and taking his son aside, said to him, "O my son, we have proved his wife and know her to be a traitress; and now I mean to prove him and see if he be a man of honour and manliness, or a fool." "How so?" asked Kamar al-Zaman; and Abd al-Rahman answered, "I mean to urge him to make peace with his wife, and if he consent thereto and forgive her, I will smite him with a sword and slay him and kill her after, her and her maid, for there is no good in the life of a fool and a quean;[1] but, if he turn from her with aversion I will marry him to thy sister and give him more of wealth than that thou tookest from him." Then he went back to Obayd and said to him, "O master, verily the way of women requireth patience and magnanimity, and whoso loveth them hath need of fortitude, for that they order themselves viper-wise towards men and evilly entreat them, by reason of their superiority over them in beauty and loveliness: wherefore they magnify themselves and belittle men. This is notably the case when their husbands show them affection; for then they requite them with hauteur and coquetry and harsh dealing of all kinds. But, if a man be wroth whenever he seeth in his wife aught that offendeth him, there can be no fellowship between them; nor can any hit it off with them who is not

---

[1] This is taking the law into one's own hands with a witness; yet amongst races who preserve the Pundonor in full and pristine force, *e.g.* the Afghans and the Persian Ilyát, the killing, so far from being considered murder or even justifiable homicide, would be highly commended by public opinion.

magnanimous and long-suffering; and unless a man bear with his wife and requite her faults with forgiveness, he shall get no good of her conversation. Indeed, it hath been said of them:—Were they in the sky, the necks of men would incline themwards; and he who hath the power and pardoneth, his reward is with Allah. Now this woman is thy wife and thy companion and she hath long consorted with thee; wherefore it behoveth that thou entreat her with indulgence which in fellowship is of the essentials of success. Furthermore, women fail in wit and Faith,[1] and if she have sinned she repenteth, and Inshallah she will not again return to that which she whilome did. So 'tis my rede that thou make peace with her and I will restore thee more than the good she took; and if it please thee to abide with me, thou art welcome, thou and she, and ye shall see naught but what shall joy you both; but, an thou seek to return to thine own land I will send thee. For that which falleth out between a man and his wife is manifold, and it behoveth thee to be indulgent and not take the way of the violent." Said the jeweller, "O my lord, and where is my wife?" and said Abd al-Rahman, "She is in that upper chamber, go up to her and be easy with her for my sake, and trouble her not; for, when my son brought her hither, he would have married her, but I forbade him from her and shut her up in yonder room, and locked the door upon her, saying in myself:—Haply her husband will come and I will hand her over to him safe; for she is fair of favour; and when a woman is like unto this one, it may not be that her husband will let her go. What I counted on is come about and praised be Allah Almighty for thy reunion with thy wife! As for my son, I have sought him another woman in marriage and have married him to her: these banquets and rejoicings are for his wedding, and to-night I bring him to his bride. So here is the key of the chamber where thy wife is: take it and open the door and go to her." Cried Obayd, "May Allah requite thee for me with all good, O my lord!" and taking the key, went up, rejoicing. The other thought his words had pleased him and that he consented thereto; so he took the sword and following him unseen, stood to espy what should happen between him and his wife. This is how it fared with the merchant Abd al-Rahman; but as for the jeweller, when he came to the chamber-door, he heard his wife weeping with sore weeping for that Kamar al-Zaman had married another than her, and the handmaid saying to her, "O my lady, how

---

[1] Arab. "Nákisátu 'aklin wa dín": the words are attributed to the Prophet, whom we find saying, "Verily in your wives and children ye have an enemy, wherefore beware of them" (Koran lxiv. 14): compare 1 Cor. vii. 28, 32.

often have I warned thee and said, Thou wilt get no good of this youth: so do thou leave his company. But thou heededst not my words and spoiledst thy husband of all his goods and gavest them to him. After the which thou forsookest thy place, of thy fondness and infatuation for him, and camest with him to this country. And now he hath cast thee out from his thought and married another and hath made the issue of thy foolish fancy for him to be durance vile." Cried Halimah, "Be silent, O accursed! Though he be married to another, yet some day needs must I recur to his thought. I cannot forget the time I have spent in his company and in any case I console myself with his saying who said:—

O my lords, shall he to your mind occur * Who recurs to you only sans other mate?
Grant Heaven you ne'er shall forget his state * Who for state of you forgot own estate!

It cannot be but he will bethink him of my affect and converse and ask for me, wherefore I will not turn from loving him nor change from passion for him, though I perish in prison; for he is my love and my leach,[1] and my reliance is on him that he will yet return to me and deal fondly with me." When the jeweller heard his wife's words, he went in to her and said to her, "O traitress, thy hope in him is as the hope of Iblis,[2] in Heaven. All these vices were in thee and I knew not thereof; for, had I been ware of one single vice, I had not kept thee with me an hour. But now I am certified of this in thee, it behoveth me to do thee die, although they put me to death for thee, O traitress!" and he clutched her with both hands and repeated these two couplets:—

O fair ones forth ye cast my faithful love * With sin, nor had ye aught regard for right:
How long I fondly clung to you, but now * My love is loathing and I hate your sight.

Then he pressed hardly upon her windpipe and brake her neck,

---

[1] Arab. "Habíbí wa tabíbí," the common jingle.

[2] Iblis and his connection with Diabolos has been noticed. The word is foreign as well as a P.N. and therefore is imperfectly declined, although some authorities deduce it from "ablasa" = he despaired (of Allah's mercy). Others call him Al-Háris (the Lion), hence Eve's first-born was named in his honour Abd al-Haris. His angelic name was Azázíl before he sinned by refusing to prostrate himself to Adam, as Allah had commanded the heavenly host for a trial of faith, not to worship the first man, but to make him a Kiblah or direction of prayer addressed to the Almighty. Hence Iblis was ejected from Heaven and became the arch-enemy of mankind (Koran xviii. 48). He was an angel but related to the Jinn: Al-Bayzáwi, however (on Koran ii. 82), opines that angelic by nature he became a Jinn by act.

whereupon her handmaid cried out "Alas, my mistress!" Said he, "O wretch, 'tis thou who art to blame for all this, for that thou knewest this evil inclination to be in her and toldest me not." Then he seized upon her and strangled her. All this happened while Abd al-Rahman stood, brand in hand, behind the door espying with his eyes and hearing with his ears. Now when Obayd the jeweller had done this, apprehension came upon him and he feared the issue of his affair and said to himself, "As soon as the merchant learneth that I have killed them in his house, he will surely slay me; yet I beseech Allah that He appoint the taking of my life to be while I am in the True Belief!" And he abode bewildered about his case and knew not what to do; but, as he was thus, behold, in came Abd al-Rahman from his lurking-place without the door and said to him, "No harm shall befal thee, for indeed thou deservest safety. See this sword in my hand. 'Twas in my mind to slay thee, hadst thou made peace with her and restored her to favour, and I would also have slain her and the maid. But since thou hast done this deed, welcome to thee and again welcome! And I will reward thee by marrying thee to my daughter, Kamar al-Zaman's sister." Then he carried him down and sent for the woman who washed the dead: whereupon it was bruited abroad that Kamar al-Zaman had brought with him two slave-girls from Bassorah and that both had deceased. So the people began to condole with him saying, "May thy head live!" and "May Allah compensate thee!" And they washed and shrouded them and buried them, and none knew the truth of the matter. Then Abd al-Rahman sent for the Shaykh al-Islam and all the notables and said, "O Shaykh, draw up the contract of marriage between my daughter Kaukab al-Sabáh[1] and Master Obayd the jeweller, and set down that her dowry hath been paid to me in full." So he wrote out the contract and Abd al-Rahman gave the company to drink of sherbets, and they made one wedding festival for the two brides, the daughter of the Shaykh al-Islam and Kamar al-Zaman's sister; and paraded them in one litter on one and the same night; after which they carried Kamar al-Zaman and Obayd in procession together and brought them in to their brides.[2] Then Obayd abode with them awhile in pleasance and joyance, after

[1] *i.e.* Star of the Morning: the first word occurs in Bar Cokba, or Barchocheba = Son of the Star, *i.e.* which was to come out of Jacob (Numbers xxiv. 17). The root, which does not occur in Heb., is Kaukab to shine. This Rabbi Akilah was also called Bar Cozla = Son of the Lie.

[2] Here some excision has been judged advisable as the names of the bridegrooms and the brides recur too often.

which he began to yearn for his native land: so he went in to Abd al-Rahman and said to him, "O uncle, I long for my own country, for I have there estates and effects, which I left in charge of one of my prentices; and I am minded to journey thither that I may sell my properties and return to thee. So wilt thou give me leave to go to my country for that purpose?" Answered the merchant, "O my son, I give thee leave to do this and there be no fault in thee or blame to thee for these words, for 'Love of mother-land is a part of Religion'; and he who hath not good in his own country hath none in other folk's country. But, haply, an thou depart without thy wife, when thou art once come to thy native place, it may seem right to thee to settle there, and thou wilt be perplexed between returning to thy wife and sojourning in thine own home; so it were the better rede that thou carry thy wife with thee; and after, an thou desire to return to us, return and welcome to you both; for we are folk who know not divorce and no woman of us marrieth twice, nor do we lightly discard a man."[1] Quoth Obayd, "Uncle, I fear me thy daughter will not consent to journey with me to my own country." Replied Abd al-Rahman, "O my son, we have no women amongst us who gainsay their spouses, nor know we a wife who is wroth with her man." The jeweller cried, "Allah bless you and your women!" and going in to his wife, said to her, "I am minded to go to my country: what sayst thou?" Quoth she, "Indeed, my sire had the ordering of me whilst I was a maid, and when I married the ordering all passed into the hands of my lord and master, nor will I gainsay him." Quoth Obayd, "Allah bless thee and thy father!" Then he cut his thongs[2] and applied himself to making ready for his journey. His father-in-law gave him much wealth and they took leave each of other, after which the jeweller and his wife journeyed on without ceasing till they reached Bassorah, where his kinsmen and comrades came out to meet him, doubting not but that he had been in Al-Hijáz. Some rejoiced at his return, whilst others were vexed, and the folk said one to another, "Now will he straiten us again every Friday, as before, and we shall be shut up in the mosques and houses, even to our cats and our dogs." On such wise it fared with him; but as regards the King of Bassorah, when he heard of his return, he was wroth with him and, sending for him, upbraided him and said to him, "Why

[1] See the note by Lane's Shaykh at the beginning of the tale. The contrast between the vicious wife of servile origin and the virtuous wife of noble birth is fondly dwelt upon but not exaggerated.

[2] *i.e.* those of his water skins for the journey, which as usual required patching and supplying with fresh handles after long lying dry.

didst thou depart without letting me know of thy departure? Was I unable to give thee somewhat wherewith thou mightest have succoured thyself in thy pilgrimage to the Holy House of Allah?" Replied the jeweller, "Pardon, O my lord! By Allah, I went not on the pilgrimage! but there have befallen me such and such things." Then he told him all that had betided him with his spouse and with Abd al-Rahman of Cairo and how the merchant had given him his daughter to wife, ending with these words, "And I have brought her to Bassorah." Said the King, "By the Lord, did I not fear Allah the Most High, I would slay thee and marry this noble lady after thy death, though I spent on her mints of money, because she befitteth none but Kings. But Allah hath appointed her of thy portion and may He bless thee in her! So look thou use her well." Then he bestowed largesse on the jeweller, who went out from before him and abode with his wife five years, after which he was admitted to the mercy of the Almighty. Presently the King sought his widow in wedlock; but she refused, saying, "O King, never among my kindred was a woman who married again after her husband's death; wherefore I will never take another husband, nor will I marry thee; no, though thou kill me." Then he sent to her one who said, "Dost thou seek to go to thy native land?" And she answered, "An thou do good, thou shalt be requited therewith." So he collected for her all the jeweller's wealth and added unto her of his own, after the measure of his degree. Lastly he sent with her one of his Wazirs, a man famous for goodness and piety, and an escort of five hundred horse, who journeyed with her till they brought her to her father; and in his home she abode, without marrying again, till she died and they died all. So, if this woman would not consent to replace her dead husband with a Sultan, how shall she be compared with one who replaced her husband, whilst he was yet alive, with a youth of unknown extraction and condition? Wherefore he who deemeth all women alike,[1] there is no remedy for the disease of his insanity. And glory be to Him to whom belongeth the Empire of the Seen and the Unseen, and He is the Living, who dieth not! And among the tales they tell, O auspicious King, is one of

---

[1] A popular saying also applied to men. It is usually accompanied with showing the open hand and a reference to the size of the fingers.

THE Caliph Harun al-Rashid was one day examining the tributes of his various provinces and viceroyalties, when he observed that the contributions of all the countries and regions had come into the treasury, except that of Bassorah, which had not arrived that year. So he held a Divan because of this and said, "Hither to me with the Wazir Ja'afar;" and when they brought him into the presence he thus bespoke him, "The tributes of all the provinces have come into the treasury save that of Bassorah, no part whereof hath arrived." Ja'afar replied, "O Commander of the Faithful, belike there hath befallen the Governor of Bassorah something that hath diverted him from sending the tribute." Quoth the Caliph, "The time of the coming of the tribute was twenty days ago; what, then, can be his excuse, for that in this time, he hath neither sent it nor sent to show cause for not doing so?" And quoth the Minister, "O Commander of the Faithful, if it please thee, we will send him a messenger." Rejoined the Caliph, "Send him Abu Ishak al-Mausili,[2] the boon companion; and Ja'afar, "Hearkening and obedience to Allah and to thee, O Prince of True Believers!" Then he returned to his house and summoning Abu Ishak, wrote him a royal writ and said to him, "Go to Abdullah bin Fazil, Viceroy of Bassorah, and see what hath diverted him from sending the tribute. If it be ready, do thou receive it from him in full and bring it to me in haste, for the Caliph hath examined the tributes of the provinces and findeth that they are all come in, except that of Bassorah: but an thou see that it is not ready and he make an excuse to thee, bring him back with thee, that he may report his excuse to the Caliph with his own tongue." Answered Abu Ishak, "I hear and I obey;" and taking with him five thousand horse of Ja'afar's host set out for Bassorah. Now when Abdullah bin Fazil heard of his approach, he went out to meet him with his troops, and led him into the city and carried him to his palace, whilst the escort encamped without the town-walls,

---

[1] Lane owns that this is "one of the most entertaining tales in the work," but he omits it "because its chief and best portion is essentially the same as 'The Story of the First of the Three Ladies of Baghdad.'" The truth is he was straitened for space by his publisher and thus compelled to cut out some of the best stories in The Nights.

[2] *i.e.* Ibrahim of Mosul, the musician poet often mentioned in The Nights. I must again warn the reader that the name is pronounced Is-hák (like Isaac with a central aspirate) not Ishák. This is not unnecessary when we hear Tait-shill for Tait's hill and "Frederick-shall" for Friedrichshall.

where he appointed to them all whereof they stood in need. So Abu Ishak entered the audience-chamber and sitting down on the throne, seated the Governor beside himself, whilst the notables sat round him according to their several degrees. After salutation with the salam Abdullah bin Fazil said to him, "O my lord, is there for thy coming to us any cause?" and said Abu Ishak, "Yes, I come to seek the tribute; for the Caliph enquireth of it and the time of its coming is gone by." Rejoined Abdullah bin Fazil, "O my lord, would Heaven thou hadst not wearied thyself nor taken upon thyself the hardships of the journey! For the tribute is ready in full tale and complete, and I purpose to despatch it to-morrow. But, since thou art come, I will entrust it to thee, after I have entertained thee three days; and on the fourth day I will set the tribute between thine hands. But it behoveth us now to offer thee a present in part requital of thy kindness and the goodness of the Commander of the Faithful." "There is no harm in that," said Abu Ishak. So Abdullah bin Fazil dismissed the Divan, and carrying him into a saloon that had not its match, bade set a tray of food before him and his companions. They ate and drank and made merry and enjoyed themselves; after which the tray was removed and there came coffee and sherbets. They sat conversing till a third part of the night was past, when they spread for Abu Ishak bedding on an ivory couch inlaid with gold glittering sheeny. So he lay down and the Viceroy lay down beside him on another couch; but wakefulness possessed Abu Ishak and he fell to meditating on the metres of prosody and poetical composition, for that he was one of the primest of the Caliph's boon-companions and he had a mighty fine fore-arm[1] in producing verses and pleasant stories; nor did he leave to lie awake improvising poetry until half the night was passed. Presently, behold, Abdullah bin Fazil arose, and girding his middle, opened a locker,[2] whence he brought out a whip; then, taking a lighted waxen taper, he went forth by the door of the saloon——And Shahrazad was surprised by the dawn of day and ceased saying her permitted say.

## Now when it was the Nine Hundred and Seventy-ninth Night,

She said, It hath reached me, O auspicious King, that when Abdullah bin Fazil went forth by the door of the saloon deeming Abu

[1] *i.e.* he was a proficient, an adept.
[2] Arab. from Pers. Dúláb = a waterwheel, a buttery, a cupboard.

Ishak asleep, the Caliph's cup-companion, seeing this, marvelled and said in himself, "Whither wendeth Abdullah bin Fazil with that whip? Perhaps he is minded to punish somebody. But needs must I follow him and see what he will do this night." So he arose and went out after him softly, very softly, that he might not be seen, and presently saw him open a closet and take thence a tray containing four dishes of meat and bread and a gugglet of water. Then he went on, carrying the tray and secretly followed by Abu Ishak, till he came to another saloon and entered, whilst the cup-companion stood behind the door and, looking through the chink, saw a spacious saloon, furnished with the richest furniture and having in its midst a couch of ivory plated with gold glittering sheeny, to which two dogs were made fast with chains of gold. Then Abdullah set down the tray in a corner and tucking up his sleeves, loosed the first dog, which began to struggle in his hands and put its muzzle to the floor, as it would kiss the ground before him, whining the while in a weak voice. Abdullah tied its paws behind its back and throwing it on the ground, drew forth the whip and beat it with a painful beating and a pitiless. The dog struggled, but could not get free, and Abdullah ceased not to beat it with the same whip till it left groaning and lay without consciousness. Then he took it and tied it up in its place, and unbinding the second dog, did with him as he had done with the first; after which he pulled out a kerchief and fell to wiping away their tears and comforting them, saying, "Bear me not malice; for by Allah, this is not of my will, nor is it easy to me! But it may be Allah will grant you relief from this strait and issue from your affliction." And he prayed for the twain what while Abu Ishak the cup-companion stood hearkening with his ears and espying with his eyes, and indeed he marvelled at his case. Then Abdullah brought the dogs the tray of food and fell to morselling them with his own hand, till they had enough, when he wiped their muzzles and lifting up the gugglet, gave them to drink; after which he took up the tray, gugglet and candle and made for the door. But Abu Ishak forewent him and making his way back to his couch, lay down; so that he saw him not, neither knew that he had walked behind him and watched him. Then the Governor replaced the tray and the gugglet in the closet, and returning to the saloon, opened the locker and laid the whip in its place; after which he doffed his clothes and lay down. But Abu Ishak passed the rest of that night pondering this affair, neither did sleep visit him for excess of wonderment, and he ceased not to say in himself, "I wonder what may be the meaning of this!" Nor did he leave wondering till daybreak, when they arose and prayed the dawn-prayer. Then they set the breakfast[1] before them and they ate and drank coffee, after which they went out to the Divan. Now Abu Ishak's thought was occupied with this mystery all day long, but he concealed the matter and questioned not Abdullah thereof. Next night, he again followed the Governor and saw him do with the two dogs as on the previous night, first beating them and then making his peace with them and giving them to eat and to drink; and so also he did the third night. On the fourth day Abdullah brought his tribute to Abu Ishak who took it and departed, without opening the matter to him. He fared on, without ceasing, till he came to Baghdad, where he delivered the tribute to the Caliph, who questioned him of the cause of its delay. Replied he, "O Commander of the Faithful, I found that the Governor of Bassorah had made ready the tribute and was about to despatch it; and had I delayed a day, it would have met me on the road. But, O Prince of True Believers, I had a wondrous adventure with Abdullah bin Fazil; never in my life saw I its like." "And what was it, O Abu Ishak?" asked the Caliph. So he replied, "I saw such and such;" and, brief, acquainted him with that which the Governor had done with the two dogs, adding, "After such fashion I saw him do three successive nights, first beating the dogs, then making his peace with them and comforting them and giving them to eat and drink, I watching him, and he seeing me not." Asked the Caliph, "Didst thou question him of the cause of this?" and the other answered, "No, as thy head liveth, O Commander of the Faithful." Then said Al-Rashid, "O Abu Ishak, I command thee to return to Bassorah and bring me Abdullah bin Fazil and the two dogs." Quoth he, "O Commander of the Faithful, excuse me from this; for indeed Abdullah entertained me with exceedingly hospitable entertainment and I became ware of this case by chance undesigned and acquainted thee therewith. So how can I go back to him and bring him to thee? Verily, if I return to him, I shall find me no face for shame of him: wherefore 'twere meet that thou send him another than myself, with a letter under thine own hand, and he shall bring him to thee, him and the two dogs." But quoth the Caliph, "If I send him other than thyself, peradventure he will deny the whole affair and say, I have no dogs. But if I send thee and thou say to him, I saw them with mine own eyes, he will not be able to deny

[1] Arab. "Futúr," the Chhotí háziri of Anglo-India or break-fast proper, eaten by Moslems immediately after the dawn-prayer except in Ramázán. Amongst sensible people it is a substantial meal of bread and boiled beans, eggs, cheese, curded milk and the pastry called fatírah, followed by coffee and a pipe. See Lane M.E. chapt. v. and my Pilgrimage ii. 48.

that. Wherefore nothing will serve but that thou go and fetch him and the two dogs; otherwise I will surely slay thee."[1]——And Shahrazad perceived the dawn of day and ceased to say her permitted say.

## Now when it was the Nine Hundred and Eightieth Night,

She continued, It hath reached me, O auspicious King, that the Caliph Harun al-Rashid said to Abu Ishak, "Nothing will serve but that thou go and fetch him and the two dogs; otherwise I will surely slay thee." Abu Ishak replied, "Hearing and obeying, O Commander of the Faithful: Allah is our aidance and good is the Agent. He spake sooth who said, 'Man's wrong is from the tongue;'[2] and 'tis I who sinned against myself in telling thee. But write me a royal rescript[3] and I will go to him and bring him back to thee." So the Caliph gave him an autograph and he took it and repaired to Bassorah. Seeing him come in, the Governor said, "Allah forfend us from the mischief of thy return, O Abu Ishak! How cometh it I see thee return in haste! Peradventure the tribute is deficient and the Caliph will not accept it?" Answered Abu Ishak, "O Emir Abdullah, my return is not on account of the deficiency of the tribute, for 'tis full measure and the Caliph accepteth it; but I hope that thou wilt excuse me, for that I have failed in my duty as thy guest and indeed this lapse of mine was decreed of Allah Almighty." Abdullah enquired, "And what may be the lapse?" and he replied, "Know that when I was with thee, I followed thee three following nights and saw thee rise at midnight and beat the dogs and return; whereat I marvelled, but was ashamed to question thee thereof. When I came back to Baghdad, I told the Caliph of thine affair, casually and without design, whereupon he charged me to return to thee, and here is a letter under his hand. Had I known that the affair would lead to this, I had not told him, but Destiny foreordained thus." And he went on to excuse himself to him; whereupon said Abdullah, "Since thou hast told him this, I will bear out thy report with him, lest he deem thee a liar, for thou art my friend. Were it other than thou, I had denied the affair and

---

[1] This "off-with-his-head" style must not be understood literally. As I have noted, it is intended by the writer to show the kingship and the majesty of the "Vicar of Allah."

[2] Lit. "the calamity of man (insán) is from the tongue" (lisán).

[3] For Khatt Sharif, lit. = a noble letter.

given him the lie. But now I will go with thee and carry the two dogs with me, though this be to me ruin-rife and the ending of my term of life." Rejoined the other, "Allah will veil[1] thee, even as thou hast veiled my face with the Caliph!" Then Abdullah took a present beseeming the Commander of the Faithful and mounting the dogs with him, each on a camel, bound with chains[2] of gold, journeyed with Abu Ishak to Baghdad, where he went in to the Caliph and kissed ground before him. He deigned bid him sit; so he sat down and brought the two dogs before Al-Rashid, who said to him, "What be these dogs, O Emir Abdullah?" Whereupon they fell to kissing the floor between his hands and wagging their tails and weeping, as if complaining to him. The Caliph marvelled at this and said to the Governor, "Tell me the history of these two dogs and the reason of thy beating them and after entreating them with honour." He replied, "O Vicar of Allah, these be no dogs, but two young men, endowed with beauty and seemliness, symmetry and shapeliness, and they are my brothers and the sons of my father and mother." Asked the Caliph, "How is it that they were men and are become dogs?" and he answered, "An thou give me leave, O Prince of True Believers, I will acquaint thee with the truth of the circumstance." Said Al-Rashid, "Tell me and 'ware of leasing, for 'tis of the fashion of the hypocrites; and look thou speak truth, for that is the Ark[3] of safety and the mark of virtuous men." Rejoined Abdullah, "Know then, O Vice-regent of Allah, when I tell thee the story of these dogs, they will both bear witness against me: an I speak sooth they will certify it and if I lie they will give me the lie." Cried the Caliph, "These are of the dogs; they cannot speak nor answer; so how can they testify for thee or against thee?" But Abdullah said to them, "O my brothers, if I speak a lying word, do ye lift your heads and stare with your eyes; but an sooth I say, hang down your heads and lower your eyes." Then said he to the Caliph:—Know, O Commander of the Faithful, that we are three brothers by one mother and the same father. Our sire's

---

[1] Arab. "Allah yastura-k" = protect thee by hiding what had better be hidden.

[2] Arab. "Janázír" = chains, an Arabised plural of the Pers. Zanjír with the metathesis or transposition of letters peculiar to the vulgar; "Janázír" for "Zanájír."

[3] Arab. "Safínah" = (Noah's) Ark, a myth derived from the Baris of Egypt with subsequent embellishments from the Babylonian deluge legends: the latter may have been survivals of the days when the waters of the Persian Gulf extended to the mountains of Eastern Syria. Hence I would explain the existence of extinct volcanoes within sight of Damascus (see Unexplored Syria i. p. 159) visited, I believe, for the first time by my late friend Charles F. Tyrwhitt Drake and myself in May, 1871.

name was Fazil and he was so named because his mother bare two sons at one birth, one of whom died forthright and the other twin remained alive, wherefore his sire named him Fazil—the Remainder. His father brought him up and reared him well till he grew to manhood, when he married him to our mother and died. Our mother conceived a first time and bare this my first brother, whom our sire named Mansúr; then she conceived again and bare this my second brother, whom he named Násir[1]; after which she conceived a third time and bare me, whom he named Abdullah. My father reared us all three till we came to man's estate, when he died, leaving us a house and a shop full of coloured stuffs of all kinds, Indian and Greek and Khorásáni and what not, besides sixty thousand dinars. We washed him and buried him to the ruth of his Lord, after which we built him a splendid monument and let pray for him prayers for the deliverance of his soul from the fire and held perlections of the Koran and gave alms on his behalf, till the forty days[2] were past; when I called together the merchants and nobles of the folk and made them a sumptuous entertainment. As soon as they had eaten, I said to them, "O merchants, verily this world is ephemeral, but the next world is eternal, and extolled be the perfection of Him who endureth always after His creatures have passed away! Know ye why I have called you together this blessed day?" And they answered, "Extolled be Allah, sole Scient of the hidden things."[3] Quoth I, "My father died, leaving much of money, and I fear lest any have a claim against him for a debt or a pledge[4] or what not else, and I desire to discharge my father's obligations towards the folk. Accordingly whoso hath any demand on him, let him say:—He oweth me so and so, and I will satisfy it to him, that I may acquit the responsibility of my sire."[5] The merchants replied, "O Abdullah, verily the goods of this world stand not in

---

[1] Mansúr and Násir are passive and active participles from the same root, Nasr = victory; the former means triumphant and the latter triumphing.

[2] The normal term of Moslem mourning, which Mohammed greatly reduced disliking the abuse of it by the Jews, who even in the present day are the strictest in its observance.

[3] An euphuistic and euphemistic style of saying, "No, we don't know."

[4] Arab. "Rahan," an article placed with him in pawn.

[5] A Moslem is bound, not only by honour but by religion, to discharge the debts of his dead father and mother and so save them from punishment on Judgment-day. Mohammed, who enjoined mercy to debtors while in the flesh (chapt. ii. 280, etc.), said, "Allah covereth all faults except debt;" that is to say, there will be punishment therefor. Also "A martyr shall be pardoned every fault but debt." On one occasion he refused to pray for a Moslem who died insolvent. Such harshness is a curious contrast with the leniency which advised the creditor to remit debts by way of alms; and practically this mild view of indebtedness renders it highly unadvisable to oblige a Moslem friend with a loan.

stead of those of the world to come, and we are no fraudful folk, but all of us know the lawful from the unlawful and fear Almighty Allah and abstain from devouring the substance of the orphan. We know that thy father (Allah have mercy on him !) still let his money lie with the folk,[1] nor did he suffer any man's claim on him to go unquitted, and we have ever heard him declare :—I am fearful of the people's substance. He used always to say in his prayers, O my God, Thou art my stay and my hope! Let me not die while in debt. And it was of his wont that, if he owed anyone aught, he would pay it to him, without being pressed, and if any owed him aught he would not dun him, but would say to him, At thy leisure. If his debtor were poor, he would release him from his liability and acquit him of responsibility ; and if he were not poor and died in his debt, he would say, "Allah forgive him what he owed me ! And we all testify that he owed no man aught." Quoth I, "May Allah bless you !" Then I turned to these my brothers and said, "Our father owed no man aught and hath left us much money and stuffs, besides the house and the shop. Now we are three and each of us is entitled to one third part. So shall we agree to waive division and dwell copartners in our wealth and eat together and drink together, or shall we apportion the stuffs and the money and take each his part?" Said they, "We will divide them and take each his share." (Then Abdullah turned to the two dogs and said to them, "Did it happen thus, O my brothers?" and they bowed their heads and lowered their eyes, as to say, "Yes.") Abdullah continued :—I called in a departitor from the Kazi's court, O Prince of True Believers, and he distributed amongst us the money and the stuffs and all our father had left, allotting the house and shop to me in exchange for a part of the coin and clothes to which I was entitled. We were content with this ; so the house and shop fell to my share, whilst my brothers took their portion in money and stuffs. I opened the shop and stocking it with my stuffs bought others with the money apportioned to me, over and above the house and shop, till the place was full, and I sat selling and buying. As for my brothers, they purchased stuffs and hiring a ship, set out on a voyage to the far abodes of folk. Quoth I, "Allah aid them both ! As for me, my livelihood is ready to my hand and peace is priceless." I abode thus a whole year, during which time Allah opened the door of fortune to me and I gained great gains, till I became possessed of the like of that which

---

[1] *i.e.* he did not press them for payment ; and, it must be remembered, he received no interest upon his moneys, this being forbidden in the Koran.

our father had left us. One day, as I sat in my shop, with two fur pelisses on me, one of sable and the other of meniver,[1] for it was the season of winter and the time of the excessive cold, behold, there came up to me my two brothers, each clad in a ragged shirt and nothing more, and their lips were white with cold, and they were shivering. When I saw them in this plight, it was grievous to me and I mourned for them——And Shahrazad was surprised by the dawn of day and ceased saying her permitted say.

## Now when it was the Nine Hundred and Eighty-first Night,

She pursued, It hath reached me, O auspicious King, that Abdullah bin Fazil continued to the Caliph:—When I saw them in this plight, it was grievous to me and I mourned for them and my reason fled my head. So I rose and embraced them and wept over their condition: then I put on one of them the pelisse of sable and on the other the fur coat of meniver[1] and, carrying them to the Hammam, sent thither for each of them a suit of apparel such as befitted a merchant worth a thousand.[2] When they had washed and donned each his suit, I carried them to my house where, seeing them well nigh famished, I set a tray of food before them and ate with them, caressing them and comforting them. (Then he again turned to the two dogs and said to them, "Was this so, O my brothers?" and they bent their heads and lowered their eyes.) So Abdullah continued:—When they had eaten, O Vicar of Allah, quoth I to them, "What hath befallen you and where are your goods?" and quoth they, "We fared up the river,[3] till we came to a city called Cufa, where we sold for ten dinars the piece of stuff that had cost half a ducat and that which cost us a ducat for twenty. So we profited greatly and bought Persian stuffs at the rate of ten sequins per piece of silk worth forty at Bassorah. Thence we

---

[1] Al-Mas'údi (chap. xvii.) alludes to furs of sable (Samúr), hermelline (Al-Farwah) and Bortás (Turkish) furs of black and red foxes. Sïnjáb is Persian for the skin of the grey squirrel (*Mus lemmus* the lemming), the meniver, erroneously miniver (menu vair), as opposed to the ermine = *Mus Armenius*, or *mustela erminia*. I never visit England without being surprised at the vile furs worn by the rich, and the folly of the poor in not adopting the sheepskin with the wool inside and the leather well tanned which keeps the peasant warm and comfortable between Croatia and Afghanistan.

[2] Arab. "Tájir Alfi," which may mean a thousand dinars (£500) or a thousand purses (= £5,000). "Alfi" is not an uncommon P.N., meaning that the bearer (Pasha or pauper) had been bought for a thousand, left indefinite.

[3] Tigris-Euphrates.

removed to a city called Al-Karkh[1] where we sold and bought and made gain galore and amassed of wealth great store." And they went on to set forth to me the places and the profits. So I said to them, "Since ye had such good luck and lot, how cometh it that I see you return naked?" They sighed and answered, "O our brother, someone must have evil-eyed us, and in travel there is no trusting. When we had gotten together these moneys and goods, we freighted a ship therewith and set sail, intending for Bassorah. We fared on three days, and on the fourth day we saw the sea rise and fall and roar and foam and swell and dash, whilst the waves clashed together with a crash, striking out sparks like fire[2] in the darks. The winds blew contrary for us and our craft struck upon the point of a hill-projected rock, when it brake up and plunged us into the river, and all we had with us was lost in the waters. We abode struggling on the surface a day and a night, till Allah sent us another ship, whose crew picked us up and we begged our way from town to town, suffering mighty sore hardships and selling our body-clothes piecemeal, to buy us food, till we drew near Bassorah; nor did we make the city till we had drained the draught of a thousand miseries. Indeed, had we come safely off with that which was by us, we had brought back riches that might be evened with those of the King: but this was fore-ordained to us of Allah." I said, "O my brothers, let not your hearts be grieved, for wealth is the ransom of bodies and safety is property. Since Allah hath written you of the saved, this is the end of desire, for want and wealth are but as it were illusions of dreams, and God-gifted is he who said:—

An a man from destruction can save his head * Let him hold his wealth as a slice of nail.

I continued, "O my brothers, we will suppose that our sire died to-day and left us all this wealth that is with me, for I am right willing to share it with you equally." So I fetched a departitor from the Kazi's court and brought out to him all my money, which he distributed into three equal parts, and we each took one. Then said I to them, "O my brothers, Allah blesseth a man in his daily bread, if he be in his own country: so let each of you open him a shop and sit therein to get his living; and he to whom aught is ordained in the Secret Purpose,[3] needs must he get it." Accordingly,

[1] Possibly the quarter of Baghdad so called and mentioned in The Nights more than once.

[2] For this fiery sea see Sind Revisited, i. 19.

[3] Arab. "Al-Ghayb," which may also mean "in the future" (unknown to man).

I helped each of them to open a shop and filled it for him with goods, saying to them, "Sell and buy and keep your moneys and spend naught thereof; for all ye need of meat and drink and so forth I will furnish to you." I continued to entreat them generously, and they fell to selling and buying by day and returning at eventide to my house where they lay the night; nor would I suffer them to expend aught of their own substance. But, whenever I sat talking with them, they would praise travel and proclaim its pleasures and vaunt the gains they had made therein; and they ceased not to urge me to accompany them in travelling over foreign parts. (Then he said to the dogs, "Was this so, O my brothers?" and they again bowed their heads and lowered their eyes in confirmation of his words.) He continued:—On such wise, O Vicar of Allah, they continued to urge me and tempt me to travel by vaunting the great gains and profits to be obtained thereby, till I said to them, "Needs must I fare with you for your sake!" Then I entered into a contract of partnership with them and we chartered a ship, and packing up all manner of precious stuffs and merchandise of every manner, freighted her therewith; after which we embarked in her all we needed and, setting sail from Bassorah, launched out into the dashing sea, swollen with clashing surge, whereinto whoso entereth is lone and lorn and whence whoso cometh forth is as a babe new-born. We ceased not sailing till we came to a city of the cities, where we sold and bought and made great cheape. Thence we went on to another place, and we ceased not to pass from land to land and port to port, selling and buying and profiting, till we had gotten us great wealth and much advantage. Presently, we came to a mountain,[1] where the captain cast anchor and said to us, "O passengers, go ye ashore; ye shall be saved from this day,[2] and make search; it may be ye shall find water." So all landed, I amongst the crowd, and dispersed about the island in search of water. As for me, I climbed to the top of the mountain, and whilst I went along, lo and behold! I saw a white snake fleeing and followed by a black dragon foul of favour and frightful of form, hotly pursuing her. Presently he overtook her and catching her, seized her by the head and wound his tail about her, whereupon she cried out and I knew that he purposed to kill her. So I was moved to ruth for her, and taking up a lump of granite,[3] five pounds or more in weight, hurled it at the dragon.

---

[1] "Arab. "Jabal"; here a mountainous island.

[2] *i.e.* ye shall be spared this day's miseries. See my Pilgrimage, vol. i. 314, and the delight with which we glided into Marsá Damghah.

[3] Arab. "Súwán" = "Syenite" (-granite), also used for flint and other hard stones.

It smote him on the head and crushed it, and ere I knew, the white snake changed and became a young girl bright with beauty and loveliness and brilliancy and perfect grace, as she were the shining full moon, who came up to me, and, kissing my hands, said to me, "Allah veil thee with two-fold veils, one from shame in this world and the other from the flame in the world to come on the day of the Great Upstanding, the day when neither wealth nor children shall avail save to him who shall come to Allah with a sound heart!"[1] And presently she continued, "O mortal, thou hast saved my life and I am indebted to thee for kindness, wherefore it behoveth me to requite thee." So saying, she signed with her hand to the earth, which opened and she descended thereinto: then it closed up again over her and by this I knew that she was of the Jinn. As for the dragon, fire was kindled in him and consumed him and he became ashes. I marvelled at this and returned to my comrades, whom I acquainted with whatso I had seen, and we passed the night on the island. When the morrow came the captain weighed anchor and spread the sails and coiled the ropes and we sailed till the shore faded from our gaze. We fared on twenty days, without seeing or land or bird, till our drink was at an end, and quoth the Rais to us, "O folk, our fresh water is spent." Quoth we, "Let us make for land; haply we shall find water." But he exclaimed, "By Allah, I have lost my way and I know not what course will bring me to the seaboard." Thereupon betided us sore chagrin and we wept and besought Almighty Allah to guide us into the right course. We passed that night in the sorriest case: but God-gifted is he who said:—

How many a night have I spent in woes * That would grizzle the suckling-babe with fear:
But morrowed not morn ere to me there came * 'Aidance from Allah and victory near.'[2]

But when the day arose in its sheen and shone, we caught sight of a high mountain and rejoiced therein, and when we came to its skirts, the captain said to us, "O folk, go ashore and seek for water." So we all landed and sought water but found none, whereat we were

---

[1] Koran xxiv. Male children are to the Arab as much prized an object of possession as riches, since without them wealth is of no value to him. Mohammed, therefore, couples wealth with children as the two things wherewith one wards off the ills of this world, though they are powerless against those of the world to come.

[2] An exclamation derived from the Surat Nasr (cx. 1) one of the most affecting in the Koran. It gave Mohammed warning of his death and caused Al-Abbás to shed tears; the Prophet sings a song of victory in the ixth year of the Hijrah (he died in the xth) and implores the pardon of his lord.

sore afflicted because we were suffering for want of it. As for me, I climbed up to the mountain-top and on the other side thereof I saw a spacious circle[1] distant from us an hour's journey or more. Presently I called my companions and as soon as they all rejoined me, said to them, "Look at yonder basin behind this mountain; for I see therein a city high of base and a strong-cornered place girt with sconce and rampartry, pasturage and lea, and doubtless it wanteth not water and good things. So hie we thither and fetch drink therefrom and buy what we need of provisions, meat and fruit, and return." But they said, "We fear lest the city-folk be Kafirs ascribing to Allah partners and they be foes of The Faith and lay hand on us and take us captive or else slay us; so should we cause the loss of our own lives, having cast ourselves into destruction and evil emprise. Indeed, the proud and presumptuous are never praiseworthy, for that they ever fare in danger of calamities, even as saith of such an one a certain poet:—

Long as earth is earth, long as sky is sky, * The o'erproud is blamed tho' from risk he fly!

So we will not expose ourselves to peril." I replied, "O folk, I have no authority over you; so I will take my brothers and go to yonder city." But my brothers said to me, "We also fear this thing and will not go with thee." Quoth I, "As for me, I am resolved to go thither, and I put my trust in Allah and accept whatsoever He shall decree to me. Do ye therefore await me, whilst I wend thither and return to you twain."——And Shahrazad perceived the dawn of day and ceased to say her permitted say.

## Now when it was the Nine Hundred and Eighty-second Night,

She resumed, It hath reached me, O auspicious King, that Abdullah said, "Do ye twain await me whilst I wend thither and return to you." So I left them and walked on till I came to the gate of the place and saw it a city of building wondrous and projection marvellous, with boulevards high-towering and towers strong-builded and palaces high-soaring. Its portals were of Chinese iron, rarely gilded and graven on such wise as confounded the wit. I entered the gateway and saw there a stone bench, whereon sat a man bearing on his forearm a chain of brass, whereto hung fourteen keys; so I knew

[1] Arab. "Dáirah," a basin surrounded by hills. The words which follow may mean, "An hour's journey or more in breadth."

him to be the porter of the city and that it had fourteen gates. I drew near him and said to him, "Peace be with thee!" but he returned not my salam and I saluted him a second and a third time; but he made me no reply. Then I laid my hand on his shoulder and said to him, "Ho thou, why dost thou not return my salam? Art thou asleep or deaf or other than a Moslem, that thou refrainest from exchanging the salutation?" But he answered me not, neither stirred; so I considered him and saw that he was stone. Quoth I, "Verily an admirable matter! This is a stone wroughten in the semblance of a son of Adam and wanting in naught save speech!" Then I left him and entering the city, beheld a man standing in the road: so I went up to him and scrutinised him and found him stone. Presently, as I walked adown the broadways and saw that this was everywhere the case, I met an old woman bearing on her head a bundle of clothes ready for washing; so I went up to her and examining her, saw that she was stone, and the bundle of clothes on her head was stone also.[1] Then I fared for the market, where I sighted an oilman with his scales set up and fronted by various kinds of wares such as cheese and so forth, all of stone. Moreover, I espied all manner of tradesmen seated in their shops, and men and women and children, some standing and some sitting; but they were all stone; and the stuffs were like spiders' webs. I amused myself with looking upon them, and as often as I laid hold upon a piece of stuff, it powdered in my hands like dust dispread. Presently I beheld some chests, and opening one of them, found it full of gold in bags; so I laid hold upon the bags, but they crumbled away in my grasp, whilst the gold abode unchanged. I carried off of it what I could carry and said to myself, "Were my brothers with me, they might take of this gold their fill and possess themselves of these hoards which have no owner." Then I entered another shop and found therein more than this, but could bear away no more than I had borne. I left this market and went on to another and thence to another and another, much enjoying the sight of all manner of creatures of various kinds, all several stones, even to the dogs and the cats, till I came to the goldsmiths' bazar, where I found men sitting in their shops, with their stock-in-trade about them, some in their hands and others in crates of wicker-work. When I saw this, O Commander of the Faithful, I threw down the gold and loaded myself with goldsmiths' ware, as much as I could carry. Then I went on to the jewel-market and sighted there the jewellers seated in their shops, each with a tray before

---

[1] These petrified folk have occurred in the "Eldest Lady's Tale," where they are of "black stone."

him, full of all sorts of precious stones, jacinths and diamonds and emeralds and balass rubies and so forth: but all the shop-keepers were stones; whereupon I threw away the goldsmiths' ware and carried off as many jewels as I could carry, regretting that my brothers were not with me, so they might take what they would of those costly gems. Then I left the jewel-market and went on till I came to a great door, quaintly gilded and decorated after the fairest fashion, within which were wooden benches, and in the porch sat eunuchs and body-guards, horsemen, and footmen and officers of police, each and every robed in the richest of raiment; but they were all stones. I touched one of them and his clothes crumbled away from his body like cobwebs. Then I passed through the door and saw a palace without equal for its building and the goodliness of the works that were therein. Here I found an audience-chamber, full of Grandees and Wazirs and Officers and Emirs, seated upon chairs and every one of them stone. Moreover, I espied a throne of red gold, crusted with pearls and gems, and seated thereon a son of Adam arrayed in the most sumptuous raiment and bearing on his head a Chosröan[1] crown, diademed with the finest stones that shed a light like the light of day; but, when I came up to him, I found him stone. Then I went on to the gate of the Harim and entering, found myself in the Queen's presence-chamber, wherein I saw a throne of red gold, inlaid with pearls and gems, and the Queen seated thereon. On her head she wore a crown diademed with finest jewels, and round about her were women like moons, seated upon chairs and clad in the most sumptuous clothing of all colours. There also the eunuchry, with their hands upon their breasts, were standing in the attitude of service, and indeed this hall confounded the beholder's wits with what was therein of quaint gilding and rare painting and curious carving and fine furniture. There hung the most brilliant lustres[3] of limpid crystal, and in every globe[4] of the crystal was an unique jewel, whose price money might not fulfil. So I threw down that which was with me, O Prince of True Believers, and fell to taking of these jewels what I could carry, bewildered as to what I should bear away and what I should

---

[1] Arab. "Táj Kisrawi," such as was worn by the Chosröes Kings.

[2] The familiar and far-famed Napoleonic pose, with the arms crossed over the breast is throughout the East the attitude assumed by slave and servant in presence of his master. Those who send statues to Anglo-India should remember this.

[3] Arab. "Ta' álík" = hanging lamps, often in lantern shape with coloured glass and profuse ornamentation: the Maroccan are now familiar to England.

[4] Arab. "Kidrah," lit. = a pot, kettle: it can hardly mean "an interval."

leave; for indeed I saw the place as it were a treasure of the treasures of the cities. Presently I espied a wicket[1] standing open and within it a staircase: so I entered and mounting forty steps, heard a human voice reciting the Koran in a low tone. I walked towards that sound till I came to the main door hung with a silken curtain, laced with wires of gold whereon were strung pearls and coral and rubies and cut emeralds which gave forth a light like the light of stars. The voice came from behind the curtain: so I raised it and discovered a gilded door, whose beauty amazed the mind. I passed through the door and found myself in a saloon as it were a hoard upon earth's surface[2] and therein a girl as she were the sun shining fullest sheen in the zenith of a sky serene. She was robed in the costliest of raiment and decked with ornaments the most precious that could be, and withal she was of passing beauty and loveliness, a model of symmetry and seemliness, of elegance and perfect grace, with waist slender and dewy lips such as heal the sick; and eyelids lovely in their languour, as it were she of whom the sayer spake when he said:—

My best salam to what that robe enrobes of symmetry, * And what that blooming garth of cheek enguards of rosy blee:
It seems as though the Pleiades depend upon her brow; * And other lights of Night in knots upon her breast we see:
Did she but don a garment weft of Rose's softest leaf, * The leaf of Rose would draw her blood[3] when pluckt that fruit from tree:

---

[1] The wicket or small doorway, especially by the side of a gate or portal, is called "the eye of the needle" and explains Matt. xix. 24, and Koran vii. 38. In the Rabbinic form of the proverb the camel becomes an elephant. Some have preferred to change the Koranic Jamal (camel) for Habl (cable) and much ingenuity has been wasted by commentators on Mark x. 25, and Luke xviii. 25.

[2] *i.e.* a "Kanz" (enchanted treasury) usually hidden underground but opened by a counter-spell and transferred to earth's face. The reader will note the gorgeousness of the picture.

[3] "Oriental writers, Indian and Persian, as well as Arab, lay great stress upon the extreme delicacy of the skin of the fair ones celebrated in their works, constantly attributing to their heroines bodies so sensitive as to brook with difficulty the contact of the finest gauze. Several instances of this will be found in the present collection, and we may fairly assume that the skin of an Eastern beauty, under the influence of constant seclusion and the unremitting use of cosmetics and the bath, would in time attain a pitch of delicacy and sensitiveness such as would in some measure justify the seemingly extravagant statements of their poetical admirers, of which the following anecdote (quoted by Ibn Khellikan from the historian Et Teberi) is a fair specimen. Ardeshir ibn Babek (Artaxerxes I.), the first Sassanian King of Persia (A.D. 226–242), having long unsuccessfully besieged El Hedr, a strong city of Mesopotamia belonging to the petty King Es Satiroun, at last obtained possession of it by the treachery of the owner's daughter Nezireh and married the latter, this having been the price stipulated by her for the betrayal to him of the place. It happened afterwards that, one night, as she was unable to sleep and turned from side to side in the bed, Ardeshir asked her what prevented her from sleeping. She replied, 'I never yet slept on a rougher bed than this;

And did she spit in Ocean's face, next morn would see a change * To sweeter than the honeycomb of what was briny sea:
And did she deign her hand to grant to grey-beard staff enpropped, * He'd wake and rend the lion's limbs for might and valiancy.

Then Abdullah continued:—O Prince of True Believers, as soon as I saw that girl I fell passionately in love with her and, going straight up to her, found her seated on a high couch, reciting by heart and in grateful memory the Book of Allah, to whom belong honour and glory! Her voice was like the harmony of the gates of Heaven, when Rizwan openeth them, and the words came from her lips like a shower of gems; whilst her face was with beauty dight, bright and blossom-white, even as saith the poet of a similar sight:—

O thou who gladdenest man by speech and rarest quality; * Grow longing and repine for thee and grow beyond degree!
In thee two things consume and melt the votaries of Love: * The dulcet song of David joined with Joseph's brilliancy.

When I heard her voice of melody reciting the sublime Koran, my heart quoted from her killing glances, 'Peace, a word from a compassionating Lord;'[1] but I stammered[2] in my speech and could not

---

I feel something irk me.' He ordered the bed to be changed, but she was still unable to sleep. Next morning she complained of her side, and on examination, a myrtle-leaf was found adhering to a fold of the skin, from which it had drawn blood. Astonished at this circumstance, Ardeshir asked her if it was this that had kept her awake and she replied in the affirmative. 'How then,' asked he, 'did your father bring you up?' She answered, 'He spread me a bed of satin and clad me in silk and fed me with marrow and cream and the honey of virgin bees and gave me pure wine to drink.' Quoth Ardeshir, 'The same return which you made your father for his kindness would be made much more readily to me;' and bade bind her by the hair to the tail of a horse, which galloped off with her and killed her." It will be remembered that the true princess, in the well-known German popular tale, is discovered by a similar incident to that of the mrytle-leaf. I quote this excellent note from Mr. Payne (ix. 148) only regretting that annotation did not enter into his plan of producing The Nights. Amongst Hindu story-tellers a phenomenal softness of the skin is a *lieu commun;* see Vikram and the Vampire (p. 285, "Of the marvellous delicacy of three Queens"); and the Tale of the Sybarite might be referred to in the lines given above.

[1] "(55) Indeed joyous on that day are the people of Paradise in their employ; (56) In shades, on bridal couches reclining they and their wives; (57) Fruits have they therein and whatso they desire; (58) 'Peace!' shall be a word from a compassionating Lord." See Koran xxxvi. 55–58, the famous Chapt. "Yá Sín," which most educated Moslems learn by heart. In addition to the proofs there offered that the Moslem Paradise is not wholly sensual, I may quote, "No soul wotteth what coolth of the eyes is reserved (for the good) in recompense of their works" (Koran lxx. 17). The Paradise of eating, drinking and revelling was preached solely to the baser sort of humanity which can understand and appreciate only the pleasures of the flesh. To talk of spiritual joys before the Badawin would have been a *non-sens,* even as it would be to the roughs of our great cities.

[2] Arab. "Lajlaj," lit. = rolling anything round the mouth when eating; hence speaking inarticulately, being tongue-tied, stuttering, etc.

say the salam-salutation aright, for my mind and sight were confounded and I was become as saith the bard:—

Love-longing urged me not except to trip in speech o'er free; * Nor, save to shed my blood I passed the campment's boundary:
I ne'er will hear a word from those who love to rail, but I * Will testify to love of him with every word of me.

Then I hardened myself against the horrors of repine and said to her, "Peace be with thee, O noble lady and treasured jewel! Allah grant endurance to the foundation of thy fortune fair and upraise the pillars of thy glory rare!" Said she, "And on thee from me be peace and salutation and high honour, O Abdullah, O son of Fazil! Well come and welcome and fair welcome to thee, O dearling mine and coolth of mine eyne!" Rejoined I, "O my lady, whence wottest thou my name and who art thou and what case befel the people of this city that they are become stones? I would have thee tell me the truth of the matter, for indeed I am admiring at this city and its citizens, and that I have found none alive therein save thyself. So, Allah upon thee, tell me the cause of all this, according to the truth!" Quoth she, "Sit, O Abdullah, and Inshallah, I will talk with thee and acquaint thee in full with the facts of my case and of this place and its people; and there is no Majesty and there is no Might save in Allah, the Glorious, the Great!" So I sat me down by her side and she said to me, "Know, O Abdullah (may Allah have mercy on thee!), that I am the daughter of the King of this city, and that it is my sire whom thou sawest seated on the high stead in the Divan, and those who are round about him were the Lords of his land and the Guards of his empery. He was a King of exceeding prowess, and had under his hand a thousand thousand and sixty thousand troopers. The number of the Emirs of his Empire was four-and-twenty thousand, all of them Governors and Dignitaries. He was obeyed by a thousand cities, besides towns, hamlets and villages; and sconces and citadels, and the Emirs[1] of the wild Arabs under his hand were a thousand in number, each commanding twenty thousand horse. Moreover, he had moneys and treasures and precious stones and jewels and things of price, such as eye never saw nor of which ear ever heard.——And Shahrazad was surprised by the dawn of day and ceased saying her permitted say.

[1] The classical "Phylarchs," who had charge of the Badawin.

## Now when it was the Nine Hundred and Eighty-third Night,

She said, It hath reached me, O auspicious King, that the Princess, daughter to the King of the Stone-city, thus continued:—Verily, O Abdullah, my father had moneys and hoards, such as eye never saw and of which ear never heard. He used to debel Kings and do to death champions and braves in battle and in the field of fight, so that the Conquerors feared him and the Chosroës[1] humbled themselves to him. For all this, he was a miscreant in creed, ascribing to Allah partnership and adoring idols, instead of the Lord of worship; and all his troops were of images fain in lieu of the All-knowing Sovereign. One day of the days as he sat on the throne of his Kingship, compassed about with the Grandees of his realm, suddenly there came in to him a Personage, whose face illumined the whole Divan with its light. My father looked at him and saw him clad in a garb of green,[2] tall of stature and with hands that reached beneath his knees. He was of reverend aspect and awesome and the light[3] shone from his face. Said he to my sire, "O rebel, O idolater, how long wilt thou take pride in worshipping idols and abandoning the service of the All-knowing King? Say:—I testify that there is no god but *the* God and that Mohammed is His servant and His messenger. And embrace Al-Islam, thou and thy tribe; and put away from you the worship of idols, for they neither suffice man's need nor intercede. None is worshipful save Allah alone, who raised up the heavens without columns and spread out the earths like carpets in mercy to His creatures."[4] Quoth my father, "Who art thou, O man who rejectest the worship of idols, that thou sayst thus? Fearest thou not that the idols will be wroth with thee?" He replied, "The idols are stones; their anger cannot prejudice me nor their favour profit me. So do thou set in my presence thine idol which thou adorest and bid all thy folk bring each his image: and when they are all present, do ye pray them to be wroth with me and I will pray my Lord to be wroth with them, and ye shall descry the difference between the anger of the creature and that of the Creator. For your idols, ye fashioned them yourselves and the Satans clad

---

[1] "The Jabábirah" (giant-rulers of Syria) and the "Akásirah" (Chosröes-Kings of Persia).

[2] This shows (and we are presently told) that the intruder was Al-Khizr, the "Green Prophet."

[3] *i.e.* of salvation supposed to radiate from all Prophets, esp. from Mohammed.

[4] This formula which has occurred from the beginning is essentially Koranic: See Chapt. li. 18-19 and passim.

themselves therewith as with clothing, and they it is who spake to you from within the bellies of the images,[1] for your idols are made and the maker is my God to whom naught is impossible. An the True appear to you, do ye cleave to it, and if the False appear to you, do ye leave it." Cried they, "Give us a proof of thy god, that we may see it;" and quoth he, "Give me proof of *your* gods." So the King bade everyone who worshipped his Lord in image-form to bring it, and all the armies brought their idols to the Divan. Thus fared it with them; but as for me, I was sitting behind a curtain, whence I could look upon my father's Divan, and I had an idol of emerald whose bigness was as the bigness of a son of Adam. My father demanded it, so I sent it to the Divan, where they set it down beside that of my sire, which was of jacinth, whilst the Wazir's idol was of diamond.[2] As for those of the Grandees and Notables, some where of balass-ruby and some of carnelian, others of coral or Comorin aloes-wood and yet others of ebony or silver or gold; and each had his own idol, after the measure of his competence; whilst the idols of the common soldiers and of the people were some of granite, some of wood, some of pottery and some of mud; and all were of various hues, yellow and red; green, black and white. Then said the Personage to my sire, "Pray your idol and these idols to be wroth with me." So they aligned the idols in a Divan,[3] setting my father's idol on a chair of gold at the upper end, with mine by its side, and ranking the others each according to the condition of him who owned it and worshipped it. Then my father arose and prostrating himself to his own idol, said to it, "O my god, thou art the Bountiful Lord, nor is there among the idols a greater than thyself. Thou knowest that this person cometh to me, attacking thy divinity and making mock of thee; yea, he avoucheth that he hath a god stronger than thou and he ordereth us leave adoring thee and adore his god. So be thou

---

[1] This trick of the priest hidden within the image may date from the days of the vocal Memnon, and was a favourite in India, esp. at the shrine of Somnauth (Soma-náth), the Moon-god, Atergatis, Aphrodite, etc.

[2] Arab. "Almás" = Gr. Adamas. In opposition to the learned ex-Professor Maskelyne I hold that the cutting of the diamond is of very ancient date. Mr. W. M. Flinders Petrie (The Pyramids and Temples of Gizah, London: Field and Tuer, 1884) whose studies have thoroughly demolished the freaks and unfacts, the fads and fancies of the "Pyramidists," and who may be said to have raised measurement to the rank of a fine art, believes that the euritic statues of old Egypt such as that of Khufu (Cheops) in the Bulak Museum were drilled by means of diamonds. Athenæus tells us (lib. v.) that the Indians brought pearls and diamonds to the procession of Ptolemy Philadelphus; and this suggests cutting, as nothing can be less ornamental than the uncut stone.

[3] *i.e.* as if they were holding a "Durbar"; the King's idol in the Sadr or place of honour and the others ranged about it in their several ranks.

wrath with him, O my god!" And he went on to supplicate the idol; but the idol returned him no reply neither bespoke him with aught of speech: whereupon quoth he, "O my god, this is not of thy wont, for thou usedst to answer me, when I addressed thee. How cometh it that I see thee silent and speaking not? Art thou unheeding or asleep?[1] Awake; succour me and speak to me!" And he shook it with his hand; but it spake not neither stirred from its stead. Thereupon quoth the Personage, "What aileth thine idol that it speaketh not?" and quoth the King, "Methinks he is absent-minded or asleep." Exclaimed the other, "O enemy of Allah, how canst thou worship a god that speaketh not nor availeth unto aught and not worship my God, who to prayers deigns assent and who is ever present and never absent, neither unheeding nor sleeping, whom conjecture may not ween, who seeth and is not seen and who over all things terrene is omnipotent? Thy god is powerless and cannot guard itself from harm; and indeed a stoned Satan had clothed himself therewith as with a coat that he might debauch thee and delude thee. But now hath its devil departed: so do thou worship Allah and testify that there is no god but He and that none is worshipful nor worshipworth but Himself; neither is there any good but His good. As for this thy god, it cannot ward off hurt from itself: so how shall it ward off harm from thee? See with thine own eyes its impotence." So saying, he went up to the idol and dealt it a cuff on the neck, that it fell to the ground; whereupon the King waxed wroth and cried to the bystanders, "This froward atheist hath smitten my god. Slay him!" So they would have arisen to smite him, but none of them could stir from his place. Then he propounded to them Al-Islam; but they refused to become Moslems, and he said, "I will show you the wroth of my Lord." Quoth they, "Let us see it!" So he spread out his hands and said, "O my God and my Lord, Thou art my stay and my hope; answer Thou my prayer against these lewd folk, who eat of Thy good and worship other gods. O Thou the Truth, O Thou of All-might, O Creator of Day and Night, I beseech Thee to turn these people into stones, for Thou art the Puissant nor is aught impossible to Thee, and Thou over all things art omnipotent!" And Allah transformed the people of this city into

[1] These words are probably borrowed from the taunts of Elijah to the priests of Baal (1 Kings xviii. 27). Both Jews and Moslems wilfully ignored the proper use of the image or idol which was to serve as a Kiblah or direction of prayer and an object upon which to concentrate thought, and looked only to the abuse of the ignobile vulgus who believe in its intrinsic powers. Christendom has perpetuated the dispute: Romanism affects statues and pictures; Greek orthodoxy pictures and not statues, and Protestantism ousts both.

stones; but, as for me, when I saw the manifest proof of His deity, I submitted myself to Him and was saved from that which befel the rest. Then the Personage drew near me and said "Felicity[1] was fore-ordained of Allah to thee and in this a purpose had He." And he went on to instruct me and I took unto him the oath and covenant.[2] I was then seven years of age and am now thirty years old. Presently said I to him, "O my lord, all that is in the city and all its citizens are become stones by thine effectual prayer, and I am saved, for that I embraced Al-Islam at thy hands. Wherefore thou art become my Shaykh; so do thou tell me thy name and succour me with thy security and provide me with provision whereon I may subsist." Quoth he, "My name is Abu al-'Abbás al-Khizr;" and he planted me a pomegranate-tree, which forthright grew up and foliaged, flowered and fruited, and bare one pomegranate; whereupon quoth he, "Eat of that wherewith Allah the Almighty provideth thee and worship Him with the worship which is His due." Then he taught me the tenets of Al-Islam and the canons of prayer and the way of worship, together with the recital of the Koran, and I have now worshipped Allah in this place three-and-twenty years. Each day the tree yieldeth me a pomegranate which I eat and it sustaineth me from tide to tide; and every Friday, Al-Khizr (on whom be Peace!) cometh to me and 'tis he who acquainted me with thy name and gave me the glad tidings of thy soon coming hither, saying to me, "When he shall come to thee, entreat him with honour and obey his bidding and gainsay him not; but be thou to him wife and he shall be to thee man, and wend with him whitherso he will." So, when I saw thee, I knew thee, and such is the story of this city and of its people, and—the Peace! Then she showed me the pomegranate-tree, whereon was one granado, which she took, and eating one-half thereof herself, gave me the other to eat, and never did I taste aught sweeter or more savoury or more satisfying than that pomegranate. After this, I said to her, "Art thou content, even as the Shaykh Al-Khizr charged thee, to be my wife and take me to mate; and art thou ready to go with me to my own country and abide with me in the city of Bassorah?" She replied, "Yes, Inshallah—an it please Almighty Allah—I hearken to thy word and obey thy hest without gainsaying." Then I made a binding covenant with her and she carried me into her father's treasury,

---

[1] Arab. "Sa'ádah" = worldly prosperity and future happiness.

[2] Arab. "Al-'Ahd wa al-Mísák," the troth pledged between the Muríd or apprentice-Darwaysh and the Shaykh or Master-Darwaysh, binding the former to implicit obedience, etc.

whence we took what we could carry, and going forth that city, walked on till we came to my brothers, whom I found searching for me. They asked, "Where hast thou been? Indeed thou hast tarried long from us, and our hearts were troubled for thee." And the captain of the ship said to me, "O merchant Abdullah, the wind hath been fair for us this great while, and thou hast hindered us from setting sail." Whereto I answered, "There is no harm in that: ofttimes slow[1] is sure, and my absence hath wrought us naught but advantage, for indeed, there hath betided me therein the attainment of our hopes, and God-gifted is he who said:—

I weet not, whenas to a land I wend * In quest of good, what I shall there obtain;
Or gain I fare with sole desire to seek; * Or loss that seeketh me when seek I gain.

Then said I to them, "See what hath fallen to me in this mine absence;" and displayed to them all that was with me of treasures, and told them what I had beheld in the City of Stone, adding, "Had ye hearkened to me and gone with me, ye had gotten of these things great gain."——And Shahrazad perceived the dawn of day and ceased to say her permitted say.

## Now when it was the Nine Hundred and Eighty-fourth Night,

She continued, it hath reached me, O auspicious King, that Abdullah bin Fazil said to his shipmates and to his two brothers, "Had ye gone with me, ye had gotten of these things great gain." But they said, "By Allah, had we gone, we had not dared to go in to the King of the city!" Then I said to my brothers, "No harm shall befal you; for that which I have will suffice us all and this is our lot."[2] So I divided my booty into four parts according to our number and gave one to each of my brothers and to the Captain, taking the fourth for myself, setting aside somewhat for the servants and sailors, who rejoiced and blessed me: and all were content with what I gave them, save my brothers, who changed countenance and rolled their eyes. I perceived that lust of lucre had gotten hold of them both; so I said to them, "O my brothers, methinketh what I have given you doth not satisfy you;

[1] Arab. "Taakhír," lit. postponement and meaning acting with deliberation as opposed to "Ajal" (haste) precipitate action condemned in the Koran lxv. 38.
[2] *i.e.* I have been lucky enough to get this and we will share it amongst us.

but we are brothers and there is no difference between us. My good and yours are one and the same thing, and if I die none will inherit of me but you." And I went on to soothe them. Then I bore the Princess on board the galleon and lodged her in the cabin, where I sent her somewhat to eat, and we sat talking, I and my brothers. Said they, "O our brother, what wilt thou do with that damsel of surpassing beauty?" And I replied, "I mean to contract marriage with her as soon as I reach Bassorah, and make a splendid wedding and marry her there." Exclaimed one of them, "O my brother, verily this young lady excelleth in beauty and loveliness, and the love of her is fallen on my heart; wherefore I desire that thou give her to me and I will espouse her." And the other cried, "I too desire this: give her to me, that I may espouse her." "O my brothers," answered I, "indeed she took of me an oath and a covenant that I would marry her myself; so, if I give her to one of you, I shall be false to my oath and to the covenant between me and her, and haply she will be broken-hearted, for she came not with me but on condition that I marry her. So how can I wed her to other than myself? As for your both loving her, I love her more than you twain, for she is my treasure-trove, and as for my giving her to one of you, that is a thing which may not be. But, if we reach Bassorah in safety, I will look you out two girls of the best of the damsels of Bassorah and demand them for you in marriage and pay the dower of my own moneys and make one wedding, and we will all three be married on the same day. But leave ye this damsel, for she is of my portion." They held their peace, and I thought they were content with that which I had said. Then we fared onwards for Bassorah, and every day I sent her meat and drink; but she came not forth of the cabin, whilst I slept between my brothers on deck. We sailed thus forty days, till we sighted Bassorah city and rejoiced that we were come near it. Now I trusted in my brothers, and was at my ease with them, for none knoweth the hidden future save Allah the Most High; so I lay down to sleep that night; but, as I abode drowned in slumber, I suddenly found myself caught up by these my brothers, one seizing me by the legs and the other by the arms, for they had taken counsel together to drown me in the sea for the sake of the damsel. When I saw myself in their hands, I said to them, "O my brothers, why do ye this with me?" And they replied, "Ill-bred that thou art, wilt thou barter our affection for a girl? we will cast thee into the sea, because of this." So saying, they threw me overboard. (Here Abdullah turned to the dogs and said to them, "Is this that I have said true, O my brothers, or not?" and they bowed their heads and fell a-whining, as if confirming his speech; whereat the Caliph wondered). Then Abdullah resumed: O Commander of the Faithful, when they threw me into the sea, I sank to the bottom; but the water bore me up again to the surface, and before I could think, behold, a great bird, the bigness of a man, swooped down upon me and snatching me up, flew up with me into upper air. I fainted, and when I opened my eyes I found myself in a strong-pillared place, a high-builded palace, adorned with magnificent paintings and pendants of gems of all shapes and hues. Therein were damsels standing with their hands crossed over their breasts, and, behold, in their midst was a lady seated on a throne of red gold, set with pearls and gems, and clad in apparel whereon no mortal might open his eyes, for the lustre of the gems wherewith they were decked. About her waist she wore a girdle of jewels no money could pay their worth, and on her head a three-fold tiara dazing thought and wit and dazzling heart and sight. Then the bird which had carried me thither shook and became a young lady bright as sun raying light. I fixed my eyes on her and behold, it was she whom I had seen in snake form on the mountain and had rescued from the dragon which had wound his tail around her. Then said to her the lady who sat upon the throne, "Why hast thou brought hither this mortal?" and she replied, "O my mother, this is he who was the means of saving my life among the maidens of the Jinn." Then quoth she to me, "Knowest thou who I am?" and quoth I, "No." Said she, "I am she who was on such a mountain, where the black dragon strave with me and would have killed me, but thou slewest him." And I said, "I saw but a white snake with the dragon." She rejoined, "'Tis I who was the white snake; but I am the daughter of the Red King, Sovran of the Jann and my name is Sa'ídah.[1] She who sitteth there is my mother and her name is Mubárakah, wife of the Red King. The black dragon who attacked me and would have killed me was Wazir to the Black King, Darfíl by name, and he was foul of favour. It chanced that he saw me and fell in love with me; so he sought me in marriage of my sire, who sent to him to say, "Who art thou, O scum of Wazirs, that thou shouldst wed with Kings' daughters?" Whereupon he was wroth and sware an oath that he would assuredly kill me to spite my father. Then he fell to tracking my steps and following me whithersoever I went, designing to kill me; wherefore there befel between him and my parent mighty fierce wars and bloody jars, but my sire

---

[1] Sa'ídah = the auspicious (fem.): Mubárakah, = the blessed; both names showing that the bearers were Moslemahs.

could not prevail against him, for that he was fierce as fraudful, and as often as my father pressed hard upon him and seemed like to conquer, he would escape from him, till my sire was at his wits' ends. Every day I was forced to take new form and hue; for, as often as I assumed a shape, he would assume its contrary, and to whatsoever land I fled he would snuff my fragrance and follow me thither, so that I suffered sore affliction of him. At last I took the form of a snake and betook myself to the mountain where thou sawest me: whereupon he changed himself to a dragon and pursued me, till I fell into his hands, when he strove with me and I struggled with him, till he wearied me and overcame me, meaning to kill me but thou camest and smotest him with the stone and slewest him. Then I returned to my own shape and showed myself to thee, saying:—I am indebted to thee for a service such as is not lost save with the son of evil.[1] So, when I saw thy brothers do with thee this treachery and throw thee into the sea, I hastened to thee and saved thee from destruction, and now honour is due to thee from my mother and my father." Then she said to the Queen, "O my mother, do thou honour him as deserveth he who saved my life." So the Queen said to me, "Welcome, O mortal! Indeed thou hast done us a kindly deed which meriteth honour." Presently she ordered me a treasure-suit,[2] worth a mint of money, and store of gems and precious stones, and said, "Take him and carry him in to the King." Accordingly, they carried me to the King in his Divan, where I found him seated on his throne, with his Marids and guards before him; and when I saw him my sight was blent for that which was upon him of jewels, but when he saw me, he rose to his feet and all his officers rose also, to do him worship. Then he saluted me and welcomed me and entreated me with the utmost honour, and gave me of that which was with him of good things; after which he said to some of his followers, "Take him and carry him back to my daughter, that she may restore him to the place whence she brought him." So they carried me back to the Lady Sa'idah, who took me up and flew away with me and my treasures. On this wise fared it with me and the Princess; but as regards the captain of the galleon, he was aroused by the splash of my fall, when my brothers cast me into the sea, and said, "What is that which hath fallen overboard?" Whereupon my brothers fell to weeping and beating of breasts and replied, "Alas, for our

---

[1] *i.e.* the base-born, from whom base deeds may be expected.

[2] Arab. "Badlat Kunúzíyah = such a dress as would be found in enchanted hoards (Kunúz); *e.g.* Prince Esterhazy's diamond jacket.

brother's loss! He thought to look over the ship's side and fell into the water!" Then they laid their hands on my good, but there befel dispute between them because of the damsel, each saying, "None shall have her but I." And they abode jangling and wrangling each with other and remembered not their brother nor his drowning, and their mourning for him ceased. As they were thus, behold Sa'idah alighted with me in the midst of the galleon,——And Shahrazad was surprised by the dawn of day and ceased saying her permitted say.

## Now when it was the Nine Hundred and Eighty-fifth Night,

She pursued, It hath reached me, O auspicious King, that Abdullah bin Fazil continued:—As they were thus, behold, Sa'idah alighted with me in the midst of the galleon, and when my brothers saw me, they embraced me and rejoiced in me, saying, "O our brother, how hast thou fared in that which befel thee? Indeed our hearts have been occupied with thee." Quoth Sa'idah, "Had ye any heart-yearnings for him or had ye loved him, ye had not cast him into the sea; but choose ye now what death ye will die." Then she seized on them and would have slain them: but they cried out, saying, "In thy safeguard, O our brother!" Thereupon I interceded and said to her, "I claim of thine honour not to kill my brothers." Quoth she, "There is no help but that I slay them, for they are traitors." However, I ceased not to speak her fair and conciliate her till she said, "To content thee, I will not kill them, but I will enchant them." So saying, she brought out a cup and filling it with sea-water, pronounced over it words that might not be understood; then saying, "Quit this human shape for the shape of a dog;" she sprinkled them with the water, and immediately they were transmewed into dogs, as thou seest them, O Vicar of Allah. (Hereupon he turned to the dogs and said to them, "Have I spoken the truth, O my brothers?" and they bowed their heads, as they would say, "Thou hast spoken sooth.") At this he continued:—Then she said to those who were in the galleon, "Know ye that Abdullah bin Fazil here present is become my brother and I shall visit him once or twice every day; so, whoso of you crosseth him or gainsayeth his bidding or doth him hurt with hand or tongue, I will do with him even as I have done with these two traitors and bespell him to a dog, and he shall end his days in that form, nor shall he find deliverance." And they all said to her, "O our lady, we are his slaves and his servants every one of us, and will not disobey him in aught." Moreover, she said to me, "When thou comest to Bassorah, examine all thy property, and if there lack aught thereof, tell me and I will bring it to thee, in whose hands and in what place soever it may be, and will change him who took it into a dog. When thou hast magazined thy goods, clap a collar [1] of wood on the neck of each of these two traitors and tie them to the leg of a couch and shut them up by themselves. Moreover, every night at midnight, do thou go down to them and beat each of them a bout till he swoon away; and if thou suffer a single night to pass without beating them, I will come to thee and drub thee a sound drubbing, after which I will drub them." And I answered, "To hear is to obey." Then said she, "Tie them up with ropes till thou come to Bassorah." So I tied a rope about each dog's neck and lashed them to the mast, and she went her way. On the morrow we entered Bassorah and the merchants came out to meet me and saluted me, and no one of them enquired of my brothers. But they looked at the dogs and said to me, "Ho, Such-and-such,[2] what wilt thou do with these two dogs thou hast brought with thee?" Quoth I, "I reared them on this voyage and have brought them home with me." And they laughed at them, knowing not that they were my brothers. When I reached my house, I put the twain in a closet and busied myself all that night with the unpacking and disposition of the bales of stuffs and jewels. Moreover, the merchants were with me, being minded to offer me the salam; wherefore I was occupied with them and forgot to beat the dogs or chain them up. Then without doing them aught of hurt, I lay down to sleep, but suddenly and unexpectedly there came to me the Red King's daughter Sa'idah and said to me, "Did I not bid thee clap chains on their necks and give each of them a bout of beating?" So saying, she seized me and pulling out a whip, flogged me till I fainted away, after which she went to the place where my brothers were, and with the same scourge beat them both till they came nigh upon death. Then said she to me, "Beat each of them a like bout every night, and if thou let a night pass without doing this, I will beat thee." I replied, "O my lady, to-morrow I will put chains on their necks, and next night I will beat them, nor will I leave them

---

[1] Arab. "Ghull," a collar of iron or other metal, sometimes made to resemble the Chinese Kza or Cangue, a kind of ambulant pillory, serving like the old stocks which still show in England the veteris vestigia ruris. See Davis, "The Chinese," i. 241. According to Al-Siyúti (p. 362) the Caliph Al-Mutawakkil ordered the Christians to wear these Ghulls round the neck, yellow head-gear and girdles, to use wooden stirrups and to place figures of devils before their houses. The writer of The Nights presently changes Ghull to "chains" and "fetters of iron."

[2] Arab. "Yá fulán," O certain person!

one night unbeaten." And she charged me strictly to beat them and disappeared. When the morning morrowed it being no light matter for me to put fetters of iron on their necks, I went to a goldsmith and bade him make them collars and chains of gold. He did this and I put the collars on their necks and chained them up, as she bade me; and next night I beat them both in mine own despite. This befel in the Caliphate of Al-Mahdi,[1] third of the sons of Al-Abbas, and I commended myself to him by sending him presents, so he invested me with the government and made me Viceroy of Bassorah. On this wise I abode some time, and after a while I said to myself, "Haply her wrath is grown cool," and left them a night unbeaten; whereupon she came to me and beat me a bout whose burning I shall never forget as long as I live. So, from that time to this I have never left them a single night unbeaten during the reign of Al-Mahdi; and when he deceased and thou camest to the succession, thou sentest to me, confirming me in the government of Bassorah. These twelve years past have I beaten them every night, in mine own despite, and after I have beaten them, I excuse myself to them and comfort them and give them to eat and drink; and they have remained shut up, nor did any of the creatures of Allah know of them, till thou sentest to me Abu Ishak the boon-companion, on account of the tribute, and he discovered my secret, and returning to thee acquainted thee therewith. Then thou sentest him back to fetch me and them; so I answered with "Hearkening and obedience," and brought them before thee, whereupon thou questionedst me and I told thee the truth of the case; and this is my history. The Caliph marvelled at the case of the two dogs and said to Abdullah, "Hast thou at this present forgiven thy two brothers the wrong they did thee, yea or nay?" He replied, "O my lord, may Allah forgive them and acquit them of responsibility in this world and the next! Indeed, 'tis I who stand in need of their forgiveness, for that these twelve years past I have beaten

---

[1] Father of Harun al-Rashid A.H. 158-169 (= 775-785) third Abbaside, who both in the Mac. and in the Bul. Edits. is called "the fifth of the sons of Al-Abbas." He was a good poet and a man of letters, also a fierce persecutor of the "Zindiks" (Al-Siyuti 278), a term especially applied to those who read the Zend books and adhered to Zoroastrianism, although afterwards given to any heretic or atheist. He made many changes at Meccah and was the first who had a train of camels laden with snow for his refreshment along a measured road of 700 miles (Gibbon, chapt. lii). He died of an accident when hunting: others say he was poisoned after leaving his throne to his sons Musa al-Hadi and Harun al-Rashid. The name means "Heaven-directed" and must not be confounded with the title of the twelfth Shi'ah Imám Mohammed Abu al-Kásim born at Sarramanrai A.H. 255, whom Sale (sect. iv.) calls "Mahdi or Director," and whose expected return has caused and will cause so much trouble in Al-Islam.

them a grievous bout every night!" Rejoined the Caliph, "Inshallah, O Abdullah, I will endeavour for their release and that they may become men again, as they were before, and I will make peace between thee and them; so shall you live the rest of your lives as brothers loving one another; and like as thou hast forgiven them, so shall they forgive thee. But now take them and go down with them to thy lodging and this night beat them not, and to-morrow there shall be naught save weal." Quoth Abdullah, "O my lord, as thy head liveth, if I leave them one night unbeaten, Sa'idah will come to me and beat me, and I have no body to brook beating." Quoth the Caliph, "Fear not, for I will give thee a writing under my hand.[1] An she come to thee, do thou give her the paper and if, when she has read it, she spare thee, the favour will be hers; but, if she obey not my bidding, commit thy business to Allah and let her beat thee a bout and suppose that thou hast forgotten to beat them for one night and that she beateth thee because of that: and if it fall out thus and she thwart me, as sure as I am Commander of the Faithful, I will be even with her." Then he wrote her a letter on a piece of paper, two fingers broad, and sealing it with his signet-ring, gave it to Abdullah, saying, "O Abdullah, if Sa'idah come, say to her:—The Caliph, King of mankind, hath commanded me to leave beating them and hath written me this letter for thee; and he saluteth thee with the salam. Then give her the warrant and fear no harm." After which he exacted of him an oath and a solemn pledge that he would not beat them. So Abdullah took the dogs and carried them to his lodging, saying to himself, "I wonder what the Caliph will do with the daughter of the Sovran of the Jinn, if she cross him and trounce me to-night! But I will bear with a bout of beating for once and leave my brothers at rest this night, though for their sake I suffer torture." Then he bethought himself awhile, and his reason said to him, "Did not the Caliph rely on some great support, he had never forbidden me from beating them." So he entered his lodging and doffed the collars from the dogs' necks, saying, "I put my trust in Allah," and fell to comforting them and saying, "No harm shall befal you; for the Caliph, fifth[2] of the sons

---

[1] This speciosum miraculum must not be held a proof that the tale was written many years after the days of Al-Rashid. Miracles grow apace in the East and a few years suffice to mature them. The invasion of Abraha the Abyssinian took place during the year of Mohammed's birth; and yet in an early chapter of the Koran (No. cv.) written perhaps forty-five years afterwards, the small-pox is turned into a puerile and extravagant miracle. I myself became the subject of a miracle in Sind which is duly chronicled in the family annals of a certain Pir or religious teacher. See History of Sindh (p. 230) and Sind Revisited (i. 156).

[2] In the texts, "Sixth."

of Al-Abbas, hath pledged himself for your deliverance and I have forgiven you. An it please Allah the Most High, the time is come and ye shall be delivered this blessed night; so rejoice ye in the prospect of peace and gladness." When they heard these words, they fell to whining with the whining of dogs,——And Shahrazad perceived the dawn of day and ceased to say her permitted say.

## Now when it was the Nine Hundred and Eighty-sixth Night,

She resumed, It hath reached me, O aupicious King, that Abdullah bin Fazil said to his brothers, "Rejoice ye in the prospect of comfort and gladness." And when they heard his words they fell to whining with the whining of dogs, and rubbed their jowls against his feet, as if blessing him and humbling themselves before him. He mourned over them and took to stroking their backs till supper time; and when they set on the trays he bade the dogs sit. So they sat down and ate with him from the tray, whilst his officers stood gaping and marvelling at his eating with dogs and all said, "Is he mad or are his wits gone wrong? How can the Viceroy of Bassorah city, he who is greater than a Wazir, eat with dogs? Knoweth he not that the dog is unclean?"[1] And they stared at the dogs, as they ate with him as servants eat with their lords,[2] knowing not that they were his brothers; nor did they cease staring at them, till they had made an end of eating, when Abdullah washed his hands and the dogs also put out their paws and washed; whereupon all who were present began to laugh at them and to marvel, saying, one to other, "Never in our lives saw we dogs eat and wash their paws after eating!" Then the dogs sat down on the divans beside Abdullah, nor dared any ask him of this; and thus the case lasted till midnight, when he dismissed the attendants and lay down to sleep and the dogs with him, each on a couch; whereupon the servants said one to other, "Verily, he hath lain down to sleep and the two dogs are lying with him." Quoth another, "Since he hath eaten with the dogs from the same tray, there is no harm in their sleeping with him; and this is naught save the fashion of madmen." Moreover, they ate not anything of the

[1] Arab. "Najis" = ceremonially impure, especially the dog's mouth, like the cow's mouth amongst the Hindus; and requiring after contact the Wuzu-ablution before the Moslem can pray.

[2] Arab. "Akl al-hashamah" (hashamah = retinue; hishmah = reverence, bashfulness) which may also mean "decorously and respectfully," according to the vowel-points.

food which remained in the tray, saying, "'Tis unclean." Such was their case; but as for Abdullah, ere he could think, the earth clave asunder and out rose Sa'idah, who said to him, "O Abdullah, why hast thou not beaten them this night and why hast thou undone the collars from their necks? Hast thou acted on this wise perversely and in mockery of my commandment? But I will at once beat thee and spell thee into a dog like them." He replied, "O my lady, I conjure thee by the graving upon the seal-ring of Solomon David-son (on the twain be the Peace!) have patience with me till I tell thee my cause and after do with me what thou wilt." Quoth she, "Say on;" and quoth he, "The reason of my not punishing them is only this. The King of mankind, the Commander of the Faithful, the Caliph Harun al-Rashid, ordered me not to beat them this night and took of me oaths and covenants to that effect; and he saluteth thee with the salam and hath committed to me a mandate under his own hand, which he bade me give thee. So I obeyed his order, for to obey the Commander of the Faithful is obligatory; and here is the mandate. Take it and read it and after work thy will." She replied, "Hither with it!" So he gave her the letter and she opened it and read as follows, "In the name of Allah, the Compassionating, the Compassionate! From the King of mankind, Harun al-Rashid, to the daughter of the Red King, Sa'idah! But, after. Verily, this man hath forgiven his brothers and hath waived his claim against them, and we have enjoined them to reconciliation. Now, when reconciliation ruleth, retribution is remitted, and if you of the Jinn contradict us in our commandments, we will contrary you in yours and traverse your ordinances; but, an ye obey our bidding and further our orders, we will indeed do the like with yours. Wherefore I bid thee hurt them no hurt, and if thou believe in Allah and in His Apostle, it behoveth thee to obey and us to command.[1] So an thou spare them, I will requite thee with that whereto my Lord shall enable me; and the token of obedience is that thou remove thine enchantment from these two men, so they may come before me to-morrow, free. But an thou release them not, I will release them in thy despite, by the aid of Almighty Allah." When she had read the letter, she said, "O Abdullah, I will do naught till I go to my sire and show him the mandate of the monarch of mankind and return to thee with the answer in haste." So saying, she signed with her hand to the earth, which clave open and she disappeared therein, whilst Abdullah's heart

---

[1] *i.e.* as the Vice-regent of Allah and Vicar of the Prophet.

was like to fly for joy and he said, "Allah advance the Commander of the Faithful!" As for Sa'idah, she went in to her father; and, acquainting him with that which had passed, gave him the Caliph's letter, which he kissed and laid on his head. Then he read it and understanding its contents said, "O my daughter, verily, the ordinance of the monarch of mankind obligeth us, and his commandments are effectual over us, nor can we disobey him; so go thou and release the two men forthwith and say to them:—Ye are freed by the intercession of the monarch of mankind. For, should he be wroth with us, he would destroy us to the last of us; so do not thou impose upon us that which we are unable." Quoth she, "O my father, if the monarch of mankind were wroth with us, what could he do with us?" and quoth her sire, "He hath power over us for several reasons. In the first place, he is a man and hath thus pre-eminence over us; secondly he is the Vicar of Allah; and thirdly, he is constant in praying the dawn-prayer of two bows;[1] therefore were all the tribes of the Jinn assembled together against him from the Seven Worlds they could do him no hurt. But he, should he be wroth with us would pray the dawn-prayer of two bows and cry out upon us one cry, when we should all present ourselves before him obediently and stand before him as sheep before the butcher. If he would, he could command us to quit our abiding-places for a desert country wherein we might not endure to sojourn; and if he desired to destroy us, he would bid us destroy ourselves, whereupon we should destroy one another. Wherefore we may not disobey his bidding for, if we did this, he would consume us with fire nor could we flee from before him to any asylum. Thus it is with every True Believer who is persistent in praying the dawn-prayer of two bows; his commandment is effectual over us: so be not thou the means of our destruction because of two mortals, but go forthright and release them ere the anger of the Commander of the Faithful fall upon us." So she returned to Abdullah and acquainted him with her father's words, saying, "Kiss for us the hands of the Prince of True Believers and seek his approval for us." Then she brought out the tasse and filling it with water, conjured over it and uttered words which might not be understood; after which she sprinkled the dogs with the water, saying, "Quit the form of dogs and return to the shape of men!" Whereupon they became men as before and the spell of the enchantment was loosed from them. Quoth they, "I testify that

---

[1] According to Al-Siyuti, Harun Al-Rashid prayed every day a hundred bows.

there is no god but *the* God and I testify that Mohammed is the Apostle of God!" Then they fell on their brother's feet and hands, kissing them and beseeching his forgiveness : but he said, "Do ye forgive me;" and they both repented with sincere repentance, saying, "Verily, the damned Devil lured us and covetise deluded us: but our Lord hath requited us after our deserts, and forgiveness is of the signs of the noble." And they went on to supplicate their brother and weep and profess repentance for that which had befallen him from them.[1] Then quoth he to them, "What did ye with my wife whom I brought from the City of Stone?" Quoth they, "When Satan tempted us and we cast thee into the sea, there arose strife between us, each saying, I will have her to wife. Now when she heard these words and beheld our contention, she knew that we had thrown thee into the sea; so she came up from the cabin and said to us:—Contend not because of me, for I will not belong to either of you. My husband is gone into the sea and I will follow him. So saying, she cast herself overboard and died." Exclaimed Abdullah, "In very sooth she died a martyr! But there is no Majesty and there is no Might save in Allah, the Glorious, the Great!" Then he wept for her with sore weeping and said to his brothers, "It was not well of you to do this deed and bereave me of my wife." They answered, "Indeed, we have sinned, but our Lord hath requited us our misdeed and this was a thing which Allah decreed unto us ere He created us." And he accepted their excuse; but Sa'idah said to him, "Have they done all these things to thee and wilt thou forgive them?" He replied, "O my sister, whoso hath power[2] and spareth, for Allah's reward he prepareth." Then said she, "Be on thy guard against them, for they are traitors;" and farewelled him and fared forth.—— And Shahrazad was surprised by the dawn of day and ceased saying her permitted say.

## Now when it was the Nine Hundred and Eighty-seventh Night,

She said, It hath reached me, O auspicious King, that Abdullah, when Sa'idah warned him and blessed him and went her ways, passed the rest of the night with his brothers, and on the morrow he

---

[1] As the sad end of his betrothed was still to be accounted for.

[2] *i.e.* if he have the power to revenge himself. The sentiment is Christian rather than Moslem.

sent them to the Hammam and clad each of them, on his coming forth, in a suit worth a hoard of money. Then he called for the tray of food and they set it before him and he ate, he and his brothers. When his attendants saw the twain and knew them for his brothers they saluted them and said to him, "O our lord, Allah give thee joy of thy reunion with thy dear brothers! Where have they been this while?" He replied, "It was they whom ye saw in the guise of dogs; praise be to Allah who hath delivered them from prison and grievous torment!" Then he carried them to the Divan of the Caliph and, kissing ground before Al-Rashid, wished him continuance of honour and fortune and surcease of evil and enmity. Quoth the Caliph, "Welcome, O Emir Abdullah! Tell me what hath befallen thee." And quoth he:—O Commander of the Faithful (whose power Allah increase!) when I carried my brothers home to my lodging, my heart was at rest concerning them, because thou hadst pledged thyself to their release and I said in myself, "Kings fail not to attain aught for which they strain, inasmuch as the divine favour aideth them." So I took off the collars from their necks, putting my trust in Allah, and ate with them from the same tray, which when my suite saw, they made light of my wit and said one to other, "He is surely mad! How can the Governor of Bassorah, who is greater than the Wazir, eat with dogs?" Then they threw away what was in the tray, saying, "We will not eat the dogs' orts." And they went on to befool my reason, whilst I heard their words, but returned them no reply because of their unknowing that the dogs were my brothers. When the hour of rest came, I sent them away and addressed myself to sleep; but, ere I was ware, the earth clave in sunder and out came Sa'idah, the Red King's daughter, enraged against me, with eyes like fire. And he went on to relate to the Caliph all that had passed between him and her and her father, and how she had transmewed his brothers from canine to human form, adding, "And here they are before thee, O Commander of the Faithful!" The Caliph looked at them and, seeing two young men like moons, said, "Allah requite thee for me with good, O Abdullah, for that thou hast acquainted me with an advantage[1] I knew not! Henceforth, Inshallah, I will never leave to pray these two-bow orisons before the breaking of the dawn, what while I live." Then he reproved Abdullah's brothers for their past transgressions against him and they excused themselves before the

---

[1] *i.e.* the power acquired (as we afterwards learn) by the regular praying of the dawn-prayer. It is not often that The Nights condescend to point a moral or inculcate a lesson as here; and we are truly thankful for the immunity.

Caliph, who said, "Join hands[1] and forgive one another and Allah pardon what is past!" Upon which he turned to Abdullah and said to him, "O Abdullah, make thy brothers thine assistants and be careful of them." Then he charged them to be obedient to their brother and bade them return to Bassorah after he had bestowed on them abundant largesse. So they went down from the Caliph's Divan, whilst he rejoiced in this advantage he had obtained by the action aforesaid, to wit, persistence in praying two inclinations before dawn, and exclaimed, He spake truth who said, "The misfortune of one tribe fortuneth another tribe."[2] On this wise befel it to them from the Caliph; but as regards Abdullah, he left Baghdad carrying with him his brothers in all honour and dignity and increase of quality, and fared on till they drew near Bassorah, when the notables and chief men of the place came out to meet them, and after decorating the city, brought them thereinto with a procession which had not its match, and all the folk shouted out blessings on Abdullah as he scattered amongst them silver and gold. None, however, took heed to his brothers; wherefore jealousy and envy entered their hearts, for all he entreated them tenderly as one tenders an ophthalmic eye; but the more he cherished them, the more they redoubled in envy and hatred of him: and indeed it is said on the subject:—

I'd win good will of every one, but whoso envies me * Will not be won on any wise and makes mine office hard:
How gain the gree of envious wight who coveteth my good, * When naught will satisfy him save to see my good go marr'd?

Then he gave each a slave-girl that had not her like, and eunuchs and servants and slaves white and black, of each kind forty. He also gave each of them fifty steeds, all thoroughbreds, and they got them guards and followers; and he assigned to them revenues and appointed them solde and stipends and made them his assistants, saying to them, "O my brothers, I and you are equal and there is no distinction between me and you twain,——And Shahrazad perceived the dawn of day and ceased to say her permitted say.

---

[1] Arab. "Musáfahah," which, I have said, serves for our shaking hands: and extends over wide regions. They apply the palms of the right hands flat to each other without squeezing the fingers and then raise the latter to the forehead Pilgrimage ii. 332, has also been quoted.

[2] Equivalent to our saying about an ill wind, etc.

## Now when it was the Nine Hundred and Eighty-eighth Night,

She continued, It hath reached me, O auspicious King, that Abdullah assigned stipends to his brothers and made them his assistants, saying, "O my brothers, I and you are equal and there is no distinction between me and you twain, and after Allah and the Caliph, the commandment is mine and yours. So rule you at Bassorah in my absence and in my presence, and your commandments shall be effectual; but look that ye fear Allah in your ordinances and beware of oppression, which if it endure depopulateth; and apply yourselves to justice, for justice, if it be prolonged, peopleth a land. Oppress not the True Believers, or they will curse you and ill report of you will reach the Caliph, wherefore dishonour will betide both me and you. Go not therefore about to violence any, but whatso ye greed for of the goods of the folk, take it from my goods, over and above that whereof ye have need; for 'tis not unknown to you what is handed down in the Koran of prohibition versets on the subject of oppression, and Allah-gifted is he who said these couplets:—

Oppression ambusheth in sprite of man * Whom naught withholdeth save the lack of might:
The sage shall ne'er apply his wits to aught * Until befitting time direct his sight:
The tongue of wisdom woneth in the heart; * And in his mouth the tongue of foolish wight.
Who at Occasion's call lacks power to rise * Is slain by feeblest who would glut his spite.
A man may hide his blood and breed, but aye * His deeds on darkest hiddens cast a light.
Wights of ill strain with ancestry as vile * Have lips which never spake one word aright;
And who committeth case to hands of fool * In folly proveth self as fond and light;
And who his secret tells to folk at large * Shall rouse his foes to work him worst despight.
Suffice the generous what regards his lot * Nor meddles he with aught regards him not.

And he went on to admonish his brothers and bid them to equity and forbid them from tyranny, doubting not but they would love him the better for his boon of good counsel,[1] and he relied upon them and honoured them with the utmost honour; but notwith-

[1] A proof of his extreme simplicity and bonhomie.

standing all his generosity to them, they only waxed in envy and hatred of him, till, one day, the two being together alone, quoth Nasir to Mansur, "O my brother, how long shall we be mere subjects of our brother Abdullah, and he in this estate of lordship and worship? After being a merchant he is become an Emir, and from being little he is grown great: but we, we grow not great nor is there aught of respect or degree left us; for, behold, he laugheth at us and maketh us his assistants! What is the meaning of this? Is it not that we are his servants and under his subjection? But, long as he abideth in good case, our rank will never be raised nor shall we be aught of repute; wherefore we shall not fulfil our wish, except we slay him and win to his wealth, nor will it be possible to get his gear save after his death. So, when we have slain him, we shall become lords and will take all that is in his treasuries of gems and things of price and divide them between us. Then will we send the Caliph a present and demand of him the government of Cufah, and thou shalt be Governor of Cufah and I of Bassorah. Thus each of us shall have formal estate and condition, but we shall never effect this, except we put him out of the world!" Answered Mansur, "Thou sayest sooth, but how shall we do to kill him?" Quoth Nasir, "We will make an entertainment in the house of one of us and invite him thereto and serve him with the uttermost service. Then will we sit through the night with him in talk and tell him tales and jests and rare stories till his heart melteth with sitting up, when we will spread him a bed, that he may lie down to sleep. When he is asleep, we will kneel upon him and throttle him and throw him into the river; and on the morrow we will say:—His sister the Jinniyah came to him, as he sat chatting with us, and said to him:—O thou scum of mankind, who art thou that thou shouldst complain of me to the Commander of the Faithful? Deemest thou that we dread him? As he is a King, so we too are Kings, and if he mend not his manners in our regard we will do him die by the foulest of deaths. But meantime I will slay thee, that we may see what the hand of the Prince of True Believers availeth to do. So saying, she caught him up and clave the earth and disappeared with him, which when we saw, we swooned away. Then we revived and we reck not what is become of him. And saying this we will send to the Caliph and tell him the case and he will invest us with the government in his room. After a while, we will send him a sumptuous present and seek of him the government of Cufah, and one of us shall abide in Bassorah and the other in Cufah. So shall the land be pleasant to us and we will be down upon the True Believers and win our wishes." And quoth Mansur, "Thou counsellest well, O my brother," and they agreed upon the murther. So Nasir made an entertainment and said to Abdullah "O my brother, verily I am thy brother, and I would have thee hearten my heart, thou and my brother Mansur, and eat of my banquet in my house, so I may boast of thee and that it may be said, The Emir Abdullah hath eaten of his brother Nasir's guest-meal; when my heart will be solaced by this best of boons." Abdullah replied, "So be it, O my brother; there is no distinction between me and thee, and thy house is my house; but since thou invitest me, none refuseth hospitality save the churl." Then he turned to Mansur and said to him, "Wilt thou go with me to thy brother Nasir's house and we will eat of his feast and heal his heart?" Replied Mansur, "As thy head liveth, O my brother, I will not go with thee, unless thou swear to me that, after thou comest forth of our brother Nasir's house, thou wilt enter my home and eat of my banquet! Is Nasir thy brother and am not I thy brother? So even as thou heartenest his heart, do thou hearten mine." Answered Abdullah, "There is no harm in that: with love and gladly gree! When I come out from Nasir's house, I will enter thine, for thou art my brother even as he." So he kissed his hand and going forth of the Divan, made ready his feast. On the morrow, Abdullah took horse and repaired, with his brother Mansur and a company of his officers, to Nasir's house, where they sat down, he and Mansur and his many. Then Nasir set the trays before them and welcomed them; so they ate and drank and sat in mirth and merriment; after which the trays and the platters were removed and they washed their hands. They passed the day in feasting and wine-drinking and diversion and delight till nightfall, when they supped and prayed the sundown prayers, and the night orisons; after which they sat conversing and carousing, and Nasir and Mansur fell to telling stories, whilst Abdullah hearkened. Now they three were alone in the pavilion, the rest of the company being in another place, and they ceased not to tell quips and tales and rare adventures and anecdotes, till Abdullah's heart was dissolved within him for watching, and sleep overcame him.——And Shahrazad was surprised by the dawn of day and ceased saying her permitted say.

## Now when it was the Nine Hundred and Eighty-ninth Night,

She pursued, It hath reached me, O auspicious King, that when Abdullah was a-wearied with watching and wanted to sleep, they also lay beside him on another couch and waited till he was drowned in slumber, and when they were certified thereof they arose and knelt upon him: whereupon he awoke and seeing them kneeling on his breast, said to them, "What is this, O my brothers?" Cried they, "We are no brothers of thine, nor do we know thee, unmannerly that thou art! Thy death is become better than thy life." Then they gripped him by the throat and throttled him, till he lost his senses and abode without motion; so that they deemed him dead. Now the pavilion wherein they were overlooked the river; so they cast him into the water; but when he fell, Allah sent to his aid a dolphin[1] who was accustomed to come under that pavilion because the kitchen had a window that gave upon the stream; and, as often as they slaughtered any beast there, it was their wont to throw the refuse into the river, and the dolphin came and picked it from the surface of the water; wherefore he ever resorted to the place. That day they had cast out much offal by reason of the banquet; so the dolphin ate more than of wont and gained strength. Hearing the splash of Abdullah's fall, he hastened to the spot, where he saw a son of Adam, and Allah guided him so that he took the man on his back, and crossing the current made with him for the other bank, where he cast his burthen ashore. Now the place where the dolphin threw up Abdullah was a well-beaten highway, and presently up came a caravan, and finding him lying on the river bank, said, "Here is a drowned man, whom the river hath cast up;" and the travellers gathered around to gaze at the corpse. The Shaykh of the caravan was a man of worth, skilled in all sciences and versed in the mystery of medicine, and withal sound of judgment: so he said to them, "O folk, what is the news?" They answered, "Here is a drowned man;" whereupon he went up to Abdullah and examining him, said to them, "O folk, there is life yet in this young man, who is a person of condition and of the sons of the great, bred in honour and fortune, and, Inshallah, there is still hope of him." Then he took him and clothing him in dry clothes warmed him before the fire; after which he nursed him and tended him during three days' march till he revived; but he was passing feeble by reason of the shock, and the chief of the caravan proceeded to medicine him with such simples as he knew, what while they ceased not faring on till they had travelled thirty days' journey from Bassorah and came to a city in the land of the Persians, by name

[1] Arab. "Dárfil = the Gr. δελφίς, later δελφίν, suggesting that the writer had read of Arion in Herodotus i. 23.

'Aúj.[1] Here they alighted at a Khan and spread Abdullah a bed, where he lay groaning all night and troubling the folk with his moans. And when morning morrowed the concierge of the Khan came to the chief of the caravan and said to him, "What is this sick man thou hast with thee? Verily, he disturbeth us." Quoth the chief, "I found him by the way, on the river-bank and well nigh drowned; and I have tended him, but to no effect, for he recovereth not." Said the porter, "Show him to the Shaykhah[2] Rájihah." "Who is this Religious?" asked the chief of the caravan, and the door-keeper answered, "There is with us a holy woman, a clean maid and a comely, called Rajihah, to whom they present whoso hath any ailment; an he pass a single night within her house he awaketh on the morrow whole and ailing naught." Quoth the chief, "Direct me to her;" and quoth the porter, "Take up thy sick man." So he took up Abdullah and the door-keeper forewent him till he came to a hermitage, where he saw folk entering with many an ex voto offering and other folk coming forth, rejoicing. The porter went in, till he came to the curtain,[3] and said, "Permission, O Shaykhah Rajihah! Take this sick man." Said she, "Bring him within the curtain;" and the porter said to Abdullah, "Enter." So he entered and looking upon the holy woman, saw her to be his wife whom he had brought from the City of Stone. And when he knew her she also knew him and saluted him and he returned her salam. Then said he, "Who brought thee hither?" and she answered, "When I saw that thy brothers had cast thee away and were contending concerning me, I threw myself into the sea; but my Shaykh Al-Khizr Abu al-'Abbás took me up and brought me to this hermitage, where he gave me leave to heal the sick and bade cry in the city:—Whoso hath any ailment, let him repair to the Shaykhah Rajihah; and he also said to me:—Tarry in this hermitage till the time betide, and thy husband shall come to thee here. So all the sick used to flock to me and I rubbed them and shampoo'd them and they awoke on the morrow whole and sound; whereby the report of me became noised abroad

[1] 'Aúj; I can only suggest, with due diffidence, that this is intended for Kúch, the well-known Baloch city in Persian Carmania (Kirmán) and meant by Richardson's "Koch u Buloch." But as the writer borrows so much from Al-Mas'udi it may possibly be Aúk in Sístán, where stood the heretical city "Shádrak," chapt. cxxii.

[2] *i.e.* The excellent (or surpassing) Religious. Shaykhah, the fem. of Shaykh, is a she-chief: even the head of the dancing-girls will be entitled "Shaykhah."

[3] The curtain would screen her from the sight of men-invalids and probably hung across the single room of the "Záwiyah" or hermit's cell. This concealment is noticed in the tales of two other reverend women.

among the folk, and they brought me votive gifts, so that I have with me abundant wealth. And now I live here in high honour and worship, and all the people of these parts seek my prayers." Then she rubbed him and by the ordinance of Allah the Most High, he became whole. Now Al-Khizr used to come to her every Friday night, and it chanced that the day of Abdullah's coming was a Thursday.[1] Accordingly, when the night darkened he and she sat, after a supper of the richest meats, awaiting the coming of Al-Khizr, who made his appearance anon, and carrying them forth of the hermitage, set them down in Abdullah's palace at Bassorah, where he left them and went his way. As soon as it was day, Abdullah examined the palace and knew it for his own ; then, hearing the folk clamouring without, he looked forth of the lattice and saw his brothers crucified, each on his own cross. Now the reason of this was as ensueth. When they had thrown him into the Tigris, the twain arose on the morrow, weeping and saying, " Our brother! the Jinniyah hath carried off our brother ! " Then they made ready a present and sent it to the Caliph, acquainting him with these tidings and suing from him the government of Bassorah. He sent for them and questioned them and they told him the false tale we have recounted, whereupon he was exceeding wroth.[2] So that night he prayed a two-bow prayer before daybreak, as of his wont, and called upon the tribes of the Jinn, who came before him subject-wise, and he questioned them of Abdullah : when they sware to him that none of them had done him aught of hurt and said, " We know not what is become of him." Then came Sa'idah, daughter of the Red King, and acquainted the Caliph with the truth of Abdullah's case, and he dismissed the Jinn. On the morrow, he subjected Nasir and Mansur to the bastinado till they confessed, each against other : whereupon the Caliph was enraged with them and cried, "Carry them to Bassorah and crucify them there before Abdullah's palace." Such was their case ; but as regards Abdullah, when he saw his brothers crucified, he commanded to bury them, then took horse and repairing to Baghdad, acquainted the Caliph, with that which his brothers had done with him, from first to last, and told him how he had recovered his wife ; whereat Al-Rashid marvelled, and summoning the Kazi and the witnesses, bade draw up the marriage-contract between Abdullah and the damsel whom he had brought from the City of Stone. So he married her and

[1] Abdullah met his wife on Thursday, the night of which would, amongst Moslems, be Friday night.
[2] *i.e.* with Sa'idah.

woned with her at Bassorah till there came to them the Destroyer of delights and the Severer of societies; and extolled be the perfection of the Living, who dieth not! Moreover, O auspicious King, I have heard a tale anent

## *MA'ARUF THE COBBLER AND HIS WIFE FATIMAH.*

THERE dwelt once upon a time in the God-guarded city of Cairo a cobbler who lived by patching old shoes.[1] His name was Ma'aruf[2] and had a wife called Fatimah, whom the folk had nicknamed "The Dirt;"[3] for that she was a worthless wretch, scanty of shame and mickle of mischief. She ruled her spouse and used to abuse him and curse him a thousand times a day; and he feared her malice and dreaded her misdoings; for that he was a sensible man and careful of his repute, but poor-conditioned. When he earned much, he spent it on her, and when he gained little, she revenged herself with her tongue that night, leaving him no peace and making his night black as her book;[4] for she was even as of one like her saith the poet:—

How manifold nights have I passed with my wife * In the saddest plight with all misery rife:
Would Heaven when first I did look on her * With a cup of cold poison I'd ta'en her life.

Amongst other afflictions which befel him from her one day she said to him, "O Ma'aruf, I wish thee to bring me this night a vermicelli-cake dressed with bees' honey."[5] He replied, "So Allah

---

[1] Arab. "Zarábín" (pl. of zarbún), lit. slaves' shoes or sandals, the chaussure worn by Mamelukes. Here the word is used in its modern sense of stout shoes or walking boots.

[2] The popular word means goodness, etc., *e.g.* "A'mil al-Ma'arúf" = have the kindness; do me the favour.

[3] Dozy translates "'Urrah" = Une Mégère: Lane terms it a "vulgar word signifying a wicked, mischievous shrew." But it is the fem. form of 'Urr = dirt; not a bad name for a daughter of Billingsgate; and reminds us of the term applied by the amiable Hallgerda to her enemy's sons. (The Story of Burnt Njal.)

[4] *i.e.* black like the book of her actions which would be shown to her on Doomsday. (See Night dccclxxi.) The ungodly hold it in the left hand, the right being bound behind their backs, and they appear in foul forms, apes, swine, etc., for which see Sale, sect. iv.

[5] The "Kunáfah" (vermicelli-cake) is a favourite dish of wheaten flour, worked somewhat finer than our vermicelli, fried with Samn (butter melted and clarified) and sweetened with honey or sugar. See Lane M. E. chapt. v. Bees' honey is opposed to various syrups which are used as sweeteners.

Almighty aid me to its price, I will bring it thee. By Allah, I have no dirhams to-day, but our Lord will make things easy."[1] Rejoined she,——And Shahrazad perceived the dawn of day and ceased to say her permitted say.

## Now when it was the Nine Hundred and Ninetieth Night,

She resumed, It hath reached me, O auspicious King, that Ma'arut the Cobbler said to his spouse, "If Allah aid me to its price, I will bring it to thee this night. By Allah, I have no dirhams to-day, but our Lord will make things easy to me!" She rejoined, "I wot naught of these words; whether He aid thee or aid thee not, look thou never come to me save with the vermicelli and bees' honey; and if thou come without it I will make thy night black as thy fortune whenas thou marriedst me and fellest into my hand." Quoth he, "Allah is bountiful!" and going out with grief scattering itself from his body, prayed the dawn-prayer and opened his shop, saying, "I beseech thee, O Lord, to vouchsafe me the price of the Kunafah and ward off from me the mischief of yonder wicked woman this night!" After which he sat in the shop till noon, but no work came to him and his fear of his wife redoubled. Then he arose and locking his shop, went out perplexed as to how he should do in the matter of the vermicelli-cake, seeing he had not even the wherewithal to buy bread. Presently he came up to the shop of the Kunafah-seller and stood before it distraught, whilst his eyes brimmed with tears. The pastry-cook glanced at him and said, "O Master Ma'aruf, why dost thou weep? Tell me what hath befallen thee." So he acquainted him with his case, saying, "My wife is a shrew, a virago, who would have me bring her a Kunafah; but I have sat in my shop till past mid-day and have not gained even the price of bread; wherefore I am in fear of her." The cook laughed and said, "No harm shall come to thee. How many pounds wilt thou have?" "Five pounds," answered Ma'aruf. So the man weighed him out five pounds of vermicelli-cake and said to him, "I have clarified butter, but no bees' honey. Here is drip-honey,[2] however, which is better than bees' honey; and what harm will there be, if it be with

[1] *i.e.* will send us aid. The shrew's rejoinder is highly impious in Moslem opinion.

[2] Arab. "Asal Katr," "a fine kind of black honey, treacle" says Lane; but it is afterwards called cane-honey ('Asal Kasab). I have never heard it applied to "the syrup which exudes from ripe dates, when hung up."

drip-honey?" Ma'aruf was ashamed to object, because the pastry-cook was to have patience with him for the price, and said, "Give it me with drip-honey." So he fried a vermicelli-cake for him with butter and drenched it with drip-honey, till it was fit to present to Kings. Then he asked him, "Dost thou want bread[1] and cheese?" and Ma'aruf answered, "Yes." So he gave him four half dirhams worth of bread and one of cheese, and the vermicelli was ten nusfs. Then said he, "Know, O Ma'aruf, that thou owest me fifteen nusfs, so go to thy wife and make merry and take this nusf for the Hammam; and thou shalt have credit for a day or two or three till Allah provide thee with thy daily bread. And straiten not thy wife, for I will have patience with thee till such time as thou shalt have dirhams to spare." So Ma'aruf took the vermicelli-cake and bread and cheese and went away, with a heart at ease, blessing the pastry-cook and saying, "Extolled be Thy perfection, O my Lord! How bountiful art Thou!" When he came home, his wife enquired of him, "Hast thou brought the vermicelli-cake?" and, replying, "Yes," he set it before her. She looked at it and seeing that it was dressed with cane-honey,[2] said to him, "Did I not bid thee bring it with bees' honey? Wilt thou contrary my wish and have it dressed with cane-honey?" He excused himself to her, saying, I bought it not save on credit;" but said she, "This talk is idle; I will not eat Kunafah save with bees' honey." And she was wroth with it and threw it in his face, saying, "Begone, thou rogue, and bring me other than this!" Then she dealt him a buffet on the cheek and knocked out one of his teeth. The blood ran down upon his breast and for stress of anger he smote her on the head a single blow and a slight; whereupon she clutched his beard and fell to shouting out and saying, "Help, O Moslems!" So the neighbours came in and freed his beard from her grip; then they reproved and reproached her, saying, "We are all content to eat Kunafah with cane-honey. Why, then, wilt thou oppress this poor man thus? Verily, this is disgraceful in thee!" And they went on to soothe her till they made peace between her and him. But, when the folk were gone, she sware that she would not eat of the vermicelli, and Ma'aruf, burning with hunger, said in himself, "She sweareth that she will not eat; so I will e'en eat." Then he ate, and when she saw him eating, she said, "Inshallah, may the eating of it be poison

---

[1] Arab. "'Aysh," lit. = that on which man lives: "Khubz" being the more popular term. "Hubz and Joobn" is well known at Malta.

[2] Arab. "Asal Kasab," *i.e.* sugar, possibly made from sorgho-stalks *Holcus sorghum* of which I made syrup in Central Africa.

to destroy the far one's body."[1] Quoth he, "It shall not be at thy bidding," and went on eating, laughing and saying, "Thou swarest that thou wouldst not eat of this; but Allah is bountiful, and to-morrow night, an the Lord decree, I will bring thee Kunafah dressed with bees' honey, and thou shalt eat it alone." And he applied himself to appeasing her, whilst she called down curses upon him; and she ceased not to rail at him and revile him with gross abuse till the morning, when she bared her forearm to beat him. Quoth he, "Give me time and I will bring thee other vermicelli-cake." Then he went out to the mosque and prayed, after which he betook himself to his shop and opening it, sat down; but hardly had he done this when up came two runners from the Kazi's court and said to him, "Up with thee, speak with the Kazi, for thy wife hath complained of thee to him and her favour is thus and thus." He recognised her by their description; and saying, "May Allah Almighty torment her!" walked with them till he came to the Kazi's presence, where he found Fatimah standing with her arm bound up and her face-veil besmeared with blood; and she was weeping and wiping away her tears. Quoth the Kazi, "Ho man, hast thou no fear of Allah the Most High? Why hast thou beaten this good woman and broken her forearm and knocked out her tooth and entreated her thus?" And quoth Ma'aruf, "If I beat her or put out her tooth, sentence me to what thou wilt; but in truth the case was thus and thus and the neighbours made peace between me and her." And he told him the story from first to last. Now this Kazi was a benevolent man; so he brought out to him a quarter dinar, saying, "O man, take this and get her Kunafah with bees' honey and do ye make peace, thou and she." Quoth Ma'aruf, "Give it to her." So she took it and the Kazi made peace between them, saying, "O wife, obey thy husband; and thou, O man, deal kindly with her."[2] Then they left the court, reconciled at the Kazi's hands, and the woman went one way, whilst her husband returned by another way to his shop and sat there, when, behold, the runners came up to him and said, "Give us our fee." Quoth he, "The Kazi took not of me aught; on the contrary, he gave me a quarter dinar." But quoth they, "'Tis no concern of ours whether the Kazi took of thee or gave to thee, and if thou give us not our fee, we will exact it in

---

[1] This unpleasant euphemy has been previously explained.

[2] This is a true picture of the leniency with which women were treated in the Kazi's court at Cairo; and the effect was simply deplorable. I have noted that matters have grown even worse since the English occupation, for history repeats herself; and the same was the case in Afghanistan and in Sind. We govern too much in these matters, which should be directed not changed, and too little in other things, especially in exacting respect for the conquerors from the conquered.

despite of thee." And they fell to dragging him about the market; so he sold his tools and gave them half a dinar, whereupon they let him go and went away, whilst he put his hand to his cheek and sat sorrowful, for that he had no tools wherewith to work. Presently, up came two ill-favoured fellows and said to him, "Come, O man, and speak with the Kazi; for thy wife hath complained of thee to him." Said he, "He made peace between us just now." But said they, "We come from another Kazi, and thy wife hath complained of thee to our Kazi." So he arose and went with them to their Kazi, calling on Allah for aid against her; and when he saw her, he said to her, "Did we not make peace, good woman?" Whereupon she cried, "There abideth no peace between me and thee." Accordingly he came forward and told the Kazi his story, adding, "And indeed the Kazi Such-an-one made peace between us this very hour." Whereupon the Kazi said to her, "O wretch, since ye two have made peace with each other, why comest thou to me complaining?" Quoth she, "He beat me after that;" but quoth the Kazi, "Make peace each with other, and beat her not again, and she will cross thee no more." So they made peace and the Kazi said to Ma'aruf, "Give the runners their fee." So he gave them their fee and going back to his shop, opened it and sat down, as he were a drunken man for excess of the chagrin which befel him. Presently, while he was still sitting, behold, a man came up to him and said, "O Ma'aruf, rise and hide thyself, for thy wife hath complained of thee to the High Court[1] and Abu Tabak[2] is after thee." So he shut his shop and fled towards the Gate of Victory.[3] He had five nusfs of silver left of the price of the lasts and gear; and therewith he bought four worth of bread and one of cheese, as he fled from her. Now it was the winter season and the hour of mid-afternoon prayer; so, when he came out among the rubbish-mounds the rain descended upon him, like water from the mouths of water-skins, and his clothes were drenched. He therefore entered the 'Ádiliyah,[4] where he saw a ruined place and therein a deserted cell without a door; and in it he took refuge and

---

[1] Arab. "Báb al-'Áli" = the high gate or Sublime Porte; here used of the Chief Kazi's court: the phrase is a descendant of the Coptic "Per-ao," whence "Pharaoh."

[2] "Abú Tabak," in Cairene slang, is an officer who arrests by order of the Kazi and means "Father of whipping" (= tabaka, a low word for beating, thrashing, whopping), because he does his duty with all possible violence *in terrorem*.

[3] Bab al-Nasr, the Eastern or Desert Gate.

[4] This is a mosque outside the great gate built by Al-Malik al-'Ádil Tuman Bey in A.H. 906 (= 1501). The date is *not* worthy of much remark, as these names are often inserted by the scribe—for which see Terminal Essay.

found shelter from the rain. The tears streamed from his eyelids, and he fell to complaining of what had betided him and saying, "Whither shall I flee from this wretch? I beseech Thee, O Lord, to vouchsafe me one who shall conduct me to a far country, where she shall not know the way to me!" Now while he sat weeping, behold, the wall clave and there came forth to him therefrom one of tall stature, whose aspect caused his hair to bristle and his flesh to creep, and said to him, "O man, what aileth thee that thou disturbest me this night? These two hundred years have I dwelt here and have never seen any enter this place and do as thou dost. Tell me what thou wishest and I will accomplish thy need, as ruth for thee hath gotten hold upon my heart." Quoth Ma'aruf, "Who and what art thou?" and quoth he, "I am the Haunter[1] of this place." So Ma'aruf told him all that had befallen him with his wife and he said, "Wilt thou have me convey thee to a country where thy wife shall know no way to thee?" "Yes," said Ma'aruf; and the other, "Then mount my back." So he mounted on his back and he flew with him from after supper-tide till daybreak, when he set him down on the top of a high mountain——And Shahrazad was surprised by the dawn of day and ceased saying her permitted say.

## Now when it was the Nine Hundred and Ninety-first Night,

She said, It hath reached me, O auspicious King, that the Marid having taken up Ma'aruf the Cobbler, flew off with him and set him down upon a high mountain and said to him, "O mortal, descend this mountain and thou wilt see the gate of a city. Enter it, for therein thy wife cannot come at thee." He then left him and went his way, whilst Ma'aruf abode in amazement and perplexity till the sun rose, when he said to himself, "I will up with me and go down into the city: indeed there is no profit in my abiding upon this highland." So he descended to the mountain-foot and saw a city girt by towering walls, full of lofty palaces and gold-adorned buildings, which was a delight to beholders. He entered in at the gate and found it a place such as lightened the grieving heart; but as he walked through the streets the townsfolk stared at him as a

---

[1] Arab. "'Ámir" lit. = one who inhabiteth, a peopler; here used in technical sense. As has been seen, ruins and impure places, such as lavatories and Hammám-baths are the favourite homes of the Jinn. The fire-drake in the text was summoned by the Cobbler's exclamation, and even Marids at times do a kindly action.

curiosity and gathered about him, marvelling at his dress, for it was unlike theirs. Presently, one of them said to him, "O man, art thou a stranger?" "Yes." "What countryman art thou?" "I am from the city of Cairo the Auspicious." "And when didst thou leave Cairo?" "I left it yesterday, at the hour of afternoon-prayer." Whereupon the man laughed at him and cried out, saying, "Come look, O folk, at this man and hear what he saith!" Quoth they, "What doth he say?" and quoth the townsman, "He pretendeth that he cometh from Cairo and left it yesterday at the hour of afternoon-prayer!" At this they all laughed and gathering round Ma'aruf, said to him, "O man, art thou mad to talk thus? How canst thou pretend that thou leftest Cairo at mid-afternoon yesterday and foundedst thyself this morning here, when the truth is that between our city and Cairo lieth a full year's journey?" Quoth he, "None is mad but you. As for me, I speak sooth, for here is bread which I brought with me from Cairo, and see, 'tis yet new." Then he showed them the bread and they stared at it, for it was unlike their country bread. So the crowd increased about him and they said to one another, "This is Cairo bread: look at it;" and he became a gazing-stock in the city and some believed him, whilst others gave him the lie and made mock of him. Whilst this was going on, behold, up came a merchant, riding on a she-mule and followed by two black slaves, and brake a way through the people, saying, "O folk, are ye not ashamed to mob this stranger and make mock of him and scoff at him?" And he went on to rate them, till he drave them away from Ma'aruf, and none could make him any answer. Then he said to the stranger, "Come, O my brother, no harm shall betide thee from these folk. Verily they have no shame."[1] So he took him and carrying him to a spacious and richly-adorned house, seated him in a speak-room fit for a King, whilst he gave an order to his slaves, who opened a chest and brought out to him a dress such as might be worn by a merchant, worth a thousand.[2] He clad him therewith and Ma'aruf, being a seemly man, became as he were consul of the merchants. Then his host called for food and they set before them a tray of all manner exquisite viands. The twain ate and drank and the merchant said to Ma'aruf, "O my brother, what is thy name?" "My name is Ma'aruf and I am a cobbler by trade and patch old shoes." "What countryman art thou?" "I am from Cairo." "What quarter?" "Dost thou know

[1] The style is modern Cairene jargon.
[2] Purses or gold pieces.

Cairo?" "I am of its children.[1] I come from the Red Street.[2]" "And whom dost thou know in the Red Street?" I know Such-an-one and Such-an-one," answered Ma'aruf, and named several people to him. Quoth the other, "Knowest thou Shaykh Ahmad the druggist?"[3] "He was my next neighbour, wall to wall." "Is he well?" "Yes." "How many sons hath he?" "Three, Mustafà, Mohammed, and Ali." "And what hath Allah done with them?" "As for Mustafa, he is well and he is a learned man, a professor:[4] Mohammed is a druggist and opened him a shop beside that of his father, after he had married, and his wife hath borne him a son named Hasan." "Allah gladden thee with good news!" said the merchant; and Ma'aruf continued, "As for Ali, he was my friend, when we were boys, and we always played together, I and he. We used to go in the guise of the children of the Nazarenes and enter the church and steal the books of the Christians and sell them and buy food with the price. It chanced once that the Nazarenes caught us with a book; whereupon they complained of us to our folk and said to Ali's father:—An thou hinder not thy son from troubling us, we will complain of thee to the King. So he appeased them and gave Ali a thrashing; wherefore he ran away none knew whither and he hath now been absent twenty years and no man hath brought news of him." Quoth the host, "I am that very Ali, son of Shaykh Ahmad the druggist, and thou art my playmate Ma'aruf."[5] So they saluted each other and after the salam Ali said, "Tell me why, O Ma'aruf, thou camest from Cairo to this city." Then he told him all that had befallen him of ill-doing with his wife Fatimah the Dirt, and said, "So, when her annoy waxed on me, I fled from her towards the Gate of Victory and went forth the city. Presently, the rain fell heavy on me; so I entered a ruined cell in the Adiliyah and sat there, weeping; whereupon there came forth to me the Haunter of the place, which was an Ifrit of the Jinn, and questioned me. I acquainted him with my case and he took me on his back and flew with me all night between heaven and earth, till he set me upon

---

[1] *i.e.* I am a Cairene.

[2] Arab. "Darb al-Ahmar," a street still existing near to and outside the noble Bab Zuwaylah.

[3] Arab. "'Attár," perfume seller and druggist; the word is connected with our "Ottar" ('Atr).

[4] Arab. "Mudarris," lit. = one who gives lessons or lectures (dars) and pop. applied to a professor in a collegiate mosque like Al-Azhar of Cairo.

[5] This thoroughly dramatic scene is told with a charming naïveté. No wonder that The Nights has been made the basis of a national theatre amongst the Turks.

yonder mountain and gave me to know of this city. So I came down from the mountain and entered the city, when the people crowded about me and questioned me. I told them that I had left Cairo yesterday, but they believed me not, and presently thou camest up and driving the folk away from me, carriedst me to this house. Such, then, is the cause of my quitting Cairo; and thou, what object brought thee hither?" Quoth Ali, "The giddiness[1] of folly turned my head when I was seven years old, from which time I wandered from land to land and city to city, till I came to this city, the name whereof is Ikhtiyán al-Khatan.[2] I found its people an hospitable folk and a kindly, compassionate for the poor man and selling to him on credit and believing all he said. So quoth I to them:—I am a merchant and have preceded my packs and I need a place wherein to bestow my baggage. And they believed me and assigned me a lodging. Then quoth I to them:—Is there any of you will lend me a thousand dinars till my loads arrive, when I will repay it to him; for I am in want of certain things before my goods come?" They gave me what I asked and I went to the merchants' bazar, where, seeing goods, I bought them and sold them next day at a profit of fifty gold pieces and bought others.[3] And I consorted with the folk and entreated them liberally, so that they loved me, and I continued to sell and buy, till I grew rich. Know, O my brother, that the proverb saith, "The world is show and trickery: and the land where none wotteth thee, there do whatso liketh thee. Thou too, an thou say to all who ask thee, I'm a cobbler by trade and poor withal, and I fled from my wife and left Cairo yesterday, they will not believe thee and thou wilt be a laughing-stock among them as long as thou abidest in the city; whilst, an thou tell them, An Ifrit brought me hither, they will take fright at thee and none will come near thee; for they will say, This man is possessed of an Ifrit and harm will betide whoso approacheth him. And such public

---

[1] Arab. "Taysh," lit. = vertigo, swimming of head.

[2] Here Trébutien (iii. 265) reads "la ville de Khaïtan (so the Mac. Edit. iv. 708) capital du royaume de Sohatan." Ikhtiyán, Lane suggests to be fictitious: Khatan is a district of Tartary, east of Káshgar, so called by Sádik al-Isfaháni, p. 24.

[3] This is a true picture of the tact and *savoir faire* of the Cairenes. It was a study to see how, under the late Khedive, they managed to take precedence of Europeans who found themselves in the background before they knew it. For instance, every Bey, whose degree is that of a Colonel, was made an "Excellency" and ranked accordingly at Court, whilst his father, some poor Fellah, was ploughing the ground. Taufík Pasha began his ill-omened rule by always placing natives close to him in the place of honour, addressing them first and otherwise snubbing Europeans who, when English, were often too obtuse to notice the petty insults lavished upon them.

report will be dishonouring both to thee and to me, because they ken I come from Cairo." Ma'aruf asked :—How then shall I do?" and Ali answered, "I will tell thee how thou shalt do, Inshallah! To-morrow I will give thee a thousand dinars and a she-mule to ride and a black slave, who shall walk before thee and guide thee to the gate of the merchants' bazar; and do thou go in to them. I will be there sitting amongst them, and when I see thee, I will rise to thee and salute thee with the salam and kiss thy hand and make a great man of thee. Whenever I ask thee of any kind of stuff, saying, Hast thou brought with thee aught of such a kind? do thou answer, Plenty.[1] And if they question me of thee, I will praise thee and magnify thee in their eyes and say to them, Get him a store-house and a shop. I also will give thee out for a man of great wealth and generosity; and if a beggar come to thee, bestow upon him what thou mayst; so will they put faith in what I say and believe in thy greatness and generosity and love thee. Then will I invite thee to my house and invite all the merchants on thy account and bring together thee and them, so that all may know thee and thou know them,——And Shahrazad perceived the dawn of day and ceased to say her permitted say.

## Now when it was the Nine Hundred & Ninety-second Night,

She continued, it hath reached me, O auspicious King, that the merchant Ali said to Ma'aruf, "I will invite thee to my house and invite all the merchants on thy account and bring together thee and them, so that all may know thee and thou know them, whereby thou shalt sell and buy and take and give with them; nor will it be long ere thou become a man of money." Accordingly, on the morrow he gave him a thousand dinars and a suit of clothes and a black slave, and mounting him upon a she-mule, said to him, "Allah give thee quittance of responsibility for all this,[2] inasmuch as thou art my friend and it behoveth me to deal generously with thee. Have no care; but put away from thee the thought of thy wife's misways and name her not to any." "Allah requite thee with good!" replied Ma'aruf and rode on, preceded by his blackamoor till the slave brought him to the gate of the merchants' bazar, where

---

[1] Arab. "Kathír" (pron. Katir) = much: here used in its slang sense, "no end."

[2] *i.e.* "May the Lord soon make thee able to repay me; but meanwhile I give it to thee for thy own free use."

they were all seated, and amongst them Ali, who when he saw him, rose and threw himself upon him, crying, "A blessed day, O Merchant Ma'aruf, O man of good works and kindness!"[1] And he kissed his hand before the merchants and said to them, "Our brothers, ye are honoured by knowing[2] the merchant Ma'aruf." So they saluted him, and Ali signed to them to make much of him, wherefore he was magnified in their eyes. Then Ali helped him to dismount from his she-mule and saluted him with the salam; after which he took the merchants apart, one after other, and vaunted Ma'aruf to them. They asked, "Is this man a merchant?" and he answered, "Yes; and indeed he is the chiefest of merchants; there liveth not a wealthier than he, for his wealth and the riches of his father and forefathers are famous among the merchants of Cairo. He hath partners in Hind and Sind and Al-Yaman and is high in repute for generosity. So know ye his rank and exalt ye his degree and do him service, and wot also that his coming to your city is not for the sake of traffic, and none other save to divert himself with the sight of folk's countries: indeed, he hath no need of strangerhood for the sake of gain and profit, having wealth that fires cannot consume, and I am one of his servants." And he ceased not to extol him, till they set him above their heads and began to tell one another of his qualities. Then they gathered round him and offered him junkets[3] and sherbets, and even the Consul of the Merchants came to him and saluted him; whilst Ali proceeded to ask him, in the presence of the traders, "O my lord, haply thou hast brought with thee somewhat of such and such a stuff?" and Ma'aruf answered, "Plenty." Now Ali had that day shown him various kinds of costly cloths and had taught him the names of the different stuffs, dear and cheap. Then said one of the merchants, "O my lord, hast thou brought with thee yellow broad cloth?" and Ma'aruf said, "Plenty!" Quoth another, "And gazelles' blood red?"[4] and quoth the Cobbler, "Plenty;" and as often as he asked him of aught, he made him the same answer. So the other said, "O Merchant Ali had thy countryman a mind to transport a thousand loads of costly stuffs, he could do so;" and Ali said, "He would take them from a single one of his store-houses,

---

[1] Punning upon his name. Much might be written upon the significance of names as ominous of good and evil; but the subject is far too extensive for a footnote.

[2] "Lane translates "Anisa-kum" by "he hath delighted you by his arrival;" Mr. Payne "I commend him to you."

[3] Arab. "Fatúrát,"= light food for the early breakfast, of which the "Fatírah"-cake was a favourite item.

[4] A dark red dye (Lane).

and miss naught thereof." Now whilst they were sitting, behold, up came a beggar and went the round of the merchants. One gave him a half dirham and another a copper,[1] but most of them gave him nothing, till he came to Ma'aruf who pulled out a handful of gold and gave it to him, whereupon he blessed him and went his ways. The merchants marvelled at this and said, "Verily, this is a King's bestowal, for he gave the beggar gold without count, and were he not a man of vast wealth and money without end, he had not given an asker a handful of gold." After a while there came to him a poor woman and he gave her another handful of gold, whereupon she went away, blessing him, and told the other beggars, who came to him, one after other, and he gave them each a handful of gold, till he disbursed the thousand dinars. Then he struck hand upon hand and said, Allah is our sufficient aid and excellent is the Agent!" Quoth the Consul, "What aileth thee, O Merchant Ma'aruf?" and quoth he, "It seemeth that the most part of the people of this city are poor and needy; and had I known their misery I would have brought with me a large sum of money in my saddle-bags and given largesse thereof to the poor. I fear me I may be long abroad[2] and 'tis not in my nature to baulk a beggar; and I have no gold left: so, if a pauper come to me, what shall I say to him?" Quoth the Consul, "Say, Allah will send thee thy daily bread!"[3] but Ma'aruf replied, "That is not my practice and I am care-ridden because of this. Would I had other thousand dinars, wherewith to give alms till my baggage come!" "Have no care for that," quoth the Consul, and, sending one of his dependents for a thousand dinars, handed them to Ma'aruf, who went on giving them to every beggar who passed till the call to noon-prayer. Then they entered the cathedral-mosque and prayed the noon-prayers, and what was left him of the thousand gold pieces he scattered upon the heads of the worshippers. This drew the people's attention to him and they blessed him, whilst the merchants marvelled at the abundance of his generosity and openhandedness. Then he turned to another trader and, borrowing of him another thousand ducats, gave these also away, whilst Merchant Ali looked on at what he did, but could not speak. He ceased not to do thus till the call to mid-afternoon prayer, when he entered the mosque and prayed and distributed the rest of the money. On this wise, by the time they locked the doors of the

---

[1] Arab. "Jadíd."

[2] Both the texts read thus, but the reading has little sense. Ma'aruf probably would say, "I fear that my loads will be long coming."

[3] One of the many formulas of polite refusal.

bazar,[1] he had borrowed five thousand sequins and given them away, saying to every one of whom he took aught. "Wait till my baggage come, when, if thou desire gold, I will give thee gold, and if thou desire stuffs, thou shalt have stuffs, for I have no end of them." At eventide Merchant Ali invited Ma'aruf and the rest of the traders to an entertainment and seated him in the upper end, the place of honour, where he talked of nothing but cloths and jewels, and whenever they made mention to him of aught, he said, "I have plenty of it." Next day, he again repaired to the market-street where he showed a friendly bias towards the merchants and borrowed of them more money, which he distributed to the poor; nor did he leave doing thus twenty days, till he had borrowed threescore thousand dinars, and still there came no baggage, no, nor a burning plague.[2] At last folk began to clamour for their money and say, "The merchant Ma'aruf's baggage cometh not. How long will he take people's moneys and give them to the poor?" And quoth one of them, "My rede is that we speak to Merchant Ali." So they went to him and said, "O Merchant Ali, Merchant Ma'aruf's baggage cometh not." Said he, "Have patience, it cannot fail to come soon." Then he took Ma'aruf aside and said to him, "O Ma'aruf, what fashion is this? Did I bid thee brown[3] the bread or burn it? The merchants clamour for their coin and tell me that thou owest them sixty thousand dinars, which thou hast borrowed and given away to the poor. How wilt thou satisfy the folk, seeing that thou neither sellest nor buyest?" Said Ma'aruf, "What matters it[4] and what are threescore thousand dinars? When my baggage shall come, I will pay them in stuffs or in gold and silver, as they will." Quoth Merchant Ali, "Allah is Most Great! Hast thou then any baggage?" and he said, "Plenty." Cried the other, "Allah and the Hallows[5] requite thee thine impudence! Did I teach thee this saying, that thou shouldst repeat it to me? But I will acquaint the folk with thee." Ma'aruf rejoined, "Begone and prate no more! Am I a poor man? I have endless wealth in my baggage and as soon as

---

[1] Each bazar, in a large city like Damascus, has its tall and heavy wooden doors, which are locked in the evening and opened in the morning by the Ghafir or guard. The "silver key," however, always lets one in.

[2] Arab. "Wa lá Kabbata hámiyah," a Cairene vulgarism meaning "There came nothing to profit him nor to rid the people of him."

[3] Arab. "Hammir," *i.e.* brown it before the fire, toast it.

[4] It is insinuated that he had lied till he himself believed the lie to be truth—not an uncommon process, I may remark.

[5] Arab. "Rijál" = the Men, equivalent to the Walis, Saints or Santons; with perhaps an allusion to the Rijál al-Ghayb, the Invisible Controls, concerning whom I have quoted Herklots.

it cometh, they shall have their money's worth, two for one. I have no need of them." At this Merchant Ali waxed wroth and said, "Unmannerly wight that thou art, I will teach thee to lie to me and be not ashamed!" Said Ma'aruf, "E'en work the worst thy hand can do! They must wait till my baggage come, when they shall have their due and more." So Ali left him and went away, saying in himself, "I praised him whilome and if I blame him now, I make myself out a liar and become of those of whom it is said:—Whoso praiseth and then blameth lieth twice."[1] And he knew not what to do. Presently, the traders came to him and said, "O Merchant Ali, hast thou spoken to him?" Said he, "O folk, I am ashamed and, though he owe me a thousand dinars, I cannot speak to him. When ye lent him your money ye consulted me not; so ye have no claim on me. Dun him yourselves, and if he pay you not, complain of him to the King of the city, saying:—He is an impostor who hath imposed upon us. And he will deliver you from the plague of him." Accordingly, they repaired to the King and told him what had passed, saying, "O King of the age, we are perplexed anent this merchant, whose generosity is excessive; for he doeth thus and thus, and all he borroweth he giveth away to the poor by handsful. Were he a man of naught, his sense would not suffer him to lavish gold on this wise; and were he a man of wealth his good faith had been made manifest to us by the coming of his baggage; but we see none of his luggage, although he avoucheth that he hath a baggage-train, and hath preceded it. Now some time hath past, but there appeareth no sign of such baggage-train, and he oweth us sixty thousand gold pieces, all of which he hath given away in alms." And they went on to praise him and extol his generosity. Now this King was a very covetous man, a more covetous than Ash'ab;[2] and when he heard tell of Ma'aruf's generosity and openhandedness, greed of gain got the better of him and he said to his Wazir, "Were not this merchant a man of

[1] A saying attributed to Al-Hariri (Lane). It is good enough to be his: the Persians say, "Cut not down the tree thou plantedst," and the idea is universal throughout the East.

[2] A quotation from Al-Hariri (Ass. of the Badawin). Ash'ab (ob. A.H. 54), a Medinite servant of Caliph Osman, was proverbial for greed and sanguine with Micawber-like expectation of "windfalls." The Scholiast Al-Sharishi (of Xeres) describes him in Theophrastic style. He never saw a man put hand to pocket without expecting a present, or a funeral go by without hoping for a legacy, or a bridal procession without preparing his own house, hoping they might bring the bride to him by mistake. * * * When asked if he knew aught greedier than himself he said "Yes; a sheep I once kept upon my terrace-roof seeing a rainbow mistook it for a rope of hay and jumping to seize it broke its neck!" Hence "Ash'ab's sheep" became a by-word (Preston tells the tale in full, p. 288).

immense wealth, he had not shown all this munificence. His baggage-train will assuredly come, whereupon these merchants will flock to him and he will scatter amongst them riches galore. Now I have more right to this money than they; wherefore I have a mind to make friends with him and profess affection for him, so that, when his baggage cometh, whatso the merchants would have gotten I shall get of him; and I will give him my daughter to wife and join his wealth to my wealth." Replied the Wazir, "O King of the age, methinks he is naught but an impostor, and 'tis the impostor who ruineth the house of the covetous;"——And Shahrazad was surprised by the dawn of day and ceased saying her permitted say.

## Now when it was the Nine Hundred & Ninety-third Night.

She pursued, It hath reached me, O auspicious King, that when the Wazir said to the King, "Methinks he is naught but an impostor, and 'tis the impostor who ruineth the house of the covetous;" the King said, "O Wazir, I will prove him and soon know if he be an impostor or a true man and whether he be a rearling of Fortune or not." The Wazir asked, "And how wilt thou prove him?" and the King answered, "I will send for him to the presence and entreat him with honour and give him a jewel which I have. An he know it and wot its price, he is a man of worth and wealth; but an he know it not, he is an impostor and an upstart and I will do him die by the foulest fashion of deaths." So he sent for Ma'aruf, who came and saluted him. The King returned his salam and seating him beside himself, said to him, "Art thou the merchant Ma'aruf?" and said he, "Yes." Quoth the King, "The merchants declare that thou owest them sixty thousand ducats. Is this true?" "Yes," quoth he. Asked the King, "Then why dost thou not give them their money?" and he answered, "Let them wait till my baggage come and I will repay them twofold. An they wish for gold, they shall have gold; and should they wish for silver, they shall have silver; or an they prefer merchandise, I will give them merchandise; and to whom I owe a thousand I will give two thousand in requital of that wherewith he hath veiled my face before the poor; for I have plenty." Then said the King, "O merchant, take this and look what is its kind and value." And he gave him a jewel the bigness of a hazel-nut, which he had bought for a thousand sequins and not having its fellow, prized it highly. Ma'aruf took it and pressing it between his thumb and forefinger brake it, for it was brittle and would not brook the squeeze. Quoth the King, "Why hast thou broken the jewel?" and Ma'aruf laughed and said, "O King of the age, this is no jewel. This is but a bittock of mineral worth a thousand dinars; why dost thou style it a jewel? A jewel I call such as is worth threescore and ten thousand gold pieces and this is called but a piece of stone. A gem that is not of the bigness of a walnut hath no worth in my eyes and I take no account thereof. How cometh it, then, that thou, who art King, stylest this thing a jewel, when 'tis but a bit of mineral worth a thousand dinars? But ye are excusable, for that ye are poor folk and have not in your possession things of price." The King asked, "O merchant, hast thou stones such as those whereof thou speakest?" and he answered, "Plenty." Whereupon avarice overcame the King and he said, "Wilt thou give me real jewels?" Said Ma'aruf, "When my baggage-train shall come, I will give thee no end of gems; and all that thou canst desire I have in plenty and will give thee, without price." At this the King rejoiced and said to the traders, "Wend your ways and have patience with him, till his baggage arrive, when do ye come to me and receive your moneys from me." So they fared forth and the King turned to his Wazir and said to him, "Pay court to Merchant Ma'aruf and take and give with him in talk and bespeak him of my daughter, Princess Dunyá, that he may wed her and so we gain these riches he hath." Said the Wazir, "O King of the age, this man's fashion misliketh me and methinketh he is an impostor and a liar: so leave this whereof thou speakest lest thou lose thy daughter for naught." Now this Minister had sued the King aforetime to give him his daughter to wife, and he was willing to do so, but when she heard of it she consented not to marry him. Accordingly, the King said to him, "O traitor, thou desirest no good for me, because in past time thou soughtest my daughter in wedlock, but she would none of thee; so now thou wouldst cut off the way of her marriage and wouldst have the Princess lie fallow, that thou mayst take her. But hear from me one word—Thou hast no concern in this matter. How can he be an impostor and a liar, seeing that he knew the price of the jewel, even that for which I bought it, and brake it because it pleased him not? He hath jewels in plenty, and when he goeth to my daughter and seeth her to be beautiful, she will captivate his reason and he will love her and give her gems and things of price: but, as for thee, thou wouldst forbid my daughter and myself these good things." So the Minister was silent, for fear of the King's anger, and said to himself, "Set the curs on the cattle[1]!" Then, with show of friendly

---

[1] *i.e.* "Show a miser money and hold him back, if you can."

bias, he betook himself to Ma'aruf and said to him, "His Highness the King loveth thee and hath a daughter, a winsome lady and a lovesome, to whom he is minded to marry thee. What sayst thou?" Said he, "No harm in that; but let him wait till my baggage come, for marriage settlements on Kings' daughters are large and their rank demandeth that they be not endowed save with a dowry befitting their degree. At this present I have no money with me till the coming of my baggage, but I have wealth in plenty, and needs must I make her marriage-portion five thousand purses. Then I shall need a thousand purses to distribute amongst the poor and needy on my wedding-night and other thousand to give to those who walk in the bridal procession and yet other thousand wherewith to provide provaunt for the troops and others;[1] and I shall want an hundred jewels to give to the Princess on the wedding-morning[2] and other hundred gems to distribute among the slave-girls and eunuchs, for I must present to each of them a jewel in honour of the bride; and I need wherewithal to clothe a thousand naked paupers, and alms too must perforce be given. All this cannot be done till my baggage come; but I have plenty and, once it is here, I shall make no account of all this outlay." The Wazir returned to the King and told him what Ma'aruf said, whereupon quoth he, "Since this is his wish, how canst thou style him impostor and liar?" Replied the Minister, "And I cease not to say this." But the King chid him angrily and threatened him, saying, "By the life of my head, an thou cease not this talk, I will slay thee. Go back to him and fetch him to me and I will manage matters with him myself." So the Wazir returned to Ma'aruf and said to him, "Come and speak with the King." "I hear and I obey," said Ma'aruf, and went in to the King, who said to him, "Thou shalt not put me off with these excuses, for my treasury is full; so take the keys and spend all thou needest and give what thou wilt and clothe the poor and do thy desire and have no care for the girl and the handmaids. When the baggage shall come, do what thou wilt with thy wife by way of generosity, and we will have patience with thee anent the marriage-portion till then, for there is no manner of difference betwixt me and thee; none at all." Then he sent for the Shaykh Al-Islam[3] and bade him write out the marriage-contract between his daughter and Merchant Ma'aruf, and he did so; after which the King gave the signal for beginning the wedding festivities, and bade decorate the city. The

---

[1] He wants £40,000 to begin with.

[2] Arab. "Sabíhat al-'urs," *i.e.* the morning after the wedding.

[3] Another sign of modern composition, as in Kamar al-Zaman II.

kettle drums beat and the tables were spread with meats of all kinds and there came performers who paraded their tricks. Merchant Ma'aruf sat upon a throne in a parlour and the players and gymnasts and dancing-men of wondrous movements and posture-makers of marvellous cunning came before him, whilst he called out to the Treasurer and said to him, "Bring gold and silver." So he brought gold and silver and Ma'aruf went round among the spectators and largessed each performer by the handful; and he gave alms to the poor and needy, and clothes to the naked, and it was a clamorous festival and a right merry. The treasurer could not bring money fast enough from the treasury, and the Wazir's heart was like to burst for rage; but he dared not say a word, whilst Merchant Ali marvelled at this waste of wealth, and said to Merchant Ma'aruf, "Allah and the Hallows visit this upon thy head-sides![1] Doth it not suffice thee to squander the traders' money, but thou must squander that of the King to boot?" Replied Ma'aruf, "'Tis none of thy concern: whenas my baggage shall come, I will requite the King manifold." And he went on lavishing money and saying in himself, "A burning plague! What shall happen will happen, and there is no flying from that which is foreordained." The festivities ceased not for the space of forty days, and on the one-and-fortieth day, they made the bride's cortège, and all the Emirs and troops walked before her. When they brought her in before Ma'aruf, he began scattering gold on the people's heads, and they made her a mighty fine procession, whilst Ma'aruf expended in her honour vast sums of money. Then they brought him in to Princess Dunya, and he sat down on the high divan; after which they let fall the curtains and shut the doors and withdrew, leaving him alone with his bride; whereupon he smote hand upon hand and sat awhile sorrowful and saying, "There is no Majesty and there is no Might save in Allah, the Glorious, the Great!" Quoth the Princess, "O my lord, Allah preserve thee! What aileth thee that thou art troubled?" Quoth he, "And how should I be other than troubled, seeing that thy father hath embarrassed me and done with me a deed which is like the burning of green corn?" She asked, "And what hath my father done with thee? Tell me!" and he answered, "He hath brought me in to thee before the coming of my baggage, and I want at very least an hundred jewels to distribute among thy handmaids, to each a jewel, so she might rejoice therein and

---

[1] Lane translates this, "May Allah and the Rijal retaliate upon thy temple!"

say, My lord gave me a jewel on the night of his marriage to my lady. This good deed would I have done in honour of thy station and for the increase of thy dignity; and I have no need to stint myself in lavishing jewels, for I have of them great plenty." Rejoined she, "Be not concerned for that. As for me, trouble not thyself about me, for I will have patience with thee till thy baggage shall come; and as for my women, have no care for them."——And Shahrazad perceived the dawn of day and ceased to say her permitted say.

## Now when it was the Nine Hundred and Ninety-fourth Night,

She resumed, It hath reached me, O auspicious King, that the Princess Dunya comforted Merchant Ma'aruf till the dawn of day, when he arose and entered the Hammam, whence, after donning a suit for sovrans suitable, he betook himself to the King's divan. All who were there rose to him and received him with honour and worship, giving him joy and invoking blessings upon him; and he sat down by the King's side and asked, "Where is the Treasurer?" They answered, "Here he is, before thee," and he said to him, "Bring robes of honour for all the Wazirs and Emirs and dignitaries and clothe them therewith." The Treasurer brought him all he sought and he sat giving to all who came to him and lavishing largesse upon every man according to his station. On this wise he abode twenty days, whilst no baggage appeared for him nor aught else, till the Treasurer was straitened by him to the uttermost and going in to the King, as he sat alone with the Wazir in Ma'aruf's absence, kissed ground between his hands and said, "O King of the age, I must tell thee somewhat, lest haply thou blame me for not acquainting thee therewith. Know that the treasury is being exhausted; there is none but a little money left in it and in ten days more we shall shut it upon emptiness." Quoth the King, "O Wazir, verily my son-in-law's baggage-train tarrieth long and there appeareth no news thereof." The Minister laughed and said, "Allah be gracious to thee, O King of the age! Thou art none other but heedless with respect to this impostor, this liar. As thy head liveth, there is no baggage for him, no, nor a burning plague to rid us of him! Nay, he hath but imposed on thee without surcease, so that he hath wasted thy treasures and married thy daughter for naught. How long therefore wilt thou be heedless of this liar?" Then quoth the King, "O Wazir, how shall we do to learn the truth of his case!" and quoth the Wazir, "O King of the age, none may come at a man's secret but his wife; so send for thy daughter and let her come behind the curtain, that I may question her of the truth of his estate, to the intent that she may make question of him and acquaint us with his case." Cried the King, "There is no harm in that; and, as my head liveth, if it be proved that he is a liar and an impostor, I will verily do him die by the foulest of deaths!" Then he carried the Wazir into the sitting-chamber and sent for his daughter, who came behind the curtain, her husband being absent, and said, "What wouldst thou, O my father?" Said he "Speak with the Wazir." So she asked, "Ho thou, the Wazir, what is thy will?" and he answered, "O my lady, thou must know that thy husband hath squandered thy father's substance and married thee without a dower; and he ceaseth not to promise us and break his promises, nor cometh there any tidings of his baggage; in short we would have thee inform us concerning him." Quoth she, "Indeed his words be many, and he still cometh and promiseth me jewels and treasures and costly stuffs; but I see nothing." Quoth the Wazir, "O my lady, canst thou this night take and give with him in talk and whisper to him:—Say me sooth and fear from me naught, for thou art become my husband and I will not transgress against thee. So tell me the truth of the matter and I will devise thee a device whereby thou shalt be set at rest. And do thou play near and far[1] with him in words and profess love to him and win him to confess and after tell us the facts of his case." And she answered, "O my papa, I know how I will make proof of him." Then she went away and after supper her husband came in to her, according to his wont, whereupon Princess Dunya rose to him and wheedled him with winsomest wheedling (and all-sufficient[2] are woman's wiles whenas she would aught of men); and she ceased not to caress him and beguile him with speech sweeter than the honey-comb till she stole his reason; and when she saw that he altogether inclined to her, she said to him, "O my beloved, O coolth of my eyes and fruit of my vitals, Allah never desolate me by less of thee nor Time sunder us twain, me and thee! Indeed, the love of thee hath homed in my heart, nor will I ever forsake thee or transgress against thee. But I would have thee tell me the truth, for that the sleights of falsehood profit not, nor do they secure credit at all seasons. How long wilt thou impose upon my father and lie to him? I fear lest thine affair be discovered to him, ere we can

[1] As we should say, "play fast and loose."

[2] Arab. "Náhi-ka," lit. = thy prohibition, but idiomatically used = let it suffice thee!

devise some device and he lay violent hands upon thee? So acquaint me with the facts of the case, for naught shall befal thee save that which shall begladden thee; and, when thou shalt have spoken sooth, fear not harm shall betide thee. How often wilt thou declare that thou art a merchant and a man of money and hast a luggage-train? This long while past thou sayest, My baggage! my baggage! but there appeareth no sign of thy baggage, and visible in thy face is anxiety on this account. So an there be no worth in thy words, tell me and I will contrive thee a contrivance whereby thou shalt come off safe, Inshallah!" He replied, "I will tell thee the truth, and then do thou whatso thou wilt." Rejoined she, "Speak and look thou speak soothly; for sooth is the ark of safety, and beware of lying, for it dishonoureth the liar, and God-gifted is he who said:—

'Ware that truth thou speak, albe sooth when said * Shall cause thee in threatenèd fire to fall:
And seek Allah's approof, for most foolish he * Who shall anger his Lord to make friends with thrall."

He said, "Know then, O my lady, that I am no merchant and have no baggage, no, nor a burning plague; nay, I was but a cobbler in my own country and had a wife called Fatimah the Dirt, with whom there befel me this and that." And he told her his story from beginning to end; whereat she laughed and said, "Verily, thou art clever in the practice of lying and imposture!" Whereto he answered, "O my lady, may Allah Almighty preserve thee to veil sins and countervail chagrins!" Rejoined she, "Know, that thou imposedst upon my sire and deceivedst him by dint of thy deluding vaunts, so that of his greed for gain he married me to thee. Then thou squanderedst his wealth and the Wazir beareth thee a grudge for this. How many a time hath he spoken against thee to my father, saying, Indeed, he is an impostor, a liar! But my sire hearkened not to his say, for that he had sought me in wedlock and I consented not that he be baron and I femme. However, the time grew longsome upon my sire and he became straitened and said to me, Make him confess. So I have made thee confess and that which was covered is discovered. Now my father purposeth thee a mischief because of this; but thou art become my husband and I will never transgress against thee. An I told my father what I have learnt from thee, he would be certified of thy falsehood and imposture and that thou imposest upon Kings' daughters and squanderest royal wealth: so would thine offence find with him no pardon and he would slay thee sans a doubt: wherefore it would be bruited among the folk that I married a man which was a liar, an impostor, and this would smirch mine honour. Furthermore an he kill thee, most like he will require me to wed another, and to such thing I will never consent; no, not though I die?"[1] So rise now and don a Mameluke's dress and take these fifty thousand dinars of my moneys and mount a swift steed and get thee to a land whither the rule of my father doth not reach. Then make thee a merchant and send me a letter by a courier who shall bring it privily to me, that I may know in what land thou art, so I may send thee all my hand can attain. Thus shall thy wealth wax great and if my father die, I will send for thee, and thou shalt return in respect and honour; and if we die, thou or I, and go to the mercy of God the Most Great, the Resurrection shall unite us. This, then, is the rede that is right: and while we both abide alive and well, I will not cease to send thee letters and moneys. Arise ere the day wax bright and thou be in perplexed plight and perdition upon thy head alight!" Quoth he, "O my lady, I beseech thee of thy favour to bid me farewell with thine embracement." So he embraced her. Then, donning the dress of a white slave, he bade the syces saddle him a thoroughbred steed. Accordingly, they saddled him a courser and he mounted, and farewelling his wife, rode forth the city at the last of the night, whilst all who saw him deemed him one of the Mamelukes of the Sultan going abroad on some business. Next morning, the King and his Wazir repaired to the sitting-chamber and sent for Princess Dunya, who came behind the curtain; and her father said to her, "O my daughter, what sayest thou?" Said she, "I say, Allah blacken thy Wazir's face, because he would have blackened my face in my husband's eyes!" Asked the King, "How so?" and she answered, "He came in to me yesterday; but, before I could name the matter to him, behold, in walked Faraj the Chief Eunuch, letter in hand, and said:—Ten white slaves stand under the palace window and have given me this letter, saying Kiss for us the hands of our lord, Merchant Ma'aruf, and gave him this letter, for we are of his Mamelukes with the baggage, and it hath reached us that he hath wedded the King's daughter, so we are come to acquaint him with that which befel us by the way. Accordingly I took the letter and read as follows:—From the five hundred Mamelukes to his highness our lord, Merchant Ma'aruf. But further.

[1] A character-sketch like that of Princess Dunya makes ample amends for a book full of abuse of women. And yet the superficial say that none of the characters have much personal individuality.

We give thee to know that, after thou quittedst us, the Arabs[1] came out upon us and attacked us. They were two thousand horse and we five hundred mounted slaves and there befel a mighty sore fight between us and them. They hindered us from the road thirty days doing battle with them, and this is the cause of our tarrying from thee.——And Shahrazad was surprised by the dawn of day and ceased saying her permitted say.

## Now when it was the Nine Hundred and Ninety-fifth Night,

She said, It hath reached me, O auspicious King, that Princess Dunya said to her sire, "My husband received a letter from his dependents ending with:—The Arabs hindered us from the road thirty days, which is the cause of our being behind time. They also took from us of the luggage two hundred loads of cloth and slew of us fifty Mamelukes. When the news reached my husband, he cried, Allah disappoint them! What ailed them to wage war with the Arabs for the sake of two hundred loads of merchandise? What are two hundred loads? It behoved them not to tarry on that account, for verily the value of the two hundred loads is only some seven thousand dinars. But needs must I go to them and hasten them. As for that which the Arabs have taken, 'twill not be missed from the baggage, nor doth it weigh with me a whit, for I reckon it as if I had given it to them by way of an alms. Then he went down from me, laughing and taking no concern for the wastage of his wealth nor the slaughter of his slaves. As soon as he was gone, I looked out from the lattice and saw the ten Mamelukes who had brought him the letter, as they were moons, each clad in a suit of clothes worth two thousand dinars; there is not with my father a chattel to match one of them. He went forth with them to bring up his baggage, and hallowed be Allah who hindered me from saying to him aught of that thou badest me, for he would have made mock of me and thee, and haply he would have eyed me with the eye of disparagement and hated me. But the fault is all with thy Wazir,[2] who speaketh against my husband words that

---

[1] As we are in Tartary "Arabs" here means plundering nomades, like the Persian "Iliyát" and other shepherd races.

[2] The very cruelty of love which hates nothing so much as a rejected lover. The Princess, be it noted, is not supposed to be merely romancing, but speaking with the second sight, the clairvoyance, of perfect affection. Men seem to know very little upon this subject, though everyone has at times been more or less startled by the abnormal introvision and divination of things hidden which are the property and prerogative of perfect love.

besit him not." Replied the King, "O my daughter, thy husband's wealth is indeed endless and he recketh not of it; for, from the day he entered our city, he hath done naught but give alms to the poor. Inshallah, he will speedily return with the baggage, and good in plenty shall betide us from him." And he went on to appease her and menace the Wazir, being duped by her device. So fared it with the King; but as regards Merchant Ma'aruf he rode on into waste lands, perplexed and knowing not to what quarter he should betake him; and for the anguish of parting he lamented and in the pangs of passion and love-longing he recited these couplets:—

Time falsed our Union and divided who were one in tway; * And the sore tyranny of Time doth melt my heart away:
Mine eyes ne'er cease to drop the tear for parting with my dear; * When shall Disunion come to end and dawn the Union-day?
O favour like the full moon's face of sheen, indeed I'm he * Whom thou didst leave with bosom torn when faring on thy way,
Would I had never seen thy sight, or met thee for an hour; * Since after sweetest taste of thee to bitters I'm a prey.
Ma'arúf will never cease to be enthralled by Dunyá's[1] charms * And long live she albe die he whom love and longing slay,
O brilliance, like resplendent sun of noontide, deign them heal * His heart for kindness[2] and the fire of longing love allay!
Would Heaven I wot an e'er the days shall deign conjoin our lots, * Join us in pleasant talk o' nights, in Union glad and gay:
Shall my love's palace hold two hearts that savour joy, and I * Strain to my breast the branch I saw upon the sand-hill[3] sway?
O favour of full moon in sheen, never may sun o' thee * Surcease to rise from Eastern rim with all-enlightening ray!
I'm well content with passion-pine and all its bane and bate, * For luck in love is evermore the butt of jealous Fate.

And when he ended his verses, he wept with sore weeping, for indeed the ways were walled up before his face and death seemed to him better than dreeing life, and he walked on like a drunken man for stress of distraction, and stayed not till noontide, when he came to a little town and saw a plougher hard by, ploughing with a yoke of bulls. Now hunger was sore upon him; and he went up to the ploughman and said to him, "Peace be with thee!" and he returned his salam and said to him, "Welcome, O my lord! Art thou one of the Sultan's Mamelukes?" Quoth Ma'aruf, "Yes;"

---

[1] The name of the Princess meaning "The World," not unusual amongst Moslem women.
[2] Another pun upon his name "Ma'aruf."
[3] Arab. "Naká," the mound of pure sand which delights the eye of the Badawi leaving a town.

and the other said, "Alight with me for a guest-meal." Whereupon Ma'aruf knew him to be of the liberal and said to him, "O my brother, I see with thee naught wherewith thou mayest feed me: how is it, then, that thou invitest me?" Answered the husbandman, "O my lord, weal is well nigh.[1] Dismount thee here: the town is near hand and I will go and fetch thee dinner and fodder for thy stallion." Rejoined Ma'aruf, "Since the town is near at hand, I can go thither as quickly as thou canst and buy me what I have a mind to in the bazar and eat." The peasant replied, "O my lord, the place is but a little village[2] and there is no bazar there, neither selling nor buying. So I conjure thee by Allah, alight here with me and hearten my heart, and I will run thither and return to thee in haste." Accordingly he dismounted and the Fellah left him and went off to the village, to fetch dinner for him whilst Ma'aruf sat awaiting him. Presently he said in himself, "I have taken this poor man away from his work; but I will arise and plough in his stead, till he come back, to make up for having hindered him from his work."[3] Then he took the plough and starting the bulls, ploughed a little, till the share struck against something and the beasts stopped. He goaded them on, but they could not move the plough; so he looked at the share and finding it caught in a ring of gold, cleared away the soil and saw that it was set centre-most a slab of alabaster, the size of the nether millstone. He strave at the stone till he pulled it from its place, when there appeared beneath it a souterrain with a stair. Presently he descended the flight of steps and came to a place like a Hammam, with four daïses, the first full of gold, from floor to roof, the second full of emeralds and pearls and coral also from ground to ceiling; the third of jacinths and rubies and turquoises and the fourth of diamonds and all manner other preciousest stones. At the upper end of the place stood a coffer of clearest crystal, full of union-gems each the size of a walnut, and upon the coffer lay a casket of gold, the bigness of a lemon. When he saw this, he marvelled and rejoiced with joy exceeding and said to himself, "I wonder what is in this casket?" So he opened it and found therein a seal-ring of gold, whereon were graven names and talismans, as they were the tracks of creeping ants. He rubbed the ring and behold, a voice said, "Adsum! Here

---

[1] Euphemistic: "I will soon fetch thee food." To say this bluntly might have brought misfortune.

[2] Arab. "Kafr" = a village in Egypt and Syria, *e.g.* Capernaum (Kafr Nahum).

[3] He has all the bonhomie of the Cairene and will do a kindness whenever he can.

am I, at thy service, O my lord! Ask and it shall be given unto thee. Wilt thou raise a city or ruin a capital or kill a king or dig a river-channel or aught of the kind? Whatso thou seekest, it shall come to pass, by leave of the King of All-might, Creator of day and night." Ma'aruf asked, "O creature of my lord, who and what art thou?" and the other answered, "I am the slave of this seal-ring standing in the service of him who possesseth it. Whatsoever he seeketh, that I accomplish for him, and I have no excuse in neglecting that he biddeth me do; because I am Sultan over two-and-seventy tribes of the Jinn, each two-and-seventy thousand in number every one of which thousand ruleth over a thousand Marids, each Marid over a thousand Ifrits, each Ifrit over a thousand Satans and each Satan over a thousand Jinn: and they are all under command of me and may not gainsay me. As for me, I am spelled to this seal-ring and may not thwart whoso holdeth it. Lo! thou hast gotten hold of it and I am become thy slave; so ask what thou wilt, for I hearken to thy word and obey thy bidding; and if thou have need of me at any time, by land or by sea, rub the signet-ring and thou wilt find me with thee. But beware of rubbing it twice in succession, or thou wilt consume me with the fire of the names graven thereon; and thus wouldst thou lose me and after regret me. Now I have acquainted thee with my case and—the Peace!"——And Shahrazad perceived the dawn of day and ceased to say her permitted say.

## Now when it was the Nine Hundred and Ninety-sixth Night

She continued, It hath reached me, O auspicious King, that when the Slave of the Signet-ring acquainted Ma'aruf with his case, the Merchant asked him, "What is thy name?" and the Jinni answered, "My name is Abú al-Sa'á'dát."[1] Quoth Ma'aruf, "O Abu al-Sa'adat what is this place and who enchanted thee in this casket?" and quoth he, "O my lord, this is a treasure called the Hoard of Shaddád son of Ad, him who the base of 'Many-columned Iram, laid, the like of which in the lands was never made.[2] I was his slave in his lifetime and this is his seal-ring, which he laid up in his treasure; but it hath fallen to thy lot." Ma'aruf enquired, "Canst thou transport that which is in this hoard to the surface of the

[1] *i.e.* the Father of Prosperities: pron. Aboosa'ádát; as in the tale of Hasan of Bassorah.
[2] Koran lxxxix. "The Daybreak," which also mentions Thamud and Pharaoh.

earth?" and the Jinni replied, "Yes! Nothing were easier." Said Ma'aruf, "Bring it forth and leave naught." So the Jinni signed with his hand to the ground, which clave asunder, and he sank and was absent a little while. Presently, there came forth young boys full of grace and fair of face, bearing golden baskets filled with gold which they emptied out and going away, returned with more; nor did they cease to transport the gold and jewels, till ere an hour had sped they said, "Naught is left in the hoard." Thereupon out came Abu al-Sa'adat and said to Ma'aruf, "O my lord, thou seest that we have brought forth all that was in the hoard." Ma'aruf asked, "Who be these beautiful boys?" and the Jinni answered, "They are my sons. This matter merited not that I should muster for it the Marids, wherefore my sons have done thy desire and are honoured by such service. So ask what thou wilt beside this." Quoth Ma'aruf, "Canst thou bring me he-mules and chests and fill the chests with the treasure and load them on the mules?" Quoth Abu al-Sa'adat, "Nothing easier," and cried a great cry; whereupon his sons presented themselves before him, to the number of eight hundred, and he said to them, "Let some of you take the semblance of he-mules and others of muleteers and handsome Mamelukes, the like of the least of whom is not found with any of the Kings; and others of you be transmewed to muleteers, and the rest to menials." So seven hundred of them changed themselves into bât-mules and other hundred took the shape of slaves. Then Abu al-Sa'adat called upon his Marids, who presented themselves between his hands and he commanded some of them to assume the aspect of horses saddled with saddles of gold crusted with jewels. And when Ma'aruf saw them do as he bade he cried, "Where be the chests?" They brought them before him and he said, "Pack the gold and the stones, each sort by itself." So they packed them and loaded three hundred he-mules with them. Then asked Ma'aruf, "O Abu al-Sa'adat, canst thou bring me some loads of costly stuffs?" and the Jinni answered, "Wilt thou have Egyptian stuffs or Syrian or Persian or Indian or Greek?" Ma'aruf said, "Bring me an hundred loads of each kind, on five hundred mules;" and Abu al-Sa'adat, "O my lord, accord me delay that I may dispose my Marids for this and send a company of them to each country to fetch an hundred loads of its stuffs and then take the form of he-mules and return, carrying the stuffs." Ma'aruf enquired, "What time dost thou want?" and Abu al-Sa'adat replied, "The time of the blackness of the night, and day shall not dawn ere thou have all thou desirest." Said Ma'aruf, "I grant thee this time," and bade them pitch him a pavilion. So they pitched it and he sat down therein and they brought him a table of food. Then said Abu al-Sa'adat to him, "O my lord, tarry thou in this tent and these my sons shall guard thee: so fear thou nothing; for I go to muster my Marids and despatch them to do thy desire." So saying, he departed, leaving Ma'aruf seated in the pavilion, with the table before him and the Jinni's sons attending upon him, in the guise of slaves and servants and suite. And while he sat in this state behold, up came the husbandman, with a great porringer of lentils [1] and a nose-bag full of barley, and seeing the pavilion pitched and the Mamelukes standing, hands upon breasts, thought that the Sultan was come and had halted on that stead. Hereat he stood open-mouthed and said in himself, "Would I had killed a couple of chickens and fried them red with clarified cow-butter for the Sultan!" And he would have turned back to kill the chickens as a regale for the King; but Ma'aruf saw him and cried out to him and said to the Mamelukes, "Bring him hither." So they brought him and his porringer of lentils before Ma'aruf, who said to him, "What is this?" Said the peasant, "This is thy dinner and thy horse's fodder! Excuse me, for I thought not that the Sultan would come hither; and, had I known that, I would have killed a couple of chickens and entertained him in goodly guise." Quoth Ma'aruf, "The Sultan is not come: I am his son-in-law and was vexed with him. However he hath sent his officers to make his peace with me, and now I am minded to return to the city. But thou hast made me this guest-meal without knowing me, and I accept it from thee, lentils though it be, and will not eat save of thy cheer." Accordingly he bade him set the porringer amiddlemost the table and ate of it his sufficiency, whilst the Fellah filled his maw with those rich meats. Then Ma'aruf washed his hands and gave the Mamelukes leave to eat; so they fell upon the remains of the meal and ate; and, when the porringer was empty, he filled it with gold and gave it to the peasant, saying, "Carry this to thy dwelling and come to me in the city, and I will entreat thee with honour." Thereupon the peasant took the porringer full of gold and returned to the village, driving the bulls before him and deeming himself akin to the King. Meanwhile, they brought Ma'aruf girls of the Brides of the Treasure,[2] who smote on instruments of music and danced before him, and he passed that night in joyance and delight, a night not to be reckoned among lives. Hardly had dawned the day when there

[1] In Egypt the cheapest and poorest of food, never seen at a table d'hôte or in a wealthy house.

[2] The beautiful girls who guard ensorcelled hoards.

arose a great cloud of dust which, presently lifting, discovered seven hundred mules laden with stuffs and attended by muleteers and baggage-tenders and cresset-bearers. With them came Abu al-Sa'adat, riding on a she-mule, in the guise of a caravan-leader, and before him was a travelling-litter, with four corner-terminals[1] of glittering red gold, set with gems. When Abu al-Sa'adat came up to the tent, he dismounted and, kissing the earth, said to Ma'aruf, "O my lord, thy desire hath been done to the uttermost and in the litter is a treasure-suit which hath not its match among Kings' raiment: so don it and mount the litter and bid us do what thou wilt." Quoth Ma'aruf, "O Abu al-Sa'adat, I wish thee to go to the city of Ikhtiyan al-Khutan and present thyself to my father-in-law the King; and go thou not in to him but in the guise of a mortal courier;" and quoth he, "To hear is to obey." So Ma'aruf wrote a letter to the Sultan and sealed it and Abu al-Sa'adat took it and set out with it; and when he arrived, he found the King saying, "O Wazir, indeed my heart is concerned for my son-in-law and I fear lest the Arabs slay him. Would Heaven I wot whither he was bound, that I might have followed him with the troops! Would he had told me his destination!" Said the Wazir, "Allah be merciful to thee for this thy heedlessness! As thy head liveth, the wight saw that we were awake to him and feared dishonour and fled, for he is nothing but an impostor, a liar." And behold, at this moment in came the courier and kissing ground before the Sultan, wished him permanent glory and prosperity and length of life. Asked the King, "Who art thou and what is thy business?" "I am a courier," answered the Jinni, "and thy son-in-law who is come with the baggage sendeth me to thee with a letter, and here it is!" So he took the writ and read therein these words, "After salutations galore to our uncle[2] the glorious King! Know that I am at hand with the baggage-train: so come thou forth to meet me with the troops." Cried the King, "Allah blacken thy brow, O Wazir! How often wilt thou defame my son-in-law's name and call him liar and impostor? Behold, he is come with the baggage-train and thou art naught but a traitor." The Minister hung his head ground-wards in shame and confusion and replied, "O King of the age, I said not this save because of the long delay of the baggage and because I feared the

---

[1] Arab. "Asákir," the ornaments of litters, which are either plain balls of metal or tapering cones based upon crescents or upon balls and crescents. See in Lane (M. E. chapt. xxiv.) the sketch of the Mahmal.

[2] Arab. "'Amm" = father's brother, courteously used for "father-in-law." Thus by a pleasant fiction the husband represents himself as having married his first cousin.

loss of the wealth he hath wasted." The King exclaimed, "O traitor, what are my riches! Now that his baggage is come he will give me great plenty in their stead." Then he bade decorate the city and going to his daughter, said to her, "Good news for thee! Thy husband will be here anon with his bales; for he hath sent me a letter to that effect and here am I now going forth to meet him." The Princess Dunya marvelled at this and said in herself, "This is a wondrous thing! Was he laughing at me and making mock of me, or had he a mind to try me, when he told me that he was a pauper? But Alhamdolillah, Glory to God, for that I failed not of my duty to him!" On this wise fared it in the Palace; but as regards Merchant Ali, the Cairene, when he saw the decoration of the city and asked the cause thereof, they said to him, "The baggage-train of Merchant Ma'aruf, the King's son-in-law, is come." Said he, "Allah is Almighty! What a calamity is this man![1] He came to me, fleeing from his wife, and he was a poor wight. Whence then should he get a baggage-train? But haply this is a device which the King's daughter hath contrived for him, fearing his disgrace, and Kings are not unable to do anything. May Allah the Most High veil his fame and not bring him to public shame!"——And Shahrazad was surprised by the dawn of day and ceased saying her permitted say.

## Now when it was the Nine Hundred and Ninety-seventh Night

She pursued, It hath reached me, O auspicious King, that when Merchant Ali asked the cause of the decorations, they told him the truth of the case; so he blessed Merchant Ma'aruf and cried, "May Allah Almighty veil his fame and not bring him to public shame!" And all the merchants rejoiced and were glad for that they would get their moneys. Then the King assembled his troops and rode forth, whilst Abu al Sa'adat returned to Ma'aruf and acquainted him with the delivering of the letter. Quoth Ma'aruf, "Bind on the loads;" and when they had done so, he donned the treasure-suit, and mounting the litter became a thousand times greater and more majestic than the King. Then he set forward; but when he had gone half-way, behold, the Sultan met him with the troops, and, seeing him riding in the Takhtrawan and clad in the dress aforesaid, threw himself upon him and saluted him, and giving him joy of his safety, greeted him with the greeting of peace. Then all the Lords

---

[1] *i.e.* a calamity to the enemy.

of the land saluted him and it was made manifest that he had spoken the truth and that in him was no lie. Presently he entered the city in such state-procession as would have caused the gall-bladder of the lion to burst[1] for envy, and the traders pressed up to him and kissed his hands, whilst Merchant Ali said to him, "Thou hast played off this trick and it hath prospered to thy hand, O Shaykh of Impostors! But thou deservest it and may Allah the Most High increase thee of His bounty!" whereupon Ma'aruf laughed. Then he entered the palace and sitting down on the throne said, "Carry the loads of gold into the treasury of my uncle the King and bring me the bales of cloth." So they brought them to him and opened them before him, bale after bale, till they had unpacked the seven hundred loads, whereof he chose out the best and said, "Bear these to Princess Dunya that she may distribute them among her slave-girls, and carry her also this coffer of jewels that she may divide them among her handmaids and eunuchs." Then he proceeded to make over to the merchants in whose debt he was stuffs by way of payment for their arrears, giving him whose due was a thousand stuffs' worth two thousand or more; after which he fell to distributing to the poor and needy, whilst the King looked on with greedy eyes and could not hinder him; nor did he cease largesse till he had made an end of the seven hundred loads, when he turned to the troops and proceeded to apportion amongst them emeralds and rubies and pearls and coral and other jewels by handsful, without count, till the King said to him, "Enough of this giving, O my son! There is but little left of the baggage." But he said, "I have plenty." Then, indeed, his good faith was become manifest and none could give him the lie; and he had come to reck not of giving, for that the Slave of the Seal-ring brought him whatsoever he sought. Presently, the treasurer came in to the King, and said, "O King of the age, the treasury is full indeed and will not hold the rest of the loads. Where shall we lay that which is left of the gold and jewels?" And he assigned to him another place. As for the Princess Dunya, when she saw this, her joy redoubled and she marvelled and said in herself, "Would I wot how came he by all this wealth!" In like manner the traders rejoiced in that which he had given them and blessed him; whilst Merchant Ali marvelled and said to himself, "I wonder how he hath lied and swindled, that he hath gotten him all these treasures?[2] Had they come

[1] Both texts read "Asad" (Lion) and Lane accepts it: there is no reason to change it for "Hásid" (Envier), the Lion being the Sultan of the Beasts and the most majestic.

[2] The Cairene knew his fellow-Cairene and was not to be taken in by him.

from the King's daughter, he had not wasted them on this wise! But how excellent is his saying who said :—

When the kings' King giveth, in reverence pause * And venture not to enquire the cause :
Allah gives His gifts unto whom He will, * So respect and abide by His Holy Laws!"

So far concerning him; but as regards the Sultan, he also marvelled with passing marvel at that which he saw of Ma'aruf's generosity and open-handedness in the largesse of wealth. Then the merchant went in to his wife, who met him, smiling and laughing-lipped and kissed his hand, saying, "Didst thou mock me or hadst thou a mind to prove me with thy saying :—I am a poor man and a fugitive from my wife? Praised be Allah for that I failed not of my duty to thee! for thou art my beloved and there is none dearer to me than thou, whether thou be rich or poor. But I would have thee tell me what didst thou design by these words." Said Ma'aruf, "I wished to prove thee and see whether thy love were true or for the sake of wealth and the greed of worldly good. But now 'tis become manifest to me that thine affection is sincere and as thou art a true woman, so welcome to thee! I know thy worth." Then he went apart into a place by himself and rubbed the seal-ring, whereupon Abu al-Sa'adat presented himself and said to him, "Adsum, at thy service! Ask what thou wilt." Quoth Ma'aruf, "I want a treasure-suit and treasure-trinkets for my wife, including a necklace of forty unique jewels." Quoth the Jinni, "To hear is to obey," and brought him what he sought, whereupon Ma'aruf dismissed him, and carrying the dress and ornaments in to his wife, laid them before her and said, "Take these and put them on and welcome!" When she saw this, her wits fled for joy, and she found among the ornaments a pair of anklets of gold set with jewels of the handiwork of the magicians, and bracelets and earrings and a belt[1] such as no money could buy. So she donned the dress and ornaments and said to Ma'aruf, "O my lord, I will treasure these up for holidays and festivals." But he answered, "Wear them always, for I have others in plenty." And when she put them on and her women beheld her, they rejoiced and bussed his hands. Then he left them and going

[1] Arab. "Hizám": Lane reads "Khizam" = a nose-ring, for which see appendix to Lane's M. E. The untrained European eye dislikes these decorations, and there is certainly no beauty in the hoops which Hindu women insert through the nostrils, camel-fashion, as if to receive the cord acting bridle. But a drop-pearl hanging to the septum is at least as pretty as the heavy pendants by which some European women lengthen their ears.

apart by himself, rubbed the seal-ring whereupon its Slave appeared and he said to him, " Bring me an hundred suits of apparel, with their ornaments of gold." "Hearing and obeying," answered Abu al-Sa'adat and brought him the hundred suits, each with its ornaments wrapped up within it. Ma'aruf took them and called aloud to the slave-girls, who came to him and he gave them each a suit: so they donned them and became like the black-eyed girls of Paradise, whilst the Princess Dunya shone amongst them as the moon among the stars. One of the handmaids told the King of this and he came in to his daughter and saw her and her women dazzling all who beheld them; whereat he wondered with passing wonderment. Then he went out and calling his Wazir, said to him, "O Wazir, such and such things have happened; what sayest thou now of this affair?" Said he, "O King of the age, this be no merchant's fashion; for a merchant keepeth a piece of linen by him for years and selleth it not but at a profit. How should a merchant have generosity such as this generosity, and whence should he get the like of these moneys and jewels, of which but a slight matter is found with the Kings? So how should loads thereof be found with merchants? Needs must there be a cause for this; but, an thou wilt hearken to me, I will make the truth of the case manifest to thee." Answered the King, "O Wazir, I will do thy bidding." Rejoined the Minister, "Do thou foregather with thy son-in-law and make a show of affect to him and talk with him and say:—O my son-in-law, I have a mind to go, I and thou and the Wazir, but no more, to a flower-garden that we may take our pleasure there. When we come to the garden, we will set on the table wine, and I will ply him therewith and compel him to drink; for when he shall have drunken, he will lose his reason and his judgment will forsake him. Then we will question him of the truth of his case, and he will discover to us his secrets, for wine is a traitor and Allah-gifted is he who said:—

When we drank the wine, and it crept its way * To the place of Secrets, I cried, 'O stay!'
In my fear lest its influence stint my wits * And my friends spy matters that hidden lay.

When he hath told us the truth we shall ken his case and may deal with him as we will; because I fear for thee the consequences of this his present fashion: haply he will covet the kingship and win over the troops by generosity and lavishing money and so depose thee and take the kingdom from thee." "True," answered the King.——And Shahrazad perceived the dawn of day and ceased to say her permitted say.

## Now when it was the Nine Hundred and Ninety-eighth Night,

She resumed, It hath reached me, O auspicious King, that when the Wazir devised this device the King said to him, "Thou hast spoken sooth!" and they passed the night on this agreement. And when morning morrowed the King went forth and sat in the guest-chamber, when lo and behold! the grooms and serving-men came in to him in dismay. Quoth he, "What hath befallen you?" and quoth they, "O King of the age, the Syces curried the horses and foddered them and the he-mules which brought the baggage; but, when we arose in the morning, we found that thy son-in-law's Mamelukes had stolen the horses and mules. We searched the stables, but found neither horse nor mule; so we entered the lodging of the Mamelukes and saw none there, nor wot we how they fled." The King marvelled at this, unknowing that the horses and Mamelukes were all Ifrits, the subjects of the Slave of the Spell, and asked the grooms, "O accursed, how could a thousand beasts and five hundred slaves and servants flee without your knowledge?" Answered they, "We know not how it happened," and he cried, "Go, and when your lord cometh forth of the Harim, tell him the case." So they went out from before the King and sat down bewildered, till Ma'aruf came out and seeing them chagrined enquired of them, "What may be the matter?" They told him all that had happened and he said, "What is their worth that ye should be concerned for them? Wend your ways." And he sat laughing and was neither angry nor grieved concerning the case; whereupon the King looked in the Wazir's face and said to him, "What manner of man is this, with whom wealth is of no worth? Needs must there be a reason for this!" Then they talked with him awhile and the King said to him, "O my son-in-law, I have a mind to go, I and thou and the Wazir, to a garden, where we may divert ourselves." "No harm in that," said Ma'aruf. So they went forth to a flower-garden, wherein every sort of fruit was of kinds twain and its waters were flowing and its trees towering and its birds carolling. There they entered a pavilion, whose sight did away sorrow from the soul, and sat talking, whilst the Minister entertained them with rare tales and quoted merry quips and mirth-provoking sayings, and Ma'aruf attentively listened, till the time of dinner came, when they set on a tray of meats and a flagon of wine. As soon as they had eaten and washed hands, the Wazir filled the cup and gave it to the King, who drank it off; then he filled a second and handed it to Ma'aruf, saying, "Take the cup of the drink to which Reason boweth neck in reverence." Quoth Ma'aruf, "What is this, O Wazir?" and quoth he, "This is the grizzled[1] virgin and the old maid long kept at home,[2] the giver of joy to hearts, whereof saith the poet :—

The feet of sturdy Miscreants[3] went trampling heavy tread, * And she hath ta'en a vengeance dire on every Arab's head.
A Káfir youth like fullest moon in darkness hands her round * Whose eyne are strongest cause of sin by him inspirited.

And Allah-gifted is he who said :—

'Tis as if wine and he who bears the bowl, * Rising to show her charms for man to see,[4]
Were dancing forenoon-Sun whose face the moon * Of night adorned with stars of Gemini.
So subtle is her essence it would seem * Through every limb like course of soul runs she.

And how excellent is the saying of the poet :—

Slept in mine arms full Moon of brightest blee * Nor did that sun eclipse in goblet see :
I nighted spying fire whereto bow down * Magians, which bowed from ewer's lip to me.

And that of another :

It runs through every joint of them as runs * The surge of health returning to the sick.

And yet another :—

I marvel at its pressers, how they died * And left us *aqua vitæ*—lymph of life !

And yet goodlier is the saying of Abu Nowas :—

Cease then to blame, because thy blame doth anger bring, * And with the draught that madded me come med'cining :
A yellow girl[5] whose court cures every carking care ; * Did a stone touch it 'twould with joy and glee upspring :

---

[1] Arab. "Shamta," one of the many names of wine, the "speckled" alluding to the bubbles which dance upon the freshly filled cup.

[2] *i.e.* in the cask. These "merry quips" strongly suggest the dismal toasts of our not remote ancestors.

[3] Arab. "A'láj" plur. of "'Ilj" and rendered by Lane, "the stout foreign infidels." The next line alludes to the cupbearer who was generally a slave and a non-Moslem.

[4] As if it were a bride. The stars of Jauzá (Gemini) are the cup-bearer's eyes.

[5] *i.e.* light-coloured wine.

She riseth in her ewer during darkest night, * The house with brightest, sheeniest light illumining;
And going round of youths to whom the world inclines[1] * Ne'er, save in whatso way they please, their hearts shall wring.

But best of all is the saying of Ibn al-Mu'tazz[2]:—

On the shaded woody island[3] His showers Allah deign * Shed on Convent hight Abdún[4] drop and drip of railing rain:
Oft the breezes of the morning have awakened me therein * When the Dawn shows her blaze,[5] ere the bird of flight was fain;
And the voices of the monks that with chants awoke the walls * Black-frocked shavelings ever wont the cup amorn to drain.[6]
Then I rose and spread my cheek like a carpet on his path * In homage, and with skirts wiped his trail from off the plain;
But threatening disgrace rose the Crescent in the sky * Like the paring of a nail, yet with light would never wane.

And gifted of God is he who saith:—

In the morn I am richest of men * And in joy at good news I start up.
For I look on the liquid gold[7] * And I measure it out by the cup.

And how goodly is the saying of the poet:—

By Allah, this is th' only alchemy: * All said of other science false we see!
Carat of wine on hundredweight of woe * Transmuteth gloomiest grief to joy and glee.

And that of another:—

The glasses are heavy when empty brought, * Till we charge them all with unmixèd wine.
Then so light are they that to fly they're fain * As bodies lightened by soul divine.

---

[1] The usual homage to youth and beauty.

[2] Abdallah ibn al-Mu'tazz, son of Al-Mu'tazz bi 'llah, the 13th Abbaside, and great-great-grandson of Harun al-Rashid. He was one of the most renowned poets of the third century (A.H.) and died in A.D. 908, strangled by the partisans of his nephew Al-Muktadir bi 'llah, 18th Abbaside.

[3] Jazírat ibn Omar, an island and town on the Tigris north of Mosul. "Some versions of the poem, from which these verses are quoted, substitute El-Mutireh, a village near Samara (a town on the Tigris, 60 miles north of Baghdad), for El-Jezireh, *i.e.* Jeziret ibn Omar." (Payne.)

[4] The Convent of Abdun on the east bank of the Tigris opposite the Jezirah was so called from a statesman who caused it to be built. For a variant of these lines see Ibn Khallikan, vol. ii. 42; here we miss "the shady groves of Al-Matírah."

[5] Arab. "Ghurrah," the white blaze on a horse's brow. In Ibn Khallikan the bird is the lark.

[6] Arab. "Táy'i" = thirsty, used with Jáy'i = hungry.

[7] *i.e.* gold-coloured wine, as the Vino d'Oro.

And yet another :—

Wine-cup and ruby-wine high worship claim ; * Dishonour 'twere to see their honour waste :
Bury me, when I'm dead, by side of vine * Whose veins shall moisten bones in clay misplaced ;
Nor bury me in wold and wild, for I * Dread only after death no wine to taste." [1]

And he ceased not to egg him on to the drink, naming to him such of the virtues of wine as he thought fit and reciting to him what occurred to him of poetry and pleasantries on the theme, till Ma'aruf addressed himself to sucking the cup-lips and cared no longer for aught else. The Wazir ceased not to fill for him and he to drink and enjoy himself and make merry, till his wits wandered and he could not distinguish right from wrong. When the Minister saw that drunkenness had attained in him to utterest and the bounds transgressed, he said to him, "By Allah, O Merchant Ma'aruf, I admire whence thou gottest these jewels whose like the Kings of the Chosroës possess not! In all our lives never saw we a merchant that had heaped up riches like unto thine or more generous than thou, for thy doings are the doings of Kings, and not merchants' doings. Wherefore, Allah upon thee, do thou acquaint me with this, that I may know thy rank and condition." And he went on to test him with questions and cajole him, till Ma'aruf, being reft of reason, said to him, "I'm neither merchant nor King," and told him his whole story from first to last. Then said the Wazir, "I conjure thee, by Allah, O my lord Ma'aruf, show us the ring, that we may see its make." So, in his drunkenness, he pulled off the ring and said, "Take it and look upon it." The Minister took it and turning it over, said, "If I rub it, will its Slave appear?" Replied Ma'aruf, "Yes. Rub it and he will appear to thee, and do thou divert thyself with the sight of him."

---

[1] Compare the charming song of Abu Miján, translated from the German of Dr. Weil in Bohn's Edit. of Ockley (p. 149),

When the Death-angel cometh mine eyes to close,
Dig my grave 'mid the vines on the hill's fair side ;
For though deep in earth may my bones repose,
The juice of the grape shall their food provide.
Ah, bury me not in a barren land,
Or Death will appear to me dread and drear !
While fearless I'll wait what he hath in hand
An the scent of the vineyard my spirit cheer.

The glorious old drinker! Compare also Omar-i-Khayyám, the quatrain beginning, "Ah, with the grape my fading life provide," etc. The idea is universal in the Moslem East and it has a secondary mystical sense.

Thereupon the Wazir rubbed the ring and behold, forthright appeared the Jinni and said, "Adsum, at thy service, O my lord! Ask and it shall be given to thee. Wilt thou ruin a city or raise a capital or kill a king? Whatso thou seekest, I will do for thee, sans fail." The Wazir pointed to Ma'aruf and said, "Take up yonder wretch and cast him down in the most desolate of desert lands, where he shall find nothing to eat nor drink, so he may die of hunger and perish miserably, and none know of him." Accordingly, the Jinni snatched him up and flew with him betwixt heaven and earth, which when Ma'aruf saw, he made sure of destruction and wept and said, "O Abu al-Sa'adat, whither goest thou with me?" Replied the Jinni, "I go to cast thee down in the Desert Quarter,[1] O ill-bred wight of gross wits. Shall one have the like of this talisman and give it to the folk to gaze at? Verily, thou deservest that which hath befallen thee; and but that I fear Allah, I would let thee fall from a height of a thousand fathoms, nor shouldst thou reach the earth, till the winds had torn thee to shreds." Ma'aruf was silent[2] and did not again bespeak him till Abu al-Sa'adat reached the Desert Quarter, and casting him down there, went away and left him in that horrible place.——And Shahrazad was surprised by the dawn of day and ceased saying her permitted say.

## Now when it was the Nine Hundred and Ninety-ninth Night,

She said, It hath reached me, O auspicious King, that the Slave of the Seal-ring took up Ma'aruf and cast him down in the Desert Quarter, where he left him and went his ways. So much concerning him; but returning to the Wazir, who was now in possession of the talisman, he said to the King, "How deemest thou now? Did I not tell thee that this fellow was a liar, an impostor, but thou wouldst not credit me?" Replied the King, "Thou wast in the right, O my Wazir, Allah grant thee weal! But give me the ring, that I may solace myself with the sight." The Minister looked at him angrily and spat in his face, saying, "O lack-wits, how shall I give it to thee and abide thy servant, after I am become thy

---

[1] Arab. "Rub'a al-Kharáb," in Ibn al-Wardi, Central Africa south of the Nile-sources, one of the richest regions in the world. Here it prob. alludes to the Rub'a al-Khálí, or Great Arabian Desert; for which see Night dclxxvi. In rhetoric it is opposed to the "Rub'a Maskún," or populated fourth of the world, the rest being held to be ocean.

[2] This is the noble resignation of the Moslem. What a dialogue there would have been in a European book between man and devil!

master? But I will spare thee no more on life." Then he rubbed the seal-ring and said to the Slave, "Take up this ill-mannered churl and cast him down by his son-in-law the swindler-man." So the Jinni took him up and flew off with him, whereupon quoth the King to him, "O creature of my Lord, what is my crime?" Abu al-Sa'adat replied, "That wot I not, but my master hath commanded me and I cannot cross whoso hath compassed the enchanted ring." Then he flew on with him, till he came to the Desert Quarter and, casting him down where he had cast Ma'aruf left him and returned. The King hearing Ma'aruf weeping, went up to him and acquainted him with his case; and they sat weeping over that which had befallen them and found neither meat nor drink. Meanwhile the Minister, after driving father-in-law and son-in-law from the country, went forth from the garden and summoning all the troops held a Divan, and told them what he had done with the King and with Ma'aruf and acquainted them with the affair of the talisman, adding, "Unless ye make me Sultan over you, I will bid the Slave of the Seal-ring take you up one and all and cast you down in the Desert Quarter where you shall die of hunger and thirst." They replied, "Do us no damage, for we accept thee as Sultan over us and will not anywise gainsay thy bidding." So they agreed, in their own despite, to his being Sultan over them, and he bestowed on them robes of honour, seeking all he had a mind to of Abu al-Sa'adat, who brought it to him forthwith. Then he sat down on the throne and the troops did homage to him; and he sent to Princess Dunya, the King's daughter, saying, "Make thee ready, for I mean to wed thee this day, because I long for thee with love." When she heard this she wept, for the case of her husband and father was grievous to her, and sent to him saying, "Have patience with me till my period of widowhood[1] be ended: then draw up thy contract of marriage with me and wed me according to law." But he sent back to say to her, "I know neither period of widowhood nor to delay have I a mood; and I need not a contract, nor know I lawful from unlawful; but needs must I wed thee this day." She answered him saying, "So be it, then, and welcome to thee!" but this was a trick on her part. When the answer reached the Wazir, he rejoiced and his breast was broadened, for that he was passionately in love with her. He bade set food before all the folk, saying, "Eat; this is my bride-

[1] Arab. "Al-'Iddah," the period of four months and ten days which must elapse before she could legally marry again. But this was a palpable wile: she was not sure of her husband's death and he had not divorced her; so that although a "grass widow," a "Strohwitwe" as the Germans say, she could not wed again either with or without interval.

feast; for I purpose to wed the Princess Dunya this day." Quoth the Shaykh al-Islam, "It is not lawful for thee to wed her till her days of widowhood be ended and thou have drawn up thy contract of marriage with her." But he answered, "I know neither days of widowhood nor other period: so multiply not words on me." The Shaykh Al-Islam was silent,[1] fearing his mischief, and said to the troops, "Verily this man is a Kafir, a Miscreant, and hath neither creed nor religious conduct." As soon as it was evenfall, he went in to her and found her robed in her richest raiment and decked with her goodliest adornments. When she saw him, she came to meet him, laughing and said, "A blessed day! Withal, hadst thou slain my father and my husband, it had been more to my mind." And he said, "There is no help but I slay them." Then she made him sit down and began to jest with him and make show of love, caressing him and smiling in his face so that his reason fled; but she cajoled him with her coaxing and cunning only that she might get possession of the ring and change his joy into calamity on the mother of his forehead:[2] nor did she deal thus with him but after the rede of him who said[3]:—

I attained by my wits * What no sword had obtained,
And return wi' the spoils * Whose sweet pluckings I gained.

When he saw her caress him and smile upon him he besought her to kiss him; but, when he approached her, she drew away from him and burst into tears, saying, "O my lord, seest thou not the man looking at us? I conjure thee by Allah, screen me from his eyes! How canst thou kiss me what while he looketh on us?" When he heard this he was angry and asked, "Where is the man?" and answered she, "There he is, in the bezel of the ring; putting out his head and staring at us!" He thought that the Jinni was looking at them and said laughing, "Fear not; this is the Slave of the Seal-ring, and he is subject to me." Quoth she, "I am afraid of Ifrits; pull it off and throw it afar from me." So he plucked it off and laying it on the cushion, drew near to her, but she dealt him a kick, and he fell over on his back senseless; whereupon she cried out to her attendants, who came to her in haste, and said to them, "Seize him!" So forty slave-girls laid hold on him, whilst she hurriedly

---

[1] Here the silence is of cowardice and the passage is a fling at the "time-serving" of the Olema, a favourite theme, like "banging the bishops" among certain Westerns.

[2] Arab. "Umm al-raas," the poll, crown of the head, here the place where a calamity coming down from heaven would first alight.

[3] From Al-Hariri (Lane); the lines are excellent.

snatched up the ring from the cushion and rubbed it; whereupon Abu al-Sa'adat presented himself, saying, "Adsum, at thy service, O my mistress." Cried she, "Take up yonder Infidel and clap him in jail and shackle him heavily." So he took him and throwing him into the Prison of Wrath,[1] returned and reported, "I have laid him in limbo." Quoth she, "Whither wentest thou with my father and my husband?" and quoth he, "I cast them down in the Desert Quarter." Then cried she, "I command thee to fetch them to me forthwith." He replied, "I hear and I obey," and taking flight at once, stayed not till he reached the Desert Quarter, where he lighted down upon them and found them seated, weeping and complaining each to other. Quoth he, "Fear not, for relief is come to you;" and he told them what the Wazir had done, adding, "Indeed I imprisoned him with my own hands in obedience to her, and she hath bidden me bear you back." And they rejoiced in his news. Then he took them both up and flew home with them; nor was it more than an hour before he brought them in to Princess Dunya, who rose and saluted sire and spouse. Then she made them sit down and brought them meat and sweetmeats, and they passed the rest of the night with her. On the next day she clad them in rich clothing and said to the King, "O my papa, sit thou upon thy throne and be King as before and make my husband thy Wazir of the Right and tell thy troops that which hath happened. Then send for the Minister out of prison and do him die, and after burn him; for that he is a Miscreant, and would have married me against the law of God, and he hath testified against himself that he is an Infidel and believeth in no religion. And do tenderly by thy son-in-law, whom thou makest thy Wazir of the Right." He replied, "Hearing and obeying, O my daughter. But do thou give me the ring or give it to thy husband." Quoth she, "It behoveth not that either thou or he have the ring. I will keep the ring myself, and belike I shall be more careful of the ring than you. Whatso ye wish seek it of me and I will demand it for you of the Slave of the Seal-ring. So fear no harm so long as I live and after my death, do what ye twain will with the ring." Quoth the King, "This is the right rede, O my daughter," and taking his son-in-law went forth to the Divan. Now the troops had passed the night in sore chagrin for Princess Dunya and that which the Wazir had done and for his ill-usage of the King and Ma'aruf, and they feared lest the law of Al-Islam be dishonoured, because it was manifest to them

---

[1] Arab. "Sijn al-Ghazab," the dungeons appropriated to the worst of criminals, where they suffer penalties far worse than hanging or guillotining.

that he was a Kafir. So they assembled in the Divan and fell to reproaching the Shaykh al-Islam, saying, "Why didst thou not forbid him from wedding the Princess?" Said he, "O folk, the man is a Miscreant and hath gotten possession of the ring and I and you may not prevail against him. But Almighty Allah will requite him his deed, and be ye silent, lest he slay you." And as the host was thus engaged in talk, behold the King and Ma'aruf entered the Divan.—— And Shahrazad perceived the dawn of day and ceased to say her permitted say.

## Now when it was the Thousandth Night,

She continued, It hath reached me, O auspicious King, that when the troops sorely chagrined sat in the Divan talking over the ill-deeds done by the Wazir to their Sovran, his son-in-law and his daughter, behold, the King and Ma'aruf entered. Then the King bade decorate the city and sent to fetch the Wazir from the place of duresse. So they brought him, and as he passed by the troops, they cursed him and abused him and menaced him, till he came to the King, who commanded to do him dead by the vilest of deaths. Accordingly, they slew him and after burned his body, and he went to Hell after the foulest of plights; and right well quoth one of him:—

The Compassionate show no ruth to the tomb where his bones shall lie * And
Munkar and eke Nakír[1] ne'er cease to abide thereby.

The King made Ma'aruf his Wazir of the Right and the times were pleasant to them and their joys were untroubled. They abode thus five years till, in the sixth year, the King died and Princess Dunya made Ma'aruf Sultan in her father's stead, but she gave him not the seal-ring. During this time she had borne him a boy of passing loveliness, excelling in beauty and perfection, who ceased not to be reared in the laps of nurses till he reached the age of five, when his mother fell sick of a deadly sickness and calling her husband to her, said to him, "I am ill." Quoth he, "Allah preserve thee, O dearling of my heart!" But quoth she, "Haply I shall die and thou needest not that I commend to thy care thy son: wherefore I charge

---

[1] According to some modern Moslems Munkar and Nakir visit the graves of Infidels (non-Moslems) and Bashshir and Mubashshir ("Givers of glad tidings") those of Mohammedans. Petis de la Croix (Les Mille et un Jours, vol. iii. 258) speaks of the "Zoubanya," black angels who torture the damned under their chief Dabilah.

thee, but be careful of the ring, for thine own sake and for the sake of this thy boy." And he answered, "No harm shall befal him whom Allah preserveth!" Then she pulled off the ring and gave it to him, and on the morrow she was admitted to the mercy of Allah the Most High,[1] whilst Ma'aruf abode in possession of the kingship and applied himself to the business of governing. Now it chanced that one day, as he shook the handkerchief[2] and the troops withdrew to their places that he betook himself to the sitting-chamber, where he sat till the day departed and the night advanced with murks bedight. Then came in to him his cup-companions of the notables according to their custom, and sat with him by way of solace and diversion, till midnight, when they craved permission to withdraw. He gave them leave and they retired to their houses; after which there came in to him a slave-girl affected to the service of his bed, who spread him the mattress, and doffing his apparel clad him in his sleeping-gown. Then he lay down and she kneaded his feet, till sleep overpowered him; whereupon she withdrew to her own chamber and slept. But suddenly he felt something beside him in the bed and awaking started up in alarm and cried, "I seek refuge with Allah from Satan the stoned!" Then he opened his eyes and seeing by his side a woman foul of favour, said to her, "Who art thou?" Said she, "Fear not, I am thy wife Fatimah al-Urrah." Whereupon he looked in her face and knew her by her loathly form and the length of her dog-teeth: so he asked her, "Whence camest thou in to me and who brought thee to this country?" "In what country art thou at this present?" "In the city of Ikhtiyan al-Khutan; and thou, when didst thou leave Cairo?" "But now." "How can that be?" "Know," said she, "that, when I fell out with thee and Satan prompted me to do thee a damage, I complained of thee to the magistrates, who sought for thee and the Kazis enquired of thee, but found thee not. When two days were passed, repentance gat hold upon me and I knew that the fault was with me; but penitence availed me not, and I abode for some time weeping for thy loss, till what was in my hand failed and I was obliged to beg my bread. So I fell to asking of all, from the courted rich to the contemned poor, and since thou leftest me, I have eaten of the bitterness of beggary and have been in the sorriest of conditions. Every night I sat beweeping our separation

---

[1] Very simple and pathetic is this short sketch of the noble-minded Princess's death.

[2] In sign of dismissal. I have noted that "throwing the kerchief" is not an Eastern practice: the idea probably arose from the Oriental practice of sending presents in richly embroidered napkins and kerchiefs.

and that which I suffered, since thy departure, of humiliation and ignominy, of abjection and misery." And she went on to tell him what had befallen her, whilst he stared at her in amazement, till she said, "Yesterday, I went about begging all day but none gave me aught; and as often as I accosted anyone and craved of him a crust of bread, he reviled me and gave me naught. When night came, I went to bed supperless, and hunger burned me and sore on me was that which I suffered: and I sat weeping when, behold, one appeared to me and said, O woman why weepest thou? Said I, Erst I had a husband who used to provide for me and fulfil my wishes; but he is lost to me and I know not whither he went and have been in sore straits since he left me. Asked he, What is thy husband's name? and I answered, His name is Ma'aruf. Quoth he, I ken him. Know that thy husband is now Sultan in a certain city, and if thou wilt, I will carry thee to him. Cried I, I am under thy protection: of thy bounty bring me to him! So he took me up and flew with me between heaven and earth, till he brought me to this pavilion and said to me:—Enter yonder chamber, and thou shalt see thy husband asleep on the couch. Accordingly I entered and found thee in this state of lordship. Indeed I had not thought thou wouldst forsake me, who am thy mate, and praised be Allah who hath united thee with me!" Quoth Ma'aruf, "Did I forsake thee or thou me? Thou complainedst of me from Kazi to Kazi and endedst by denouncing me to the High Court and bringing down on me Abú Tabak from the Citadel: so I fled in mine own despite." And he went on to tell her all that had befallen him and how he was become Sultan and had married the King's daughter and how his beloved Dunya had died leaving him a son who was then seven years old. She rejoined, "That which happened was fore-ordained of Allah; but I repent me and I place myself under thy protection, beseeching thee not to abandon me, but suffer me to eat bread with thee by way of an alms." And she ceased not to humble herself to him and to supplicate him till his heart relented towards her and he said, "Repent from mischief and abide with me, and naught shall betide thee save what shall pleasure thee: but, an thou work any wickedness, I will slay thee nor fear anyone. And fancy not that thou canst complain of me to the High Court and that Abu Tabak will come down on me from the Citadel; for I am become Sultan and the folk dread me; but I fear none save Allah Almighty, because I have a talismanic ring, which when I rub, the Slave of the Signet appeareth to me. His name is Abu al-Sa'adat, and whatsoever I demand of him he bringeth to me. So, an thou desire to return to thine own country, I will give thee what shall suffice thee all thy life long and will send thee thither speedily; but, an thou desire to abide with me, I will clear for thee a palace and furnish it with the choicest of silks and appoint thee twenty slave-girls to serve thee and provide thee with dainty dishes and sumptuous suits, and thou shalt be a Queen and live in all delight till thou die or I die. What sayest thou of this?" "I wish to abide with thee," she answered and kissed his hand and vowed repentance from frowardness. Accordingly, he set apart a palace for her sole use and gave her slave-girls and eunuchs, and she became a Queen. The young Prince used to visit her as he visited his sire; but she hated him for that he was not her son; and when the boy saw that she looked on him with the eye of aversion and anger, he shunned her and took a dislike to her. As for Ma'aruf, he bethought him not of his wife Fatimah the Dirt, for that she was grown a grizzled old fright, foul-favoured to the sight, a bald-headed blight, loathlier than the snake speckled black and white; the more that she had beyond measure evil entreated him aforetime; and as saith the adage, "Ill-usage the root of affection disparts and sows aversion in the soil of hearts;" and God-gifted is he who saith:—

Beware of losing hearts of men by thine injurious deed; * For whenas Hatred takes his place none may dear Love restore:
Hearts, when affection flies from them, are likest unto glass, * Which broken cannot whole be made,—'tis breached for evermore.

And indeed Ma'aruf had not given her shelter by reason of any praiseworthy quality in her, but he dealt with her thus generously only of desire for the approval of Allah Almighty.——Here Dunyazad interrupted her sister Shahrazad, saying, "How winsome are these words of thine which win hold of the heart more forcibly than enchanters' eyne; and how beautiful are these wondrous books thou hast cited and the marvellous and singular tales thou hast recited!" Quoth Shahrazad, "And where is all this compared with what I shall relate to thee on the coming night, an I live and the King deign spare my days?" So when morning morrowed and the day brake in its sheen and shone, the King arose from his couch with breast broadened and in high expectation for the rest of the tale; and saying, "By Allah, I will not slay her till I hear the last of her story," repaired to his Durbár while the Wazir, as was his wont, presented himself at the palace, shroud under arm. Shahriyar tarried abroad all that day, bidding and forbidding between man and man; after which he returned to his Harim and, according to his custom, went in to his wife Shahrazad.[1]

## Now when it was the Thousand and First Night,

Dunyazad said to her sister, "Do thou finish for us the History of Ma'aruf." She replied, "With love and goodly gree, an my lord deign permit me recount it." Quoth the King, "I permit thee; for that I am fain of hearing it." So she said:—It hath reached me, O auspicious King, that Ma'aruf would have naught to do with his wife by way of conjugal love. Now when she saw that he held aloof from her, she hated him and jealousy gat the mastery of her and Iblis prompted her to take the seal-ring from him and slay him and make herself Queen in his stead. So she went forth one night from her pavilion, intending for that wherein was her husband King Ma'aruf. And it was his wont, of the excellence of his piety, that, when he was minded to sleep, he would doff the enchanted seal-ring from his finger, in reverence to the Holy Names graven thereon, and lay it on the pillow. Moreover, when he went to the Hammam he locked the door of the pavilion till his return, when he put on the ring, and after this, all were free to enter according to custom. His wife Fatimah the Dirt knew of all this and went not forth from her place till she had certified herself of the case. So she sallied out, when the night was dark, purposing to go in to him, whilst he was drowned in sleep, and steal the ring unseen of him. Now it chanced at this time that the King's son had gone out to take the air, leaving the door open. Presently, he saw Fatimah come forth of her pavilion and make stealthily for that of his father and said in himself, "What aileth this witch to leave her lodging in the dead of the night and make for my father's pavilion? Needs must there be some reason for this;" so he went out after her and followed in her steps unseen of her. Now he had a short sword of watered steel, which he held so dear that he went not to his father's Divan, except he were girt therewith; and his

[1] Curious to say, both Lane and Payne omit this passage which appears in both texts (Mac. and Bul.). The object is evidently to prepare the reader for the ending by reverting to the beginning of the tale; and its prolixity has its effect, as in the old Romances of Chivalry from Amadis of Ghaul to the Seven Champions of Christendom. If it provoke impatience, it also heightens expectation: "it is like the long elm-avenues of our forefathers; we wish ourselves at the end; but we know that at the end there is something great."

father used to laugh at him and exclaim, "Mashallah![1] This is a mighty fine sword of thine, O my son! But thou hast not gone down with it to battle nor cut off a head therewith." Whereupon the boy would reply, "I will not fail to cut off with it some head which deserveth[2] cutting." And Ma'aruf would laugh at his words. Now when treading in her track he drew the sword from its sheath and he followed her till she came to his father's pavilion and entered, whilst he stood and watched her from the door. He saw her searching about and heard her say to herself, "Where hath he laid the seal-ring?" whereby he knew that she was looking for the ring, and he waited till she found it and said, "Here it is." Then she picked it up and turned to go out; but he hid behind the door. As she came forth, she looked at the ring and turned it about in her grasp; but when she was about to rub it, he raised his hand with the sword and smote her on the neck; and she cried a single cry and fell down dead. With this Ma'aruf awoke, and seeing his wife strown on the ground, with her blood flowing, and his son standing with the drawn sword in his hand, said to him, "What is this, O my son?" He replied, "O my father, how often hast thou said to me, Thou hast a mighty fine sword; but thou hast not gone down with it to battle nor cut off a head. And I have answered thee, saying, I will not fail to cut off with it a head which deserveth cutting. And now, behold, I have therewith cut off for thee a head well worth the cutting!" And he told him what had passed. Ma'aruf sought for the seal-ring, but found it not; so he searched the dead woman's body till he saw her hand closed upon it; whereupon he took it from her grasp and said to the boy, "Thou art indeed my very son, without doubt or dispute; Allah ease thee in this world and in the next, even as thou hast eased me of this vile woman! Her attempt led only to her own destruction, and Allah-gifted is he who said:—

When Allah's aid deigns further man's intent, * Man's wish in every case shall find consent:
But an that aid of Allah be refused, * Man's first attempt shall do him damagement.

Then King Ma'aruf called aloud to some of his attendants, who came in haste, and he told them what his wife Fatimah the Dirt had done and bade them to take her and lay her in a place till the morning. They did his bidding, and next day he gave her in

---

[1] Here the exclamation wards off the Evil Eye from the Sword and the wearer. Mr. Payne notes, "The old English exclamation 'Cock's 'ill!' (*i.e.*, God's will, thus corrupted for the purpose of evading the statute of 3 Jac. i. against profane swearing exactly corresponds to the Arabic"—with a difference, I add.

[2] Arab. "Mustahakk" = deserving (Lane) or worth (Payne) the cutting.

charge to a number of eunuchs, who washed her and shrouded her and made her a tomb[1] and buried her. Thus her coming from Cairo was but to her grave, and Allah-gifted is he who said[2]:—

We trod the steps appointed for us: and he whose steps are appointed must tread them.
He whose death is decreed to take place in one land shall not die in any land but that.

And how excellent is the saying of the poet:—

I wot not, whenas to a land I fare, * Good luck pursuing, what my lot shall be:
Whether boon fortune I perforce pursue * Or the misfortune which pursueth me."

After this, King Ma'aruf sent for the husbandman, whose guest he had been when he was a fugitive, and made him his Wazir of the Right and his Chief Counsellor.[3] Then, learning that he had a daughter of passing beauty and loveliness, of qualities nature-ennobled at birth and exalted of worth, he took her to wife; and in due time he married his son. So they abode awhile in all solace of life and its enjoyment, and their days were serene and their joys untroubled, till there came to them the Destroyer of delights and the Sunderer of societies, the Depopulator of populous places and the Orphaner of sons and daughters. And glory be to the Living who dieth not and in whose hand are the Keys of the Seen and the Unseen!

## Conclusion.

Now, during this time, Shahrazad had borne the King three boy children: so, when she had made an end of the story of Ma'aruf, she rose to her feet and kissing ground before him, said, "O King of the time and unique one[4] of the age and the tide, I am thine handmaid; and these thousand nights and a night have I entertained thee with stories of folk gone before and admonitory instances of the men of yore. May I then make bold to crave a boon of thy Highness?" He replied, "Ask, O Shahrazad, and it shall be

---

[1] Arab. "Mashhad" the same as "Sháhid" = the upright stones at the head and foot of the grave. Lane mistranslates, "Made for her a funeral procession."

[2] These lines have occurred before. I quote Lane.

[3] There is nothing strange in such sudden elevations amongst Moslems, and even in Europe we still see them occasionally. The family in the East, however humble, is a model and miniature of the state, and learning is not always necessary to wisdom.

[4] Arab. "Faríd," which may also mean "union-pearl."

granted to thee."[1] Whereupon she cried out to the nurses and the eunuchs, saying, "Bring me my children." So they brought them to her in haste, and they were three boy children, one walking, one crawling, and one sucking. She took them and setting them before the King, again kissed the ground and said, "O King of the age, these are thy children and I crave that thou release me from the doom of death, as a dole to these infants; for, an thou kill me, they will become motherless and will find none among women to rear them as they should be reared." When the King heard this, he wept and straining the boys to his bosom, said, "By Allah, O Shahrazad, I pardoned thee before the coming of these children, for that I found thee chaste, pure, ingenuous, pious! Allah bless thee and thy father and thy mother and thy root and thy branch! I take the Almighty to witness against me that I exempt thee from aught that can harm thee." So she kissed his hands and feet and rejoiced with exceeding joy, saying, "The Lord make thy life long and increase thee in dignity and majesty![2] presently adding, "Thou marvelledst at that which befel thee on the part of women; yet there betided the Kings of the Chosroës before thee greater mishaps and more grievous than that which hath befallen thee, and indeed I have set forth unto thee that which happened to Caliphs and Kings and others with their women, but the relation is longsome and hearkening groweth tedious, and in this is all-sufficient warning for the man of wits and admonishment for the wise." Then she ceased to speak, and when King Shahriyar heard her speech and profited by that which she said, he summoned up his reasoning powers and cleansed his heart and caused his understanding revert and turned to Allah Almighty and said to himself "Since there befel the Kings of the Chosroës more than that which hath befallen me, never, whilst I live, shall I cease to blame myself for the past. As for this Shahrazad, her like is not found in the lands; so praise be to Him who appointed her a means for delivering His creatures from oppression and slaughter!" Then he arose from his séance and kissed her head, whereat she rejoiced, she and her sister Dunyazad, with exceeding joy. When the morning morrowed, the King went forth and sitting down on the throne of the Kingship, summoned the Lords of his land; whereupon the Chamberlains and Nabobs and Captains of the host went

---

[1] Trébutien (iii 497) cannot deny himself the pleasure of a French touch, making the King reply, "C'est assez; qu'on lui coupe la tête, car ces dernières histoires surtout m'ont causé un ennui mortel." This reading is found in some of the MSS.

[2] After this I borrow from the Bresl. Edit. inserting, however, passages from the Mac. Edit.

in to him and kissed ground before him. He distinguished the Wazir, Shahrazad's sire, with special favour and bestowed on him a costly and splendid robe of honour and entreated him with the utmost kindness, and said to him, "Allah protect thee for that thou gavest me to wife thy noble daughter, who hath been the means of my repentance from slaying the daughters of folk. Indeed I have found her pure and pious, chaste, ingenuous, and Allah hath vouchsafed me by her three boy children; wherefore praised be He for his passing favour. Then he bestowed robes of honour upon his Wazirs and Emirs and Chief Officers, and he set forth to them briefly that which had betided him with Shahrazad and how he had turned from his former ways and repented him of what he had done and proposed to take the Wazir's daughter, Shahrazad, to wife and let draw up the marriage-contract with her. When those who were present heard this, they kissed the ground before him and blessed him, and his betrothed[1] Shahrazad and the Wazir thanked her. Then Shahriyar made an end of his sitting in all weal, whereupon the folk dispersed to their dwelling-places and the news was bruited abroad that the King purposed to marry the Wazir's daughter, Shahrazad. So he proceeded to make ready the wedding gear, and presently he sent after his brother, King Shah Zaman, who came, and King Shahriyar went forth to meet him with the troops. Furthermore they decorated the city after the goodliest fashion and diffused scents from censers and burnt aloes-wood and other perfumes in all the markets and thoroughfares and rubbed themselves with saffron,[2] what while the drums beat and the flutes and pipes sounded and mimes and mountebanks played and plied their arts and the King lavished on them gifts and largesse; and in very deed it was a notable day. When they came to the palace, King Shahriyar commanded to spread the tables with beasts roasted whole and sweetmeats and all manner of viands and bade the crier cry to the folk that they should come up to the Divan and eat and drink and that this should be a means of reconciliation between him and them. So, high and low, great and small came up unto him and they abode on that wise, eating and drinking, seven days with their nights. Then the King shut himself up with his brother and related to him that which had betided him with the Wazir's daughter, Shahrazad,

---

[1] *i.e.* whom he intended to marry with regal ceremony.

[2] The use of coloured powders in sign of holiday-making is not obselete in India. See Herklots for the use of "Huldee" (Haldi) or turmeric powder. pp. 64-65.

during the past three years and told him what he had heard from her of proverbs and parables, chronicles and pleasantries, quips and jests, stories and anecdotes, dialogues and histories and elegies and other verses; whereat King Shah Zaman marvelled with the uttermost marvel and said, "Fain would I take her younger sister to wife, so we may be two brothers-german to two sisters-german, and they on like wise be sisters to us; for that the calamity which befel me was the cause of our discovering that which befel thee and all this time of three years past I have taken no delight in love save that I wed each night with a damsel of my kingdom, and every morning I do her to death; but now I desire to marry thy wife's sister Dunyazad." When King Shahriyar heard his brother's words, he rejoiced with joy exceeding and arising forthright, went in to his wife Shahrazad and acquainted her with that which his brother purposed, namely that he sought her sister Dunyazad in wedlock; whereupon she answered, "O King of the age, we seek of him one condition, to wit, that he take up his abode with us, for that I cannot brook to be parted from my sister an hour, because we were brought up together and may not endure separation each from other.[1] If he accept of this pact, she is his handmaid." King Shahriyar returned to his brother and acquainted him with that which Shahrazad had said; and he replied, "Indeed, this is what was in my mind, for that I desire nevermore to be parted from thee one hour. As for the kingdom, Allah the Most High shall send to it whomso He chooseth, for that I have no longer a desire for the Kingship." When King Shahriyar heard his brother's words, he rejoiced exceedingly and said, "Verily, this is what I wished, O my brother. So Alhamdolillah—Praised be Allah—who hath brought about union between us." Then he sent after the Kazis and Olema, Captains and Notables, and they married the two brothers to the two sisters. The contracts were written out and the two Kings bestowed robes of honour of silk and satin on those who were present, whilst the city was decorated and the rejoicings were renewed. The King commanded each Emir and Wazir and Chamberlain and Nabob to decorate his palace and the folk of the city were gladdened by the presage of happiness and contentment. King Shahriyar also bade slaughter sheep and set up kitchens and made bride-feasts and fed all comers, high and low; and he gave alms to the poor and needy and extended his bounty to great and small. Then the eunuchs went

[1] Many Moslem families insist upon this before giving their girls in marriage, and the practice is still popular amongst many Mediterranean peoples.

forth, that they might perfume the Hammam for the brides; so they scented it with rose-water and willow-flower-water and pods of musk and fumigated it with Kákilí[1] eagle-wood and ambergris. Then Shahrazad entered, she and her sister Dunyazad, and they cleansed their heads and clipped their hair. When they came forth of the Hammam-bath, they donned raiment and ornaments, such as men were wont to prepare for the Kings of the Chosroës; and among Shahrazad's apparel was a dress purfled with red gold and wrought with counterfeit presentments of birds and beasts. And the two sisters encircled their necks with necklaces of gems of price, in the like whereof Iskander[2] rejoiced not, for therein were great jewels such as amazed the wit and dazzled the eye; and the imagination was bewildered at their charms, for indeed each of them was brighter than the sun and the moon. Before them they lighted brilliant flambeaux of wax in candelabra of gold, but their faces outshone the flambeaux, for that they had eyes sharper than unsheathed swords and the lashes of their eyelids bewitched all hearts. Their cheeks were rosy red and their necks and shapes gracefully swayed and their eyes wantoned like the gazelle's, as the slave-girls came out to meet them with instruments of music. Then the two Kings entered the Hammam-bath, and when they fared forth, they sat down on a couch set with pearls and gems, whereupon the two sisters came up to them and stood between their hands, as they were moons, bending and leaning from side to side in their beauty and loveliness. Presently they brought forward Shahrazad and displayed her in a red suit for the first dress; whereupon King Shahriyar rose to look upon her, and the wits of all present, men and women, were bewitched for that she was even as saith of her one of her describers[3]:—

A sun on wand in knoll of sand she showed, * Clad in her cramoisy-hued chemisette:
Of her lips honey-dew she gave me drink * And with her rosy cheeks quencht fire she set.

Then they attired Dunyazad in a dress of blue brocade and she became as she were the full moon when it shineth forth. So they displayed her in this, for the first dress, before King Shah Zaman, who rejoiced in her and well-nigh swooned away for love, yea, he was distraught with passion for her whenas he saw her, because she was as saith of her one of her describers in these couplets[3]:—

---

[1] *i.e.* Sumatran.
[2] *i.e.* Alexander, according to the Arabs.
[3] These lines occur before.

She comes apparelled in an azure vest, * Ultramarine as skies are deckt and dight:
I view'd th' unparallel'd sight, which showed my eyes * A Summer-moon upon a Winter-night.

Then they returned to Shahrazad and displayed her in the second dress, a suit of surpassing goodliness, and veiled her face with her hair like a chin-veil.[1] Moreover, they let down her side locks and she was even as saith of her one of her describers in these couplets:—

O hail to him whose locks his cheeks o'ershade * Who slew my life by cruel hard despight:
Said I, "Hast veiled the Morn in Night?" He said, * "Nay, I but veil the Moon in hue of Night."

Then they displayed Dunyazad in a second and a third and a fourth dress and she paced forward like the rising sun, and swayed to and fro in the insolence of beauty; and she was even as saith the poet of her in these couplets[2]:—

The sun of beauty she to all appears * And, lovely coy, she mocks all loveliness:
And when he fronts her favour and her smile * A-morn, the sun of day in clouds must dress.

Then they displayed Shahrazad in the third dress and the fourth and the fifth and she became as she were a Bán-branch snell or a thirsting gazelle, lovely of face and perfect in attributes of grace, even as saith of her one in these couplets[2]:—

She comes like fullest moon on happy night * Taper of waist, with shape of magic might:
She hath an eye whose glances quell mankind, * And ruby on her cheeks reflects his light:
Enveils her hips the blackness of her hair; * Beware of curls that bite with viper-bite!
Her sides are silken-soft, what while the heart * Mere rock behind that surface 'scapes our sight:
From the fringed curtains of her eyne she shoots * Shafts that at furthest range on mark alight.

Then they returned to Dunyazad and displayed her in the fifth dress and in the sixth, which was green, when she surpassed with her love-

---

[1] All these coquetries require as much inventiveness as a cotillon; the text alludes to fastening the bride's tresses across her mouth giving her the semblance of beard and mustachios.

[2] Quoted before.

liness the fair of the four quarters of the world and outvied, with the brightness of her countenance, the full moon at rising tide; for she was even as saith of her the poet in these couplets:—

A damsel 'twas the tirer's art had decked with snare and sleight * And robed with rays as though the sun from her had borrowed light:
She came before us wondrous clad in chemisette of green, * As veilèd by his leafy screen Pomegranate hides from sight:
And when he said, "How callest thou the fashion of thy dress?" * She answered us in pleasant way with double meaning dight,
"We call this garment *crève-cœur;* and rightly is it hight, * For many a heart wi' this we brake and harried many a sprite."

Then they displayed Shahrazad in the sixth and seventh dresses and clad her in youth's clothing, whereupon she came forward swaying from side to side and coquettishly moving and indeed she ravished wits and hearts and ensorcelled all eyes with her glances. She shook her sides and swayed her hips, then put her hand on sword-hilt and went up to King Shahriyar, who embraced her as hospitable host embraceth guest, and threatened her in her ear with the taking of the sword; and she was even as saith of her the poet in these words:—

Were not the Murk[1] of gender male, * Than feminines surpassing fair,
Tirewomen they had grudged the bride, * Who made her beard and whiskers wear!

Thus also they did with her sister Dunyazad, and when they had made an end of the display, the King bestowed robes of honour on all who were present and sent the brides to their own apartments. Then Shahrazad paid the first visit to King Shahriyar and Dunyazad to King Shah Zaman, and each of them solaced himself with the company of his beloved consort and the hearts of the folk were comforted. When morning morrowed, the Wazir came in to the two Kings and kissed ground before them; wherefore they thanked him and were large of bounty to him. Presently they went forth and sat down upon their couches of Kingship, whilst all the Wazirs and Emirs and Grandees and Lords of the land presented themselves and kissed ground. King Shahriyar ordered them dresses of honour and largesse and they prayed for the permanence and prosperity of the King and his brother. Then the two Sovrans appointed their sire-in-law the Wazir to be Viceroy in Samarcand and assigned him five of the Chief Emirs to accompany him, charging them attend him and do him service. The Minister kissed the

---

[1] Arab. "Sawád" = the blackness of the hair.

ground and prayed that they might be vouchsafed length of life: then he went in to his daughters, whilst the Eunuchs and Ushers walked before him, and saluted them and farewelled them. They kissed his hands and gave him joy of the Kingship and bestowed on him immense treasures; after which he took leave of them and setting out, fared days and nights, till he came near Samarcand, where the townspeople met him at a distance of three marches and rejoiced in him with exceeding joy. So he entered the city and they decorated the houses and it was a notable day. He sat down on the throne of his kingship and the Wazirs did him homage and the Grandees and Emirs of Samarcand, and all prayed that he might be vouchsafed justice and victory and length of continuance. So he bestowed on them robes of honour and entreated them with distinction and they made him Sultan over them. As soon as his father-in-law had departed for Samarcand, King Shahriyah summoned the Grandees of his realm and made them a stupendous banquet of all manner of delicious meats and exquisite sweetmeats. He also bestowed on them robes of honour and guerdoned them and divided the kingdoms between himself and his brother in their presence, whereat the folk rejoiced. Then the two Kings abode, each ruling a day in turn, and they were ever in harmony each with other while on similar wise their wives continued in the love of Allah Almighty and in thanksgiving to Him; and the peoples and the provinces were at peace and the preachers prayed for them from the pulpits, and their report was bruited abroad and the travellers bore tidings of them to all lands. In due time King Shahriyah summoned chroniclers and copyists and bade them write all that had betided him with his wife, first and last; so they wrote this and named it "The Stories of the Thousand Nights and a Night." The book came to fill thirty volumes and these the King laid up in his treasury. And the two brothers abode with their wives in all pleasance and solace of life and its delights, for that indeed Allah the Most High had changed their annoy into joy; and on this wise they continued till there took them the Destroyer of delights and the Severer of societies, the Desolator of dwelling-places and Garnerer of grave-yards, and they were translated to the ruth of Almighty Allah; their houses fell waste and their palaces lay in ruins[1] and the Kings inherited their riches. Then there reigned after them a wise ruler, who was just, keen-witted and accomplished and who loved tales and legends, especially those which chronicle the doings of Sovrans and Sultans, and he found in the

[1] Because Easterns build, but never repair.

treasury these marvellous stories and wondrous histories, contained in the thirty volumes aforesaid. So he read in them a first book and a second and a third and so on to the last of them, and each book astounded and delighted him more than that which preceded it, till he came to the end of them. Then he admired whatso he had read therein of description and discourse and rare traits and anecdotes and moral instances and reminiscences and bade the folk copy them and dispread them over all lands and climes; wherefore their report was bruited abroad and the people named them "**The marvels and wonders of the Thousand Nights and a Night,**" This is all that hath come down to us of the origin of this book, and Allah is All-knowing.[1] So Glory be to Him whom the shifts of Time waste not away, nor doth aught of chance or change affect His sway: whom one case diverteth not from other case and Who is sole in the attributes of perfect grace. And prayer and peace be upon the Lord's Pontiff and Chosen One among His creatures, our lord MOHAMMED, the Prince of mankind, through whom we supplicate Him for a goodly and a godly

FINIS,

والسلام

[1] *i.e.* God only knows if it be true or not.

# Terminal Essay.

## PRELIMINARY.

THE reader who has reached this terminal stage will hardly require my assurance that he has seen the mediæval Arab at his best and, perhaps, at his worst. In glancing over the myriad pictures of this panorama, those who can discern the soul of goodness in things evil will note the true nobility of the Moslem's mind in the Moyen Age, and the cleanliness of his life from cradle to grave. As a child he is devoted to his parents, fond of his comrades and respectful to his "pastors and masters," even schoolmasters. As a lad he prepares for manhood with a will and this training occupies him throughout youthtide: he is a gentleman in manners without awkwardness, vulgar astonishment or mauvaise-honte. As a man he is high-spirited and energetic, always ready to fight for his Sultan, his country and, especially, his Faith: courteous and affable, rarely failing in temperance of mind and self-respect, self-control and self-command: hospitable to the stranger, attached to his fellow-citizens, submissive to superiors and kindly to inferiors—if such classes exist: Eastern despotisms have arrived nearer the idea of equality and fraternity than any republic yet invented. As a friend he proves a model to the Damons and Pythiases. As a lover an examplar to Don Quijote without the noble old Caballero's touch of eccentricity. As a knight he is the mirror of chivalry, doing battle for the weak and debelling the strong, while ever "defending the honour of women." As a husband his patriarchal position causes him to be loved and fondly loved by more than one wife. As a father affection for his children rules his life: he is domestic in the highest degree and he finds few pleasures beyond the bosom of his family. Lastly, his death is simple, pathetic and edifying as the life which led to it.

Considered in a higher phase, the mediæval Moslem mind displays, like the ancient Egyptian, a most exalted moral idea, the deepest reverence for all things connected with his religion and a sublime conception of the Unity and Omnipotence of the Deity. Noteworthy too is a proud resignation to the decrees of Fate and Fortune (Kazá wa Kadar), of Destiny and Predestination—a feature which ennobles the low aspect of Al-Islam even in these her days of comparative degeneration and local decay. Hence his moderation in prosperity, his fortitude in adversity, his dignity, his perfect self-dominance and, lastly, his lofty quietism which sounds the true heroic ring. This again is softened and tempered by a simple faith in the supremacy of Love over Fear, an unbounded humanity and charity for the poor and helpless; an unconditional forgiveness of the direst injuries ("which is the note of the noble"); a generosity and liberality which at times seem impossible, and an enthusiasm for universal benevolence and beneficence which, exalting kindly deeds done to man above every form of holiness, constitute the root and base of Oriental, nay, of all, courtesy. And the whole is crowned by pure trust and natural confidence in the progress and perfectibility of human nature, which he exalts instead of degrading; this he holds to be the foundation-stone of society and indeed the very purpose of its existence. His Pessimism resembles far more the optimism which the so-called Books of Moses borrowed from the Ancient Copt than the mournful and melancholy creed of the true Pessimist, as Solomon the Hebrew, the Indian Buddhist and the esoteric European imitators of Buddhism. He cannot but sigh when contemplating the sin and sorrow, the pathos and bathos of the world ; and feel the pity of it, with its shifts and changes ending in nothingness, its scanty happiness and its copious misery. But his melancholy is expressed in—

> "A voice divinely sweet, a voice no less
> Divinely sad."

Nor does he mourn as they mourn who have no hope. He has an absolute conviction in future compensation ; and, meanwhile, his lively poetic impulse, the poetry of ideas, not of formal verse, and his radiant innate idealism breathe a soul into the merest matter of squalid work-a-day life and awaken the sweetest harmonies of Nature epitomised in Humanity.

Such was the Moslem at a time when "the dark clouds of ignorance and superstition hung so thick on the intellectual horizon of Europe as to exclude every ray of learning that darted from the East and when all that was polite or elegant in literature was classed among the *Studia Arabum.*"[1]

Nor is the shady side of the picture less notable. Our Arab at his worst is a mere barbarian who has not forgotten the savage. He is a model mixture of childishness and astuteness, of simplicity and cunning, concealing levity of mind under solemnity of aspect. His stolid instinctive conservatism grovels before the tyrant rule of routine, despite that turbulent and licentious independence which ever suggests revolt against the ruler: his mental torpidity, founded upon physical indolence, renders immediate action and all manner of exertion distasteful : his conscious weakness shows itself in overweening arrogance and intolerance. His crass and self-satisfied ignorance makes him glorify the most ignoble superstitions, while acts of revolting savagery are the natural results of a malignant fanaticism and a furious hatred of every creed beyond the pale of Al-Islam.

It must be confessed that these contrasts make a curious and interesting tout ensemble.

---

[1] Ouseley's Orient. Collect. I, vii.

## § I.

## THE ORIGIN OF THE NIGHTS.

### A.—THE BIRTHPLACE.

HERE occur the questions, Where and When was written and to Whom do we owe a prose-poem which, like the dramatic epos of Herodotus, has no equal?

I proceed to lay before the reader a procès-verbal of the sundry pleadings already in court as concisely as is compatible with intelligibility, furnishing him with references to original authorities and warning him that a fully-detailed account would fill a volume. Even my own reasons for decidedly taking one side and rejecting the other must be stated briefly. And before entering upon this subject I would distribute the prose-matter of our Recueil of Folk-lore under three heads.

1. The Apologue or Beast-fable proper, a theme which may be of any age, as it is found in the hieroglyphs and in the cuneiforms.

2. The Fairy-tale, as for brevity we may term the stories based upon supernatural agency: this was a favourite with olden Persia; and Mohammed, most austere and puritanical of the "Prophets," strongly objected to it because preferred by the more sensible of his converts to the dry legends of the Talmud and the Koran, quite as fabulous without the halo and glamour of fancy.

3. The Histories and historical anecdotes, analects, and acroamata, in which the names, when not used achronistically by the editor or copier, give unerring data for the earliest date à quo, and which, by the mode of treatment, suggest the latest.

Each of these constituents will require further notice when the subject-matter of the book is discussed. The metrical portion of The Nights may also be divided into three categories, viz. :—

1. The oldest and classical poetry of the Arabs, *e.g.* the various quotations from the "Suspended Poems."

2. The mediæval, beginning with the laureates of Al-Rashid's court, such as Al-Asma'í and Abú Nowás; and ending with Al-Harírí, A.H. 446–516 = 1030–1100.

3. The modern quotations and the *pièces de circonstance* by the editors or copyists of the Compilation.[1]

Upon this metrical portion also further notices must be offered at the end of this Essay.

In considering the unde derivatur of The Nights we must carefully separate subject-matter from language-manner. The neglect of such essential difference has caused the remark, "It is not a little curious that the origin of a work which has been known to Europe and has been studied by many during nearly two centuries, should still be so

---

[1] This three-fold distribution occurred to me many years ago and when far beyond reach of literary authorities; I was, therefore, much pleased to find the subjoined classification with minor details made by Baron von Hammer-Purgstall (Preface to Contes Inédits, etc., of G. S. Trébutien, Paris, mdcccxxviii.) (1) The older stories which serve as a base to the collection, such as the Ten Wazirs ("Malice of Women") and Voyages of Sindbad (?) which may date from the days of Mahommed. These are distributed into two sub-classes; (*a*) the marvellous and purely imaginative (*e.g.* Jamasp and the Serpent Queen) and (*b*) the realistic mixed with instructive fables and moral instances. (2) The stories and anecdotes peculiarly Arab, relating to the Caliphs and especially to Al-Rashíd; and (3) The tales of Egyptian provenance, which mostly date from the times of the puissant "Aaron the Orthodox." Mr. John Payne (Villon Translation, vol. ix. pp. 367-73) distributes the stories roughly under five chief heads as follows: (1) Histories or long Romances, as King Omar bin Al-Nu'man. (2) Anecdotes or short stories dealing with historical personages and with incidents and adventures belonging to the every-day life of the period to which they refer: *e.g.* those concerning Al-Rashíd and Hátim of Tayy. (3) Romances and romantic fictions comprising three different kinds of tales; (*a*) purely romantic and supernatural; (*b*) fictions and *nouvelles* with or without a basis and background of historical fact; and (*c*) contes fantastiques. (4) Fables and Apologues; and (5) Tales proper, as that of Tawaddud.

mysterious, and that students have failed in all attempts to detect the secret." Hence also the chief authorities at once branched off into two directions. One held the work to be practically Persian : the other as persistently declared it to be purely Arab.

Professor Galland, in his Epistle Dedicatory to the Marquise d'O, daughter of his patron M. de Guillerague, showed his literary acumen and unfailing sagacity by deriving The Nights from India viâ *Persia;* and held that they had been reduced to their present shape by an *Auteur Arabe inconnu.* This reference to India, also learnedly advocated by M. Langlès, was inevitable in those days : it had not then been proved that India owed all her literature to far older civilisations, and even that her alphabet the Nágari, erroneously called Devanágari, was derived through Phœnicia and Himyar-land from Ancient Egypt. So Europe was contented to compare The Nights with the Fables of Pilpay for upwards of a century. At last the Pehlevi or old Iranian origin of the work found an able and strenuous advocate in Baron von Hammer-Purgstall,[1] who worthily continued what Galland had begun : although a most inexact writer, he was extensively read in Oriental history and poetry. His contention was that the book is an Arabisation of the Persian Hazár Afsánah or Thousand Tales and he proved his point.

Von Hammer began by summoning into Court the "Herodotus of the Arabs," (Ali Abú al-Hasan) Al-Mas'údi who, in A.H. 333 (= 944), about one generation before the founding of Cairo, published at Bassorah the first edition of his far-famed Murúj al-Dahab wa Ma'ádin al-Jauhar, Meads of Gold and Mines of Gems. The Styrian Orientalist[2] quotes with sundry misprints[3] an ampler version of a passage in

---

[1] Journal Asiatique (Paris, Dondey-Dupré, 1826) "Sur l'origine des Mille et une Nuits."

[2] Baron von Hammer-Purgstall's château is near Styrian Graz; and, when I last saw his library, it had been left as it was at his death.

[3] At least, in Trébutien's Preface, pp. xxx.-xxxi., reprinted from the Journ. Asiat. August, 1839: for corrections see De Sacy's "Mémoire," p. 39.

chapter lxviii., which is abbreviated in the French translation of M. C. Barbier de Meynard.[1]

"And, indeed, many men well acquainted with their (Arab) histories [2] opine that the stories above mentioned and other trifles were strung together by men who commended themselves to the Kings by relating them, and who found favour with their contemporaries by committing them to memory and by reciting them. Of such fashion [3] is the fashion of the books which have come down to us translated from the Persian (Fárasiyah), the Indian (Hindíyah),[4] and the Græco-Roman (Rúmíyah)[5]: we have noted the judgment which should be passed upon compositions of this nature. *Such is the book entituled Hazár Afsánah, or The Thousand Tales, which word in Arabic signifies Khuráfah (Facetiæ): it is known to the public under the name of the Book of a Thousand Nights and a Night (Kitab Alf Laylah wa Laylah).*[6] This is an history of a King and his Wazir, the minister's daughter and a slave-girl (járiyah) who are named Shírzád (lion-born), and Dínár-zád (ducat-born).[7] Such also is the tale of Farzah[8]

---

[1] Vol. iv. pp. 89-90, Paris, mdccclxv. Trébutien quotes, chapt. lii. (for lxviii.) one of Von Hammer's manifold inaccuracies.

[2] Alluding to Iram the many-columned, etc.

[3] In Trébutien "Sihá," for which the Editor of the Journ. Asiat. and De Sacy rightly read "Sabíl-há."

[4] For this some MSS. have "Fahlawíyah" = Pehlevi.

[5] *i.e.* Lower Roman, Grecian, of Asia Minor, etc., the word is still applied throughout Marocco, Algiers and Northern Africa to Europeans in general.

[6] De Sacy (Dissertation prefixed to the Bourdin Edition) notices the "thousand and one," and in his Mémoire "a thousand:" Von Hammer's MS. reads a thousand, and the French translation a thousand and one. Evidently no stress can be laid upon the numerals.

[7] These names are noticed by me. According to De Sacy some MSS. read "History of the Wazir and his Daughters."

[8] Lane (iii. 735) has Wizreh or Wardeh, which guide us to Wird Khan, the hero of the tale. Von Hammer's MS. prefers Djilkand (Jilkand), whence probably the Isegil or Isegild of Langlès (1814), and the Tséqyl of De Sacy (1833). The mention of "Simás" (Lane's Shemmas) identifies it with "King Jalí'ád of Hind," etc. (Night dcccxcix.). Writing in A.D. 961 Hamzah Isfaháni couples with the libri Sindbad and Schimas, the libri Baruc and Barsinas, fou nouvelles out of nearly seventy. See also Al-Makri'zi's Khitat or Topography (ii. 485) for a notice of the Thousand or Thousand and one Nights.

(alii Firza), and Simás, containing details concerning the Kings and Wazirs of Hind: the Book of Al-Sindibád[1] and others of a similar stamp."

Von Hammer adds, quoting chapt. cxvi. of Al-Mas'údi, that Al-Mansúr (second Abbaside, A.H. 136–158 = 754-775, and grandfather of Al-Rashíd) caused many translations of Greek and Latin, Syriac and Persian (Pehlevi) works to be made into Arabic, specifying the Kalílah wa Damnah,"[2] the Fables of Bidpái (Pilpay), the Logic of Aristotle, the Geography of Ptolemy and the elements of Euclid. Hence he concludes "L'original des Mille et une Nuits * * * selon toute vraisemblance, a été traduit au temps du Khalife Mansur, c'est-à-dire trente ans avant le règne du Khalife Haroun al-Raschid, qui, par la suite, devait lui-même jouer un si grand rôle dans ces histoires." He also notes that, about a century after Al-Mas'udi had mentioned the Hazár Afsánah, it was versified and probably remodelled by one "Rásti," the Takhallus or nom de plume of a bard at the Court of Mahmúd, the Ghaznevite Sultan who, after a reign of thirty-three years, ob. A.D. 1030.[3]

Von Hammer some twelve years afterwards (Journ. Asiat. August, 1839) brought forward, in his "Note sur l'origine Persane des Mille et une Nuits," a second and an even more

---

[1] Alluding to the "Seven Wazirs" alias "The Malice of Women" (Night dlxxviii.), which Von Hammer and many others have carelessly confounded with Sindbad the Seaman. We find that two tales once separate have now been incorporated with The Nights, and this suggests the manner of its composition by accretion.

[2] Arabised by a most "elegant" stylist, Abdullah ibn al-Mukaffá (the shrivelled), a Persian Guebre named Roz-bih (Day good), who islamised and was barbarously put to death in A.H. 158 (= 775) by command of the Caliph Al-Mansur (Al-Siyuti, p. 277). "He also translated from Pehlevi the book entitled *Sekiseran*, containing the annals of Isfandiyar, the death of Rustam, and other episodes of old Persic history," says Al-Mas'udi, chapt. xxi. See also Ibn Khallikan (I, 43) who dates the murder in A.H. 142 (= 759-60).

[3] "Notice sur Le Schah-namah de Firdoussi, a posthumous publication of M. de Wallenbourg, Vienna, 1810, by M. A. de Bianchi. In sect. iii. I shall quote another passage of Al-Mas'udi (viii. 175) in which I find a distinct allusion to the Gaboriau-detective tales" of The Nights.

important witness: this was the famous Kitab al-Fihrist,[1] or Index List of (Arabic) works, written (in A.H. 387=987) by Mohammed bin Isháḱ al-Nadím (cup companion or equerry), "popularly known as Ebou Yacoub el-Werrek."[2] The following is an extract (p. 304) from the Eighth Discourse which consists of three arts (funún.)[3] "The first section on the history of the confabulatores nocturni (tellers of night-tales) and the relaters of fanciful adventures, together with the names of books treating upon such subjects. Mohammed ibn Isháḱ saith:—The first who indited themes of imagination and made books of them, consigning these works to the libraries, and who ordered some of them as though related by the tongues of brute beasts, were the palæo-Persians (and the Kings of the First Dynasty). The Ashkanian Kings of the Third Dynasty appended others to them and they were augmented and amplified in the days of the Sassanides" (the fourth and last royal house). The Arabs also translated them into Arabic, and the loquent and eloquent polished and embellished them and wrote others resembling them. The first work of such kind was entituled 'The Book of Hazár Afsán,' signifying Alf Khuráfah, the argument whereof was as follows. A King of their Kings was wont, when he wedded a woman, to slay her on the next morning. Presently he espoused a damsel of the daughters of the Kings, Shahrázád[4] hight, one endowed with intellect and eruditon, and she fell to telling him tales of

---

[1] Here Von Hammer shows his customary inexactitude. As we learn from Ibn Khallikan (Fr. Tr. i. 630), the author's name was Abu al-Faraj Mohammed ibn Is'hak, popularly known as Ibn Ali Ya'kúb al-Warrák, the bibliographe, librarian, copyist. It was published (vol. i. Leipzig, 1871) under the editorship of G. Fluegel, J. Roediger, and A. Müller.

[2] See also the Journ. Asiat., August, 1839, and Lane iii. 736-37.

[3] Called "Afsánah" by Al-Mas'udi, both words having the same sense = tale, story, parable, "facetiæ." Moslem fanaticism renders it by the Arab "Khuráfah" = silly fables, and in Hindostan it = a jest:—"Bát-kí bát; khurafát-ki khurafát (a word for a word, a joke for a joke.)

[4] Al-Mas'údi (chapt. xxi.) makes this a name of the Mother of Queen Humáí or Humáyah, for whom see below.

fancy; moreover she used to connect the story at the end of the night with that which might induce the King to preserve her alive and to ask her of its ending on the next night until a thousand nights had passed over her. Meanwhile he dwelt with her till she was blest by boon of child of him, when she acquainted him with the device she had wrought upon him; wherefore he admired her intelligence and inclined to her and preserved her life. That King had also a Kahramánah (nurse and duenna), hight Dínárzád (Dunyázád?), who aided the wife in this (artifice). It is also said that this book was composed for (or by) Humái, daughter of Bahman[1] and in it were included other matters. Mohammed bin Is'hak adds:—And the truth is, Inshallah,[2] that the first who solaced himself with hearing night-tales was Al-Iskandar (he of Macedon) and he had a number of men who used to relate to him imaginary stories and provoke him to laughter: he, however, designed not therein merely to please himself, but that he might thereby become the more cautious and alert. After him the Kings in like fashion made use of the book entitled 'Hazár Afsán.' It containeth a thousand nights, but less than two hundred night-stories, for a single history often occupied several nights. I have seen it complete sundry times; and it is, in truth, a corrupted book of cold tales."[3]

---

[1] The preface of a copy of the Shah-nameh (by Firdausi, ob. A.D. 1021), collated in A.H. 829 by command of Bayisunghur Bahadur Khán (Atkinson p. x.) informs us that the Hazar Afsanah was composed for or by Queen Humái, whose name is Arabised to Humáyah. This Persian Marguerite de Navarre was daughter and wife to (Ardashir) Bahman, sixth Kayanian and surnamed Dirazdast (Artaxerxes Longimanus) Abu Sásán from his son, the Eponymus of the Sassanides who followed the Kayanians when these were extinguished by Alexander of Macedon. Humai succeeded her husband as seventh Queen, reigned thirty-two years, and left the crown to her son Dárá or Dáráb 1st = Darius Codomanus. She is better known to Europe (through Herodotus) as Parysatis = Peri-zádeh or the Fairy-born.

[2] *i.e.* if Allah allow me to say sooth.

[3] *i.e.* of silly anecdotes: here speaks the good Moslem!

A writer in *The Athenæum*,[1] objecting to Lane's modern date for The Nights, adduces evidence to prove the greater antiquity of the work. (Abu al-Hasan) Ibn Sa'id (bin Musa al-Gharnáti = of Granada) born in A.D. 1218 and ob. Tunis in 1286, left his native city and arrived at Cairo in 1241. This Spanish poet and historian wrote Al-Muhallá bi-al-Ash'ár (The Adorned with Verses), a Topography of Egypt and Africa, which now is apparently lost. In this he quotes from Al-Kurtubi, the Cordovan;[2] and he in his turn is quoted by the Arab historian of Spain, Abú al-Abbás Ahmad bin Mohammed al-Makkári, in the "Windwafts of Perfume from the Branches of Andalusia the Blooming"[3] (A.D. 1628-29). Mr. Payne (x. 301) thus translates from Dr. Dozy's published text:—

"Ibn Said (may God have mercy upon him!) sets forth in his book, El Muhella bi-l-ashar, quoting from El Curtubithe story of the building of the Houdej in the Garden of Cairo," the which was of the magnificent pleasaunces of the Fatimite Khalifs, the rare of ordinance and surpassing, to wit that the Khalif El Aamir bi-ahkam-illah[4] let build it for a Bedouin woman, the love of whom had gotten the mastery of him, in the neighbourhood of the 'Chosen Garden'[5] and used to resort often thereto and was slain as he went thither; and it ceased not to be a pleasuring-place for the Khalifs after him.

---

[1] No. 622, Sept. 29, '39; a review of Torrens which appeared shortly after Lane's vol. i. The author quotes from a MS. in the British Museum, No. 7334, fol. 136.

[2] There are many Spaniards of this name: Mr. Payne (ix. 302) proposes Abu Ja'afar ibn Abd al-Hakk al-Khazraji, author of a History of the Caliphs about the middle of the twelfth century.

[3] The well-known Rauzah, or Garden-island, of old Al-Saná'ah for Dár al-Saná'ah, the Darsana, the Arsenal (Ibn Khall. iii. 573); (Al-Mas'udi, chapt. xxxi.), which is more than once noticed in The Nights. The name of the pavilion Al-Haudaj = a camel-litter, was probably intended to flatter the Badawi girl.

[4] He was the Seventh Fatimite Caliph of Egypt: regn. A.D. 1101—1129.

[5] Suggesting a private pleasaunce in Al-Rauzah which has ever been and is still a succession of gardens.

The folk abound in stories of the Bedouin girl and Ibn Meyyah[1] of the sons of her uncle (cousin ?) and what hangs thereby of the mention of El-Aamir, so that the tales told of them on this account became like unto the story of El Bettál[2] and the *Thousand Nights and a Night* and what resembleth them."

The same passage from Ibn Sa'id, corresponding in three MSS., occurs in the famous Khitat[3] attributed to Al-Makrizi (ob. A.D. 1444) and was thus translated from a MS. in the British Museum by Mr. John Payne (ix. 303).

"The Khalif El-Aamir bi-ahkam-illah set apart, in the neighbourhood of the Chosen Garden, a place for his beloved the Bedouin maid (Aaliyah)[4] which he named El Houdej. Quoth Ibn Said, in the book El-Muhella bi-l-ashar, from the History of El Curtubi, concerning the traditions of the folk of the story of the Bedouin maid and Ibn Menah (Meyyah) of the sons of her uncle and what hangs thereby of the mention of the Khalif El Aamír bi-ahkam-illah, so that their traditions (or tales) upon the garden became like unto El Bettál[5] and the *Thousand Nights* and what resembleth them."

This evidently means either that The Nights existed in the days of Al-'Ámir (xiith cent.) or that the author compared them with a work popular in his own age. Mr. Payne attaches much importance to the discrepancy of titles, which

---

[1] The writer in *The Athenæum* calls him Ibn Miyyah, and adds that the Badawiyah wrote to her cousin certain verses complaining of her thraldom, which the youth answered, abusing the Caliph. Al-'Ámir found the correspondence and ordered Ibn Meyyah's tongue to be cut out, but he saved himself by timely flight.

[2] In Night dccclxxxv. we have the passage "He was a wily thief: none could avail against his craft as he were Abu Mohammed Al-Battál" : the word etymologically means The Bad ; but see infra.

[3] Amongst other losses which Orientalists have sustained by the death of Rogers Bey, I may mention his proposed translation of Al-Makrízi's great topographical work.

[4] The name appears only in a later passage.

[5] Mr. Payne notes (viii. 137) "apparently some famous brigand of the time" (of Charlemagne). But the title may signify The Brave as well as the Bad, and the tale may be much older.

appears to me a minor detail. The change of names is easily explained. Amongst the Arabs, as amongst the wild Irish, there is divinity (the proverb says luck) in odd numbers and, consequently, the others are inauspicious. Hence, as Sir Wm. Ouseley says (Travels ii. 21), the number Thousand and One is a favourite in the East (Olivier, Voyages vi. 385, Paris, 1807), and quotes the Cistern of the "Thousand and One Columns" at Constantinople. Kaempfer (Amœn. Exot. p. 38) notes of the Takiyahs or Dervishes' Convents and the Mazárs or Santons' tombs near Koníah (Iconium), "Multa seges sepulchralium quæ virorum ex omni ævo doctissimorum exuvias condunt, mille et unum recenset auctor Libri qui inscribitur Hassaaer we jek mesaar (Hazár ve yek Mezár), *i.e.* mille et unum mausolea." A book, The Hazar o yek Rúz (= 1001 Days), was composed in the mid-xviith century by the famous Dervaysh Mukhlis, Chief Sufi of Isfahan: it was translated into French by Petis de la Croix, with a preface by Cazotte, and was Englished by Ambrose Phillips. Lastly, in India and throughout Asia where Indian influence extends, the number of cyphers not followed by a significant number is indefinite; for instance, to determine hundreds the Hindus affix the required figure to the end and for 100 write 101; for 1000, 1001. But the grand fact of the Hazár Afsánah is its being the archetype of The Nights, unquestionably proving that the Arab work borrows from the Persian bodily its cadre or frame-work, the principal characteristic; its exordium and its dénoûement, whilst the two heroines still bear the old Persic names.

Baron Silvestre de Sacy[1]—clarum et venerabile nomen—

---

[1] In his "Mémoire sur l'origine du Recueil des Contes intitulé Les Mille et une Nuits" (Mém. d'Hist. et de Littér. Orientale, extrait des tomes ix. et x. des Mémoires de l'Inst. Royal Acad. des Inscriptions et Belles Lettres, Paris, Imprimerie Royale, 1833). He read the Memoir before the Royal Academy on July 31, 1829. See also his Dissertation "Sur les Mille et une Nuits" (pp. i.–viii), prefixed to the Bourdin Edit. When the first Arabist in Europe landed at Alexandria, he could not exchange a word with the people; the same is told of Golius the lexicographer at Tunis.

is the chief authority for the Arab provenance of The Nights. Apparently founding his observations upon Galland,[1] he is of opinion that the work, as now known, was originally composed in Syria[2] and written in the vulgar dialect; that it was never completed by the author, whether he was prevented by death or by other cause; and that imitators endeavoured to finish the work by inserting romances which were already known but which formed no part of the original recueil, such as the Travels of Sindbad the Seaman, the Book of the Seven Wazirs and others. He accepts the Persian scheme and cadre of the work, but no more. He contends that no considerable body of præ-Mohammedan or non-Arabic fiction appears in the actual texts;[3] and that all the tales, even those dealing with events localised in Persia, India, China and other Infidel lands and dated from anti-islamitic ages, mostly with the naïvest anachronism, confine themselves to depicting the people, manners and customs of Baghdad and Mosul, Damascus and Cairo, during the Abbaside epoch; and he makes a point of the whole being impregnated with the strongest and most zealous spirit of Mohammedanism. He points out that the language is the popular or vulgar dialect, differing widely from the classical and literary; that it contains many words in common modern use and that generally it suggests the decadence of Arabian literature. Of one tale he remarks:—The History of the loves of Camaralzaman and Budour, Princess of China, is no more Indian or Persian than the others. The prince's father has Moslems for subjects, his mother is named Fatimah and, when imprisoned, he solaces himself with reading the Koran.

---

[1] Lane, Nights ii. 218.

[2] This origin had been advocated a decade of years before by Shaykh Ahmad al-Shirawání: Editor of the Calc. text. (1814-18): his Persian preface opines that the author was an Arabic-speaking Syrian who designedly wrote in a modern and conversational style, none of the purest withal, in order to instruct non-Arabists. Here we find the genus "Professor" pure and simple.

[3] Such an assertion makes us enquire, Did de Sacy ever read through The Nights in Arabic?

The Genii who interpose in these adventures are, again, those who had dealings with Solomon. In fine, all that we here find of the City of the Magians, as well as of the fire-worshippers, suffices to show that one should not expect to discover in it anything save the production of a Moslem writer.

All this, with due deference to so high an authority, is very superficial. Granted, which nobody denies, that the archetypal Hazár Afsánah was translated from Persic into Arabic nearly a thousand years ago, it had ample time and verge enough to assume another and a foreign dress; the corpus, however, remaining untouched. Under the hands of a host of editors, scribes and copyists, who have no scruples anent changing words, names and dates, abridging descriptions and attaching their own decorations, the florid and rhetorical Persian would readily be converted into the straightforward, business-like, matter-of-fact Arabic. And what easier than to islamise the old Zoroasterism, to transform Ahrimán into Iblís the Shaytán, Ján bin Ján into Father Adam, and the Divs and Peris of Kayomars and the olden Guebre Kings into the Jinns and Jinniyahs of Sulayman? Volumes are spoken by the fact that the Arab adapter did not venture to change the Persic names of the two heroines and of the royal brothers or to transfer the mise-en-scène any whither from Khorasan or outer Persià. Where the story has not been too much worked by the literato's pen, for instance the "Ten Wazirs" (in the Bresl. Edit. vi. 191-343), which is the Guebre Bakhtiyár-námah, the names and incidents are old Iranian and, with few exceptions, distinctly Persian. And at times we can detect the process of transition, *e.g.* when the Mázin of Khorásán,[1] of the Wortley Montague MS., becomes the Hasan of Bassorah of the Turner Macan MS. (Mac. Edit.).

Evidently the learned Baron had not studied such works as the Totá-kaháni or Parrot-chat which, notably translated

---

[1] Dr. Jonathan Scott's "translation," vi. 283.

by Nakhshabi from the Sanskrit Suka-Saptati, has now become as orthodoxically Moslem as The Nights. The old Hindu Rajah becomes Ahmad Sultan of Balkh, the Prince is Maymún and his wife Khujisteh Another instance of such radical change is the later Syriac version of Kalílah wa Dimnah,[1] old "Pilpay" converted to Christianity. We find precisely the same process in European folk-lore; for instance, the Gesta Romanorum, wherein, after five hundred years, the life, manners and customs of the classical Romans lapse into the knightly and chivalrous, the Christian and ecclesiastical developments of mediæval Europe. Here, therefore, I hold that the Austrian Arabist has proved his point whilst the Frenchman has failed.

Mr. Lane, during his three years' labour of translation, first accepted Von Hammer's view and then came round to that of De Sacy; differing, however, in minor details, especially concerning the native country of The Nights. Syria had been chosen because then the most familiar to Europeans: "the Wife of Bath" had made three pilgrimages to Jerusalem; but few cared to visit the barbarous and dangerous Nile-Valley. Mr. Lane, however, was an enthusiast for Egypt or rather for Cairo, the only part of it he knew; and, when he pronounces The Nights to be of purely "Arab," that is, of Nilotic origin, his opinion is entitled to no more deference than his deriving the sub-African and negroid Fellah from Arabia, the land per excellentiam of pure and noble blood. Other authors have wandered still further afield. Some finding Mosul idioms in the Recueil, propose "Middlegates" for its birth-place and Mr. W. G. P. Palgrave boldly says, "The original of this entertaining work appears to have been composed in Baghdad about the eleventh century; another

---

[1] In the annotated translation by Mr. I. G. N. Keith-Falconer, Cambridge University Press. I regret to see the wretched production called the "Fables of Pilpay" in the "Chandos Classics" (London, F. Warne). The words are so mutilated that few will recognise them, *e.g.* Carchenas for Kár-shínás, Chaschmanah for Chashmey-e-Máh (Fountain of the Moon), etc.

less popular but very spirited version is probably of Tunisian authorship and somewhat later."[1]

## B.—The Date.

The next point to consider is the date of The Nights in its present form; and here opinions range between the tenth and the sixteenth centuries. Professor Galland began by placing it arbitrarily in the middle of the thirteenth. De Sacy, who abstained from detailing reasons and who, forgetting the number of editors and scribes through whose hands it must have passed, argued only from the nature of the language and the peculiarities of style, proposed as its latest date, le milieu du neuvième siècle de l'hégire (= A.D. 1445-6). Mr. Hole, who knew The Nights only through Galland's version, had already advocated in his "Remarks" the close of the fifteenth century; and M. Caussin (de Perceval, vol. viii., p. viii.), upon the authority of a MS. note in Galland's MS.[2] (vol. iii. fol. 20, verso), declares the compiler to have been living in the seizième siècle, A.D. 1548 and 1565. Mr. Lane says, "Not begun earlier than the last fourth of the fifteenth century nor ended before the first

[1] Article Arabia in Encyclop. Brit., 9th Edit., p. 263, col. 2. I do not quite understand Mr. Palgrave, but presume that his "other version" is the Bresl. Edit., the MS. of which was brought from Tunis; see its Vorwort (vol. i. p. 3),

[2] There are three distinct notes according to De Sacy (Mém., p. 50). The first (in MS. 1508) says, "This blessed book was read by the weak slave, etc., Wahabah son of Rizkallah the Kátib (secretary, scribe) of Tarábulus al-Shám (Syrian Tripoli), who prayeth long life for its owner (li máliki-h). This tenth day of the month First Rabí'a A.H. 955 ( = 1548)." A similar note by the same Wahabah occurs at the end of vol. ii. (MS. 1507) dated A.H. 973 (=1565) and a third (MS. 1506) is undated. Evidently M. Caussin has given undue weight to such evidence. For further information see "Tales of the East," to which is prefixed an Introductory Dissertation (vol. i. pp. 24-26, note) by Henry Webber, Esq., Edinburgh, 1812, in 3 vols. M. Zotenberg has also pointed out to me the earliest inscription by Rizkallah b. Yohanná b. Shaykh al-Nájj, father of Wahabah, dated Jamádà ii. A.H. 943=1537-8: it is in four lines at the end of vol. ii. There is also a fifth, and the latest, by Mohammed ibn Mahmúd, A.H. 1030 = A.D. 1592.

fourth of the sixteenth," *i.e.* soon after Egypt was conquered by Selim, Sultan of the Osmanli Turks in A.D. 1517. Lastly the learned Dr. Weil says in his far too scanty Vorwort (p. ix. 2nd Edit.) :—" Das wahrscheinlichste dürfte also sein, das im 15. Jahrhundert ein Egyptier nach altern Vorbilde Erzählungen für 1001 Nächte theils erdichtete, theils nach mündlichen Sagen, oder frühern schriftlichen Aufzeichnungen bearbeitete, dass er aber entweder sein Werk nicht vollendete, oder dass ein Theil desselben verloren ging, so dass das Fehlende von Andern bis ins 16. Jahrhundert hinein durch neue Erzählungen ergänzt wurde."

But, as justly observed by Mr. Payne, the first step when enquiring into the original date of The Nights is to determine the nucleus of the Repertory by a comparison of the four printed texts and the dozen MSS. which have been collated by scholars.[1] This process makes it evident that the tales common to all are the following thirteen :—

1. The Introduction (with a single incidental story " The Bull and the Ass").
2. The Trader and the Jinni (with three incidentals).
3. The Fisherman and the Jinni (with four).
4. The Porter and the Three Ladies of Baghdad.
5. The Tale of the Three Apples.
6. The Tale of Núr al-Dín Ali and his son Badr al-Dín Hasan.
7. The Hunchback's Tale (with eleven).
8. Nur al-Dín and Anís al-Jalís.
9. Tale of Ghánim bin 'Ayyúb (with two).
10. Alí bin Bakkár and Shams al-Nahár (with two).
11. Tale of Kamar al-Zaman.
12. The Ebony Horse ; and
13. Julnár the Seaborn.

These forty-two tales, occupying one hundred and twenty

---

[1] "Notice sur les douze manuscrits connus des Milles et une Nuits, qui existent en Europe." Von Hammer in Trébutien, Notice, vol. i.

Nights, form less than a fifth part of the whole collection which, in the Mac. Edit.,[1] contains a total of two hundred and sixty-four. Hence Dr. Patrick Russell,[2] the Natural Historian of Aleppo,[3] whose valuable monograph amply deserves study even in this our day, believed that the original Nights did not outnumber two hundred, to which subsequent writers added till the total of a thousand and one was made up. Dr. Jonathan Scott,[4] who quotes Russell, "held it highly probable that the tales of the original Arabian Nights did not run through more than two hundred and eighty Nights, if so many." To this suggestion I may subjoin, "Habent sua fata libelli." Galland, who preserves in his Mille et une Nuits only about one fourth of The Nights, ends them in No. cclxiv[5] with the seventh voyage of Sindbad, after which he intentionally omits the dialogue between the sisters and the reckoning of time, to proceed uninterruptedly with the tales. And so his imitator, Petis de la Croix,[6] in his Mille et un Jours, reduces the thousand to two hundred and thirty-two.

The internal chronological evidence offered by the Collection is useful only in enabling us to determine that the

---

[1] Printed from the M.S. of Major Turner Macan, Editor of the Shahnamah: he bought it from the heirs of Mr. Salt, the historic Consul-General of England in Egypt, and after Macan's death it became the property of the now extinct Allens, then of Leadenhall Street (Torrens, Preface, i). I have vainly enquired of the present house about its later adventures.

[2] The short paper by "P. R." in the Gentleman's Magazine (Feb. 19th, 1799, vol. lxix. p. 61) tells us that MSS. of The Nights were scarce at Aleppo and that he found only two vols. (280 Nights) which he had great difficulty in obtaining leave to copy. He also noticed (in 1771) a MS., said to be complete, in the Vatican and another in the "King's Library" (Bibliothèque Nationale), Paris.

[3] Aleppo has been happy in finding such monographers as Russell and Maundrell, while poor Damascus fell into the hands of Mr. Missionary Porter and suffered accordingly.

[4] Vol. vi. Appendix, p. 452.

[5] The numbers, however, vary with the Editions of Galland: some end the formula with Night cxcvii; others with the ccxxxvi.; I adopt that of the De Sacy Edition.

[6] Contes Persans; suivis des Contes Turcs. Paris, Béchet Ainé, 1826.

tales were not written *after* a certain epoch; the actual dates and, consequently, all deductions from them, are vitiated by the habits of the scribes. For instance we find the Tale of the Fisherman and the Jinni (vol. i. 35) placed in A.D. 785,[1] which is hardly possible. The immortal Barber in the "Tailor's Tale" (vol. i. 265) dates his adventure with the unfortunate lover on Safar 10, A.H. 653 (= March 25th 1255) and 7,320 years of the era of Alexander.[2] This is supported in his Tale of Himself (vol. i. pp. 280-282), where he places his banishment from Baghdad during the reign of the penultimate Abbaside, Al-Mustansir bi 'llah[3] (A.D. 1225-1242), and his return to Baghdad after the accession of another Caliph who can be no other but Al-Muntasim bi 'llah (A.D. 1242–1258). Again at the end of the tale he is described as "an ancient man, past his ninetieth year," and "a very old man" in the days of Al-Mustansir; so that the Hunchback's adventure can hardly be placed earlier than A.D. 1265, or seven years after the storming of Baghdad by Huláku Khan, successor of Janghíz Khan, a terrible catastrophe which resounded throughout the civilised world. Yet there is no allusion to this crucial epoch and the total silence suffices to invalidate the date.[4] Could we assume it to be true, by adding to A.D. 1265 half a century for the composition of

---

[1] In the old translation we have "eighteen hundred years since the prophet Solomon died," (B.C. 975) = A.D. 825.

[2] Meaning the era of the Seleucides. Dr. Jonathan Scott shows (vol. ii. 324) that A.H. 653 and A.D. 1255 would correspond with 1557 of that epoch; so that the scribe has here made a little mistake of 5,763 years. Ex uno disce.

[3] The *Saturday Review* (Jan 2nd, '86), writes, "Captain Burton has fallen into a mistake by not distinguishing between the names of the by no means identical Caliphs Al-Muntasir and Al-Mustansir." Quite true: it was an ugly confusion of the melancholy madman and parricide with one of the best and wisest of the Caliphs. I can explain (not extenuate) my mistake only by a misprint in Al-Siyúti (p. 554).

[4] In the Galland MS. and the Bresl. Edit. (ii. 253), we find the Barber saying that the Caliph (Al-Mustansir) was *at that time* (yaumaizin) in Baghdad; and this has been held to imply that the Caliphate had fallen. But such conjecture is evidently based upon insufficient grounds.

the Hunchback's story and its incidentals, we should place the earliest date in A.D. 1315.

As little can we learn from inferences which have been drawn from the body of the book: at most they point to its several editions or redactions. In the Tale of the "Ensorcelled Prince" Mr. Lane (i. 135) conjectured that the four colours of the fishes were suggested by the sumptuary laws of the Mameluke Soldan, Mohammed ibn Kala'un, "subsequently to the commencement of the eighth century of the Flight, or fourteenth of our era." But he forgets that the same distinction of dress was enforced by the Caliph Omar after the capture of Jerusalem in A.D. 636; that it was revived by Harun al-Rashid, a contemporary of Carolus Magnus, and that it was noticed as a long-standing grievance by the so-called Maundeville in A.D. 1322. In the Tale of the Porter and the Ladies of Baghdad the "Sultáni oranges" have been connected with Sultáníyah city in Persian Irák, which was founded about the middle of the thirteenth century: but "Sultáni" may simply mean "royal," a superior growth. The same story makes mention of Kalandars or religious mendicants, a term popularly corrupted, even in writing, to Karandal."[1] Here again "Kalandar" may be due only to the scribes, as the Bresl. Edit. reads Sa'alúk = asker, beggar. The Khan al-Masrúr in the Nazarene Broker's Story (i. 231) was a ruin during the early ninth century, A.D. 1420; but the Báb Zuwaylah dates from A.D. 1087. In the same tale occurs the Darb al-Munkari (or Munakkari), which is probably the Darb al-Munkadi of Al-Makrizi's careful topography, the Khitat (ii. 40). Here we learn that in his time (about A.D. 1430) the name had become obsolete, and the highway was known as Darb al-

---

[1] De Sacy makes the "Kalandar" order originate in A.D. 1150; but the Shaykh Sharíf bú Ali Kalandar died in A.D. 1323-24. In Sind the first Kalandar, Osmán-i-Marwándí surnamed Lál Sháhbáz, the Red Goshawk, from one of his miracles, died and was buried at Sehwán in A.D. 1274: see my "History of Sindh," chapt. viii. for details. The dates, therefore, run wild.

Amír Baktamír al-Ustaddar, from one of two high officials who both died in the fourteenth century (circ. A.D. 1350). And lastly we have the Khan al-Jáwali built about A.D. 1320. In Badr al-Din Hasan, "Sáhib" is given as a Wazírial title and it dates only from the end of the fourteenth century.[1] In Sindbad the Seaman, there is an allusion to the great Hindu kingdom, Vijayanagar of the Narasimha,[2] the paramount power of the Deccan; but this may be due to editors or scribes, as the despotism was founded only in the fourteenth century (A.D. 1320). The Ebony Horse apparently dates before Chaucer; and "The Sleeper and the Waker" (Bresl. Edit. iv. 134-189) may precede Shakespeare's "Taming of the Shrew": no stress, however, can be laid upon such resemblances, the nouvelles being world-wide. But when we come to the last stories, especially to Kamar al-Zaman II. and the tale of Ma'arúf, we are apparently in the fifteenth and sixteenth centuries. The first contains (Night cmlxvii.) the word Láwandiyah = Levantine, the mention of a watch = Sá'ah in the next Night;[3] and, further on (cmlxxvi.), the "Shaykh Al-Islam," an officer invented by Mohammed II. after the capture of Stambul in A.D. 1453.

---

[1] In this same tale H. H. Wilson observes that the title of Sultan of Egypt was not assumed before the middle of the xiith century.

[2] Popularly called Bisnagar of the Narsingha.

[3] Time-measurers are of very ancient date. The Greeks had clepsydræ and the Romans gnomons, portable and ring-shaped, besides large standing town-dials as at Aquileja and San Sabba near Trieste. The "Saracens" were the perfecters of the clepsydra: Bosseret (p. 16) and the Chronicon Turense (Beckmann ii. 340 *et seq.*) describe the water-clock sent by Al-Rashid to Karl the Great as a kind of "cuckoo-clock." Twelve doors in the dial opened successively and little balls dropping on brazen bells told the hour: at noon a dozen mounted knights paraded the face and closed the portals. Trithonius mentions an horologium presented in A.D. 1232 by Al-Malik al-Kámil, the Ayyubite Soldan, to the Emperor Frederick II.: like the Strasbourg and Padua clocks, it struck the hours, told the day, month and year, showed the phases of the moon, and registered the position of the sun and the planets. Towards the end of the fifteenth century Gaspar Visconti mentions in a sonnet the watch proper (certi orologii piccioli e portativi); and the "animated eggs" of Nuremburg became famous. The earliest English watch (Sir Ashton Lever's) dates from 1541; and in 1544 the portable chronometer became common in France.

In Ma'arúf the 'Adilayah is named—the mosque founded outside the Bab al-Nasr by Al-Malik al-'Ádil Túmán Bey, in A.D. 1501. But, I repeat, all these names may be mere interpolations.

On the other hand, a study of the vie intime in Al-Islam and of the manners and customs of the people proves that the body of the work, as it now stands, must have been written before A.D. 1400. The Arabs use wines, ciders and barley-beer, not distilled spirits; and they have neither coffee nor tobacco. The battles in The Nights are fought with bows and javelins, swords, spears (for infantry) and lances (for cavalry): and, whenever fire-arms are mentioned, we must suspect the scribe. This consideration would determine the work to have been written before the fourteenth century. We ignore the invention-date and the inventor of gunpowder, as of all old discoveries which have affected mankind at large: all we know is that the popular ideas betray great ignorance and here we are led to suspect that an explosive compound, having been discovered in the earliest ages of human society, was utilised by steps so gradual that history has neglected to trace the series. According to Demmin,[1] bullets for stuffing with some incendiary composition, in fact bombs, were discovered by Dr. Keller in the Palafites or Crannogs of Switzerland; and the Hindu's Agni-Astar ("fire-weapon"), Agni-bán ("fire-arrow") and Shatagni ("hundred-killer"), like the Roman Phalarica, and the Greek fire of Byzantium, suggest explosives. Indeed, Dr. Oppert[2] accepts the statement of Flavius Philostratus that when Appolonius of Tyana, that grand semi-mythical figure, was travelling in India, he learned the reason why Alexander of Macedon desisted from attacking the Oxy-

---

[1] An illustrated History of Arms and Armour, etc. (p. 59); London: Bell and Sons, 1877. The best edition is the Guide des Amateurs d'Armes; Paris: Renouard, 1879.

[2] Chapt. iv. Dr. Gustav. Oppert, "On the Weapons, etc., of the Ancient Hindus;" London: Trubner and Co., 1880.

dracæ who live between the Ganges and the Hyphasis (Satadru or Sutledge):—"These holy men, beloved by the gods, overthrew their enemies with tempests and thunderbolts shot from their walls." Passing over the Arab sieges of Constantinople (A.D. 668) and Meccah (A.D. 690) and the disputed passage in Firishtah touching the Tufang or musket during the reign of Mahmúd the Ghaznevite[1] (ob. A.D. 1030), we come to the days of Alphonso the Valiant, whose long and short guns, used at the Siege of Madrid in A.D. 1084, are preserved in the Armeria Real. Viardot has noted that the African Arabs first employed cannon in A.D. 1200 and that the Maghribis defended Algeciras near Gibraltar with great guns in A.D. 1247, and utilised them to besiege Seville in A.D. 1342. This last feat of arms introduced the cannon into barbarous Northern Europe, and it must have been known to civilised Asia for many a decade before that date.

The mention of wine in The Nights, especially the Nabíz or fermented infusion of raisins well known to the præ-Mohammedan Badawis, perpetually recurs. As a rule, except only in the case of holy personages and mostly of the Caliph Al-Rashid, the "service of wine" appears immediately after the hands are washed; and women, as well as men, drink, like true Orientals, for the honest purpose of getting drunk—la recherche de l'idéal, as the process had been called. Yet distillation became well known in the fourteenth century. Amongst the Greeks and Romans it was confined to manufacturing aromatic waters, and Nicander the poet (B.C. 140) used for a still the term ἄμβιξ, like the Irish "pot" and its produce "poteen." The simple art of converting salt water into fresh, by boiling the former and passing the steam through a cooled pipe into a recipient, would not have escaped the students of the Philosophers' "stone;" and thus we find

---

[1] I have given other details on this subject in pp. 631-637 of "Camoens, his Life and his Lusiads."

throughout Europe the Arabic modifications of Greek terms Alchemy, Alembic (Al-ἄμβιξ), Chemistry and Elixir; while "Alcohol" (Al-Kohl), originally meaning "extreme tenuity or impalpable state of pulverulent substances," clearly shows the origin of the article. Avicenna, who died in A.D. 1036, nearly two hundred years before we read of distillation in Europe, compared the human body with an alembic, the belly being the cucurbit and the head the capital. Spirits of wine were first noticed in the xiiith century, when the Arabs had overrun the Western Mediterranean, by Arnaldus de Villa Nova, who dubs the new invention a universal panacea; and his pupil, Raymond Lully (nat. Majorca A.D. 1236), declared this essence of wine to be a boon from the Deity. Now The Nights, even in the latest adjuncts, never allude to the "white coffee" of the "respectable" Moslem, the Ráki (raisin-brandy) or Ma-hayát (aqua vitæ) of the modern Mohametan: the drinkers confine themselves to wine like our contemporary Dalmatians, one of the healthiest and the most vigorous of seafaring races in Europe.

The Nights, I have said, belongs to the days before coffee (A.D. 1550) and tobacco (A.D. 1650) had overspread the East. The former, which derives its name from the Káfá or Káffá province, lying south of Abyssinia proper and peopled by the Sidáma Gallas, was introduced to Mokha of Al-Yaman in A.D. 1429–30 by the Shaykh al-Sházili who lies buried there, and found a congenial name in the Arabic Kahwah = old wine.[1] In The Nights (Mac. Edit.) it is mentioned twelve times[2]; but never in the earlier tales: except in the case of

[1] For another account of the transplanter and the casuistical questions to which coffee gave rise, see my "First Footsteps in East Africa" (p. 76).

[2] The first mention of coffee proper (not of Kahwah or old wine) is in Night cdxxvi. where the coffee-maker is called Kahwahjiyyah, a mongrel term showing the modern date of the passage in Ali the Cairene. As the work advances notices become thicker, *e.g.* in Night dccclxvi., where Ali Nur al-Din and the Frank King's daughter seems to be a modernisation of the story "Ala al-Din Abu al-Shámát," and in Abu Kir and Abu Sir (Nights cmxxx. and cmxxxvi.) where coffee is drunk with sherbet after present fashion. The use culminates in Kamar al-

Kamar al-Zaman II. it evidently does not belong to the epoch and we may fairly suspect the scribe. In the xvith century coffee began to take the place of wine in the nearer East; and the barbarous gradually ousted the classical drink from daily life and from folk-tales.

It is the same with tobacco, which is mentioned only once by The Nights (cmxxxi.), in conjunction with meat, vegetables and fruit and where it is called "Tábah." Lane (iii. 615) holds it to be the work of a copyist; but in the same tale of Abu Kir and Abu Sir, sherbet and coffee appear to have become en vogue, in fact, to have gained the ground they now hold. The result of Lord Macartney's Mission to China was a suggestion that smoking might have originated spontaneously in the Old World.[1] This is undoubtedly true. The Bushmen and other wild tribes of Southern Africa threw their Dakhá (*cannabis indica*) on the fire and sat round it inhaling the intoxicating fumes. Smoking without tobacco was easy enough. The North American Indians of the Great Red Pipe Stone Quarry and those who lived above the line where nicotiana grew, used the kinni-kinik or bark of the red willow and some seven other succedanea."[2] But tobacco proper, which soon superseded all materials except hemp and opium, was first adopted by the Spaniards of Santo Domingo in A.D. 1496 and reached England in 1565. Hence the word, which, amongst the so-called Red Men, denoted the pipe, the container, not the contained, spread over the Old World as a generic term with additions, like "Tutun,"[3] for

Zaman II., where it is mentioned six times (Nights cmlxvi., cmlxx., cmlxxi. twice; cmlxxiv. and cmlxxvii.), as being drunk after the dawn-breakfast and following the meal as a matter of course. The last notices are in Abdullah bin Fazil, Nights cmlxxviii. and cmlxxix.

[1] It has been suggested that Japanese tobacco is an indigenous growth, and sundry modern travellers in China contend that the potato and the maize, both white and yellow, have there been cultivated from time immemorial.

[2] For these see my "City of the Saints," p. 136.

[3] Lit. meaning smoke: hence the Arabic "Dukhán," with the same signification.

especial varieties. The change in English manners brought about by the cigar after dinner has already been noticed; and much of the modified sobriety of the present day may be attributed to the influence of the Holy Herb en cigarette. Such, we know from history was its effect amongst Moslems; and the normal wine-parties of The Nights suggest that the pipe was unknown even when the latest tales were written.

## C.

We know absolutely nothing of the author or authors who produced our marvellous Recueil. Galland justly observes (Epist. Dedic.), "Probably this great work is not by a single hand; for how can we suppose that one man alone could own a fancy fertile enough to invent so many ingenious fictions?" Mr. Lane, and Mr. Lane alone, opined that the work was written in Egypt by one person, or at most by two, one ending what the other had begun, and that he or they had re-written the tales and completed the collection by new matter composed or arranged for the purpose. It is hard to see how the distinguished Arabist came to such a conclusion: at most it can be true only of the editors and scribes of MSS. evidently copied from each other, such as the Mac. and the Bul. texts. As the Reviewer (Forbes Falconer?) in the "Asiatic Journal" (vol. xxx., 1839) says, "Every step we have taken in the collation of these agreeable fictions has confirmed us in the belief that the work called the *Arabian Nights* is rather a vehicle for stories, partly fixed and partly arbitrary, than a collection fairly deserving, from its constant identity with itself, the name of the distinct work, and the reputation of having wholly emanated from the same inventive mind; to say nothing of the improbability of supposing that one individual, with every licence to build upon the foundation of popular stories, a work which had once received a definite form from a single writer, would have been multiplied by the copyist with some regard at least to his arrangement of words as well as matter. But the various copies we have seen bear about as much mutual resemblance as if they had passed through the famous process recommended for disguising a plagiarism: 'Translate your English author into French and again into English.'"

Moreover, the style of the several tales, which will be considered in a future page, so far from being homogeneous is heterogeneous in the extreme. Different nationalities show themselves; West Africa, Egypt and Syria are all represented, and while some authors are intimately familiar with Baghdad, Damascus and Cairo, others are equally ignorant. All copies, written and printed, absolutely differ in the last tales and a measure of the divergence can be obtained by comparing the Bresl. Edit. with the Mac. text: indeed it is my conviction that the MSS. preserved in Europe would add sundry volumes full of tales to those hitherto translated; and here the Wortley-Montague copy can be taken as a test. We may I believe, safely compare the history of The Nights with the so-called Homeric poems, the Iliad and the Odyssey, a collection of immortal ballads and old Epic formulæ and verses traditionally handed down from rhapsode to rhapsode, incorporated in a slowly-increasing body of poetry and finally welded together about the age of Pericles.

To conclude. From the data above given I hold myself justified in drawing the following deductions:—

1. The framework of the book is purely Persian perfunctorily arabised; the archetype being the Hazár Afsánah.[1]

2. The oldest tales, such as Sindibad (the Seven Wazirs) and King Jilíád, may date from the reign of Al-Mansur, eighth century A.D.

3. The thirteen tales mentioned above as the nucleus of

[1] Unhappily the book is known only by name: for years I have vainly troubled friends and correspondents to hunt for a copy. Yet I am sanguine enough to think that some day we shall succeed: Mr. Sidney Churchill, of Teheran, is ever on the look-out.

the Repertory, together with "Dalilah the Crafty,"[1] may be placed in our tenth century.

4. The most modern tales, notably Kamar al-Zaman the Second and Ma'aruf the Cobbler, are as late as the sixteenth century.

5. The work assumed its present form in the thirteenth century.

6. The author is unknown for the best reason ; there never was one: for information touching the editors and copyists we must await the fortunate discovery of some MSS.

---

[1] In § 3 I shall suggest that this tale also is mentioned by Al-Mas'udi.

## § II.

## THE NIGHTS IN EUROPE.

THE history of The Nights in Europe is one of slow and gradual development. The process was begun (1704–17) by Galland a Frenchman, continued (1823) by Von Hammer an Austro-German, and finished by Mr. John Payne (1882–84) an Englishman. But we must not forget that it is wholly and solely to the genius of the Gaul that Europe owes the "Arabian Nights' Entertainments" over which Western childhood and youth have spent so many spelling hours. Antoine Galland was the first to discover the marvellous fund of material for the story-teller buried in the Oriental mine; and he had in a high degree that art of telling a tale which is far more captivating than culture or scholarship. Hence his delightful version (or perversion) became one of the world's classics and at once made "Scheherazade" and "Dinarzarde," "Haroun Alraschid," the "Calendars" and a host of other personages as familiar to the home reader as Prospero, Robinson Crusoe, Lemuel Gulliver and Dr. Primrose. Without the name and fame won for the work by the brilliant paraphrase of the learned and single-minded Frenchman, Lane's curious hash and latinized English, at once turgid and empty, would have found few readers. Mr. Payne's admirable version appeals to the Orientalist and the "stylist," not to the many-headed; and mine to the anthropologist and student of Eastern manners and customs. Galland did it and alone he did it: his fine literary *flaire*, his pleasing style, his polished taste and perfect tact at once made his work take high rank in the republic of letters, nor will the immortal fragment ever be superseded in the infallible judgment of childhood. As the Encyclopædia Britannica has been pleased to ignore this excellent man and admirable Orientalist, numismatologist and littérateur, the reader may not be unwilling to see a short sketch of his biography.[1]

Antoine Galland was born in A.D. 1646 of peasant parents "poor and honest" at Rollot, a little bourg in Picardy some two leagues from Montdidier. He was a seventh child, and his mother, left a widow in early life and compelled to earn her livelihood, saw scant chance of educating the boy who was but four years old, when the kindly assistance of a Canon of the Cathedral and the President of the Collége de Noyon relieved her difficulties. In this establishment Galland studied Latin, Greek and Hebrew for nine or ten years, after which he lost his patrons, and the "strait thing at home" apprenticed him to a trade. But he was made for letters; he hated manual labour, and after a twelvemonth of Purgatory, he removed *en cachette* to Paris, where he knew only an ancient kinswoman. She introduced him to a priestly relative of the Canon of Noyon, who in turn recommended him to the "Sous-principal" of the Collége du Plessis, Here he made such notable progress in Oriental studies, that M. Petitpied, a "Doctor of Sorbonne," struck by his abilities, enabled him to study at the Collége Royal and eventually to catalogue the Eastern MSS. in the great ecclesiastical Society. Thence he passed to the Collége Mazarin, where a Professor, M. Godouin, was making an experiment which might be revived to advantage in our present schools. He collected a class of boys, aged about four, the Duc de Meilleraye amongst the number, and proposed to teach them Latin speedily and easily by making them converse in the classical language as well as read and write it.[2] Galland, his

---

[1] I have extracted it from many books, especially from Hoeffer's Biographie Générale, Paris, Firmin Didot, mdccclvii.; Biographie Universelle, Paris, Didot, 1816, etc. etc. All are taken from the work of M. de Boze, his "Bozzy," the Secrétaire Perpétual de l'Acad. des Inscriptions, etc.

[2] As learning a language is an affair of pure memory, almost without other exercise of the mental faculties, it should be assisted by the ear and the tongue as

assistant, had not time to register success or failure before he was appointed attaché-secretary to M. de Nointel named in 1670 Ambassadeur de France for Constantinople. His special province was to study the dogmas and doctrines and to obtain official attestations concerning the articles of the Orthodox (or Greek) Christianity, which had then been a subject of lively discussion amongst certain Catholics, especially Arnaud (Antoine) and Claude the Minister, and which even in our day occasionally crops up amongst "Protestants."[1] Galland, by frequenting the cafés and listening to the tale-tellers, soon mastered Romaic and grappled with the religious question, under the tuition of a deposed Patriarch and of sundry Matráns or Metropolitans, whom the persecutions of the Pashas had driven for refuge to the Palais de France. M. de Nointel, after settling certain knotty points in the Capitulations, visited the harbour-towns of the Levant and the "Holy Places," including Jerusalem, where Galland copied epigraphs, sketched monuments and collected antiques, such as the marbles in the Baudelot Gallery of which Père Dom Bernard de Montfaucon presently published specimens in his "Palæographia Græca," etc. (Parisiis, 1708).

In Syria Galland was unable to buy a copy of The Nights: as he expressly states in his Epistle Dedicatory, *il a fallu le faire venir de Syrie.* But he prepared himself for translating it by studying the manners and customs, the religion and superstitions of the people; and in 1676, leaving his chief who was ordered back to Stambul, he returned to France. In Paris his numismatic fame recommended him to MM. Vaillant, Carcavy and Giraud, who strongly urged a second

---

well as the eyes. I would invariably make pupils talk, during lessons, Latin and Greek, no matter how badly at first; but unfortunately I should have to begin with teaching the pedants who, as a class, are far more unwilling and unready to learn than are those they teach.

[1] The late Dean Stanley was notably trapped by the wily Greek who had only political purposes in view. In religions as a rule the minimum of difference breeds the maxium of disputation, dislike and disgust.

visit to the Levant, for the purpose of collecting, and he set out without delay. In 1679 he made a third journey, travelling at the expense of the Compagnie des Indes orientales, with the main object of making purchases for the Library and Museum of Colbert the Magnificent. The commission ended eighteen months afterwards with the changes of the Company, when Colbert and the Marquis de Louvois caused him to be created "Antiquary to the King," Louis le Grand, and charged him with collecting coins and medals for the royal cabinet. As he was about to leave Smyrna, he had a narrow escape from the earthquake and subsequent fire which destroyed some fifteen thousand of the inhabitants: he was buried in the ruins; but, his kitchen being cold as becomes a philosopher's, he was dug out unburnt.[1]

Galland again returned to Paris where his familiarity with Arabic and Hebrew, Persian and Turkish recommended him to MM. Thevenot and Bignon: this first President of the Grand Council acknowledged his services by a pension. He also became a favourite with D'Herbelot whose Bibliothèque Orientale, left unfinished and but half printed at his death, he had the honour of completing and prefacing.[2] He also furnished materials for the first volume of the "Ménagiana" and sundry translations from Turkish and other Eastern tongues. President Bignon died within the twelvemonth, which made Galland attach himself in 1697 to M. Foucault, Councillor of State and Intendant (Governor) of Caen in Lower Normandy, then famous for its academy: in his new patron's fine library and numismatic collection he found materials for a long succession of works, including a version of the Koran.[3] They recommended him strongly to

---

[1] See in Trébutien (Avertissement iii.) how Baron von Hammer escaped drowning by the blessing of The Nights.

[2] He signs his name to the Discours pour servir de Préface.

[3] I need not trouble the reader with their titles, which fill up nearly a column and a half in M. Hoeffer. His collection of maxims from Arabic, Persian and Turkish authors appeared in English in 1695.

the literary world and in 1701 he was made a member of the Académie des Inscriptions et Belles Lettres.

At Caen Galland issued in 1704,[1] the first part of his *Mille et une Nuits, Contes Arabes traduits en François*, which at once became famous as "The Arabian Nights' Entertainments." Abridged to one-fourth, mutilated, fragmentary and paraphrastic though the tales were, the glamour of imagination, the marvel of the miracles and the gorgeousness and magnificence of the scenery at once secured an exceptional success: it was a revelation in romance, and the public recognised that it stood in presence of a monumental literary work. France was a-fire with delight at a something so new, so unconventional, so entirely without purpose, religious, moral or philosophical; the Oriental wanderer in his stately robes was a startling surprise to the easy-going and utterly corrupt Europe of the *ancien régime* with its indecently tight garments and perfectly loose morals. "Ils produisirent," said Charles Nodier, a genius in his way, "dès le moment de leur publication, cet effet qui assure aux productions de l'esprit une vogue populaire, quoiqu'ils appartinssent à une littérature peu connue en France; et que ce genre de composition admit ou plutôt exigeât des détails de moeurs, de caractère, de costume et de localités absolument étrangers à toutes les idées établies dans nos contes et nos romans. On fut étonné du charme que résultait du leur lecture. C'est que la vérité des sentimens, la nouveauté des tableaux, une imagination féconde en prodiges, un coloris plein de chaleur, l'attrait d'une sensibilité sans prétention, et le sel d'un comique sans caricature, c'est que l'esprit et le naturel enfin plaisent partout, et plaisent à tout le monde."[2]

---

[1] Galland's version was published by Barbin of Paris in 1704—1717 in 12 vols. (M. de Boze says 10 vols.) 12mo. (Hoeffer's Biographie; Graesse's Trésor de Livres rares and Encyclop. Britannica, ixth Edit.) This Edit. Princeps is extraordinarily rare: even the Bibliothèque Nationale of Paris (the Bib. du Roi) has not a copy; thus rivalling in neglect the British Museum.

[2] See also Leigh Hunt "The Book of the Thousand Nights and one Night," etc., etc. London and Westminster Review, Art. iii., No. lxiv., mentioned in Lane, iii. 746.

The Contes Arabes at once made Galland's name, and a popular tale is told of them and him, known to all reviewers, who, however, mostly mangle it. In the Biographie Universelle of Michaud[1] we find:—Dans les deux premiers volumes de ces contes l'exorde était toujours, "Ma chère sœur, si vous ne dormez pas, faites-nous un de ces contes que vous savez." Quelques jeunes gens, ennuyés de cette plate uniformité allèrent une nuit qu'il faisait très-grand froid, frapper à la porte de l'auteur, qui courut en chemise à sa fenêtre. Après l'avoir fait morfondre quelque temps par diverses questions insignificantes, ils terminèrent en lui disant, "Ah, Monsieur Galland, si vous ne dormez pas, faites-nous un de ces beaux contes que vous savez si bien." Galland profita de la leçon et supprima dans les volumes suivants le préambule qui lui avait attiré la plaisanterie. This legend has the merit of explaining why the Professor so soon gave up the Arab framework which he had deliberately adopted.

England at once annexed The Nights from France,[2] though when, where and by whom the work was done no authority seems to know. In Lowndes' "Bibliographer's Manual" the English Editio Princeps is thus noticed: "Arabian Nights' Entertainments, translated from the French, London, 1724, 12mo, 6 vols." and a footnote states that this translation, very inaccurate and vulgar in its diction, was often reprinted. In 1712 Addison introduced into the *Spectator* (No. 535, Nov. 13) the "Story of Alnaschar" (= Al-Nashshár, the Sawyer) and says that his remarks on Hope "may serve as a moral to an Arabian tale which I find translated into French by M. Galland." His version appears, from the tone and

---

[1] Edition of 1856, vol. xv.

[2] To France England also owes her first translation of the Koran, a poor and mean version by Andrew Ross of that made from the Arabic (No. iv.) by André du Reyer, Consul de France for Egypt. It kept the field till ousted in 1734 by the learned lawyer George Sale, whose conscientious work, including the Preliminary Discourse and Notes (4to London), a mine of reference for all subsequent writers, brought him the ill-fame of having "turned Turk."

style, to have been made by himself, and yet in that year a second English edition had appeared. The nearest approach to the Edit. Prin. in the British Museum [1] is a set of six volumes bound in three and corresponding with Galland's first half dozen (decade?). Tomes i. and ii. are from the fourth edition of 1713, Nos. iii. and iv. are from the second of 1712, and v. and vi. are from the third of 1715. It is conjectured that the first two volumes were reprinted several times, apart from their subsequents, as was the fashion of the day; but all is mystery. We (my friends and I) have turned over scores of books in the British Museum, the University Library, and the Advocates' Libraries of Edinburgh and Glasgow: I have been permitted to put the question in "Notes and Queries," and in the "Antiquary;" but all our researches hitherto have been in vain.

The popularity of The Nights in England must have rivalled their vogue in France, judging from the fact that in 1713, or nine years after Galland's Edit. Prin. appeared, they had already reached a fourth issue. Even the ignoble national jealousy which prompted Sir William Jones grossly to abuse that valiant scholar, Anquetil du Perron, could not mar their popularity. But as there are men who cannot read Pickwick, so they were not wanting who spoke of "Dreams of the distempered fancy of the East." [2] "When the work

---

[1] Catalogue of Printed Books, 1884, p. 159, col. i. I am ashamed to state this default in the British Museum, concerning which Englishmen are apt to boast and which so carefully mulcts modern authors in unpaid copies. But it is only a slight specimen of the sad state of art and literature in England, neglected equally by Conservatives, Liberals and Radicals. What has been done for the endowment of research? What is our equivalent for the Prix de Rome? Since the death of Dr. Birch, who can fairly deal with a Demotic papyrus? Contrast the Société Anthropologique and its palace and professors in Paris with our "Institute" *au second* in a corner of Hanover Square and its skulls in the cellar! In speaking thus of the British Museum, I would by no means reflect upon any of the officials, to whose kindness and attention I am greatly indebted, and notably to Mr. Ellis, M.A., Assistant in the Dep. of Printed Books, who lent me valuable assistance in finding Hindi versions of The Nights.

[2] Art. vii. pp. 139-168, "On the Arabian Nights and translators, Weil, Torrens

first appeared in England," says Henry Weber,[1] "it seems to have made a considerable impression upon the public. Pope [in 1720] sent a copy [two volumes: French? or English?] to Bishop Atterbury, without making any remarks on it; but, from his very silence, it may be presumed that he was not displeased with the perusal. The bishop, who does not appear to have joined a relish for the flights of imagination to his other estimable qualities, expressed his dislike of these tales pretty strongly, and stated it to be his opinion, formed on the frequent description of female dress, that they were the work of some Frenchman [*i.e.* Petis de la Croix, a mistake afterwards corrected by Warburton]. The *Arabian Nights*, however, quickly made their way to public favour. We have been informed of a singular instance of the effect they produced soon after their first appearance. Sir James Stewart, Lord Advocate for Scotland, having one Saturday evening found his daughters employed in reading these volumes, he seized them, with a rebuke for spending the evening before the sabbath in such worldly amusements; but the grave advocate became himself a prey to the fascination of these tales, being found up on the morning of the sabbath itself employed in their perusal, from which he had not risen the whole of the night." As late as 1780 Dr. Beattie professed himself uncertain whether they were translated or fabricated by M. Galland; and, while Dr. Pusey wrote of them "Noctes Mille et Una dictæ, quæ in omnium firmè populorum cultiorum linguas conversæ, in deliciis omnium habentur, manibusque omnium

---

and Lane (vol. i.) with the Essai of A. Loisseleur Deslongchamps." The Foreign Quarterly Review, vol. xxiv., Oct. 1839—Jan. 1840: London, Black and Armstrong, 1840.

[1] Introduction to his Collection "Tales of the East," 3 vols. Edinburgh, 1812; vol. i. pp. xxi. xxii. note. He was the first to point out the resemblance between the introductory adventures of Shahryar and Shah Zaman and those of Astolfo and Giacondo in the Orlando Furioso (Canto xxviii.). M. E. Lévêque in Les Mythes et les Légendes de l'Inde et la Perse (Paris, 1880), gives French versions of the Arabian and Italian narratives, side by side in p. 543 ff. (Clouston)

terentur,"[1] the amiable Carlyle, in the gospel according to Saint Froude, characteristically termed them "downright lies" and forbade the house to such "unwholesome literature." What a sketch of character in two words!

The only fault found in France with the Contes Arabes was that their style is *peu correcte;* in fact they want classicism. Yet all Gallic imitators, Trébutien included, have carefully copied their leaders and Charles Nodier remarks:—"Il me semble que l'on n'a pas rendu assez de justice au style de Galland. Abondant sans être prolixe, naturel et familier sans être lâche ni trivial, il ne manque jamais de cette élégance qui résulte de la facilité, et qui présente je ne sais quel mélange de la naïveté de Perrault et de la bonhomie de La Fontaine."

Our Professor, with a name now thoroughly established, returned in 1706 to Paris, where he was an assiduous and efficient member of the Société Numismatique, and corresponded largely with foreign Orientalists. Three years afterwards he was made Professor of Arabic at the Collége Royal de France, succeeding Pierre Dippy; and, during the next half decade, he devoted himself to publishing his valuable studies. Then the end came. In his last illness, an attack of asthma complicated with pectoral mischief, he sent to Noyon for his nephew Julien Galland[2] to assist in ordering his MSS. and in making his will after the simplest military fashion: he bequeathed his writings to the Bibliothèque du Roi, his Numismatic Dictionary to the Academy, and his Alcoran to the Abbé Bignon. He died, aged sixty-nine,[3] on

---

[1] Notitiæ Codicis MI. Noctium. Dr. Pusey studied Arabic to familiarise himself with Hebrew, and was very different from his predecessor at Oxford in my day, who, when applied to for instruction in Arabic, refused to lecture except to a class.

[2] This nephew was the author of "Recueil des Rits et Cérémonies du Pélérinage de la Mecque," etc., etc. Paris and Amsterdam, 1754, in 12mo.

[3] M. de Doze says, "Il avait soixante-dix-neuf ans," which his own dates contradict.

February 17, 1715, leaving his Second Part of The Nights unpublished.[1]

Professor Galland was a French littérateur of the good old school which is rapidly becoming extinct. Homme vrai dans les moindres choses (as his Éloge stated); simple in life and manners and single-hearted in his devotion to letters, he was almost childish in worldly matters, while notable for penetration and acumen in his studies. He would have been as happy, one of his biographers remarks, in teaching children the elements of education as he was in acquiring his immense erudition. Briefly, truth and honesty, exactitude and indefatigable industry characterised his most honourable career.

Galland informs us (Epist. Ded.) that his MS. consisted of four volumes, only three of which are extant,[2] bringing the

---

[1] The concluding part did not appear, I have said, till 1717: his "Contes et Fables Indiennes de Bidpaï et de Lokman," were first printed in 1724, 2 vols. in 12mo. Hence, I presume, Lowndes' mistake.

[2] M. Caussin (de Perceval), Professor of Arabic at the Imperial Library, who edited Galland in 1806, tells us that he found there only two MSS., both imperfect. The first (Galland's) is in three small vols. 4to, each of about pp. 140. The stories are more detailed, and the style, more correct than that of other MSS., is hardly intelligible to many Arabs, whence he presumes that it contains the original (an early?) text which has been altered and vitiated. The date is supposed to be circa A.D. 1600. The second Parisian copy is a single folio of some 800 pages, and is divided into 29 sections and cmv. Nights, the last two sections being reversed. The MS. is very imperfect, the 12th, 15th, 16th, 18th, 20th, 21st-23rd, 25th and 27th parts are wanting; the sections which follow the 17th contain sundry stories repeated, there are anecdotes from Bidpai, the Ten Wazirs and other popular works, and lacunæ everywhere abound. Galland's Arab. copy of The Nights in the Bibliothèque Nationale (Cat. MSS. Bibl. Reg., Tome i. 258) is attributed by the learned M. Hermann Zotenberg *to the xivth century.* It is inversely numbered in the catal.; for instance, "MDVI. Codex bombycinus, olim Gallandianus, quo continetur fabula romanensis inscripta Noctes Mille et Una; incipit a centesima sexagesima septima," is vol. iii.; "MDVII." is vol. ii., and "MDVIII." is vol. i. The first volume proper (70 feuillets, date of registering, Jan. 22, 1876) contains 25 lines to the page (19 centimètres × 12); white paper with 15 yellow leaves at the end; titles in red ink: no vowel-points; marginal corrections in rare places; a few notes (Latin and French) and scribblings at the beginning, not at the end (suggesting that it was originally the first half of what is now vol. ii.). This tome ends with half-Night lxvii. The second volume (76

work down to Night cclxxxii., or about the beginning of "Camaralzaman." The missing portion, if it contained, like the other volumes, 140 pages, would end that tale, together with the Stories of Ghánim and the Enchanted (Ebony) Horse; and such is the disposition in the Bresl. Edit. which mostly favours in its ordinance the text used by the first translator. But this would hardly have filled more than two-thirds of his volumes; for the other third he interpolated, or is supposed to have interpolated, the ten[1] following tales:—

1. Histoire du Prince Zeyn Al-asnam et du Roi des Génies.[2]
2. " de Codadad et de ses frères (including *La Princesse de Deryabar*).
3. " de la Lampe Merveilleuse (Aladdin).
4. " de l'Aveugle Baba Abdalla.
5. " de Sidi Nouman.
6. " de Cogia Hassan Alhabbal.
7. " d'Ali Baba et de Quarante Voleurs exterminés par une Esclave.
8. " d'Ali Cogia, marchand de Bagdad.

---

feuillets, Jan. 22, 1876) is the largest, the edges having been less trimmed (yet cuttings show in verso. p. 64); 25 lines to page and 26 to first page (20 cent. × 12); yellow paper; only 18 leaves white; few marginal corrections (a long one in p. 30), and inscription of Rizkallah, four lines, in p. 60, with erasure and hiatus between it and p. 61; scribblings on pp. 64, 65. Begins by ending Night lxvii. and ends Night clxvi. all but two lines. The third volume, 81 feuillets, Jan. 22, 1876) same format as vol. i. (page 19 cent. × 12); edges much cut; of total 81 leaves 34 are yellow and the rest white; few marginal corrections, vowel-points as everywhere omitted, long inscription p. 20; ends Night cclxxxii. and begins the next; colophon reads, "Here endeth the third Juz (= section) of the wondrous and marvellous Tales of a Thousand Nights and a Night, and Allah is the Aider," —proving a defective codex.

[1] Mr. Payne (ix. 264) makes eleven, including the Histoire du Dormeur éveillé = The Sleeper and the Waker, which he afterwards translated from the Bresl. Edit. in his "Tales from the Arabic" (vol. i. 5, etc.).

[2] Mr. E. J. W. Gibb has come upon this tale in a Turkish story-book, from which he drew his "Jewád." I have printed it in vol. iii "Supplemental Nights."

9. Histoire du Prince Ahmed et de la fée Peri-Banou.
10. „ de deux Sœurs jalouses de leur Cadette.[1]

Concerning these interpolations (?) which contain two of the best and most widely known stories in the work, Alaeddin[2] and the Forty Thieves, conjectures have been manifold, but they mostly ran upon three lines. De Sacy held that they were found by Galland in the public libraries of Paris. Mr. Chenery, whose acquaintance with Arabic grammar was ample, suggested that the Professor had borrowed them from the recitations of the Rawis, rhapsodists or professional story-tellers, in the bazars of Smyrna and other ports of the Levant. The late Mr. Henry Charles Coote (in the "Folk-Lore Record," vol. iii. part ii. p. 178 et seq.), "On the Source of some of M. Galland's Tales," quotes from popular Italian, Sicilian and Romaic stories incidents identical with those in Prince Ahmad, Alaeddin, Ali Baba and the Envious Sisters, suggesting that the Frenchman had heard these *paramythia* in Levantine coffee-houses and had inserted them into his unequalled *corpus fabularum.* Mr. Payne (ix. 268) conjectures the probability "of their having been composed at a comparatively recent period by an inhabitant of Baghdad, in imitation of the legends of Haroun er Rashid and other well-known tales of the original work;" and adds, "It is possible that an exhaustive examination of the various MS. copies of the Thousand and One Nights known to exist in the public libraries of Europe might yet cast some light upon the question of the origin of the interpolated tales." I quite agree with him, taking "The Sleeper and the Waker" and "Zeyn Al-asnam" as cases in point; but I should expect, for reasons before given,

[1] A littérateur lately assured me that Nos. ix. and x. have been found in the Bibliothèque Nationale (du Roi) Paris; but two friends were kind enough to enquire and ascertained that it was a mistake. Such Persianisms as Codadad (Khudadad), Baba Cogia (Khwájah) and Peri (fairy) suggest a Persic MS.

[2] I shall prefer this form when translating the tale even to M. de Sacy' "Ala-eddin."

to find the stories in a Persic rather than an Arabic MS. And I feel convinced that all will be recovered: Galland was not the man to commit a literary forgery.

As regards Alaeddin, the most popular tale of the whole work, I am convinced that it is genuine, although my unfortunate friend, the late Professor Palmer, doubted its being an Eastern story. It is laid down upon all the lines of Oriental fiction. The mise-en-scène is China, "where they drink a certain warm liquor" (tea); the hero's father is a poor tailor; and, as in "Judar and his Brethren," the Maghrabi Magician presently makes his appearance, introducing the Wonderful Lamp and the Magical Ring. Even the Sorcerer's cry, "New lamps for old lamps!"—a prime point—is paralleled in the Tale of the Fisherman's Son,[1] where the Jew asks in exchange only old rings, and the Princess, recollecting that her husband kept a shabby, well-worn ring in his writing-stand, and he being asleep, took it out and sent it to the man. In either tale the palace is transported to a distance, and both end with the death of the wicked magician and the hero and heroine living happily together ever after.[2]

All Arabists have remarked the sins of omission and commission, of abridgment, amplification and substitution, and the audacious distortion of fact and phrase in which Galland

---

[1] Vol. vi. 212, "The Arabian Nights' Entertainments (London: Longmans, 1811) by Jonathan Scott, with the Collection of New Tales from the Wortley Montague MS. in the Bodleian." I regret to see that Messieurs Nimmo in reprinting Scott have omitted his sixth volume. The Rev. George F. Townsend, M.A. "The Arabian Nights' Entertainments," (London: Warne, 1866 and 1869) has followed in his so-called "Revised Edition" Dr. Scott's text, "as being at once more accurate (!) than that of M. Galland; less diffuse and verbose than that of Forster; less elevated (!), difficult (!!) and abstruse (!!!) than that of Lane." (Pref.)

[2] Since this was written M. Hermann Zotenberg, the well-known translator of Tabari, bought for the Bibliothèque Nationale, Paris, two Arabic folios containing Zayn al-Asnam and Alaeddin. The learned Arabist kindly lent me his transcript for my translation (Supplemental Volumes No. iii.), and is printing the text in Paris.

freely indulged, whilst his knowledge of Eastern languages proves that he knew better. But literary licence was the order of his day, and at that time French, always the most *bégueule* of European languages, was bound by a rigorisme of the narrowest and the straightest of lines from which the least *écart* condemned a man as a barbarian and a *tudesque*. If we consider Galland fairly we shall find that he errs mostly for a purpose, that of popularising his work; and his success has indeed justified his means. He has been derided (by scholars) for "Hé Monsieur!" and "Ah Madame!" but he could not write "O mon sieur" and "O ma dame;" although we can borrow from biblical and Shakespearean English, "O my lord!" and "O my lady!" "Bon Dieu! ma sœur" (which our translators english by "O heavens," Night xx.) is good French for Wa 'lláhi—by Allah; and "cinquante cavaliers bien faits" ("fifty handsome gentlemen on horse-back") is a more familiar picture than fifty knights. "L'officieuse Dinarzade" (Night lxi.), and "Cette plaisante querelle des deux frères" (Night lxxii.), become ridiculous only in translation—"the officious Dinarzade" and "this pleasant quarrel;" while "ce qu'il y a de remarquable" (Night lxxiii.) would relieve the Gallic mind from the mortification of "Destiny decreed." "Plusieurs sortes de fruits et de bouteilles de vin" (Night ccxxxi., etc.) europeanises flasks and flagons; and the violent convulsions in which the girl dies (Night cliv., her head having been cut off by her sister) is mere Gallic squeamishness: France laughs at "le shoking" in England, but she has only to look at home, especially during the reign of Galland's contemporary—Roi Soleil. The terrible "Old man" (Shaykh) "of the Sea" (-board) is badly described by "l'incommode vieillard" ("the ill-natured old fellow"): "Brave Maimune" and "Agréable Maimune" are hardly what a Jinni would say to a Jinniyah (ccxiii.); but they are good Parisian. The same may be noted of "Plier les voiles pour marque qu'il se rendait" (Night ccxxxv.), a European practice; and of the false note struck in two passages. " Je m'estimais heureuse d'avoir fait une si belle conquête " (Night lxvii.) gives a Gaulois turn; and " Je ne puis voir sans horreur cet abominable barbier que voilà : quoiqu'il soit né dans un pays où tout le monde est blanc, il ne laisse pas à resembler à un Éthiopien ; mais il à l'âme encore plus noire et horrible que le visage " (Night clvii.), is a mere affectation of Orientalism. Lastly, " Une vieille dame de leur connaissance " (Night clviii.) puts French polish upon the matter-of-fact Arab's "old woman."

The list of absolute mistakes, not including violent liberties, can hardly be held excessive. Professor Weil and Mr. Payne (ix. 271) justly charged Galland with making the Trader (Night i.) throw away the *shells* (*écorces*) of the date, which has only a pellicle, as Galland certainly knew ; but dates were not seen every day in France, while almonds and walnuts were of the quatre mendiants. He preserves the écorces, which later issues have changed to noyaux, probably in allusion to the jerking practice called Inwá. Again in the " First Shaykh's Story " (vol. i. 24) the " maillet " is mentioned as the means of slaughtering cattle, because familiar to European readers : at the end of the tale it becomes "le couteau funeste." In Badr al-Din a " tarte à la crême," so well known to the West, displaces, naturally enough, the outlandish " mess of pomegranate-seeds." Though the text especially tells us the hero removed his bag-trousers (not only " son habit ") and placed them under the pillow, a crucial fact in the history, our Professor sends him to bed fully dressed, apparently for the purpose of informing his readers in a foot-note that Easterns " se couchent en caleçon " (Night lxxx.). It was mere ignorance to confound the arbalète or cross-bow with the stone-bow (Night xxxviii.), but this has universally been done, even by Lane, who ought to have known better ; and it was an unpardonable carelessness or something worse to turn Nár (fire) and Dún (in lieu of) into " le faux dieu Nardoun " (Night lxv.) : as this has been untouched by De Sacy, I cannot but conclude that he never read the text with the translation. Nearly as bad also to make the Jewish physician remark, when the youth gave him the left wrist (Night cl.), "Voilà une grande ignorance de ne savoir pas que l'on presente la main droite à un médecin et non pas la gauche"—whose exclusive use all travellers in the East must know. I have noticed the incuriousness which translates "along the Nile-shore" by "up towards Ethiopia" (Night cli.), and the "Islands of the *Children* of Khaledan" (Night ccxi.) instead of the Khálidatáni or Khálidát, the Fortunate Islands. It was by no means "des petits soufflets" ("some tips from time to time with her fingers") which the sprightly dame administered to the Barber's second brother (Night clxxi.), but sound and heavy "cuffs" on the nape; and the sixth brother (Night clxxx.) was not "aux lèvres fendues" ("he of the hair-lips"), for they had been cut off by the Badawi jealous of his fair wife. Abu al-Hasan would not greet his beloved by saluting "le tapis à ses pieds:" he would kiss her hands and feet. Haïatalnefous (Hayat al-Nufús, Night ccxxvi.) would not "throw cold water in the Princess's face:" she would sprinkle it with eau-de-rose. "Camaralzaman" I. addresses his two abominable wives in language purely European (ccxxx.), "et de la vie il ne s'approche d'elles," missing one of the fine touches of the tale which shows its hero a weak and violent man, hasty and lacking the pundonor. "La belle Persienne," in the Tale of Nur al-Din, was no Persian; nor would her master address her "Venez çà, impertinente" ("come hither, impertinence"). In the story of Badr, one of the Comoro Islands becomes "L'île de la Lune." "Dog" and "dog-son" are not "injures atroces et indignes d'un grand roi:" the greatest Eastern kings allow themselves far more energetic and significant language. Fitnah[1] is by no means "Force de cœurs:" our author

[1] Dr. Scott, who uses Fitnah (iv. 42), makes it worse by adding "Alcolom (Al-Kulúb?), signifying Ravisher of Hearts," and his names for the six slave-girls (vol. iv. 37), such as "Zohorob Bostan" (Zahr al-Bústán), which Galland

misread "Kút al-Kulúb" (Food of Hearts) and made it "Kuwwat al-Kulúb = Force of Hearts. Lastly the *dénoûement* of The Nights is widely different in French and in Arabic; but that is not Galland's fault, as he never saw the original ending, and indeed he deserves high praise for having invented so pleasant and sympathetic a close, inferior only to the Oriental device.[1]

Galland's fragment has a strange effect upon the Orientalist and those who take the scholastic view, be it wide or narrow. De Sacy does not hesitate to say that the work owes much to his fellow-countryman's hand; but I venture to judge otherwise: it is necessary to dissociate the two works and to regard Galland's paraphrase, which contains only a quarter of The Thousand Nights and a Night, as a wholly different book. Its attempts to amplify beauties and to correct or conceal the defects and the grotesqueness of the original, absolutely suppress much of the local colour, clothing the bare body in the best of Parisian suits. It ignores the rhymed prose and excludes the verse, rarely, and very rarely, rendering a few lines in a balanced style. It generally rejects the proverbs, epigrams and moral reflections which form the pith and marrow of the book; and, worse still, it disdains those finer touches of character which are often Shakesperian in their depth and delicacy, and which, applied to a race of familiar ways and thoughts, manners and customs, would have been

---

rightly renders by "Fleur du Jardin," serve only to heap blunder upon blunder. Indeed the Anglo-French translations are below criticism: it would be waste of time to notice them. The characteristic is a servile suit paid to the original, *e.g.* rendering hair "accommodé en boucles" by "hair festooned in buckles" (Night ccxiv.), and Île d'Ébène (Jazírat al-Abnús, Night xliii.) by "the Isle of Ebene." That surly old littérateur Henry Reeve tells me that he prefers these wretched versions to Mr. Payne's. Padrone! as the Italians say: I cannot envy his taste or his temper.

[1] De Sacy (Mémoire, p. 52) notes that in some MSS., the Sultan, ennuyé by the last tales of Shahrázad, proposes to put her to death, when she produces her three children and all ends merrily without marriage-bells. Von Hammer prefers this version as the more dramatic, the Frenchman rejects it on account of certain difficulties of detail, and here he strains at the gnat—a common process.

the wonder and delight of Europe. It shows only a single side of the gem that has so many facets. By deference to public taste it was compelled to expunge the often repulsive simplicity, the childish indecencies and the wild revels of the original, contrasting with the gorgeous tints, the elevated morality and the religious tone of passages which crowd upon them. We miss the odeur du sang which taints the parfums du harem; also the humoristic tale and the Rabelaisian outbreak which relieve and throw out into strong relief the splendour of Empire and the havoc of Time. Considered in this light it is a caput mortuum, a magnificent texture seen on the wrong side; and it speaks volumes for the genius of the man who could recommend it in such blurred and caricatured condition to readers throughout the civilised world. But those who look only at Galland's picture, his effort to "transplant into European gardens the magic flowers of Eastern fancy," still compare his tales with the sudden prospect of magnificent mountains seen after a long desert-march: they arouse strange longings and indescribable desires; their marvellous imaginativeness produces an insensible brightening of mind and an increase of fancy-power, making one dream that behind them lies the new and unseen, the strange and unexpected—in fact, all the glamour of the unknown.

The Nights has been translated into every far-extending Eastern tongue, Persian, Turkish and Hindostani. The latter entitles them Hikáyát al-Jalílah or Noble Tales, and the translation was made by Munshi Shams al-Din Ahmad for the use of the College of Fort George in A.H. 1252 = 1836.[1] All these versions are direct from the Arabic; my search for a translation of Galland into any Eastern tongue has hitherto been fruitless.[2]

---

[1] See Journ. Asiatique, iii. série, vol. viii., Paris, 1839.

[2] Since this was written I have found no less than three in Hindostani alone; and these will be noticed in my "Supplemental Nights," vol. iii.

I was assured by the late Bertholdy Seemann that the "language of Hoffmann and Heine" contained a literal and complete translation of The Nights; but personal enquiries at Leipzig and elsewhere convinced me that the work still remains to be done. The first attempt to improve upon Galland and to show the world what the work really is was made by Dr. Max Habicht and was printed at Breslau (1824-25), in fifteen small square volumes.[1] Thus it appeared before the "Tunis Manuscript,"[2] of which it purports to be a translation. The German version is, if possible, more condemnable than the Arabic original. It lacks every charm of style; it conscientiously shirks every difficulty; it abounds in the most extraordinary blunders and it is utterly useless as a picture of manners or a book of reference. We can explain its lâches only by the theory that the eminent Professor left the labour to his collaborateurs and did not take the trouble to revise their careless work.

The next German translation was by Aulic Councillor J. von Hammer-Purgstall[3] who, during his short stay at Cairo

---

[1] "Tausend und Eine Nacht: Arabische Erzählungen. Zum erstenmale aus einer Tunesischen Handschrift ergänzt und vollständig übersetzt," Von Max. Habicht, F. H. von der Hagen und Karl Schall (the offenders?)

[2] Dr. Habicht informs us (Vorwort iii., vol. ix. 7) that he obtained his MS. with other valuable works from Tunis, through a personal acquaintance, a learned Arab, Herr M. Annagar (Mohammed Al-Najjár?) and was aided by Baron de Sacy, Langlès and other savants in filling up the lacunæ by means of sundry MSS. The editing was a prodigy of negligence: the corrigenda (of which brief lists are given) would fill a volume; and, as before noticed, the indices of the first four tomes were printed in the fifth, as if the necessity of a list of tales had just struck the dense editor. After Habicht's death in 1839 his work was completed in four vols. (ix.—xii.) by the well-known Prof. H. J. Fleischer, who had shown some tartness in his "Dissertatio Critica de Glossis Habichtianis." He carefully imitated all the shortcomings of his predecessor and even omitted the Verzeichniss, etc., the Varianten and the Glossary of Arabic words not found in Golius, which formed the only useful part of the first eight volumes.

[3] Der Tausend und Eine Nacht noch nicht übersetzte Märchen, Erzählungen und Anekdoten, zum erstenmale aus dem Arabischen in's Französische übersetzt von Joseph von Hammer, und aus dem Französischen in's Deutsche von Aug. E. Zinserling, Professor. Stuttgart und Tübingen, 1823. Drei Bände. 8°. Trebutien's, therefore, is the translation of a translation of a translation.

and Constantinople, turned into French the tales neglected by Galland. After some difference with M. Caussin (de Perceval) in 1810, the Styrian Orientalist entrusted his MS. to Herr Cotta the publisher of Tubingen. Thus a German version appeared, the translation of a translation, at the hand of Professor Zinserling, while the French version was unaccountably lost en route to London. Finally the "Contes inédits," etc., appeared in a French translation by G. S. Trébutien (Paris, mdcccxxviii.). Von Hammer took liberties with the text which can compare only with those of Lane: he abridged and retrenched till the likeness in places entirely disappeared; he shirked some difficult passages and he misexplained others. In fact the work did no honour to the amiable and laborious historian of the Turks.

The only good German translation of The Nights is due to Dr. Gustav Weil who, born on April 24, 1808, is still (1886) professing at Heidelburg.[1] His originals (he tells us) were the Breslau Edition, the Bulak text of Abd al-Rahman al-Safati, and a MS. in the library of Saxe Gotha. The venerable savant, who has rendered such service to Arabism, informs me that Aug. Lewald's "Vorhalle" (pp. i.—xv.)[2] was written without his knowledge. Dr. Weil neglects the division of days which enables him to introduce any number of tales: for instance, Galland's decade occupies a large part of vol. iii. The Vorwort wants development; the notes, confined to a few words, are inadequate and verse is every-

[1] Tausend und Eine Nacht: Arabische Erzahlungen. Zum Erstenmale aus dem Urtext vollständig und treu uebersetzt von Dr. Gustav Weil. He began his work on return from Egypt in 1836 and completed his first version of the Arabische Meisterwerk in 1838—42 (3 vols. roy. oct.). I have the Zweiter Abdruck der dritten Auflage (2nd reprint of 3rd) in 4 vols. 8vo., Stuttgart, 1872. It has more than a hundred woodcuts, all of that art fashionable in Europe till Lane taught what Eastern illustrations should be.

[2] My learned friend Dr. Wilhelm Storck, to whose admirable translations of Camoens I have often borne witness, also notes that this Vorhalle, or Porch to the first edition, a rhetorical introduction addressed to the general public, is held in Germany to be valueless, and that it was noticed only for the Bemerkung concerning the offensive passages which Professor Weil had toned down in his translation. In the Vorwort of the succeeding editions (Stuttgart) it is wholly omitted.

where rendered by prose, the Saj'a or assonance being wholly ignored. On the other hand the scholar shows himself by a correct translation, contrasting strongly with those which preceded him, and by a strictly literal version, save where the treatment required to be modified in a book intended for the public. Under such circumstances it cannot well be other than longsome and monotonous reading.

Although Spain and Italy have produced many and remarkable Orientalists, I cannot find that they have taken the trouble to translate The Nights for themselves: cheap and gaudy versions of Galland seem to have satisfied the public.[1] Notes on the Romaic, Icelandic, Russian (?) and other versions will be found in Appendix No. II.

Professor Galland has never been forgotten in France, where, amongst a host of editions, four have claims to distinction;[2] and his success did not fail to create a host of imitators, and to attract what De Sacy justly terms "une prodigieuse importation de marchandise de contrabande." As early as 1823 Von Hammer numbered seven in France (Trébutien, Préface xviii.), and during later years they have grown prodigiously. Mr. William F. Kirby, who has made a special study of the subject, has favoured me with detailed bibliographical notes on Galland's imitators which are printed in Appendix No. II.

---

[1] The older are, "Novelle Arabe divise in Mille ed una Notte, tradotte dall' idioma Francese nel volgare Italiano": in Bingen, mdccxxiii., per Sebastiano Coleti (12 vols. 8vo); and "Le Mille ed una Notte: Novelle Arabe; Milano presso la Libraria Ferrario Editria. The most popular are now "Mille ed una Notte. Novelle Arabe." Napoli, 1867, 8vo, illustrated, 4 francs; the "Mille ed una Notte. Novelle Arabe, versione italiana nuovamente emendata e corredata di note;" 4 vols. in-32 (dateless) Milano, 8vo, 4 francs; and Prof. Pietro Malan's so-called "translation" (Persur, Perino, 1882). It is not a little curious that the illustrations are almost the same in Weil, De Sacy, Malan, and Mr. W. F. Kirby's "New Arabian Nights;" and I may add that nothing could be more grotesque—Orientalism drawn from the depths of European self-consciousness.

[2] These are—(1) by M. Caussin (de Perceval), Paris, 1806, 9 vols. 12mo, now exceedingly rare and expensive; (2) Edouard Gauttier, Paris, 1822—24, 7 vols. 8vo, valued for its hideous illustrations, yet I procured a good copy for 15 francs; (3) M. Destain, Paris, 1823—25, 6 vols. 8vo; and (4) Baron de Sacy Paris, 1838 (?) 3 vols. large 8vo, illustrated (and vilely illustrated).

## § III.

# THE MATTER AND THE MANNER OF THE NIGHTS.

## A.—The Matter.

Returning to my threefold distribution of this Prose Poem (§ 1) into Fable, Fairy Tale and Historical Anecdote,[1] let me proceed to consider these sections more carefully.

The Apologue or Beast-fable, which apparently antedates all other subjects in The Nights, has been called "One of the earliest creations of the awakening consciousness of mankind." I should regard it, despite a monumental antiquity, as the offspring of a comparatively civilised age, when a jealous despotism or a powerful oligarchy threw difficulties and dangers in the way of speaking "plain truths" A hint can be given and a friend or foe can be lauded or abused as Belins the sheep or Isengrim the wolf, when the Author is debarred the higher enjoyment of praising him or dispraising him by name. And, as the purposes of fables are twofold—

> Duplex libelli dos est: quod risum movet,
> Et quod prudenti vitam consilio monet—

the speaking of brute beasts would give a piquancy and a pleasantry to moral design as well as to social and political satire.

The literary origin of the fable is not Buddhistic: we must especially shun that "Indo-Germanic" school which goes to India for its origins, when Pythagoras, Solon, Herodotus,

---

[1] The number of fables and anecdotes varies in the different texts, but may assumed to be upwards of four hundred, about half of which were translated or abridged by Lane.

Plato, Aristotle and possibly Homer sat for instruction at the feet of the Hir-seshtha, the learned grammarians of the pharaohnic court. Nor was it Æsopic: evidently Æsop inherited the hoarded wealth of ages. As Professor Lepsius taught us, "In the olden times within the memory of man, we know of only *one* advanced culture; of only *one* mode of writing, and of only *one* literary development, viz. those of Egypt." The invention of an alphabet, as opposed to a syllabary, unknown to Babylonia, to Assyria and to that extreme bourne of their civilising influences, China, would for ever fix their literature—poetry, history and criticism,[1] the apologue and the anecdote. To mention no others, The Lion and the Mouse appears in a Leyden papyrus dating from B.C. 1200—1166 the days of Rameses III. (Rhampsinitus) or Hak On, not as a rude and early attempt, but in a finished form, postulating an ancient origin and illustrious ancestry. The dialogue also is brought to perfection in the discourse between the Jackal Koufi and the Ethiopian Cat (Revue Égyptologique ivme. année, Part i.). Africa, therefore, was the home of the Beast-fable; not, as Professor Mahaffy thinks, because it was the chosen land of animal worship, where

Oppida tota canem venerantur nemo Dianam;[2]

but simply because the Nile-land originated every form of literature from Fabliau to Epos.

---

[1] I have noticed these points more fully in the beginning of chapt. iii., "The Book of the Sword."

[2] A notable instance of Roman superficiality, incuriousness and ignorance. Every old Egyptian city had its idols (images of metal, stone or wood), in which the Deity became incarnate as in the Catholic Host; besides its own symbolic animal used as a Kiblah or prayer-direction (Jerusalem or Meccah), the visible means of fixing and concentrating the thoughts of the vulgar, like the crystal of the hypnotist or the disk of the electro-biologist. And goddess Diana was in no way better than goddess Pasht. For the true view of idolatry see Koran xxxix. 4. I am deeply grateful to Mr. P. le Page Renouf (Soc. of Biblic. Archæology, April 6, 1886), for identifying the Manibogh, Michabo or Great Hare of the American indigenes with Osiris Unnefer ("Hare God"). These are the lines upon which scientific investigation should run.

From Kemi the Black-land it was but a step to Phœnicia, Judæa,[1] Phrygia and Asia Minor, whence a ferry led over to Greece. Here the Apologue found its populariser in Αἴσωπος, Æsop, whose name, involved in myth, possibly connects with Αιθιοψ:—"Æsopus et Aithiops idem sonant" say the sages. This would show that the Hellenes preserved a legend of the land where the beast-fable arose, and we may accept the fabulist's æra as contemporary with Crœsus and Solon (B.C. 570), about a century after Psammeticus (Psamethik 1st) threw Egypt open to the restless Greek.[2] From Africa too the Fable would in early ages migrate eastwards and make for itself a new home in the second great focus of civilisation formed by the Tigris-Euphrates Valley. The late Mr. George Smith found amongst the cuneiforms fragmentary beast-fables, such as dialogues between the Ox and the Horse, the Eagle and the Sun. In after centuries, when the conquests of Macedonian Alexander completed what Sesostris and Semiramis had begun, and mingled the manifold families of mankind by joining the eastern to the western world, the Orient became formally hellenised. Under the Seleucidæ and during the life of the independent Bactrian kingdom (B.C. 255–125), Grecian art and science, literature and even language overran the old Iranic reign and extended eastwards throughout northern India. Porus sent two embassies to Augustus in B.C. 19, and in one of them the herald Zarmanochagas (Shramanácharya) of Bargosa, the modern Baroch in Gujarat, bore an epistle upon vellum written in Greek (Strabo xv. 1 § 78). "Videtis gentes populosque mutasse sedes," says Seneca (De Cons. ad Helv.

---

[1] See Jotham's fable of the Trees and King Bramble (Judges lxi. 8) and Nathan's parable of the Poor Man and his little ewe Lamb (2 Sam. ix. 1).

[2] Herodotus (ii. c. 134) notes that "Æsop the fable-writer (ὁ λογόποιος) was one of her (Rhodopis) fellow slaves." Aristophanes (Vespæ, 1446) refers to his murder by the Delphians and his fable beginning, "Once upon a time there was a fight;" while the Scholiast finds an allusion to The Serpent and the Crab in Pax 1084; and others in Vespæ 1401, and Aves 651.

c. vi.). Quid sibi volunt in mediis barbarorum regionibus Græcæ artes? Quid inter Indos Persasque Macedonicus sermo? Atheniensis in Asia turba est." Upper India, in the Macedonian days, would have been mainly Buddhistic, possessing a rude alphabet borrowed from Egypt through Arabia and Phœnicia, but still in a low and barbarous condition: her buildings were wooden, and she lacked, as far as we know, stone-architecture—the main test of social development. But the Bactrian kingdom gave an impulse to her civilisation and the result was classical opposed to vedic Sanskrit. From Persia Greek letters, extending southwards to Arabia, would find indigenous imitators, and there Æsop would be represented by the sundry sages who share the name Lokman.[1] One of these was of servile condition,

---

[1] There are three distinct Lokmans who are carefully confounded in Sale (Koran, chapt. xxxi.) and in Smith's Dict. of Biography, etc., art. Æsopus. The first or eldest Lokman, entitled Al-Hakím (the Sage) and the hero of the Koranic chapter which bears his name, was son of Bá'úrá of the Children of Azar, sister's son to Job or son of Job's maternal aunt; he witnessed David's miracles of mail-making and when the tribe of 'Ád was destroyed, he became King of the country. The second, also called the Sage, was a slave, an Abyssinian negro, sold to the Israelites during the reign of David or Solomon, synchronous with the Persian Kay Káús and Kay Khusrau, also with Pythagoras the Greek (!) His physique is alluded to in the saying, "Thou resemblest Lokman (in black ugliness) but not in wisdom" (Ibn Khallikan i. 145). This negro or negroid, after a godly and edifying life, left a volume of "Amsál," proverbs and exempla (not fables or apologues); and Easterns still say, "One should not pretend to teach Lokman"—in Persian, "Hikmat ba Lokman ámokhtan." Three of his apothegms dwell in the public memory: "The heart and the tongue are the best and worst parts of the human body." "I learned wisdom from the blind, who make sure of things by touching them" (as did St. Thomas); and, when he ate the colocynth offered by his owner, "I have received from thee so many a sweet that 'twould be surprising if I refused this one bitter." He was buried (says the Tárikh Muntakhab) at Ramlah in Judæa, with the seventy Prophets stoned in one day by the Jews. The youngest Lokman "of the vultures" was a prince of the tribe of 'Ád who lived 3,500 years, the age of seven vultures (Tabari). He could dig a well with his nails; hence the saying, "Stronger than Lokman" (A.P. i. 701); and he loved the arrow-game, hence "More gambling than Lokman" (ibid. ii. 938). "More voracious than Lokman" (ibid. i. 134) alludes to his eating one camel for breakfast and another for supper. His wife Barákish also appears in proverb, *e.g.* "Camel us and camel thyself" (ibid. i. 295), *i.e.* give us camel flesh to eat,

tailor, carpenter or shepherd; and a "Habashi" (Æthiopian) meaning a negro slave with blubber lips and splay feet, so far showing a superficial likeness to the Æsop of authentic history.

The Æsopic fable, carried by the Hellenes to India, might have fallen in with some rude and fantastic barbarian of Buddhistic "persuasion" and indigenous origin: so Reynard the Fox has its analogue amongst the Kafirs and the Vái tribe of Mandengan negroes in Liberia,[1] amongst whom one Doalu invented or rather borrowed a syllabarium. The modern Gypsies are said also to have beast-fables which have never been traced to a foreign source (Leland). But I cannot accept the refinement of difference which Professor Benfey, followed by Mr. Keith-Falconer, discovers between the Æsopic and the Hindu apologue:—"In the former animals are allowed to act as animals: the latter makes them act as men in the form of animals." The essence of the beast-fable is a reminiscence of Homo primigenius with erected ears and hairy hide, and its expression is to make the brother brute behave, think and talk like him with the superadded experience of ages. To early man the "lower animals," which are born, live and die like himself, showing all the same affects and disaffects, loves and hates, passions, prepossessions and prejudices, must have seemed quite human enough and on an equal level to become his substitutes. The savage, when he began to reflect, would regard the carnivor and the serpent with awe, wonder and dread; and would soon suspect the same mysterious potency in the brute as in himself: so the Malays still look upon the Uran-utan, or Wood-man, as the possessor of superhuman wisdom. The hunter and the herdsman, who had few other

---

said when her son by a former husband brought her a fine joint which she and her husband relished. Also "Barákish hath sinned against her kin" (ibid. ii. 89). More of this in Chenery's Al-Hariri, p. 422; but the three Lokmans are there reduced to two.

[1] I have noticed them elsewhere: see "To the Gold Coast for Gold."

companions, would presently explain the peculiar relations of animals to themselves by material metamorphosis, the bodily transformation of man to brute, giving increased powers of working him weal and woe. A more advanced stage would find the step easy to metempsychosis, the beast containing the Ego (*alias* soul) of the human: such instinctive belief explains much in Hindu literature, but it was not wanted at first by the Apologue.

This blending of blood, this racial baptism, would produce a fine robust progeny; and, after our second century, Ægypto-Græco-Indian stories overran the civilized globe between Rome and China. Tales have wings and fly farther than the jade hatchets of proto-historic days. And the result was a book which has had more readers than any other except the Bible. Its original is unknown.[1] The volume, which in Pehlevi became the Jávidán Khirad ("Wisdom of Ages") or the Testament of Hoshang, that ancient guebre King, and in Sanskrit the Panchatantra ("Five Chapters"), is a recueil of apologues and anecdotes related by the learned Brahman, Vishnu Sharmá, for the benefit of his pupils, the sons of an Indian Rajah. The Hindu original has been adapted and translated, under a host of names, into a number of languages Arabic, Hebrew and Syriac, Greek and Latin, Persian and Turkish.[2] Voltaire[3] wisely remarks of this venerable production:—Quand on

---

[1] I can hardly accept the dictum that the Katha Sarit Sagara, of which more presently, is the "earliest representation of the first collection."

[2] The Pehlevi version of the days of King Anushirwan (A.D. 531-72) became the Humáyun-námeh ("August Book"), turned into Persian for Bahram Shah the Ghaznavite: the Hitopadesa ("Friendship-boon") of Prakrit, avowedly compiled from the "Panchatantra," became the Hindu Panchopakhyan, the Hindostani Akhlák-i-Hindi ("Moralities of Ind"), and in Persia and Turkey the Anvar-i-Suhayli ("Lights of Canopus"). Arabic, Hebrew and Syriac writers entitle their version Kalilah wa Damnah, or Kalilaj wa Damnaj, from the name of the two jackal-heroes, and Europe knows the recueil as the Fables of Pilpay or Bidpay (Bidyá-pati, Lord of learning?), a learned Brahman reported to have been Premier at the Court of the Indian King Dabishlím.

[3] Dict. Philosoph. s. v. Apocryphes.

fait réflexion que presque toute la terre a été enfatuée de pareils contes, et qu'ils ont fait l'éducation du genre humain, on trouve les fables de Pilpay, de Lokman,[1] d'Ésope, bien raisonnables. But methinks the sage of Ferney might have said far more. These fables speak with the large utterance of early man; they have also their own especial beauty—the charms of well-preserved and time-honoured old age. There is in their wisdom a perfume of the past, homely and ancient-fashioned like a whiff of *pot pourri*, wondrous soothing withal to olfactories agitated by the patchoulis and jockey clubs of modern pretenders and petit-maîtres, with their grey young heads and pert intelligence the motto of whose ignorance is "Connu!" Were a dose of its antique, mature experience adhibited to the Western before he visits the East, those few who could digest it might escape the normal lot of being twisted round the fingers of every rogue they meet from Dragoman to Rajah. And a quotation from them tells at once: it shows the quoter to be a man of education, not a "Jangalí," a sylvan or savage, as the Anglo-Indian official is habitually termed by his more civilised "fellow-subject."

The main difference between the classical apologue and the fable in the Nights is that while Æsop and Gabrias write laconic tales with a single event and a simple moral, the Arabian fables are often "long-continued novelle involving a variety of events, each characterised by some social or political aspect, forming a narrative highly interesting in itself, often exhibiting the most exquisite moral, and yet preserving, with rare ingenuity, the peculiar characteristics of the actors."[2] And the distinction between the ancient and the mediæval apologue, including the modern, which, since "Reineke Fuchs," is mainly German, appears equally

[1] The older Arab writers, I repeat, do not ascribe fables or beast-apologues to Lokman; they record only "dictes" and proverbial sayings.

[2] Professor Taylor Lewis: Preface to Pilpay.

pronounced. The latter is humorous enough and rich in the wit which results from superficial incongruity; but it ignores the deep underlying bond which connects man with beast. Again, the main secret of its success is the strain of pungent satire, especially in the Renardine Cycle, which the people could apply to all unpopular "lordes and prelates, gostly and worldly."

Our Recueil contains two distinct sets of apologues.[1] The first (vol. ii.) consists of eleven, alternating with five anecdotes (Nights cxlvi.—cliii.), following the lengthy and knightly romance of King Omar bin al Nu'uman and followed by the melancholy love tale of Ali bin Bakkár. The second series in vol. v., consisting of eight fables, not including ten anecdotes (Nights cmi.—cmxxiv.), is injected into the romance of King Jali'ád and Shimas mentioned by Al-Mas'údi as independent of The Nights. In both places the beast-fables are introduced with some art and add variety to the subject-matter, obviating monotony—the deadly sin of such works—and giving repose to the hearer or reader after a climax of excitement such as the murder of the Wazirs. And even these are not allowed to pall upon the mental palate, being mingled with anecdotes and short tales, such as The Hermits (ii. 227), with biographical or literary episodes, acroamata, table-talk and analects where humorous Rabelaisian anecdote finds a place; in fact the fabliau or novella. This style of composition may be as ancient as the apologues. We know that it dates as far back as Rameses III., from the history of the Two Brothers in the Orbigny papyrus,[2] the prototype of Yusuf and Zulaykha, the

---

[1] In the Katha Sarit Sagara the beast-apologues are more numerous, but they can be reduced to two great nuclei; the first in chapter lx. (lib. x.) and the second in the same book, chapters lxii-lxv. Here too they are mixed up with anecdotes and acroamata after the fashion of The Nights, suggesting great antiquity for this style of composition.

[2] Brugsch, History of Egypt, vol. i. 266 *et seq.* This fabliau is interesting in more ways than one. Anepu the elder (Potiphar) understands the language of cattle, an idea ever cropping up in Folk-lore; and Bata (Joseph), his "little

Koranic Joseph and Potiphar's wife. It is told with a charming naïveté and sharp touches of local colour.

Some of the apologues in The Nights are pointless enough, rien moins qu'amusants; but in the best specimens, such as the Wolf and the Fox[1] (the wicked man and the wily man), both characters are carefully kept distinct, and neither action nor dialogue ever flags. Again the Flea and the Mouse (ii. 251), of a type familiar to students of the Pilpay cycle, must strike the home-reader as peculiarly quaint.

Next in date to the Apologue comes the Fairy Tale proper, where the natural universe is supplemented by one of purely imaginative existence. "As the active world is inferior to the rational soul," says Bacon with his normal sound sense, "so Fiction gives to Mankind what History denies and in some measure satisfies the Mind with Shadows when it cannot enjoy the Substance. And as real History gives us not the success of things according to the deserts of vice and virtue, Fiction corrects it and presents us with the fates and fortunes of persons rewarded and punished according to merit." But I would say still more. History paints or attempts to paint life as it is, a mighty maze with or without a plan: Fiction shows or would show us life as it should be, wisely ordered

---

brother," who becomes a "panther of the South (Nubia) for rage," at the wife's wicked proposal, takes the form of a bull—metamorphosis full blown. It is not, as some have called it, the "oldest book in the world;" that name was given by M. Chabas to a MS. of Proverbs, dating from B.C. 2200. See also the "Story of Saneha," a novel earlier than the popular date of Moses, in the Contes Populaires d'Égypte.

[1] The fox and the jackal are confounded by the Arabic dialects, not by the Persian, whose "Rubáh" can never be mistaken for "Shaghál." "Sa'lab" among the Semites is locally applied to either beast and we can distinguish the two only by the fox being solitary and rapacious, and the jackal gregarious and a carrion-eater. In all Hindu tales the jackal seems to be an awkward substitute for the Grecian and classical fox, the Giddar or Kolá (*Canis aureus*) being by no means sly and wily as the Lomri (*Vulpes vulgaris*). This is remarked by Weber (Indische Studien) and Prof. Benfey's retort about "King Nobel," the lion, is by no means to the point. See Katha Sarit Sagara, ii. 28.

I may add that in Northern Africa jackal's gall, like jackal's grape (*Solanum nigrum*=black nightshade), ass's milk and melted camel-hump, is used as an unguent by both sexes.

and laid down on fixed lines. Thus Fiction is not the mere handmaid of History: she has a household of her own and she claims to be the triumph of Art, which, as Goëthe remarked, is "Art because it is not Nature." Fancy, *la folle du logis,* is "that kind and gentle portress who holds the gate of Hope wide open, in opposition to Reason, the surly and scrupulous guard."[1] As Palmerin of England says, and says well, "For that the report of noble deeds doth urge the courageous mind to equal those who bear most commendation of their approved valiancy; this is the fair fruit of Imagination and of ancient histories." And, last but not least, the faculty of Fancy takes count of the cravings of man's nature for the Marvellous, the Impossible, and of his higher aspirations for the Ideal, the Perfect: she realises the wild dreams and visions of his generous youth and portrays for him a portion of that "other and better world," with whose expectation he would fain console his age.

The imaginative varnish of The Nights serves admirably as a foil to the absolute realism of the picture in general. We enjoy being carried away from trivial and commonplace characters, scenes and incidents; from the matter-of-fact surroundings of a work-a-day world, a life of eating and drinking, sleeping and waking, fighting and loving, into a society and a mise-en-scène which we suspect can exist and which we know does not. Every man at some turn or term of his life has longed for supernatural powers and a glimpse of Wonderland. Here he is in the midst of it. Here he sees mighty spirits summoned to work the human mite's will, however whimsical; who can transport him in an eye-twinkling whithersoever he wishes; who can ruin cities and build palaces of gold and silver, gems and jacinths; who can serve up delicate viands and delicious drinks in priceless chargers and impossible cups and bring the choicest fruits from farthest Orient; here he finds

[1] Rambler, No. lxvii.

magas and magicians who can make kings of his friends, slay armies of his foes and bring any number of beloveds to his arms. And from this outraging probability and outstripping possibility arises not a little of that strange fascination exercised for nearly two centuries upon the life and literature of Europe by The Nights, even in their mutilated and garbled form. The reader surrenders himself to the spell, feeling almost inclined to enquire "And why may it not be true?"[1] His brain is dazed and dazzled by the splendours which flash before it, by the sudden procession of Jinns and Jinniyahs, demons and fairies, some hideous, others preternaturally beautiful; by good wizards and evil sorcerers, whose powers are unlimited for weal and for woe; by mermen and mermaids, flying horses, talking animals, and reasoning elephants; by magic rings and their slaves and by talismanic couches which rival the Carpet of Solomon. Hence, as one remarks, these Fairy Tales have pleased and still continue to please almost all ages, all ranks and all different capacities.

Dr. Hawkesworth[2] observes that these Fairy Tales find favour "because even their machinery, wild and wonderful as it is, has its laws; and the magicians and enchanters perform nothing but what was naturally to be expected from such beings, after we had once granted them existence." Mr. Heron "rather supposes the very contrary is the truth of the fact. It is surely the strangeness, the unknown nature, the anomalous character of the supernatural agents here employed, that make them to operate so powerfully on our hopes, fears, curiosities, sympathies, and, in short, on all the feelings of our hearts. We see men and women, who possess qualities to recommend them to our favour, subjected

---

[1] Some years ago I was asked by my old landlady if ever in the course of my travels I had come across Captain Gulliver.

[2] In "The Adventurer," quoted by Mr. Heron, "Translator's Preface to the Arabian Tales of Chaves and Cazotte."

to the influence of beings whose good or ill will, power or weakness, attention or neglect, are regulated by motives and circumstances which we cannot comprehend: and hence, we naturally tremble for their fate, with the same anxious concern as we should for a friend wandering, in a dark night, amidst torrents and precipices; or preparing to land on a strange island, while he knew not whether he should be received on the shore by cannibals waiting to tear him piecemeal and devour him, or by gentle beings, disposed to cherish him with fond hospitality." Both writers have expressed themselves well, but meseems each has secured, as often happens, a fragment of the truth and holds it to be the whole Truth. Granted that such spiritual creatures as Jinns walk the earth, we are pleased to find them so very human, as wise and as foolish in word and deed as ourselves: similarly we admire in a landscape natural forms like those of Staffa or the Palisades, which favour the works of architecture. Again, supposing such preternaturalisms to be around and amongst us, the wilder and more capricious they prove, the more our attention is excited and our forecasts are baffled to be set right in the end. But this not all. The grand source of pleasure in Fairy Tales is the natural desire to learn more of the Wonderland which is known to many as a word and nothing more, like Central Africa before the last half century: thus the interest is that of the "Personal Narrative" of a grand exploration to one who delights in travels. The pleasure must be greatest where faith is strongest; for instance amongst imaginative races like the Kelts and especially Orientals, who imbibe supernaturalism with their mothers' milk. "I am persuaded," writes Mr. Bayle St. John,[1] "that the great scheme of preternatural energy, so fully developed in The Thousand and One Nights, is believed

---

[1] "Life in a Levantine Family," chapt. xi. Since the able author found his "family" firmly believing in The Nights, much has been changed in Alexandria; but the faith in Jinn and Ifrit, ghost and vampire is lively as ever.

in by the majority of the inhabitants of all the religious profession both in Syria and Egypt." He might have added "by every reasoning being from prince to peasant, from Mullah to Badawi, between Marocco and Outer Ind."

The Fairy Tale in The Nights is wholly and purely Persian. The gifted Iranian race, physically the noblest and the most beautiful of all known to me, has exercised upon the world-history an amount of influence which has not yet been fully recognised. It repeated for Babylonian art and literature what Greece had done for Egyptian, whose dominant idea was that of working for eternity a κτῆμα εἰς ἀεί. Hellas and Iran instinctively chose as their characteristic the idea of Beauty, rejecting all that was exaggerated and grotesque; and they made the sphere of Art and Fancy as real as the world of Nature and Fact. The innovation was hailed by the Babylonian Hebrews. The so-called Book of Moses deliberately and ostentatiously ignored the future state of rewards and punishments, the other world which ruled the life of the Egyptian in this world: the lawgiver, whoever he may have been, Osarsiph or Moshe, apparently held the tenet to be unworthy of a race whose career he was directing to conquest and isolation in dominion. But the Jews, removed to Mesopotamia, the second cradle of the creeds, presently caught the infection of their Asiatic media; superadded Babylonian legend to Egyptian myth; stultified The Law by supplementing it with the "absurdities of foreign fable," and ended, as the Talmud proves, with becoming the most wildly superstitious and "other-worldly" of mankind.

The same change befel Al-Islam. The whole of its supernaturalism is borrowed bodily from Persia, which had "imparadised earth by making it the abode of angels." Mohammed, a great and commanding genius blighted and narrowed by surroundings and circumstance to something little higher than a Covenanter or a Puritan, declared to his followers,

> "I am sent to 'stablish the manners and customs;"

and his deficiency of imagination made him dislike everything but "women, perfumes and prayers," with an especial aversion to music and poetry, plastic art and fiction. Yet his system, unlike that of Moses, demanded thaumaturgy and metaphysical entities, and these he perforce borrowed from the Jews who had borrowed them from the Babylonians: his soul and spirit, his angels and devils, his cosmogony, his heavens and hells, even the Bridge over the Great Depth, are all either Talmudic or Iranian. But there he stopped and would have stopped others. His enemies among the Koraysh were in the habit of reciting certain Persian fabliaux and of extolling them as superior to the silly and equally fictitious stories of the "Glorious Koran." The leader of these scoffers was one Nazr ibn Haris who, taken prisoner after the Battle of Bedr, was incontinently decapitated, by apostolic command, for what appears to be a natural and sensible preference. It was the same furious fanaticism and one-idea'd intolerance which made Caliph Omar destroy all he could find of the Alexandrian Library and prescribe burning for the Holy Books of the Persian Guebres. And the taint still lingers in Al-Islam: it will be said of a pious man, "He always studies the Koran, the Traditions and other books of Law and Religion; and he never reads poems nor listens to music or to stories."

Mohammed left a dispensation or rather a reformation so arid, jejune and material that it promised little more than the "Law of Moses," before this was vivified and racially baptised by Mesopotamian and Persic influences. But human nature was stronger than the Prophet and, thus outraged, took speedy and absolute revenge. Before the first century had elapsed, orthodox Al-Islam was startled by the rise of Tasawwuf or Sufyism,[1] a revival of classic Platonism and Christian Gnosticism, with a mingling of modern Hylozoism; which, quickened by the glowing imagination

[1] The name dates from the second century A.H. or before A.D. 815.

of the East, speedily formed itself into a creed the most poetical and impractical, the most spiritual and the most transcendental ever invented; satisfying all man's hunger for "belief," which, if placed upon a solid basis of fact and proof, would forthright cease to be belief.

I will take from The Nights, as a specimen of the true Persian Romance, "The Queen of the Serpents" (vol. iii. 337), the subject of Lane's Carlylean denunciation. The first gorgeous picture is the Session of the Snakes, which, like their Indian congeners the Nága kings and queens, have human heads and reptile bodies, an Egyptian myth that engendered the "old serpent" of Genesis. The Sultánah welcomes Hásib Karím al-Dín, the hapless lad who had been left in a cavern to die by the greedy woodcutters; and, in order to tell him her tale, introduces the "Adventures of Bulúkiyá:" the latter is an Israelite converted by editor and scribe to Mohammedanism; but we can detect under his assumed faith the older creed. Solomon is not buried by authentic history "beyond the Seven (mystic) Seas," but at Jerusalem or Tiberias; and his seal-ring suggests the Jám-i-Jam, the crystal cup of the great King Jamshíd. The descent of the Archangel Gabriel, so familiar to Al-Islam, is the manifestation of Bahman, the First Intelligence, the mightiest of the Angels, who enabled Zarathustra-Zoroaster to walk like Bulukiya, over the Dálatí or Caspian Sea.[1] Amongst the sights shown to Bulukiya, as he traverses the Seven Oceans, is a battle royal between the believing and the unbelieving Jinns, true Magian dualism, the eternal duello of the Two Roots or antagonistic Principles, Good and Evil, Hormuzd and Ahriman, which Milton has debased into a commonplace modern combat fought also with cannon. Sakhr the Jinni is Eshem, chief of the Divs, and Kaf, the encircling mountain, is a later edition of Persian Alborz. So in the Mantak al-Tayr (Colloquy of the Flyers) the Birds, emblems of souls, seeking the presence of the gigantic

[1] Dabistan i. 231, etc.

feathered biped Simurgh, their god, traverse seven Seas (according to others seven Wadys) of Search, of Love, of Knowledge, of Competence, of Unity, of Stupefacation, and of Altruism (*i.e.* annihilation of self), the several stages of contemplative life. At last, standing upon the mysterious island of the Simurgh and "casting a clandestine glance at him they saw thirty birds[1] in him; and when they turned their eyes to themselves the thirty birds seemed one Simurgh: they saw in themselves the entire Simurgh; they saw in the Simurgh the thirty birds entirely." Therefore they arrived at the solution of the problem "*We* and *Thou;*" that is, the identity of God and Man; they were for ever annihilated in the Simurgh and the shade vanished in the sun (ibid.) The wild ideas concerning Khalít and Malít (vol. iii. 393) are again Guebre. "From the seed of Kayomars (the androgyne, like pre-Adamite man) sprang a tree shaped like two human beings and thence proceeded Meshia and Meshianah, first man and woman, progenitors of mankind;" who, though created for "Shídistán, Lightland," were seduced by Ahriman. This "two-man-tree" is evidently the duality of Physis and Anti-physis, Nature and her counterpart, the battle between Mihr, Izad or Mithra with his Surush and Feristeh (Seraphs and Angels) against the Divs, who are the children of Time led by the arch-demon Eshem. Thus when Hormuzd created the planets, the dog, and all useful animals and plants, Ahriman produced the comets, the wolf, noxious beasts and poisonous growths. The Hindus represent the same metaphysical idea by Bramhá the Creator and Visva-karma, the Anti-creator,[2] miscalled by Europeans Vulcan:

[1] Because Sí = thirty and Murgh = bird. In McClenachan's Addendum to Mackay's Encyclopædia of Freemasonry we find the following definition: "Simorgh, a monstrous griffin, guardian of the Persian mysteries."

[2] For a poor and inadequate description of the festivals commemorating this "Architect of the Gods" see vol. iii. 177, "View of the History, etc., of the Hindus," by the learned Dr. Ward, who could see in them only the "low and sordid nature of idolatry." But we can hardly expect better things from a missionary in 1822, when no one took the trouble to understand what "idolatry" means.

the former fashions a horse and a bull and the latter caricatures them with an ass and a buffalo,—"evolution" turned topsy turvy. After seeing nine angels and obtaining an explanation of the Seven Stages of Earth, which is supported by the Gáv-i-Zamín, the energy, symbolised by a bull, implanted by the Creator in the mundane sphere, Bulukiya meets the four Archangels, to wit Gabriel who is the Persian Rawánbakhsh or Life-giver; Michael or Beshter, Raphael or Isráfil alias Ardibihisht, and Azazel or Azrail who is Dumá or Mordád, the Death-giver; and the four are about to attack the Dragon, that is, the demons hostile to mankind who were driven behind Alborz-Káf by Tahmuras the ancient Persian king. Bulukiya then recites an episode within an episode, the "Story of Jánsháh," itself a Persian name and accompanied by two others (vol. iii. 401), the *mise-en-scène* being Kabul and the King of Khorasan appearing in the proem. Janshah, the young Prince, no sooner comes to man's estate than he loses himself out hunting and falls in with cannibals whose bodies divide longitudinally, each moiety going its own way: these are the Shikk (split ones) which the Arabs borrowed from the Persian Ním-chihrah or Half-faces. They escape to the Ape-island whose denizens are human in intelligence and speak articulately, as the universal East believes they can: these Simiads are at chronic war with the Ants, alluding to some obscure myth which gave rise to the gold-diggers of Herodotus and other classics, "emmets in size somewhat less than dogs but bigger than foxes."[1] The episode then falls into the banalities of Oriental folk-lore. Janshah, passing the Sabbation river and reaching the Jews' city, is per-

[1] Rawlinson (ii. 491) on Herod. iii. c. 102. Nearchus saw the skins of these formicæ Indicæ, by some rationalists explained as "jackals," whose stature corresponds with the text, and by others as "pangolins" or ant-eaters (*manis pentedactyla*). The learned Sanskritist, Horace H. Wilson, quotes the name Pippilika = ant-gold, given by the people of Little Thibet to the precious dust thrown up in the emmet heaps.

suaded to be sewn up in a skin and is carried in the normal way to the top of the Mountain of Gems where he makes acquaintance with Shaykh Nasr, Lord of the Birds: he enters the usual forbidden room; falls in love with the pattern Swan-maiden; wins her by the popular process; loses her and recovers her through the Monk Yaghmús, whose name, like that of King Teghmús, is a burlesque of the Greek; and, finally, when she is killed by a shark, determines to mourn her loss till the end of his days. Having heard this story Bulukiya quits him; and, resolving to regain his natal land, falls in with Khizr; and the Green Prophet, who was Wazir to Kay Kobad (sixth century B. C.) and was connected with Macedonian Alexander (!), enables him to win his wish. The rest of the tale calls for no comment.

Thirdly and lastly we have the histories, historical stories and the "Ana" of great men, in which Easterns as well as Westerns delight: the gravest writers do not disdain to relieve the dulness of chronicles and annals by means of such discussions, humorous or pathetic, moral or grossly indecent. The dates must greatly vary: some of the anecdotes relating to the early Caliphs appear almost contemporary; others, like Ali of Cairo and Abu al-Shámát, may be as late as the Ottoman Conquest of Egypt (sixteenth century). All are distinctly Sunnite and show fierce animus against the Shi'ah heretics, suggesting that they were written after the destruction of the Fatimite dynasty (twelfth century) by Salah al-Din (Saladin the Kurd) one of the latest historical personages and the last king named in The Nights.[1] These anecdotes are so often connected with what a learned Frenchman terms the

---

[1] A writer in the *Edinburgh Review* (July, '86), of whom more, and much more, presently, suggests that The Nights assumed essentially their present shape during the general revival of letters, arts and requirements which accompanied the Kurdish and Tartar irruptions into the Nile Valley, a golden age which embraced the whole of the thirteenth, fourteenth and fifteenth centuries and ended with the Ottoman Conquest in A.D. 1527.

"regne féerique de Haroun er-Réschid,"[1] that the Great Caliph becomes the hero of this portion of The Nights. Aaron the Orthodox was the central figure of the most splendid empire the world had seen, the Viceregent of Allah combining the powers of Cæsar and Pope, and wielding them right worthily according to the general voice of historians. To quote a few: Ali bin Tálib al-Khorásáni described him, in A.D. 934, a century and-a-half after his death, when flattery would be tougue-tied, as "one devoted to war and pilgrimage, whose bounty embraced the folk at large." Sa'adi (ob. A.D. 1291) tells a tale highly favourable to him in the "Gulistan" (lib. i. 36). Fakhr al-Din[2] (fourteenth century) lauds his merits, eloquence, science and generosity; and Al-Siyuti (nat. A.D. 1445) asserts, "He was one of the most distinguished of Caliphs and the most illustrious of the Princes of the Earth" (p. 290). The Shaykh al-Nafzáwi (sixteenth century) in his Rauz al-'Átir fí Nazáh al-Khátir = the Scented Garden Man's Heart to gladden, calls Harun (chapt. vii.) the "Master of munificence and bounty, the best of the generous." And even the latest writers have not ceased to praise him. Says Alí Azíz Efendi, the Cretan, in the Story of Jewád[3] (p. 81), "Harun was the most bounteous, illustrious and upright of the Abbaside Caliphs."

The fifth Abbaside was fair and handsome, of noble and majestic presence, a sportsman and an athlete who delighted in polo and archery. He showed sound sense and true wisdom in his speech to the grammarian-poet Al-Asma'í, who

---

[1] Let us humbly hope not again to hear of the golden prime of

"The good (fellow?) Haroun Alrasch'id,"

a mispronunciation which suggests only a rasher of bacon. Why will not poets mind their quantities, in lieu of stultifying their lines by childish ignorance? What can be more painful than Byron's

"They laid his dust in Ar'qua (for Arqua') where he died"?

[2] See De Sacy's Chrestomathie Arabe (Paris, 1826), vol. i.

[3] Translated by a well-known Turkish scholar, Mr. E. J. W. Gibb, Glasgow, Wilson and McCormick, 1884).

had undertaken to teach him :—" Ne m'enseignez jamais en public, et ne vous empressez pas trop de me donner des avis en particulier. Attendez ordinairement que je vous interroge, et contentez-vous de me donner une réponse précise à ce que je vous demanderai, sans y rien ajouter de superflu. Gardez vous surtout de vouloir me préoccuper pour vous attirer ma créance, et pour vous donner de l'autorité. Ne vous étendez jamais trop en long sur les histoires et les traditions que vous me raconterez, si je ne vous en donne la permission. Lorsque vous verrai que je m'eloignerai de l'équité dans mes jugements, ramenez-moi avec douceur, sans user de paroles fâcheuses ni de réprimandes. Enseignez-moi principalement les choses qui sont les plus nécessaries pour les discours que je dois faire en public, dans les mosquées et ailleurs ; et ne parlez point en termes obscurs ou mystérieux, ni avec des paroles trop recherchées." [1]

He became well read in science and letters, especially history and tradition, for " his understanding was as the understanding of the learned ;" and, like all educated Arabs of his day, he was a connoisseur of poetry which at times he improvised with success."[2] He made the pilgrimage every alternate year and sometimes on foot, while " his military expeditions almost equalled his pilgrimages." Day after day during his Caliphate he prayed a hundred " bows," never neglecting them, save for some especial reason, till his death ; and he used to give from his privy purse alms to the extent of a hundred dirhams per diem. He delighted in panegyry and liberally rewarded its experts, one of whom, Abd al-Sammák the Preacher, fairly said of him, " Thy humility in thy greatness is nobler than thy greatness." " No Caliph," says Al-Niftawayh, " had been

---

[1] D'Herbelot (s. v. " Asmai "): I am reproached by a dabbler in Orientalism for using this admirable writer, who shows more knowledge in one page than my critic ever did in a whole volume.

[2] For specimens see Al-Siyutí, pp. 301 and 304 ; and the Shaykh al-Nafzawi, pp. 134-35.

so profusely liberal to poets lawyers and divines, although as the years advanced he wept over his extravagance amongst other sins." There was vigorous manliness in his answer to the Grecian Emperor who had sent him an insulting missive: —"In the name of Allah! From the Commander of the Faithful, Harun al-Rashid, to Nicephorus the Roman dog. I have read thy writ, O son of a miscreant mother! Thou shalt not hear, thou shalt see my reply." Nor did he cease to make the Byzantine feel the weight of his arm till he "nakh'd"[1] his camel in the imperial court-yard; and this was only one instance of his indomitable energy and hatred of the Infidel. Yet, if the West is to be believed, he forgot his fanaticism in his diplomatic dealings and courteous intercourse with Carolus Magnus.[2] Finally, his civilised and well regulated rule contrasted as strongly with the barbarity and turbulence of occidental Christendom, as the splendid Court and the luxurious life of Baghdad and its carpets and hangings devanced the quasi-savagery of London and Paris whose palatial halls were spread with rushes.

The great Caliph ruled twenty-three years and a few months (A. H. 170–193 = A.D. 786–808); and, as his youth was chequered and his reign was glorious, so was his end

---

[1] The word "nakh" (to make a camel kneel) has been explained.

[2] The present of the famous horologium-clepsydra-cuckoo-clock, the dog Becerillo and the elephant Abu Lubábah sent by Harun to Charlemagne is not mentioned by Eastern authorities and consequently no reference to it will be found in my late friend Professor Palmer's little volume "Haroun Alraschid," London, Marcus Ward, 1881. We have allusions to many presents, the clock and elephant, tent and linen hangings, silken dresses, perfumes, and candelabra of auricalch brought by the Legati (Abdalla, Georgius Abba et Felix) of Aaron Amiralmumminim Regis Persarum who entered the Port of Pisa (A.D. 801) in (vol. v. 178) Recueil des Hist. des Gaules et de la France, etc., par Dom Martin Bouquet, Paris mdccxliv. The author also quotes the lines:—

Persarum Princeps illi devinctus amore
Præcipuo fuerat, nomen habens Aaron.
Gratia cui Caroli præ cunctis Regibus atque
Illis Principibus tempora cara fuit.

obscure.[1] After a vision foreshadowing his death,[2] which happened, as becomes a good Moslem, during a military expedition to Khorasan, he ordered his grave to be dug and himself to be carried to it in a covered litter. When sighting the fosse he exclaimed, "O son of man, thou art come to this!" Then he commanded himself to be set down and a perlection of the Koran to be made over him in the litter on the edge of the grave. He was buried (æt. forty-five) at Sanábád, a village near Tús.

Aaron the Orthodox appears in The Nights as a headstrong and violent autocrat, a right royal figure according to the Moslem ideas of his day. But his career shows that he was not more tyrannical nor more sanguinary than the normal despot of the East or the contemporary Kings of the West: in most points, indeed, he was far superior to the historic misrulers who have afflicted the world from Spain to furthest China. But a single great crime, a tragedy whose details are almost incredibly horrible, marks his reign with the stain of infamy, with a blot of blood never to be washed away. This tale, "full of the waters of the eye," as Firdausi sings, is the massacre of the Barmecides; a story which has often been told and which cannot here be passed over in silence. The ancient and noble Iranian house, belonging to the "Ebná" or Arabised Persians, had long served the Ommiades, till, early in our eighth century, Khálid bin Bermek,[3] the chief, entered the service of the first Abbaside and became Wazir and Intendant of Finance to Al-Saffáh. The most remarkable and distinguished of the

---

[1] Many have remarked that the actual date of the decease is unknown.

[2] See Al-Siyuti (p. 305) and Dr. Jonathan Scott's "Tales, Anecdotes, and Letters" (p. 296).

[3] I have given the vulgar derivation of the name; and D'Herbelot (s. v. Barmakian) quotes some Persian lines alluding to the "supping up." Al-Mas'udi's account of the family's early history is unfortunately lost. This Khálid succeeded Abu Salámah, first entitled "Wazir" under Al-Saffah (Ibn Khallikan i. 468).

family, he was in office when Al-Mansur transferred the capital from Damascus, the head-quarters of the hated Ommiades, to Baghdad, built ad hoc. After securing the highest character in history by his personal gifts and public services, he was succeeded by his son and heir Yáhyá (John), a statesman famed from early youth for prudence and profound intelligence, liberality and nobility of soul.[1] He was charged by the Caliph Al-Mahdi with the education of his son Harun, hence the latter was accustomed to call him father; and, until the assassination of the fantastic tyrant Al-Hádi, who proposed to make his own child Caliph, he had no little difficulty in preserving the youth from death in prison. The Orthodox, once seated firmly on the throne, appointed Yahya his Grand Wazir. This great administrator had four sons, Al-Fazl, Ja'afar, Mohammed, and Musa,[2] in whose time the house of Bermek rose to that height from which decline and fall are, in the East, well nigh certain and imminent Al-Fazl was a foster-brother of Harun, an exchange of suckling infants having taken place between the two mothers for the usual object, a tightening of the ties of intimacy: he was a man of exceptional mind, but he lacked the charm of temper and manner which characterised Ja'afar. The poets and rhetoricians have been profuse in their praises of the cadet who appears in The Nights as an adviser of calm sound sense, an intercessor and a peace-maker, and even more remarkable than the rest of his family for an almost incredible magnanimity and generosity—une générosité effrayante. Mohammed was famed for exalted views and nobility of sentiment, and Musa for bravery and energy: of both it was justly said, "They did good and harmed not."[3]

For ten years (not including an interval of seven) from the time of Al-Rashid's accession (A.D. 786) to the date of their

[1] For his poetry see Ibn Khallikan iv. 103.

[2] Their flatterers compared them with the four elements.

[3] Al-Mas'udi, chapt. cxii.

fall (A.D. 803), Yahya and his sons Al-Fazl and Ja'afar were virtually rulers of the great heterogeneous empire which extended from Mauritania to Tartary, and they did notable service in arresting its disruption. Their downfall came sudden and terrible like "a thunderbolt from the blue." As the Caliph and Ja'afar were halting in Al-'Umr (the convent) near Anbár-town on the Euphrates, after a convivial evening spent in different pavilions, Harun during the dead of the night called up his page Yásir al-Rikhlah [1] and bade him bring Ja'afar's head. The messenger found Ja'afar still carousing with the blind poet Abú Zakkár [2] and the Christian physician Gabriel ibn Bakhtiashú, and was persuaded to return to the Caliph and report his death; the Wazir adding, "An he express regret I shall owe thee my life; and if not, whatso Allah will, be done." Ja'afar followed to listen and heard only the Caliph exclaim, "O slave, if thou answer me another word, I will send thee before him!" whereupon he at once bandaged his own eyes and received the fatal blow. Al-Asma'í, who was summoned to the presence shortly after, recounts that when the head was brought to Harun he gazed at it, and summoning two witnesses commanded them to decapitate Yasir, crying, "I cannot bear to look upon the slayer of Ja'afar!" His vengeance did not cease with the death: he ordered the head to be gibbetted at one end and the trunk at the other abutment of the Tigris Bridge, where the corpses of the vilest malefactors used to be exposed, and, some months afterwards, he insulted the remains by having them burned—the last and worst indignity which can be offered to a Moslem. There are indeed pity and terror in the difference between two such items in the Treasury-

---

[1] Ibn Khallikan (i. 310) says the Eunuch Abú Háshim Masrúr, the Sworder of Vengeance, who is so pleasantly associated with Ja'afar in many nightly disguises; but the Eunuch survived the Caliph. Fakhr al-Din (p. 27) adds that Masrur was an enemy of Ja'afar; and gives further details concerning the execution.

[2] For the verses which Abú Zakkár was singing at the time, see De Sacy, Chrest., iii. 519.

accounts as these: "Four hundred thousand dinars (£200,000) to a robe of honour for the Wazir Ja'afar bin Yahya;" and "Ten kírát (5 shillings) to naphtha and reeds for burning the body of Ja'afar the Barmecide."

Meanwhile Yahya and Al-Fazl, seized by the Caliph Harun's command at Baghdad, were significantly cast into the prison "Habs al-Zanádikah"—of the Guebres—and their immense wealth, which, some opine, hastened their downfall, was confiscated. According to the historian Tabari (vol. iv. 468), who, however, is not supported by all the annalists, the whole Barmecide family, men, women, and children, numbering over a thousand, were slaughtered with only three exceptions; Yahya, his brother Mohammed, and his son Al-Fazl. The Caliph's foster-father, who lived to the age of seventy-four, was allowed to die in jail (A.H. 805) after two years' imprisonment at Rakkah. Al-Fazl, after having been tortured with two hundred blows in order to make him produce concealed property, survived his father three years and died in Nov. A.H. 808, some four months before his terrible foster-brother. A pathetic tale is told of the son warming water for the old man's use by pressing the copper ewer to his own stomach.

The motives of this terrible massacre are variously recounted, but no sufficient explanation has yet been, or possibly ever will be given. The popular idea is embodied in The Nights.[1] Harun, wishing Ja'afar to be his companion even in the Harem, had wedded him, pro formâ, to his eldest sister Abbásah, "the loveliest woman of her day," and brilliant in mind as in body; but he had expressly said, "I will marry thee to her, that it may be lawful for thee to look upon her, but thou shalt not touch her." Ja'afar bound himself by a solemn oath; but his mother Attábah was mad enough

[1] Bresl. Edit., Night dlxvii., translated in Mr. Payne's "Tales from the Arabic," vol. i. 189, and headed "Al-Rashid and the Barmecides." It is far less lively and dramatic than the account of the same event given by Al-Mas'udi, chapt. cxii., by Ibn Khallikan, by Tabari and by Fakhr al-Din.

to deceive him in his cups and the result was a boy (Ibn Khallikan) or, according to others, twins. The issue was sent under the charge of a confidential eunuch and a slave-girl to Meccah for concealment; but the secret was divulged to Zubaydah, who had her own reasons for hating husband and wife and who cherished an especial grievance against Yahya.[1] Thence it soon found its way to head-quarters. Harun's treatment of Abbásah supports the general conviction: according to the most credible accounts she and her child were buried alive in a pit under the floor of her apartment.

But, possibly, Ja'afar's perjury was only "the last straw." Already Al-Fazl bin Rabí'a, the deadliest enemy of the Barmecides, had been entrusted (A.D. 786) with the Wazirate, which he kept seven years. Ja'afar had also acted generously but imprudently in abetting the escape of Yahya bin Abdillah, Sayyid and Alide, for whom the Caliph had commanded confinement in a close dark dungeon: when charged with disobedience the Wazir had made full confession and Harun had (they say) exclaimed, "Thou hast done well!" but was heard to mutter, "Allah slay me an I slay thee not."[2] The great house seems at times to have abused its powers by being too peremptory with Harun and Zubaydah, especially in money matters;[3] and its very greatness would have created for it many and powerful enemies and detractors who plied the Caliph with anonymous verse and prose. Nor was it forgotten that, before the spread of Al-Islam, they had presided over the Naubehár or Pyræthrum of Balkh; and Harun is said to have remarked anent Yahya, "The zeal for magianism, rooted in his heart, induces him to save all the monuments connected with his faith."[4] Hence

---

[1] Al-Mas'udi, chapt. cxi.

[2] See Dr. Jonathan Scott's extracts from Major Ouseley's "Tarikh-i-Barmaki."

[3] Al-Mas'udi, chapt. cxii. For the liberties Ja'afar took see Ibn Khall. i. 303.

[4] Ibid. chapt. xxiv. For Al-Rashid's hatred of the Zindiks see Al-Siyuti, pp. 292, 301; and as regards the religious troubles, ibid. p. 362 and passim.

the charge that they were "Zanádikah," a term properly applied to those who study the Zend scripture, but popularly meaning Mundanists, Positivists, Reprobates, Agnostics (know-nothings), Atheists; and, it may be noted that, immediately after Al-Rashid's death, violent religious troubles broke out in Baghdad. Ibn Khallikan[1] quotes Sa'íd ibn Sálim, a well-known grammarian and traditionist, who philosophically remarked, "Of a truth the Barmecides did nothing to deserve Al-Rashid's severity, but the day (of their power and prosperity) had been long and whatso endureth long waxeth longsome." Fakhr al-Din says (p. 27), "On attribue encore leur ruine aux manières fières et orgueilleuses de Djafar (Ja'afar) et de Fadhl (Al-Fazl), manières que les rois ne sauroient supporter." According to Ibn Badrún the poet, when the Caliph's sister 'Olayyah asked him, "O my lord, I have not seen thee enjoy one happy day since putting Ja'afar to death: wherefore didst thou slay him?" he answered, "My dear life, an I thought that my shirt knew the reason I would tear it in tatters!" I therefore hold with Al-Mas'udi, "As regards the intimate cause (of the catastrophe) it is unknown, and Allah is Omniscient."

Aaron the Orthodox appears sincerely to have repented his enormous crime. From that date he never enjoyed refreshing sleep: he would have given his whole realm to recall Ja'afar to life; and, if any spoke slightingly of the Barmecides in his presence, he would exclaim, "Allah curse your fathers! Cease to blame them, or fill the void they have left." And he had ample reason to mourn the loss. After the extermination of the wise and enlightened family, the affairs of the Caliphate never prospered: Fazl bin Rabí'a, though a man of intelligence and devoted to letters, proved a poor substitute for Yahya and Ja'afar; and the Caliph is reported to have applied to him the couplet:—

No sire to your sire,[2] I bid you spare * Your calumnies or their place replace.

---

[1] Biogr. Dict. i. 309.

[2] *i.e.* Perdition to your fathers, Allah's curse on your ancestors.

His unwise elevation of his two rival sons filled him with fear of poison, and, lastly, the violence and recklessness of the popular mourning for the Barmecides,[1] whose echo has not yet died away, must have added poignancy to his tardy penitence. The crime still "sticks fiery off" from the rest of Harun's career: it stands out in ghastly prominence as one of the most terrible tragedies recorded by history, and its horrible details make men write passionately on the subject to this our day.[2]

As of Harun so of Zubaydah it may be said that she was far superior in most things to contemporary royalties, and she was not worse at her worst than the normal despot-queen of the Morning-land. We must not take seriously the tales of her jealousy in The Nights, which mostly end in her selling off or burying alive her rivals; but, even were all true, she acted after the recognised fashion of her exalted sisterhood. The secret history of Cairo, during the last generation, tells of many a viceregal dame who committed all the crimes, without any of the virtues, which characterised Harun's cousin-spouse. And the difference between the manners of the Caliphate and the "respectability" of the nineteenth century may be measured by the Tale called "Al-Maamun and Zubaydah."[3] The lady, having won a game of forfeits from her husband, and being vexed with him for imposing unseemly conditions when he had been the winner, condemned him to marry the foulest and filthiest kitchen-wench in the palace; and thus was begotten the Caliph who succeeded and destroyed her son.

Zubaydah was the grand-daughter of the second Abbaside

---

[1] See "Ja'afar and the Bean-seller;" where the great Wazir is said to have been "crucified." Also Roebuck's Persian Proverbs, i. 2, 346, "This also is through the munificence of the Barmecides."

[2] I especially allude to my friend Mr. Payne's admirably written account of it in his concluding Essay (vol. ix.) From his views of the Great Caliph and the Lady Zubaydah I must differ in every point except the destruction of the Barmecides.

[3] Bresl. Edit., vol. vii. 261-62.

Al-Mansur, by his son Ja'afar, whom The Nights persistently term Al-Kasim: her name was Amat al-Azíz or Handmaid of the Almighty; her cognomen was Umm Ja'afar as her husband's was Abú Ja'afar; and her popular name "Creamkin" derives from Zubdah,[1] cream or fresh butter, on account of her plumpness and freshness. She was as majestic and munificent as her husband; and the hum of prayer was never hushed in her palace. Al-Mas'udi[2] makes a historian say to the dangerous Caliph Al-Káhir, "The nobleness and generosity of this Princess, in serious matters as in her diversions, place her in the highest rank;" and he proceeds to give ample proof. Al-Siyuti relates how she once filled a poet's mouth with jewels which he sold for twenty thousand dinars. Ibn Khallikan (i. 523) affirms of her, "Her charity was ample, her conduct virtuous, and the history of her pilgrimage to Meccah and of what she undertook to execute on the way is so well known that it were useless to repeat it." I have noted (Pilgrimage iii. 2) how the Darb al-Sharki or Eastern road from Meccah to Al-Medinah was due to the piety of Zubaydah, who dug wells from Baghdad to the Prophet's burial place and built not only cisterns and caravanserais, but even a wall to direct pilgrims over the shifting sands. She also supplied Meccah, which suffered severely from want of water, with the chief requisite for public hygiene by connecting it, through levelled hills and hewn rocks, with the Ayn al-Mushásh in the Arafat subrange; and the fine aqueduct, some ten miles long, was erected at a cost of 1,700,000 to 2,000,000 of gold pieces.[3] We cannot wonder that her name is still famous among the Badawin and the "Sons of the Holy

---

[1] Mr. Grattan Geary, in a work previously noticed, informs us (i. 212), "The Sitt al-Zobeide, or the Lady Zobeide, was so named from the great Zobeide tribe of Arabs occupying the country East and West of the Euphrates near the Hindi'ah Canal; she was the daughter of a powerful Sheik of that tribe." Can this explain the "Kásim"?

[2] Vol. viii. 296.

[3] Burckhardt, "Travels in Arabia," vol. i. 185.

Cities." She died at Baghdad, after a protracted widowhood, in A.H. 216, and her tomb, which still exists, was long visited by the friends and dependents who mourned the loss of a devout and most liberal woman.

The reader will bear with me while I run through the tales and add a few remarks to the notices given in the notes: the glance must necessarily be brief, however extensive be the theme. The admirable introduction follows, in all the texts and MSS. known to me, the same main lines, but differs greatly in minor details, as will be seen by comparing Mr. Payne's translation with Lane's and mine. In the tale of the Sage Dúbán appears the speaking head which is found in the Kámil, in Mirkhond and in the Kitáb al-Uyún: M. C. Barbier de Meynard (v. 503) traces it back to an abbreviated text of Al-Mas'udi. I would especially recommend to students The Porter and the Three Ladies of Baghdad (i. 73), whose mighty revel ends in general marriage. To judge by the style and changes of person, some of the most "archaic" expressions suggest the hand of the Ráwi or professional tale-teller. The next tale, sometimes called "The Two Wazírs," is notable for its regular and genuine drama-intrigue, which, however, appears still more elaborate and perfected in other pieces. The richness of this Oriental plot-invention contrasts strongly with all European literatures except the Spaniard's, whose taste for the theatre determined his direction, and the Italian's, which in Boccaccio's day had borrowed freely through Sicily from the East. And the remarkable deficiency lasted till the romantic movement dawned in France, when Victor Hugo and Alexander Dumas showed their marvellous powers of faultless fancy, boundless imagination and scenic luxuriance, "raising French poetry from the dead and *not* mortally wounding French prose."[1] The Two Wazirs is

---

[1] The reverse has been remarked by more than one writer; and contemporary French opinion seems to be that Victor Hugo's influence on French prose was, on the whole, not beneficial.

followed by the gem of the volume, The Adventure of the Hunchback-jester, also containing an admirable surprise and a fine development of character, while its "wild but natural simplicity" and its humour are so abounding that it has echoed through the world to the farthest West. It gave to Addison the Story of Alnaschar[1] and to Europe the term "Barmecide Feast," from the "Tale of Shacabac." The adventures of the corpse were known to the Occident long before Galland, as shown by three fabliaux in Barbazan. I have noticed that the Barber's Tale of Himself is historical, and I may add that it is told in detail by Al-Mas'udi (chap. cxiv).

Follows the tale of Núr al-Dín Alí, and what Galland miscalls "The Fair Persian," a brightly written historiette with not a few touches of true humour. Noteworthy are the Slaver's address, the fine description of the Baghdad garden, the drinking-party, the Caliph's frolic and the happy end of the hero's misfortunes. Its brightness is tempered by the gloomy tone of the tale which succeeds, and which has variants in the Bágh o Bahár, a Hindustani version of the Persian "Tale of the Four Darwayshes;" and in the Turkish Kirk Vezir or "Book of the Forty Vezirs." Its dismal péripéties are relieved only by the witty tale of Eunuch Bukhayt and the admirable humour of Eunuch Káfur, whose "half-lie" is known throughout the East. Here also the lover's agonies are piled upon him for the purpose of unpiling at last: the Oriental

---

[1] Mr. W. S. Clouston, the "Storiologist," who has lately published an excellent work entitled "Popular Tales and Fictions; their Migrations and Transformations," informs me the first to adapt this witty anecdote was Jacques de Vitry, the crusading bishop of Accon (Acre), who died at Rome in 1240, after setting the example of "Exempla" or instances in his sermons. He had probably heard it in Syria, and he changed the day-dreamer into a Milkmaid and her Milk-pail to suit his "flock." It then appears as an "Exemplum" in the Liber de Donis or de Septem Donis (or De Dono Timoris from Fear, the first gift) of Stephanus de Borbone, the Dominican, ob. Lyons, 1261: the book treated of the gifts of the Holy Spirit (Isaiah xi. 2, 3), Timor, Pietas, Scientia, Fortitudo, Consilium, Intellectus et Sapientia; and was plentifully garnished with narratives for the use of preachers.

tale-teller knows by experience that, as a rule, doleful endings "don't pay."

The next is the long romance of chivalry, "King Omar bin al-Nu'uman," etc., which occupies an eighth of the whole repertory and the best part of two volumes. Mr. Lane omits it because "obscene and tedious," showing the licence with which he translated; and he was set right by a learned reviewer,[1] who truly declared that "the omission of half-a-dozen passages out of four hundred pages would fit it for printing in any language and the charge of tediousness could hardly have been applied more unhappily." The tale is interesting as a picture of mediæval Arab chivalry and has many other notable points; for instance, the lines beginning "Allah holds the kingship!" are a lesson to the manichæanism of Christian Europe. It relates the doings of three royal generations and has all the characteristics of Eastern art: it is a phantasmagoria of Holy Places, palaces and Harems, convents, castles and caverns, here restful with gentle landscapes, and there bristling with furious battle-pictures and tales of princely prowess and knightly derring-do. The characters stand out well. King Nu'uman is an old villain who deserves his death; the ancient Dame Zát al-Dawáhí merits her title Lady of Calamities (to her foes); Princess Abrízah appears as a charming Amazon, doomed to a miserable and pathetic end; Zau al-Makán is a wise and pious royalty; Nuzhat al-Zamán, though a longsome talker, is a model sister; the Wazir Dandán, a sage and sagacious counsellor, contrasts with the Chamberlain, an ambitious miscreant; Kánmakán is the typical Arab knight, gentle and brave:—

> Now managing the mouthes of stubborne steedes,
> Now practising the proof of warlike deedes:

and the kind-hearted, simple-minded Stoker serves as a foil

[1] The Asiatic Journal and Monthly Register (new series, vol. xxx. Sept.-Dec. 1830, London, Allens, 1839); p. 69, Review of the Arabian Nights, the Mac. Edit. vol. i., and H. Torrens.

to the villains, the kidnapping Badawi and Ghazbán the detestable negro. The fortunes of the family are interrupted by two episodes, both equally remarkable. Táj al-Mulúk is the model lover whom no difficulties or dangers can daunt. In "Azíz and Azízah" we have the beau idéal of a loving maiden: the writer's object was to represent a "softy" who had the luck to win the love of a beautiful and clever cousin and the mad folly to break her heart. The poetical justice which he receives at the hands of women of quite another stamp leaves nothing to be desired. Finally the plot of "King Omar" is well worked out; and the gathering of all the actors upon the stage before the curtain drops may be improbable but is highly artistic.

The long Crusading Romance is relieved by a sequence of sixteen fabliaux, partly historiettes of men and beasts and partly apologues proper—a subject already noticed. We have then the saddening and dreary love-tale of Ali bin Bakkár, a Persian youth, and the Caliph's concubine Shams al-Nahár. Here the end is made doleful enough by the deaths of the "two martyrs," who are killed off, like Romeo and Juliet,[1] a lesson that the course of true Love is sometimes troubled and that men as well as women *can* die of the so-called "tender passion." It is followed by the long tale of Kamar al-Zamán, or Moon of the Age, the first of that name, the "Camaralzaman" whom Galland introduced into the best European society, Like "The Ebony Horse" it seems to have been derived from a common source with "Peter of Provence" and "Cleomades and Claremond"; and we can hardly wonder at its wide diffusion: the tale is brimful of life, change, movement; containing as much character and incident as would fill a modern three-volumer and the Supernatural pleasantly jostles

[1] I have lately found these lovers at Schloss Sternstein near Cilli in Styria, the property of my excellent colleague. Mr. Consul Faber, of Fiume, dating from A.D. 1300 when Jobst of Reichenegg and Agnes of Sternstein were aided and abetted by a Capuchin of Seizkloster.

the Natural; Dahnash the Jinn and Maymúnah daughter of Al-Dimiryát, a renowned King of the Jann, being as human in their jealousy about the virtue of their lovers as any children of Adam, and so their metamorphosis to fleas has all the effect of a surprise. The *troupe* is again drawn with a broad firm touch. Prince Charming, the hero, is weak and wilful, shifty and immoral, hasty and violent: his two spouses are rivals in abominations, as his sons Amjad and As'ad are examples of a fraternal affection rarely found in half-brothers by sister-wives. There is at least one fine melodramatic situation; and marvellous feats of indelicacy, a practical joke which would occur only to the canopic mind, emphasise the recovery of her husband by that remarkable "blackguard," the Lady Budúr. The interpolated tale of Ni'amah and Naomi, a simple and pleasing narrative of youthful amours, contrasts well with the boiling passions of the murderous Queens, and serves as a pause before the grand *dénoûement* when the parted meet, the lost are found, the unwedded are wedded and all ends merrily as a xixth century "society novel."

The long tale of Alá al-Dín, our old friend "Aladdin," is wholly out of place in its present position: it is a counterpart of Ali Núr al-Dín and Miriam the Girdle-girl; and the mention of the Shahbandar or Harbour-master, the Kunsúl or Consul, the Kaptán (Capitano), the use of cannon at sea and the choice of Genoa-city prove that it belongs to the xvth or xvith century and should accompany Kamar al-Zamán II. and Ma'aruf at the end of The Nights. Despite the lutist Zubaydah being carried off by the Jinn, the Magic Couch, a modification of Solomon's carpet, and the murder of the King who refused to Islamize, it is evidently a European tale, and I believe with Dr. Bacher that it is founded upon the legend of "Charlemagne's" daughter Emma and his secretary Eginhardt, as has been noted in the counterpart.

This quasi-historical fiction is followed by a succession of fabliaux, novelle and historiettes till we reach the terminal story, The Queen of the Serpents. It appears to me that most of them are historical and could easily be traced. Not a few are in Al-Mas'udi; for instance the grim Tale of Hatim of Tayy is given bodily in "Meads of Gold" (iii. 327); and the two adventures of Ibrahim al-Mahdi with the barber-surgeon (vol. iv. 103) and the Merchant's sister are also in his pages (vol. vii. pp. 68 and 18). The City of Lubtayt embodies the legend of Don Rodrigo, last of the Goths, and may have reached the ears of Washington Irving; Many-columned Iram is held by all Moslems to be factual; and sundry writers have recorded the tricks played by Al-Maamun with the Pyramids of Jízah which still show his handiwork.[1] The germ of Isaac of Mosul is found in Al-Mas'udi who (vii. 65) names "Burán" the poetess (Ibn Khall. i. 268); and the Tale of Harun al-Rashid and the Slave-girl is told by a host of writers. Ali the Persian is a rollicking bit of fun from some Iranian jest-book: Abu Mohammed hight Lazybones belongs to the cycle of "Sindbad the Seaman," with a touch of Whittington and his Cat; and Zumurrud ("Smaragdine") in Ali Shar shows at her sale the impudence of Miriam the Girdle-girl and the curious device of the Lady Budur. The "Ruined Man who became Rich," etc., is historical and Al-Mas'udi (vii. 281) relates the coquetry of Mahbúbah the concubine: the historian also quotes four couplets, two identical with Nos. 1 and 2 in The Nights, and adding:—

Then see the slave who lords it o'er her lord * In lover privacy and public site:
Behold these eyes that one like Ja'afar saw: * Allah on Ja'afar reign boons infinite!

---

[1] Omitted by Lane for some reason unaccountable as usual. A correspondent sends me his version of the lines which occur in The Nights.

Behold the Pyramids and hear them teach
What they can tell of Future and of Past:
They would declare, had they the gift of speech,
The deeds that Time hath wrought from first to last.

* * * *

My friends, and is there aught beneath the sky
Can with th' Egyptian Pyramids compare?
In fear of them strong Time hath passèd by;
And everything dreads Time in earth and air.

Uns al Wújúd is a love tale which has been translated into a host of Eastern languages; and The Lovers of the Banu Ozrah belong to Al-Mas'udi's "Martyrs of Love" (vii. 355), with the "Ozrite love" of Ibn Khallikan (iv. 537). "Harun and the Three Poets" has given to Cairo a proverb which Burckhardt renders "The day obliterates the word or promise of the Night," for

The promise of night is effaced by day.

The Simpleton and the Sharper, like the Foolish Dominie, is an old Joe Miller in Hindu as well as Moslem folk-lore. "Kisra Anushirwán" is "The King, the Owl and the Villages" of Al-Mas'údi (iii. 171), who also notices the Persian monarch's four seals of office; and "Masrur the Eunuch and Ibn Al-Káribi" (vol. iii. 221) is from the same source as Ibn al-Magházili the Reciter and a Eunuch belonging to the Caliph Al-Mu'tazad. In the Tale of Tawaddud we have the fullest development of the disputations and displays of learning then so common in Europe, teste the "Admirable Crichton"; and these were affected not only by Eastern tale-tellers but even by sober historians. To us it is much like "padding" when Nuzhat al-Zamán fags her hapless hearers with a discourse covering sixteen mortal pages; when the Wazir Dandan reports at length the cold speeches of the five high-bosomed maids and the Lady of Calamities; and when Wird Khan, in presence of his papa, discharges his patristic exercitations and heterogeneous knowledge. Yet Al-Mas'udi also relates, at dreary extension (vol. vi. 369) the disputation of the twelve sages in presence of Barmecide Yahya upon the origin, the essence, the accidents and the omnes res of Love; and in another place (vii. 181) shows Honayn, author of the Book of Natural Questions, undergoing a long examination before the Caliph Al-Wásik (Vathek) and describing, amongst other things, the human teeth. See also the dialogue or catechism of Al-Hajjáj and Ibn al-Kirríya in Ibn Khallikan (vol. i. 238–240).

These disjecta membra of tales and annals are pleasantly relieved by the seven voyages of Sindbad the Seaman. The "Arabian Odyssey" may, like its Greek brother, descend from a noble family, the "Shipwrecked Mariner," a Coptic travel-tale of the twelfth dynasty (B.C. 3500) preserved on a papyrus at St. Petersburg. In its actual condition "Sindbad" is a fanciful compilation, like De Foe's "Captain Singleton," borrowed from travellers' tales of an immense variety with extracts from Al-Idrísi, Al-Kazwíni and Ibn al-Wardi. Here we find the Polyphemus, the Pygmies and the cranes of Homer and Herodotus; the escape of Aristomenes; the Plinian monsters well known in Persia; the magnetic mountain of Saint Brennan (Brandanus); the aeronautics of "Duke Ernest of Bavaria"[1] and sundry cuttings from Moslem writers dating between our ninth and fourteenth centuries.[2] The "Shaykh of the Seaboard," the true reading of The Old Man of the Sea, appears in the Persian romance of Kámarupa, translated by Francklin, all the particulars absolutely corresponding. The "Odyssey" is valuable because it shows how far Eastward the mediæval Arab had extended: already in The Ignorance he had reached China and had formed a centre of trade at Canton. But the higher merit of the cento is to produce one of the most charming books of travel ever written, like Robinson Crusoe, the delight of children and the admiration of all ages.

The hearty life and realism of Sindbad are made to stand out in strong relief by the deep melancholy which pervades

---

[1] A rhyming Romance by Henry of Waldeck (flor. A.D. 1160) with a Latin poem on the same subject by Odo and a prose version still popular in Germany. (Lane's Nights, iii. 81; and Weber's "Northern Romances.")

[2] *e.g.* 'Ajáib al-Hind (=Marvels of Ind) ninth century, translated by J. Marcel Devic, Paris, 1878; and about the same date the Two Mohammedan Travellers, translated by Renaudot. In the eleventh century we have the famous Sayyid al-Idrisi; in the thirteenth the 'Ajáib al-Makhlúkát of Al-Kazwíni (see De Sacy, vol. iii.), and in the fourteenth the Kharídat al-Ajáib of Ibn al-Wardi. Lane (in loco) traces most of Sindbad to the two latter sources.

"The City of Brass," a dreadful book for a dreary day. It is curious to compare the doleful verses with those spoken to Caliph Al-Mutawakkil by Abu al-Hasan Ali (Al-Mas'udi, vii. 246). We then enter upon the venerable Sindibad-nameh, the Malice of Women, of which, according to the Kitab al-Fihrist, there were two editions, a greater (Sinzibád al-Kabír) and a lesser (Sinzibád al-Saghír), the latter being probably an epitome of the former. This bundle of legends, I have shown, was incorporated with The Nights as an editor's addition; and as an independent work it has made the round of the world. Space forbids any detailed notice of this choice collection of anecdotes, for which a volume would be required. I may, however, note that the "Wife's Device" has its analogues in the Kathá (chapt. xiii.), in the Gesta Romanorum (No. xxviii.) and in Boccaccio (Day iii. 6 and Day vi. 8), modified by La Fontaine to Richard Minutolo (Contes, lib. i. tale 2); and it is quoted almost in the words of The Nights by the Shaykh al-Nafzáwi. Another form of that witty tale The Three Wishes is found in the Arab proverb "More luckless than Basús" (Kamus), a fair Israelite who persuaded her husband, also a Jew, to wish that she might become the loveliest of women. Allah granted it, spitefully as Jupiter; the consequence was that her contumacious treatment of her mate made him pray that the beauty might be turned into a dog; and the third wish restored her to her original state.

The Story of Júdar is Egyptian, to judge from its local knowledge together with its absolute ignorance of Marocco. It shows a contrast, in which Arabs delight, of an almost angelical goodness and forgiveness with a well-nigh diabolical malignity, and we find the same extremes in Abú Sír the noble-minded Barber and the hideously inhuman Abú Kír. The excursion to Mauritania is artfully managed and gives a novelty to the *mise-en-scène.* Gharíb and Ajíb belongs to the cycle of Antar and King Omar bin al-Nu'uman: its exaggerations make it a fine type of Oriental Chauvinism, pitting the superhuman virtues, valour, nobility and success of all that is Moslem, against the scum of the earth which is non-Moslem. Like the exploits of Friar John of the Chopping-knives (Rabelais i. c. 27), it suggests ridicule cast on impossible battles and tales of giants, paynims and paladins. The long romance is followed by thirteen historiettes all apparently historical: compare "Hind, daughter of Al-Nu'uman" and "Isaac of Mosul and the Devil" with Al-Mas'udi v. 365 and vi. 340. They end in two long detective-tales like those which M. Gaboriau has popularised: the Rogueries of Dalilah and the Adventures of Mercury Ali, being based upon the principle, "One thief wots another." The former, who has appeared before, seems to have been a noted character: Al-Mas'udi says (viii. 175) "In a word this Shaykh (Al-'Ukáb) outrivalled in his rogueries and the ingenuities of his wiles *Dállah* (Dalilah ?) the *Crafty* and other tricksters and coney-catchers, ancient and modern."

The Tale of Ardashir lacks originality: we are now entering upon a series of pictures which are replicas of those preceding. This is not the case with that charming Undine, Julnár the Sea-born, which, like Abdullah of the Land and Abdullah of the Sea, describes the vie intime of mermen and merwomen. Somewhat resembling Swift's inimitable creations, the Houyhnhnms for instance, they prove, amongst other things, that those who dwell in a denser element can justly blame and severely criticise the contradictory prejudices and unreasonable predilections of mankind. Sayf al-Mulúk, the romantic tale of two lovers, shows by its introduction that it was originally an independent work, and it is known to have existed in Persia during the eleventh century; this novella has found its way into every Moslem language of the East even into Sindi, which calls the hero "Sayfal." Here we again meet the "Old Man of the Sea" and make acquaintance with a Jinni whose soul is outside his body: thus he resembles Hermotimos of Klazamunæ in Apollonius, whose spirit left his mortal frame à discrétion. The author, philanthropically remarking "Knowest thou not that a single mortal is better, in Allah's sight, than a thousand Jinn?" brings the wooing to a happy end which leaves a pleasant savour upon the mental palate.

Hasan of Bassorah is a Master Shoetie on a large scale like Sindbad, but his voyages and travels extend into the supernatural and fantastic rather than the natural world. Though long, the tale is by no means wearisome and the characters are drawn with a fine firm hand. The hero with his hen-like persistency of purpose, his weeping, fainting and versifying, is interesting enough and proves that "Love can find out the way." The charming adopted sister, the model of what the feminine friend should be; the silly little wife who never knows that she is happy till she loses happiness; the violent and hard-hearted queen with all the cruelty of a good woman, and the manners and customs of Amazon-land are outlined with a life-like vivacity. Khalífah, the next tale, is valuable as a study of Eastern life, showing how the fisherman emerges from the squalor of his surroundings and becomes one of the Caliph's favourite cup-companions. Ali Nur al-Din and King Jali'ad have been noticed elsewhere and there is little to say of the concluding stories which bear the evident impress of a more modern date.

Dr. Johnson thus sums up his notice of The Tempest. "Whatever might have been the intention of their author, these tales are made instrumental to the production of many characters, diversified with boundless invention, and preserved with profound skill in nature; extensive knowledge of opinions, and accurate observation of life. Here are exhibited princes, courtiers and sailors, all speaking in their real characters. There is the agency of airy spirits and of earthy goblin, the operations of magic, the tumults of a storm, the adventures on a desert island, the native effusion of untaught affection, the punishment of guilt, and the final happiness of those for whom our passions and reason are equally interested."

We can fairly say this much and far more for our Tales. Viewed as a tout ensemble in full and complete form, they are a drama of Eastern life, and a Dance of Death made sublime by faith and the highest emotions, by the certainty of expiation and the fulness of atoning equity; where virtue is victorious, vice is vanquished and the ways of Allah are justified to man. They are a panorama which remains kenspeckle upon the mental retina. They form a phantasmagoria in which archangels and angels, devils and goblins, men of air, of fire, of water, naturally mingle with men of earth; where flying horses and talking fishes are utterly realistic; where King and Prince meet fisherman and pauper, lamia and cannibal; where citizen jostles Badawi, eunuch meets knight; the Kazi hob-nobs with the thief; the pure and pious sit down to the same tray with the pander and the procuress; where the professional religionist, the learned Koranist and the strictest moralist consort with the wicked magician, the scoffer and the debauchee-poet like Abu Nowas; where the courtier jests with the boor and where the sweep is wedded with the noble lady. And the characters are "finished and quickened by a few touches swift and sure as the glance of sunbeams." The work is a kaleidoscope where everything falls into picture; gorgeous palaces and pavilions; grisly underground caves and deadly wolds; gardens fairer than those of the Hesperid; seas dashing with clashing billows upon enchanted mountains; valleys of the Shadow of Death; air-voyages and promenades in the abysses of ocean; the duello, the battle and the siege; the wooing of maidens and the marriage-rite. All the splendour and squalor, the beauty and baseness, the glamour and grotesqueness, the magic and the mournfulness, the bravery and the baseness of Oriental life are here: its pictures of the three great Arab passions, love, war and fancy, entitle it to be called "Blood, Musk and Hashish."[1] And still more,

[1] So Hector France proposed to name his admirably realistic volume "Sous le Burnous" (Paris, Charpentier, 1886).

the genius of the story-teller quickens the dry bones of history, and by adding Fiction to Fact revives the dead past: the Caliphs and the Caliphate return to Baghdad and Cairo, whilst Asmodeus kindly removes the terrace-roof of every tenement and allows our curious glances to take in the whole interior. This is perhaps the best proof of their power. Finally, the picture-gallery opens with a series of weird and striking adventures and shows as a tail-piece an idyllic scene of love and wedlock in halls before reeking with lust and blood.

I have noticed in my Foreword that the two main characteristics of The Nights are Pathos and Humour, alternating with highly artistic contrast, and carefully calculated to provoke tears and smiles in the coffee-house audience which paid for them. The sentimental portion mostly breathes a tender passion and a simple sadness: such are the Badawi's dying farewell; the lady's broken heart on account of her lover's hand being cut off; the Wazir's death; the mourner's song and the "tongue of the case"; the murder of Princess Abrízah with the babe sucking its dead mother's breast; and, generally, the last moments of good Moslems, which are described with inimitable terseness and naïveté. The sad and the gay mingle in the character of the good Hammam-stoker who becomes Roi Crotte; and the melancholy deepens in the Tale of the Mad Lover, the Blacksmith who could handle fire without hurt, the Devotee Prince and the whole Tale of Azízah, whose angelic love is set off by the sensuality and selfishness of her more fortunate rivals. A new note of absolutely tragic dignity seems to be struck in the Sweep and the Noble Lady, showing the piquancy of sentiment which can be evolved from the common and the unclean. The pretty conceit of the Lute is afterwards carried out in a Song which is a masterpiece of originality[1] and (in the Arabic) of exquisite

---

[1] I mean in European literature, not in Arabic where it is a lieu commun. See three several forms of it in one page (505) of Ibn Khallikan, vol. iii.

tenderness and poetic melancholy, the wail over the past and the vain longing for reunion. And the very depths of melancholy, of majestic pathos and of true sublimity are reached in Many-columned Iram and the City of Brass: the metrical part of the latter shows a luxury of woe; it is one long wail of despair which echoes long and loud in the hearer's heart.

In my Foreword I have compared the humorous vein of the comic tales with our northern "wut," chiefly for the dryness and slyness which pervade it. But it differs in degree as much as the pathos varies. The staple article is Cairene "chaff," a peculiar banter possibly inherited from their pagan forefathers: instances of this are found in the Cock and Dog, the Eunuch's address to the Cook, the Wazir's exclamation "Too little pepper!" the self-communing of Judar the Hashish-eater in Ali Shár, the scene between the brother-Wazirs, the treatment of the Gobbo, the water of Zemzem and the Eunuchs Bukhayt and Kafur.[1] At times it becomes a masterpiece of fun, of rollicking Rabelaisian humour underlaid by the caustic mother-wit of Sancho Panza, as in the revel of the ladies of Baghdad, the Holy Ointment applied to the beard of Luka the Knight, "unxerunt regem Salomonem," and Ja'afar and the old Badawi with its reminiscence of "chaffy" King Amasis. This reaches its acme in the description of ugly old age, in The Three Wishes, in Ali the Persian, in the Lady and her Five Suitors, which corresponds and contrasts with the dully told Story of Upakosa and her Four Lovers of the Kathá; and in The Man of Al-Yaman, where we find the true Falstaffian touch. But there is sterling wit, sweet and bright, expressed without any artifice of words, in the immortal Barber's tales of his brothers, especially the second, the fifth and the sixth. Finally, wherever the honest and independent old debauchee Abu Nowas makes his appearance the fun becomes fescennine and milesian.

---

[1] My attention has been called to the resemblance between the half-lie and Job (i. 13-19), an author who seems to be growing more modern with every generation of commentators.

## B.—The Manner of The Nights.

And now, after considering the matter, I will glance at the language and style of The Nights. The first point to remark is the peculiarly happy framework of the Receuil, which I cannot but suspect set an example to the Decamerone and its host of successors.[1] The admirable Introduction, a perfect mise-en-scène, gives the amplest raison d'être of the work, which thus has all the unity required for a great romantic cento. We perceive this when reading the contemporary Hindu work the Kathá Sarit Ságara,[2] which is at once so like and so unlike The Nights: here the preamble is insufficient; the whole is clumsy

---

[1] Boccaccio (ob. Dec. 2, 1375) may easily have heard of The Thousand Nights and a Night or of its archetype the Hazár Afsánah. He was followed by the Piacevoli Notti of Giovan Francisco Straparola (A.D. 1550), translated into almost all European languages but English; the original Italian is now rare. Then came the Heptameron ou Histoire des Amans fortunez of Marguerite d'Angoulême, Reyne de Navarra and only sister of Francis I. She died in 1549 before the Days were finished: in 1558 Pierre Boaistuan published the Histoire des Amans fortunez, and in 1559 Claude Guiget the "Heptameron." Next is the Hexameron of A. de Torquemada, Rouen, 1610; and lastly, the Pentamerone, or El Cunto de li Cunte of Giambattista Basile (Naples, 1637), known by the meagre abstract of J. E. Taylor and the caricatures of George Cruikshank (London, 1847-50). I propose to translate this Pentamerone direct from the Neapolitan and have already finished half the work.

[2] Translated and well annotated by Prof. Tawney, who, however, affects asterisks and has considerably bowdlerised sundry of the tales, *e.g.* the Monkey who picked out the Wedge (vol. ii. 28). This tale, by the by, is found in the Khirad Afroz (i. 128) and in the Anwar-i-Suhayli (chapt. i.) and gave rise to the Persian proverb, "What has a monkey to do with carpentering?" It is curious to compare the Hindu with the Arabic work whose resemblances are as remarkable as their differences, while even more notable is their correspondence in impressionising the reader. The Thaumaturgy of both is the same: the Indian is profuse in demonology and witchcraft; in transformation and restoration; in monsters as wind-men, fire-men and water-men; in air-going elephants and flying horses (i. 541-43); in the wishing cow, divine goats and laughing fishes (i. 24) and in the speciosa miracula of magic weapons. He delights in fearful battles (i. 400) fought with the same weapons as the Moslem and rewards his heroes with a "turband of honour" (i. 266) in lieu of a robe. There is a quaint family likeness arising from similar stages and states of society: the city is adorned for

for want of a thread upon which the many independent tales and fables could be strung;[1] and the consequent disorder

gladness; men carry money in a robe-corner and exclaim "Ha! good!" (for "Good, by Allah!"); lovers die with exemplary facility; the "soft-sided" ladies drink spirits (i. 61) and princesses get drunk (i. 476); whilst the Eunuch, the Hetaira and the Mercury (Kuttini) play the same preponderating parts as in The Nights. Our Brahman is strong in love-making; he complains of the pains of separation in this phenomenal universe; he revels in youth, "twin-brother to mirth," and beauty which has illuminating powers; he foully reviles old age and he alternately praises and abuses the sex, concerning which more presently. He delights in truisms, the fashion of contemporary Europe (see Palmerin of England, chapt. vii.), such as, "It is the fashion of the heart to receive pleasure from those things which ought to give it," etc., etc. "What is there the wise cannot understand?" and so forth. He is liberal in trite reflections and frigid conceits (i. 19, 55, 97, 103, 107, in fact everywhere); and his puns run through whole lines; this in fine Sanskrit style is inevitable. Yet some of his expressions are admirably terse and telling, *e.g.*, Ascending the swing of Doubt: Bound together (lovers) by the leash of gazing: Two babes looking like Misery and Poverty: Old Age seized me by the chin: (A lake) first essay of the Creator's skill: (A vow) difficult as standing on a sword-edge: My vital spirits boiled with the fire of woe: Transparent as a good man's heart: There was a certain convent full of fools: Dazed with scripture-reading: The stones could not help laughing at him: The Moon kissed the laughing forehead of the East: She was like a wave of the Sea of Love's insolence (ii. 127), a wave of the Sea of Beauty tossed up by the breeze of Youth: The King played dice, he loved slave-girls, he told lies, he sat up o' nights, he waxed wroth without reason, he took wealth wrongously, he despised the good and honoured the bad (i. 562); with many choice bits of the same kind. Like the Arab the Indian is profuse in personification; but the doctrine of pre-existence, of incarnation and emanation and an excessive spiritualism, ever aiming at the infinite, makes his imagery run mad. Thus we have Immoral Conduct embodied; the God of Death; Science; the Svarga-heaven; Evening; Untimeliness; and the Earthbride, while the Ace and Deuce of dice are turned into a brace of Demons. There is also that grotesqueness which the French detect even in Shakespeare, *e.g.* She drank in his ambrosial form with thirsty eyes like partridges (i. 476), and it often results from the comparison of incompatibles, *e.g.* a row of birds likened to a garden of nymphs; and from forced allegories, the favourite figure of contemporary Europe. Again, the rhetorical Hindu style differs greatly from the sobriety, directness and simplicity of the Arab, whose motto is "Brevity combined with Precision," except where the latter falls into "fine writing." And, finally, there is a something in the atmosphere of these Tales which is unfamiliar to the West and which makes them, as more than one has remarked to me, very hard reading.

[1] The Introduction (i. 1–5) leads to the Curse of Pushpadanta and Mályaván who live on Earth as Vararúchi and Gunádhya, and this runs through lib. i. Lib. ii. begins with the Story of Udáyana to whom we must be truly grateful as our only guide: he and his son Naraváhanadatta fill up the rest and end with

and confusion tell upon the reader, who cannot remember the sequence without taking notes.

As was said in my Foreword, "without the Nights no Arabian Nights!" and now, so far from holding the pauses "an intolerable interruption to the narrative," I attach additional importance to these pleasant and restful breaks introduced into long and intricate stories. Indeed, beginning again, I should adopt the plan of the Calc. Edit. opening and ending every division with a dialogue between the sisters. Upon this point, however, opinions will differ and the critic will remind me that the consensus of the MSS. would be wanting: The Bresl. Edit. in many places merely interjects the number of the night without interrupting the tale; and Galland ceases to use the division after the ccxxxvith Night and in some editions after the cxcviith.[1] A fragmentary MS., according to Scott, whose friend J. Anderson found it in Bengal, breaks away after Night xxix.; and in the Wortley Montague, the Sultan relents at an early opportunity, the stories, as in Galland, continuing only as an amusement. I have been careful to preserve the balanced sentences with which the tales open; the tautology and the prose-rhyme serving to attract attention, *e.g.* "In days of yore and in times long gone before there was a King," etc.; in England where we strive not to waste words this becomes "Once upon a time." The closings also are artfully calculated, by striking a minor chord after the rush and hurry of the incidents, to suggest repose: "And they led the most pleasurable of lives and the most delectable, till there came to them the Destroyer of delights and the Severer of societies and they became as though they had never been." Place

---

lib. xviii. Thus the want of the clew or plot compels a division into books, which begin for instance with "We worship the elephantine proboscis of Ganesha" (lib. x. 1), a reverend and awful object to a Hindu, but to Englishmen mainly suggesting the "Zoo." The "Bismillah" etc. of The Nights is much more satisfactory.

[1] See pp. 5-6 Avertissement des Editeurs, Le Cabinet des Fées, vol. xxxviii.: Geneva, 1788. Galland's Edit. of mdccxxvi. ends with Night ccxxxiv. and the English translations with ccxxxvi. and cxcvii. See retro. p. 82.

this by the side of Boccaccio's favourite formulæ :—Egli conquistò poi la Scozia, e funne re coronato (ii. 3) ; Et onorevolmente visse infino àlla fine (ii. 4) ; Molte volte goderono del loro amore : Iddio faccia noi goder del nostro (iii. 6) ; E cosi nella sua grossezza si rimase e ancor vi si sta (vi. 8). We have further docked this tail into :—" And they lived happily ever after."

I cannot take up The Nights, in their present condition, without feeling that the work has been written down from the Káwi or Nakkál,[1] the conteur or professional story-teller, also called Kassás and Maddáh, corresponding with the Hindu Bhat or Bard. To these men my learned friend Baron A. von Kremer would attribute the Mu'allakát, vulgarly called the Suspended Poems, as being " indited from the relation of the Ráwi." Hence in our text the frequent interruption of the formula Kál' al-Ráwi = quotes the reciter ; *dice Turpino.* Moreover, The Nights read in many places like a hand-book or guide for the professional, who would learn them by heart ; here and there introducing his " gag " and " patter." To this " business " possibly we may attribute much of the ribaldry which starts up in unexpected places : it was meant simply to provoke a laugh. How old the custom is and how unchangeable is Eastern life is shown, a correspondent suggests, by the Book of Esther which might form part of The Alf Laylah. " On that night (we read in chap. vi. 1) could not the King sleep, and he commanded to bring the book of records of the chronicles ; and they were read before the King." The Ráwi would declaim the recitative somewhat in conversational style ; he would intone the Saj'a or prose-rhyme and he would chant to the twanging of the Rabáb, a

[1] There is a shade of difference in the words ; the former is also used for Reciters of Traditions—a serious subject. But in the case of Hammád surnamed Al-Ráwiyah (the Rhapsode) attached to the Court of Al-Walíd, it means simply a conteur. So the Greeks had Homeristæ = reciters of Homer, as opposed to the Homeridæ or School of Homer.

one-stringed viol, the poetical parts. Dr. Scott[1] borrows from the historian of Aleppo a life-like picture of the Story-teller. "He recites walking to and fro in the middle of the coffee-room, stopping only now and then, when the expression requires some emphatical attitude. He is commonly heard with great attention; and not unfrequently in the midst of some interesting adventure, when the expectation of the audience is raised to the highest pitch, he breaks off abruptly and makes his escape, leaving both his hero or heroine and his audience in the utmost embarrassment. Those who happen to be near the door endeavour to detain him, insisting upon the story being finished before he departs; but he always makes his retreat good;[2] and the auditors suspending their curiosity are induced to return at the same time next day to hear the sequel. He has no sooner made his exit than the company in separate parties fall to disputing about the characters of the drama or the event of an unfinished adventure. The controversy by degrees becomes serious and opposite opinions are maintained with no less warmth than if the fall of the city depended upon the decision."

At Tangier, where a murder in a "coffee-house" had closed these hovels,[3] pending a sufficient payment to the Pasha; and where, during the hard winter of 1885–86, the poorer classes were compelled to puff their Kayf (Bhang, *cannibis indica*) and sip their black coffee in the muddy streets under a rainy sky, I found the Ráwi active on Sundays and Thursdays, the

---

[1] Vol. i. Preface, p. v. He notes that Mr. Dallaway ("Constantinople, Ancient and Modern") describes the same scene at Stamboul, where the Story-teller was used, like the modern "Organs of Government" in newspaper shape, for "reconciling the people to any recent measure of the Sultan and Vizier." There are women Ráwiyahs for the Harems, and some have become famous like the Mother of Hasan al-Basri (Ibn Khall. i. 370).

[2] Hence the Persian proverb, "Báki-e-dastán fardá" = the rest of the tale to-morrow, said to askers of silly questions.

[3] This was in 1885-6; in 1887 His Shereefian Majesty has peremptorily forbidden the smoking of "Kayf" (Bhang) and tobacco, and the result has been the crowding of prisons by the energy of the corrupt police.

market-days. The favourite place was the "Soko de Barra," or large bazar, outside the filthy town, whose condition is that of Suez and Bayrut half a century ago. The stage is a foul slope; now slippery with viscous mud, then powdery with fetid dust, dotted with graves and decaying tombs, unclean booths, gargottes and tattered tents, and frequented by women, mere bundles of unclean rags, and by men wearing the haik or burnús, a Franciscan frock, tending their squatting camels and chaffering over cattle for Gibraltar beef-eaters. Here the market-people form ring about the reciter, a stalwart man affecting little raiment besides a broad waist-belt into which his lower chiffons are tucked, and noticeable only for his shock hair, wild eyes, broad grin and generally disreputable aspect. He usually handles a short stick; and, when drummer and piper are absent, he carries a tiny tomtom shaped like an hour-glass, upon which he taps the periods. This "Scealuidhe," as the Irish call him, opens the drama with extempore prayer, proving that he and the audience are good Moslems: he speaks slowly and with emphasis, varying the diction with breaks of animation, abundant action and the most comical grimace: he advances, retires and wheels about, illustrating every point with pantomime; and his features, voice and gestures are so expressive that even Europeans, who cannot understand a word of Arabic, divine the meaning of his tale. The audience stands breathless and motionless, surprising strangers [1] by the ingenuousness and freshness of feeling hidden under their hard and savage exterior. The performance usually ends with the embryo actor going round for alms and flourishing in air every silver bit, the usual honorarium being a few "f'lús," that marvellous money of Barbary, big coppers worth one-twelfth of a penny. All the tales I heard were purely

[1] The scene is excellently described in, "Morocco: Its People and Places," by Edmondo de Amicis (London: Cassell, 1882), a most refreshing volume after the enforced platitudes and commonplaces of English travellers.

local, but Fakhri Bey, a young Osmanli domiciled for some time in Fez and Mequinez, assured me that The Nights are still recited there.

Many travellers, including Dr. Russell, have complained that they failed to find a complete MS. copy of The Nights. Evidently they never heard of the popular superstition which declares that no one can read through the said series without dying—it is only fair that my patrons should know this. Yacoub Artín Pasha declares that the superstition dates from the fourteenth and fifteenth centuries and he explains it in two ways. Firstly, it is a facetious exaggeration, meaning that no one has leisure or patience to wade through the long repertory. Secondly, the work is condemned as futile. When Egypt produced savants and legists like Ibn al-Hajar, Al-'Ayni, and Al-Kastallání, to mention no others, the taste of the country inclined to dry factual studies and positive science; nor, indeed, has this taste wholly died out: there are not a few who, like Khayri Pasha, contend that the mathematic is more useful even for legal studies than history and geography; and at Cairo the chief of the Educational Department has always been an engineer, *i.e.* a mathematician. The Olema declared war against all "futilities," in which they included not only stories but also what is politely entitled Authentic History. From this to the fatal effect of such lecture is only a step. Society, however, cannot rest without light literature; so the novel-reading class was thrown back upon writings which had all the indelicacy and few of the merits of The Nights.[1]

Turkey is the only Moslem country which has dared to produce a regular drama[2] and to arouse the energies of such

[1] About the close of the last century Col. James Capper, "Observations on a Passage to India through Egypt" (London, 1785, 1 vol. 8vo), tells us that "They (the Arabian Nights) are universally read and admired throughout Asia by all ranks of men, both young and old." Duhalde (vol. iii.) mentions them in China, and Capt. Lyons (ii. 44 Fr. Transl.) in Inner Africa.

[2] It began, however, in Persia, where the celebrated Darwaysh Mukhlis, Chief

brilliant writers as Munír Pasha, statesman and scholar; Ekrem Bey, literato and professor; Kemál Bey, held by some to be the greatest writer in modern Osmanli-land and Abd al-Hakk Hamíd Bey, first Secretary of the London Embassy. The theatre began in its ruder form by taking subjects bodily from The Nights; then it annexed its plays as we do—the Novel having ousted the Drama—from the French; and lastly it took courage to be original. Many years ago I saw Harun al-Rashid and the Three Kalandars, with deer-skins and all their properties de rigueur, in the court-yard of Government House, Damascus, declaiming to the extreme astonishment and delight of the audience. It requires only to glance at The Nights for seeing how much histrionic matter they contain.

In considering the style of The Nights we must bear in mind that the work has never been edited according to our ideas of the process. Consequently there is no just reason for translating the whole verbatim et literatim, as has been done by Torrens, Lane and Payne in his "Tales from the Arabic."[1] This conscientious treatment is required for

---

Sofi of Isfahan in the xviith century, translated into Persian tales certain Hindu plays, of which a MS. entitled Alfaraga Badal-Schidda (Al-Faraj ba'd Al-Shiddah = Joy after Annoy) exists in the Bibliothèque Nationale, Paris. But to give an original air to his work, he entitled it, "Hazár o yek Ruz"=Thousand and One Days, and in 1675 he allowed his friend Petis de la Croix, who happened to be at Isfahan, to copy it. Le Sage (of Gil Blas) is said to have converted many of the tales of Mukhlis into comic operas, which were performed at the Théâtre Italien. I still hope to see The Nights at the Lyceum.

[1] This author, however, when hazarding a change of style which is, I think, regretable, has shown abundant art by filling up the frequent deficiencies of the text after the fashion of Baron McGuckin de Slane in Ibn Khallikan. As regards the tout ensemble of his work, a noble piece of English, my opinion will ever be that expressed in my Foreword. A carping critic has remarked that the translator, "as may be seen in every page, is no Arabic scholar." If I be a judge, the reverse is the case: the brilliant and beautiful version thus ignobly traduced is almost entirely free from the blemishes and carelessness which disfigure Lane's, and thus it is far more faithful to the original. But it is no secret that on the staff of that journal the translator of Villon has sundry enemies, *vrais diables enjuponés*, who take every opportunity of girding at him because he does not belong to the

versions of an author like Camoens, whose works were carefully corrected and arranged by a competent littérateur, but it is not merited by The Nights as they now are. The Macnaghten, the Bulak and the Bayrut texts, though printed from MSS. identical in order, often differ in minor matters. Many friends have asked me to undertake the work: but, even if lightened by the aid of Shaykhs, Munshis and copyists, the labour would be severe, tedious and thankless: better leave the holes open than patch them with fancy work or with heterogeneous matter. The learned, indeed, as Lane tells us (i. 74; iii. 740), being thoroughly dissatisfied with the plain and popular, the ordinary and "vulgar" note of the language, have attempted to refine and improve it and have more than once threatened to remodel it, that is, to make it odious. This would be to dress up Robert Burns in plumes borrowed from Dryden and Pope.

The first defect of the texts is in the distribution and arrangement of the matter, as I have noticed in the case of Sindbad the Seaman. Moreover, many of the earlier Nights are overlong and not a few of the others are overshort; this, however, has the prime recommendation of variety. Even the vagaries of editor and scribe will not account for all the incoherences, disorder and inconsequence, and for the vain iterations which suggest that the author has forgotten what he said. In places there are dead allusions to persons and tales which are left dark. The digressions are abrupt and useless, leading nowhere, while sundry pages are wearisome for excess of prolixity or hardly intelligible for extreme conciseness. The perpetual recurrence of mean colloquialisms and of words and idioms peculiar to Egypt and Syria[1] also

---

clique and because he does good work and theirs is mostly sham. The sole fault I find with Mr. Payne is that his severe grace of style treats an unclassical work as a classic, when the romantic and irregular would have been a more appropriate garb. But this is a mere matter of private judgment.

[1] Here I offer a few, but very few, instances from the Breslau text which is the greatest sinner in this respect. Mas. for fem., vol. i. p. 9, and three

takes from the pleasure of the perusal. Yet we cannot deny that it has its use: this unadorned language of familiar conversation in its day, adapted for the understanding of the people, is best fitted for the Rawi's craft in the camp and caravan, the Harem, the bazar and the coffee-house. Moreover, as has been well said, The Nights is the only written half-way house between the literary and colloquial Arabic which is accessible to readers, and thus it becomes necessary to all students who would qualify themselves for service in Moslem lands from Mauritania to Mesopotamia. It freely uses Turkish words like "Khátún" and Persian terms as "Sháhbandar," thus requiring for translation not only a somewhat archaic touch, but also a vocabulary borrowed from various sources: otherwise the effect would not be reproduced. In places, however, the style rises to the highly ornate, approaching the

---

times in seven pages. Ahná and nahná for nahnú (iv. 370, 372): Aná ba-ashtarí = I will buy (iii. 109): and Aná 'Ámil = I will do (v. 367): Alaykí for Alayki (i. 18): Antí for Anti (iii. 66) and generally long í for short ĭ. 'Ammál (from 'amala = he did) tahlam = certainly thou dreamest, and 'Ammálín yaakulú = they were about to eat (ix. 315): Aywá, a time-honoured corruption, for Ay wa'lláhí = yes, by Allah (passim): Bitá, = belonging to, *e.g.* Sára bitá'k = it is become thine (ix. 352) and Matá' with the same sense (iii. 80): Dá 'l-khurj = this saddle-bag (ix. 336) and Dí (for hazah) = this woman (iii. 79) or this time (ii. 162): Fayn as ráha fayn = whither is he gone? (iv. 323): Káma badri = he rose early (ix. 318): Kamán = also, a word known to every European (ii. 43): Katt = never (ii. 172): Kawám (pronounced 'awám) = fast, at once (iv. 385): and Rih ásif kawí (pron. 'awí) = a wind, strong very. Laysh, *e.g.* bi-tasalní laysh (ix. 324) = why do you ask me? a favourite form for li ayya shayyin, also an old form: so Máfish = má fihi shayyun (there is no thing) in which Herr Landberg (p. 425) makes "Sha, le présent de pouvoir": Min ajalí = for my sake; and Li-ajal al-taudí'a = for the sake of taking leave (Mac. Edit. i. 384): Rijál nautiyah = men sailors when the latter word would suffice: Shuwayh (dim. of shayy) = a small thing, a little (iv. 309) like Moyyah (dim. of Má) a little water: Waddúní = they carried me (ii. 172) and lastly the abominable Wáhid gharíb = one (for *a*) stranger. These few must suffice: the tale of Judar and his Brethren, which in style is mostly Egyptian, will supply a number of others. It must not, however, be supposed, as many have done, that vulgar and colloquial Arabic is of modern date: we find it in the first century of Al-Islam, as is proved by the tale of Al-Hajjáj and Al-Shabi (Ibn Khallikan, ii. 6). The former asked "Kam ataa-k?" (= how much is thy pay?) to which the latter answered, "Alfayn!" (= two thousand!) "Tut," cried the Governor, "Kam atau-ka?" to which the poet replied as correctly and classically, "Alfáni."

pompous; *e.g.* the Wazirial addresses in the tale of King Jali'ad. The battle-scenes, mostly admirable, are told with the conciseness of a despatch and the vividness of an artist; the two combining to form perfect "word-pictures." Of the Badí'a or euphuistic style, "parleying euphuism," and of Al-Saj'a, the prose rhyme, I shall speak in a future page.

The characteristics of the whole are naïveté and simplicity, clearness and a singular concision. The gorgeousness is in the imagery, not in the language; the words are weak while the sense, as in the classical Scandinavian books, is strong; and here the Arabic differs diametrically from the florid exuberance and turgid amplifications of the Persian story-teller, which sound so hollow and unreal by the side of a chaster model. It abounds in formulæ such as repetitions of religious phrases which are unchangeable. There are certain stock comparisons, as Lokman's wisdom, Joseph's beauty, Jacob's grief, Job's patience, David's music, and Maryam the Virgin's chastity. The eyebrow is a Nún; the eye a Sád, the mouth a Mím. A hero is more prudent than the crow, a better guide than the Katá-grouse, more generous than the cock, warier than the crane, braver than the lion, more aggressive than the panther, finer sighted than the horse, craftier than the fox, greedier than the gazelle, more vigilant than the dog, and thriftier than the ant. The cup-boy is a sun rising from the dark underworld symbolised by his collar; his cheek-mole is a crumb of ambergris, his nose is a scymitar grided at the curve; his lower lip is a jujube; his teeth are the Pleiades, or hailstones; his browlocks are scorpions; his young hair on the upper lip is an emerald; his side beard is a swarm of ants or a Lám (l-letter) enclosing the roses or anemones of his cheek. The cup-girl is a moon who rivals the sheen of the sun; her forehead is a pearl set off by the jet of her "idiot-fringe;" her eyelashes scorn the sharp sword; and her glances are arrows shot from the bow of the eyebrows. A mistress necessarily belongs, though living in the next street, to the Wady Liwá in Al-Naja, the Arabian

Arcadia; also to a hostile clan of Badawin whose blades are ever thirsting for the lover's blood and whose malignant tongues aim only at the "defilement of separation." Youth is upright as an Alif ( ا ), or slender and bending as a branch of the Bán tree which we should call a willow-wand,[1] while Age, crabbed and crooked, stoops groundward, vainly seeking in the dust his lost juvenility. As Baron de Slane says of these stock comparisons (Ibn Khall. i. xxxvi.), "The figurative language of Moslem poets is often difficult to be understood. The *narcissus* is the eye; the *feeble* stem of that plant bends *languidly* under its flower, and thus recalls to mind the languor of the eyes. *Pearls* signify both *tears* and *teeth*; the latter are sometimes called *hailstones*, from their whiteness and moisture; the *lips* are *cornelians* or *rubies*; the *gums*, a *pomegranate flower*; the dark *foliage* of the *myrtle* is synonymous with the *black hair* of the beloved, or with the first down on the cheeks of puberty. The *down* itself is called the *izâr*, or head-stall of the bridle, and the curve of the izar is compared to the letters lâm (ل) and nûn (ن).[2] Ringlets trace on the cheek or neck the letter Wâw (و); they are called *Scorpions* (as the Greek σκορπιος), either from their dark colour or their agitated movements; the *eye* is a *sword;* the *eyelids scabbards;* the *whiteness* of the complexion, *camphor;* and a *mole* or *beauty-spot*, *musk*, which term denotes also *dark hair*. A *mole* is sometimes compared also to an *ant* creeping on the cheek towards the *honey* of the mouth; a *handsome face* is both a *full moon* and *day; black hair* is *night;* the *waist* is a *willow-branch* or a *lance;* the *water of the face*[3] is *self-respect:* a poet *sells the water of his face* when he bestows mercenary praises on a rich patron."

---

[1] In Russian folk-songs a young girl is often compared with this tree, *e.g.*—

Ivooshka, ivooshka zelonaia moia—
(O Willow, O green Willow mine!)

[2] So in Hector France ("La Vache enragée") "Le sourcil en accent circonflexe et l'œil en point d'interrogation."

[3] In Persian "Áb-i-rú," by Indians pronounced Ábrú.

This does not sound promising: yet, as has been said of Arab music, the persistent repetition of the same notes in the minor key is by no means monotonous and ends with haunting the ear, occupying the thought and touching the soul. Like the distant frog-concert and chirp of the cicada, the creak of the water-wheel and the stroke of hammers upon the anvil from afar, the murmur of the fountain, the sough of the wind and the plash of the wavelet, they occupy the sensorium with a soothing effect, forming a barbaric music full of soothing sweetness and peaceful pleasure.

## § IV.

## SOCIAL CONDITION.

I HERE propose to treat of the Social Condition which The Nights discloses and of Al-Islam at the earlier period of its development.

### A.—AL-ISLAM.

A splendid and glorious life was that of Baghdad in the days of the mighty Caliph,[1] when the capital had towered to the zenith of grandeur and was already trembling and tottering to the fall. The centre of human civilisation, which was then confined to Greece and Arabia, and the metropolis of an Empire exceeding in extent the widest limits of Rome, it was essentially a city of pleasure, a Paris of the ninth century. The "Palace of Peace" (Dár al-Salám), worthy successor of Babylon and Nineveh, which had outrivalled Damascus, the "Smile of the Prophet," and Kufah, the successor of Hira and the magnificent creation of Caliph Omar, possessed unrivalled advantages of site and climate. The Tigris-Euphrates Valley, where the fabled Garden of Eden has been placed, in early ages succeeded the Nile-Valley as a great centre of human development: and the prerogative of a central and commanding position still promises it, even in the present state of decay and desolation under the unspeakable Turk, a magnificent future,[2] when railways and canals shall connect it with Europe. The city of palaces and government offices,

---

[1] For further praises of his poetry and eloquence see the extracts from Fakhr al-Din of Rayy (an annalist of the xivth century A.D.) in De Sacy's Chrestomathie Arabe, vol. i.

[2] After this had been written I received "Babylonien, das reichste Land in der Vorzeit und das lohnendste Kolonisationsfeld für die Gegenwart," by my learned friend Dr. Aloys Sprenger, Heidelberg, 1886.

hôtels and pavilions, mosques and colleges, kiosks and squares, bazars and markets, pleasure grounds and orchards, adorned with all the graceful charms which Saracenic architecture had borrowed from the Byzantines, lay couched upon the banks of the Dijlah-Hiddekel under a sky of marvellous purity and in a climate which makes mere life a "Kayf"—the luxury of tranquil enjoyment. It was surrounded by far-extending suburbs, like Rusáfah (the Dyke) on the Eastern side and villages like Baturanjah, dear to the votaries of pleasure; and with the roar of a gigantic capital mingled the hum of prayer, the trilling of birds, the thrilling of harp and lute, the shrilling of pipes, the minstrel's lay, and the witching strains of the professional Almah.

The population of Baghdad must have been enormous when the smallest number of her sons who fell victims to Huláku Khan in 1258 was estimated at eight hundred thousand, while other authorities more than double that terrible "butcher's bill." Her policy and polity were unique. A well-regulated routine of tribute and taxation, personally inspected by the Caliph; a network of waterways and canaux d'arrosage; a noble system of highways, provided with viaducts, bridges and caravanserais, and a postal service of mounted couriers enabled it to collect as in a reservoir the wealth of the outer world. The facilities for education were upon the most extended scale; large sums, from private as well as public sources, were allotted to Mosques, each of which, by the admirable rule of Al-Islam, was expected to contain a school: these establishments were richly endowed and stocked with professors collected from every land between Khorasan and Marocco,[1] and immense libraries[2] attracted the learned of all

---

[1] The first school for Arabic literature was opened by Ibn Abbas who lectured to multitudes in a valley near Meccah; this rude beginning was followed by public teaching in the great Mosque of Damascus. For the rise of the "Madrasah," Academy or College, see Introd. to Ibn Khallikan, pp. xxvii.-xxxii.

[2] When Ibn Abbád the Sáhib (Wazir) was invited to visit one of the Samanides, he refused, one reason being that he would require 400 camels to carry only his books.

nations. It was a golden age for poets and panegyrists, koranists and literati, preachers and rhetoricians, physicians and scientists who, besides receiving high salaries and fabulous presents, were treated with all the honours of Chinese Mandarins ; and, like these, the humblest Moslem—fisherman or artizan—could aspire through knowledge of savoir faire to the highest offices of the Empire. The effect was a grafting of Egyptian and old Mesopotamian, of Persian and Græco-Latin fruits, by long Time deterioriated, upon the strong young stock of Arab genius; and the result, as usual after such imping, was a shoot of exceptional luxuriance and vitality. The educational establishments devoted themselves to the three main objects recognized by the Moslem world, Theology, Civil Law and Belles Lettres ; and a multitude of trained Councillors enabled the ruling powers to establish and enlarge that complicated machinery of government, at once concentrated and decentralized, a despotism often fatal to the wealthy great but never neglecting the interests of the humbler lieges, which forms the beau idéal of Oriental administration. Under the Chancellors of the empire the Kazis administered law and order, justice and equity; and from their decisions the poorest subject, Moslem or miscreant, could claim with the general approval of the lieges, access and appeal to the Caliph who, as Imám or Antistes of the Faith, was High President of a Court of Cassation.

Under wise administration Agriculture and Commerce, the twin pillars of national prosperity, necessarily flourished. A scientific canalisation, with irrigation-works inherited from the ancients, made the Mesopotamian Valley a rival of Kemi the Black Land, and rendered cultivation a certainty of profit, not a mere speculation as it must ever be to those who perforce rely upon the fickle rains of Heaven. The remains of extensive mines prove that this source of public wealth was not neglected ; navigation laws encouraged transit and traffic ; and ordinances for the fisheries aimed at developing a branch of industry which is still backward even during the xixth century. Most substantial encouragement was given to trade and commerce, to manufactures and handicrafts, by the flood of gold which poured in from all parts of earth; by the presence of a splendid and luxurious court, and by the call for new arts and industries which such a civilisation would necessitate. The crafts were distributed into guilds and syndicates under their respective chiefs, whom the Government did not "govern too much:" these Shahbandars, Mukaddams and Nakíbs regulated the several trades, rewarded the industrious, punished the fraudulent, and were personally answerable, as we still see at Cairo, for the conduct of their constituents. Public order, the sine quâ non of stability and progress, was preserved, first, by the satisfaction of the lieges, who, despite their characteristic turbulence, had few if any grievances; and, secondly, by a well-directed and efficient police, an engine of statecraft which in the West seems most difficult to perfect. In the East, however, the Wali or Chief Commissioner can reckon more or less upon the unsalaried assistance of society: the cities are divided into quarters shut off one from other by night, and every Moslem is expected, by his law and religion, to keep watch upon his neighbours, to report their delinquencies and, if necessary, himself to carry out the penal code. But in difficult cases the guardians of the peace were assisted by a body of private detectives, women as well as men: these were called Tawwábún = the Penitents, because like our Bow-street runners, they had given up an even less respectable calling. Their adventures still delight the vulgar, as did the Newgate Calendar of past generations; and to this class we owe the tales of Calamity Ahmad, Dalilah the Wily One, Saladin with the three Chiefs of Police (vol. iii. 116), and Al-Malik al-Záhir with the Sixteen Constables (Bresl. Edit. xi. pp. 321-99). Here and in many other places we also see the origin of that "picaresque" literature which arose in Spain and overran Europe; and which begat Le Moyen de Parvenir.[1]

[1] This "Salmagondis" by François Beroalde de Verville was afterwards worked by Tabarin, the pseudo-Bruscambille d'Aubigné and Sorel.

I need say no more on this heading, the civilization of Baghdad contrasting with the barbarism of Europe then Germanic, The Nights itself being the best expositor. On the other hand the action of the state-religion upon the state, the condition of Al-Islam during the reign of Al-Rashid, its declension from the primitive creed and its relation to Christianity and Christendom, require a somewhat extended notice.

Al-Islam, it has been said, is essentially a fighting faith and never shows to full advantage save in the field. The exceeding luxury of a wealthy capital, the debauchery and variety of vices which would spring up therein, naturally as weeds in a rich fallow, and the cosmopolitan views which suggest themselves in a meeting-place of nations, were sore trials to the primitive simplicity of the "Religion of Resignation"—the saving faith. Harun and his cousin-wife, as has been shown, were orthodox and even fanatical; but the Barmecides were strongly suspected of heretical leanings; and while the many-headed showed itself, as usual, violent, and ready to do battle about an Azan-call, the learned, who sooner or later leaven the masses, were profoundly dissatisfied with the dryness and barrenness of Mohammed's creed, so acceptable to the vulgar, and were devising a series of schisms and innovations.

In the Tale of Tawaddud the reader has seen a fairly extended catechism of the Creed (Dín), the ceremonial observances (Mazhab) and the apostolic practices (Sunnat) of the Shafi'í school which, with minor modifications, applies to the other three orthodox. Europe has by this time clean forgotten some tricks of her former bigotry, such as "Mawmet" (an idol!) and "Mahommerie" (mummery[1]), a

[1] I prefer this derivation to Strutt's adopted by the popular, "*mumm* is said to be derived from the Danish word *mumme*, or *momme* in Dutch (Germ. = larva) and signifies disguise in a mask, hence a mummer." In the Promptorium Parvulorum we have "Mummynge, mussacio, vel mussatus:" it was a pantomime in dumb show, *e.g.* "I mumme in a mummynge;" "Let us go mumme

place of Moslem worship: educated men no longer speak with Ockley of the "great impostor Mahomet," nor believe with the learned and violent Dr. Prideaux that he was foolish and wicked enough to dispossess "certain poor orphans, the sons of an inferior artificer" (the Banú Najjár!). A host of books has attempted, though hardly with success, to enlighten popular ignorance upon a crucial point; namely, that the Founder of Al-Islam, like the Founder of Christianity, never pretended to establish a new religion. His claims, indeed, were limited to purging the "School of Galilee" of the dross of ages and of the manifold abuses wherewith long use had infected its early constitution: hence to the unprejudiced observer his reformation seems to have brought it nearer the primitive and original doctrine than any subsequent attempts, especially the Judaizing tendencies of the so-called neo-"Protestant" churches. The Meccan Apostle preached that the Hanafíyyah or orthodox belief, which he subsequently named Al-Islam, was first taught by Allah, in all its purity and perfection, to Adam, and consigned to certain inspired volumes now lost; and that this primal Holy Writ received additions in the days of his descendants Shís (Seth) and Idrís (Enoch?), the founder of the Sabian (not "Sabæan") faith. Here, therefore, Al-Islam at once avoided the deplorable assumption of the Hebrews and the Christians,—an error which has been so injurious to their science and their progress,—of placing their "first man" in circa B.C. 4000, or somewhat subsequent to the building of the Pyramids: the Pre-Adamite[1] races and dynasties of the

---

(mummer) to nyghte in women's apparayle." "Mask" and "Mascarade," for persona, larva or vizard, also derive, I have noticed, from an Arabic word—Maskharah.

[1] The Pre-Adamite doctrine has been preached but with scant success in Christendom. Peyrère, a French Calvinist, published (A.D. 1655) his Præadamitæ, sive exercitatio supra versibus 12, 13, 14, cap. v. Epist. Paul ad Romanos," contending that Adam was called the first man because with him the law began. It brewed a storm of wrath and the author was fortunate to escape with only imprisonment for belief in "Adam Kadmon."

Moslems remove a great stumbling-block and square with the anthropological views of the present day. In process of time, when the Adamite religion demanded a restoration and a supplement, its pristine virtue was revived, restored and further developed by the books communicated to Abraham, whose dispensation thus takes the place of the Hebrew Noah and his Noachidæ. In due time the Torah, or Pentateuch, superseded and abrogated the Abrahamic dispensation; the "Zabúr" of David (a book not confined to the Psalms) reformed the Torah; the Injíl or Evangel reformed the Zabur and was itself purified, quickened and perfected by the Koran which means *κατ᾽ἐξοχήν* The Reading or The Recital. Hence Locke, with many others, held Moslems to be unorthodox, that is anti-Trinitarian Christians who believe in the immaculate Conception, in the Ascension and in the divine mission of Jesus; and when Priestley affirmed that "Jesus was sent from God," all Moslems do the same. Thus they are, in the main point of doctrine connected with the Deity, simply Arians as opposed to Athanasians. History proves that the former was the earlier faith which, though formally condemned in A.D. 325 by Constantine's Council of Nice,[1] overspread the Orient beginning with Eastern Europe, where Ulphilas converted the Goths; which extended into Africa with the Vandals, claimed a victim or martyr as late as in the sixteenth century[2] and has by no means died out in this our day,

The Talmud had been completed a full century before Mohammed's time and the Evangel had been translated into Arabic; moreover travel and converse with his Jewish and Christian friends and companions must have convinced the Meccan apostle that Christianity was calling as loudly for reform as Judaism had done. An exaggerated Trinitarianism

---

[1] According to Socrates the verdict was followed by a free fight of the Bishop-voters over the word "consubstantiality."

[2] Servetus burnt (in A.D. 1553 for publishing his Arian tractate) by Calvin.

or rather Tritheism, a "Fourth Person," and Saint-worship had virtually dethroned the Deity; whilst Mariolatry had made the faith a religio muliebris, and superstition had drawn from its horrid fecundity an incredible number of heresies and monstrous absurdities. Even ecclesiastic writers draw the gloomiest pictures of the Christian Church in the fourth and seventh centuries, and one declares that the "Kingdom of Heaven had become a Hell." Egypt, distracted by the blood-thirsty religious wars of Copt and Greek, had been covered with hermitages by a gens æterna of semi-maniacal superstition. Syria, ever "feracious of heresies," had allowed many of her finest tracts to be monopolised by monkeries and nunneries.[1] After many a tentative measure Mohammed seems to have built his edifice upon two bases, the unity of the Godhead and the priesthood of the paterfamilias. He abolished for ever the "sacerdos, alter Christus" whose existence, as someone acutely said, is the best proof of Christianity, and whom all know to be its weakest point. The Moslem family, however humble, was to be the model in miniature of the State, and every father in Al-Islam was made priest and pontiff in his own house, able unaided to marry himself, to circumcise (to baptise as it were) his children, to instruct them in the law and canonically to bury himself. Ritual, properly so called, there was none; congregational prayers were merely those of the individual en masse and the only admitted approach to a sacerdotal order were the Olema or scholars learned in the legistic and the Mullah or schoolmaster. By thus abolishing the priesthood Mohammed reconciled ancient with modern wisdom. "Scito dominum," said Cato, "pro totâ familiâ rem divinam facere:" "No priest at a birth, no priest at a marriage, no priest at a death," is the aspiration of the present Rationalistic School.

---

[1] It was the same in England before the "Reformation," and in France where, during our days, a returned priesthood collected in a few years "Peter-pence" to the tune of five hundred millions of francs. And these men wonder at being turned out!

The Meccan apostle wisely retained the compulsory sacrament of circumcision and the ceremonial ablutions of the Mosaic law; and the five daily prayers not only diverted man's thoughts from the world but tended to keep his body pure. These two institutions had been practised throughout life by the Founder of Christianity; but the followers who had never even seen him, abolished them for purposes evidently political and propagandist. By ignoring the truth that cleanliness is next to godliness they paved the way for such saints as Simon Stylites and Sabba who, like the lowest Hindu orders of ascetics, made filth a concomitant and an evidence of piety: even now English Catholic girls are at times forbidden by Italian priests a frequent use of the bath as a penance against the sin of "luxury." Mohammed would have accepted the morals contained in the Sermon on the Mount much more readily than did the Jews from whom its matter was borrowed.[1] He did something to abolish the use of wine, which in the East means only its abuse; and he denounced games of chance, well knowing that the excitable races of sub-tropical climates cannot play with patience, fairness or moderation. He set aside certain sums for charity to be paid by every Believer and he was the first to establish a poor-rate (Zakát): thus he avoided the shame and scandal of mendicancy which, beginning in the Catholic countries of Southern Europe, extends to Syria and as far East as Christianity is found. By these and other measures of the same import he made the ideal Moslem's life physically clean, moderate and temperate.

But Mohammed, the "master mind of the age," had, we must own, a "genuine prophetic power, a sinking of self in the Divine, not distinguishable in kind from the inspiration of the Hebrew prophets," especially in that puritanical and pharisaic narrowness which, with characteristic simplicity,

---

[1] Deutsch on the Talmud: Quarterly Review, 1867.

can see no good outside its own petty pale. He had insight as well as outsight, and the two taught him that personal and external reformation were mean matters compared with elevating the inner man. In the "purer Faith," which he was commissioned to abrogate and to quicken, he found two vital defects equally fatal to its energy and to its longevity. These were (and are) its egoism and its degradation of humanity. Thus it cannot be a "pleroma:" it needs a Higher Law. As Judaism promised the good Jew all manner of temporal blessings, issue, riches, wealth, honour, power, length of days, so Christianity offered the good Christian, as a bribe to lead a godly life, personal salvation and a future state of happiness, in fact, the Kingdom of Heaven, with an alternative threat of Hell. It never rose to the height of the Hindu Brahmans and Lao-Tse (the "Ancient Teacher"), of Zeno the Stoic and his disciples the noble Pharisees[1] who believed and preached that Virtue is its own reward. It never dared to say "Do good for Good's sake;"[2] even now it does not declare with Cicero, "The sum of all is, that what is right should be sought for its own sake, because it is right, and not because it is enacted." It does not even now venture to say with Philo Judæus, "The good man seeks the day for the sake of the day, and the light for the light's sake: and he labours to acquire what is good for the sake of the Good itself, and not

[1] These Hebrew Stoics would justly charge the Founder of Christianity with preaching a more popular and practical doctrine, but a degradation from their own far higher and more ideal standard.

[2] Dr. Theodore Christlieb ("Modern Doubt and Christian Belief," Edinburgh: Clark, 1874) can even now write:—"So then the 'full age' to which humanity is at present supposed to have attained, consists in man's doing good purely for goodness sake! Who sees not the hollowness of this bombastic talk? *That* man has yet to be born whose practice will be regulated by this insipid theory (*dieser grauen Theorie*). What is the idea of goodness per se? * * * The abstract idea of goodness is not an effectual motive for well-doing" (p. 104). My only comment is *c'est ignoble!* His reverence acts the part of Satan in Holy Writ, "Does Job serve God for naught?" Compare this selfish, irreligious, and immoral view with Philo Judæus (On the Allegory of the Sacred Laws, cap. lviii.), to measure the extent of the fall from Pharisaism to Christianity.

of anything else." So far for the egotism, naïve and unconscious, of Christianity, whose burden is, "Do good to escape Hell and gain Heaven."

A no less defect in the "School of Galilee" is its low view of human nature. Adopting as sober and authentic history an Osirian-Hebrew myth which Philo and a host of Rabbis explain away, each after his own fashion, Christianity dwells, lovingly, as it were, upon the "Fall" of man[1] and seems to revel in the contemptible condition to which "original sin" condemned him; thus grovelling before God ad majorem Dei gloriam. To such a point was and is this carried that the Synod of Dort declared, Infantes infidelium morientes in infantiâ reprobatos esse statuimus; nay, many of the orthodox still hold a Christian babe dying unbaptised to be unfit for a higher existence, and some have even created a "limbo" expressly to domicile the innocents, "of whom is the Kingdom of Heaven." Here, if anywhere, the cloven foot shows itself and teaches us that the only solid stratum underlying priestcraft is one composed of £ s. d.

> And I never can now believe it, my Lord! (Bishop) we come to this earth
> Ready damned, with the seeds of evil sown quite so thick at our birth,

sings Edwin Arnold.[2] We ask, can infatuation or hypocrisy, for it must be the one or the other, go farther? But the Adamical myth is opposed to all our modern studies. The deeper we dig into the Earth's "crust," the lower are the specimens of human remains which occur; and hitherto not a single "find" has come to revive the faded glories of

> Adam the goodliest man of men since born (!)
> His sons, the fairest of her daughters Eve.

Thus Christianity, admitting like Judaism, its own saints and

---

[1] Of the doctrine of the Fall the heretic Marcion wrote: "The Deity must either be deficient in goodness if he willed, in prescience if he did not foresee, or in power if he did not prevent it."

[2] In his charming book, "India Revisited."

santons, utterly ignores the Progress of Humanity, perhaps the only belief in which the wise man can take unmingled satisfaction. Both have proposed an originally perfect being with hyacinthine locks, from whose type all the subsequent humans are degradations physical and moral. We on the other hand hold, from the evidence of our senses, that early man was a savage very little superior to the brute; that during man's millions of years upon earth there has been a gradual advance towards perfection, at times irregular and even retrograde, but in the main progressive; and that a comparison of man in the xixth century with the caveman[1] affords us the means of measuring past progress and of calculating the future of humanity.

Mohammed was far from rising to the moral heights of the ancient sages: he did nothing to abate the egotism of Christianity; he even exaggerated the pleasures of its Heaven and the horrors of its Hell. On the other hand he did much to exalt human nature. He passed over the "Fall" with a light hand; he made man superior to the angels: he encouraged his fellow-creatures to be great and good by dwelling upon their nobler not their meaner side; he acknowledged, even in this world, the perfectability of mankind, including womankind, and in proposing the loftiest ideal he acted unconsciously upon the grand dictum of chivalry—Honneur oblige.[2] His prophets were mostly faultless men; and, if Adam, the "Pure of Allah," sinned, he "sinned against himself." Lastly, he made Allah predetermine the career and fortunes, not only of empires, but of every created being; thus inculcating sympathy and tolerance of others, which is true humanity, and a proud resignation to evil as to good fortune. This is the doctrine which teaches the vulgar Moslem a dignity observed even by the

---

[1] This is the answer to those who contend with much truth that the moderns are by no means superior to the ancients of Europe: they look at the results of only 3,000 years instead of 30,000 or 300,000.

[2] As a maxim the saying is attributed to the Duc de Lévis, but it is much older.

"blind traveller," and which enables him to display a moderation, a fortitude, and a self-command rare enough amongst the followers of the "purer creed."

Christian historians explain variously the portentous rise of Al-Islam and its marvellous spread over vast regions not only of pagans and idolaters but of Christians. Prideaux disingenuously suggests that it "seems to have been purposely raised up by God, to be a scourge to the Christian church for not living in accordance with their most holy religion." The popular excuse is by the free use of the sword; this, however, is mere ignorance: in Mohammed's day and early Al-Islam only actual fighters were slain [1]: the rest were allowed to pay the Jizyah, or capitation tax, and to become tributaries, enjoying almost all the privileges of Moslems. But even had forcible conversion been most systematically practised, it would have afforded an insufficient explanation of the phenomenal rise of an empire which covered more ground in eighty years than Rome had gained in eight hundred. During so short a time the grand revival of Christian Monotheism had consolidated into a mighty nation, despite their eternal blood-feuds, the scattered Arab tribes; a six-years' campaign had conquered Syria, and a lustre or two utterly overthrew Persia, humbled the Græco-Roman, subdued Egypt and extended The Faith along northern Africa as far as the Atlantic. Within three generations the Copts of Nile-land had formally cast out Christianity, and the same was the case with Syria, the cradle of the Nazarene, and Mesopotamia, one of his strongholds although both were backed by all the remaining power of the Byzantine empire. North-Western Africa, which had rejected the idolatro-philosophic system of pagan and imperial Rome, and had accepted, after lukewarm fashion, the Arian Christianity

[1] There are a few, but only a few, frightful exceptions to this rule, especially in the case of Khálid bin Walíd, the Sword of Allah, and his ferocious friend, Darár ibn al-Azwar. But their cruel excesses were loudly blamed by the Moslems, and Caliph Omar only obeyed the popular voice in superseding the fierce and furious Khalid by the mild and merciful Abú Obaydah.

imported by the Vandals, and the "Nicene mystery of the Trinity," hailed with enthusiasm the doctrines of the Koran and has never ceased to be most zealous in its Islam. And while Mohammedanism speedily reduced the limits of Christendom by one-third, while throughout the Arabian, Saracenic and Turkish invasions whole Christian peoples embraced the monotheistic faith, there are hardly any instances of defection from the new creed, and, with the exception of Spain and Sicily, it has never been suppressed in any land where once it took root. Even now, when Mohammedanism no longer wields the sword, it is spreading over wide regions in China, in the Indian Archipelago, and especially in Western and Central Africa, propagated only by self-educated individuals, trading travellers, while Christianity makes no progress and cannot exist on the Dark Continent without strong support from Government. Nor can we explain this honourable reception by the "licentiousness" ignorantly attributed to Al-Islam, one of the most severely moral of institutions; or by the allurements of polygamy and concubinage, slavery,[1] and a "wholly sensual Paradise" devoted to eating, drinking[2] and the pleasures of the sixth sense. The true and simple explanation is that this grand Reformation of Christianity was urgently wanted when it appeared, that it suited the people better than the creed which it superseded, and that it has not ceased to be sufficient for their requirements, social, sexual and vital. As the practical Orientalist Dr. Leitner well observes from his own experience, "The Mohammedan religion can

---

[1] This too when St. Paul sends the Christian slave Onesimus back to his unbelieving (?) master Philemon; which in Al-Islam would have created a scandal.

[2] This too when the Founder of Christianity talks of "Eating and drinking at his table!" (Luke xxii. 29). My notes have often touched upon this inveterate prejudice, the result, like the soul-less woman of Al-Islam, of ad captandum, pious fraud. "No soul knoweth what joy of the eyes is reserved for the good in recompense for their works" (Koran xxxii. 17) is surely as "spiritual" as St. Paul (1 Cor. ii. 9). Some lies, however, are very long-lived, especially those begotten by self-interest.

adapt itself better than any other, and has adapted itself to circumstances and to the needs of the various races which profess it, in accordance with the spirit of the age."[1] Hence, I add, its wide diffusion and its impregnable position. "The dead hand, stiff and motionless" is a forcible simile for the present condition of Al-Islam; but it results from limited and imperfect observation and it fails in the sine quâ non of similes and metaphors, a solid foundation of fact.

I cannot quit this subject without a passing reference to an admirably written passage in Mr. Palgrave's travels[2] which is essentially unfair to Al-Islam. The author has had ample opportunities of comparing creeds; of Jewish blood and born a Protestant, he became a Catholic and a Jesuit (Père Michel Cohen)[3] in a Syrian convent; he crossed Arabia as a good Moslem and he finally returned to his premier amour, Anglicanism. But his picturesque depreciation of Mohammedanism, which has found due appreciation in more than one popular volume,[4] is a notable specimen of special pleading, of the ad captandum in its modern and least honest form. The writer begins by assuming the arid and barren Wahhabi-ism, which he had personally studied, as a fair expression of the Saving Faith. What should we say to a Moslem traveller who would make the Calvinism of the sourest Covenanter, model, genuine

---

[1] I have elsewhere noted its strict conservatism which, however, it shares with all Eastern faiths in the East. But progress, not quietism, is the principle which governs humanity and it is favoured by events of most different nature. In Egypt the rule of Mohammed Ali the Great and in Syria the Massacre of Damascus (1860) have greatly modified the constitution of Al-Islam throughout the nearer East.

[2] Chapt. viii. "Narrative of a Year's Journey through Central and Eastern Arabia;" London, Macmillan, 1865.

[3] The Soc. Jesu has, I believe, a traditional conviction that converts of Israelitic blood bring only misfortune to the Order.

[4] I especially allude to an able but most superficial book, the "Ten Great Religions," by James F. Clarke (Boston, Osgood, 1876), which caricatures and exaggerates the false portraiture of Mr. Palgrave. The writer's admission that, "Something is always gained by learning what the believers in a system have to say in its behalf," clearly shows us the man we have to deal with and the "depths of his self-consciousness."

and ancient Christianity? What would sensible Moslems say to these propositions of Professor Maccovius and the Synod of Dort:—Good works are an obstacle to salvation. God does by no means will the salvation of all men: He does will sin and He destines men to sin, as sin? What would they think of the Inadmissible Grace, the Perseverance of the Elect, the Supralapsarian and the Sublapsarian and, finally, of a Deity, the author of man's existence, temptation and fall, who deliberately pre-ordains sin and ruin? "Father Cohen" carries out into the regions of the extreme his strictures on the one grand vitalising idea of Al-Islam, "There is no god but God;"[1] and his deduction concerning the Pantheism of Force sounds unreal and unsound, compared with the sensible remarks upon the same subject by Dr. Badger,[2] who sees the abstruseness of the doctrine and does not care to include it in hard and fast lines or to subject it to mere logical analysis. Upon the subject of "predestination" Mr. Palgrave quotes, not from the Koran, but from the Ahádís or Traditional Sayings of the Apostle; what importance, however, attaches to a legend in the Mischnah, or Oral Law, of the Hebrews utterly ignored by the Written Law? He joins the many in complaining that even the mention of "the love of God" is absent from Mohammed's theology, burking the fact that it never occurs in the Jewish scriptures, and that the genius of Arabic, like Hebrew, does not admit the expression: worse still; he keeps from his reader such Koranic passages as, to quote no other, "Allah loveth you and will forgive your sins" (iii. 29). He pities Allah for having "no son, companion or counsellor" and, of course, he must equally commiserate Jehovah. Finally

---

[1] But how could the Arabist write such hideous grammar as "La Ilāh illa Allāh" for Lá iláha (accus.) ill' Allah?

[2] p. 996 "Muhammad" in vol. iii. Dictionary of Christian Biography. See also the Illustration of the Mohammedan Creed, etc. from Al-Ghazáli introduced (pp. 72—77) into Bell and Sons' "History of the Saracens" by Simon Ockley, B.D. (London, 1878). I regret that some Orientalist did not correct the proofs: everybody will not detect "Al-Lauh al-Mahfúz" (the Guarded Tablet) in "Allauh ho'hnehphoud" (p. 171); and this but a pinch out of a camel-load.

his views of the lifelessness of Al-Islam are directly opposed to the opinions of Dr. Leitner and the experience of all who have lived in Moslem lands. Such are the ingenious but not ingenuous distortions of fact, the fine instances of the pathetic fallacy, and the noteworthy illustrations of the falsehood of extremes, which have engendered "Mohammedanism a Relapse: the worst form of Monotheism,"[1] and which have been eagerly seized upon and further deformed by the authors of popular books, that is, volumes written by those who know little for those who know less.

In Al-Rashid's day a mighty change had passed over the primitive simplicity of Al-Islam, the change to which faiths and creeds, like races and empires and all things sublunary, are subject. The proximity of Persia and the close intercourse with the Græco-Romans had polished and greatly modified the physiognomy of the rugged old belief: all manner of metaphysical subtleties had cropped up, with the usual disintegrating effect, and some of these threatened even the unity of the Godhead. Musaylimah, Al-Aswad and Aywalah bin Ka'b had left traces of their handiwork; whilst Karmat was about to preach and the Mutazilites (separatists or secessors) actively propagated their doctrine of a created and temporal Koran. The Khárijí or Ibázi, who rejects and reviles Abú Turáb (Caliph Ali), contended passionately with the Shí'ah who reviles and rejects the other three "Successors;" and these sectarians, favoured by the learned, and by the Abba-

---

[1] The word should have been Arianism. This "heresy" of the early Christians was much aided by the "Discipline of the Secret," supposed to be of apostolic origin, which concealed from neophytes, catechumens and penitents all the higher mysteries, like the Trinity, the Incarnation, the Metastoicheiosis (transubstantiation), the Real Presence, the Eucharist and the Seven Sacraments; when Arnobius could ask, Quid Deo cum vino est? and when Justin, fearing the charge of Polytheism, could expressly declare the inferior nature of the Son to the Father. Hence the creed was appropriately called Symbol, *i.e.*, Sign of the Secret. This "mental reservation" lasted till the Edict of Toleration, issued by Constantine in the fourth century, held Christianity secure when divulging her "mysteries"; and it allowed Arianism to become *the* popular creed.

sides in their jealous hatred of the Ommiades, went to the extreme length of the Ali-Iláhi—the God-makers of Ali—whilst the Dahrí and the Zindík, the Mundanist and the Agnostic, proposed to sweep away the whole edifice. The neo-Platonism and Gnosticism, which had not essentially affected Christendom,[1] found in Al-Islam a rich fallow and gained strength and luxuriance by the solid materialism and stolid conservatism of its basis. Such were a few of the distracting and resolving influences which Time had brought to bear upon the True Believer, and which, after some half a dozen generations, had separated the several schisms by a wider breach than that which yawns between Orthodox Romanist and Lutheran. Nor was this scandal in Al-Islam abated until the Tartar sword applied to it the sharpest remedy.

## B.—Woman.

The next point I propose to consider is the position of womanhood in The Nights, so curiously at variance with the stock ideas concerning the Moslem home and domestic polity still prevalent, not only in England but throughout Europe. Many readers of these volumes have remarked to me with much astonishment that they find the female characters more remarkable for decision, action and manliness than the male; and are wonderstruck by their masterful attitude and by the supreme influence they exercise upon public and private life. I have glanced at the subject of the sex in Al-Islam to such an extent throughout my notes that little remains here to be added. Women, all the world over, are what men make them; and the main charm of Amazonian fiction is to see how they

---

[1] The Gnostics played rather a fantastic rôle in Chistianity with their Demiurge, their Æonogony, their Æons by syzygies or couples, their Maio and Sabscho and their beatified bride of Jesus, Sophia Achamoth; and some of them descended to absolute absurdities, *e.g.* the Tascodrugitæ and the Pattalorhinchitæ who during prayers placed their fingers upon their noses or in their mouths, &c., reading literally Psalm cxli. 3.

live and move and have their being without aid masculine. But it is the old ever-new fable

> "Who drew the lion vanquished? 'Twas a man!"

The books of the Ancients, written in that stage of civilisation when the sexes are at civil war, make women even more than in real life the creatures of their masters: hence from the dawn of literature to the present day the sex has been the subject of disappointed abuse and eulogy almost as unmerited. Ecclesiastes, perhaps the strangest specimen of an "inspired volume" the world has yet produced, boldly declares "One (upright) man among a thousand I have found; but a woman among all have I not found" (vol. vii. 28), thus confirming the pessimism of Petronius:—

> Femina nulla bona est, et si bona contigit ulla,
> Nescio quo fato res mala facta bona est.

In the Psalms again (xxx. 15) we have the old sneer at the three insatiables, Hell, Earth and the Feminine; and Rabbinical learning has embroidered these and other texts, producing a truly hideous caricature. A Hadis attributed to Mohammed runs, "They (women) lack wits and faith. When Eve was created Satan rejoiced saying:—Thou art half of my host, the trustee of my secret and my shaft wherewith I shoot and miss not!" Another tells us, "I stood at the gate of Heaven, and lo! most of its inmates were poor, and I stood at the gate of Hell, and lo! most of its inmates were women."[1] "Take care of the glass-phials!" cried the Prophet to a camel-guide singing with a sweet voice. Yet the Meccan apostle made, as has been seen, his own household produce two perfections. The blatant popular voice follows with such "dictes" as, "Women are made of nectar and poison;" "Women have long hair and short wits," and so forth. Nor are the Hindus behindhand. Woman has fickleness implanted in

---

[1] "Kitáb al-'Unwán fi Makáid al-Niswán" = The Book of the Beginnings on the Wiles of Womankind (Lane i. 38.)

her by Nature like the flashings of lightning (Kathá, ss. i. 147); she is valueless as a straw to the heroic mind (169); she is hard as adamant in sin and soft as flour in fear (170); and, like the fly, she quits camphor to settle on compost (ii. 17). "What dependence is there in the crowing of a hen?" (women's opinions) says the Hindi proverb: also "A virgin with grey hairs!" (*i.e.* a monster), and "Wherever wendeth a fairy face a devil wendeth with her." The same superficial view of holding woman to be lesser (and very inferior) man is taken generally by the classics; and Euripides distinguished himself by misogyny, although he drew the beautiful character of Alcestis. Simonides, more merciful than Ecclesiastes, after naming swine-women, dog-women, cat-women, etc., ends the decade with the admirable bee-woman thus making ten per cent. honest. In mediæval or Germanic Europe the doctrine of the Virgin mother gave the sex a status unknown to the ancients except in Egypt, where Isis was the help-mate and completion of Osiris, in modern parlance "The Woman clothed with the Sun." The kindly and courtly Palmerin of England, in whose pages "gentlemen may find their choice of sweet inventions and gentlewomen be satisfied with courtly expectations," suddenly blurts out, "But in truth women are never satisfied by reason, being governed by accident or appetite" (chapt. xlix).

The Nights, as might be expected from the emotional East, exaggerate these views. Women are mostly "Sectaries of the god Wünsch;" beings of impulse, blown about by every gust of passion; stable only in instability; constant only in inconstancy. The false ascetic, the perfidious and murderous crone and the old hag-go-between who misleads like Umm Kulsum,[1] for mere pleasure, are drawn with an experienced and loving

---

[1] This person was one of the Amsál or Exempla of Arabian history, and she lived a life of peculiar infamy. These proverbial models will be found quoted and explained by those who care to study the subject in the Arabum Proverbia, *Arabice et Latine*, Commentarii illustravit Freytag, 3 vols. Bonnæ, 1831-43.

hand. Yet not the less do we meet with examples of the dutiful daughter, the model lover matronly in her affection, the devoted wife, the perfect mother, the saintly devotee, the learned preacher, Univira the chaste widow and the self-sacrificing heroic woman. If we find (vol. iii. 216) the sex described as—

> An offal cast by kites where'er they list,

and the studied insults of sundry tales, we also come upon admirable sketches of conjugal happiness; and, to mention no other, Shahryar's attestation to Shahrazad's excellence in the last charming pages of The Nights. And modern Moslem feeling upon the subject has apparently undergone a change. Ashraf Khan, the Afghan poet, sings,

> Since I, the parted one, have come the secrets of the world to ken,
> Women in hosts therein I find, but few (and very few) of men.

And the Osmanli proverb is, "Of ten men nine are women!"

It is the same with the Kathá, whose praise and dispraise are equally enthusiastic; *e.g.* "Women of good family are guarded by their own virtue, the sole efficient chamberlain; but the Lord himself can hardly guard the vicious. Who can stem a furious stream and a frantic woman?" (i. 328). "Excessive love in woman is your only hero for daring" (i. 339). "Thus fair ones, naturally feeble, bring about a series of evil actions which engender discontent and aversion to the world; but here and there you will find a virtuous woman who adorneth a glorious house as the streak of the moon arrayeth the breadth of the Heavens" (i. 346.) "So you see, King, honourable matrons are devoted to their husbands and 'tis not the case that women are always bad" (ii. 624). And there is true wisdom in that even balance of feminine qualities advocated by our Hindu-Hindi class-book the Toti-námeh or Parrot volume. The perfect woman has seven requisites. She must not always be merry (1) nor sad (2); she must not always be talking (3) nor silently musing (4); she must not always be adorning herself (5) nor neglecting her person (6); and (7) at all times she must be moderate and self-possessed.

The legal status of womankind in Al-Islam is exceptionally high, a fact of which Europe has often been assured, although the truth has not even yet penetrated into the popular brain. Nearly a century ago one Mirza Abú Tálib Khán, an Amildár or revenue collector, after living two years in London, wrote an "apology" for, or rather a vindication of, his Indian countrywomen which is still worth reading and quoting.[1] Nations are but superficial judges of one another: where customs differ they often remark only the salient distinctive points which, when examined, prove to be of minor importance. Europeans seeing and hearing that women in the East are "cloistered" as the Grecian matron was wont ἔνδον μένειν and οἰκουρεῖν; that wives may not walk out with their husbands and cannot accompany them to "balls and parties;" moreover, that they are always liable, like the ancient Hebrew, to the mortification of the "sister-wife," have most ignorantly determined that they are mere serviles and that their lives are not worth living. Indeed, a learned lady, Miss Martineau, once visiting a Harem went into ecstasies of pity and sorrow because the poor things knew nothing of—say trigonometry and the use of the globes. Sonnini thought otherwise, and my experience, like that of all old dwellers in the East, is directly opposed to this conclusion.

I have noted (Night cmlxii.) that Mohammed, in the fifth year of his reign[2], after his ill-advised and scandalous mar-

---

[1] His Persian paper "On the Vindication of the Liberties of the Asiatic Women" was translated and printed in the Asiatic Annual Register for 1801 (pp. 100-107); it is quoted by Dr. Jon. Scott (Introd. vol. i. p. xxxiv. *et seq.*) and by a host of writers. He also wrote a book of Travels translated by Prof. Charles Stewart in 1810 and re-issued (3 vols. 8vo.) in 1814.

[2] The beginning of which I date from the Hijrah, lit. = the separation, popularly "The Flight." Stating the case broadly, it has become the practice of modern writers to look upon Mohammed as an honest enthusiast at Meccah and an unscrupulous despot at Al-Medinah, a view which appears to me eminently unsound and unfair. In a private station the Meccan Prophet was famed as good citizen, *teste* his title Al-Amín = the Trusty. But when driven from his home by the pagan faction, he became de facto as de jure a king: nay a royal pontiff; and the preacher was merged in the Conqueror of his foes and the Commander of the Faithful.

riage[1] with his foster-daughter Zaynab, established the Hijáb or veiling of women: probably an exaggeration of local usage, a modified separation of the sexes, which extended and still extends even to the Badawi; it must long have been customary in Arabian cities, and its object was to deliver the sexes from temptation, as the Koran says (xxxii. 32), "Purer will this (practice) be for your hearts and their hearts."[2] The women, who all the world over delight in restrictions which tend to their honour, accepted it willingly and still affect it; they do not desire a liberty or rather a licence which they have learned to regard as inconsistent with their time-honoured notions of feminine decorum and delicacy, and they would think very meanly of a husband who permitted them to be exposed, like hetairæ, to the public gaze.[3] As Zubayr Pasha, exiled to Gibraltar for another's treason, said to my friend General Buckle, after visiting quarters evidently laid out by a jealous husband, "We Arabs think that when a man has a precious jewel, 'tis wiser to lock it up in a box than to leave it about for anyone to take." The Eastern adopts the instinctive, the Western prefers the rational method. The former jealously guards his treasure, surrounds it with all precautions, fends

---

[1] It was not, however, "incestuous:" the scandal came from its ignoring the Arab "pundonor."

[2] The "opportunism" of Mohammed has been made a matter of obloquy by many who have not reflected and discovered that time-serving is the very essence of "Revelation." Says the Rev. W. Smith ("Pentateuch" chapt. xiii.), "As the journey (Exodus) proceeds, so laws originate from the accidents of the way," and he applies this to successive decrees (Numbers xxvi. 32—36; xxvii. 8—11 and xxxvi. 1—9) holding it indirect internal evidence of Mosaic authorship (?) Another tone, however, is used in the case of Al-Islam. "And now, that he might not stand in awe of his wives any longer, *down comes a revelation*," says Ockley in his bluff and homely style, which admits such phrases as, "the impostor has the impudence to say." But why, in common honesty, refuse to the Koran the concessions freely made to the Torah? It is a mere petitio principii to argue that the latter is "inspired" while the former is not; moreover, although we may be called upon to believe things *beyond* Reason, it is hardly fair to require our behalf in things *contrary* to Reason.

[3] This is noticed in my wife's volume on The Inner Life of Syria, chapt. xii. vol. i. 155.

off from it all risks, and if the treasure go astray, kills it. The latter, after placing it *en evidence* upon an eminence in ball dress with back and bosom bared to the gaze of society, a bundle of charms exposed to every possible seduction, allows it to take its own way, and if it be misled, he kills or tries to kill the misleader. It is a fiery trial; and the few who safely pass through it may claim a higher standpoint in the moral world than those who have never been sorely tried. But the crucial question is whether Christian Europe has done wisely in offering such temptations.

The second and main objection to Moslem custom is the marriage-system which begins with a girl being wedded to a man whom she knows only by hearsay. This was the habit of our forbears not many generations ago, and it still prevails amongst noble houses in Southern Europe, where a lengthened study of it leaves me doubtful whether the "love-marriage," as it is called, or wedlock with an utter stranger, evidently the two extremes, is likely to prove the happier. The "sister-wife" is or would be a sore trial to monogamic races like those of Northern Europe, where Caia, all but the equal of Caius in most points, mental and physical, and superior in some, not unfrequently proves herself the "man of the family," the "only man in the boat." But in the East, where the sex is far more delicate, where a girl is brought up in polygamy, where religious reasons separate her from her husband during pregnancy and lactation; and where often enough, like the Mormon damsel, she would hesitate to "nigger it with a one-wife-man," the case assumes a very different aspect and the load, if burden it be, falls comparatively light. Lastly, the "patriarchal household" is mostly confined to the grandee and the richard, whilst Holy Law and public opinion, neither of which can openly be disregarded, assign command of the household to the *equal* or first wife and jealously guard the rights and privileges of the others.

Mirza Abu Talib, "the Persian Prince,"[1] offers six reasons why "the liberty of the Asiatic women appears less than that of the Europeans," ending with,

> I'll fondly place on either eye
> The man that can to this reply.

He then lays down eight points in which the Moslem wife has greatly the advantage over her Christian sisterhood; and we may take his first as a specimen. Custom, not contrary to law, invests the Mohammedan mother with despotic government of the homestead, slaves, servants and children, especially the latter: she alone directs their early education, their choice of faith, their marriage and their establishment in life; and in case of divorce she takes the daughters, the sons going to the sire. She has also liberty to leave her home, not only for one or two nights, but for a week or a fortnight, without consulting her husband; and whilst she visits a strange household, the master and all males above fifteen are forbidden the Harem. But the main point in favour of the Moslem wife is her being a "legal sharer": inheritance is secured to her by Koranic law: she must be dowered by the bridegroom to legalise marriage and all she gains is secured to her; whereas in England a "Married Woman's Property Act" was completed only in 1882 after many centuries of the grossest abuses.

---

[1] Mirza preceding the name means Mister and following it Prince. Addison's "Vision of Mirza" (Spectator, No. 159), is therefore "The Vision of Mister."

## § V.

## ON THE PROSE-RHYME AND THE POETRY OF THE NIGHTS.

### A.—THE SAJ'A.

ACCORDING to promise in my Foreword (p. xiv.), I here proceed to offer a few observations concerning the Saj'a or rhymed prose, and the Sh'ir or measured sentence, that is, the verse of The Nights. The former has in composition, metrical or unmetrical, three distinct forms. Saj'a mutawázi (parallel), the most common, is when the ending words of sentences agree in measure, assonance and final letter, in fact our full rhyme; next is Saj'a mutarraf (the affluent), when the periods, hemistichs or couplets end in words whose terminal letters correspond, although differing in measure and number; and thirdly, Saj'a muwázanah (equilibrium) is applied to the balance which affects words corresponding in measure but differing in final letters.[1]

Al Saj'a, the fine style or style fleuri, also termed Al-Badí'a, or euphuism, is the basis of all Arabic euphony. The whole of the Koran is written in it; and the same is the case with the Makámát of Al-Hariri and the prime master-pieces of rhetorical composition: without it no translation of the Holy Book can be satisfactory or final; and where it is not, the Assemblies become the prose of prose. Thus universally used the assonance has necessarily been abused, and its excess has given rise to the saying "Al-Saj'a faj'a"—prose rhyme 's a pest. English translators have, unwisely I think, agreed in rejecting it, while Germans have not. Mr. Preston assures us that "rhyming

---

[1] For detailed examples and specimens see p. 10 of Gladwin's "Dissertations on Rhetoric," etc., Calcutta, 1801.

prose is extremely ungraceful in English and introduces an air of flippancy:" this was certainly not the case with Friedrich Rückert's version of the great original, and I see no reason why it should be so or become so in our tongue. Torrens (Pref. p. vii.) declares that "the effect of the irregular sentence with the iteration of a jingling rhyme is not pleasant in our language:" he therefore systematically neglects it and gives his style the semblance of being "scamped" with the object of saving study and trouble. Mr. Payne (ix. 379) deems it an "excrescence born of the excessive facilities for rhyme afforded by the language," and of Eastern delight in antithesis of all kinds, whether of sound or of thought; and, aiming elaborately at grace of style, he omits it wholly, even in the proverbs.

The weight of authority was against me but my plan compelled me to disregard it. The dilemma was simply either to use the Saj'a or to follow Mr. Payne's method and "arrange the disjecta membra of the original in their natural order;" that is to remodel the text. Intending to produce a faithful copy of the Arabic, I was compelled to adopt the former and still hold it to be the better alternative. Moreover I question Mr. Payne's dictum (ix. 383) that "the Seja-form is utterly foreign to the genius of English prose, and that its preservation would be fatal to all vigour and harmony of style." The English translator of Palmerin of England, Anthony Munday, attempted it in places with great success as I have before noted; and my late friend Edward Eastwick made artistic use of it in his Gulistan. Had I rejected the "Cadence of the cooing-dove" because un-English, I should have adopted the balanced periods of the Anglican marriage service[1] or the

[1] For instance: I, M. | take thee N. | to my wedded wife, | to have and to hold | from this day forward, | for better for worse, | for richer for poorer, | in sickness and in health, | to love and to cherish, | till death do us part, etc. Here it becomes mere blank verse which is, of course, a defect in prose style. In that delightful old French the Saj'a frequently appeared when attention was solicited for the titles of books: *e.g.* Le Romant de la Rose, où tout l'art d'amours est enclose.

essentially English system of alliteration, requiring some such artful aid to distinguish from the vulgar recitative style the elevated and classical tirades in The Nights. My attempt has found with reviewers more favour than I expected; and a kindly critic writes of it, "These melodious fragments, these little eddies of song set like gems in the prose, have a charming effect on the ear. They come as dulcet surprises and mostly recur in highly-wrought situations, or they are used to convey a vivid sense of something exquisite in nature or art. Their introduction seems due to whim or caprice, but really it arises from a profound study of the situation, as if the Tale-teller felt suddenly compelled to break into the rhythmic strain."

## B.—The Verse.

The Shi'r or metrical part of The Nights is considerable, amounting to not less than ten thousand lines, and these I could not but render in rhyme or rather in monorhyme. This portion has been a bugbear to translators. De Sacy noticed the difficulty of the task (p. 283). Lane held the poetry untranslatable because abounding in the figure Tajnís, our paronomasia or paragram, of which there are seven distinct varieties,[1] not to speak of other rhetorical flourishes. He therefore omitted the greater part of the verse as tedious, and, through the loss of measure and rhyme, "generally intolerable to the reader." He proved his position by the bald literalism of the passages which he rendered in truly prosaic prose and succeeded in changing the facies and presentment of the work. For the Shi'r, like the Saj'a, is not introduced arbitrarily; and its unequal distribution throughout The Nights may be accounted for by rule of art. Some tales, like Omar bin al Nu'uman and Tawaddud, contain very little because the theme is historical or realistic; whilst in stories of love and courtship,

---

[1] See Gladwin loc. cit. p. 8: Tajnís also is = alliteration (Ibn Khall. ii. 316).

as that of Rose-in-hood, the proportion may rise to one-fifth of the whole. And this is true to nature. Love, as Addison said, makes even the mechanic (the British mechanic!) poetical, and Joe Hume of material memory once fought a duel about a fair object of dispute.

Before discussing the verse of The Nights it may be advisable to enlarge a little upon the prosody of the Arabs. We know nothing of the origin of their poetry, which is lost in the depths of antiquity, and the oldest bards of whom we have any remains belong to the famous epoch of the war Al-Basús, which would place them about A.D. 500. Moreover, when the Muse of Arabia first shows, she is not only fully developed and mature, she has lost all her first youth, her beauté du diable, and she is assuming the characteristics of an age beyond "middle age." No one can study the earliest poetry without perceiving that it results from the cultivation of centuries and that it has already assumed that artificial type and conventional process of treatment which presages inevitable decay. Its noblest period is included in the century preceding the Apostolate of Mohammed, and the oldest of that epoch is the prince of Arab songsters, Imr al-Kays, "The Wandering King." The Christian Fathers characteristically termed poetry Vinum Dæmonorum. The stricter Moslems called their bards "enemies of Allah;" and when the Prophet, who hated verse and could not even quote it correctly, was asked who was the best poet of the Peninsula he answered that the "Man of Al-Kays," *i.e.* the worshipper of the Lampsacus-idol, would usher them all into Hell. Here he only echoed the general verdict of his countrymen who loved poetry, and, as a rule, despised poets. The earliest complete pieces of any volume and substance saved from the wreck of old Arabic literature and familiar in our day are the seven Kasídahs (purpose-odes or tendence-elegies) which are popularly known as the Gilded or the Suspended Poems; and in all of these we find, with an elaboration of material and formal art which can go no further, a subject-matter of trite imagery and stock ideas which suggest a long ascending line of model ancestors and predecessors.

Scholars are agreed upon the fact that many of the earliest and best Arab poets were, as Mohammed boasted himself, unalphabetic[1] or rather could neither read nor write. They addressed the ear and the mind, not the eye. They "spoke verse," learning it by rote and dictating it to the Ráwi, and this reciter again transmitted it to the musician whose pipe or zither accompanied the minstrel's song. In fact the general practice of writing began only at the end of the first century after The Flight.

The rude and primitive measure of Arab song, upon which the most complicated system of metres subsequently arose, was called Al-Rajaz, literally "the trembling," because it reminded the highly imaginative hearer of a pregnant she-camel's weak and tottering steps. This was the carol of the camel-driver, the lover's lay and the warrior's chaunt of the heroic ages; and its simple, unconstrained flow adapted it well for extempore effusions. Its merits and demerits have been extensively discussed amongst Arab grammarians, and many, noticing that it was not originally divided into hemistichs, make an essential difference between the Shá'ir who speaks poetry and the Rájiz who speaks Rajaz. It consisted, to describe it technically, of iambic dipodia (⏑ - ⏑ -), the first three syllables being optionally long or short. It can generally be read like our iambs and, being familiar, is pleasant to the English ear. The dipodia are repeated either twice or thrice; in the former

[1] He called himself "Nabiyun ummí" = illiterate prophet; but only his most ignorant followers believe that he was unable to read and write. His last words, accepted by all traditionists, were "Aatíní dawáta wa kalam" (bring me ink-case and pen); upon which the Shi'ah or Persian sectaries base, not without probability, a theory that Mohammed intended to write down the name of Ali as his Caliph or successor, when Omar, suspecting the intention, exclaimed, "The Prophet is delirious; have we not the Koran?" thus impiously preventing the precaution. However that may be, the legend proves that Mohammed could read and write even when not "under inspiration." The vulgar idea would arise from a pious intent to add miracle to the miraculous style of the Koran.

case Rajaz is held by some authorities, as Al-Akhfash (Sa'íd ibn Másadah), to be mere prose. Although Labíd and Antar composed in iambics, the first Kásídah or regular poem in Rajaz was by Al-Aghlab al-Ajibi, temp. Mohammed: the Alfíyah-grammar of Ibn Málik is in Rajaz Muzdawij, the hemistichs rhyming and the assonance being confined to the couplet. Al-Hariri also affects Rajaz in the third and fifth Assemblies. So far Arabic metre is true to Nature: in impassioned speech the movement of language is iambic: we say, "I *will*, I *will*," not "I will."

For many generations the Sons of the Desert were satisfied with Nature's teaching; the fine perceptions and the nicely trained ear of the bard needing no aid from art. But in time came the inevitable prosodist under the formidable name of Abu Abd al-Rahmán al-Khalíl, i. Ahmad, i. Amrú, i. Tamím al-Faráhidi (of the Faráhid sept), al-Azdi (of the Azd clan), al-Yahmadi (of the Yahmad tribe), popularly known as Al-Khalíl ibn Ahmad al-Basri of Bassorah, where he died æt. 68, scanning verses they say, in A.H. 170 (= 786—87). Ibn Khallikán relates (i. 493) on the authority of Hamzah al-Isfaháni how this "father of Arabic grammar and discoverer of the rules of prosody" invented the science as he walked past a coppersmith's shop on hearing the strokes of a hammer upon a metal basin: "two objects devoid of any quality which could serve as a proof and an illustration of anything else than their own form and shape and incapable of leading to any other knowledge than that of their own nature."[1] According to others

---

[1] I cannot but vehemently suspect that this legend was bodily taken from much older traditions. We have Jubal the semi-mythical, who, "by the different falls of his hammer on the anvil, discovered by the ear the first rude music that pleased the antediluvian fathers." Then came Pythagoras, of whom Macrobius (lib. ii.) relates how this Græco-Egyptian philosopher, passing by a smithy, observed that the sounds were grave or acute according to the weights of the hammers; and he ascertained by experiment that such was the case when different weights were hung by strings of the same size. The next discovery was that two strings of the same substance and tension, the one being double the length of the other, gave the diapason-interval or an eighth; and the same was effected from two strings

he was passing through the Fullers' Bazar at Basrah when his ear was struck by the Dak-dak (دق دق) and the Dakak-dakak (دقق دقق) of the workmen. In these two onomapoetics we trace the expression which characterises the Arab tongue: all syllables are composed of consonant and vowel, the latter long or short as Bā and Bă; or of a vowelled consonant followed by a consonant as Bal, Bau (بو).

The grammarian, true to the traditions of his craft, which looks for all poetry to the Badawi,[1] adopted for metrical details the language of the Desert. The distich, which amongst Arabs is looked upon as one line, he named "Bayt," nighting-place, tent or house; and the hemistich Misrá'ah, the one leaf of a folding door. To this "scenic" simile all the parts of the verse were more or less adapted. The metres, our feet, were called "Arkán," the stakes and stays of the tent; the syllables were "Usúl" or roots divided into three kinds: the first or "Sabab" (the tent-rope) is composed of two letters, a vowelled and a quiescent consonant, as "Lam."[2] The "Watad" or tent-peg of three letters is of two varieties; the Majmú', or united, a foot (iamb) in which the two first consonants are moved by vowels and the last is jazmated or made quiescent by apocope as "Lakad" (trochee); and the Mafrúk, or disunited, when the two moved consonants are separated by one jazmated, as "Kabla". And lastly the "Fásilah" or intervening space, applied to the main pole of the tent, consists of four letters (anapæst).

The metres were called Buhúr or "seas" (plur. of Bahr),

---

of similar length and size, the one having four times the tension of the other. Belonging to the same cycle of invention-anecdotes are Galileo's discovery of the pendulum by the lustre of the Pisan Duomo; and the kettle-lid, the falling apple and the copper hook which inspired Watt, Newton and Galvani.

[1] To what an absurd point this has been carried we may learn from Ibn Khallikán (i. 114). A poet addressing a single individual does not say "My friend!" or "My friends!" but "My two friends!" (in the dual) *because* a Badawi required a pair of companions, one to tend the sheep and the other to pasture the camels.

[2] For further details concerning the Sabab, Watad and Fasilah, see at the end of this Essay the learned remarks of Dr. Steingass.

also meaning the space within the tent-walls, the equivoque alluding to pearls and other treasures of the deep. Al-Khalil the systematiser, found in general use only five Dáirah (circles, classes or groups of metre); and he characterised the harmonious and stately measures, all built upon the original Rajaz, as Al-Tawíl (the long),[1] Al-Kámil (the complete), Al-Wáfir (the copious), Al-Basít (the extended) and Al-Khafíf (the light).[2] These embrace all the Mu'allakát and the Hamásah, the great Anthology of Abú Tammám; but the crave for variety and the extension of foreign intercourse had multiplied wants, and Al-Khalil deduced, from the original five Dáirah, fifteen, to which Al-Akhfash (ob. A.D. 830) added a sixteenth, Al-Khabab. The Persians extended the number to nineteen. The first four were peculiarly Arab; the fourteenth, the fifteenth and seventeenth peculiarly Persian, and all the rest were Arab and Persian.[3]

Arabic metre so far resembles that of Greece and Rome that the value of syllables depends upon the "quantity" or position of their consonants, not upon accent as in English and the Neo-Latin tongues. Al-Khalil was doubtless familiar with the classic prosody of Europe, but he rejected it as unsuited to the genius of Arabic and like a true Eastern Gelehrte he adopted a process devised by himself. Instead of scansion by pyrrhics and spondees, iambs and trochees, anapæsts and similar simplifications he invented a system of weights ("wuzún"). Of these there are nine[4] memorial words used as quantitive signs, all built upon

---

[1] *e.g.* the Mu'allakáts of "Amriolkais," Tarafah and Zuhayr compared by Mr. Lyall (Introduction to Translations) with the metre of Abt Vogler, *e.g.*

Ye know why the forms are fair, ye hear how the tale is told.

[2] *e.g.* the Poem of Hareth, which often echoes the hexameter.

[3] Gladwin, p. 80.

[4] Gladwin (p. 77) gives only eight, omitting Fă'ŭl, which he or his author probably considers the Muzáhaf, imperfect or apocopêd form of Fă'ŭlŭn, as Măfă'il of Măfă'īlŭn. For the infinite complications of Arabic prosody the Khafíf (soft breathing) and Sahíh (hard breathing); the Sadr and Arúz (first and

the root "fa'l" which has rendered such notable service to Arabic and Hebrew[1] grammar and varying from the simple "fa'ál," in Persian "fa'úl," (⏑ -) to the complicated "Mutafá'ilun"(⏑⏑ - ⏑ -), anapæst + iamb. Thus the prosodist would scan the Shahnámeh of Firdausi as

Fa'úlun, fa'úlun, fa'úlun, fa'úl.
⏑ - - ⏑ - - ⏑ - - ⏑ -

These weights also show another peculiarity of Arabic verse. In English we have few if any spondees: the Arabic contains about three longs to one short; hence its gravity, stateliness and dignity. But these longs again are peculiar, and sometimes strike the European ear as shorts, thus adding a difficulty for those who would represent Oriental metres by western feet, ictus and accent. German Arabists can register an occasional success in such attempts: Englishmen none. My late friend Professor Palmer of Cambridge tried the tour de force of dancing on one leg instead of two and notably failed: Mr. Lyall also strove to imitate Arabic metre and produced only prose bewitched.[2] Mr. Payne appears to me to have wasted trouble in "observing the exterior form of the stanza, the movement of the rhyme and (as far as possible) the identity in number of the syllables composing the beits." There is only one part of his admirable

---

last feet), the Ibtidá and Zarb (last foot of every line); the Hashw (cushion-stuffing) or body-part of verse; the 'Amúd al-Kasídah or Al-Musammaț (the strong) and other details I must refer readers to such specialists as Freytag and Sam. Clarke (Prosodia Arabica), and to Dr. Steingass's notes infra.

[1] The Hebrew grammarians of the Middle Ages wisely copied their Arab cousins by turning Fa'la into Pael and so forth.

[2] Mr. Lyall, whose "Ancient Arabic Poetry" (Williams and Norgate, 1885) I reviewed in *The Academy* of Oct. 3, '85, did the absolute reverse of what is required: he preserved the metre and sacrificed the rhyme even when it naturally suggested itself. For instance, in the last four lines of No. xli. what would be easier than to write,

Ah sweet and soft wi' thee her ways: bethink thee well! The day shall be
When someone favoured as thyself shall find her fair and fain and free;
And if she swear that parting ne'er shall break her word of constancy,
When did rose-tinted finger-tip with pacts and pledges e'er agree?

version concerning which I have heard competent readers complain; and that is the metrical, because here and there it sounds strange to their ears.

I have already stated my conviction that there are two and only two ways of translating Arabic poetry into English. One is to represent it by good heroic or lyric verse as did Sir William Jones; the other is to render it after French fashion, by measured and balanced Prose, the little sister of Poetry. It is thus and thus only that we can preserve the peculiar *cachet* of the original. This old-world Oriental song is spirit-stirring as a "blast of that dread horn," albeit the words be thin. It is heady as the "Golden Wine" of Libanus, to the tongue water, and brandy to the brain—the clean contrary of our nineteenth century effusions. Technically speaking, it can be vehicled only by the verse of the old English ballad or by the prose of the Book of Job. And Badawi poetry is a perfect expositor of Badawi life, especially in the good and gladsome old Pagan days ere Al-Islam, like the creed which it abolished, overcast the minds of men with its dull grey pall of realistic superstition. They combined to form a marvellous picture—those contrasts of splendour and squalor amongst the sons of the sand. Under airs pure as æther, golden and ultramarine above and melting over the horizon into a diaphanous green which suggested a reflection of Kaf, that unseen mountain-wall of emerald, the so-called Desert changed face twice a year; now brown and dry as summer-dust; then green as Hope, beautified with infinite verdure and broad sheetings of rain-water. The vernal and autumnal shiftings of camp, disruptions of homesteads and partings of kith and kin, friends and lovers, made the life many-sided as it was vigorous and noble, the outcome of hardy frames, strong minds and spirits breathing the very essence of liberty and independence. The day began with the dawn-drink, "generous wine bought with shining ore," poured into the crystal goblet from the leather bottle swinging before the cooling breeze. The rest was spent in the practice of weapons; in the favourite arrow-game known as Al-Maysar, gambling which at least had the merit of feeding the poor; in racing for which the Badawin had a mania, and in the chase, the foray and the fray which formed the serious business of his life. And how picturesque the hunting scenes; the greyhound, like the mare, of purest blood; the falcon cast at francolin and coney; the gazelle standing at gaze; the desert ass scudding over the ground-waves; the wild cows or bovine antelopes browsing with their calves and the ostrich-chickens flocking round the parent bird! The Musámarah or night-talk round the camp-fire was enlivened by the lute-girl and the gleeman, whom the austere Prophet described as "roving distraught in every vale" and whose motto in Horatian vein was, "To-day we shall drink, to-morrow be sober; wine this day, that day work." Regularly once a year, during the three peaceful months when war and even blood revenge were held sacrilegious, the tribes met at Ukádh (Ocaz) and other fairsteads, where they held high festival and the bards strave in song and prided themselves upon doing honour to women and to the successful warriors of their tribe. Brief, the object of Arab life was to *be*—to be free, to be brave, to be wise; while the endeavours of other peoples was and is to *have*—to have wealth, to have knowledge, to have a name; and while moderns make their "epitome of life" to be, to do and to *suffer*. Lastly the Arab's end was honourable as his life was stirring: few Badawin had the crowning misfortune of dying "the straw-death."

The poetical forms in The Nights are as follows:—The Misrá'ah or hemistich is half the "Bayt" which, for want of a better word I have rendered couplet: this, however, though formally separated in MSS. is looked upon as one line, one verse; hence a word can be divided, the former part pertaining to the first and the latter to the second moiety of the distich. As the Arabs ignore blank verse, when we come upon a rhymeless couplet we know that it is an extract from a longer composition in monorhyme. The Kit'ah is a fragment, either an occasional piece or more frequently a portion of a Ghazal (ode) or Kasídah (elegy), other than the Matlá, the initial Bayt with rhyming distichs. The Ghazal and Kasídah differ mainly in length: the former is popularly limited to eighteen couplets: the latter begins at fifteen and is of indefinite number. Both are built upon monorhyme, which appears twice in the first couplet and ends all the others, *e.g.* aa + ba + ca, etc.; nor may the same assonance be repeated, unless at least seven couplets intervene. In the best poets, as in the old classic verse of France, the sense must be completed in one couplet and not run on to a second; and, as the parts cohere very loosely, separate quotation can generally be made without injuring their proper effect. A favourite form is the Rubá'í or quatrain, made familiar to English ears by Mr. Fitzgerald's masterly adaptation of Omar-i-Khayyám: the movement is generally aa + ba; but it also appears as ab + cb, in which case it is a Kit'ah or fragment. The Murabbá tetrastichs, or four-fold song, occurs once only in The Nights (vol. i. 89, 90); it is a succession of double Bayts or of four-lined stanzas rhyming aa + bc + dc + ec: in strict form the first three hemistichs rhyme with one another only, independently of the rest of the poem, and the fourth with that of every other stanza, *e.g.* aa + ab + cb + db. The Mukhammas, cinquains or pentastichs (Night cmlxiv.), represent a stanza of two distichs and a hemistich in monorhyme, the fifth line being the "bob" or burden: each succeeding stanza affects a new rhyme, except in the fifth line, *e.g.* aaaab + ccccb + ddddb, and so forth. The Muwwál is a simple popular song in four to six lines; specimens of it are given in the Egyptian grammar of my friend the late Dr. Wilhelm Spitta.[1] The Muwashshah, or ornamented

[1] See p. 439 Grammatik des Arabischen Vulgär Dialekts von Ægyptien, by Dr. Wilhelm Spitta Bey, Leipzig, 1880. In pp. 489-493 he gives specimens of eleven Mawáwíl varying in length from four to fifteen lines. The assonance mostly attempts monorhyme: in two tetrastichs it is aa + ba, and it does not disdain alternates, ab + ab + ab.

verse, has two main divisions: one applies to our acrostics in which the initials form a word or words; the other is a kind of Musaddas, or sextines, which occurs once only in The Nights (cmlxxxvii.). It consists of three couplets or six-line strophes: all the hemistichs of the first are in monorhyme; in the second and following stanzas the three first hemistichs take a new rhyme, but the fourth resumes the assonance of the first set and is followed by the third couplet of No. 1 serving as bob or refrain, *e.g.* aaaaaa + bbbaaa + cccaaa, and so forth. It is the most complicated of all the measures and is held to be of Morisco or Hispano-Moorish origin.

Mr. Lane (Lex.) lays down, on the lines of Ibn Khallikan (i. 476, etc.) and other representative literati, as our sole authorities for pure Arabic, the precedence in following order. First of all ranks the Jáhili (Ignoramus) of The Ignorance, the Αραβίας ἄρειον ἔθνος: these pagans left hemistichs, couplets, pieces and elegies which once composed a large corpus and which are now mostly forgotten. Hammád al-Ráwiyah, the Reciter, a man of Persian descent (ob. A.H. 160 = 777), who first collected the Mu'allakát, once recited by rote in a séance before Caliph Al-Walid two thousand poems of præ-Mohammedan bards.[1] After the Jáhili stands the Mukhadram or Muhadrim, the "Spurious," because half Pagan half Moslem, who flourished either immediately before or soon after the preaching of Mohammed. The Islámi or full-blooded Moslem at the end of the first century A.H. (= 720) began the process of corruption in language; and, lastly, he was followed by the Muwallad of the second century, who fused Arabic with non-Arabic and in whom purity of diction disappeared.

I have noticed (I. § A) that the versical portion of The Nights may be distributed into three categories. First are

---

[1] Al-Siyuti, p. 235, from Ibn Khallikan. Our knowledge of oldest Arab verse is drawn chiefly from the Kitáb al-Aghání (Song-book) of Abu al-Faraj the Isfaháni, who flourished A.H. 284 – 356 (= 897 – 967): it was printed at the Bulak Press in 1868.

the olden poems which are held classical by all modern Arabs; then comes the mediæval poetry, the effusions of that brilliant throng which adorned the splendid Court of Harun al-Rashid and which ended with Al-Haríri (ob. A.H. 516); and, lastly, are the various *pièces de circonstance* suggested to editors or scribes by the occasion. It is not my object to enter upon the historical part of the subject: a mere sketch would have neither value nor interest whilst a finished picture would lead too far: I must be contented to notice a few of the most famous names.

Of the præ-Islamites we have Âdi bin Zayd al-Ibádi, the "celebrated poet" of Ibn Khallikán (i. 188); Nábighat (the full-grown) al-Zubyáni, who flourished at the Court of Al-Nu'uman in A.D. 580–602, and whose poem is compared with the "Suspendeds,"[1] and Al-Mutalammis the "pertinacious" satirist, friend and intimate with Tarafah of the "Prize Poem." About Mohammed's day we find Imr al-Kays "with whom poetry began," to end with Zú al-Rummah; Amrú bin Mádi Karab al-Zubaydi, Labíd; Ka'b ibn Zuhayr, the father, one of the Mu'allakah-poets, and the son-author of the Burdah or Mantle-poem (see vol. iii. p. 2), and Abbás bin Mirdás, who lampooned the Prophet and had "his tongue cut out," *i.e.* received a double share of booty from Ali. In the days of Caliph Omar we have Alkamah bin Olátha followed by Jamíl bin Ma'mar of the Banu Ozrah (ob. A.H. 82), who loved Azzá. Then came Al-Kuthayyir (the dwarf, *ironicè*), the lover of Buthaynah, "who was so lean that birds might be cut to bits with her bones:" the latter was also a poetess (Ibn Khall. i. 87), like Hind bint al-Nu'man, who made herself so disagreeable to Al-Hajjáj (ob. A.H. 95). Jarír al-Khatafah, the noblest of the Islami poets in the first century, is noticed at full length by Ibn Khallikan (i. 294), together with his rival in poetry and debauchery, Abú Firás Hammám or Homaym bin Ghalib

[1] See Lyall loc. cit. p. 97.

al-Farazdak, the Tamími, the Ommiade poet "without whose verse half Arabic would be lost:"[1] he exchanged satires with Jarír and died forty days before him (A.H. 110). Another contemporary, forming the poetical triumvirate of the period, was the debauched Christian poet Al-Akhtal al-Taghlibi. They were followed by Al-Ahwas al-Ansári, whose witty lampoons banished him to Dahlak Island in the Red Sea (ob. A.H. 179 = 795); by Bashshár ibn Burd and by Yúnus ibn Habib (ob. A.H. 182).

The well-known names of the Harun-cycle are Al-Asma'i, rhetorician and poet, whose epic with Antar for hero is not forgotten (ob. A.H. 216); Isaac of Mosul (Ishak bin Ibrahim of Persian origin); Al-'Utbi "the Poet" (ob. A.H. 228); Abu al-Abbas al-Rakáshi; Abu al-Atahiyah, the lover of Otbah; Muslim bin al-Walíd al-Ansari; Abú Tammám of Tay, compiler of the Hamásah (ob. A.H. 230), "a Muwallad of the first class" (says Ibn Khallikan, i. 392); the famous or infamous Abu Nowás; Abu Mus'ab (Ahmad ibn Ali), who died in A.H. 242; the satirist Dibil al Khuzáí (ob. A.H. 246), and a host of others quos nunc perscribere longum est. They were followed by Al-Bohtori "the Poet" (ob. A.H. 286); the royal author Abdullah ibn al-Mu'tazz (ob. A.H. 315); Ibn Abbád the Sahib (ob. A.H. 334); Mansúr al-Halláj, the martyred Sufi; the Sahib ibn Abbad; Abu Faras al-Hamdáni (ob. A.H. 357); Al-Námi (ob. A.H. 399), who had many encounters with that model Chauvinist Al-Mutanabbi, nicknamed Al-Mutanabbih (the "wide-awake"), killed A.H. 354; Al-Manázi of Manazjird (ob. 427); Al-Tughrai, author of the Lámiyat al-Ajam (ob. A.H. 375); Al-Haríri, the model rhetorician (ob. A.H. 516); Al-Hájiri al-Irbili, of Arbela (ob. A.H. 632); Bahá al-Din al-Sinjari (ob. A.H. 622); Al-Kátib or the Scribe (ob. A.H. 656); Abdun al-Andalúsi the Spaniard (our xiith century), and about the same time Al-Náwaji,

[1] His Diwán has been published with a French translation, par R. Boucher. Paris, Labitte, 1870.

author of the Halbat al-Kumayt or "Race-course of the Bay-Horse"—poetical slang for wine.[1]

Of the third category, the pièces d'occasion, little need be said: I may refer readers to my notes on the doggrels in preceding volumes.

Having a mortal aversion to the details of Arabic prosody, I have persuaded my friend Dr. Steingass to undertake in the following pages the subject as far as concerns the poetry of The Nights. He has been kind enough to collaborate with me from the beginning, and to his minute lexicographical knowledge I am deeply indebted for discovering not a few blemishes which would have been "nuts to the critic." The learned Arabist's notes will be highly interesting to students: mine (§ V.) are intended to give a superficial and popular idea of the Arab's verse-mechanism.

The principle of Arabic Prosody (called 'Arúz, pattern standard, or 'Ilm al-'Arúz, science of the 'Arúz), in so far resembles that of classical poetry, as it chiefly rests on metrical weight, not on accent, or in other words a verse is measured by short and long quantities, while the accent only regulates its rhythm. In Greek and Latin, however, the quantity of

---

[1] I find also minor quotations from the Imám Abu al-Hasan al-Askari (of Sarra man raa) ob. A.D. 868; Ibn Makúla (murdered in A.D. 862?); Ibn Durayd (ob. A.D. 933); Al-Zahr the Poet (ob. A.D. 963); Abu Bakr al-Zubaydi (ob. A.D. 989); Kábús ibn Wushmaghir (murdered in A.D. 1012-13); Ibn Nabatah the Poet (ob. A.D. 1015); Ibn al-Sa'ati (ob. A.D. 1028); Ibn Zaydun al-Andalusi, who died at Hums (Emessa, the Arab name for Seville) in A.D. 1071; Al-Mu'tasim ibn Sumadih (ob. A.D. 1091); Al-Murtaza ibn al-Shahrozuri the Sufi (ob. A.D. 1117); Ibn Sara al-Shantaráni (of Santarem), who sang of Hind and died A.D. 1123; Ibn al-Kházin (ob. A.D. 1124); Ibn Kalakis (ob. A.D. 1172); Ibn al-Ta'wizi (ob. A.D. 1188); Ibn Zabádah (ob. A.D. 1198); Bahá al-Dín Zuhayr (ob. A.D. 1249); Muwaffak al-Din Muzaffar (ob. A.D. 1266), and sundry others. Notices of Al-Utayyah (vol. i. 10), of Ibn al-Sumám (vol. i. 81) and of Ibn Sáhib al-Ishbíli of Seville (vol. i. 91), are deficient. The most notable point in Arabic verse is its savage satire, the language of excited "destructiveness" which characterises the Badawi: he is "keen for satire as a thirsty man for water;" and half his poetry seems to consist of foul innuendo, of lampoons, and of gross personal abuse.

the syllables depends on their vowels, which may be either naturally short or long, or become long by position, *i.e.* if followed by two or more consonants. We all remember from our school-days what a fine string of rules had to be committed to and kept in memory, before we were able to scan a Latin or Greek verse, without breaking its neck by tripping over false quantities. In Arabic, on the other hand, the answer to the question, what is metrically long or short, is exceedingly simple, and flows with stringent cogency from the nature of the Arabic alphabet. This, strictly speaking, knows only consonants (Harf, pl. Hurúf). The vowels which are required, in order to articulate the consonants, were at first not represented in writing at all. They had to be supplied by the reader, and are not improperly called "motions" (Harakát), because they move or lead on as it were, one letter to another. They are three in number, a (Fathah), i (Kasrah), u (Zammah), originally sounded as the corresponding English vowels in bat, bit and butt respectively, but in certain cases modifying their pronunciation under the influence of a neighbouring consonant. When the necessity made itself felt to represent them in writing, especially for the sake of fixing the correct reading of the Koran, they were rendered by additional signs, placed above or beneath the consonant, after which they are pronounced in a similar way as it is done in some systems of English shorthand. A consonant followed by a short vowel is called a "moved letter" (Muharrakah); a consonant without such vowel is called "resting" or "quiescent" (Sákinah), and can stand only at the end of a syllable or word.

And now we are able to formulate the *one* simple rule, which determines the prosodical quantity in Arabic: any moved letter, as ta, li, mu, is counted short; any moved letter followed by a quiescent one, as taf, lun, mus, *i.e.* any closed syllable beginning and terminating with a consonant and having a short vowel between, forms a long quantity. This is certainly a relief in comparison with the numerous rules of classical Prosody, proved by not a few exceptions, which, for instance, in Dr. Smith's Elementary Latin Grammar fill eight closely printed pages.

Before I proceed to show how from the prosodical unities, the moved and the quiescent letter, first the metrical elements, then the feet, and lastly the metres are built up, it will be necessary to obviate a few misunderstandings, to which our mode of transliterating Arabic into the Roman character might give rise.

The line:

"Love in my heart they lit and went their ways," (vol. i. 204).

runs in Arabic:

"Akámú al-wajda fí kalbí wa sárú." (Mac. Ed. i. 179).

Here, according to our ideas, the word akámú would begin with a short vowel a, and contain two long vowels á and ú; according to Arabic views neither is the case. The word begins with "Alif," and its second syllable ká closes in Alif after Fathah (a), in the same way, as the third syllable mú closes in the letter Wáw (w) after Zammah (u).

The question, therefore, arises, what is "Alif." It is the first of the twenty-eight Arabic letters, and has through the medium of the Greek Alpha nominally entered into our alphabet, where it now plays rather a misleading part. Curiously enough, however, Greek itself has preserved for us the key to the real nature of the letter. In 'Αλφα the initial a is preceded by the so-called spiritus lenis ('), a sign which must be placed in front or at the top of any vowel beginning a Greek word, and which represents that slight aspiration or soft breathing almost involuntarily uttered, when we try to pronounce a vowel by itself. We need not go far to find how deeply rooted this tendency is and to what exaggerations it will sometimes lead. Witness the gentleman, who after mentioning that he had been visiting his "favourite haunts" on the scenes of his early life, was sympathetically asked how the dear old ladies were. This spiritus lenis is the silent h of the French "homme" and the English "honour," corresponding exactly to the Arabic Hamzah, whose mere prop the Alif is, when it stands at the beginning of a word : a native Arabic Dictionary does not begin with Báb al-Alif (Gate or Chapter of the Alif), but with Báb al-Hamzah. What the Greeks call Alpha and have transmitted to us as a name for the vowel a, is in fact nothing else but the Arabic Hamzah-Alif (أ), moved by Fathah, *i.e.* bearing the sign َ for a at the top (أَ), just as it might have the sign Zammah ( ُ ), superscribed to express u (أُ), or the sign Kasrah ( ِ ) subjoined to represent i (إ). In each case the Hamzah-Alif, although scarcely audible to our ear, is the real letter and might fitly be rendered in transliteration by the above-mentioned silent h, wherever we make an Arabic word begin with a vowel not preceded by any other sign. This latter restriction refers to the sign ', which in Sir Richard Burton's translation of The Nights, as frequently in books published in this country, is used to represent the Arabic letter ع in whose very name 'Ayn it occurs. The 'Ayn is "described as produced by a smart compression of the upper part of the windpipe and forcible emission of breath," imparting a guttural tinge to a following or preceding vowel-sound ; but it is by no means a mere guttural vowel, as Professor Palmer styles it. For Europeans, who do not belong to the Israelitic dispensation, as well as for Turks and Persians, its exact pronunciation is most difficult, if not impossible to acquire.

In reading Arabic from transliteration for the purpose of scanning poetry, we have therefore in the first instance to keep in mind that no Arabic word or syllable can begin with a vowel. Where our mode of rendering Arabic in the Roman character would make this appear to be the case, either Hamzah (silent h), or 'Ayn (represented by the sign ') is the real initial, and the only element to be taken in account as a *letter*. It follows as a self-evident corollary that wherever a single consonant stands between two vowels, it never closes the previous syllable, but always opens the next one. The word "Akámú," for instance, can only be divided into the syllables: A (properly Ha)-ká-mú, never into Ak-á-mú or Ak-ám-ú.

It has been stated above that the syllable ká is closed by the letter Alif after Fathah, in the same way as the syllable mú is closed by the letter Wáw, and I may add now, as the word fí is closed by the letter Yá (y). To make this perfectly clear, I must repeat that the Arabic alphabet, as it was originally written, deals only with consonants. The signs for the short vowel-sounds were added later for a special purpose, and are generally not represented even in printed books, *e.g.* in the various editions of The Nights, where only quotations from the Koran or poetical passages are provided with the vowel-points. But among those consonants there are three, called weak letters (Hurúf al-'illah), which have a particular organic affinity to these vowel-sounds: the guttural Hamzah, which is akin to a, the palatal Yá, which is related to i, and the labial Wáw, which is homogeneous with u. Where any of the weak letters follows a vowel of its own class, either at the end of a word or being itself followed by another consonant, it draws out or lengthens the preceding vowel and is in this sense called a letter of prolongation (Harf al-Madd). Thus, bearing in mind that the Hamzah is in reality a silent h, the syllable ká might be written kah, similarly to the German word "sah," where the h is not pronounced either, but imparts a lengthened sound to the a. In like manner mú and fí are written in Arabic muw and fiy respectively, and form long quantities not because they contain a vowel long by nature, but because their initial "Muharrakah" is followed by a "Sákinah," exactly as in the previously mentioned syllables taf, lun, mus.[1] In the Roman transliteration, Akámú forms a word of five letters, two of which are consonants, and three vowels; in Arabic it represents the combination

---

[1] If the letter preceding Wáw or Yá is moved by Fathah, they produce the diphthongs au (aw), pronounced like ou in "bout," and ai, pronounced as i in "bite."

H(a)k(a)hm(u)w, consisting also of five letters but all consonants, the intervening vowels being expressed in writing either merely by superadded external signs, or more frequently not at all. Metrically it represents one short and two long quantities (⏑ - -), forming in Latin a trisyllabic foot called Bacchíus, and in Arabic a quinqueliteral "Rukn" (pillar) or "Juz" (part, portion), the technical designation for which we shall introduce presently.

There is one important remark more to be made with regard to the Hamzah: at the beginning of a word it is either conjunctive, Hamzat al-Wasl, or disjunctive, Hamzat al Kat'. The difference is best illustrated by reference to the French so-called aspirated h, as compared with the above-mentioned silent h. If the latter, as initial of a noun, is preceded by the article, the article loses its vowel, and, ignoring the silent h altogether, is read with the following noun almost as one word: le homme becomes l'homme (pronounced lomme), as le ami becomes l'ami. This resembles very closely the Arabic Hamzah Wasl. If, on the other hand, a French word begins with an aspirated h, as for instance héros, the article does not drop its vowel before the noun, nor is the h sounded as in the English word "hero," but the effect of the aspirate is simply to keep the two vowel sounds apart, so as to pronounce le éros with a slight hiatus between, and this is exactly what happens in the case of the Arabic Hamzah Kat'.

With regard to the Wasl, however, Arabic goes a step further than French. In the French example quoted above, we have seen it is the silent h and the *preceding* vowel, which are eliminated; in Arabic both the Hamzah and its own Harakah, *i.e.* the short vowel *following* it, are supplanted by their antecedent. Another example will make this clear. The most common instance of the Hamzah Wasl is the article al (for h(a)l = the Hebrew hal), where it is moved by Fathah. But it has this sound only at the beginning of a sentence or speech, as in "Al-hamdu" at the head of the

Fatihah, or in "Alláhu" at the beginning of the third Surah. If the two words stand in grammatical connection, as in the sentence "Praise be to God," we cannot say "Al-Hamdu li-Alláhi," but the junction (Wasl) between the dative particle li and the noun which it governs must take place. According to the French principle, this junction would be effected at the cost of the preceding element and li Alláhi would become l'Alláhí; in Arabic, on the contrary, the kasrated l of the particle takes the place of the following fathated Hamzah and we read li 'lláhi instead. Proceeding in the Fatihah we meet with the verse "Iyyáka na'budu wa iyyáka nasta'ínu," Thee do we worship and of Thee do we ask aid. Here the Hamzah of iyyáka (properly hiyyáka with silent h) is disjunctive, and therefore its pronunciation remains the same at the beginning and in the middle of the sentence, or to put it differently, instead of coalescing with the preceding wa into wa'yyáka, the two words are kept separate, by the Hamzah reading wa iyyáka, just as it was the case with the French Le héros.

If the conjunctive Hamzah is preceded by a quiescent letter, this takes generally Kasrah: "Tálat al-Laylah," the night was longsome, would become Tálati 'l-Laylah. If, however, the quiescent letter is one of prolongation, it mostly drops out altogether, and the Harakah of the next preceding letter becomes the connecting vowel between the two words, which in our parlance would mean, that the end-vowel of the first word is shortened before the elided initial of the second. Thus "fí al-bayti," in the house, which in Arabic is written f(i)y h(a)l-b(a)yt(i) and which we transliterate fí 'l-bayti, is in poetry read fil-bayti, where we must remember, that the syllable fil, in spite of its short vowel, represents a long quantity, because it consists of a moved letter followed by a quiescent one. Fíl would be over-long and could, according to Arabic prosody, stand only in certain cases at the end of a verse, *i.e.* in pause, where a natural tendency prevails to prolong a sound.

The attentive reader will now be able to fix the prosodical value of the line quoted above with unerring security. For metrical purposes it syllabifies into: A-ká-mul-vaj-da fí kal-bí wa sá-rú, containing three short and eight long quantities. The initial unaccented a is short, for the same reason why the syllables da and wa are so, that is, because it corresponds to an Arabic letter, the Hamzah or silent h, moved by Fathah. The syllables ká, fí, bí, sá, rú, are long for the same reason why the syllables mul, waj, kal are so, that is, because the accent in the transliteration corresponds to a quiescent Arabic letter, following a moved one. The same simple criterion applies to the whole list, in which I give in alphabetical order the first lines and the metre of all the poetical pieces contained in the Mac. edition, and which will be found at the end of Sir R. Burton's tenth volume.

The prosodical unities, then, in Arabic are the moved and the quiescent letter, and we are now going to show how they combine into metrical elements, feet, and metres.

i. The metrical elements (Usúl) are:

1. The Sabab,[1] which consists of *two* letters and is either khafíf (light) or sakíl (heavy). A moved letter followed by a quiescent, *i.e.* a closed syllable, like the afore-mentioned taf, lun, mus, to which we may now add fá = fah, 'í = 'iy, 'ú = 'uw, form a Sabab khafíf, corresponding to the classical long quantity (-). Two moved letters in succession, like muta 'ala, constitute a Sabab sakíl, for which the classical name would be Pyrrhic (⏑ ⏑). As in Latin and Greek, they are equal in weight and can frequently interchange, that is to say, the Sabab khafíf can be evolved into a sakíl by moving its second Harf, or the latter contracted into the former by making its second letter quiescent.

2. The Watad, consisting of *three* letters, one of which is quiescent. If the quiescent follows the two moved ones, the

[1] For the explanation of this name and those of the following terms, see Terminal Essay, p. 344.

Watad is called majmú' (collected or joined), as fa'ú (= fa'uw), mafá (= mafah), 'ilun, and it corresponds to the classical Iambus ( ⏑ - ). If, on the contrary, the quiescent intervenes between or separates the two moved letters, as in fá'i (= fah'i), látu (= lahtu), taf'i, the Watad is called mafrúk (separated), and has its classical equivalent in the Trochee ( - ⏑ ).

3. The Fásilah,[1] containing *four* letters, *i.e.* three moved ones followed by a quiescent, and which, in fact, is only a shorter name for a Sabab sakíl followed by Sabab khafíf, as muta + fá, or 'ala + tun, both of the measure of the classical Anapæst, ( ⏑ ⏑ -).

ii. These three elements, the Sabab, Watad and Fásilah, combine further into feet Arkán, pl. of Rukn, or Ajzá, pl. of Juz, two words explained supra p. 358. The technical terms by which the feet are named are derivatives of the root fa'l, to do, which as the student will remember, serves in Arabic Grammar to form the Auzán or weights, in accordance with which words are derived from roots. It consists of the three letters Fá (f), 'Ayn ('), Lám (l), and, like any other Arabic root, cannot strictly speaking be pronounced, for the introduction of any vowel-sound would make it cease to be a root and change it into an individual word. The above fa'l, for instance, where the initial Fá is moved by Fathah (a), is the Infinitive or verbal noun, "to do," "doing." If the 'Ayn also is moved by Fathah, we obtain fa'al, meaning in colloquial Arabic "he did" (the classical or literary form would be fa'ala). Pronouncing the first letter with Zammah (u), the second with Kasrah (i), *i.e.* fu'il, we say "it was done" (classically fu'ila). Many more forms are derived by prefixing, inserting or subjoining certain additional letters called Hurúf al-Ziyádah (letters of increase) to the original radicals:

---

[1] This Fásilah is more accurately called sughrà, the smaller one; there is another Fásilah kubrà, the greater, consisting of four moved letters followed by a quiescent, or of a Sabab sakíl followed by a Watad majmú'. But it occurs only as a variation of a normal foot, not as an integral element in its composition, and consequently no mention of it was needed in the text.

fá'il, for instance, with an Alif of prolongation in the first syllable, means "doer;" maf'úl (=maf'uwl), where the quiescent Fá is preceded by a fathated Mím (m), and the zammated 'Ayn followed by a lengthening Waw, means "done"; Mufá'alah, where in addition to a prefixed and inserted letter, the feminine termination ah is subjoined after the Lám, means "to do a thing reciprocally." Since these and similar changes are with unvarying regularity applicable to all roots, the grammarians use the derivatives of Fa'l as model-forms for the corresponding derivations of any other root, whose letters are in this case called its Fá, 'Ayn and Lám. From a root, *e.g.* which has Káf (k) for its first letter or Fá, Tá (t) for its second letter or 'Ayn, and Bá (b) for its third letter or Lám,

fa'l would be katb = to write, writing;
fa'al would be katab = he wrote;
fu'il would be kutib = it was written;
fá'il would be kátib = writer, scribe;
maf'úl would be maktúb = written, letter;
mufá'alah would be mukátabah = to write reciprocally, correspondence.

The advantage of this system is evident. It enables the student, who has once grasped the original meaning of a root, to form scores of words himself, and in his readings, to understand hundreds, nay thousands, of words, without recourse to the Dictionary, as soon as he has learned to distinguish their radical letters from the letters of increase, and recognises in them a familiar root. We cannot wonder, therefore, that the inventor of Arabic Prosody readily availed himself of the same plan for his own ends. The Taf'íl, as it is here called, that is the representation of the metrical feet by current derivatives of fa'l, has in this case, of course, nothing to do with the etymological meaning of those typical forms. But it proves none the less useful in another direction: in simply naming a particular foot it shows at the same time its prosodical measure and character, as will now be explained in detail.

We have seen supra p. 357 that the word Akámú consists of a short syllable followed by two long ones ( ᴗ - - ), and consequently forms a foot, which the classics would call Bacchíus. In Latin there is no connection between this name and the metrical value of the foot: we must learn both by heart. But if we are told that its Taf'íl in Arabic is Fa'úlun, we understand at once that it is composed of the Watad majmú' fa'ú ( ᴗ - ) and the Sabab khafíf lun ( - ), and as the Watad contains three, the Sabab two letters, it forms a quinqueliteral foot or Juz khamásí.

In combining into feet, the Watad has the precedence over the Sabab and the Fásilah, and again the Watad majmú' over the Watad mafrúk. Hence the Prosodists distinguish between Ajzá aslíyah or primary feet (from Asl, root), in which this precedence is observed, and Ájzá far'íyah or secondary feet (from Far' = branch), in which it is reversed. The former are four in number:—

1. Fa'ú.lun, consisting, as we have just seen, of a Watad majmú' followed by a Sabab khafíf, = the Latin Bacchíus ( ᴗ - - ).

2. Mafá.'í.lun, *i.e.* Watad majmú' followed by two Sabab khafíf = the Latin Epitritus primus ( ᴗ - - - ).

3. Mufá.'alatun, *i.e.* Watad majmú' followed by Fásilah = the Latin Iambus followed by Anapæst ( ᴗ - ᴗ ᴗ - ).

4. Fá'i.lá.tun, *i.e.* Watad mafrúk followed by two Sabab khafíf = the Latin Epitritus secundus ( - ᴗ - - ).

The number of the secondary feet increases to six, for as No. 2 and 4 contain two Sabab, they "branch out" into two derived feet each, according to both Sabab or only one changing place with regard to the Watad. They are:

5. Fá.'ilun, *i.e.* Sabab khafíf followed by Watad majmú' = the Latin Creticus ( - ᴗ - ). The primary Fa'ú.lun becomes by transposition Lun.fa'ú. To bring this into conformity with a current derivative of fa'l, the initial Sabab must be

made to contain the first letter of the root, and the Watad the two remaining ones in their proper order. Fá is therefore substituted for lun, and 'ilun for fa'ú, forming together the above Fá.'ilun. By similar substitutions, which it would be tedious to specify in each separate case, Mafá.'í.lun becomes:

6. Mus.taf.'ilun, for 'Í.lun.mafá, *i.e.* two Sabab khafíf followed by Watad majmú' = the Latin Epitritus tertius (- - ᴗ -), or:

7. Fá.'ilá.tun, for Lun.mafá.'í, *i.e.* Watad majmú' between two Sabab khafíf = the Latin Epitritus secundus ( - ᴗ - - ).

8. Mutafá.'ilun (for 'Alatun.mufá, the reversed Mufá.'alatun) *i.e.* Fásilah followed by Watad majmú' = the Latin Anapaest succeeded by Iambus ( ᴗ ᴗ - ᴗ - ). The last two secondary feet are transpositions of No. 4, Fá'.ilá.tun, namely:

9. Maf.'ú.látu, for Lá.tun.fá'i, *i.e.* two Sabab khafíf followed by Watad mafrúk = the Latin Epitritus quartus ( - - - ᴗ ).

10. Mus.taf'i.lun, for Tun.fá'i.la, *i.e.* Watad mafrúk between two Sabab khafíf = the Latin Epitritus tertius ( - - ᴗ - ).[1]

The "branch"-foot Fá.'ilun (No. 5), like its "root" Fa'úlun (No. 1), is quinqueliteral. All other feet, primary or secondary, consist necessarily of seven letters, as they contain a triliteral Watad (see supra i. 2) with either two biliteral Sabab khafíf (i. 1) or a quadriliteral Fásilah (i. 3). They are, therefore, called Sabá'í = seven lettered.

iii. The same principle of the Watad taking precedence over Sabab and Fásilah, rules the arrangement of the Arabic metres, which are divided into five circles (Dawáir, pl. of Dáirah) so called for reasons presently to be explained. The first is named:

---

[1] It is important to keep in mind that the seemingly identical feet 10 and 6, 7 and 3, are distinguished by the relative positions of the constituting elements in either pair. For as it will be seen that Sabab and Watad are subject to *different* kinds of alterations, it is evident that the effect of such alteration upon a foot will vary, if Sabab and Watad occupy *different* places with regard to each other.

A. Dáirat al-Mukhtalif, circle of "the varied" metre, because it is composed of feet of various length, the five-lettered Fa'úlun (supra ii. 1) and the seven-lettered Mafá'ílun (ii. 2) with their secondaries Fá'ilun, Mustaf.'ilun and Fá.'ilátun (ii. 5-7), and it comprises three Buhúr or metres (pl. of Bahr, sea), the Tawíl, Madíd and Basít.

1. Al-Tawíl, consisting of twice

Fa'ú.lun Mafá.'ílun Fa'ú.lun Mafá.'ílun,

the classical scheme for which would be

⏑ - - | ⏑ - - - | ⏑ - - | ⏑ - - - |

If we transfer the Watad Fa'ú from the beginning of the line to the end, it would read:

Lun.mafá'í Lun.fa'ú Lun.mafá'í Lun.fa'ú, which, after the substitutions indicated above (ii. 7 and 5), becomes:

2. Al-Madíd, consisting of twice

Fá.'ilátun Fá.'ilun Fá.'ilátun Fá.'ilun,

which may be represented by the classical scheme

- ⏑ - - | - ⏑ - | - ⏑ - - | - ⏑ - |

If again, returning to the Tawíl, we make the break after the Watad of the second foot we obtain the line:

'Ílun.fa'ú. Lun.mafá 'Ílun.fa'u Lun.mafá, and as metrically 'Ílun.fa'ú (two Sabab followed by Watad) and Lun.mafá (one Sabab followed by Watad) are ='Ílun.mafá and Lun.fa'ú respectively, their Taf'íl is effected by the same substitutions as in ii. 5 and 6, and they become:

3. Basít, consisting of twice

Mastaf.'ilun Fá.'ilun Mustaf.'ilun Fá.'ilun,

in conformity with the classical scheme:

- - ⏑ - | - ⏑ - | - - ⏑ - | - ⏑ - |

Thus one metre evolves from another by a kind of rotation, which suggested to the Prosodists an ingenious device of representing them by circles (hence the name Dáirah), round the circumference of which on the outside the complete Taf'íl of the original metre is written, while each moved letter is faced by a small loop, each quiescent by a small vertical stroke[1] inside the circle. Then, in the case of this present Dáirat al-Mukhtalif, for instance, the loop corresponding to the initial f of the first Fa'úlun is marked as the beginning of the Tawíl, that corresponding to its l (of the Sabab lun) as the beginning of the Madid, and that corresponding to the 'Ayn of the next Mafá'ílun as the beginning of the Basít. The same process applies to all the following circles, but our limited space compels us simply to enumerate them, together with their Buhúr, without further reference to the mode of their evolution.

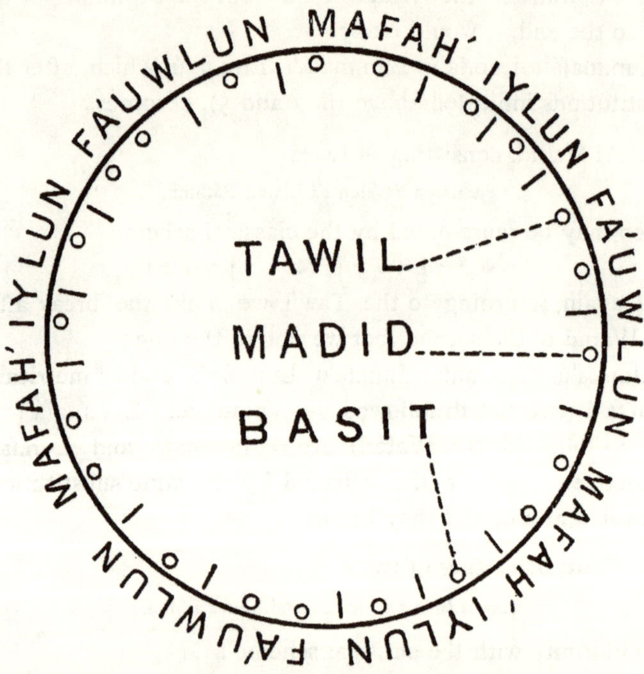


B. Dáirat al-Mútalif, circle of "the agreeing" metre, so called because all its feet agree in length, consisting of seven letters each. It contains:

[1] *i.e.* vertical to the circumference.

1. Al-Wáfir, composed of twice

Mufá.'alatun Mufá.'alatun Mufá.'alatun (ii. 3).

= ⏑ - ⏑ ⏑ - | ⏑ - ⏑ ⏑ - | ⏑ - ⏑ ⏑ - |

where the Iambus in each foot precedes the Anapæst and its reversal:

2. Al-Kámil, consisting of twice

Mutafá.'ilun Mutafá.'ilun Mutafá.'ilun (ii. 8)

= ⏑ ⏑ - ⏑ - | ⏑ ⏑ - ⏑ - | ⏑ ⏑ - ⏑ - |

where the Anapæst takes the first place in every foot.

C. Dáirat al-Mujtalab, circle of "the brought on" metre, so called because its seven-lettered feet are brought on from the first circle.

1. Al-Hazaj, consisting of twice

Mafá.'ílun Mafá.'ílun Mafá.'ílun (ii. 2)

= ⏑ - - - | ⏑ - - - | ⏑ - - - | ⏑ - - - |

2. Al-Rajaz, consisting of twice

Mustaf 'ilun Mustaf.'ilun Mustaf.'ilun,

and, in this full form, almost identical with the Iambic Trimeter of the Greek Drama:

- - ⏑ - | - - ⏑ - | - - ⏑ - |

3. Al-Ramal, consisting of twice

Fá.'ilátun Fá.'ilátun Fa.'ilátun,

the trochaic counterpart of the preceding metre

= - ⏑ - - | - ⏑ - - | - ⏑ - - |

D. Dáirat al-Mushtabih, circle of "the intricate" metre, so called from its intricate nature, primary mingling with secondary feet, and one foot of the same verse containing a Watad majmú', another a Watad mafrúk, *i.e.* the iambic rhythm alternating with the trochaic and *vice versa*. Its Buhúr are:

1. Al-Sarí', twice

Mustaf.'ilun Mustaf.'ilun Maf'ú.látu (ii. 6 and 9),

= - - ⏑ - | - - ⏑ - | - - - ⏑ |

2. Al-Munsarih, twice

Mustaf.'ilun Mafú.látu Mustaf.'ilun (ii. 6. 9. 6)

= - - ⏑ - | - - - ⏑ | - - ⏑ - |

3. Al-Khafíf, twice

Fá.'ilátun Mustaf'i.lun Fá.'ilátun (ii. 7. 10. 7)

= - ᴗ - - | - - ᴗ - | - ᴗ - - |

4. Al-Muzári', twice

Mafá.'ilun Fá'i.látun Mafá.'ilun (ii. 2. 4. 2)

= ᴗ - - - | - ᴗ - - | ᴗ - - - |

5. Al-Muktazib, twice

Maf'ú.látu Mustaf.'ilun Maf'ú.látu (ii. 9. 6. 9)

= - - - ᴗ | - - ᴗ - | - - - ᴗ |

6. Al-Mujtass, twice

Mustaf'i.lun Fá.'ilátun Mustaf'i.lun (ii. 10. 7. 10)

= - - ᴗ - | - ᴗ - - | - - ᴗ - |

E. Dáirat al-Muttafik, circle of "the concordant" metre, so called for the same reason why circle B is called "the agreeing," *i.e.* because the feet all harmonise in length, being here, however quinqueliteral, not seven-lettered as in the Mútalif. Al-Khalíl, the inventor of the 'Ilm al-'Arúz, assigns to it only one metre:

1. Al-Mutakárib, twice

Fa'úlun Fa'úlun Fa'úlun Fa'úlun (ii. 1)

= ᴗ - - | ᴗ - - | ᴗ - - | ᴗ - - |

Later Prosodists added:

2. Al-Mútadárak, twice

Fá'ilun Fá'ilun Fá'ilun Fá'ilun (ii. 5)

= - ᴗ - | - ᴗ - | - ᴗ - | - ᴗ - |

The feet and metres as given above, are however to a certain extent merely theoretical; in practice the former admit of numerous licences and the latter of variations brought about by modification or partial suppression of the feet final in a verse. An Arabic poem (Kasídah, or if numbering less than ten couplets, Kat'ah) consists of Bayts or couplets, bound together by a continuous rhyme, which connects the first two lines and is repeated at the end of every second line throughout the poem. The *last* foot of every odd line is called 'Arúz (fem. in contradistinction of 'Arúz in the sense of Prosody which is masc.) pl. A'áriz, that of every even line is called Zarb, pl. Azrub, and the remaining feet may be termed Hashw (stuffing), although in stricter parlance a further distinction is made between the *first* foot of every odd and even line as well.

Now with regard to the Hashw on the one hand, and the 'Aruz and Zarb on the other, the changes which the normal feet undergo are of two kinds: Zuháf (deviation) and 'Illah (defect). Zuháf applies, as a rule, occasionally and optionally to the second letter of a Sabab in those feet which compose the Hashw or body-part of a verse, making a long syllable short by suppressing its quiescent final, or contracting two short quantities in a long one, by rendering quiescent a moved letter which stands second in a Sabab sakíl. In Mustaf'ilun (ii. 6. = - - ⏑ -), for instance, the s of the first syllable, or the f of the second, or both may be dropped and it will become accordingly Mutaf'ilun, by substitution, Mafá'ilun (⏑ - ⏑ -) or Musta'ilun, by substitution Mufta'ilun (- ⏑ ⏑ -), or Muta'ilun, by substitution Fa'ilatun (⏑ ⏑ ⏑ -).[1] This means that wherever the foot Mustaf.'ilun occurs in the Hashw of a poem, we can represent it by the scheme ⏓ ⏓ ⏑ - *i.e.* the Epitritus tertius can, by poetical licence change into Diiambus, Choriambus or Pæon quartus. In Mufá'alatun (ii. 3, = ⏑ - ⏑ ⏑ -) and Mutafá'ilun (ii. 8, = ⏑ ⏑ - ⏑ -) again the Sabab 'ala and muta may become khafíf by suppression of their final Harakah and thus turn into Mufá'altun, by substitution Mafá'ílun (ii. 2, = ⏑ - - -), and Mutfá'ilun, by substitution Mustaf'ilun (ii. 6, = - - ⏑ - as above. In other words the two feet correspond to the schemes ⏑ - ⏖ ⏑ - and ⏖ ⏑ - ⏑ -, where a Spondee can take the place of the Anapæst after or before the Iambus respectively.

'Illah, the second way of modifying the primitive or normal feet, applies to both Sabab and Watad, but only in the 'Aruz and Zarb of a couplet, being at the same time constant and obligatory. Besides the changes already mentioned, it consists

[1] This would be a Fásilah kubrà spoken of in the note p. 361.

in adding one or two letters to a Sabab or Watad, or curtailing them more or less, even to cutting them off altogether. We cannot here exhaust this matter any more than those touched upon until now, but must be satisfied with an example or two, to show the proceeding in general and indicate its object.

We have seen that the metre Basít consists of the two lines :

Mustaf.'ilun Fá.'ilun Mustaf'ilun Fá'ilun
Mustaf'ilun Fá'ilun Mustaf'ilun Fá'ilun.

This complete form, however, is not in use amongst Arab poets. If by the Zuháf Khabn, here acting as 'Illah, the Alif in the final Fá'ilun is suppressed, changing it into Fa'ilun (∪ ∪ -), it becomes the first 'Aruz, called makhbúnah, of the Basít, the first Zarb of which is obtained by submitting the final Fá'ilun of the second line to the same process. A second Zarb results, if in Fá'ilun the final n of the Watad 'ilun is *cut* off and the preceding l made quiescent by the 'Illah Kat' thus giving Fá'il and by substitution Fa'lun (- -). Thus the formula becomes :—

Mustaf'ilun Fá'ilun Mustaf'ilun Fa'ilun
Mustaf'ilun Fá'ilun Mustaf'ilun { Fa'ilun / Fa'lun

As in the Hashw, *i.e.* the first three feet of each line, the Khabn can likewise be applied to the medial Fá'ilun, and for Mustaf'ilun the poetical licences, explained above, may be introduced ; this first 'Arúz or Class of the Basít with its two Zarb or subdivisions will be represented by the scheme :

```
∪ ∪     | ∪     | ∪ ∪     |
- - ∪ - | - ∪ - | - - ∪ - | ∪ ∪ -

∪ ∪     | ∪     | ∪ ∪     { ∪ ∪ -
- - ∪ - | - ∪ - | - - ∪ - {  - -
```

that is to say in the first subdivision of this form of the Basít both lines of each couplet end with an Anapæst and every second line of the other subdivision terminates in a Spondee.

The Basít has four more A'áriz, three called majzúah, because each line is shortened by a Juz or foot, one called mashtúrah (halved), because the number of feet is reduced from four to two, and we may here notice that the former kind of lessening the number of feet is frequent with the hexametrical circles (B.C.D.), while the latter can naturally only occur in those circles whose couplet forms an octameter (A. E.) Besides being majzúah, the second 'Aruz is sahíhah (perfect), consisting of the normal foot Mustaf'ilun. It has three Azrub: 1. Mustaf'ilán (- - ⏑ -́, with an overlong final syllable, supra p. 359), produced by the 'Illah Tazyíl, *i.e.* addition of a quiescent letter at the end (Mustaf'ilunn, by substitution Mustaf'ilán); 2. Mustaf'ilun, like the 'Aruz; 3. Maf'úlun (- - -), produced by the 'Illah Kat' (see the preceding page; Mustaf'ilun, by dropping the final n and making the l quiescent becomes Mustaf'il and by substitution Maf'úlun). Hence the formula is:

```
Mussaf'ilun Fá'ilun Mustaf'ilun
                      ⎧ Mustaf'ilán
Mustaf'ilun Fá'ilun  ⎨ Mustaf'ilun
                      ⎩ Maf'úlun,
```

which, with its allowable licences, may be represented by the scheme:

```
⏑ ⏑       | ⏑       |
- - ⏑ -   | - ⏑ -   | - - ⏑ -
                    ⎧ ⏑ ⏑
                    ⎪ - - ⏑ -́
⏑ ⏑       | ⏑       ⎨ - - ⏑ -
- - ⏑ -   | - ⏑ -   ⎪ ⏑
                    ⎩ - - -
```

The above will suffice to illustrate the general method of the Prosodists, and we must refer the reader for the remaining classes and subdivisions of the Basít as well as the other metres to more special treatises on the subject, to which this Essay is intended merely as an introduction, with a view to facilitate the first steps of the student in an important, but I fear somewhat neglected, field of Arabic learning.

If we now turn to the poetical pieces contained in The Nights, we find that out of the fifteen metres known to al-Khalíl, or the sixteen of later Prosodists, instances of thirteen occur in the Mac. N. edition, but in vastly different proportions. The total number amounts to 1,385 pieces (some, however, repeated several times), out of which 1,128 belong to the first two circles, leaving only 257 for the remaining three. The same disproportionality obtains with regard to the metres of each circle. The Mukhtalif is represented by 331 instances of Tawíl and 330 of Basít against 3 of Madíd; the Mutalif by 321 instances of Kámil against 143 of Wáfir; the Mujtalab by 32 instances of Ramal and 30 of Rajaz against 1 of Hazaj; the Mushtabih by 72 instances of Khafíf and 52 of Sarí' against 18 of Munsarih and 15 of Mujtass; and lastly the Muttafik by 37 instances of Mutakárib. Neither the Mutadárak (E. 2), nor the Muzári' and Muktazib (D. 4, 5) are met with.

Finally it remains for me to quote a couplet of each metre, showing how to scan them, and what relation they bear to the theoretical formulas exhibited on p. 363 to p. 368.

It is characteristic for the preponderance of the Tawíl over all the other metres, that the first four lines, with which my alphabetical list begins, are written in it. One of these belongs to a poem which has for its author Bahá al-Dín Zuhayr (born A.D. 1186 at Mekkah or in its vicinity, ob. 1249 at Cairo), and is to be found in full in Professor Palmer's edition of his works, p. 164. Sir Richard Burton translates the first Bayt (vol. i. 256):

An I quit Cairo and her pleasances * Where can I hope to find so gladsome ways?

Professor Palmer renders it:

Must I leave Egypt where such joys abound?
What place can ever charm me so again.

In Arabic it scans:

⏑ – ⏑ | ⏑ – – – | ⏑ – ⏑ | ⏑ – ⏑ – |
A-arhalu 'an Misrin wa tíbi na'ímihi [1]

⏑ – ⏑ | ⏑ – – – | ⏑ – ⏑ | ⏑ – ⏑ – |
Fa-ayyu makánin ba'dahá li-ya sháiku.

---

[1] In pause that is at the end of a line, a short vowel counts either as long or is dropped, according to the exigencies of the metre. In the Hashw the u or i of

In referring to iii. A. 1, p. 365, it will be seen that in the Hashw Fa'úlun (⏑ - -) has become Fa'úlu (⏑ - ⏑) by a Zuháf called Kabz (suppression of the fifth letter of a foot if it is quiescent), and that in the 'Arúz and Zarb Mafá'ílun (⏑ - - -) has changed into Mafá'ilun (⏑ - ⏑ -) by the same Zuháf acting as 'Illah. The latter alteration shows the couplet to be of the second Zarb of the first 'Arúz of the Tawíl. If the second line did terminate in Mafá'ílun, as in the original scheme, it would be the first Zarb of the same 'Arúz; if it did end in Fa'úlun (⏑ - -) or Mafá'íl (⏑ - ⏑̄) it would represent the third or fourth subdivision of this first class respectively. The Tawíl has one other 'Arúz, Fa'úlun, with a twofold Zarb, either Fa'úlun also, or Mafá'ilun.

The first instance of the Basít occurring in The Nights are the lines translated vol. i. p. 23:

> Containeth Time a twain of days, this of blessing, that of bane *
> And holdeth Life a twain of halves, this of pleasure, that of pain.

In Arabic (Mac. N. i. 11):

- - ⏑ - | - ⏑ - | - - ⏑ - | ⏑ ⏑ - |
Al-Dahru yaumáni zá amnun wa zá hazaru.

- - ⏑ - | - ⏑ - | - - ⏑ - | ⏑ ⏑ - |
Wa 'l-'Ayshu shatráni zá safwun wa zá kadaru.

Turning back to p. 365, where the A'áríz and Azrub of the Basít are shown, the student will have no difficulty to recognise the Bayt as one belonging to the first Zarb of the first 'Arúz.

As an example of the Madíd we quote the original of the lines (vol. iii. p. 240):—

> I had a heart, and with it lived my life * 'Twas seared with fire and burnt with loving-lowe.

---

the pronominal affix for the third person sing. masc., and the final u of the enlarged pronominal plural forms, humu and kumu may be either short or long, according to the same exigencies. The end-vowel of the pronoun of the first person ana, I, is generally read short, although it is written with Alif.

They read in Arabic :—

- ⏑ - - | - ⏑ - | ⏑ ⏑ - |

Kána lí kalbun a'íshu bihi

- ⏑ - - | - ⏑ - | ⏑ - |

Fa'ktawà bi'l-nári wa'htarak.

If we compare this with the formula (iii. A. 2, p. 365), we find that either line of the couplet is shortened by a foot; it is therefore majzú. The first 'Arúz of this abbreviated metre is Fá'ilátun ( - ⏑ - - ), and is called sahíhah (perfect) because it consists of the normal third foot. In the second 'Arúz Fá'ilátun loses its end syllable tun by the 'Illah Hafz (suppression of a final Sabab khafíf), and becomes Fá'ilá ( - ⏑ - ) for which Fá'ilun is substituted. Shortening the first syllable of Fá'ilun, *i.e.* eliminating the Alif by Khabn, we obtain the third 'Arúz Fa'ilun ( ⏑ ⏑ - ) as that of the present lines, which has two Azrub: Fa'ilun, like the 'Arúz and Fa'lun ( - - ), here, again by Khabn, further reduced to Fa'al ( ⏑ - ).

Ishak of Mosul, who improvises the piece, calls it "so difficult and so rare, that it went nigh to deaden the quick and to quicken the dead;" indeed, the native poets consider the metre Madíd as the most difficult of all, and it is scarcely ever attempted by later writers. This accounts for its rare occurrence in The Nights, where only two more instances are to be found, Mac. N. ii. 244 and iii. 404.

The second and third circle will best be spoken of together, as the Wáfir and Kámil have a natural affinity to the Hazaj and Rajaz. Let us revert to the line :—

⏑ - - - | ⏑ - - - | ⏑ - - |

Akámú 'l-wajda fí kalbí wa sárú.

Translated, as it were, into the language of the Prosodists it will be :—

Mafá'ílun [1] 'Mafá'ílun Fa'úlun,

---

[1] On p. 274 the word akámú, as read by itself, was identified with the foot Fa'úlun. Here it must be read together with the following syllable as "akámulwaj," which is Mafá'ílun.

and this, standing by itself, might prima facie be taken for a line of the Hajaz (iii. C. 1), with the third Mafá'ílun shortened by Hafz (see above) into Mafá'í for which Fa'úlun would be substituted. We have seen (p. 369) that and how the foot Mufá'alatun can change into Mafá'ílun, and if in any poem which otherwise would belong to the metre Hazaj, the former measure appears even in one foot only along with the latter, it is considered to be the original measure, and the poem counts no longer as Hazaj but as Wáfir. In the piece now under consideration, it is the second Bayt where the characteristic foot of the Wáfir first appears :—

⏑ - - - | ⏑ - ⏑ ⏑ - | ⏑ - - |
Naat 'anní'l-rubú'u wa sákiníhá

⏑ - ⏑ ⏑ - | ⏑ - ⏑ ⏑ - | ⏑ - - |
Wa kad ba'uda 'l-mazáru fa-lá mazáru

Anglicè :—

Far lies the camp and those who camp therein ; * Far is her tent-shrine where I ne'er shall tent.

It must, however, be remarked that the Hazaj is not in use as a hexameter, but only with an 'Arúz majzúah or shortened by one foot. Hence it is only in the second 'Arúz of the Wáfir, which is likewise majzúah, that the ambiguity as to the real nature of the metre can arise ;[1] and the isolated couplet :—

⏑ - - - | ⏑ - - - | ⏑ - - |
Yarídu 'l-mar-u an yu'tà munáhu

⏑ - - - | ⏑ - - - | ⏑ - - |
Wa yabà 'lláhu illá má yurídu

Man wills his wish to him accorded be, * But Allah naught accords save what he wills (vol. iii. 35),

being hexametrical forms undoubtedly part of a poem in Wáfir although it does not contain the foot Mufá'alatun at all.

---

[1] Prof. Palmer, p. 328 of his Grammar, identifies this form of the Wáfir, when every Mufá'alatun of the Hashw has become Mafá'ílun, with the second form of the Rajaz. It should be Hazaj. Professor Palmer was misled, it seems, by an evident misprint in one of his authorities, the Muhít al-Dáira by Dr. Van Dayk, p. 52.

Thus the solitary instance of Hazaj in The Nights is Abú Nuwás' abomination, beginning with :—

u - - - | u - - - |

Fa-lá tas'au ilà ghayrí

u - - - | u - - - |

Fa-'indí ma'dinu 'l-khayri (Mac. N. ii. 377).

Steer ye your steps to none but me * Who hath a mine of luxury.

If in the second 'Arúz of the Wáfir Mafáílun ( u - - - ) is further shortened to Mafá'ilun ( u - u - ), the metre resembles the second 'Arúz of Rajaz, where, as we have seen, the latter foot can, by licence, take the place of the normal Mustaf'ilun ( - - u - ).

The Kámil bears a similar relation to the Rajaz, as the Wáfir bears to the Hajaz. By way of illustration we quote from Mac. N. ii. 8 the first two Bayts of a little poem taken from the 23rd Assembly of Al-Hariri :—

- - u - | - - u - | u u - u - |

Yá khátiba 'l-dunyá 'l-daniyyati innahá

u u - u - | u u - u - | - - - |

Sharaku 'l-radà wa karáratu 'l-akdári

- - u - | - - u - | - - u - |

Dárun matà má azhakat fí yaumihá

- - u - | - - u - | - - - |

Abkat ghadan bu'dan lahá min dari

In Sir Richard Burton's translation :—

O thou who woo'st a World unworthy, learn * 'Tis house of evils, 'tis Perdition's net :

A house where whoso laughs this day shall weep * The next, then perish house of fume and fret.

The 'Aruz of the first couplet is Mutafá'ilun, assigning the piece to the first or perfect (sahíhah) class of the Kámil. In the Hashw of the opening line and in that of the whole second Bayt this normal Mutafá'ilun has, by licence, become Mustaf'ilun, and the same change has taken place in the 'Arúz of the second couplet ; for it is a peculiarity which this metre shares with a few others, to allow certain alterations of the kind Zuháf in the 'Arúz and Zarb as well as in the Hashw. This class has three subdivisions: the Zarb of the first is Mutafá'ilun, like the 'Arúz; the Zarb of the second is Fa'a-látun (⏑⏑--), a substitution for Mutafá'il, which latter is obtained from Mutafá'ilun by suppressing the final n and rendering the l quiescent; the Zarb of the third is Fa'lun (- -) for Mútfá, derived from Mutafá'ilun by cutting off the Watad 'ilun and dropping the medial a of the remaining Mutafá.

If we make the 'Ayn of the second Zarb Fa'alátun also quiescent by the permitted Zuháf Izmár, it changes into Fa'látun, by substitution Maf'úlun (- - -) which terminates the rhyming lines of the foregoing quotation. Consequently the two couplets taken together, belong to the second Zarb of the first 'Arúz of the Kámil, and the metre of the poem with its licences may be represented by the scheme:

```
 -          |  -         |  -         |
⏑⏑ - ⏑ -   | ⏑⏑ - ⏑ -   | ⏑⏑ - ⏑ -   |
 -          |  -         |  -     |
⏑⏑ - ⏑ -   | ⏑⏑ - ⏑ -   | ⏑⏑ - -  |
```

Taken isolated, on the other hand, the second Bayt might be of the metre Rajaz, whose first 'Arúz Mustaf'ilun has two Azrub: one equal to the 'Arúz, the other Maf'úlun as above, but here substituted for Mustaf'il after applying the 'Illah Kat' (see p. 370) to Mustaf'ilun. If this were the metre of the poem throughout, the scheme with the licences peculiar to the Rajaz would be:

```
⏑ ⏑       | ⏑ ⏑       | ⏑ ⏑       |
- - ⏑ -   | - - ⏑ -   | - - ⏑ -   |
⏑ ⏑       | ⏑ ⏑       | ⏑       |
- - ⏑ -   | - - ⏑ -   | - - -   |
```

The pith of Al-Hariri's Assembly is that the knight errant, not to say the arrant wight of the Romance, Abú Sayd of Sarúj, accuses before the Wáli of Baghdad his pretended pupil, in reality his son, to have appropriated a poem of his by lopping off two feet of every Bayt. If this is done in the quoted lines, they read:

- - ᴗ - | - - ᴗ - |
Yá khátiba 'l-dunyá 'l-daniy.

ᴗ ᴗ - ᴗ - | ᴗ ᴗ - ᴗ - |
Yati innahá sharaku l'-radà

- - ᴗ - | - - ᴗ - |
Dárun matà má azhakat

- - ᴗ - | - - ᴗ - |
Fí yaumihá abkat ghadá,

with a different rhyme and of a different variation of metre. The amputated piece belongs to the fourth Zarb of the third 'Aruz of Kámil, and its second couplet tallies with the second sub-division of the second class of Rajaz.

The Rajaz, a iambic metre pure and simple, is the most popular, because the easiest, in which even the Prophet was caught napping sometimes, at the dangerous risk of following the perilous leadership of Imru 'l-Kays. It is the metre of improvisation, of ditties, and of numerous didactic poems. In the latter case, when the composition is called Urjúzah, the two lines of every Bayt rhyme, and each Bayt has a rhyme of its own. This is the form in which, for instance, Ibn Málik's Alfíyah is written, as well as the remarkable grammatical work of the modern native scholar, Nasíf al-Yazijí, of which a notice will be found in Chenery's Introduction to his Translation of Al-Hariri.

While the Hazaj and Rajaz connect the third circle with the first and second, the Ramal forms the link between the third and fourth Dáirah. Its measure Fá'ilátun ( - ᴗ - - ) and the reversal of it, Maf'úlátu ( - - - ᴗ), affect the trochaic rhythm, as opposed to the iambic of the two first-named metres. The iambic movement has a ring of gladness about it, the trochaic a wail of sadness: the former resembles a nimble pedestrian, striding apace with an elastic step and a cheerful heart; the latter is like a man toiling along on the desert path, where his foot is ever and anon sliding back in the burning sand (Raml, whence probably the name of the metre). Both combined in regular alternation, impart an agitated character to the verse, admirably fit to express the conflicting emotions of a passion-stirred mind.

Examples of these more or less plaintive and pathetic metres are numerous in the Tale of Uns al-Wujúd and the Wazir's Daughter, which being throughout a story of love, as has been noted vol. iii. 167, abounds in verse, and, in particular, contains ten out of the thirty-two instances of Ramal occurring in The Nights. We quote:

Ramal, first Zarb of the first 'Arúz (Mac. N. ii. 361):

- ‿ - - | ‿ ‿ - - | - ‿ - |
Inna li 'l-bulbuli sautan fí 'l-sahar

- ‿ - - | ‿ ‿ - - | - ‿ - |
Ashghala 'l-'áshika 'an husni 'l-watar

The Bulbul's note, whenas dawn is nigh * Tells the lover from strains of strings to fly (vol. iii. 180).

Sarí', second Zarb of the first 'Arúz (Mac. N. ii. 359):

‿ - ‿ - | - - ‿ - | - ‿ - |
Wa fákhitin kad kála fí nauhihi

- - ‿ - | - - ‿ - | - ‿ - |
Yá Dáiman shukran 'alà balwatí

I heard a ringdove chanting soft and plaintively, * "I thank Thee, O Eternal, for this misery" (vol. iii. 179).

Khafíf, full or perfect form (sahíh), both in Zarb and 'Arúz (Mac. N. ii. 356):

- ‿ - - | ‿ - ‿ - | - ‿ - - |
Yá li-man ashtakí 'l-gharáma 'llazí bí

‿ ‿ - - | ‿ - ‿ - | - ‿ - - |
Wa shujúní wa furkatí 'an habíbí

O to whom now of my desire complaining sore shall I * Bewail my parting from my fere compellèd thus to fly (vol. iii. 176).

Mujtass, the only 'Arúz (majzúah sahíhah, *i.e.* shortened by one foot and perfect) with equal Zarb (Mac. N. ii. 367):

- - ⏑ - | ⏑ ⏑ - - |
Ruddú 'alayya habíbí
- - ⏑ - | - ⏑ - - |
Lá hajatan lí bi-málin

To me restore my dear * I want not wealth untold (vol. iii. 186).

As an instance of the Munsarih, I give the second occurring in The Nights, because it affords me an opportunity to show the student how useful a knowledge of the laws of Prosody frequently proves for ascertaining the correct reading of a text. Mac. N. i. 33 we find the line:

- ⏑ ⏑ - | - ⏑ ⏑ - | - ⏑ ⏑ - |
Arba'atun má 'jtama'at kattu  á.

This would be Rajaz with the licence Mufta'ilun for Mustaf'ilun. But the following lines of the fragment evince, that the metre is Munsarih; hence, a clerical error must lurk somewhere in the second foot. In fact, on page 833 of the same volume, we find the piece repeated, and here the first couplet reads

- ⏑ ⏑ - | - ⏑ - ⏑ | - ⏑ ⏑ - |
Arba'atun má 'jtama'na kattu siwà
⏑ - ⏑ - | - ⏑ - ⏑ | - ⏑ ⏑ - |
Alà azá mujhatí wa safki damí

Four things which ne'er conjoin unless it be * To storm my vitals and to shed my blood.

The Mutakárib, the last of the metres employed in The Nights, has gained a truly historical importance by the part which it plays in Persian literature. In the form of trimetrical double-lines, with a several rhyme for each couplet, it has become the "Nibelungen-" stanza of the Persian epos: Firdausí's immortal "Book of Kings" and Nizámi's Iskandernámah are written in it, not to mention a host of Masnawis in which Sufic mysticism combats Mohammedan orthodoxy. On account of its warlike and heroical character, therefore, I choose for an example the knightly Jamrakán's challenge to the single fight in which he conquers his scarcely less valiant adversary Kauraján (Mac. N. iii. 296):

⏑ – – | ⏑ – ⏑ | ⏑ – – | ⏑ – – |
Aná 'l-Jamrakánu kawiyyu 'l-janáni

⏑ – – | ⏑ – ⏑ | ⏑ – – | ⏑ – – |
Jamí'u 'l-fawárisi takhshà kitálí.

Here the third syllable of the second foot in each line is shortened by licence, and the final Kasrah of the first line, standing in pause, is long, the metre being the full form of the Mutakárib as exhibited p. 368, iii. E. i. If we suppress the Kasrah of Al-Janáni, which is also allowable in pause, and make the second line to rhyme with the first, saying, for instance:

⏑ – – | ⏑ – ⏑ | ⏑ – – | ⏑ –
Aná 'l-Jamrakánu kawiyyu 'l-janán

⏑ – – | ⏑ – – | ⏑ – – | ⏑ –
La-yakshà kitálí shijá'u 'l-zamán,

we obtain the powerful and melodious metre in which the Sháhnámah sings of Rustam's lofty deeds, of the tender love of Rúdabah and the tragic downfall of Siyáwush.

Shall I confess that in writing the foregoing pages it has been my ambition to become a conqueror, in a modest way, myself: to conquer, I mean, the prejudice frequently entertained, and shared even by my accomplished countryman, Rückert, that Arabic Prosody is a clumsy and repulsive doctrine. I have tried to show that it springs naturally from the character of the language, and, intimately connected as it is with the grammatical system of the Arabs, it appears to me quite worthy of the acumen of a people, to whom, amongst other things, we owe the invention of Algebra, the stepping-stone of our whole modern system of Mathematics. I cannot refrain, therefore, from concluding with a little anecdote anent al-Khalíl, which Ibn Khallikán tells in the following words. His son went one day into the room where his father was, and on finding him scanning a piece of poetry by the rules of prosody, he ran out and told the people that his father had lost his wits. They went in immediately and related to al-Khalíl what they had heard, on which he addressed his son in these terms:

"Had you known what I was saying, you would have excused me, and had you known what you said, I should have blamed you. But you did not understand me, so you blamed me, and I knew that you were ignorant, so I pardoned you."

---

## L'Envoi.

HERE end, to my sorrow, the labours of a quarter-century, and here I must perforce say with the "poets' Poet,"

> "Behold! I see the haven nigh at hand,
> To which I mean my wearie course to bend;
> Vere the main shete, and bear up with the land
> The which afore is fairly to be ken'd."

Nothing of importance now indeed remains for me but briefly to estimate the character of my work and to take cordial leave of my readers, thanking them for the interest they have accorded to these volumes and for enabling me thus successfully to complete ten volumes.

Without over-diffidence I would claim to have fulfilled the promise contained in my Foreword. The anthropological notes and notelets, which not only illustrate and read between the lines of the text, but assist the student of Moslem life and of Arabo-Egyptian manners, customs and language in a multitude of matters, form a repertory of Eastern knowledge.

That the work contains errors, shortcomings and many a lapsus, I am the first and foremost to declare. Yet in justice to myself I must also notice that the maculæ are few and far between; even the most unfriendly and interested critics have failed to point out an abnormal number of slips. And before pronouncing the "Vos plaudite!" or, as Easterns more politely say, "I implore that my poor name may be raised aloft on the tongue of praise," let me invoke the fair field and courteous favour which the Persian poet expected from his readers.

بپوش گر بخطای رسی و طعنه مزن
که هیچ بشر خالی از خطا نبود

Veil it, an fault thou find, nor jibe nor jeer:—
None may be found of faults and failings clear!

RICHARD F. BURTON.

TRIESTE, *September* 20, '87.

# Appendix.

*A.*—INDEX TO THE TALES AND PROPER NAMES.

*B.*—BIBLIOGRAPHICAL NOTES BY MR. W. F. KIRBY.

## *INDEX TO THE TALES AND PROPER NAMES.*

N.B.—*The Roman numerals denote the volume, the Arabic the page.*

## *CONTRIBUTIONS TO THE BIBLIOGRAPHY OF THE THOUSAND AND ONE NIGHTS, AND THEIR IMITATIONS, WITH A TABLE SHOWING THE CONTENTS OF THE PRINCIPAL EDITIONS AND TRANSLATIONS OF THE NIGHTS.*

By W. F. KIRBY,

*Author of*

*"Ed-Dimiryah: an Oriental Romance," "The New Arabian Nights," &c.*

---

THE European editions of the Thousand and One Nights, even excluding the hundreds of popular editions which have nothing specially noticeable about them, are very numerous; and the following Notes must, I am fully aware, be incomplete, though they will, perhaps, be found useful to persons interested in the subject. Although I believe that editions of most of the English, French and German versions of any importance have passed through my hands, I have not had an opportunity of comparing many in other languages, some of which at least may be independent editions, not derived from Galland. The imitations and adaptations of The Nights are, perhaps, more numerous than the editions of The Nights themselves, if we exclude mere reprints of Galland; and many of them are even more difficult of access.

In the following Notes, I have sometimes referred to tales by their numbers in the Table.

### *GALLAND'S MS. AND TRANSLATION.*

The first MS. of The Nights known in Europe was brought to Paris by Galland at the close of the 17th century; and his translation was published in Paris, in twelve small volumes, under the title of "Les Mille et une Nuit: Contes Arabes, traduits en François par M. Galland." These volumes appeared at intervals between 1704 and 1717. Galland himself died in 1715, and it is uncertain how far he was responsible for the latter part of the work. Only the first six of the twelve vols. are divided into Nights, vol. 6 completing the story of Camaralzaman, and ending with

Night 234. The Voyages of Sindbad are not found in Galland's MS. though he has intercalated them as Nights 69-90 between Nos. 3 and 4. It should be mentioned, however, that in some texts (Bresl., for instance) No. 133 is placed much earlier in the series than in others.

The Stories in Galland's last six vols. may be divided into two classes, viz., those known to occur in genuine texts of The Nights, and those which do not. To the first category belong Nos. 7, 8, 59, 153 and 170; and some even of these are not found in Galland's own MS., but were derived by him from other sources. The remaining tales (Nos. 191-198) do not really belong to The Nights; and, strange to say, although they are certainly genuine Oriental tales, the actual originals have never been found. I am inclined to think that Galland may, perhaps, have written and adapted them from his recollection of stories which he himself heard related during his own residence in the East, especially as most of these tales appear to be derived rather from Persian or Turkish than from Arabian sources.

The following Preface appeared in vol. 9 which I translate from Talander's German edition, as the original is not before me:

"The two stories with which the eighth volume concludes do not properly belong to the Thousand and One Nights. They were added and printed without the previous knowledge of the translator, who had not the slightest idea of the trick that had been played upon him until the eighth volume was actually on sale. The reader must not, therefore, be surprised that the story of the Sleeper Awakened, which commences vol. 9 is written as if Scheherazade had related it immediately after the story of Ganem, which forms the greater part of vol. 8. Care will be taken to omit these two stories in a new edition, as not belonging to the work."

It is, perhaps, not to be wondered at that when the new edition was actually published, subsequently to Galland's death, the condemned stories were retained, and the preface withdrawn; though No. 170 still reads as if it followed No. 8.

The information I have been able to collect respecting the disputed tales is very slight. I once saw a MS. advertised in an auction catalogue (I think that of the library of the late Prof. H. H. Wilson) as containing two of Galland's doubtful tales, but which they were was not stated. The fourth and last volume of the MS. used by Galland is lost; but it is almost certain that it did not contain any of these tales (compare Payne ix. 265, note).

The story of Zeyn Alasnam (No. 191) is derived from the same source as that of the Fourth Durwesh, in the well-known Hindustani reading-book, the Bagh o Bahar. If it is based upon this, Galland has greatly altered and improved it, and has given it the whole colouring of a European moral fairy tale.

The story of Ali Baba (No. 195) is, I have been told, a Chinese tale. It occurs under the title of the Two Brothers and the Forty-nine Dragons in Geldart's Modern Greek Tales. It has also been stated that the late Prof. Palmer met with a very similar story among the Arabs of Sinai (Payne, ix. 266).

The story of Sidi Nouman (No. 194b) may have been based partly upon the Third Shaykh's Story (No. 1c), which Galland omits. The feast of the Ghools is, I believe, Greek or Turkish, rather than Arabian, in character, as vampires, personified plague, and similar horrors are much commoner in the folk-lore of the former peoples.

Many incidents of the doubtful, as well as of the genuine tales, are common in European folk-lore (versions of Nos. 2 and 198, for instance, occur in Grimm's Kinder und Hausmärchen), and some of the doubtful tales have their analogues in Scott's MS.

I have not seen Galland's original edition in 12 vols.; but the Stadt-Bibliothek of Frankfort-on-Main contains a copy, published at La Haye, in 12 vols. (with frontispieces), made up of two or more editions, as follows:—

Vol. i. (ed. 6) 1729; vols. ii. iii. iv. (ed. 5) 1729; vols. v. vi. viii. (ed. 5) 1728; vol. vii. (ed. 6) 1731; vols. ix. to xi. (ed. not noted) 1730; and vol. xii. (ed. not noted) 1731.

The discrepancies in the dates of the various volumes looks (as Mr. Clouston has suggested) as if separate volumes were reprinted as required, independently of the others. This might account for vols. v. vi. and viii. of the fifth edition having been apparently reprinted before vols. ii. iii. and iv.

The oldest French version in the British Museum consists of the first eight vols., published at La Haye, and likewise made up of different editions, as follows:—

i. (ed. 5) 1714; ii. iii. iv. (ed. 4) 1714; v. vi. (ed. 5) 1728; vii. (ed. 5) 1719; viii. ("suivant la copie imprimée à Paris") 1714.

Most French editions (old and new) contain Galland's Dedication, "A Madame Madame la Marquise d'O., Dame du Palais de Madame la Duchesse de Bourgogne," followed by an "Avertissement." In addition to these, the La Haye copies have Fontenelle's Approbation prefixed to several volumes, but in slightly different words, and bearing different dates:—December 27th, 1703 (vol. i.); April 14th, 1704 (vol. vi.); and October 4th, 1705 (vol. vii.). This is according to the British Museum copy; I did not examine the Frankfort copy with reference to the Approbation. The Approbation is translated in full in the old English version as follows: "I have read, by order of my Lord Chancellor, this Manuscript, wherein I find nothing that ought to hinder its being Printed. And I am of opinion that the Publick will be very well pleased with the Perusal of these Oriental Stories. Paris, 27th December, 1705 [apparently a misprint for 1703]. (Signed) FONTENELLE."

In the Paris edition of 1726 (vide infrà), Galland says in his Dedication, "Il a fallu le faire venir de Syrie, et mettre en François, le premier volume que voici, de quatre seulement qui m'ont été envoyez." So, also, in a Paris edition (in eight vols. 12mo) of 1832; but in the La Haye issue of 1714, we read not "quatre" but "six" volumes. The old German edition of Talander (vide infrà) does not contain Galland's Dedication (Epître) or Avertissement.

The earliest French editions were generally in 12 vols., or six; I possess a copy of a six-volume edition, published at Paris in 1726. The title-page of the latter designates it as "nouvelle edition, corrigée."

Galland's work was speedily translated into various European languages, and even now forms the original of all the numerous popular editions. The earliest English editions were in six volumes, corresponding to the first six of Galland, and ending with the story of Camaralzaman; nor was it till nearly the end of the 18th century that the remaining half of the work was translated into English. The date of appearance of the first edition is unknown to bibliographers; Lowndes quotes an edition of 1724 as the oldest; but the British Museum contains a set of six vols., made up of portions of the second, third and fourth editions, as follows:—

Vols. i. ii. (ed. 4) 1713; vols. iii. iv. (ed. 2) 1712; and vols. v. vi. (ed. 3) 1715.

Here likewise the separate volumes seem to have been reprinted independently of each other; and it is not unlikely that the English translation may have closely followed the French publication, being issued volume by volume, as the French appeared, as far as vol. vi. The title-page of this old edition is very quaint:

"Arabian Nights Entertainments, consisting of One thousand and one Stories, told by the Sultaness of the Indies to divert the Sultan from the Execution of a Bloody Vow he had made, to marry a Lady every day, and have her head cut off next Morning, to avenge himself for the Disloyalty of the first Sultaness, also containing a better account of the Customs, Manners and Religion of the Eastern Nations, viz., Tartars, Persians and Indians than is to be met with in any Author hitherto published. Translated into French from the Arabian MSS. by Mr. Galland of the Royal Academy, and now done into English. Printed for Andrew Bell at the Cross Keys and Bible, in Cornhill."

The British Museum has an edition in 4to published in 1772, in farthing numbers, every Monday, Wednesday and Friday. It extends to 79 numbers, forming five volumes.

The various editions of the old English version appear to be rare, and the set in the British Museum is very poor. The oldest edition which I have seen which contains the latter half of Galland's version is called the 14th edition, and was published in London in four volumes, in 1778. Curiously enough, the "13th edition," also containing the conclusion, was published at Edinburgh in three volumes in 1780. Perhaps it is a reprint of a London edition published before that of 1778. The Scotch appear to have been fond of The Nights, as there are many Scotch editions both of The Nights and the imitations.

Revised or annotated editions by Piguenit (4 vols., London, 1792) and Gough (4 vols., Edinburgh, 1798) may deserve a passing notice.

A new translation of Galland, by Rev. E. Forster, in five vols. 4to, with engravings from pictures by Robert Smirke, R.A., appeared in 1802; and now commands a higher price than any other edition of Galland.

A new edition in 8vo appeared in 1810. Most of the recent popular English versions are based either upon Forster's or Scott's.

Another translation from Galland by G. S. Beaumont (four vols. 8vo), appeared in 1811. (Lowndes writes *Wiliam* Beaumont.)

Among the various popular editions of later date we may mention an edition in two vols., 8vo, published at Liverpool (1813), and containing Cazotte's Continuation; an edition published by Griffin and Co., in 1866, to which Beckford's "Vathek" is appended; an edition "arranged for the perusal of youthful readers," by the Hon. Mrs. Sugden (Whittaker & Co., 1863); and "Five Favourite Tales from The Arabian Nights in words of one syllable, by A. & E. Warner" (Lewis, 1871).

Some of the English editions of Galland aim at originality by arranging the tales in a different order. The cheap edition published by Dicks in 1868 is one instance.

An English version of Galland was published at Lucknow, in four vols., 8vo, in 1880.

I should, perhaps, mention that I have not noticed De Sacy's "Mille et une Nuit," because it is simply a new edition of Galland; and I have not seen either Destain's French edition (mentioned by Sir R. F. Burton), nor Cardonne's Continuation (mentioned in Cabinet des Fées, xxxvii. p. 83). As Cardonne died in 1784, his Continuation, if genuine, would be the earliest of all.

The oldest German version, by Talander, seems to have appeared in volumes, as the French was issued; and these volumes were certainly reprinted when required, without indication of separate editions; but in slightly varied style, and with alteration of dates. This old German version is said to be rarer than the French. It is in twelve parts—some, however, being double. The set before me is clearly made up of different reprints, and the first title-page is as follows: "Die Tausend und eine Nacht, worinnen seltzame Arabische Historien und wunderbare Begebenheiten, benebst artigen Liebes-Intriguen, auch Sitten und Gewohnheiten der Morgenländer, auf sehr anmuthige Weise erzehlet werden; Erstlich vom Hru. Galland, der Königl. Academie Mitgliede aus der Arabischen Sprache in die Französische und aus selbiger anitzo ins Deutsche übersetzt: Erster und Anderer Theil. Mit der Vorrede Herru Talanders. Leipzig: Verlegts Moritz Georg Weidmann Sr. Königl. Maj. in Hohlen und Churfürstl. Durchl. zu Sachsen Buchhändler, Anno 1730." Talander's Preface relates chiefly to the importance of the work as illustrative of Arabian manners and customs, &c. It is dated from "Liegnitz, den 7 Sept., Anno 1710," which fixes the approximate date of publication of the first part of this translation. Vols. i. and ii. of my set (double vol. with frontispiece) are dated 1730, and have Talander's preface; vols. iii. and iv. (divided, but consecutively paged, and with only one title-page and frontispiece and reprint of Talander's preface) are dated 1719; vols. v. and vi. (same remarks, except that Talander's preface is here dated 1717) are dated 1737; vol. vii. (no frontispiece; preface dated 1710) is dated 1721; vol. viii. (no frontispiece nor preface, nor does Talander's name appear on the title-page) is dated 1729; vols. ix. and x. (divided, but consecutively paged, and with only one title-page and frontispiece; Talander's name and preface do not appear, but Galland's preface to vol. ix., already mentioned, is prefixed) are dated 1731; and vols xi. and xii. (same remarks, but no preface) are dated 1732.

Galland's notes are translated, but not his preface and dedication.

There is a later German translation (6 vols. 8vo, Bremen, 1781–1785) by J. H. Voss, the author of the standard German translation of Homer.

The British Museum has just acquired a Portuguese translation of Galland, in 4 volumes: "As Mil e uma Noites, Contos Arabes," published by Ernesto Chardron, Editor, Porto e Braga, 1881.

There are two editions of a modern Greek work in the British Museum, (1792 and 1804) published at Venice (*Ενετιηριν*) in three small volumes. The first volume contains Galland (Nos. 1–6 of the table) and vols. ii. and iii. chiefly contain the Thousand and One Days. It is, apparently, translated from some Italian work.

Several editions in Italian (Mille ed una Notte) have appeared at Naples and Milan; they are said by Sir R. F. Burton to be mere reprints of Galland.

There are, also, several in Dutch, one of which, by C. Van der Post, in 3 vols. 8vo, published at Utrecht in 1848, purports, I believe, to be a translation from the Arabic, and has been reprinted several times. The Dutch editions are usually entitled, "Arabische Vertellinge." A Danish edition appeared at Copenhagen in 1818, under the title of "Prindsesses Schehezerade. Fortällinger eller de saakatle Tusende og een Nat. Udgivna paa Dansk vid Heelegaan." Another, by Rasmassen, was commenced in 1824; and a third Danish work, probably founded on the Thousand and One Nights, and published in 1816, bears the title, "Digt og Eventyr fra Osterland, af arabiska og persischen utrykta kilder."

I have seen none of these Italian, Dutch or Danish editions; but there is little doubt that most, if not all, are derived from Galland's work.

The following is the title of a Javanese version, derived from one of the Dutch editions, and published at Leyden in 1865, "Eenige Vertellingen uit de Arabisch duizend en één Nacht. Naar de Nederduitsche vertaling in het Javaansch vertaald, door Winter-Roorda."

Mr. A. G. Ellis has shown me an edition of Galland's Aladdin (No. 193) in Malay, by M. Van der Lawan (?) printed in Batavia A.D. 1869.

## *COMPARATIVE TABLE OF THE TALES IN THE PRINCIPAL EDITIONS OF THE THOUSAND AND ONE NIGHTS, viz.:—*

1. Galland (French).
2. Caussin de Perceval (French).
3. Gauttier (French).
4. Scott's MS. (Wortley Montague) (Arabic).
5. Ditto (Anderson; marked A) (Arabic).
6. Scott's Arabian Nights (English).
7. Scott's Tales and Anecdotes (marked A) (English).
8. Von Hammer's MS. (Arabic).
9. Zinserling (German).
10. Lamb (English).
11. Trébutien (French).
12. Bul. text (Arabic).
13. Lane (English).
14. Bres. text (Arabic).
15. Habicht (German).
16. Weil (German).
17. Mac. text (Arabic).
18. Torrens (English).
19. Payne (English).
20. Payne's Tales from the Arabic (marked I. II. III.) (English).
21. Calc. (Arabic).
22. Lady Burton (English).
23. Sir R. F. Burton (Supplementary Nights marked I. II. III.) (English).

As nearly all editions of The Nights are in several volumes, the volumes are indicated throughout, except in the case of some of the texts. Only those tales in No. 5, not included in No. 4, are here indicated in the same column. All tales which there is good reason to believe do not belong to the genuine Nights are marked with an asterisk.

| | Galland. | Caussin de Perceval. | Gautier. | Scott's MS. | Scott. | Von Hammer's MS. | Zinserling. | Lamb. | Trébutien. | "Bul." Text. | Lane. | "Bres." Text. | Habicht. | Weil. | "Mac." Text. | Torrens. | Payne. | Calc. | Burton (Lady). | Burton (Sir R. F.) |
|---|---|---|---|---|---|---|---|---|---|---|---|---|---|---|---|---|---|---|---|---|
| Introduction . . . . . . . . . | 1 | ... | ... | 1 | — | (Full contents from Introd. to No. 4 not given: 3*e* and 4 are apparently wanting.) | ... | ... | ... | + | 1 | + | ... | 1 | + | 1 | 1 | + | 1 | 1 |
| Story of King Shahryar and his Brother . . | 1 | 1 | 1 | 1 | 1 | | ... | ... | ... | + | 1 | + | 1 | 1 | + | 1 | 1 | + | 1 | 1 |
| *a.* Tale of the Bull and the Ass . . . | 1 | 1 | 1 | A | 1 | | ... | ... | ... | + | 1 | + | 1 | 1 | + | 1 | 1 | + | 1 | 1 |
| 1. Tale of the Trader and the Jinni . . . . | 1 | 1 | 1 | 1 | 1 | | ... | ... | ... | + | 1 | + | 1 | 1 | + | 1 | 1 | + | 1 | 1 |
| *a.* The First Shaykh's Story . . . . | 1 | 1 | 1 | 1 | 1 | | ... | ... | ... | + | 1 | + | 1 | 1 | + | 1 | 1 | + | 1 | 1 |
| *b.* The Second Shaykh's Story . . . | 1 | 1 | 1 | 1 | 1 | | ... | ... | ... | + | 1 | + | 1 | 1 | + | 1 | 1 | + | 1 | 1 |
| *c.* The Third Shaykh's Story . . . | — | — | ... | 1 | — | | ... | ... | ... | + | 1 | + | 1 | 1 | + | 1 | 1 | — | 1 | 1 |
| 2. The Fisherman and the Jinni . . . . | 1 | 1 | 1 | 1 | 1 | | ... | ... | ... | + | 1 | + | 1 | 1 | + | 1 | 1 | + | 1 | 1 |
| *a.* Tale of the Wazir and the Sage Duban . | 1 | 1 | 1 | 1 | 1 | | ... | ... | ... | + | 1 | + | 1 | 1 | + | 1 | 1 | + | 1 | 1 |
| *ab.* Story of King Sindibad and his Falcon . | — | — | ... | ? | — | | ... | ... | ... | + | — | — | — | 1 | + | 1 | 1 | — | 1 | 1 |
| *ac.* Tale of the Husband and the Parrot . | 1 | 1 | 1 | ? | 1 | | ... | ... | ... | — | 1 | + | 1 | 1 | — | — | — | + | 1 | 1 |
| *ad.* Tale of the Prince and the Ogress . | 1 | 1 | 1 | ? | 1 | | ... | ... | ... | + | 1 | + | 1 | 1 | + | 1 | 1 | + | 1 | 1 |
| *b.* Tale of the Ensorcelled Prince . . . | 1 | 1 | 1 | 1 | 1 | | ... | ... | ... | + | 1 | + | 1 | 1 | + | 1 | 1 | + | 1 | 1 |
| 3. The Porter and the Three Ladies of Baghdad . | 1 | 1 | 1 | 1 | 1 | | ... | ... | ... | + | 1 | + | 2 | 1 | + | 1 | 1 | + | 1 | 1 |
| *a.* The First Kalandar's Tale . . . | 2 | 1 | 1 | 1 | 1 | | ... | ... | ... | + | 1 | + | 2 | 1 | + | 1 | 1 | + | 1 | 1 |
| *b.* The Second Kalandar's Tale . . . | 2 | 1 | 1 | 1 | 1 | | ... | ... | ... | + | 1 | + | 2 | 1 | + | 1 | 1 | + | 1 | 1 |
| *ba.* Tale of the Envier and the Envied . | 2 | 1 | 1 | ? | 1 | | ... | ... | ... | — | 1 | + | 2 | 1 | + | 1 | 1 | + | 1 | 1 |
| *c.* The Third Kalandar's Tale . . . | 2 | 1 | 1 | 1 | 1 | | ... | ... | ... | + | 1 | + | 2 | 1 | + | 1 | 1 | + | 1 | 1 |
| *d.* The Eldest Lady's Tale . . . . | 2 | 2 | 1 | 1 | 1 | | ... | ... | ... | + | 1 | + | 2 | 1 | + | 1 | 1 | + | 1 | 1 |
| *e.* Tale of the Portress . . . . . . | 2 | 2 | 1 | 1 | 1 | | ... | ... | ... | + | 1 | + | 2 | 1 | + | 1 | 1 | — | 1 | 1 |
| Conclusion of the Story of the Porter and Three Ladies . . . . . . . . . | 2 | 2 | 1 | 1 | 1 | | ... | ... | ... | + | 1 | + | 2 | 1 | + | 1 | 1 | + | 1 | 1 |
| 4. Tale of the Three Apples . . . . . . | 3 | 2 | 2 | ... | 2 | | ... | ... | ... | + | 1 | + | 3 | 1 | + | 1 | 1 | + | 1 | 1 |
| 5. Tale of Nur Al-Din and his Son Badr Al-Din Hasan . . . . . . . . | 3, 4 | 2 | 2 | ... | 2 | 1 | ... | ... | ... | + | 1 | + | 3 | 1 | + | 1 | 1 | + | 1 | 1 |
| 6. The Hunchback's Tale . . . . . . | 4 | 2 | 2 | 1 | 2 | 1 | ... | ... | ... | + | 1 | + | 3 | 1 | + | 1 | 1 | + | 1 | 1 |

| | | | | | | | | | | | | | | | | | | | | |
|---|---|---|---|---|---|---|---|---|---|---|---|---|---|---|---|---|---|---|---|---|
| *a.* The Nazarene Broker's Story . . . . | 4 | 2 | 2 | I | 2 | I | ... | ... | ... | + | I | + | 3 | I | + | I | I | + | I | I |
| *b.* The Reeve's Tale . . . . . . . | 4 | 2 | 2 | I | 2 | I | ... | ... | ... | + | I | + | 3 | I | + | I | I | + | I | I |
| *c.* Tale of the Jewish Doctor . . . . . | 4 | 3 | 2 | ? | 2 | I | ... | ... | ... | + | I | + | 3 | I | + | I | I | + | I | I |
| *d.* Tale of the Tailor . . . . . . | 4, 5 | 3 | 2 | I | 2 | I | ... | ... | ... | + | I | + | 3 | I | + | I | I | + | I | I |
| *e.* The Barber's Tale of Himself . . . . | 5 | 3 | 2 | I | 2 | I | ... | ... | ... | + | I | + | 3 | I | + | I | I | + | I | I |
| *ea.* The Barber's Tale of his First Brother . | 5 | 3 | 2 | I | 2 | I | ... | ... | ... | + | I | + | 4 | I | + | I | I | + | I | I |
| *eb.* The Barber's Tale of his Second Brother . | 5 | 3 | 2 | ? | 2 | I | ... | ... | ... | + | I | + | 4 | I | + | I | I | + | I | I |
| *ec.* The Barber's Tale of his Third Brother . . | 5 | 3 | 2 | I | 2 | I | ... | ... | ... | + | I | + | 4 | I | + | I | I | + | I | I |
| *ed.* The Barber's Tale of his Fourth Brother . | 5 | 3 | 2 | I | 2 | I | ... | ... | ... | + | I | + | 4 | I | + | I | I | + | I | I |
| *ee.* The Barber's Tale of his Fifth Brother . . | 5 | 3 | 2 | I | 2 | I | ... | ... | ... | + | I | + | 4 | I | + | I | I | + | I | I |
| *ef.* The Barber's Tale of his Sixth Brother . | 5 | 3 | 2 | I | 2 | I | ... | ... | ... | + | I | + | 4 | I | + | I | I | + | I | I |
| The End of the Tailor's Tale . . . | 5 | 3 | 2 | I | 2 | I | ... | ... | ... | + | I | + | 4 | I | + | I | I | + | I | I |
| 7. Nur Al-Din Ali and the Damsel Anis Al-Jalis . . | 7 | 4 | 3 | I | 3 | I | ... | ... | ... | + | I | + | 5, 6 | I | + | I | I | + | I | 2 |
| 8. Tale of Ghanim Bin Ayyub, the Distraught, the Thrall o' Love . . . . . . . . . | 8 | 4, 5 | 4 | ... | 4 | I | ... | ... | ... | + | I | + | 8 | 2 | + | I | I | ... | I | 2 |
| *a.* Tale of the First Eunuch, Bukhayt . . | ... | ... | ... | ... | ... | ? | ... | ... | ... | + | – | + | ... | 2 | + | I | I | ... | ... | 2 |
| *b.* Tale of the Second Eunuch, Kafur . . | ... | ... | ... | ... | ... | ? | ... | ... | ... | + | I | ... | ... | 2 | + | I | I | ... | I | 2 |
| 9. Tale of King Omar Bin Al-Nu'uman, and his sons Sharrkan and Zau Al-Makan . . . . . | ... | ... | ... | ... | ... | I | ... | ... | ... | + | – | ... | ... | 3 | + | I(p) | 2 | ... | I, 2 | 2, 3 |
| *a.* Tale of Taj Al-Muluk and the Princess Dunya . . . . . . . . | ... | ... | ... | ... | ... | I | ... | ... | ... | + | I | ... | ... | 3 | + | ... | 2 | ... | 2 | 2, 3 |
| *aa.* Tale of Aziz and Azizah . . . . . | ... | ... | ... | ... | ... | I | ... | ... | ... | + | I | ... | ... | 3 | + | ... | 2 | ... | 2 | 2. 3 |
| *b.* Tale of the Hashish-Eater . . . . . | ... | ... | ... | ... | ... | ? | ... | ... | ... | + | – | ... | ... | – | + | ... | 2 | ... | ... | 3 |
| *c.* Tale of Hammad the Badawi . . . . | ... | ... | ... | ... | ... | I | ... | ... | ... | + | – | ... | ... | – | + | ... | 2 | ... | 2 | 3 |
| 10. The Birds and Beasts and the Carpenter . . . | ... | ... | ... | ... | ... | Nos. 10-19 represented by 7 Fables.) | ... | ... | ... | + | 2 | ... | ... | 2 | + | ... | 3 | ... | 2 | 3 |
| 11. The Hermits . . . . . . . . | ... | ... | ... | ... | ... | | ... | ... | ... | + | – | ... | ... | 2 | + | ... | 3 | ... | 2 | 3 |
| 12. The Water-fowl and the Tortoise . . . . | ... | ... | ... | ... | ... | | ... | ... | ... | + | – | ... | ... | ... | + | ... | 3 | ... | 2 | 3 |
| 13. The Wolf and the Fox . . . . . . | ... | ... | ... | ... | ... | | ... | ... | ... | + | 2 | ... | ... | ... | + | ... | 3 | ... | 2 | 3 |
| *a.* Tale of the Falcon and the Partridge . . | ... | ... | ... | ... | ... | | ... | ... | ... | + | 2 | ... | ... | ... | + | ... | 3 | ... | 2 | 3 |
| 14. The Mouse and the Ichneumon . . . . . | ... | ... | ... | ... | ... | | ... | ... | ... | + | – | ... | ... | ... | + | ... | 3 | ... | 2 | 3 |
| 15. The Cat and the Crow . . . . . . | ... | ... | ... | ... | ... | | ... | ... | ... | + | – | ... | ... | ... | + | ... | 3 | ... | 2 | 3 |
| 16. The Fox and the Crow . . . . . . | ... | ... | ... | ... | ... | | ... | ... | ... | + | – | ... | ... | 2 | + | ... | 3 | ... | 2 | 3 |
| *a.* The Flea and the Mouse . . . . . | ... | ... | ... | ... | ... | | ... | ... | ... | + | – | ... | ... | ... | + | ... | 3 | ... | 2 | 3 |
| *b.* The Saker and the Birds . . . . . | ... | ... | ... | ... | ... | | ... | ... | ... | + | – | ... | ... | ... | + | ... | 3 | ... | 2 | 3 |
| *c.* The Sparrow and the Eagle . . . . . | ... | ... | ... | ... | ... | | ... | ... | ... | + | – | ... | ... | ... | + | ... | 3 | ... | 2 | 3 |

| | Galland. | Caussin de Perceval. | Gauttier. | Scott's MS. | Scott. | Von Hammer's MS. | Zinserling. | Lamb. | Trébutien. | "Bul." Text. | Lane. | "Bres." Text. | Habicht. | Weil. | "Mac." Text. | Torrens. | Payne. | Calc. | Burton (Lady). | Burton (Sir R. F.) |
|---|---|---|---|---|---|---|---|---|---|---|---|---|---|---|---|---|---|---|---|---|
| 17. The Hedgehog and the Wood Pigeons | ... | ... | ... | ... | ... | ... | ... | ... | ... | + | – | ... | ... | ... | + | ... | 3 | ... | 2 | 3 |
| *a.* The Merchant and the Two Sharpers | ... | ... | ... | ... | ... | ... | ... | ... | ... | + | – | ... | ... | ... | + | ... | 3 | ... | 2 | 3 |
| 18. The Thief and his Monkey | ... | ... | ... | ... | ... | ... | ... | ... | ... | + | – | ... | ... | ... | + | ... | 3 | ... | 2 | 3 |
| *a.* The Foolish Weaver | ... | ... | ... | ... | ... | ... | ... | ... | ... | + | – | ... | ... | ... | + | ... | 3 | ... | 2 | 3 |
| 19 The Sparrow and the Peacock | ... | ... | ... | ... | ... | ... | ... | ... | ... | + | – | ... | ... | ... | + | ... | 3 | ... | 2 | 3 |
| 20. Ali Bin Bakkar and Shams Al-Nahar | 5, 6 | 3 | 3 | ... | 2, 3 | 1 | ... | ... | ... | + | 2 | + | 4 | 1 | + | ... | 3 | + | 2 | 3 |
| 21. Tale of Kamar Al-Zaman | 6 | 3, 4 | 3 | 2 | 2 | 1, 2 | ... | ... | ... | + | 2 | + | 5 | 1 | + | ... | 3 | ... | 2 | 3 4 |
| *a.* Ni'amah bin Al-Rabia and Naomi his Slave-girl | ... | 9 | ... | ... | ... | ? | ... | ... | ... | + | 2 | + | 13 | 2 | + | ... | 3 | ... | 2 | 4 |
| 22. Ala Al-Din Abu Al-Shamat | ... | 9 | ... | ... | ... | 2 | ... | ... | ... | + | 2 | + | 13 | 2 | + | ... | 3 | ... | 2 | 4 |
| 23. Hatim of the Tribe of Tayy | ... | ... | ... | ... | ... | 2 | 1 | ... | 3 | + | 2 | + | ... | 2 | + | ... | 3 | ... | 2 | 4 |
| 24. Ma'an the son of Zaidah and the three Girls | ... | ... | ... | ... | ... | 2 | 1 | ... | 3 | + | 2 | + | ... | 2 | + | ... | 3 | ... | 2 | 4 |
| 25. Ma'an son of Zaidah and the Badawi | ... | ... | ... | ... | ... | 2 | 1 | ... | 3 | + | – | + | ... | 2 | + | ... | 3 | ... | 2 | 4 |
| 26. The City of Labtayt | ... | ... | ... | ... | ... | 2 | 1 | ... | 3 | + | – | + | ... | 2 | + | ... | 3 | ... | 2 | 4 |
| 27. The Caliph Hisham and the Arab Youth | ... | ... | ... | ... | ... | 2 | 1 | ... | 3 | + | – | + | ... | 2 | + | ... | 3 | ... | 2 | 4 |
| 28. Ibrahim bin Al-Mahdi and the Barber-Surgeon | ... | ... | ... | ... | ... | 2 | 1 | ... | 3 | + | 2 | + | ... | 2 | + | ... | 3 | ... | 2 | 4 |
| 29. The City of Many-columned Iram and Abdullah son of Abi Kalabah | ... | ... | ... | ... | ... | 2 | 1 | ... | 3 | + | 2 | + | ... | 2 | + | ... | 3 | ... | 2 | 4 |
| 30. Isaac of Mosul | ... | ... | 7 | ... | ... | 2 | 1 | ... | 3 | + | 2 | + | 13 | 2 | + | ... | 3 | + | 3 | 4 |
| 31. The Sweep and the Noble Lady | ... | ... | ... | ... | ... | 2 | 1 | ... | 3 | + | – | ... | ... | 4 | + | ... | 3 | ... | ... | 4 |
| 32. The Mock Caliph | ... | 9 | 2 | ... | ... | 2 | – | ... | – | + | 2 | + | 4 | 2 | + | ... | 3 | ... | 3 | 4 |
| 33. Ali the Persian | ... | ... | ... | ... | ... | 2 | 1 | ... | 3 | + | – | ... | ... | 4 | + | ... | 3 | ... | 3 | 4 |
| 34. Harun Al-Rashid and the Slave-Girl and the Imam Abu Yusuf | ... | ... | ... | ... | ... | – | – | ... | – | + | – | + | ... | 2 | + | ... | 4 | ... | 3 | 4 |
| 35. The Lover who feigned himself a Thief | ... | ... | ... | ... | ... | 2 | 1 | ... | 3 | + | 2 | + | ... | 2 | + | ... | 4 | ... | 3 | 4 |
| 36. Ja'afar the Barmecide and the Bean-Seller | ... | ... | ... | ... | ... | 2 | – | ... | – | + | 2 | ... | ... | 4 | + | ... | 4 | ... | 3 | 4 |

| | | | | | | | | | | | | | | | | | | | | |
|---|---|---|---|---|---|---|---|---|---|---|---|---|---|---|---|---|---|---|---|---|
| 37. Abu Mohammed hight Lazybones | ... | 9 | ... | ... | ... | 2 | – | ... | – | + | 2 | + | 13 | 2 | + | ... | 4 | ... | 3 | 4 |
| 38. Generous dealing of Yahya bin Khalid the Barmecide with Mansur | ... | ... | ... | ... | ... | ? | – | ... | – | + | 2 | ... | ... | ... | + | ... | 4 | ... | 3 | 4 |
| 39. Generous dealing of Yahya son of Khalid with a man who forged a letter in his name | ... | ... | ... | ... | ... | ? | – | ... | – | + | 2 | + | ... | ... | + | ... | 4 | ... | 3 | 4 |
| 40. Caliph Al-Maamun and the Strange Scholar | ... | ... | ... | ... | ... | 2 | 1 | ... | 3 | + | 2 | ... | ... | ... | + | ... | 4 | .. | 3 | 4 |
| 41. Ali Shar and Zumurrud | ... | ... | ... | ... | ... | 2 | 1 | ... | 1 | + | 2 | + | ... | 2 | + | ... | 4 | ... | 3 | 4 |
| 42. The Loves of Jubayr Bin Umayr and the Lady Budur | ... | ... | ... | ... | ... | 2 | 1 | ... | 1 | + | 2 | + | ... | 2 | + | ... | 4 | ... | 3 | 4 |
| 43. The Man of Al-Yaman and his six Slave-Girls | ... | ... | ... | ... | ... | 2 | 1 | ... | 3 | + | – | + | ... | 2 | + | ... | 4 | ... | ... | 4 |
| 44. Harun Al-Rashid and the Damsel and Abu Nowas | ... | ... | ... | ... | ... | 2 | 1 | ... | 3 | + | – | + | ... | 2 | + | ... | 4 | ... | ... | 4 |
| 45. The Man who stole the dish of gold whereon the dog ate | ... | ... | ... | ... | ... | 2 | 1 | ... | 3 | + | 2 | + | ... | 4 | + | ... | 4 | ... | 3 | 4 |
| 46. The Sharper of Alexandria and the Chief of Police | ... | ... | ... | ... | ... | 2 | 1 | ... | 3 | + | 2 | ... | ... | 4 | + | ... | 4 | ... | 3 | 4 |
| 47. Al-Malik Al-Nasir and the three Chiefs of Police | ... | ... | ... | ... | ... | 2 | 1 | ... | 3 | + | 2 | + | ... | 4 | + | ... | 4 | ... | 3 | 4 |
| *a.* Story of the Chief of the new Cairo Police | ... | ... | ... | ... | ... | 2 | 1 | ... | 3 | + | 2 | + | ... | 4 | + | ... | 4 | ... | 3 | 4 |
| *b.* Story of the Chief of the Bulak Police | ... | ... | ... | ... | ... | 2 | 1 | ... | 3 | + | 2 | + | ... | 4 | + | ... | 4 | ... | 3 | 4 |
| *c.* Story of the Chief of the Old Cairo Police | ... | ... | ... | ... | ... | 2 | 1 | ... | 3 | + | 2 | + | ... | 4 | + | ... | 4 | ... | 3 | 4 |
| 48. The Thief and the Shroff | ... | ... | ... | ... | ... | – | – | ... | – | + | 2 | + | ... | 4 | + | ... | 4 | ... | 3 | 4 |
| 49. The Chief of the Kus Police and the Sharper | ... | ... | ... | ... | ... | – | – | ... | – | + | – | ... | ... | ... | + | ... | 4 | ... | 3 | 4 |
| 50. Ibrahim bin al-Mahdi and the Merchant's Sister | ... | ... | ... | ... | ... | 2 | 1 | ... | 3 | + | 2 | + | ... | ... | + | ... | 4 | ... | 3 | 4 |
| 51. The Woman whose hands were cut off for almsgiving | ... | ... | ... | ... | ... | 2 | 1 | ... | 3 | + | 2 | + | ... | 4 | + | ... | 4 | ... | 3 | 4 |
| 52. The devout Israelite | ... | ... | ... | ... | ... | 2 | 1 | ... | 3 | + | 2 | ... | ... | 4 | + | ... | 4 | ... | 3 | 4 |
| 53. Abu Hassan Al-Ziyadi and the Khorasan Man | ... | ... | ... | ... | ... | 2 | 1 | ... | 3 | + | 2 | ... | ... | 4 | + | ... | 4 | ... | 3 | 4 |
| 54. The Poor Man and his Friend in Need | ... | ... | ... | ... | ... | – | – | ... | – | + | 2 | + | ... | 4 | + | ... | 4 | ... | 3 | 4 |
| 55. The Ruined Man who became rich again through a dream | ... | ... | ... | ... | ... | 2 | 1 | ... | 3 | + | 2 | + | ... | 4 | + | ... | 4 | ... | 3 | 4 |
| 56. Caliph Al-Mutawakkil and his Concubine Mahbubah | ... | ... | ... | ... | ... | 2 | 1 | ... | 3 | + | 2 | ... | ... | 4 | + | ... | 4 | ... | 3 | 4 |
| 57. Wardan the Butcher's Adventure with the Lady and the Bear | ... | ... | ... | ... | ... | 2 | 1 | ... | 3 | + | – | ... | ... | 4 | + | ... | 4 | ... | ... | 4 |
| 58. The King's Daughter and the Ape | ... | ... | ... | ... | ... | 2 | 1 | ... | 3 | + | – | ... | ... | .. | + | ... | 4 | ... | ... | 4 |
| 59. The Ebony Horse | 11 | 7 | 5 | ... | 5 | 2 | – | ... | – | + | 2 | + | 9 | 1 | + | ... | 4 | ... | 3 | 5 |
| 60. Uns Al-Wujud and the Wazir's Daughter Rose-in-Hood | ... | ... | 6 | 4 | 6 | 2 | 1 | ... | 1 | + | 2 | + | 11 | 2 | + | ... | 4 | ... | 3 | 5 |

| | Galland. | Caussin de Perceval. | Gauttier. | Scott's MS. | Scott. | Von Hammer's MS. | Zinserling. | Lamb. | Trébutien. | "Bul." Text. | Lane. | "Bres." Text. | Habicht. | Weil. | "Mac." Text. | Torrens. | Payne. | Calc. | Burton (Lady). | Burton (Sir R. F.) |
|---|---|---|---|---|---|---|---|---|---|---|---|---|---|---|---|---|---|---|---|---|
| 61. Abu Nowas with the Three Boys and the Caliph Harun Al-Rashid | ... | ... | ... | ... | ... | 2 | 1 | ... | – | + | – | + | ... | ... | + | ... | 4 | ... | ... | 5 |
| 62. Abdullah bin Ma'amar with the Man of Bassorah and his Slave-Girl | ... | ... | ... | ... | ... | 2 | 1 | ... | 3 | + | 2 | ... | ... | ... | + | ... | 4 | ... | 3 | 5 |
| 63. The Lovers of the Banu Ozrah | ... | ... | ... | ... | ... | – | – | ... | – | + | 2 | + | 11 | 4 | + | ... | 4 | ... | 3 | 5 |
| 64. The Wazir of Al-Yaman and his young Brother | ... | ... | ... | ... | ... | 2 | 1 | ... | 3 | + | – | ... | ... | ... | + | ... | 4 | ... | ... | 5 |
| 65. The Loves of the Boy and Girl at School | ... | ... | ... | ... | ... | 2 | 1 | ... | 3 | + | 2 | ... | ... | 4 | + | ... | 4 | ... | 3 | 5 |
| 66. Al-Mutalammis and his Wife Umaymah | ... | ... | ... | ... | ... | – | – | ... | – | + | – | + | ... | 4 | + | ... | 4 | ... | 3 | 5 |
| 67. Harun Al-Rashid and Zubaydah in the Bath | ... | ... | ... | ... | ... | 2 | 1 | ... | 3 | + | – | + | ... | ... | + | ... | 4 | ... | ... | 5 |
| 68. Harun Al-Rashid and the Three Poets | ... | ... | ... | ... | ... | 2 | 1 | ... | 3 | + | – | + | ... | 2 | + | ... | 4 | ... | ... | 5 |
| 69. Mus 'ab bin Al-Zubayr and Ayishah his Wife | ... | ... | ... | ... | ... | 2 | 1 | ... | 3 | + | – | + | ... | ... | + | ... | 4 | ... | ... | 5 |
| 70. Abu Al-Aswad and his Slave-Girl | ... | ... | ... | ... | ... | – | – | ... | ... | + | – | + | ... | ... | + | ... | 4 | ... | ... | 5 |
| 71. Harun Al-Rashid and the two Slave-Girls | ... | ... | ... | ... | ... | 2 | 1 | ... | 3 | + | – | + | ... | ... | + | ... | 4 | ... | ... | 5 |
| 72. Harun Al-Rashid and the Three Slave-Girls | ... | ... | ... | ... | ... | – | – | ... | ... | + | – | + | ... | ... | + | ... | 4 | ... | ... | 5 |
| 73. The Miller and his Wife | ... | ... | ... | ... | ... | 2 | 1 | ... | 3 | + | 2 | ... | ... | ... | + | ... | 4 | ... | 3 | 5 |
| 74. The Simpleton and the Sharper | ... | ... | ... | ... | ... | – | – | ... | – | + | 2 | + | ... | 4 | + | ... | 4 | ... | 3 | 5 |
| 75. The Kazi Abu Yusuf with Harun Al-Rashid and Queen Zubaydah | ... | ... | ... | A | A | – | – | ... | – | + | – | + | ... | ... | + | ... | 4 | ... | 3 | 5 |
| 76. The Caliph Al-Hakim and the Merchant | ... | ... | ... | ... | ... | 2 | 1 | ... | 3 | + | 2 | + | ... | 4 | + | ... | 4 | ... | 3 | 5 |
| 77. King Kisra Anushirwan and the Village Damsel | ... | ... | ... | ... | ... | 2 | 1 | ... | 3 | + | 2 | + | ... | 4 | + | ... | 4 | ... | 3 | 5 |
| 78. The Water-carrier and the Goldsmith's Wife | ... | ... | ... | ... | ... | 2 | 1 | ... | 3 | + | – | + | ... | ... | + | ... | 4 | ... | 3 | 5 |
| 79. Khusrau and Shirin and the Fisherman | ... | ... | ... | ... | ... | 2 | 1 | ... | 3 | + | 2 | + | ... | ... | + | ... | 4 | ... | 3 | 5 |
| 80. Yahya bin Khalid and the Poor Man | ... | ... | ... | ... | ... | – | – | ... | – | + | 2 | + | ... | ... | + | ... | 4 | ... | 3 | 5 |
| 81. Mohammed al-Amin and the Slave-Girl | ... | ... | ... | ... | ... | – | – | ... | – | + | 2 | + | ... | ... | + | ... | 4 | ... | 3 | 5 |
| 82. The Sons of Yahya bin Khalid and Said bin Salim | ... | ... | ... | ... | ... | – | – | ... | – | + | 2 | ... | ... | ... | + | ... | 4 | ... | 3 | 5 |
| 83. The Woman's Trick against her Husband | ... | ... | ... | ... | ... | 2 | 1 | ... | 3 | + | 2 | + | ... | ... | + | ... | 4 | ... | 3 | 5 |

| | | | | | | | | | | | | | | | | | | | | |
|---|---|---|---|---|---|---|---|---|---|---|---|---|---|---|---|---|---|---|---|---|
| 84. The Devout Woman and the Two Wicked Elders | ... | ... | ... | ... | ... | 2 | 1 | ... | 3 | + | − | + | ... | 4 | + | ... | 4 | ... | 3 | 5 |
| 85. Ja'afar the Barmecide and the old Badawi | ... | ... | ... | ... | ... | 2 | 1 | ... | 3 | + | − | + | ... | 4 | + | ... | 4 | ... | 3 | 5 |
| 86. Omar bin Al-Khattab and the Young Badawi | ... | ... | ... | ... | ... | 2 | 1 | 1 | 3 | + | 2 | ... | ... | ... | + | ... | 4 | ... | 3 | 5 |
| 87. Al-Maamun and the Pyramids of Egypt | ... | ... | ... | ... | ... | 2 | 1 | ... | 3 | + | − | ... | ... | 4 | + | ... | 4 | ... | 3 | 5 |
| 88. The Thief and the Merchant | ... | ... | ... | ... | ... | 2 | 1 | ... | 3 | + | 2 | + | ... | 4 | + | ... | 4 | ... | 3 | 5 |
| 89. Masrur the Eunuch and Ibn Al-Karibi | ... | ... | ... | ... | ... | 2 | 1 | ... | 3 | + | 2 | + | ... | 4 | + | ... | 4 | ... | 3 | 5 |
| 90. The Devotee Prince | ... | ... | ... | ... | ... | 2 | 1 | 3 | 3 | + | 2 | + | ... | 4 | + | ... | 4 | ... | 3 | 5 |
| 91. The Schoolmaster who fell in Love by Report | ... | ... | ... | ... | ... | 2 | 1 | ... | 3 | + | − | + | ... | 4 | + | ... | 4 | ... | 3 | 5 |
| 92. The Foolish Dominie | ... | ... | ... | ... | ... | − | − | ... | ... | + | − | + | ... | ... | + | ... | 4 | ... | 3 | 5 |
| 93. The Illiterate who set up for a Schoolmaster | ... | ... | ... | ... | ... | 2 | 1 | ... | 3 | + | 2 | + | ... | ... | + | ... | 4 | ... | 3 | 5 |
| 94. The King and the Virtuous Wife | ... | ... | ... | ... | ... | 2 | 1 | ... | 3 | + | − | ... | ... | 4 | + | ... | 4 | ... | ... | 5 |
| 95. Abd Al-Rahman the Maghribi's story of the Rukh | ... | ... | ... | ... | ... | 2 | 1 | ... | 3 | + | 2 | ... | ... | ... | + | ... | 4 | ... | 3 | 5 |
| 96. Adi bin Zayd and the Princess Hind | ... | ... | ... | ... | ... | 2 | 1 | ... | 3 | + | − | + | ... | ... | + | ... | 4 | ... | 3 | 5 |
| 97. Di'ibil Al-Khuza'i with the Lady and Muslim bin Al-Walid | ... | ... | ... | ... | ... | 2 | 1 | ... | 3 | + | − | + | ... | ... | + | ... | 4 | ... | 3 | 5 |
| 98. Isaac of Mosul and the Merchant | ... | ... | ... | ... | ... | 2 | 1 | ... | 3 | + | − | + | ... | ... | + | ... | 4 | ... | 3 | 5 |
| 99. The Three Unfortunate Lovers | ... | ... | ... | ... | ... | 2 | 1 | ... | 3 | + | − | + | ... | ... | + | ... | 4 | ... | 3 | 5 |
| 101. The Lovers of the Banu Tayy | ... | ... | ... | ... | ... | 2 | 1 | ... | 3 | + | 2 | + | ... | ... | + | ... | 4 | ... | 3 | 5 |
| 102. The Mad Lover | ... | ... | ... | ... | ... | 2 | 1 | ... | 3 | + | 2 | + | ... | ... | + | ... | 4 | ... | 3 | 5 |
| 103. The Prior who became a Moslem | ... | ... | ... | ... | ... | 2 | 1 | 2 | 3 | + | 2 | + | ... | 4 | + | ... | 4 | ... | 3 | 5 |
| 104. The Loves of Abu Isa and Kurrat Al-Ayn | ... | ... | ... | ... | ... | 2 | 1 | ... | 3 | + | 2 | + | ... | ... | + | ... | 4 | ... | 3 | 5 |
| 105. Al-Amin and his Uncle Ibrahim bin Al-Mahdi | ... | ... | ... | ... | ... | 2 | 1 | ... | 3 | + | − | + | ... | ... | + | ... | 4 | ... | ... | 5 |
| 106. Al-Fath bin Khakan and Al-Mutawakkil | ... | ... | ... | ... | ... | 2 | 1 | ... | 3 | + | − | + | ... | ... | + | ... | 4 | ... | ... | 5 |
| 107. The Man's dispute with the Learned Woman concerning the relative excellence of male and female | ... | ... | ... | ... | ... | 2 | 1 | ... | 3 | + | − | + | ... | ... | + | ... | 4 | ... | ... | 5 |
| 108. Abu Suwayd and the pretty Old Woman | ... | ... | ... | ... | ... | 2 | 1 | ... | 3 | + | − | + | ... | ... | + | ... | 4 | ... | ... | 5 |
| 109. Ali bin Tahir and the girl Muunis | ... | ... | ... | ... | ... | 2 | 1 | ... | 3 | + | − | + | ... | ... | + | ... | 4 | ... | ... | 5 |
| 110. The Woman who had a Boy, and the other who had a Man to lover | ... | ... | ... | ... | ... | 2 | 1 | ... | 3 | + | − | + | ... | ... | + | ... | 4 | ... | ... | 5 |
| 111. Ali the Cairene and the Haunted House in Baghdad | ... | ... | ... | ... | ... | 2 | 1 | ... | 1 | + | 2 | + | ... | 4 | + | ... | 4 | ... | 3 | 5 |
| 112. The Pilgrim Man and the Old Woman | ... | ... | ... | ... | ... | 2 | 1 | ... | 3 | + | 2 | ... | ... | ... | + | ... | 4 | ... | 3 | 5 |
| 113. Abu Al-Husn and his Slave-girl Tawaddud | ... | ... | ... | ... | ... | 2 | 1 | ... | 1 | + | − | ... | ... | ... | + | ... | 4 | ... | 3 | 5 |
| 114. The Angel of Death with the Proud King and the Devout Man. | ... | ... | ... | ... | ... | 2 | 1 | ... | 3 | + | − | ... | ... | 4 | + | ... | 5 | ... | 3 | 5 |

| | Galland. | Caussin de Perceval. | Gauttier. | Scott's MS. | Scott. | Von Hammer's MS. | Zinserling. | Lamb. | Trébutien. | "Bul." Text. | Lane. | "Bres." Text. | Habicht. | Weil. | "Mac." Text. | Torrens. | Payne. | Calc. | Burton (Lady). | Burton (Sir R.F.) |
|---|---|---|---|---|---|---|---|---|---|---|---|---|---|---|---|---|---|---|---|---|
| 115. The Angel of Death and the Rich King . . . . | ... | ... | ... | ... | ... | 2 | 1 | ... | 3 | + | — | ... | ... | 4 | + | | 5 | ... | 3 | 5 |
| 116. The Angel of Death and the King of the Children of Israel . . . . . . . . | ... | ... | ... | ... | ... | 2 | 1 | 3 | 3 | + | 2 | ... | ... | ... | + | ... | 5 | ... | 3 | 5 |
| 117. Iskandar zu Al-Karnayn and a certain Tribe of Poor Folk . . . . . . . | ... | ... | ... | ... | ... | 2 | 1 | ... | 3 | + | — | ... | ... | 4 | + | ... | 5 | ... | 3 | 5 |
| 118. The Righteousness of King Anushirwan . . . | ... | ... | ... | ... | ... | 2 | 1 | ... | 3 | + | — | ... | ... | 4 | + | ... | 5 | ... | 3 | 5 |
| 119. The Jewish Kazi and his Pious Wife . . . | ... | ... | ... | ... | ... | 2 | 1 | ... | 3 | + | — | ... | ... | 4 | + | ... | 5 | ... | 3 | 5 |
| 120. The Shipwrecked Woman and her Child . . . | ... | ... | ... | ... | ... | 2 | 1 | ... | 3 | + | — | ... | ... | 4 | + | ... | 5 | ... | 3 | 5 |
| 121. The Pious Black Slave . . . . . . | ... | ... | ... | ... | ... | 2 | 1 | ... | 3 | + | — | ... | ... | 4 | + | ... | 5 | ... | 3 | 5 |
| 122. The Devout Tray-maker and his Wife . . . | ... | ... | ... | ... | ... | 2 | 1 | ... | 3 | + | 2 | ... | ... | 4 | + | ... | 5 | ... | 3 | 5 |
| 123. Al-Hajjaj bin Yusuf and the Pious Man . . . | ... | ... | ... | ... | ... | 2 | 1 | ... | 3 | + | — | ... | ... | ... | + | ... | 5 | ... | 3 | 5 |
| 124. The Blacksmith who could Handle Fire Without Hurt . . . . . . . . | ... | ... | ... | ... | ... | 2 | 1 | ... | 3 | + | — | ... | ... | 4 | + | ... | 5 | ... | 3 | 5 |
| 125. The Devotee to whom Allah gave a Cloud for Service and the Devout King . . . . . . | ... | ... | ... | ... | ... | 2 | 1 | ... | 3 | + | — | ... | ... | 4 | + | ... | 5 | ... | 3 | 5 |
| 126. The Moslem Champion and the Christian Damsel . | ... | ... | ... | ... | ... | 2 | 1 | ... | 3 | + | 2 | ... | ... | 4 | + | ... | 5 | ... | 3 | 5 |
| 127. The Christian King's Daughter and the Moslem . | ... | ... | ... | ... | ... | 2 | 1 | ... | 3 | + | — | ... | ... | ... | + | ... | 5 | ... | 3 | 5 |
| 128. The Prophet and the Justice of Providence . . | ... | ... | ... | ... | ... | 2 | 1 | ... | 3 | + | 2 | ... | ... | 4 | + | ... | 5 | ... | 3 | 5 |
| 129. The Ferryman of the Nile and the Hermit . . | ... | ... | ... | ... | ... | 2 | 1 | ... | — | + | — | ... | ... | ... | + | ... | 5 | ... | 3 | 5 |
| 130. The Island King and the Pious Israelite . . . | ... | ... | 6 | ... | ... | 2 | 1 | ... | 3 | + | — | ... | 10 | 4 | + | ... | 5 | ... | 3 | 5 |
| 131. Abu Al-Hasan and Abu Ja'afar the Leper . . | ... | ... | ... | ... | ... | 2 | 1 | ... | 3 | + | — | ... | ... | ... | + | ... | 5 | ... | 3 | 5 |
| 132. The Queen of the Serpents . . . . . | ... | ... | ... | ... | ... | 2 | 1 | 3 | 1 | + | — | ... | ... | 4 | + | ... | 5 | ... | 3 | 5 |
| *a*. The Adventure of Bulukiya . . . . . | ... | ... | ... | ... | ... | 2 | 1 | 3 | 1 | + | — | ... | ... | 4 | + | ... | 5 | ... | 3 | 5 |
| *b*. The Story of Janshah . . . . . . | ... | ... | ... | ... | ... | 2 | 1 | 3 | 1 | + | — | ... | ... | 4 | + | ... | 5 | ... | 3 | 5 |
| 133. Sindbad the Seaman and Sindbad the Landsman . | 3 | 2 | 2 | ... | 2 | 3 | — | ... | — | + | 3 | + | 2 | 1 | + | ... | 5 | + | 3 | 6 |
| *a*. The First Voyage of Sindbad the Seaman . | 3 | 2 | 2 | ... | 2 | 3 | — | ... | — | + | 3 | + | 2 | 1 | + | ... | 5 | + | 3 | 6 |

| | | | | | | | | | | | | | | | | | | | | |
|---|---|---|---|---|---|---|---|---|---|---|---|---|---|---|---|---|---|---|---|---|
| *b.* The Second Voyage of Sindbad the Seaman | 3 | 2 | 2 | ... | 2 | 3 | – | ... | – | + | 3 | + | 2 | 1 | + | ... | 5 | + | 3 | 6 |
| *c.* The Third Voyage of Sindbad the Seaman | 3 | 2 | 2 | ... | 2 | 3 | – | ... | – | + | 3 | + | 2 | 1 | + | ... | 5 | + | 3 | 6 |
| *d.* The Fourth Voyage of Sindbad the Seaman | 3 | 2 | 2 | ... | 2 | 3 | – | ... | – | + | 3 | + | 2 | 1 | + | ... | 5 | + | 3 | 6 |
| *e.* The Fifth Voyage of Sindbad the Seaman | 3 | 2 | 2 | ... | 2 | 3 | – | ... | – | + | 3 | + | 3 | 1 | + | .. | 5 | + | 3 | 6 |
| *f.* The Sixth Voyage of Sindbad the Seaman | 3 | 2 | 2 | ... | 2 | 3 | – | ... | – | + | 3 | + | 3 | 1 | + | ... | 5 | – | 4 | 6 |
| *ff.* The Sixth Voyage of Sindbad the Seaman | ... | ... | ... | ... | ... | ... | ... | ... | ... | - | 3 | – | ... | ... | – | ... | III | + | ... | – |
| *g.* The Seventh Voyage of Sindbad the Seaman | 3 | 2 | 2 | ... | 2 | 3 | – | ... | – | + | 3 | + | 3 | 1 | + | ... | 5 | – | 4 | 6 |
| *gg.* The Seventh Voyage of Sindbad the Seaman | – | ... | ... | ... | – | – | – | ... | – | – | 3 | – | ... | – | – | ... | III | + | 4 | 6 |
| 134. The City of Brass | ... | ... | ... | .. | ... | 3 | 2 | 1 | 1 | + | 3 | + | ... | 2 | + | ... | 5 | ... | 4 | 6 |
| 135. The Craft and Malice of Women | ... | ... | ... | A | A | 3 | – | ... | – | + | 3 | + | 15 | ... | + | ... | 5 | ... | 4 | 6 |
| *a.* The King and his Wazir's Wife | ... | ... | ... | A | A | ... | – | ... | – | + | 3 | + | 15 | ... | + | ... | 5 | ... | 4 | 6 |
| *b.* The Confectioner, his Wife and the Parrot | ... | ... | ... | A | A | (Would include subordinate tales.) | – | ... | – | + | – | + | ... | ... | + | ... | 5 | ... | 4 | 6 |
| *c.* The Fuller and his Son | ... | ... | ... | A | A | | ... | ... | ... | + | – | + | 15 | ... | + | ... | 5 | ... | 4 | 6 |
| *d.* The Rake's Trick against the Chaste Wife | ... | ... | ... | ... | ... | | ... | ... | ... | + | – | + | 15 | ... | + | ... | 5 | ... | ... | 6 |
| *e.* The Miser and the Loaves of Bread | ... | ... | ... | ... | ... | | ... | ... | ... | + | – | + | 15 | ... | + | ... | 5 | ... | 4 | 6 |
| *f.* The Lady and her two Lovers | ... | ... | ... | A | A | | ... | ... | ... | + | 3 | + | 15 | ... | + | ... | 5 | ... | 4 | 6 |
| *g.* The King's Son and the Ogress | ... | ... | ... | A | A | | ... | ... | ... | + | – | + | 15 | ... | + | ... | 5 | ... | 4 | 6 |
| *h.* The Drop of Honey | ... | ... | ... | A | A | | ... | ... | ... | + | 3 | + | 15 | ... | + | ... | 5 | ... | 4 | 6 |
| *i.* The Woman who made her husband sift dust | ... | ... | ... | A | ... | | ... | ... | ... | + | 3 | + | 15 | ... | + | ... | 5 | ... | 4 | 6 |
| *i.* The Enchanted Spring | ... | ... | ... | A | A | | ... | ... | ... | + | 3 | + | 15 | ... | + | ... | 5 | ... | 4 | 6 |
| *k.* The Wazir's Son and the Hamman-keeper's Wife | ... | ... | ... | A | ... | ... | ... | ... | ... | + | – | + | ... | ... | + | ... | 5 | ... | ... | 6 |
| *l.* The Wife's Device to cheat her Husband | ... | ... | ... | A | A | ... | ... | ... | ... | + | 3 | + | 15 | ... | + | ... | 5 | ... | ... | 6 |
| *m.* The Goldsmith and the Cashmere Singing-girl | ... | ... | 1 | A | A | ... | ... | ... | ... | + | 3 | + | 1 | 1 | + | ... | 5 | ... | 4 | 6 |
| *n.* The Man who never laughed during the rest of his days | ... | ... | ... | A | A | ... | ... | ... | ... | + | 3 | + | 15 | ... | + | ... | 5 | ... | 4 | 6 |
| *o.* The King's Son and the Merchant's Wife | ... | ... | ... | A | A | ... | ... | ... | ... | + | – | + | 15 | ... | + | ... | 5 | ... | 4 | 6 |
| *p.* The Page who feigned to know the Speech of Birds | ... | ... | ... | ... | ... | ... | ... | ... | ... | + | – | ... | ... | ... | + | ... | 5 | ... | 4 | 6 |
| *q.* The Lady and her five Suitors | ... | ... | ... | A | A | ... | ... | ... | ... | + | – | ... | ... | ... | + | ... | 5 | ... | 4 | 6 |
| *r.* The Three Wishes or the Man who longed to see the Night of Power | ... | ... | ... | A | ... | ... | ... | ... | ... | + | – | + | ... | ... | + | ... | 5 | ... | 4 | 6 |
| *s.* The Stolen Necklace | ... | ... | ... | A | A | ... | ... | ... | ... | + | 3 | + | 15 | ... | + | ... | 5 | ... | 4 | 6 |
| *t.* The Two Pigeons | ... | ... | ... | ... | ... | ... | ... | ... | ... | + | 3 | ... | ... | ... | + | ... | 5 | ... | 4 | 6 |

| | Galland. | Caussin de Perceval. | Gauttier. | Scott's MS. | Scott. | Von Hammer's MS. | Zinserling. | Lamb. | Trébutien. | "Bul." Text. | Lane. | "Bres." Text. | Habicht. | Weil. | "Mac." Text. | Torrens. | Payne. | Calc. | Burton (Lady). | Burton (Sir R. F.) |
|---|---|---|---|---|---|---|---|---|---|---|---|---|---|---|---|---|---|---|---|---|
| *u.* Prince Behram and the Princess Al-Datma | ... | ... | ... | A | A | ... | ... | .. | ... | + | 3 | + | 15 | ... | + | ... | 5 | ... | 4 | 6 |
| *v.* The House with the Belvedere | ... | ... | ... | A | A | ... | ... | ... | ... | + | 3 | + | 15 | ... | + | ... | 5 | ... | 4 | 6 |
| *w.* The King's Son and the Ifrit's Mistress | ... | ... | ... | ... | ... | ... | ... | ... | .. | + | − | ... | ... | ... | + | ... | 5 | ... | 4 | 6 |
| *x.* The Sandal-wood Merchant and the Sharpers | ... | ... | ... | ... | ... | ... | ... | ... | ... | + | 3 | + | 15 | ... | + | ... | 5 | ... | 4 | 6 |
| *y.* The Debauchee and the Three-year-old Child | ... | ... | ... | ... | ... | ... | ... | ... | ... | + | − | + | ... | ... | + | ... | 5 | ... | 4 | 6 |
| *z.* The Stolen Purse | ... | ... | ... | ... | ... | ... | ... | .. | ... | + | 3 | + | 15 | ... | + | ... | 5 | ... | 4 | 6 |
| *aa.* The Fox and the Folk | ... | ... | ... | ... | ... | ... | ... | ... | ... | − | − | + | 15 | ... | − | ... | 5 | . | 4 | 6 |
| 136. Judar and his Brethren | ... | ... | ... | ... | ... | 3 | 2 | 1 | 1 | + | 3 | + | ... | 2 | + | ... | 6 | ... | 4 | 6 |
| 137. The History of Gharib and his Brother Ajib | ... | ... | ... | ... | ... | 3 | 2 | ... | 1 | + | − | + | ... | ... | + | ... | 6 | ... | 4 | 6, 7 |
| 138. Otbah and Rayya | ... | ... | ... | ... | ... | 3 | 2 | ... | 3 | + | 3 | ... | ... | ... | + | ... | 6 | ... | 4 | 7 |
| 139. Hind, daughter of Al-Nu'man and Al-Hajjaj | ... | ... | ... | ... | ... | 3 | 2 | ... | 3 | + | − | ... | ... | ... | + | ... | 6 | ... | 4 | 7 |
| 140. Khuzaymah bin Bishr and Ekrimah al-Fayyaz | ... | ... | ... | ... | ... | 3 | 2 | ... | 3 | + | 3 | .. | ... | 4 | + | ... | 6 | ... | 4 | 7 |
| 141. Yunus the Scribe and the Caliph Walid bin Sahl | ... | ... | ... | ... | ... | 3 | 2 | ... | 3 | + | − | ... | .. | 4 | + | ... | 6 | ... | 4 | 7 |
| 142. Harun Al-Rashid and the Arab Girl | ... | ... | ... | ... | ... | 3 | 2 | ... | 3 | + | − | . | ... | ... | + | ... | 6 | ... | 4 | 7 |
| 143. Al-Asma'i and the three girls of Bassorah | ... | ... | ... | ... | ... | 3 | − | ... | − | + | − | ... | ... | ... | + | ... | 6 | ... | ... | 7 |
| 144. Ibrahim of Mosul and the Devil | ... | ... | ... | ... | ... | 3 | − | ... | ... | + | − | ... | ... | ... | + | ... | 6 | ... | 4 | 7 |
| 145. The Lovers of the Banu Uzrah | ... | ... | 6 | 4 | 6 | 3 | − | ... | ... | + | 3 | ... | 11 | ... | + | ... | 6 | ... | 4 | 7 |
| 146. The Badawi and his Wife | ... | ... | ... | ... | ... | 3 | 2 | ... | 3 | + | − | ... | ... | ... | + | ... | 6 | ... | 4 | 7 |
| 147. The Lovers of Bassorah | ... | ... | ... | ... | ... | 3 | 2 | ... | 3 | + | − | .. | ... | ... | + | ... | 6 | ... | 4 | 7 |
| 148. Ishak of Mosul and his Mistress and the Devil | ... | ... | ... | ... | ... | 3 | 2 | ... | 3 | + | − | ... | ... | ... | + | ... | 6 | ... | 4 | 7 |
| 149. The Lovers of Al-Medinah | ... | ... | ... | ... | ... | 3 | 2 | ... | 3 | + | 3 | .. | ... | .. | + | ... | 6 | ... | 4 | 7 |
| 150. Al-Malik Al-Nasir and his Wazir | ... | ... | ... | ... | ... | 3 | 2 | ... | 3 | + | − | ... | ... | ... | + | . | 6 | .. | 4 | 7 |
| 151. The Rogueries of Dalilah the Crafty and her Daughter Zaynab the Coney-Catcher | ... | ... | ... | ... | ... | 3 | 2 | ... | 2 | + | − | + | ... | 4 | + | ... | 6 | ... | 4 | 7 |
| *a.* The Adventures of Mercury Ali of Cairo | ... | ... | ... | ... | ... | 3 | 2 | ... | 2 | + | − | + | ... | 4 | + | ... | 6 | ... | 4 | 7 |
| 152. Ardashir and Hayat Al-Nufus | ... | ... | ... | 7 | ... | 3 | 2 | 1 | 2 | + | − | + | ... | 2 | + | ... | 6 | ... | 4 | 7 |

| | | | | | | | | | | | | | | | | | | | | |
|---|---|---|---|---|---|---|---|---|---|---|---|---|---|---|---|---|---|---|---|---|
| 153. Julnar the Sea-born and her son King Badr Basim of Persia | 7 | 4 | 3 | … | 3, 4 | 3 | – | … | – | + | 3 | … | 6 | 3 | + | … | 7 | .. | 4 | 7 |
| 154. King Mohammed bin Sabaik and the Merchant Hasan | … | … | … | 1 | … | 3 | 2 | … | 2 | + | 3 | + | .. | – | + | .. | 7 | … | 4 | 7 |
| *a.* Story of Prince Sayf Al-Muluk and the Princess Badi'a Al-Jamal | … | … | … | 1 | … | 3, 4 | 2 | … | 2 | + | 3 | + | … | 2 | + | … | 7 | … | 4, 5 | 7, 8 |
| 155. Hasan of Bassorah | … | … | … | 3 | … | 4 | 3 | 2 | 2 | + | 3 | + | … | 2 | + | … | 7 | … | 5 | 8 |
| 156. Khalifah the Fisherman of Baghdad | … | … | … | … | … | 4 | 3 | … | 2 | + | 3 | – | … | 2 | + | … | 7 | … | 5 | 8 |
| *a.* The same from the Breslau Edition | … | … | … | … | … | … | … | … | … | … | – | + | … | … | … | … | 7 | … | 5 | 8 |
| 157. Masrur and Zayn Al-Mawassif | … | … | … | … | … | 4 | 3 | 2 | 2 | + | – | + | … | … | + | … | 8 | … | 5 | 8 |
| 158. Ali Nur al-Din and Miriam the Girdle-Girl | … | … | … | … | … | 4 | 3 | 2 | 2 | + | – | + | … | … | + | … | 8 | … | 5 | 8,9 |
| 159. The Man of Upper Egypt and his Frankish Wife | … | … | … | … | … | 4 | 3 | – | 3 | + | – | + | … | … | + | … | 8 | … | 5 | 9 |
| 160. The Ruined Man of Baghdad and his Slave-Girl | … | … | … | … | … | 4 | 3 | – | 3 | + | 3 | + | … | 4 | + | … | 8 | … | 5 | 9 |
| 161. King Jali'ad of Hind and his Wazir Shimas, followed by the history of King Wird Khan, son of King Jali'ad, with his Women and Wazirs | … | … | … | … | … | 4 | 3 | 3 | 3 | + | – | + | … | 4 | + | … | 8 | … | 5 | 9 |
| *a.* The Mouse and the Cat | … | … | … | … | … | 4 | 3 | 3 | 3 | + | – | + | … | 4 | + | … | 8 | … | 5 | 9 |
| *b.* The Fakir and his Jar of Butter | … | … | … | … | … | 4 | 3 | 3 | 3 | + | – | + | … | 4 | + | … | 8 | … | 5 | 9 |
| *c.* The Fishes and the Crab | … | … | … | … | … | 4 | 3 | 3 | 3 | + | – | + | … | 4 | + | … | 8 | … | 5 | 9 |
| *d.* The Crow and the Serpent | … | … | … | … | … | 4 | 3 | 3 | 3 | + | – | + | … | 4 | + | … | 8 | … | 5 | 9 |
| *e.* The Wild Ass and the Jackal | … | … | … | … | … | 4 | 3 | 3 | 3 | + | – | + | … | 4 | + | .. | 8 | … | 5 | 9 |
| *f.* The Unjust King and the Pilgrim Prince | … | … | … | … | … | 4 | 3 | 3 | 3 | + | – | + | … | 4 | + | … | 8 | … | 5 | 9 |
| *g.* The Crows and the Hawk | … | … | … | … | … | 4 | 3 | 3 | 3 | + | – | + | … | 4 | + | … | 8 | … | 5 | 9 |
| *h.* The Serpent-Charmer and his Wife | … | … | … | … | … | 4 | 3 | 3 | 3 | + | – | + | … | 4 | + | … | 8 | … | 5 | 9 |
| *i.* The Spider and the Wind | … | … | … | … | … | 4 | 3 | 3 | 3 | + | – | + | … | 4 | + | … | 8 | … | 5 | 9 |
| *j.* The Two Kings | … | … | … | . | … | 4 | 3 | 3 | 3 | + | – | + | … | 4 | + | … | 8 | … | 5 | 9 |
| *k.* The Blind Man and the Cripple | … | … | … | … | … | 4 | 3 | 3 | 3 | + | – | + | … | 4 | + | … | 8 | … | 5 | 9 |
| *l.* The Foolish Fisherman | … | … | … | … | … | 4 | 3 | 3 | 3 | + | – | + | … | 4 | + | … | 8 | … | 5 | 9 |
| *m.* The Boy and the Thieves | … | … | … | … | … | 4 | 3 | 3 | 3 | + | – | + | … | 4 | + | … | 8 | … | 5 | 9 |
| *n.* The Man and his Wife | … | … | … | … | … | 4 | 3 | 3 | 3 | + | – | + | … | 4 | + | … | 8 | … | 5 | 9 |
| *o.* The Merchant and the Robbers | … | … | … | … | … | 4 | 3 | 3 | 3 | + | – | + | … | 4 | + | … | 8 | … | 5 | 9 |
| *p.* The Jackals and the Wolf | … | … | … | … | … | 4 | 3 | 3 | 3 | + | – | + | … | 4 | + | … | 8 | … | 5 | 9 |
| *q.* The Shepherd and the Rogue | … | … | … | … | … | 4 | 3 | 3 | 3 | + | – | + | … | 4 | + | … | 8 | … | 5 | 9 |
| *r.* The Francolin and the Tortoises | … | … | … | … | … | 4 | 3 | 3 | 3 | + | – | + | … | 4 | + | … | 8 | … | 5 | 9 |

| | Galland. | Caussin de Perceval. | Gauttier. | Scott's MS. | Scott. | Von Hammer's MS. | Zinserling. | Lamb. | Trébutien. | "Bul." Text. | Lane. | "Bres." Text. | Habicht. | Weil. | "Mac." Text. | Torrens. | Payne. | Calc. | Burton (Lady). | Burton (Sir R.F.) |
|---|---|---|---|---|---|---|---|---|---|---|---|---|---|---|---|---|---|---|---|---|
| 162. Abu Kir the Dyer and Abu Sir the Barber | ... | ... | ... | ... | ... | 4 | 3 | 1 | 3 | + | 3 | + | ... | 4 | + | ... | 8 | ... | 5 | 9 |
| 163. Abdullah the Fisherman and Abdullah the Merman | ... | ... | ... | ... | ... | 4 | 3 | 1 | 3 | + | 3 | + | ... | ... | + | ... | 8 | ... | 5 | 9 |
| 164. Harun Al-Rashid and Abu Hasan the Merchant of Oman | ... | ... | ... | ... | ... | 4 | 3 | ... | 3 | + | — | + | ... | 2 | + | ... | 9 | ... | 6 | 9 |
| 165. Ibrahim and Jamilah | ... | ... | ... | ... | ... | 4 | 3 | 1 | 3 | + | 3 | ... | ... | ... | + | ... | 9 | ... | 6 | 9 |
| 166. Abu Al-Hasan of Khorasan | ... | ... | ... | ... | ... | 4 | 3 | 1 | 3 | + | — | ... | ... | ... | + | ... | 9 | ... | 6 | 9 |
| 167. Kamar Al-Zaman and the Jeweller's Wife | ... | ... | ... | ... | ... | 4 | 3 | 1 | 3 | + | — | ... | ... | 4 | + | ... | 9 | ... | 6 | 9 |
| 168. Abdullah bin Fazil and his Brothers | .. | ... | ... | ... | ... | 4 | 3 | ... | 3 | + | — | ... | ... | ... | + | ... | 9 | ... | 6 | 9 |
| 169. Ma'aruf the Cobbler and his wife Fatimah | ... | ... | ... | ... | ... | 4 | 3 | 3 | 3 | + | 3 | ... | ... | 4 | + | ... | 9 | .. | 6 | 10 |
| 170. Asleep and Awake | 9 | 5 | 4 | ... | 4 | ... | ... | .. | ... | ... | 2 | + | 7 | 1 | ... | ... | I. | ... | ... | I. |
| *a.* Story of the Lackpenny and the Cook | ... | ... | ... | ... | ... | ... | ... | ... | ... | ... | — | + | ... | ... | ... | ... | I. | ... | ... | I. |
| 171. The Caliph Omar ben Abdulaziz and the Poets | ... | ... | ... | ... | ... | ... | ... | ... | ... | ... | — | + | ... | 2 | ... | ... | I. | ... | ... | I. |
| 172. El Hejjaj and the Three Young Men | ... | ... | ... | ... | ... | ... | ... | ... | ... | ... | — | + | ... | ... | ... | ... | I. | ... | ... | I. |
| 173. Haroun Er Reshid and the Woman of the Barmecides | ... | ... | ... | ... | ... | ... | ... | ... | .. | ... | — | + | ... | ... | ... | ... | I. | ... | ... | I. |
| 174. The Ten Viziers, or the History of King Azadbekht and his Son | ... | 8 | 6 | ... | ... | ... | ... | ... | ... | ... | — | + | 10 | 2 | ... | ... | I. | .. | ... | I. |
| *a.* Of the uselessness of endeavour against persistent ill-fortune. | ... | ... | ... | ... | ... | ... | ... | ... | ... | ... | ... | ... | ... | ... | ... | ... | ... | ... | ... | I. |
| *aa.* Story of the Unlucky Merchant. | ... | 8 | 6 | ... | ... | ... | ... | ... | ... | ... | — | + | 10 | 2 | ... | ... | I. | ... | ... | I. |
| *b.* Of looking to the issues of affairs | ... | ... | ... | ... | ... | ... | ... | ... | ... | ... | ... | ... | ... | ... | ... | ... | ... | ... | ... | I. |
| *bb.* Story of the Merchant and his Sons | ... | 8 | 6 | ... | ... | ... | ... | ... | ... | ... | ... | + | 10 | 2 | ... | ... | I. | ... | ... | I. |
| *c.* Of the advantages of Patience. | ... | ... | ... | ... | ... | ... | ... | ... | ... | ... | ... | ... | ... | ... | ... | ... | ... | ... | ... | I. |
| *cc.* Story of Abou Sabir | ... | 8 | 6 | ... | ... | ... | ... | ... | ... | ... | ... | + | 10 | 2 | ... | ... | I. | ... | ... | I. |
| *d.* Of the ill effects of Precipitation | ... | ... | ... | ... | ... | ... | ... | ... | ... | ... | ... | ... | ... | ... | ... | ... | ... | ... | ... | I. |
| *dd.* Story of Prince Bihzad | ... | 8 | 6 | ... | ... | ... | ... | ... | ... | ... | ... | + | 10 | 2 | ... | ... | I. | ... | ... | I. |

| | | | | | | | | | | | | | | | | | | | | |
|---|---|---|---|---|---|---|---|---|---|---|---|---|---|---|---|---|---|---|---|---|
| *e.* Of the issues of good and evil actions | ... | ... | ... | ... | ... | ... | ... | ... | ... | ... | ... | ... | ... | ... | ... | ... | ... | ... | ... | ... |
| *ee.* Story of King Dabdin and his Viziers. | ... | 8 | 6 | ... | ... | ... | ... | ... | ... | ... | ... | + | 10 | 2 | ... | ... | I. | ... | ... | I. |
| *f.* Of Trust in God | ... | ... | ... | ... | ... | ... | ... | ... | ... | ... | ... | ... | ... | ... | ... | ... | ... | ... | ... | ... |
| *ff.* Story of King Bekhtzeman | ... | 8 | ... | ... | ... | . | ... | ... | ... | ... | ... | + | ... | 2 | ... | ... | I. | ... | ... | I. |
| *g.* Of Clemency | ... | ... | ... | ... | ... | ... | ... | ... | . | ... | ... | ... | ... | ... | ... | ... | ... | ... | ... | ... |
| *gg.* Story of King Bihkerd | ... | 8 | 6 | ... | ... | ... | ... | ... | .. | ... | ... | + | 10 | 2 | ... | ... | I. | ... | ... | I. |
| *h.* Of Envy and Malice | ... | ... | ... | ... | ... | ... | ... | ... | ... | ... | ... | ... | ... | ... | ... | ... | ... | ... | ... | ... |
| *hh.* Story of Ilan Shah and Abou Temam | ... | 8 | 6 | .. | ... | ... | ... | ... | ... | ... | ... | + | 10 | 2 | ... | ... | I. | ... | .. | I. |
| *i.* Of Destiny, or that which is written on the Forehead | ... | ... | ... | .. | ... | ... | ... | ... | ... | ... | ... | ... | ... | ... | ... | ... | ... | ... | ... | ... |
| *ii.* Story of King Ibrahim and his Son | .. | 8 | 7 | ... | ... | ... | .. | ... | ... | .. | ... | + | 13 | 2 | ... | ... | I. | ... | ... | I. |
| *j.* Of the appointed Term, which if it be advanced, may not be deferred, and if it be deferred, may not be advanced | ... | ... | ... | ... | ... | ... | ... | ... | ... | ... | ... | ... | ... | ... | ... | ... | ... | ... | ... | ... |
| *jj.* Story of King Suleiman Shah and his Sons | ... | 8 | ... | ... | ... | ... | ... | ... | ... | ... | ... | + | ... | 2 | ... | ... | I. | ... | ... | I. |
| *k.* Of the speedy Relief of God | ... | ... | ... | .. | .. | ... | ... | ... | .. | ... | ... | ... | ... | ... | ... | ... | ... | ... | ... | ... |
| *kk.* Story of the Prisoner, and how God gave him relief | ... | 8 | ... | ... | ... | ... | ... | ... | ... | ... | ... | + | ... | 2 | ... | ... | I. | ... | ... | I. |
| 175. Jaafer Ben Zehya and Abdulmelik Ben Salih the Abbaside | ... | ... | ... | ... | ... | ... | ... | ... | ... | ... | ... | + | ... | 2 | ... | ... | I. | ... | ... | I. |
| 176. Er Reshid and the Barmecides | ... | ... | ... | ... | ... | ... | ... | ... | ... | .. | ... | + | ... | 2 | ... | ... | I. | ... | ... | I. |
| 177. Ibn Es-Semmak and Er-Reshid | ... | ... | ... | ... | ... | ... | ... | ... | ... | ... | ... | + | ... | ... | ... | ... | I. | ... | ... | I. |
| 178. El Mamoun and Zubeideh | ... | ... | ... | ... | ... | ... | .. | ... | ... | ... | ... | + | ... | ... | ... | ... | I. | ... | ... | I. |
| 179. En Numan and the Arab of the Benou Tai | ... | ... | ... | ... | ... | ... | .. | ... | ... | ... | ... | + | ... | ... | ... | ... | I. | ... | ... | I. |
| 180. Firouz and his Wife | ... | ... | ... | ... | ... | ... | . | ... | ... | ... | ... | + | ... | ... | ... | ... | I. | ... | ... | I. |
| 181. King Shah Bekht and his Vizier Er Rehwan | ... | ... | ... | ... | ... | ... | ... | ... | ... | ... | ... | + | 14 | ... | ... | ... | I. | ... | ... | I. |
| *a.* Story of the Man of Khorassan, his son and his governor | ... | ... | ... | ... | ... | ... | ... | ... | ... | ... | ... | + | 14 | ... | ... | ... | I. | ... | ... | I. |
| *b.* Story of the Singer and the Druggist | ... | ... | ... | ... | ... | ... | ... | ... | ... | ... | ... | + | 14 | ... | ... | ... | I. | ... | ... | I. |
| *c.* Story of the King who knew the quintessence of things | ... | ... | ... | ... | ... | ... | ... | ... | ... | ... | ... | + | 14 | ... | ... | ... | I. | ... | ... | I. |
| *d.* Story of the Rich Man who gave his fair Daughter in Marriage to the Poor Old Man | ... | ... | ... | ... | ... | ... | ... | ... | ... | ... | ... | + | 14 | ... | ... | ... | I. | ... | ... | I. |
| *e.* Story of the Rich Man and his Wasteful Son | ... | ... | ... | ... | ... | ... | ... | ... | ... | ... | ... | + | 14 | ... | ... | ... | I. | ... | ... | I. |

| | Galland. | Caussin de Perceval. | Gauttier. | Scott's MS. | Scott. | Von Hammer's MS. | Zinserling. | Lamb. | Trébutien. | "Bul." Text. | Lane. | "Bres." Text. | Habicht. | Weil. | "Mac." Text. | Torrens. | Payne. | Calc. | Burton (Lady). | Burton (Sir R.F.) |
|---|---|---|---|---|---|---|---|---|---|---|---|---|---|---|---|---|---|---|---|---|
| *f.* The King's Son who fell in love with the Picture | ... | ... | ... | ... | ... | ... | ... | ... | ... | ... | ... | + | 14 | ... | ... | ... | I. | ... | ... | I. |
| *g.* Story of the Fuller and his Wife | ... | ... | ... | ... | ... | ... | ... | ... | ... | ... | ... | + | 14 | ... | ... | ... | I. | ... | ... | I. |
| *h.* Story of the Old Woman, the Merchant, and the King | ... | ... | ... | ... | ... | ... | ... | ... | ... | ... | ... | + | 14 | ... | ... | ... | I. | ... | ... | I. |
| *i.* Story of the credulous Husband | ... | ... | ... | ... | ... | ... | ... | ... | ... | ... | ... | + | 14 | ... | ... | ... | I. | ... | ... | I. |
| *j.* Story of the Unjust King and the Tither | ... | ... | ... | ... | ... | ... | ... | ... | ... | ... | ... | + | 14 | ... | ... | ... | I. | ... | ... | I. |
| *jj.* Story of David and Solomon | ... | ... | ... | ... | ... | ... | ... | ... | ... | ... | ... | + | 14 | ... | ... | ... | I. | ... | ... | I. |
| *k.* Story of the Thief and the Woman | ... | ... | ... | ... | ... | ... | ... | ... | ... | ... | ... | + | 14 | ... | ... | ... | I. | ... | ... | I. |
| *l.* Story of the Three Men and our Lord Jesus | ... | ... | ... | ... | ... | ... | ... | ... | ... | ... | ... | + | 14 | ... | ... | ... | I. | ... | ... | I. |
| *ll.* The Disciple's Story | ... | ... | ... | ... | ... | ... | ... | ... | ... | ... | ... | + | 14 | ... | ... | ... | I. | ... | ... | I. |
| *m.* Story of the Dethroned King whose kingdom and good were restored to him | ... | ... | ... | ... | ... | ... | ... | ... | ... | ... | ... | + | 14 | ... | ... | .. | I. | ... | ... | I. |
| *n.* Story of the Man whose caution was the cause of his Death | ... | ... | ... | ... | ... | ... | ... | ... | ... | ... | ... | + | 14 | ... | ... | ... | I. | ... | ... | I. |
| *o.* Story of the Man who was lavish of his house and his victual to one whom he knew not | ... | ... | ... | ... | ... | ... | ... | ... | ... | ... | ... | + | 14 | ... | ... | ... | I. | ... | ... | I. |
| *p.* Story of the Idiot and the Sharper | ... | ... | ... | ... | ... | ... | ... | ... | ... | ... | ... | + | 14 | ... | ... | ... | I. | ... | ... | I. |
| *q.* Story of Khelbes and his Wife and the Learned Man | ... | ... | ... | ... | ... | ... | ... | ... | ... | ... | ... | + | 14 | ... | ... | ... | I. | ... | ... | I. |
| *r.* Story of the Pious Woman accused of lewdness | ... | ... | ... | ... | ... | ... | ... | ... | ... | ... | ... | + | ... | ... | ... | ... | II. | ... | ... | I. |
| *s.* Story of the Journeyman and the Girl | ... | ... | ... | ... | ... | ... | ... | ... | ... | ... | ... | + | 14 | ... | ... | ... | II. | ... | ... | I. |
| *t.* Story of the Weaver who became a Physician by his Wife's commandment | ... | ... | ... | ... | ... | ... | ... | ... | ... | ... | ... | + | 14 | ... | ... | ... | II. | ... | ... | I. |
| *u.* Story of the Two Sharpers who cheated each his fellow | ... | ... | ... | ... | ... | ... | ... | ... | ... | ... | ... | + | 14 | ... | ... | ... | II | ... | ... | I. |

| | | | | | | | | | | | | | | | | | | | | |
|---|---|---|---|---|---|---|---|---|---|---|---|---|---|---|---|---|---|---|---|---|
| *v.* Story of the Sharpers with the Money-changer and the Ass | ... | ... | ... | ... | ... | ... | ... | ... | ... | ... | ... | + | 14 | ... | ... | ... | II. | ... | ... | I. |
| *w.* Story of the Sharper and the Merchants | ... | ... | ... | ... | ... | ... | ... | ... | ... | ... | ... | + | 14 | ... | ... | ... | II. | ... | ... | I |
| *wa.* Story of the Hawk and the Locust | ... | ... | ... | ... | ... | ... | ... | ... | ... | ... | ... | + | 14 | ... | ... | ... | II. | ... | ... | I. |
| *x.* Story of the King and his Chamberlain's Wife | ... | ... | ... | ... | ... | ... | ... | ... | ... | ... | ... | + | 14 | ... | ... | ... | II. | ... | ... | I |
| *xa.* Story of the Old Woman and the Draper's Wife | ... | ... | ... | ... | ... | ... | ... | ... | ... | ... | ... | + | 14 | ... | ... | ... | II. | ... | ... | I. |
| *y.* Story of the Foul-favoured Man and his Fair Wife | ... | ... | ... | ... | ... | ... | ... | ... | ... | ... | ... | + | 14 | ... | ... | ... | II. | ... | ... | I. |
| *z.* Story of the King who lost Kingdom and Wife and Wealth, and God Restored them to him. | ... | ... | ... | ... | ... | ... | ... | ... | ... | ... | ... | + | 14 | ... | ... | ... | II. | ... | ... | I. |
| *aa.* Story of Selim and Selma | ... | ... | ... | ... | ... | ... | ... | ... | ... | ... | ... | + | 14 | ... | ... | ... | II. | ... | ... | I. |
| *bb.* Story of the King of Hind and his Vizier | ... | ... | ... | ... | ... | ... | ... | ... | ... | ... | ... | + | 14 | ... | ... | ... | II. | ... | ... | I. |
| 182. El Melik Ez Zahir Rukneddin Bibers El Bunducdari, and the Sixteen Officers of Police | ... | ... | ... | ... | ... | ... | ... | ... | ... | ... | ... | + | 14 | ... | ... | ... | II. | ... | ... | II. |
| *a.* The First Officer's Story | ... | ... | ... | ... | ... | ... | ... | ... | ... | ... | ... | + | 14 | ... | ... | ... | II. | ... | ... | II. |
| *b.* The Second Officer's Story | ... | ... | ... | ... | ... | ... | ... | ... | ... | ... | ... | + | 14 | ... | ... | ... | II. | ... | ... | II. |
| *c.* The Third Officer's Story | ... | ... | ... | ... | ... | ... | ... | ... | ... | ... | ... | + | 14 | ... | ... | ... | II. | ... | ... | II. |
| *d.* The Fourth Officer's Story | ... | ... | ... | ... | ... | ... | ... | ... | ... | ... | ... | + | ... | ... | ... | ... | II. | ... | ... | II. |
| *e.* The Fifth Officer's Story | ... | ... | ... | ... | ... | ... | ... | ... | ... | ... | ... | + | 14 | ... | ... | ... | II. | ... | ... | II. |
| *f.* The Sixth Officer's Story | ... | ... | ... | ... | ... | ... | ... | ... | ... | ... | ... | + | ... | ... | ... | ... | II. | ... | ... | II. |
| *g.* The Seventh Officer's Story | ... | ... | ... | ... | ... | ... | ... | ... | ... | ... | ... | + | 14 | ... | ... | ... | II. | ... | ... | II. |
| *h.* The Eighth Officer's Story | ... | ... | ... | ... | ... | ... | ... | ... | ... | ... | ... | + | 14 | ... | ... | ... | II | ... | ... | II. |
| *ha.* The Thief's Story | ... | ... | ... | ... | ... | ... | ... | ... | ... | ... | ... | + | 14 | ... | ... | ... | II. | ... | ... | II. |
| *i.* The Ninth Officer's Story | ... | ... | ... | ... | ... | ... | ... | ... | ... | ... | ... | + | 14 | ... | ... | ... | II. | ... | ... | II. |
| *j.* The Tenth Officer's Story | ... | ... | ... | ... | ... | ... | ... | ... | ... | ... | ... | + | 14 | ... | ... | ... | II. | ... | ... | II |
| *k.* The Eleventh Officer's Story | ... | ... | ... | ... | ... | ... | ... | ... | ... | ... | ... | + | 14 | ... | ... | ... | II. | ... | ... | II. |
| *l.* The Twelfth Officer's Story | ... | ... | ... | ... | ... | ... | ... | ... | ... | ... | ... | + | 14 | ... | ... | ... | II. | ... | ... | II. |
| *m.* The Thirteenth Officer's Story | ... | ... | ... | ... | ... | ... | ... | ... | ... | ... | ... | + | 14 | ... | ... | ... | II. | ... | ... | II |
| *n.* The Fourteenth Officer's Story | ... | ... | ... | ... | ... | ... | ... | ... | ... | ... | ... | + | 14 | ... | ... | ... | II. | ... | ... | II. |
| *na.* A Merry Jest of a Thief | ... | ... | ... | ... | ... | ... | ... | ... | ... | ... | ... | + | 14 | ... | ... | ... | II | ... | ... | II. |
| *nb.* Story of the Old Sharper | ... | ... | ... | ... | ... | ... | ... | ... | ... | ... | ... | + | 14 | ... | ... | ... | II. | ... | ... | II. |
| *o.* The Fifteenth Officer's Story | ... | ... | ... | ... | ... | ... | ... | ... | ... | ... | ... | + | 14 | ... | ... | ... | II. | ... | ... | II. |
| *p.* The Sixteenth Officer's Story | ... | ... | ... | ... | ... | ... | ... | ... | ... | ... | ... | + | 14 | ... | ... | ... | II | ... | ... | II. |

| | Galland. | Caussin de Perceval. | Gautier. | Scott's MS. | Scott. | Von Hammer's MS. | Zinserling. | Lamb. | Trébutien. | "Bul." Text. | Lane. | "Bres." Text. | Habicht. | Weil. | "Mac." Text. | Torrens. | Payne. | Calc. | Burton (Lady). | Burton (Sir R.F.) |
|---|---|---|---|---|---|---|---|---|---|---|---|---|---|---|---|---|---|---|---|---|
| 183. Abdallah Ben Nafi, and the King's Son of Cashgbar | ... | ... | ... | ... | ... | ... | ... | .. | ... | ... | ... | + | 14 | ... | ... | ... | II. | ... | ... | II. |
| *a.* Story of the Damsel Tuhfet El Culoub and Khalif Haroun Er Reshid | ... | ... | ... | ... | ... | ... | ... | ... | ... | ... | .. | + | 14 | ... | ... | ... | II. | ... | ... | II. |
| 184. Women's Craft | ... | ... | 2 | 3 | 6 | ... | ... | ... | ... | ... | ... | ... | 14 | ... | ... | ... | II. | + | ... | II. |
| 185. Noureddin Ali of Damascus and the Damsel Sitt El Milah | ... | ... | ... | ... | ... | ... | ... | ... | ... | ... | ... | + | 15 | ... | ... | ... | III. | ... | ... | II. |
| 186. El Abbas and the King's Daughter of Baghdad | ... | ... | ... | ... | ... | ... | ... | ... | ... | ... | ... | + | 15 | ... | ... | ... | III. | ... | ... | II. |
| 187. The Two Kings and the Vizier's Daughters | ... | ... | ... | ... | .. | ... | ... | ... | ... | ... | ... | + | 15 | ... | ... | ... | III. | ... | ... | II. |
| 188. The Favourite and her Lover. | ... | ... | ... | ... | ... | ... | ... | ... | ... | ... | .. | + | 15 | ... | ... | ... | III. | ... | ... | II. |
| 189. The Merchant of Cairo and the Favourite of the Khalif El Mamoun El Hakim bi Amrillah | ... | ... | ... | ... | ... | ... | ... | ... | ... | ... | .. | + | 15 | ... | ... | ... | III. | ... | ... | II. |
| 190. Conclusion | ... | ... | ... | ... | ... | 4 | 3 | ... | 3 | + | 3 | + | 15 | ... | + | { | 9 & III. | ... | 6 | 10 |
| *191. History of Prince Zeyn Alasnam | 8 | 5 | 4 | ... | 4 | ... | ... | ... | ... | ... | ... | ... | 6 | 3 | ... | ... | ... | ... | ... | III. |
| *192. History of Codadad and his Brothers | 8 | 5 | 4 | ... | 4 | ... | ... | ... | ... | ... | ... | ... | 6 | 3 | ... | ... | ... | ... | ... | III. |
| **a.* History of the Princess of Deryabar | 8 | 5 | 4 | ... | 4 | ... | ... | ... | ... | ... | ... | ... | 6 | 3 | ... | ... | ... | ... | ... | III. |
| *193. Story of Aladdin, or the Wonderful Lamp | 9, 10 | 5, 6 | 4 | ... | 4, 5 | ... | ... | ... | ... | ... | ... | ... | 7, 8 | 3 | ... | ... | ... | ... | ... | III. |
| *194. Adventures of the Caliph Harun Al-Rashid | 10 | 6 | 5 | ... | 5 | ... | ... | ... | ... | ... | ... | ... | 8 | 3 | ... | ... | ... | ... | ... | III. |
| **a.* Story of the Blind Man, Baba Abdallah | 10 | 6 | 5 | ... | 5 | ... | ... | ... | ... | ... | ... | ... | 8 | 3 | ... | ... | ... | .. | ... | III. |
| **b.* Story of Sidi Numan | 10 | 6 | 5 | ... | 5 | ... | ... | ... | ... | ... | ... | ... | 8 | 3 | ... | ... | ... | ... | ... | III. |
| **c.* Story of Cogia Hassan Alhabbal | 10, 11 | 6 | 5 | .. | 5 | ... | ... | ... | ... | ... | ... | ... | 8 | 3 | ... | ... | ... | ... | ... | III. |
| *195. Story of Ali Baba and the Forty Thieves | 11 | 6 | 5 | ... | 5 | ... | ... | ... | ... | ... | ... | ... | 9 | 3 | ... | ... | ... | ... | ... | III. |
| *196. Story of Ali Cogia, a Merchant of Baghdad | 11 | 7 | 5 | ... | 5 | ... | ... | ... | ... | ... | ... | ... | 9 | 3 | ... | ... | ... | ... | ... | III. |
| *197. Story of Prince Ahmed and the Fairy Peri Banou | 12 | 7 | 5 | ... | 5 | ... | ... | ... | ... | ... | ... | ... | 9 | 3 | ... | ... | ... | ... | ... | III. |

| | | | | | | | | | | | | | | | | | | | | |
|---|---|---|---|---|---|---|---|---|---|---|---|---|---|---|---|---|---|---|---|---|
| *198. Story of the Sisters who envied their younger sister | 12 | 7 | 5 | ... | 5 | ... | ... | ... | ... | ... | ... | ... | 10 | 3 | ... | ... | ... | ... | ... | III. |
| 199. (Anecdote of Jaafar the Barmecide, = No. 39) | ... | ... | ... | ... | ... | ... | ... | ... | ... | ... | ... | ... | ... | 2 | ... | ... | ... | ... | ... | ... |
| 200. The Adventures of Ali and Zaher of Damascus | ... | ... | ... | ... | ... | ... | ... | .. | ... | ... | ... | ... | ... | 4 | ... | ... | ... | ... | ... | ... |
| 201. The Adventures of the Fisherman, Judar of Cairo, and his meeting with the Moor Mahmood and the Sultan Beibars | ... | ... | ... | ... | ... | ... | ... | ... | ... | ... | ... | ... | ... | 4 | ... | .. | ... | ... | ... | ... |
| 202. The Physician and the young man of Mosul | .. | ... | ... | 1 | ... | ... | ... | ... | ... | ... | ... | ... | ... | ... | ... | ... | ... | ... | ... | ... |
| 203. Story of the Sultan of Yemen and his three sons | ... | ... | 6 | 3 | 6 | ... | ... | ... | ... | ... | ... | ... | 11 | ... | ... | ... | ... | ... | ... | ... |
| 204. Story of the Three Sharpers and the Sultan | ... | ... | 6 | 3 | 6 | ... | ... | ... | ... | ... | ... | ... | 11 | ... | ... | ... | ... | ... | ... | ... |
| *a.* Adventures of the Abdicated Sultan | ... | ... | 6 | 3 | 6 | ... | ... | ... | ... | ... | ... | ... | 11 | ... | ... | ... | ... | ... | ... | ... |
| *b.* History of Mahummud, Sultan of Cairo | ... | ... | 6 | 3 | 6 | ... | ... | ... | ... | ... | ... | ... | 11 | ... | ... | ... | ... | ... | ... | ... |
| *c.* Story of the First Lunatic | ... | 8 | 6 | 3 | 6 | ... | ... | ... | ... | ... | ... | ... | 11 | ... | ... | ... | ... | ... | ... | ... |
| *d.* (Story of the Second Lunatic = No. 184) | ... | ... | 2 | 3 | 6 | ... | ... | ... | ... | ... | ... | ... | 11 | ... | ... | ... | ... | ... | ... | ... |
| *e.* Story of the Sage and his Pupil | ... | ... | 6 | 3 | 6 | ... | ... | ... | ... | ... | ... | ... | 11 | ... | ... | ... | ... | ... | ... | ... |
| *f.* Night Adventure of the Sultan | ... | ... | 6 | 3 | 6 | ... | ... | ... | ... | ... | ... | ... | 11 | ... | ... | ... | ... | ... | ... | ... |
| *g.* Story of the first foolish man | ... | ... | ... | 3 | ... | ... | ... | ... | ... | ... | ... | ... | ... | ... | ... | ... | ... | ... | ... | ... |
| *h.* Story of the broken-backed Schoolmaster | ... | ... | 6 | 3 | 6 | ... | ... | ... | ... | ... | ... | ... | 11 | ... | ... | ... | ... | ... | ... | ... |
| *i.* Story of the wry-mouthed Schoolmaster | ... | ... | 6 | 3 | 6 | ... | ... | ... | ... | ... | ... | ... | 11 | ... | ... | ... | ... | ... | ... | ... |
| *j.* The Sultan's second visit to the Sisters | ... | ... | 6 | 3 | 6 | ... | ... | ... | ... | ... | ... | ... | 11 | ... | ... | ... | ... | ... | ... | ... |
| *k.* Story of the Sisters and the Sultana, their mother | ... | ... | 6 | 3 | 6 | ... | ... | ... | ... | ... | ... | ... | 11 | ... | ... | ... | ... | ... | ... | ... |
| 205. Story of the Avaricious Cauzee and his wife | ... | ... | 6 | 3 | 6 | ... | ... | ... | ... | ... | ... | ... | 11 | ... | ... | ... | ... | ... | ... | ... |
| 206. Story of the Bang-Eater and the Cauzee | ... | ... | 6 | 3 | 6 | ... | ... | ... | ... | ... | ... | ... | 11 | ... | ... | ... | ... | ... | ... | ... |
| *a.* Story of the Bang-Eater and his wife | ... | ... | 6 | 3 | 6 | ... | ... | ... | ... | ... | ... | ... | 11 | ... | ... | ... | ... | ... | ... | ... |
| *b.* Continuation of the Fisherman, or Bang-Eater's Adventures | ... | ... | 6 | 3 | 6 | ... | ... | ... | ... | ... | ... | ... | 11 | ... | ... | ... | ... | ... | ... | ... |
| 207. The Sultan and the Traveller Mhamood Al Hyjemmee | ... | ... | 6 | 3 | 6 | ... | ... | ... | ... | ... | ... | ... | 11 | ... | ... | ... | ... | ... | ... | ... |
| *a.* The Kcord Robber (= No. 33) | ... | ... | ... | 3 | 6 | ... | ... | ... | ... | ... | ... | ... | ... | ... | ... | ... | ... | ... | ... | ... |
| *b.* Story of the Husbandman | ... | ... | .. | 3 | 6 | ... | ... | ... | ... | ... | ... | ... | ... | ... | ... | ... | ... | ... | ... | ... |
| *c.* Story of the Three Princes and Enchanting Bird | ... | .. | 6 | 3 | 6 | ... | ... | ... | ... | ... | ... | ... | 11 | ... | ... | ... | ... | ... | ... | ... |
| *d.* Story of a Sultan of Yemen and his three Sons | ... | ... | 6 | 4 | 6 | ... | ... | ... | ... | ... | ... | .. | 11 | ... | ... | ... | ... | ... | ... | ... |

| | Galland. | Caussin de Perceval. | Gautier. | Scott's MS. | Scott. | Von Hammer's MS. | Zinserling. | Lamb. | Trébutien. | "Bul." Text. | Lane. | "Bres." Text. | Habicht. | Weil. | "Mac." Text. | Torrens. | Payne. | Calc. | Burton (Lady). | Burton (Sir R.F.) |
|---|---|---|---|---|---|---|---|---|---|---|---|---|---|---|---|---|---|---|---|---|
| *e.* Story of the first Sharper in the Cave | ... | ... | ... | 4 | 6 | ... | ... | ... | ... | ... | ... | ... | ... | ... | ... | ... | ... | ... | ... | ... |
| *f.* Story of the second Sharper | ... | ... | ... | 4 | — | ... | ... | ... | ... | ... | ... | ... | ... | ... | ... | ... | ... | ... | ... | ... |
| *g.* Story of the third Sharper | ... | ... | ... | 4 | — | ... | ... | ... | ... | ... | ... | ... | ... | ... | ... | ... | ... | ... | ... | ... |
| *h.* History of the Sultan of Hind | ... | ... | 5 | 4 | 6 | ... | ... | ... | ... | ... | ... | ... | 10 | ... | ... | ... | ... | ... | ... | ... |
| 208. Story of the Fisherman's Son | ... | ... | ... | 4 | 6 | ... | ... | ... | ... | ... | ... | ... | ... | ... | ... | ... | ... | ... | ... | ... |
| 209 Story of Abou Neeut and Abou Neeuteen | ... | ... | 6 | 4 | 6 | ... | ... | ... | ... | ... | ... | ... | 11 | ... | ... | ... | ... | ... | ... | ... |
| 210. Story of the Prince of Sind, and Fatima, daughter of Amir bin Naomaun | ... | ... | 6 | 4 | 6 | ... | ... | ... | ... | ... | ... | ... | 11 | ... | ... | ... | ... | ... | ... | ... |
| 211. Story of the Lovers of Syria, or the Heroine | ... | ... | 6 | 4 | 6 | ... | ... | ... | ... | ... | ... | ... | 11 | ... | ... | ... | ... | ... | ... | ... |
| 212. Story of Hyjauje, the tyrannical Governor of Confeh, and the young Syed | ... | ... | ... | 4 | 6 | ... | ... | ... | ... | ... | ... | ... | ... | ... | ... | ... | ... | ... | ... | ... |
| 213. Story of the Sultan Haieshe | ... | ... | ... | 4 | — | ... | ... | ... | ... | ... | ... | ... | ... | ... | ... | ... | ... | ... | ... | ... |
| 214. Story told by a Fisherman | ... | ... | ... | 4 | — | ... | ... | ... | ... | ... | ... | ... | ... | ... | ... | ... | ... | ... | ... | ... |
| 215. The Adventures of Mazin of Khorassaun | ... | ... | 6 | 4,5 | 6 | ... | ... | ... | ... | ... | ... | ... | ... | 10 | ... | ... | ... | ... | ... | ... |
| 216. Adventure of Haroon Al Rusheed | ... | ... | 6 | 5 | 6 | ... | ... | ... | ... | ... | ... | ... | ... | 11 | ... | ... | ... | ... | ... | ... |
| *a.* Story of the Sultan of Bussorah | ... | ... | ... | 5 | — | ... | ... | ... | ... | ... | ... | ... | ... | ... | ... | ... | ... | ... | ... | ... |
| *b.* Nocturnal adventures of Haroon Al Rusheed | ... | ... | ... | 5 | 6 | ... | ... | ... | ... | ... | ... | ... | ... | ... | ... | ... | ... | ... | ... | ... |
| *c.* Story related by Munjaub | ... | ... | ... | 5 | 6 | ... | ... | ... | ... | ... | ... | ... | ... | ... | ... | ... | ... | ... | ... | ... |
| *d.* Story of the Sultan, the Dirveshe and the Barber's Son | ... | ... | ... | 5 | 6 | ... | ... | ... | ... | ... | ... | ... | ... | ... | ... | ... | ... | ... | ... | ... |
| *e.* Story of the Bedouin's Wife | ... | ... | ... | 5 | — | ... | ... | ... | ... | ... | ... | ... | ... | ... | ... | ... | ... | ... | ... | ... |
| *f.* Story of the Wife and her two Gallants | ... | ... | ... | 5 | - | ... | ... | ... | ... | ... | ... | ... | ... | ... | ... | ... | ... | ... | ... | ... |
| 217. Adventures of Aleefa, daughter of Mherejaun, Sultan of Hind, and Eusuff, son of Sohul, Sultan of Sind | ... | ... | 6 | 5 | 6 | ... | ... | ... | ... | ... | ... | ... | ... | 11 | ... | ... | ... | ... | ... | ... |
| 218. Adventures of the three Princes, sons of the Sultan of China | ... | ... | 5 | 5 | 6 | ... | ... | ... | ... | ... | ... | ... | ... | 10 | ... | ... | ... | ... | ... | ... |

| | | | | | | | | | | | | | | | | | | | | |
|---|---|---|---|---|---|---|---|---|---|---|---|---|---|---|---|---|---|---|---|---|
| 219. Story of the Gallant Officer | ... | ... | ... | 5 | — | ... | ... | ... | ... | ... | ... | ... | ... | ... | ... | ... | ... | ... | ... | ... |
| 220. Story of another officer | ... | ... | ... | 5 | — | ... | ... | ... | ... | ... | ... | ... | ... | ... | ... | ... | ... | ... | ... | ... |
| 221. Story of the Idiot and his Asses | ... | ... | ... | 5 | — | ... | ... | ... | ... | ... | ... | ... | ... | ... | ... | ... | ... | ... | ... | ... |
| 222. Story of the Lady of Cairo and the Three Debauchees | ... | ... | ... | 5 | — | ... | ... | ... | ... | ... | ... | ... | ... | ... | ... | ... | ... | ... | ... | ... |
| 223. Story of the Good Vizier unjustly imprisoned | ... | ... | 6 | 5 | 6 | ... | ... | ... | ... | ... | ... | ... | ... | 11 | ... | ... | ... | ... | ... | ... |
| 224. Story of the Prying Barber and the young man of Cairo | ... | ... | ... | 5 | — | ... | ... | ... | ... | ... | ... | ... | ... | ... | ... | ... | ... | ... | ... | ... |
| 225. Story of the Lady of Cairo and her four Gallants | ... | ... | 6 | 5 | 6 | ... | ... | ... | ... | ... | ... | ... | ... | 11 | ... | ... | ... | ... | ... | ... |
| *a.* The Cauzee's Story | ... | ... | ... | 5 | 6 | ... | ... | ... | ... | ... | ... | ... | ... | ... | ... | ... | ... | ... | ... | ... |
| *b.* The Syrian | ... | ... | ... | 5,6 | — | ... | ... | ... | ... | ... | ... | ... | ... | ... | ... | ... | ... | ... | ... | ... |
| *c.* The Caim-makaum's Wife | ... | ... | ... | 6 | — | ... | ... | ... | ... | ... | ... | ... | ... | ... | ... | ... | ... | ... | ... | ... |
| *d.* Story told by the Fourth Gallant | ... | ... | ... | 6 | — | ... | ... | ... | ... | ... | ... | ... | ... | ... | ... | ... | ... | ... | ... | ... |
| 226. Story of a Hump-backed Porter | ... | ... | ... | 6 | — | ... | ... | ... | ... | ... | ... | ... | ... | ... | ... | ... | ... | ... | ... | ... |
| 227. The aged Porter of Cairo and the Artful Female Thief | ... | ... | ... | 6 | — | ... | ... | ... | ... | ... | ... | ... | ... | ... | ... | ... | ... | ... | ... | ... |
| 228. Mhassun and his tried friend Mouseh | ... | ... | ... | 6 | — | ... | ... | ... | ... | ... | ... | ... | ... | ... | ... | ... | ... | ... | ... | ... |
| 229. Mahummud Julbee, son to an Ameer of Cairo | ... | ... | ... | 6 | — | ... | ... | ... | ... | ... | ... | ... | ... | ... | ... | ... | ... | ... | ... | ... |
| 230. The Farmer's Wife | ... | ... | ... | 6 | — | ... | ... | ... | ... | ... | ... | ... | ... | ... | ... | ... | ... | ... | ... | ... |
| 231. The Artful Wife | ... | ... | ... | 6 | — | ... | ... | ... | ... | ... | ... | ... | ... | ... | ... | ... | ... | ... | ... | ... |
| 232. The Cauzee's Wife | ... | ... | ... | 6 | — | ... | ... | ... | ... | ... | ... | ... | ... | ... | ... | ... | ... | ... | ... | ... |
| 233. Story of the Merchant, his Daugher, and the Prince of Eerauk | ... | ... | ... | 6 | 6 | ... | ... | ... | ... | ... | ... | ... | ... | ... | ... | ... | ... | ... | ... | ... |
| 234. The Two Orphans | ... | ... | ... | 6 | — | ... | ... | ... | ... | ... | ... | ... | ... | ... | ... | ... | ... | ... | ... | ... |
| 235. Story of another Farmer's Wife | ... | ... | ... | 6 | — | ... | ... | ... | ... | ... | ... | ... | ... | ... | ... | ... | ... | ... | ... | ... |
| 237. The two Wits of Cairo and Syria | ... | ... | ... | 6 | — | ... | ... | ... | ... | ... | ... | ... | ... | ... | ... | ... | ... | ... | ... | ... |
| 238. Ibrahim and Mouseh | ... | ... | ... | 6 | — | ... | ... | ... | ... | ... | ... | ... | ... | ... | ... | ... | ... | ... | ... | ... |
| 239. The Viziers Ahmed and Mahummud | ... | ... | ... | 6,7 | — | ... | ... | ... | ... | ... | ... | ... | ... | ... | ... | ... | ... | ... | ... | ... |
| 240. The Son addicted to Theft | ... | ... | ... | 7 | — | ... | ... | ... | ... | ... | ... | ... | ... | ... | ... | ... | ... | ... | ... | ... |
| 241. Adventures of the Cauzee, his Wife, &c. | ... | ... | 6 | 7 | 6 | ... | ... | ... | ... | ... | ... | ... | ... | 11 | ... | ... | ... | ... | ... | ... |
| *a.* The Sultan's Story of Himself | ... | ... | 6 | 7 | 6 | ... | ... | ... | ... | ... | ... | ... | ... | 11 | ... | ... | ... | ... | ... | ... |
| 242. Story of Shaykh Nukheet the Fisherman, who became favourite to a Sultan | ... | ... | ... | 7 | — | ... | ... | ... | ... | ... | ... | ... | ... | ... | ... | ... | ... | ... | ... | ... |
| *a.* Story of the King of Andalusia | ... | ... | ... | 7 | — | ... | ... | ... | ... | ... | ... | ... | ... | ... | ... | ... | ... | ... | ... | ... |
| 243. Story of Teilone, Sultan of Egypt | ... | ... | ... | 7 | — | ... | ... | ... | ... | ... | ... | ... | ... | ... | ... | ... | ... | ... | ... | ... |

| | Galland. | Caussin de Perceval. | Gautier. | Scott's MS. | Scott. | Von Hammer's MS. | Zinserling. | Lamb. | Trébutien. | "Bul." Text. | Lane. | "Bres." Text. | Habicht. | Weil. | "Mac." Text. | Torrens. | Payne. | Calc. | Burton (Lady). | Burton (Sir R.F.) |
|---|---|---|---|---|---|---|---|---|---|---|---|---|---|---|---|---|---|---|---|---|
| 244. Story of the Retired Man and his Servant | ... | ... | ... | 7 | 1 | ... | ... | ... | ... | ... | ... | ... | ... | ... | ... | ... | ... | ... | ... | ... |
| 245. The Merchant's Daughter who married the Emperor of China | ... | ... | ... | 7 | 1 | ... | ... | ... | ... | ... | ... | ... | ... | ... | ... | ... | ... | ... | ... | ... |
| *246. New Adventures of the Caliph Harun Al-Rashid | ... | 8 | 7 | ... | ... | ... | ... | ... | ... | ... | ... | ... | 12 | ... | ... | ... | ... | ... | ... | ... |
| *247. The Physician and the young Purveyor of Bagdad | ... | 8 | ... | ... | ... | ... | ... | ... | ... | ... | ... | ... | 13 | ... | ... | ... | ... | ... | ... | ... |
| *248. The Wise Heycar | ... | 8 | 7 | ... | ... | ... | ... | ... | ... | ... | ... | ... | 13 | ... | ... | ... | ... | ... | ... | ... |
| *249. Attaf the Generous | ... | 9 | 7 | ... | ... | ... | ... | ... | ... | ... | ... | ... | 13 | ... | ... | ... | ... | ... | ... | ... |
| *250. Prince Habib and Dorrat-al-Gawas | ... | 9 | 7 | ... | ... | ... | ... | ... | ... | ... | ... | ... | 12 | ... | ... | ... | ... | ... | ... | ... |
| *251. The Forty Wazirs | ... | ... | 1 | ... | ... | ... | ... | ... | ... | ... | ... | ... | 1 | ... | ... | ... | ... | ... | ... | ... |
| *a. Story of Shaykh Shababeddin | ... | ... | 1 | ... | ... | ... | ... | ... | ... | ... | ... | ... | 1 | ... | ... | ... | ... | ... | ... | ... |
| *b. Story of the Gardener, his Son, and the Ass | ... | ... | 1 | ... | ... | ... | ... | ... | ... | ... | ... | ... | 1 | ... | ... | ... | ... | ... | ... | ... |
| *c. The Sultan Mahmoud and his Wazir | ... | ... | 1 | ... | ... | ... | ... | ... | ... | ... | ... | ... | 1 | ... | ... | ... | ... | ... | ... | ... |
| *d. Story of the Brahman Padmanaba and the young Fyquai | ... | ... | 1 | ... | ... | ... | ... | ... | ... | ... | ... | ... | 1 | ... | ... | ... | ... | ... | ... | ... |
| *e. Story of Sultan Akshid | ... | ... | 1 | ... | ... | ... | ... | ... | ... | ... | ... | ... | 1 | ... | ... | ... | ... | ... | ... | ... |
| *f. Story of the Husband, the Lover and the Thief | ... | ... | 1 | ... | ... | ... | ... | ... | ... | ... | ... | ... | 1 | ... | ... | ... | ... | ... | ... | ... |
| *g. Story of the Prince of Carisme and the Princess of Georgia | ... | ... | 1 | ... | ... | ... | ... | ... | ... | ... | ... | ... | 1 | ... | ... | ... | ... | ... | ... | ... |
| *h. The Cobbler and the King's Daughter | ... | ... | 1 | ... | ... | ... | ... | ... | ... | ... | ... | ... | 1 | ... | ... | ... | ... | ... | ... | ... |
| *i. The Woodcutter and the Genius | ... | ... | 1 | ... | ... | ... | ... | ... | ... | ... | ... | ... | 1 | ... | ... | ... | ... | ... | ... | ... |
| *j. The Royal Parrot | ... | ... | 1 | ... | ... | ... | ... | ... | ... | ... | ... | ... | 1 | ... | ... | ... | ... | ... | ... | ... |
| *252. Story of the King and Queen of Abyssinia | ... | ... | 6 | ... | ... | ... | ... | ... | ... | ... | ... | ... | 10 | ... | ... | ... | ... | ... | ... | ... |
| *253. Story of Princess Amina | ... | ... | 7 | ... | ... | ... | ... | ... | ... | ... | ... | ... | 12 | ... | ... | ... | ... | ... | ... | ... |
| *a. Story of the Princess of Tartary | ... | ... | 7 | ... | ... | ... | ... | ... | ... | ... | ... | ... | 12 | ... | ... | ... | ... | ... | ... | ... |
| *b. Story told by the Old Man's Wife. | ... | ... | 7 | ... | ... | ... | ... | ... | ... | ... | ... | ... | 12 | ... | ... | ... | ... | ... | ... | ... |

| | | | | | | | | | | | | | | | | | | | | |
|---|---|---|---|---|---|---|---|---|---|---|---|---|---|---|---|---|---|---|---|---|
| *254. Story of Ali Johari. | ... | ... | 7 | ... | ... | ... | ... | ... | ... | ... | ... | ... | 12 | ... | ... | ... | ... | ... | ... | .. |
| *255. Story of the two Princes of Cochin China | ... | ... | 7 | ... | ... | ... | ... | ... | ... | ... | ... | ... | 12 | ... | ... | ... | ... | ... | ... | .. |
| *256. Story of the two Husbands | ... | ... | 7 | ... | ... | ... | ... | ... | ... | ... | ... | ... | 12 | ... | ... | ... | ... | ... | ... | ... |
| *a. Story of Abdallah | ... | ... | 7 | ... | ... | ... | ... | ... | ... | ... | ... | ... | 12 | ... | ... | ... | ... | ... | ... | ... |
| *b. Story of the Favourite | ... | ... | 7 | ... | ... | ... | ... | ... | ... | ... | ... | ... | 12 | ... | ... | ... | ... | ... | ... | ... |
| *257. Story of Yusuf and the Indian Merchant | ... | ... | 7 | ... | ... | ... | ... | ... | ... | ... | ... | ... | 12 | ... | ... | ... | ... | ... | ... | ... |
| *258. Story of Prince Benazir | ... | ... | 7 | ... | ... | ... | ... | | ... | ... | ... | ... | 12 | ... | ... | ... | ... | ... | ... | ... |
| *259. Story of Selim, Sultan of Egypt | ... | ... | 7 | ... | ... | ... | ... | ... | ... | ... | ... | ... | 13 | ... | ... | ... | ... | ... | ... | ... |
| *a. Story of the Cobbler's Wife | ... | ... | 7 | ... | ... | ... | ... | ... | ... | ... | ... | ... | 13 | ... | ... | ... | ... | ... | ... | ... |
| *b. Story of Adileh | ... | ... | 7 | ... | ... | ... | ... | ... | ... | ... | ... | ... | 13 | ... | ... | ... | ... | ... | ... | ... |
| *c. Story of the scarred Kalender | ... | ... | 7 | ... | ... | ... | ... | ... | ... | ... | ... | ... | 13 | ... | ... | ... | ... | ... | ... | ... |
| *d. Continuation of the story of Selim. | ... | ... | 7 | ... | ... | ... | ... | ... | ... | ... | ... | ... | 13 | ... | ... | ... | ... | ... | ... | ... |
| *260. Story of Seif Sul Yesn | ... | ... | ... | ... | ... | ... | ... | ... | ... | ... | ... | ... | 14 | ... | .. | ... | ... | ... | ... | ... |
| 261. Story of the Labourer and the Chair | ... | ... | ... | A | A | ... | .. | ... | ... | ... | ... | ... | ... | ... | ... | ... | ... | ... | ... | ... |
| 262. Story of Ahmed the Orphan | ... | ... | ... | A | A | ... | ... | ... | ... | ... | ... | ... | ... | ... | ... | ... | ... | ... | ... | ... |

N.B.—In using this Table, some allowance must be made for differences in the titles of many of the tales in different editions. For the contents of the printed text, I have followed the lists in Mr. Payne's "Tales from the Arabic," vol. iii.

W. F. KIRBY.

AND here I end this volume with repeating in other words and other tongue what was said in "L'Envoi":—

ان تجد عيبا فسدّ الخللا * جلّ من لا عيب فيه و علا

Hide thou whatever here is found of fault;
And laud The Faultless and His might exalt!

After which I have only to make my bow and to say

والسلام

# OPINIONS OF THE PRESS

## AND OF SCHOLARS

ON

## SIR RICHARD F. BURTON'S TRANSLATION

OF THE

# "ARABIAN NIGHTS."

# OPINIONS OF THE PRESS.

### Morning Advertiser.

Captain Burton, thirty-three years ago, went in the disguise of an Indian pilgrim to Meccah and Al-Medinah, and no one capable of giving the world the result of his experience has so minute, so exhaustive a knowledge of Arab and Oriental life generally. Hence the work now begun—only a limited number of students can ever see—is simply priceless to anyone who concerns himself with such subjects, and may be regarded as marking an era in the annals of Oriental translation.

---

### St. James's Gazette, *September 12th*, 1885.

One of the most important translations to which a great English scholar has ever devoted himself is now in the press. For three decades Captain Burton has been more or less engaged on his translation of the "Arabian Nights," the latest of the many versions of that extraordinary story which has been made into English, the only one at all worthy of a great original.

---

### Standard, *September 12th*, 1885.

The first volume of Captain Burton's long expected edition of the "Arabian Nights" was issued yesterday to those who are in a position to avail themselves of the wealth of learning contained in this monumental labour of the famous Eastern traveller. The book is printed for subscribers only, and is sold at a price which is not likely to be paid by any save the scholars and students for whose instruction it is intended.

Moreover, no previous editor—not even Lane himself—had a tithe of Captain Burton's acquaintance with the manners and customs of the Moslem East. Hence, not unfrequently, they made ludicrous blunders, and in no instance did they supply anything like the explanatory notes which have added so greatly to the value of this issue of "Alf Laylah wa Laylah."

On the other hand, apart from the language, the general tone of the "Nights" is exceptionally high and pure. The devotional fervour, as Captain Burton justly claims, often rises to the boiling point of fanaticism, and the pathos is sweet and deep, genuine and tender, simple and true. Its life—strong, splendid, and multitudinous—is everywhere flavoured with that unaffected pessimism and constitutional melancholy which strikes deepest root under the brightest skies. The Kazi administers poetical justice with exemplary impartiality; and so healthy is the morale that at times we descry vistas of a transcendental morality—the morality of Socrates and Plato.

In no other work is Eastern life so vividly pourtrayed. This work, illuminated with notes so full of learning, should give the nation an opportunity for wiping away that reproach of neglect which Captain Burton seems to feel more keenly than he cares to express.

---

*To the Editor of the* "PALL MALL GAZETTE."

SIR,—Your correspondent "Sigma" has forgotten the considerable number of "students" who will buy Captain Burton's translation as the only literal one, needing it to help them in what has become necessary to many—a masterly knowledge of Egyptian Arabic. The so-called "Arabian Nights" are about the only written half-way house between the literary Arabic and the colloquial Arabic, both of which they need, and need introductions too. I venture to say that its largest use will be as a grown-up school book, and that it is not coarser than the classics in which we soak all our boys' minds at school.

ANGLO-EGYPTIAN.

*September 14th,* 1885.

---

MORNING ADVERTISER, *September 15th,* 1885.

There is one work not entered in the publishers' announcements of "new books," though for years scholars and others have looked forward to it with an eagerness which has left far behind the ordinary curiosity which is bestowed on the greatest of contributions to current literature, and to-day the few fortunate possessors are examining it with an interest proportionate to the long toil which has been bestowed on its preparation. We refer to Captain Burton's "Arabian Nights." Hitherto, all the editions have been imperfect, and more or less valueless versions of the original. They throw a flood of light on hundreds of features of Oriental life on which the student has failed to be informed. But the work only a few limited students can even see, and is simply priceless to anyone thus interested in the subject, and may be regarded as marking an era in the annals of Oriental translation. Burton writes: "Many a time and oft, after the day's journey was over, I have gathered the Arabs around me and read or recited these tales to them until the tears trickled down their cheeks and they rolled on the sand in uncontrollable delight. Nor was it only in Arabia that the immortal 'Nights' did me such notable service. I found the wildlings of Somali-Land equally amenable to their discipline; no one was deaf to the charm, and the two women workers of my caravan on its way to Harar were incontinently dubbed by my men Shahrazad and Dinarzad."

---

WHITEHALL REVIEW, *September 17th*, 1885.

The publication of the first volume of Captain Burton's translation ot the "Alif Laïla" enriches the world of Oriental investigation with a monument of labour and scholarship and of research. The book is advisedly, and even inevitably, printed for private circulation, and is intended, as Captain Burton says in his preface, only for the eyes of such persons as are seriously students of Oriental life and manners, and are desirous of making a more complete acquaintance with the great masterpieces of Eastern literature than has hitherto been possible, except to finished Arabic scholars. In the name of the whole world of Oriental scholarship, we offer our heartfelt thanks and congratulations to Captain Burton upon the appearance of this first volume; and we look forward with the keenest interest for its successors.

---

HOME NEWS, *September 18th*, 1885.

Captain Burton has begun to issue the volumes of his subscription translation of the "Arabian Nights" and its fortunate possessors will now be able to realise the full flavour of Oriental feeling. They will now have the great storehouse of Eastern folk-lore opened to them, and Captain Burton's minute acquaintance with Eastern life makes his comments invaluable. In this respect, as well as in the freeness of the translation, the version will be distinguished from its many predecessors. Captain Burton's preface, it may be observed, bears traces of soreness at official neglect. Indeed it seems curious that his services could not have been utilised in the Soudan, when the want of competent Arabic scholars was so severely felt.

---

NOTTINGHAM JOURNAL, *September 19th*, 1885.

To scholars and men who have sufficient love of the soul of these sweet stories to discern the form in its true proportions, the new edition will be welcome. From an Oriental point of view the work is masterly to a degree. The quatrains and couplets, reading like verses from Elizabethan mantels, and forming a perfect rosary of Eastern lore, the constant succession of brilliant pictures, and the pleasure of meeting again our dear old friend Shahrázád, all these combine to give a unique charm and interest to this "perfect expositor of the mediæval Moslem mind."

---

DAILY EXCHANGE, *September 19th*, 1885.

The first volume of Captain Burton's "Thousand Nights and a Night," is printed at Benares by the Kamashastra Society, for private subscribers only, and has been delivered to the latter. If the other nine portions equal the first, English literature will be the richer by a work the like of which is rare. The English is strong and vitally idiomatic. It is the English of Shakespeare and Jeremy Taylor, the English of Robert Browning, with a curiously varied admixture of modern colloquial phraseology. I confess that I was not prepared, familiar as I was with Captain Burton's other work, to find so perfect a command of clear and vigorous style on the part of the great traveller and Oriental scholar. I must say that the tone of the work is singularly robust and healthy. What a treasurehouse Captain Burton has opened! Until he turned the key we knew little or nothing of the "Nights," and the notes which he has added to the work have a value that is simply unique.

---

MONTREAL DAILY HERALD, *September 21st*, 1885.

Captain Burton has translated the "Arabian Nights," but will only publish it for private distribution. A correspondent says that all these years we have been reading Lane's turgid emasculated selections we have been kept in the dark as to their singular beauty and vitally human strength. I have been amazed at the "Nights" as Englished by Captain Burton in strong, vital, picturesque prose. The stories, instead of being pieces of wild extravagance, unreal and theatrically tinselly, with the limelight instead of daylight, and paste instead of diamonds, are full of abounding life.

---

THE BAT, *September 29th*, 1885.

Captain Burton, in his way, renders a gigantic service to all students of literature who are not profound Orientalists, and to many who are, by giving them a literal, honest, and accurate translation of the "Arabian Nights."

The blatant buffoons who have spoken of Captain Burton's work indifferently, only show their own ignorance of the literature of the East. Captain Burton's work is well worth the price he charges for it to students of Eastern literatures and Eastern manners, and Eastern customs; but the misguided lunatic who invests in it in the hope of getting hold of a good thing, in the Holywell Street sense of the term, will find indeed that the fool and his money are soon parted.

---

THE LINCOLN GAZETTE, *October 10th*, 1885.

Captain Burton's first volume in sombre black and dazzling gold—the livery of the Abassides—made its appearance three weeks ago, and divided attention with the newly discovered star. It is the first volume of ten, the set issued solely to subscribers. And already, as in the case of Mr. Payne's edition, there has been a scramble to secure it, and it is no longer to be had for love or money. The fact is, it fills a void, the world has been waiting for this chef d'œuvre, and all lovers of the "Arabian Nights" wonder how they have got on without it.

---

THE LINCOLN GAZETTE, *October 10th*, 1885.

Another speciality of Captain Burton's edition is the notes. He is celebrated for sowing the bottom of his pages with curiously illuminating remarks, and he has here carried out his custom in a way to astonish. He tells us that those who peruse his notes in addition to those of Lane would be complete proficients in the knowledge of Oriental practices and customs. Lane begins with Islam, from Creation to the present day, and has deservedly won for his notes the honour of a separate reprint. Captain Burton's object in his annotations is to treat of subjects which are completely concealed from the multitude. They are utterly and entirely esoteric, and deal with matters of which books usually know nothing. Indeed, he has been assured by an Indian officer who had been 40 years in the East, that he was entirely ignorant of the matters revealed in these notes. Without these marvellous elucidations, "The Arabian Nights" would remain only half understood, but by their aid we may know as much of the Moslems as the Moslems know of themselves.

---

"*Jehu Junior*," VANITY FAIR, *October 24th*, 1885.

As a bold, astute traveller, courting danger, despising hardship, and compelling fortune, Captain Burton has few equals; as a master of Oriental languages, manners and customs, he has none. He is still very young, very vigorous, very full of anecdote and playful humour, and, what is remarkable in a linguist, he has not disdained even his own mother tongue, which he handles with a precision and a power that few can approach. He has recently crowned his literary labours by the most complete, laborious, uncompromising and perfect translation of that collection of stories known to us as the "Arabian Nights," but more correctly called "A Thousand Nights and a Night." He is a wonderful man.

## WHITEHALL REVIEW, *October 29th*, 1885.

The second volume of Captain Burton's translation of the "Arabian Nights" has just been issued to the subscribers, who had already become impatient for a second instalment of this great and fascinating contribution to literature. The new volume is, if possible, of even greater interest than the first. It contains the whole of the fantastic semi-chivalrous story of King Omar Bin al-Nu'-uman and his sons Sharrkan and Zau al-Makan, a knowledge of which has hitherto been confined chiefly to Oriental scholars, as Lane only admitted an episode from it into his version of "Alf Laila." Some of Sharrkan's adventures will remind students of other Eastern stories of some of the adventures recorded of the hero of Persian romance, Hatim Taī. As usual, Captain Burton's notes are rich, varied, and copious, of the greatest service to all serious students of Arabic manners and customs, and of Oriental life in general.

---

## SOUTH EASTERN HERALD, *October 31st.*

At Mr. Quaritch's trade sale the other day, Captain Burton made an interesting speech regarding "The Thousand and One Nights," of which the gist was to show that his translation performs a double office. It is not only a faithful and racy version of the true original, but it also represents a better text than any which has been hitherto accessible in print or manuscript. He, in fact, produced for his own use, and by collation of the existing materials, a careful, critical recension of the original, and his rendering may, therefore, claim to stand towards the Alf Laiiah in the same manner as the Latin version of Plato, by Marsilius Ficinus, towards the Greek text.

---

## LINCOLN GAZETTE, *November 2nd*, 1885.

In announcing the issue of the first volume of Captain Burton's long expected edition of the "Arabian Nights," the "Standard" reminds its readers that the book is printed for subscribers only, and is sold at a price which is not likely to be paid by any save the scholars and students for whose instruction it is intended. Many of those who know the ordinary epitome prepared for the nursery and drawing-room have little idea of the nature of the original. Galland's abridgment was a mere shadow of the Arabic. Even the editions of Lane, and Habicht, and Torrens, and Payne, represented but imperfectly the great corpus of Eastern folk-lore, which Captain Burton has undertaken to render into English. To Captain Burton, the preparation of these volumes must have been a labour of love. He began them in conjunction with his friend, Steinhaeuser, soon after his return from the Meccah pilgrimage, more than thirty years ago, and he has been doing something to them ever since. In no other work of the same nature is Eastern life so vividly pourtrayed. We see the Arab knight, his prowess and his passion for adventure, his love and his revenge, the craft of his wives and the hypocrisy of his priests, as plainly as if we had lived among them. Gilded palaces, charming women, lovely gardens, caves full of jewels, and exquisite repasts, captivate the senses and give variety to the panorama which is passing before our eyes. Indeed there is a tinge of melancholy pervading the preface in which the Editor refers to his "unsuccessful professional life," and to the knowledge of which his country has cared so little to avail itself. When the great explorer discovered the African lakes he was a captain. He is a captain still. No University has thought fit to make him a Doctor; and while knighthoods have been distributed with a profusion which has gone far to lower the value of these distinctions, the foremost of English travellers and the greatest of European Arabists is still untitled.* Even in the recent Egyptian troubles—which are referred to somewhat bitterly—his wisdom was not utilised, though after the death of Major Morice there was not an English official in the camps before Suakin capable of speaking Arabic. On this scandal, and on the ignorance of Oriental customs which was everywhere displayed, Captain Burton is deservedly severe.

There is only one "Arabian Nights" in the world, and only one Captain Burton. The general tone of the London press has been distinctly favourable, the "Standard" leading the way and other journals following suit. The "Thousand Nights and a Night" offers a complete picture of Eastern peoples. But the English reader must be prepared to find that the manners of Arabs and Moslems differ from his own. Eastern people look at things from a more natural and primitive point of view, and they say what they think with the unrestraint of children. At times their plain speaking is formidable; it is their nature to be downright, and to be communicative on subjects about which the Saxon is shy or silent, and it must be remembered that the separation of the sexes adds considerably to this freedom of expression.

It is only knowledge that knows how to observe; and it is satisfactory that Captain Burton's amazing insight into Eastern peculiarities has been put to its best use in giving a true idea of the people of the Sun and a veritable version of their book of books. The labour expended on this edition has been enormous. The work could only have been completed by the most excessive and pertinacious application. All the same we are told it has been "a labour of love," a task that has brought its exceeding great reward. There is only one regret, the circulation is limited. We cannot help hoping, at some future time, a selection may be made from the ten volumes. If the public cannot have the whole work, at least it might have a part, and not be entirely shut out from a masterpiece unparalleled.

---

* This was written some weeks before the author was made a K.C.M.G.

MORNING POST, *January 19th*, 1886.

Everything comes to him who waits—even the long-promised, eagerly-expected "Plain and Literal Translation of the Arabian Nights," by Richard F. Burton. It is a whole quarter of a century since this translation of one of the most famous books of the world was contemplated, and we are told it is the natural outcome of the well-known pilgrimage to Al-Medinah and Meccah. Of Captain Burton's fitness for the task who can doubt? It was during that celebrated journey to the Tomb of the Prophet that he proved himself to be an Arab—indeed, he says, in a previous state of existence he was a Bedouin. Did he not for months at a stretch lead the life of a Son of the Faithful, eat, drink, sleep, dress, speak, pray, like his brother devotees, the sharpest eyes failing to pierce his disguise? He knows the ways of Eastern men—and women—as he does the society of London or Trieste. How completely at home he is with his adopted brethren he showed at Cairo, when, to the amazement of some English friends who were looking on at the noisy devotions of some "howling" Dervishes, he suddenly joined the shouting, gesticulating circle, and behaved as if to the manner born. He has qualified as a "howler," he holds a diploma as a master Dervish, and he can initiate disciples. Clearly, to use a phrase of Arabian story, it was decreed by Allah from the beginning—and fate and fortune have arranged—that Captain Burton should be the one of all others to confer upon his countrymen the boon of the genuine unsophisticated "Thousand Nights and a Night." In the whole of our literature no book is more widely known. It is spread broadcast like the Bible, Bunyan, and Shakespeare; yet although it is in every house, and every soul in the kingdom knows something about it, yet nobody knows it as it really exists. We have only had what translators have chosen to give—selected, diluted, and abridged transcripts. And of late some so-called "original" books have been published, containing minor tales purloined bodily from the "Nights."

---

COURT SOCIETY, *March 4th*, 1886.

Not a little disgust has been excited by the vulgar sneer which a morning paper has indulged in at the expense of Sir Richard Burton. Long neglected by successive Governments, Captain Burton received, after 44 years, a tardy recognition of his services. Straightway, it was suggested that he is made a knight because he translated the "Arabian Nights." It need scarcely be said that his translation has nothing to do with the distinction conferred upon him, but as it is the habit in a certain quarter to denounce the literal translation of the "Nights," it cannot be too distinctly understood that Captain Burton never meant his work to fall into any hands save those of a thousand students.

### WHITEHALL REVIEW, *May 24th*, 1886.

The sixth volume of Sir Richard Burton's Arabian Nights," which has just been issued to subscribers, is one of the most interesting of the series to Anglo-Orientalists. For it contains that story—or set of stories—which is, perhaps, of all the tales of the "Arabian Nights," the dearest to legend-loving mankind, whether Oriental or Occidental—the story of the voyages of "Sindbad the Sailor," or of "Sindbad the Seaman," as Sir Richard Burton prefers to call him. Perhaps the only tale which at all competes in popularity with the wandering record of the "Eastern Odysseus" is the story of "Ali Baba," and that, unfortunately, does not belong to the "Arabian Nights" at all, and can only, as far as we know, be traced to a modern Greek origin. Lovers of the story of "Sindbad the Sailor" will be pleased to learn that their old friend remains to all intents and purposes the same in Sir Richard's literal translation as he was in the fanciful adaptation of Galland, and the more accurate rendering of Lane. He does not "suffer a sea change," but remains, what he has always been, the most wonderful wanderer in the whole range and region of romance. Sir Richard Burton's sixth volume contains, besides, that story of the "Seven Viziers," which in so many forms is a favourite in all the languages of the East.

---

### THE BAT, *July 7th*, 1886.

As regards his translation, however, Captain Burton is certainly felicitous in the manner in which he has Englished the picturesque turns of the original. One great improvement in this version over that of Mr. Lane will be found in the fact that the verses so freely interspersed throughout the "Nights" are here rendered in metre, and that an attempt also has often been made to preserve the assonants and the monorhyme of the Arabic. Mr. Lane frankly stated that he omitted the greater part of the poetry as tedious, and, through the loss of mea sure and rhyme "generally intolerable to the reader," as, in truth, the specimens inserted mostly proved to be on account of the bald literalism of the rendering. Captain Burton has naturally inserted the poetry with the rest; and has often shown much skill in doing into English verse the rippling couplets of the original. Take as an instance, the verses which Mr. Lane renders :—

> "Tell him who is oppressed with anxiety that anxiety will not last.
> As happiness passeth away, so passeth away anxiety."

Almost equally literal, and certainly more poetical, is Captain Burton, who gracefully turns this :—

> "Tell whoso hath sorrow, Grief never shall last;
> E'en as Joy hath no morrow, so Woe shall go past."

And since, in proverbs and epigrams, so much depends on the form, the spirit of the original is well observed, when, for instance, we read in a certain chronicle the lines of one Ibn al-Sumam :—

> "Hold fast thy secret, and to none unfold ;
> Lost is a secret when that secret's told.
> An fail thy breast thy secret to conceal,
> How canst thou hope another's breast shall hold ?"

Doubtless, too—and in this not following Mr. Lane—Captain Burton is right in retaining the original division into Nights : for, as he justly observes, "Without the Nights, no Arabian Nights !" And, besides this being a prime feature of the original, a grateful pause is thereby introduced into these intricate and interminable stories. In the translation Captain Burton's English is generally picturesque and always fluent. As is frankly stated, too, he has "never hesitated to coin a word when wanted." Captain Burton, who has passed the greater portion of his life in Arab-speaking countries, mixing freely in Moslem society, and often passing —as during his pilgrimage—himself for a True Believer, is naturally well qualified to translate this "Great Eastern Saga-Book." Also, since the scene of the stories is laid successively in every country of Islam, from Tangier to India, and beyond, the translator's intimate acquaintance, made during his wanderings, with all these peoples and places, stands him in good stead in elucidating peculiar manners and customs, and in this gives him the advantage over Mr. Lane, who had only seen Islam as domiciled in Egypt.

---

THE SPORTING LIFE, *July 17th*, 1886.

The more I see of this splendid translation, the more do I feel that we are indebted to the translator for the first real idea in English of the immortal original, and to him alone, for a complete reflection of the "Arabian Nights." The lustre and vigour of the English compel one's admiration at every step. . . . . It is palpable enough that, until Sir Richard Burton's wonderful work first saw the light, *we had no "Arabian Nights."*

---

# LETTERS FROM SCHOLARS.

[*Mr. Floyer, at the Telegraph Conference, has secured Egypt telegraphic independence, and an annual gain of £7,000.*]

GOVERNMENT TELEGRAPHS, BERLIN,
*16th September*, 1885.

MY DEAR CAPTAIN BURTON,

I cannot tell you how delighted I am with the translation. The language is wonderful. Only you in the world could have written it. How did you find out ensorcelled, instead of the vulgar bewitched? And how did you find out a hundred other words equally graceful and exact? It is the most wonderful translation in the whole of literature. In accuracy, in swing, it breathes Egypt to me. I could take it and read it straight out to my Effendis almost word for word. But the language is wonderful. As compared with Eastwick's Anwár-i-Suhayli it is Tennyson to Gladstone. My sense of the feelings inspired by the first pages of the Foreword it is impossible to express, and I congratulate you most sincerely on your absolutely unique achievement.

Yours very truly,
(Signed) ERNEST A. FLOYER.

---

*September 25th*, 1885.

DEAR CAPTAIN BURTON,

I have received the first volume of the "Nights," and beg you to accept my most heartfelt and sincere thanks for the valuable gift. I cannot express the pleasure which it affords me to see this wonderful book reproduced in a form which is as faithful a rendering of the original as it will remain an admirable "*monumentum aere perennius*" of the English language.

Moreover, I am not ashamed to acknowledge that in reading again the text, together with your translation, I have learned more Arabic in a few months than in as many years of former toilsome study.

---

*September 26th*, 1885.

I have been devouring your first volume of the "Nights," and cannot tell you how much I enjoyed the book, and how anxiously I am looking for the next volume.

JOHN ADDINGTON SYMONDS, *Am Hof, Davos Platz, Switzerland.*

ACADEMY, *October 3rd*, 1885.

The real question is whether a word-for-word version of the "Arabian Nights," executed with peculiar literary vigour, exact scholarship, and rare insight into Oriental modes of thought and feeling can, under any shadow of pretence, be ignored.

---

EDWARD PEACOCK, *Bottesford Manor, Brigg, October 3rd*, 1885.

I have read every word of the first volume of Captain Burton's "Arabian Nights," and, as I am not an Arabic scholar, *am very grateful to him for having given us* an English version.

---

*October 24th*, 1885.

DEAR SIR,

I do not know whether a letter which I wrote to the "Academy" about your "Arabian Nights" has come under your notice. If so, I beg you to excuse the chary words I used in commendation of a work which now, from the literary point of view, I regard as one of great original excellence.

---

*November 13th*, 1885.

I wish you *had* issued more numbers of your book, as you well deserve to be rewarded for such an admirable work. I delight in the vigour and Oriental character of the language. Even a few months in India were enough to make me appreciate and perhaps better understand the charm of the "Arabian Nights."

---

DEAR CAPTAIN,

The joy which your volume has occasioned me I will not attempt to express in a short letter. Let us meet soon and talk of nothing else.

---

DEAR BURTON,

This is merely a line of greeting in appreciation of your first volume, which I have been reading, just to say how pleased I am with everything—intrinsic and extrinsic.

---

I want to tell you how thoroughly I have enjoyed your "Arabian Nights," and how greatly they have contributed in making life endurable during these months. Your "Arabian Nights" is a revelation of Orientalism, and the finest study of words that I have ever met with. It will remain a literary text book as long as the English language lasts.

---

Volume I. awaiting me.

I congratulate Captain Burton heartily. The book looks very handsome, and the notes are most valuable. Altogether a great success.

---

Your "Nights" are admirable, fascinating—the true thing at last! I delight in my volume.

I can hardly express to you how highly I appreciate the "Nights," the first two volumes of which are to hand. The work is interesting, too, and permits another edition.

# OPINIONS OF THE PRESS

ON

## LADY BURTON'S EDITION

OF THE

# "ARABIAN NIGHTS."

# OPINIONS OF THE PRESS

ON

## LADY BURTON'S EDITION

OF THE

# "ARABIAN NIGHTS."

---

COURT JOURNAL, *June 26th*, 1886.

Book lovers will be glad to learn that Sir Richard Burton's "Thousand and One Nights" will shortly be reprinted, and that also with revision, which will remove it from the top shelf of a library to the drawing-room. Lady Burton is to be congratulated on her enterprise in taking up the matter, for unquestionably so admirable and indeed instructive a work should be placed within the reach of all. A copy of the *privately* printed edition is now worth £25, and undoubtedly its re-appearance as revised will be hailed with satisfaction by all lovers of Orientalism.

---

LITERARY WORLD, *July 2nd*, 1886.

A Bowdlerised edition of Sir Richard Burton's translation of the "Arabian Nights," for the benefit of the general public, is to be brought out by Lady Burton.

---

SHROPSHIRE READER, SHREWSBURY, *July 15th*, 1886.

The success of Sir Richard Burton's privately printed version of "The Thousand Nights and a Night" has been so great that he has consented to allow the issue to the general public of a "chastened" edition. The modifications that the necessity of the case demand will be confined to the removal of certain "archaic crudities" of the original; but the vigorous and simple language of the translation will otherwise be preserved throughout. Lady Burton has already made arrangements with a competent literato for the execution of this task. The mode of publication will be by subscription.

## LYTTLETON TIMES, *August 25th*, 1886.

### THE NEW "ARABIAN NIGHTS."

Sir Richard Burton's version of the "Thousand Nights and a Night," privately printed for the use of men and scholars, is now unobtainable. The edition sold off immediately, and the price has already reached twenty-six guineas. The best critics among the thousand purchasers say that the language is wonderful, the words graceful, the rendering of thought, as well as words, most accurate, and the poetry marvellous. The Oriental purchasers say that the language is wonderful, and they declare that they have learnt more Orientalism in the volumes than by long years of study. Lady Burton thinks it deplorable that this country should be deprived of this masterpiece, and believes that by removing certain archaic crudities the grand Arabian work (so infinitely superior to the "Arabian Nights Entertainments," which has been published and re-published by thousands) may be made an acceptable offering to an English public. She is, therefore, making arrangements with a competent man for fitting this work for family reading, and she proposes to print it by subscription and to publish it without delay. Details concerning numbers of volumes, price, appearance, and date of issue, will shortly be announced.

---

## ARMY AND NAVY MAGAZINE, *September*, 1886.

Lady Burton's object is to secure for the public, especially for her own sex and for scholars who have not subscribed to the original edition, the advantages of this Oriental masterpiece—the English reading, the knowledge of Eastern life, and perfect workmanship—which have been so heartily praised by the Press and by Scholars.

---

## LAND AND WATER, *September 4th*, 1886.

Lady Burton is publishing a drawing-room edition of her late husband's crude translation of the "Arabian Nights." Some time since I had occasion to speak out energetically about this same work, thinking that a book which, though running only to a small edition, might from its general interest excite the curiosity of those who saw copies of it, and that, within its luxurious covers, matters of prurient crudity might meet the prying eyes of those whom we would guard against such knowledge. Perhaps others thought with me, for Mr. Justin Huntly McCarthy, M.P., and Lady Burton give us their guarantees, in the preface of this coming three guinea edition, that "no mother shall regret her girl's reading it."

The book is most tastefully printed, and it is a matter for congratulation that they shall no longer be compelled to bar the children of this, their rightful treasure-house. Of the vigorous and poetic English of Captain Burton's translation, its freshness and virility, it is needless to speak.

ALLEN'S INDIAN MAIL, *September 4th*, 1886.

Lady Burton's edition of her husband's "Arabian Nights," translated literally from the Arabic, will shortly be issued by subscription to the public. It will consist of six volumes, demy octavo, of about 500 pages each, handsomely bound in white and gold. The price will be three guineas. Lady Burton's object is to secure for the public, especially for her own sex and for scholars who have not subscribed to the original edition, the advantages of this Oriental masterpiece—the English reading, the knowledge of Eastern life, and perfect workmanship—which have been so heartily praised by the Press and by Scholars. She has been fortunate in securing the able assistance of a literary friend, Mr. Justin Huntly McCarthy, M.P., who will prepare it for family reading, and the work will be printed by Messrs. Waterlow and Sons, Limited.

---

PALL MALL GAZETTE, *September 7th*, 1886.

*The "Arabian Nights" for "Household Reading."*—Lady Burton is preparing for publication a women's edition of her husband's translation of the "Arabian Nights." Her collaborateur in this task is Mr. Justin Huntly McCarthy, M.P. The first volume will be issued very shortly, the remaining five, "handsomely bound in white and gold," following at short intervals. Lady Burton is her own publisher, and is ready to receive orders through her bankers, Messrs. Coutts. The following is the preface to the book :—

DEAR READERS,—It is a long time since we last met. For seven years' travels, toil, and latterly weak health, have prevented my offering you any large work of my own. You have always been so kind and so indulgent that I shall never be ungrateful enough to offer you second-rate work.

In the case of my husband's "Nights," I have ever felt that to limit the work to a thousand people was squandering on a few what the many should enjoy. To secure it to you without detracting from its merits has occupied all my thoughts. It seems a pity that you should lose this deep well of reading and knowledge, beside which the flood of modern fiction flows thin and shallow.

The best critics among the thousand purchasers write me that the language is wonderful and the expression so graceful, the rendering of thought as well as words so accurate, and the poetry fresh and charming. The Orientalists tell me that in these volumes they have learnt more Orientalism than by years of hard study, and that it has greatly facilitated their study of Arabic.

There is no doubt that this faithful rendering of the grand Arabian work is in every respect superior to the "Arabian Nights Entertainments" which have been published and republished by thousands, and it would be a deplorable pity that an exaggerated mode of expressing thought should deprive the country of this masterpiece. I want to give to the English public for family reading the real thing, not the drawing-room tales which have been put before them as the "Arabian Nights" for the past 180 years, since the days of Professor Galland. The home student will thus for the first time realise what Arab life really is, and better understand those peoples, of whose "Life behind the scenes" Britons know so very little.

I can only add that the object of my colleague (Mr. Justin Huntly McCarthy, M.P.) has been to make as few omissions as possible, and that both he and I guarantee that no mother shall regret her girl's reading this "Arabian Nights." We consider that you will be deprived of nothing, and that you will have all the gain.

Therefore, dear readers, I hope that I shall find you as kind as you have ever been to

Yours, with sympathy and gratitude,

ISABEL BURTON.

LONDON, *July 15th*, 1886.

---

NOTTINGHAM JOURNAL, *September 7th*, 1886.

Lady Isabel Burton has just issued a preface and title-page of the new edition of her husband's "Arabian Nights," to the great value of which we have previously borne testimony in the columns of The Journal. The new edition is dedicated to the women of England, the authoress believing that the majority of them can appreciate fine language, exquisite poetry, and romantic Easternlife just as well as the thousand students and scholars who secured the original thousand copies. Lady Burton has been assisted in her work by Mr. Justin Huntly McCarthy, M.P., and she guarantees the work has been so edited that no mother shall regret her girl reading this "Arabian Nights."

---

WHITEHALL REVIEW, *September 8th*, 1886.

Lady Burton has just addressed a document, or rather a series of documents, to the world at large which ought by rights to give the world at large much pleasure. Lady Burton has always been a sharer in her husband's labours, a colleague in his work, and she has made her own place in contemporary literature by such books as "The Inner Life of Syria" and "Arabia, Egypt, India," which are well worthy of their companionship with the famous "Pilgrimage to Meccah." Lady Burton now proposes to issue an edition of Sir Richard Burton's translation of the "Arabian Nights," made suitable for general reading. This edition which is to be known as "Lady Burton's edition of her husband's 'Arabian Nights,'" will be edited by Mr. Justin Huntly McCarthy, M.P., whose Oriental sympathies and studies will serve him for the task. Sir

Richard Burton's translation was, by the very nature of its purpose, unfitted for general reading. It was intended solely for scholars and students of the East, and into their hands alone has it fallen. It is the aim of Lady Burton and of Mr. McCarthy to render the bulk of that book accessible to the reading public, and, above all things, to women—to give them, in fact, an edition of "The Arabian Nights" which shall be far truer to the great original than any other rendering from Galland's to Lane's, but which, at the same time, shall be absolutely suited for household reading. Mr. Podsnap himself, in his supervision of the historic "Young Person," could find nothing which he would not approve of in Lady Burton's "Arabian Nights."

---

ST. LOUIS POST DISPATCH, *September 8th*, 1886.

I am glad that this revised edition is to be published, for it would be greatly to be regretted if a certain broadness of expression, which is necessary in literal translation from the Arabic, should deprive many of so accurate a rendering of Arab thought.

---

TRUTH, *September 9th*, 1886.

Lady Burton states in the prospectus of her contemplated edition of her husband's translation of the "Arabian Nights":—

I want to give to the English public, for family reading, the real thing, not the drawing-room tales which have been put before them as the "Arabian Nights" since the days of Professor Galland. The home student will thus, for the first time, realise what Arab life really is, and better understand those peoples of whose life behind the scenes Britons know so very little.

---

LITERARY WORLD, *September 10th*, 1886.

In the preface to her forthcoming "household" edition of her husband's "Arabian Nights," which will be published by subscription (the six volumes for three guineas) Lady Burton says, "I want to give to the English public for family reading the real thing, not the drawing-room tales which have been put before them as the 'Arabian Nights' for the past one hundred and eighty years, since the days of Professor Galland. The home student will thus for the first time realise what Arab life really is, and better understand those peoples of whose 'life behind the scenes' Britons know so very little." She has been assisted in the work of preparing this edition for household reading by Mr. Justin Huntly McCarthy, M.P.

---

UNITED SERVICE GAZETTE, *September 11th*, 1886.

We are charmed to hear that Lady Burton has in rapid preparation a "family" edition of her husband's unapproachable translation of the

Arabian Nights. The work will consist of six volumes, demy 8vo, of about 500 pages each, to be issued at £3. 3s., and will be printed by Messrs. Waterlow and Sons. Mr. Justin Huntly McCarthy, M.P., collaborates with Lady Burton. We may safely prophesy for the work an undoubted success. There is a charm and fascination about Burton's translation that enchains the reader. The Eastern beauties of expression are singularly attractive, and under Lady Burton's careful editing we may rely on a rich feast of such gems of thought and poesies of imagination as only the resplendent Orient can produce. To calm the anxiety of parents we would add that Lady Burton guarantees "that no mother shall regret her girl reading this edition of the Arabian Nights."

---

THE QUEEN, *September 11th*, 1886.

Lady Burton is preparing for publication a women's edition of her husband's translation of the "Arabian Nights." Her collaborateur in this task is Mr. Justin Huntly McCarthy, M.P. The first volume will be issued shortly, the remaining five, "handsomely bound in white and gold," following at short intervals. Lady Burton is her own publisher, and is ready to receive orders through her bankers, Messrs. Coutts, 59, Strand, London.

---

ACADEMY, *September 11th*, 1886.

The following will be the title-page of the "chastened" edition of Sir Richard F. Burton's "The Thousand Nights and a Night," which we have already announced as in preparation: "Lady Burton's edition of her husband's Arabian Nights, translated literally from the Arabic; prepared for household reading by Justin Huntly McCarthy, M.P." It will be dedicated by Lady Burton to the women of England, "believing that the majority can appreciate fine language, exquisite poetry, and romantic Eastern life, just as well as the thousand students and scholars who secured the original thousand copies." The work will consist of six volumes, demy octavo, of about 500 pages each, handsomely bound in white and gold. The price will be three guineas. It will be printed by Messrs. Waterlow & Sons, Limited; but it will only be sold to subscribers, who should address themselves to Lady Burton, Messrs. Coutts & Co., Strand, London.

---

ECHO, *September 11th*, 1886.

The following is the title-page of Lady Burton's "The Thousand and One Nights:"—"Lady Burton's edition of her husband's Arabian Nights, translated literally from the Arabic; prepared for household reading by Justin Huntly McCarthy, M.P." It will be dedicated by Lady Burton to the women of England, "believing that the majority can appreciate fine language, exquisite poetry, and romantic Eastern life, just as well as the thousand students and scholars who secured the original thousand copies."

---

THE GAZETTE, *September 11th*, 1886.

*Lady Burton's "Arabian Nights."*—The book of the coming "publishers'" season is to be Lady Burton's edition of her husband's "Arabian Nights," dedicated to the women of England. The original thousand subscribers need not be startled, their rights and privileges have been held sacred; there is no infringement of learned dues, and they will still retain the monopoly of the exact and literal translation from the Arabic, together with the notes and commentaries intended solely for the instruction of the scholar and Oriental student. With the aid of Mr. Justin Huntly McCarthy, M.P., Lady Burton intends "to give to the English public for family reading the real thing, not the drawing-room tales which have been put before them as the 'Arabian Nights' since the days of Professor Galland." Her prepared edition will be in six volumes, the price £3 3s., and as Lady Burton is her own publisher, applications for copies should be made to her address, British Consulate, Triest. For the countless folk who at Christmas will be at their wits' end for a gift book, the problem is here solved. What could be better for the rising generation than these wonderful stories here born afresh and re-told by the scholar of all others fitted for the task. It is to be expected that there will be a revived zest for this Book of the East, for this complete and all-round record of the lives of the followers of Mohammed, Apostle of Allah. For years past Lane's edition has hel the field, and now comes a formidable rival to dispute possession, and, inevitably, to take precedence. For the future, there will be no "Arabian Nights" except those to which the name of Burton is attached.

---

BROAD ARROW, *September 11th*, 1886.

"Lady Burton's edition of her husband's Arabian Nights, translated literally from the Arabic," will shortly be issued by subscription. It will consist of six volumes, demy octavo, of about 500 pages each, handsomely bound in white and gold. Lady Burton's object is to secure for the public, especially for her own sex and for scholars who have not subscribed to the original edition, the advantages of this Oriental masterpiece—the English reading, the knowledge of Eastern life, and perfect workmanship—which has been so heartily praised by the Press and by scholars. Mr. Justin Huntly McCarthy, M.P., has assisted to prepare it for family reading. Under these favourable conditions, there is no doubt that the work will be a success.

### FIGARO, *September 11th*, 1886.

Lady Burton's edition of her husband's "Arabian Nights" is exciting much interest. As the price is reasonable—three guineas—and the book is to be completed in six volumes, there is no doubt that the number of subscribers will be considerable.

---

### COURT CIRCULAR, *September 11th*, 1886.

Sir Richard Burton's translation of "The Arabian Nights" is a work of marvellous erudition, and a perpetual delight to Arabic scholars and all who care to read these famous stories as accurately reproduced as possible. But they contain much that is not fit reading for women and for young people. We are glad, therefore, to announce that Lady Burton has determined to issue an expurgated edition, as it were, which can be placed in the hands of families. Lady Burton's object, she tells us in the prospectus, is to secure for the public, especially for her own sex and for scholars who have not subscribed to the original edition, the advantages of this Oriental masterpiece—the English reading, the knowledge of Eastern life, and perfect workmanship—which have been so heartily praised by the Press and by scholars. This popular edition will assuredly be in great demand, and we most heartily commend it to our readers.

---

### WEEKLY DESPATCH, *September 12th*, 1886.

It is delightful to hear that Lady Burton (Mr. Justin Huntly McCarthy collaborating) is preparing an edition of her husband's translation of the "Arabian Nights" for family reading. The young person, says Lady Burton, will be able to read her version without raising the proverbial blush. If Lady Burton can accomplish her task with success, we ought not to despair of the Bowdlerising business. "Wycherley for the Home Circle," "Every Girl's Catullus," and "Boccaccio for Boys" ought to become popular in the lending libraries and the class-room.

---

### SUN, *September 12th*, 1886.

Shortly will come before the public, "Lady Burton's edition of her husband's Arabian Nights" (Waterlow & Sons). As the sun rises in the east to open and enliven the day, so comes this Oriental masterpiece—which originally created so much observation not long ago—now prepared for household reading by Justin Huntly McCarthy, M.P., and Lady Burton, to open and enlighten our minds to the true graces, beauties, and poetry of real Arab life.

BIRMINGHAM DAILY MAIL, *September 15th*, 1886.

The following will be the title-page of the "chastened" edition of Sir Richard F. Burton's "The Thousand Nights and a Night," which are in preparation: "Lady Burton's edition of her husband's Arabian Nights, translated literally from the Arabic; prepared for household reading by Justin Huntly McCarthy, M.P." It will be dedicated by Lady Burton to the women of England, "believing that the majority can appreciate fine language, exquisite poetry, and romantic Eastern life, just as well as the thousand students and scholars who secured the original thousand copies." The work will consist of six volumes, demy octavo, of about 500 pages each, handsomely bound in white and gold. The price will be three guineas. It will be printed by Messrs. Waterlow & Sons, Limited; but it will only be sold to subscribers, who should address themselves to Lady Burton, Messrs. Coutts & Co., Strand, London.

---

HASTINGS ADVERTISER, *September 16th*, 1886.

Sir Richard Burton's translation of "The Arabian Nights" is a work of marvellous erudition, and a perpetual delight to Arabic scholars and all who care to read these famous stories as accurately reproduced as possible. But they contain much that is not fit reading for women and for young people. We are glad, therefore, to announce that Lady Burton has determined to issue an expurgated edition, as it were, which can be placed in the hands of families. Lady Burton's object, she tells us in the prospectus, is to secure for the public, especially for her own sex and for scholars who have not subscribed to the original piece, the English reading, the knowledge of Eastern life, and perfect workmanship which have been so heartily praised by the Press and by scholars. This popular edition will assuredly be in great demand, and we most heartily commend it to our readers.

---

SCHOOLMISTRESS, *September 16th*, 1886.

Lady Burton's "The Thousand and One Nights" will be dedicated to the women of England, her ladyship believing "that the majority can appreciate fine language, exquisite poetry, and romantic Eastern life, just as well as the thousand students and scholars who secured the original thousand copies." The title-page of the work runs as follows: "Lady Burton's edition of her husband's Arabian Nights, translated literally from the Arabic; prepared for household reading by Justin Huntly McCarthy, M.P."

LEKLEY FREE PRESS, *September 17th*, 1886.

The following is the title-page of Lady Burton's "The Thousand and One Nights, translated literally from the Arabic: prepared for household reading by Justin Huntly McCarthy, M.P." It will be dedicated by Lady Burton to the women of England, "believing that the majority can appreciate fine language, exquisite poetry, and romantic Eastern life, just as well as the thousand students and scholars who secured the original thousand copies." The work will consist of six volumes, demy octavo, of about 500 pages each, handsomely bound in white and gold.

---

HOME NEWS, *September 17th*, 1886.

Lady Burton, in collaboration with Mr. Justin Huntly McCarthy, M.P., is about to issue an expurgated edition of the Arabian Nights in six volumes. In the preface, of which we have received an advance copy, Lady Burton declares that her object is "to give to the English public for family reading the real thing, not the drawing-room tales which have been put before them as the 'Arabian Nights' for the past one hundred and eighty years. I can only add that the object of my colleague has been to make as few omissions as possible, and that both he and I guarantee that no mother shall regret her girl's reading this 'Arabian Nights.'"

---

LONDON AND WESTMINSTER SPORTING LIFE, *September 18th*, 1886.

From a private note which I have received from Sir Richard Burton I judge that the supplementary volumes to the "Thousand Nights and a Night" will be of great and peculiar interest. Indeed the entire set will form a library of Oriental lore of unique value. The scheme of Lady Burton for popularising her husband's translation of the "Arabian Nights" approaches completion. Her partner in the plan is Mr. Justin Huntly McCarthy, M.P., and with reference to him Lady Burton says that our object has been "to make as few omissions as possible, and that both he and I have guaranteed that no mother shall regret her girl's reading this 'Arabian Nights.'" Well, although I agree with Lady Burton that "it seems a pity that the public should lose this deep well of learning and knowledge, beside which the flood of modern fiction flows thin and shallow," and am with "the best critics among the thousand purchasers" of the original edition who have declared that "the language is wonderful, and the expressions so graceful, the rendering of thought as well as words so accurate, and the poetry fresh and charming," the excisions for the family reader will have to be made with a bold hand. Who is to revise the sheets for the press? "The British Matron"?

NORTHERN WHIG, BELFAST, *September 20th*, 1886.

The following is the title-page of Lady Burton's "The Thousand and One Nights":—"Lady Burton's edition of her husband's Arabian Nights, translated literally from the Arabic; prepared for household reading by Justin Huntly McCarthy, M.P." It will be dedicated by Lady Burton to the women of England, "believing that the majority can appreciate fine language, exquisite poetry, and romantic Eastern life just as well as the thousand students and scholars who secured the original thousand copies." The work will consist of six volumes, demy octavo, of about five hundred pages each, handsomely bound in white and gold. The price will be three guineas.

---

NOTTINGHAM JOURNAL, *October 6th*, 1886.

Lady Burton's household edition of her husband's translation of the "Arabian Nights" is making satisfactory progress. That it gives delight to the subscribers may be inferred from their encomiums. One writes, "I would give passages of it to the Board Schools"; another goes so far as to say, "It is like a new Bible for beauty of expression, and can you fancy a more wondrous gift than a second inspired Book?" I don't feel quite so enthusiastic as this, but it is fair to say that the difficult task which Lady Burton and Mr. Justin Huntly McCarthy have set themselves is being performed with singular skill and success.

---

CIVIL SERVICE GAZETTE, *November 2nd*, 1886.

Lady Burton, laudably desirous of enabling British subjects of all ranks and sexes to enjoy the enchanting Arabian tales in their entirety, and translated in pure English direct and literally from the Arabic, has undertaken the task, with the assistance of Mr. Justin Huntly McCarthy, M.P., of preparing for publication an edition of her husband's superb work, from which every word, sentiment, and expression to which exception can be made by the most critical has been expunged. We have been favoured with an advance copy of the first volume—now ready for publication—and we can affirm that it is an elegant and perfectly innocent version, in which is preserved, with the utmost delicacy of phraseology the wondrous fictions of Araby without any detraction from the grace and spirit of the original.

---

FUN, *November 2nd*, 1886.

NEW LEAVES.

*Lady Burton's edition of her husband's Arabian Nights, prepared for household reading by Justin Huntly McCarthy, M.P.*—Apart from the learning and labour so lavishly bestowed upon the original edition, and the careful eliminations in preparing this, there is ever a charm of seeming enchantment surrounding these wondrous stories, which age does not abate, nor time destroy—yet the truthfulness of this translation enriches and enhances them. Lady Burton deserves all praise and many thanks for putting her husband's work before the public in the present pleasingly pure and elegant form, thus making it available to the many.

---

LAND AND WATER, *November 13th*, 1886.

Lady Burton sends me to-day the first volume of her ladyship's edition of Sir Richard's "Arabian Nights." She is very happy in her choice of season for issuing this work, for a pleasanter present than such volumes as may have been published before Christmas, together with a promise of their successors to follow in due course, would be about as delightful a gift as Santa Claus could bring mother or daughter. The binding is of nuptial-white, a white all too nuptial, methinks; for, like wedded bliss, it too readily loses its pristine charm, and grows soiled and finger-marked. Lady Burton presents her own portrait to her subscribers as a photographic frontispiece.

---

COURT AND SOCIETY, *November 18th*, 1886.

Between emblematic covers of purest white, on which the "spotless lily" and the "chaste crescent of the young moon" are the only ornaments. Lady Burton has brought out the first volume of her edition of her husband's "Arabian Nights," "prepared for household reading" by Justin Huntly McCarthy, M.P. Of the contents, what need be said? In substance, they are those of Sir Richard's noble work. But of the truly exquisite workmanship of the book itself much might be said, and yet not exhaust the full measure of its merit. Lady Burton herself designed the cover and the beautifully Arabic title-page, and Waterlow & Sons have printed the work in such type and on such paper as makes reading a luxury, and her ladyship's volumes an artistic delight.

o o o o o o o

By excision only some two hundred out of three thousand pages are lost; but the result of the omission is that Lady Burton guarantees that no mother shall regret her girl's reading this "Arabian Nights."

---

DAILY TELEGRAPH, *November 18th*, 1886.

Though, no doubt, it is possible that some very erudite translations may be literary caviar—beyond the taste and sympathy of uncultivated palates —yet this does not hold good of such a popular work as the one recently translated by Sir Richard Burton; and Lady Burton, in issuing a more popular edition of her husband's "Arabian Nights," (Waterlow), has put us under a debt of gratitude. Of the first issue only a thousand copies were printed, and these passed at once into the hands of scholars and linguists. There was, however, no reason why so learned and careful a translation of a delightful classic should be restricted within narrow limits, and, with ample justification on her side, Lady Burton, assisted by Mr. Justin McCarthy, has revised the work for home reading, and published it in a new and cheaper form. This "wondrous treasury of Moslem folk-lore," is, in the words of its scholarly translator, something more than a fairy book for small boys—"the pathos is sweet, deep, and genuine, tender, simple, and true, utterly unlike much of our modern tinsel. Its life is strong, splendid, and multitudinous; the moral is sound and healthy, and at times we descry vistas of a transcendental morality, the morality of Socrates in Plato." It is, indeed, this unique contrast of a quaint element, childish crudities jostling the finest and highest views of life and character, shown in the kaleidoscopic shiftings of the marvellous picture, which forms the chiefest charm of the "Nights." It is not necessary to speak of the translator's fitness for his task. It has been a standing pity that there should be no English equivalent to some of the sterling German translations—of which, by the way, no mention is made here—and Lady Burton's public-spirited enterprise, will enable the great company of readers to whom she dedicated it, to go to the fountain head, and form their own opinion of the wealth and worth, the dignity and the richness of this wonderful diadem of romance.

---

THE QUEEN, *November 20th*, 1886.

Lady Burton's edition of her husband's very literal translation of the "Arabian Nights," volume I., has been published. Mr. J. H. McCarthy, M.P., has helped her to prepare it for household reading. The edition is dedicated to "the women of England," in the belief that "the majority can appreciate fine language, exquisite poetry, and romantic Eastern life, just as well as the thousand students and scholars who secured the original thousand copies."

---

CIVIL SERVICE GAZETTE, *November 20th*, 1886.

We are of opinion that the Arabian tales, which are so universally pleasing to the people, should be placed within reach of the people, and not be withheld from them, as they would be practically if shut up in glass cases, among the éditions de luxe of connoisseurs. Lady Burton, laudably desirous of enabling British subjects of all ranks and sexes to enjoy the enchanting Arabian tales in their entirety, and translated into pure English direct and literally from the Arabic, has undertaken the task, with the assistance of Mr. Justin McCarthy, M.P., of preparing for publication an edition of her husband's superb work, from which every word, sentiment and expression to which exception can be made by the most critical has been expunged. We have been favoured with an advance copy of the first volume—now ready for publication—and we can affirm that it is an elegant and perfectly innocent version, in which is preserved with the utmost delicacy of phraseology, the wondrous fictions of Araby without any detraction from the grace and spirit of the original.

---

BAT, *November 23rd*, 1886.

Sir Richard Burton's translation of these famous tales was enthusiastically received by the book-loving world. The whole edition was speedily disposed of, and when complete it will probably be worth more than double its original price. Still, the edition was a small one, and the fact that the renderings were always literal—that what was a spade in the Arabic remained a spade in the new version—made it a book which could not be left about upon the drawing-room table. Anxious to afford her countrywomen opportunities of studying the beauties of Arabic lore and legend, Lady Burton has undertaken the issue of a new edition, with the original improprieties carefully expurgated, and this she dedicates "To the Women of England." A more beautiful and interesting work than this has seldom been offered to the public. It is a handsome gift suitable to the whole world. The type and paper are admirable, and the chastity of the white binding is appropriately symbolical of the purity which prompted its contents.

---

COUNTY GENTLEMAN, *November 27th*, 1886.

In making this offering of priceless Oriental treasures to her sisters of the West, Lady Burton guarantees "that no mother shall regret her girl's reading this Arabian Nights," coupling the guarantee with the assurance that "you will be deprived of nothing of the original save 215 out of 3,215 pages, and you will have all the gain." We are very glad to find that the present editor has preserved her husband's most eloquent and characteristic "Foreword" to the unabridged version. Sir Richard Burton's work has been criticised in some quarters for a too obvious straining after the literal reproduction of the original. In our opinion, such a course deserves rather praise than censure. And, indeed, we would demur to the phrase "obvious straining" in connection with the great Orientalist and explorer's wonderfully successful representation to English eyes and ears of both the meaning and the form of this marvellous mosaic of Eastern fancy and imagination. That certain words and phrases Sir Richard makes use of are unfamiliar to the British reader is perfectly true. But it must be remembered that they have been made the means of rendering intelligible unfamiliar modes of thought and feeling which are entirely beyond the reach of smug literary conventions and forms of expression. For ourselves, we can honestly say that these very outrages upon Philistine sensibility have been amongst the principal charms of this unequal and unrivalled translation—adding vastly to the vicissitudes and seeming fidelity of the work. The marvel to us has been rather—remarking the uniformly level execution of the whole—that so few verbal ingenuities of the kind referred to have been found necessary, and that so much of the translated prose is English undefiled, albeit of the vigorous and vertebrate order, and so much of the translated poetry has the ring of genuine English verse. We might. however, write pages in explanation of our view of the manner in which Sir Richard has discharged his task without approaching his definition of his work as "a faithful copy of the great Eastern Saga-book by preserving intact not only the spirit, but even the *mécanique*, the manner, and the matter." Of the tales themselves, we can, of course, say nothing true that is new, or nothing new that is also true. No romances of intrigue and adventure, of wealth and poverty, of luxury and love, have had such universal acceptance, or received so much of that homage which is said to be the sincerest—the flattery of imitation. And this by means of the garbled and imperfect versions which have hitherto obtained currency in the Western world. Lady Burton deserves the thanks of all English women and children—from whom, for obvious reasons, her husband's complete work must ever be a sealed book—for giving "to the English public, for family reading, the real thing, not the drawing-room tales which have been put before them as the 'Arabian Nights' for the past one hundred and eighty years, since the days of Professor Galland." The present volume—the initial portion of a most sumptuous édition de luxe—contains the introduction and nine of the immortal tales, by the recital of which Shahrázád induced the "pious and auspicious" King to forego the fulfilment of his sanguinary vow.

---

JUDY, *December 1st*, 1886.

*Lady Burton's edition of her husband's "Arabian Nights" translated literally from the Arabic, and prepared for household reading by Justin Huntly McCarthy*, will, I think, find a warm welcome among English readers. There has been of late a visible tendency to over-Bowdlerize the classics; but, I hardly see how any sensible objection can be made to this truly excellent version of a book, that in all sorts of shapes has for so many years retained its undying popularity. The paper, print, and binding are perfect in their way, and this edition of the "Arabian Nights" will form a very desirable Christmas present.

---

MORNING POST, *December 2nd*, 1886.

The Lady Burton book—in the preparation of which she has been helped by Mr. Justin Huntly McCarthy—is all that the "Arabian Nights" was to us in its old guise, with the addition of many characteristic specialities of Orientalism. The work on which this book is founded has been so thoroughly reviewed, that it is not necessary to enlarge upon merits which have been simply reproduced here.

---

GRAPHIC, *December 4th*, 1886.

It was a happy thought of Lady Burton to issue a household edition of her husband's scholarly translation of the "Arabian Nights." The thoroughness with which Sir Richard Burton had carried out his task necessitated the introduction of matter of considerable value to the scholar and Oriental student, but which was scarcely fitted for household reading. Lady Burton, therefore, aided by Mr. Justin Huntly McCarthy, M.P., unwilling that such excellent work should be confined to a select few, has eliminated everything from her husband's book that could in any way be found objectionable to the ordinary reader, and at the sacrifice only of 215 pages out of 3,215 pages, has been enabled to publish what is certainly the best and most characteristic English rendering of the "Arabian Nights." Lady Burton guarantees that "no mother shall regret her girl reading this edition," but it must not be assumed that the work is a mere collection of drawing-room tales. All the vigour of the original is there, and the language is unaltered, save for the few omissions which were necessary. A more complete insight into the manners and customs of the Easterns, with all their religious fervour and their love of romance and poetry, could scarcely have been afforded, the stories being told in a picturesque and realistic style, which impresses the reader with the idea that he is sitting in a Baghdad bazaar listening to the original narrator.

---

KENT HERALD, *December 9th*, 1886.

Among the numerous literary delights of Christmas, even as an édition de luxe, surely this expurgated sample of the Arabian Nights, time-honoured and familiar as the title of the entertainment may appear to be, ought to claim a distinguished place ; for not only have Lady Burton and her collaborateur, Mr. McCarthy, done more than ample as well as conscientious justice to the work of Sir Richard Burton, but the Messrs. Waterlow also have vied with the editors in clothing their language and labour in a dress of virgin white and in an excellence of type which are a credit to the publishing trade.

Vulgarity, far less sensuality, will be searched for in vain, while those who will search for the beauties of language and of thought, which the translator has indicated as the true guide towards a due estimation of the "Arabian Nights," will experience a rich and lasting treat by the perusal of the wondrous tales of Shahrazad, and be as eager for their continuation as was Shahryar himself. In fact the noble-minded daughter of the Wazir—not Vizier, as the cheap edition vainly talks—

would have made an admirable editor of a monthly magazine, so well did she understand the art of leaving off at the interesting point in her narrative, and the value of the information "to be continued in our next." ○ ○ ○

We confess to a strong partiality for much of the poetry with which many of the tales are interlarded, while we are astonished at the spontaneity and aptness of its rendering as exactly suitable to the individual case.

---

THE ACADEMY, *December 11th*, 1886.

Under Lady Burton's auspices, "The Book of the Thousand Nights and a Night" becomes once again the dear old "Arabian Nights" of our youth. The title strikes the key-note of the situation. Sir Richard Burton's famous translation was made for scholars, and strictly limited to one thousand copies; Lady Burton's household edition is made for all who run and read—that is to say, for the whole English-speaking and English-reading world. It, therefore, demands no special gift of second-sight to prophecy for the abridgment a circulation many times larger than that of the original work. And this not only because the Alf Laylah wa Laylah is one of the most popular books in the world—beloved by old and young, learned and unlearned, Christian and Infidel, but because the great, composite, heterogeneous, public, notwithstanding its omnivorous appetite, does heartily relish and appraise at its just value whatever is best in literature, whether in the way of matter or manner. ○ ○ ○ It is, therefore, as an addition to English literature proper, that Lady Burton's "Arabian Nights" now comes before the public; and it is in that sense that we welcome it, not merely as a book to be read by the fireside on a winter's night, or as one of the few companions to be selected for a vacation tour or a long sea voyage; not merely as a suitable gift for young folk, free libraries, and mechanics' institutes, nor even as an inexhaustible storehouse of Oriental legends, superstitions, proverbs, poetry, manners, customs, and the like, but as a most remarkable tour de force in the way of literary workmanship.

The book (to which Lady Burton's photograph lends an added grace) is beautifully printed on a creamy rough-edged paper, and is clad in a most attractive garb of white and gold. The foot-notes, without being obtrusively many or lengthy, are full of excellent and learned and interesting matter. In a word, we owe Lady Burton a large debt of gratitude for the happy thought which places an inaccessible work at the disposal of all sorts and conditions of readers.

---

CHRISTMAS BOOKSELLERS, *December 18th*, 1886.

*Lady Burton's edition of her husband's "Arabian Nights," translated literally from the Arabic. Prepared for household reading by Justin Huntly McCarthy.*—Many thanks are due to Lady Burton for the appearance of this book. Outwardly, even, it is beautiful in its way, with pure white cover, relieved by the Moslem Crescent and group of golden lilies, and Arabic ornamentation, and, within, will be found that "kaleidoscopic shifting of the marvellous picture" of fable and fancy, and humour. and pathos enclosed in its setting of Eastern imagery, that we know by the name of "The Thousand and One Nights." With the assistance of Mr. Justin Huntly McCarthy, Lady Burton has, in short, prepared an edition of her husband's translation, not only in such a form that it may be read by all, but also may be procured, the original edition having been issued to subscribers only, and having already more than doubled in price since its publication. We may, therefore, look upon the present edition as that which will be the one generally known to the reading world, and we are glad to find that it in every way correctly represents Sir Richard Burton's original version, minus the omitted portions, which, it appears, form after all only a small fraction of the whole. It is, as Lady Burton says, "the real thing," and, as such, we wish to give the publication the prominence it deserves. Since Galland astonished and delighted the world at the beginning of last century, with the first translation (or, rather, adaptation) of the "Nights," there have been various versions, the latest being Lane's well-known work, and Torrens' (both appearing about the same time), and, still later. the translation by Mr. John Payne, published only a few years since. While availing himself of these later versions, Sir Richard's rendering is his own, equally "avoiding the hideous hag-like nakedness of Torrens, and the bald literalism of Lane," and he claims for his work, the right to be considered "a faithful copy of the great Eastern Saga-book, not only in the spirit, but in the mécanique, the manner and the matter."

---

THE GAZETTE, *Saturday, December 18th,* 1886.

"*Lady Burton's edition of her husband's Arabian Nights.*"--That the outer host of readers may not be excluded, and that with certain reservations they may benefit by this remarkable translation, is the object of "Lady Burton's edition of her husband's Arabian Nights." Lady Burton deputed Mr. Justin Huntly McCarthy, M.P., who has earned his laurels as historian and poet, to undertake for her the task of revision, she herself finally looking over the proofs, making sure that neither too much nor too little is excised. The amount of material withdrawn from text and notes is really inconsiderable, and although ten volumes are compressed into six, only 215 pages out of 3.,215 are cancelled, and the omissions chiefly concern Orientalists and anthropologists. General readers are to be congratulated on the fact that they now have access to Sir Richard Burton's translation, that under the guidance of this omniscient Professor they may know the East, not as well, but much better, than if they journeyed thither and trusted to their own eyes. The most widely circulated translations of the "Nights," the countless cheap editions, many of them illustrated, give no idea whatever of the true East, and are mere burlesques of Galland's French version. If only parents could distinguish between the genuine and the spurious, these unsatisfactory imitations would cease to be acceptable, and children in the nursery would be allowed to drink from the real fountain. It would be quite as easy, and far better for the juveniles, to follow the story of an Ensorcelled Prince, of a Magic Horse, or a Bottled Jinni, where the colour is all true, as it is to swallow make-believe attempts of Eastern imagery. But a better time is coming for children, and for children of a greater growth. To know the "Arabian Nights" in all their perfection, in all their gorgeous setting, in all their bewildered variety, and in all their truth, we must look to the latest translator. For the last fifty years it is Lane's version that has held the field, and many people, not knowing there could be anything better, accepted him as final. But, like the Horseman of Brass on the Horse of Brass in the Sea of Peril, the time has come for dethronement, and Lane must yield to a scholar of wider research, to an Orientalist who, during one part of his career, lived as a veritable Moslem, and was indistinguishable from other Moslems. Lane's idea was to give but a portion of the "Nights," to please himself and his printer and publisher as to what should be selected, what omitted. If a story resembled another story, he rejected it on the score that it might prove wearisome. For instance, he leaves out "Nur al-Din and Miriam the Girdle Girl!"—despite its great historical interest as connected with Charlemagne and his daughter—because it bears a family likeness to "Ali Shar and Zamurrud;" and because he himself felt unsympathetic he altogether discards the lively story of "Masrur and Zayn al-Mawásif," a tale full of poetical merits with lute scenes nowhere excelled, and with the most beautiful of all the many gardens in the Nights. He passes over the truly Rabelasian tale of "Ali the Persian, and his marvellous Carpet Bag;" he omits the chivalric story of "King Omar bin al Nu'uman and his Sons"—like cutting "Ivanhoe" out of "Waverley" novels—and for fear of ruffling susceptibilities he suppresses "The Rogueries of Dalilah;" and "Mercury Ali of Cairo," most characteristic of stories, full of fun, frisk and frolic, and devilry, opening up new ideas of Eastern human nature. These are but indications of Lane's arbitrary method, and people have submitted because quite unconscious they have been defrauded, and that treasures have been withheld. At length, however, they have the entire and perfect chrysolite. Sir Richard Burton does not pick and choose.

Various novelties distinguish the Burton edition. To begin with, a strict account is kept of the separate Nights, and the interest of the opening drama is sustained throughout. On each individual Night of the whole Thousand and One we learn exactly the amount and quality of incident related. The dramatic idea which binds the whole sheaf of stories together is kept artistically in view. It is a peculiarity of the stories that so many of them are told when the speaker is on the edge of doom—hardly the moment for collected oration—and the story saves the story-teller's life. The mighty Ifrit who cuts off the hands and feet of his lady with four strokes, and then sends her head flying, because he thinks she has betrayed him, is diverted from instant vengeance on the suspected lover by the prospect of a story.

Lady Burton's edition is accessible to everybody. Her white volumes are certain soon to be seen in every library and every well-furnished book-case in the kingdom, and the study of these volumes will give a fresh impetus to the never-dying taste for the "Arabian Nights."

---

LINCOLN GAZETTE, *December 18th*, 1886.

Lady Burton's edition of her husband's "Arabian Nights," translated literally from the Arabic, and prepared for household reading (Waterlow and Sons, London Wall), ought, assuredly, to have a great circulation. Nothing essential is omitted, but it is so scrupulously revised and expurgated that we think the reviser is right in saying that the most careful of mothers may safely place it in the hands of her daughters.

---

SCOTCH NEWS, GLASGOW, *December 23rd*, 1886.

The first issue of Sir Richard Burton's "Arabian Nights," limited to one thousand copies, was quickly absorbed by scholars and linguists. It would have been a subject of regret had so remarkable a work remained comparatively unknown. Thus gratitude is due to Lady Burton for publishing, with a spirit of enterprise worthy of praise, a new and popular edition of her husband's "Arabian Nights," which she has carefully revised with the assistance of Mr. Justin McCarthy. English versions of the "Arabian Nights" have hitherto chiefly represented them as charming fairy tales. It remained to Sir R. Burton to fully accentuate their wider meaning. In the translator's words, their "pathos is sweet, deep and genuine, tender, simple and true."

The morale is sound and healthy, and at times we descry vistas of a transcendental morality, the morality of Socrates in Plato.

---

MORNING ADVERTISER, *December 25th*, 1886.

Replete with poetry, and expressed in the graceful, fluent language of the Orientals, this rendering by a master scholar is a real boon for household reading, and may be taken as a typical specimen of the perfection to be obtained in translation by the power of an author's research and enthusiasm.

---

WHITEHALL REVIEW, *December 30th*, 1886.

Books on Eastern subjects appear to be popular just now, and the publishing season has produced a number of them, Lady Burton's edition of Sir Richard Burton's translation of the "Arabian Nights" taking the lead.

FIGARO, *January 1st*, 1887.

The fact that Her Majesty has accepted the first copy issued of Lady Burton's edition of the "Arabian Nights" will be regarded as conclusive proof of the admirable manner in which the wife of the distinguished traveller has done her work. I have received the first volume of the edition, which is published by Messrs. Waterlow and Sons, London Wall. Its appearance is altogether in its favour; it is bound in vellum and beautifully printed. But, better still, the contents are all that could be desired. Not only may fathers of families safely purchase "Lady Burton's edition," but in preparing her husband's book for household reading, Lady Burton—who was assisted by Mr. J. H. McCarthy—has been able to furnish what she incisively calls "the real thing," not the "Arabian Nights" as they are popularly known, without any of the grosser expressions which appear in Sir Richard's edition.

---

BROAD ARROW, *January 1st*, 1887.

We fancy that even Mr. Stead, who was so horrified at the edition of this perennial work, translated by Sir R. Burton, would allow that Lady Burton's edition is *sans reproche* from the high moral point of view of the *Pall Mall Gazette*. In fact, to puritans of that class Lady Burton expressly says, "I guarantee that no mother shall regret her girl's reading this Arabian Nights." Suffice it to add, that full justice is done in this translation to the beauty and picturesqueness of the original; and the son of the famous leader writer of the *Daily News* has evidently laboured hard to assist in this. The work is very handsomely got up, the binding being most chaste, whilst the paper and print are of an appropriate semi-antique character. A striking portrait of Lady Burton is prefixed to this volume. We rather regret that this portrait has not been engraved instead of resorting to photography. When complete this work will form a very handsome Bowdlerised edition of the Arabian Nights, the elegant binding making it particularly suited for a wedding or other present.

---

MORNING POST, *January 2nd*, 1887.

Her Royal Highness the Princess of Wales has been graciously pleased to accept a copy of Lady Burton's edition of the "Arabian Nights."

---

LUNES, *January 3rd*, 1887.

Lady Burton's edition of her husband's "Arabian Nights," translated literally from the Arabic and prepared for household reading (Waterlow and Sons, London Wall), ought assuredly to have a great circulation. Nothing essential is omitted, but it is so scrupulously revised and expurgated that we think the reviser is right in saying that the most careful of mothers may safely place it in the hands of her daughters. Few people know anything of the trouble and the travelling which Sir Richard Burton has undertaken in the accomplishment of his tremendous task. He has ransacked all the libraries of the East and West, and has often undertaken a roving but idle quest in the hope of throwing clearer light on a single disputed passage. His profound acquaintance with Oriental languages and literature is shown at every turn, and, preserving the romantic colouring of the original in a poetic rhythm of expression, he has cast his finished version in a form which is singularly picturesque.

---

## ALLEN'S INDIAN MAIL, *January 17th*, 1887.

### LADY BURTON'S "ARABIAN NIGHTS."

The reason is not far to seek, since there never has been a really good translation of this most untranslatable of Oriental works. From such a sweeping assertion must be excluded the happy and successful effort of Mr. John Payne; but this latter work was printed for the Villon Society, and the issue being restricted to five hundred copies, while the author bound himself "not to reproduce the work in its complete form," the version is and must ever be "caviare to the general." Such being the case Sir Richard Burton bethought himself that he would employ his leisure hours in presenting to the public a trustworthy and withal picturesque translation of the Thousand and One Nights: and who more fitted for such task?

But the new translation, valuable and sound as it was, possessed the demerit that the indelicacy of the original text appeared in all their glaring hideousness. His wife has now come to the rescue and presented a "readable" version of tales, "beside which the flood of Moslem fiction flows thin and shallow." Associating with herself Mr. Justin McCarthy as a colleague in the task of purification, she has succeeded in so far as success was possible, for it is a truism to state that her husband's edition is far more full of fire, life and pithiness than the more refined bantling for which his wife has stood sponsor. This was absolutely unavoidable, alike by the nature of the tales as by the circumstances of the case. Could some of Dickens' inimitable sketches of lower life be rendered in grammatical English and retain the charm of the original? Could baby-talk be Anglicised and keep its simplicity? Equally could Orientalism be purified and preserve the racy brusqueness of the original.

We have no hesitation in pronouncing the present version of the "Arabian Nights" to be incontestably the best extant. Perfection is not given to mortals, but the tales now appear in as satisfactory a garb as is possible; and henceforth there will be no excuse should the English public fail to become familiar with a work which all should read—the time-honoured "Thousand and One Nights."

---

THE QUEEN, *January 27th*, 1887.

The volume before us is beautifully printed, on excellent paper, and elegantly bound with cloth resembling vellum. A photograph portrait of Lady Burton herself faces the handsomely-designed title-page. As regards the text, the poetical portions are exhibited in a metrical form, and all divisions and breaks are carefully indicated. The foot-notes are both numerous and important, and they should by no means be lightly passed over, giving, as they do, much valuable information, explanatory and illustrative, which the "home student" will profit by. This great effort will be extensively appreciated, and not a few will read and learn more than otherwise they would or could have done respecting those wonderful tribes and nations, among whom still linger so much of the lore which instructs as well as fascinates, not only themselves, but the children of the West. We have read considerable portions of this volume, and compared them with a popular English edition, and, without hesitation, we say that the style of this is far better, and the arrangement very much to be preferred. The colloquial terms and homely phrases, we presume, truly reflect the original, as do some other unusual forms of expression. Meanwhile, we regard the book with much satisfaction, and hope it will receive a hearty welcome from the well-instructed and inquiring reader who seeks wisdom as well as recreation.

---

SPORTING LIFE, *January 29th*, 1887.

Beautiful exceedingly is the second volume of the Lady Burton edition of her husband's "Thousand Nights and a Night." I described the sumptuous binding and extolled the fine typography of the work in a note on the first tome. With regard to the second it is only necessary to add that it is embellished with a striking portrait of Sir Richard Burton in semi-oriental costume which, as the ghost of George Robins would say, only in more ornate phraseology, "is alone worth the money." The volume contains 516 pages, or the stories told by Shahrazad during 275 nights.

---

COUNTY GENTLEMAN, *February*, 1887.

The second volume of Lady Burton's household version of her husband's "Arabian Nights" contains twenty complete tales, besides the conclusion of the tale of King Omar Bin Al-Nu'uman and his Sons, which was commenced in the first volume. Several of the stories now issued are in the form of apologues or fables, in which the inferior animals are the chief actors and interlocutors. Amongst these we may mention, the tales of the Water Fowl and the Tortoise, the Wolf and the Fox, the Mouse and the Ichneumon, the Cat and the Crow, the Hedgehog and the Wood Pigeons, and the Sparrow and the Peacock. There is, of course, here a suggestion or a reminiscence of Æsop, but the Arabian fabulists take a line of their own. There are striking differences between the two authors or sets of authors, both in the narrative form and in the ethical quality of the moral conveyed. And this difference may, we think, on examination, be traced to national idiosyncrasy and modes of thought. The fables of the Arabian Nights have less point and conciseness, and less of harmonious subservience of details to unity of effect and impression than those of the great Ethiopian. On the other hand, they have greater perfection of literary form, far more splendid imagery, and in some instances more psychological subtlety in the somewhat long-drawn disquisitive, and, indeed, disputatious dialogues in which the chief characters indulge. For our own part, we have found this introduction of the lower animal element an interesting temporary departure from the comprehensive and elaborate, and, sooth to say, somewhat monotonous representations of men and their affairs which form the staple of these gorgeous productions of an ancient Oriental loom. In the story of the Wolf and the Fox we have an example of the justification of the lex talionis, which mingles somewhat curiously with the general exhortations to mercy and forgiveness, founded on the maxims of the Sacred Books. In our notice of the first volume we made some inadequate attempt to express our admiration of the virile beauty and force of Sir Richard Burton's translation. Only captious critics will consider that he has strained a point in his use of obsolete words and phrases, or in his happy invention of new collocations. As these are invariably conceived and expressed in the spirit of the original Arabic, they present to our mind the aspect of beauties rather than blemishes, and indisputably add to the Oriental flavour of this fine translation. The notes are in themselves a liberal education in respect of Persian and Arabian manners and customs, old and new. Again, we thank Lady Burton most sincerely for her great gift to our British householders. Her share of the work demands no little patience and judgment, and reminds us in its successful result of the pure and sparkling gems which, in their freedom from native or acquired impurities and disfigurements, bear eloquent testimony to the skill and industry of the lapidary who has contrived, not certainly to gild refined gold, but to add a lustre to the diamond.

---

BAT, *February 8th*, 1887.

BOWDLERISED BURTON.

Between them, Lady Burton and Mr. J. H. McCarthy, M.P., have done a good work, and done it well, as the first two volumes of their production now presented to the public show. Thanks to their collaboration, the most marvellous collection of stories in the world is for the first time placed before the English readers. Positively for the first time. Those who know the Arabian Nights, through the charming, but ludicrously unoriental, paraphrase of Galland, or through the solid, and perhaps slightly stolid, rendering of Lane, cannot be said to know the Arabian Nights at all. It would be indeed a thousand pities if such a book as Sir Richard has made were to be entirely tabooed to the world at large and to women. The matchless wealth of fancy of the Arabian Nights, the amazing wealth of knowledge which Sir Richard Burton has accumulated about it, the glowing virile prose in which these Eastern tales have been imbued with a new vitality, all these should be the possession, not of a poor thousand students and scholars, but of all the myriad readers of books who speak the English speech. It was, therefore, a happy inspiration which led Lady Burton, herself a great traveller, herself a writer of delightful books, herself a lover of the East, to believe that the real Arabian Nights might be given to her countrywomen well-nigh in its entirety. The inspiration has been happily acted upon ; the dream has become an accomplished fact, with the assistance of the young journalist and author whose Oriental studies made him an appropriate colleague. Lady Burton has, as it were, made the Thousand Nights and One Night, for the first time, citizens of the great Republic of English literature. Now, for the first time, all that enchanted Eastern world is open to everyone. Jean Paul Richter, most delightful of German writers, has dwelt, in his great essay on education, on the importance of Oriental fiction in the education of the young. It is easy to imagine the delight with which he would have welcomed the masterpieces of Oriental fancy which Lady Burton has, for the first time, placed within the reach of all who care to read.

Between the fair, white covers of her volumes the reader passes at once into the most exquisite world of fancy, where enchanted princesses, caliphs and mock caliphs, wizards, ghouls, jinns, barmecides, kalendars, sultans, slaves, moolahs, and dancing-girls jostle one another in a mad merry world of their own, by the yellow Nile or the yellow Tigris. All the life of the East—vivid, passionate, fantastic, poetic—lives in these entrancing pages, and the reader who knows them, and knows them well, knows more about Oriental life and Oriental thought than many who have passed half their lives in Cairo or Bagdad. All the life of the East, indeed the readers of Lady Burton's volumes must not expect to know. Lady Burton's edition is a work that may be placed with safety in the hands of any school-girl, and yet, at the same time—a fact which speaks well for the East—it contains almost everything to be found in the original text, and it contains the vast bulk of Sir Richard Burton's annotations. Lady Burton's edition is, indeed, a work of which she and her colleague, and all lovers of English literature, may well be proud.

---

MORNING POST, *February 14th*, 1887.

"THE ARABIAN NIGHTS."—Messrs. Waterlow and Sons publish the second volume of Lady Burton's edition of her husband's translation of the popular work. It has been expurgated and prepared for household reading by Mr. J. H. McCarthy, M.P. and Lady Burton. There is a great difference between the paraphrase known to the public as "The Arabian Nights" and the text now offered to the reader, which is a literal translation from the Arabic. In the volume under notice are comprised the tales from the 78th to the 275th night inclusive. They are remarkable for their originality and poetic sentiment, and the spirit of chivalry which animates the heroes. The tales of birds and beasts are fables containing a wholesome moral. The volume is handsomely bound and printed in clear type, and Lady Burton has done her work well, there being nothing objectionable in the book. It includes numerous explanatory notes and a portrait of Sir Richard Burton.

---

MORNING POST, *February 14th*, 1887.

There is a great difference between the paraphrase known to the public as "The Arabian Nights" and the text now offered to the reader, which is a literal translation from the Arabic. They are remarkable for their originality and poetic sentiment, and the spirit of chivalry which animates the heroes. The tales of birds and beasts are fables containing a wholesome moral.

---

JUDY, *February 16th*, 1887.

The second volume of Lady Burton's charming edition of the "Arabian Nights" has reached me. This may really be said to be the first time that this wonderful work has ever been properly placed before the English public, and a better present for a lady could not be imagined.

---

MORNING ADVERTISER, *February 26th*, 1887.

The poetic imagery of the Arabic masterpiece is presented in all its naïve and native charm, almost as far as such a thing is possible, when we remember the immense gulf which sunders the ideas and tongues of the Orients from our own mental methods and modes of speech. The use of rhymed prose by the translator is most judicious, and enhances the impression produced by the Arabic simile and metaphor, as in the following, where Sulayman Shah prepares to send forth his Wazir to sue for the hand of the daughter of Zahr Shah :—"Then he hied to his own house and bade make ready presents befitting Kings, of precious stones and things of price, and other matters light of load but weighty of worth, besides Arab steeds and coats of mail, such as David made, and chests of treasure for which speech hath no measure". Again we find the same use of rhyme in the Wazir's mention to the celibate King of the charms of the Princess:—"Know, O King, it hath come to my knowledge that King Zahr Shah, Lord of the White Land, hath a daughter of surpassing loveliness, whose charms talk and tale fail to express. She hath not her equal in this age, for she is perfect in proportion and symmetry, black-eyed as if kohl-dyed and long-locked, wee of waist and full of form." The couplets in which many of the characters after composing their minds unbind their tongues put the resources of the Queen's English to some strain. Here is a specimen of how the emissary of Sulayman Shah "displayed the oratory of Wazirs and saluted the King in the language of eloquence." When it is remembered, however, that the Arabic verse is improvised, we can afford to be charitable to the not unsuccessful effort of the translator, who has no small difficulties to cope with. It runs as follows :—

He cometh robed and bending gracefully :
O'er face and figure dews of grace sheds he :
He charms ; nor characts, spells, nor grammarye
May fend the glances of those eyne from thee.
O heart ! th' art not the sole that loveth him,
So live with him while I desertion dree.
There's naught to joy mine eyes with joyous sound
Save praise of King Zahr Shah in jubilee :
A King ! albeit thou leave thy life to win
One look, that look were all sufficiency ;
And if a pious prayer thou breathe for him,
Shall join all faithful in such pious gree :
Folk of his realm ! If any shirk his right for other
hoping, gross unfaith I see.

Still, though the English is a little quaint, and every period in the history of the language is laid under contribution to supply material of verbiage, this very circumstance heightens the effect upon the mind of the reader of the strange scenery, the bizarre situations, and the eccentricity—according to our notions—of the characters. Generally, we think that the thanks of the public are due to Lady Burton for placing within the reach of everyone this correct version of so renowned a mass of Eastern folk-lore as is the "Arabian Nights." Men who as children have revelled in this narrative of wonders, and then accepted them with implicit and ingenuous trust, will return to it again to find light shed on the customs and manners of the East. The very instructive notes elucidate the text, and so the reader may, as he peruses, not only discover delight for his fancy, but gain information about the social life of lands which, though the Western world has varied and altered over and over again, have for ages remained in their main social features unchanged, so much so as to lead many observers to regard them as unchangeable. Down at the bottom of all we read, however, the great truth that human nature is much the same all the world over, and in all ages, in its joys and griefs, its gratifications and its heartburnings. The volume before us is very handsomely put out of hand, and for its letterpress and general get-up much praise is due to both printer and publisher. The frontispiece is a fine photograph of the distinguished translator, Sir Richard Burton, whose face and form in no way belie the tale of his exploits. In conclusion, we may add that this work may with safety be introduced within the precincts of the family circle.

---

CLAPHAM OBSERVER, *February 26th*, 1887.

The second volume of Lady Burton's edition of her husband's translation of "The Arabian Nights" has just been published by Messrs. Waterlow and Sons, Limited. It is produced in the same sumptuous style as the first volume, and contains a portrait of Sir Richard Burton. The volume has been specially prepared for ladies and children, who may now peruse these charming Eastern stories without meeting with any of the coarseness of the original.

---

ARMY AND NAVY GAZETTE, *February 26th*, 1887.

Although so much merit belongs to Sir Richard's translation, its very character, drawn literally from the original, rendered it unsuitable for the general reader, and Lady Burton has now accomplished an excellent labour in issuing these two first volumes of a rendering of it adapted for the perusal of the young, which retains all the admirable features of her husband's work, while it seems to improve upon it in some small particulars. The text has been revised by Mr. Justin Huntly McCarthy, M.P., who has been quite successful in his task. When complete, it will certainly be the best translation we have for general use of "The Thousand Nights and One Night," and we hope to welcome the succeeding volumes, and to say something about them. The edition is an excellent specimen of typography, and is very pleasant to read. To the first volume is prefixed a very good Woodbury-type portrait of Lady Burton, and to the second a similar one of her husband.

---

MORNING ADVERTISER, *February 26th*, 1887.

We think that the thanks of the public are due to Lady Burton and her collaborateur for placing within the reach of everyone this correct version of so renowned a mass of Eastern folk-lore as in "The Arabian Nights." Men who as children have revelled in this narrative of wonders, and then accepted them with implicit and ingenuous trust, will return to it again to find light shed on the customs and manners of the East. The very instructive notes elucidate the text, and so the reader may as he peruses not only discover delight for his fancy, but gain information about the social life of lands which, though the Western world has varied and altered over and over again, have for ages remained in their main social features unchanged, so much so as to lead many observers to regard them as unchangeable. Down at the bottom of all we read, however, the great truth that human nature is much the same all the world over, and in all ages, in its joys and griefs, its gratifications and its heartburnings. The volume before us is very handsomely put out of hand, and for its letterpress and general get-up much praise is due to both printer and publisher.

---

FIGARO, *February 26th*, 1887.

The publishers of Lady Burton's edition of her husband's translation of "The Arabian Nights"—Messrs. Waterlow and Sons, Limited—have sent me the second and third volumes of this splendid work. The second volume contains an excellent portrait of Sir Richard Burton, and both are, in all respects, equal to the first. As the Queen and the Princess of Wales have acknowledged the value of the edition, there is no need to say more than that this volume closes with the fifth adventure of Sindbad the Seaman.

---

JUDY, *March 2nd*, 1887.

The third volume of Lady Burton's delightful edition of the Arabian Nights Entertainments has reached me. I can only repeat what I have said before, no more welcome addition to a lady's library could well be chosen.

---

FUN, *March 2nd*, 1887.

The third volume of "Lady Burton's edition of her husband's Arabian Nights" has followed quickly upon the second. We readily repeat our expression of the high estimation in which we hold the superiority of this translation over all others. Many stories are included which have hitherto been left untold.

---

BOOKSELLER, *March 4th*, 1887.

*Lady Burton's Arabian Nights.*—The progress of this charming work continues apace, in the appearance of a further volume going down to the "Five Hundred and Fifty-Seventh Night" of Shahrazad's world-famous tales. Within the limits of the new instalment will be found several old favourites, such as Harun al-Rashid and the Slave Girl, The Ebony (Flying) Horse, and The Voyages of Sindbad the Sailor. Sir Richard Burton's notes, which liberally accompany the text, are by no means the least entertaining portion of the book, leading, as they do, to many suggestive comparisons with Scriptural and mythological analogies, and to points of etymology as curious as they are instructive. The story of the "Death-Angel and the Rich King," by the way, is so closely akin to the Parables of the Rich Fool and The Unjust Steward of the Gospels, that it is difficult to believe that they did not serve as the original of the Arabian counterpart.

---

ALLEN'S INDIAN MAIL, *March 7th*, 1887.

On reading the first volume of "Lady Burton's edition of the Arabian Nights," again and again the reflection occurred, how little—how very little—the general public know, as to the tales of which the name is familiar in every circle of society. Still more does this fact force itself into notice in the second volume. Not a story do we meet which bears a name linked with the memoirs of youth or the recollections of early age. What is the explanation? Are all the tales, which for generation after generation have played their part in the nursery, merely idle dreams of a fanciful edition of the "Thousand and One Nights" or are the well-known stories reserved for the last? We cannot say; but we avow with some trepidation, that we have not hitherto met with a single friendly face amongst the two hundred and fifty divisions as yet presented to the public.

If, however, we have expected against expectation for some landmark to show us the road whereon we are travelling, it must notwithstanding, be avowed that in the present continuation of the tales there is much to interest, and perhaps, more to instruct. Apart from this, there is such a vast array of wisdom contained in this storehouse of experience and knowledge that the world should be wiser, and therefore happier, in learning what dangers to avoid, what virtues to cultivate, what vices to eradicate. Then, too, as regards the notes by Sir Richard Burton. It would be impossible to exaggerate their worth, their depth, or the insight that they afford into the inner life of the Arabian natives, a life of which so little is known, though so much is talked—a life which has much to recommend it—albeit Exeter Hall is loud in its dispraise, and the advocates of women's rights are passionate in denunciation thereof. Like all other nations the people of the East have their faults, but who are they which presume to cast the first stone? So we gladly welcome this further instalment of Eastern lore, with an expression of thanks that Lady Burton has enabled our daughters to enjoy what, save for her labours, would have been a closed book for those who have cheeks to blush, feelings to suffer, or modesty to shame.

---

THE QUEEN, *March 12th*, 1887.

It is a very handsome work, and will form a very ornamental and attractive addition to the family library. The complete work will consist of six volumes, and we understand that in its entirety it will not be printed in a cheaper form. Those, therefore who would possess the work, without further abridgment, should secure this edition. The original version, as produced by Sir Richard Burton, is not in the market.

---

THE ACADEMY, *March 12th*, 1887.

The second and third volumes of this elegant edition are to the full as attractive as the first volume, which is saying a great deal. The second contains, inter alia, the delightful story of Prince Camaralzaman and the Princess Badrool Badoor, which loses none of its old charm as "The Tale of Kamar Al-Zaman," and gains incalculably by being translated into Sir Richard Burton's rich, quaint, and picturesque English. The third volume brings another, and a still more familiar favourite, in the story of "Sindbad the Seaman and Sindbad the Landsman," told with a force and vivacity which make it all seem as true as it seemed in the days of our credulous childhood. In both volumes we find a large number of minor tales which are not included in Lane's edition; as, for instance, the stories of Four Chiefs of Police, and a whole series of charming fables about beasts, birds, and "other small game." The long chivalric history of "King Omar Bin Al-Nu'uman and his sons, Sharrkan and Zau Al-Makan," begun in vol. i., and ended in vol. ii. (also one of those omitted by Lane), is a distinct gain in a collection so complete and extensive as the present. As regards Sir Richard Burton's dramatis personæ, treatment and style, we need only say that his foul fiends and ancient duennas are more variously hideous, his couplets more steeped in oriental passion, his descriptive passages more elaborately rhythmic than ever; while the footnotes are so interesting and full of information that one only regrets that they are so sparingly inserted. By way of pendant to Lady Burton's charming portrait issued with vol. i., the second volume contains a characteristic photograph of Sir Richard himself. Resolute of eye, stern of jaw, massive of brow, grave, reticent looking, dauntless, as befits one who "dares do all that may become a man," he wears Eastern frock and tarboosh, and leans easily upon a marble pedestal.

---

MANCHESTER EXAMINER, *March 16th*, 1887.

These three volumes will prove a great boon at once to the general reader and to the student of literature. However, it would have been nothing less than a misfortune if the precious and unique results of Sir Richard Burton's learning, industry, and experience had been confined to a favoured few, and, as a matter of fact, those portions which exclude it from the book-shelves visited by the youths and maidens of our families are by no means so inwrought with the fabric of the work as to be incapable of detachment without injury to the general effect. We have carefully examined some of the tales, which seemed to us almost insusceptible of successful Bowdlerisation, and we have been simply astonished at Lady Burton's success, for, while omitting everything to which the most fastidious could urge an objection, she has retained both the narrative continuity and the distinguishing literary and artistic characteristics of the unexpurgated original. Concerning the original, of which all the essential characteristics are reproduced by Lady Burton and her fellow-worker, it is not necessary to speak at length. The "Arabian Nights" is one of the great books of the world, and as a revelation of the outer and inner life of the Orient is quite unique, but it is only during quite recent years that the general reader has had any opportunity of knowing the full extent of its riches. True, English translations have been common enough for the last century, but they have been, for the most part taken, *not* immediately from the Arabic, but mediately through a French reproduction, often so garbled in substance and in form as to convey nothing like a veracious impression of the original. We have at last—thanks to the loyal enthusiasm of Lady Burton—an English version of "The Arabian Nights" which, while it may be accepted frankly as a reproduction of the great original, is free from those offences against modern habits of thought and feeling which in a student's edition cannot be, and perhaps ought not to be, ignored.

---

### THE GRAPHIC, *March 19th*, 1887.

The second and third volumes of Lady Burton's edition of her husband's masterly translation of the "Arabian Nights" have now been published, and contain fuller versions of many old friends, together with many of the subsidiary fables and shorter tales which even Lane condenses in the form of notes. Amongst the most favourite stories in these volumes are "Kamar Al-Zaman and the Princess Budur" and "Sindbad the Seaman," while, "Abu Al-Husn and his Slave Girl Tawaddud," in which the latter holds discussion with, and fairly puzzles all the learned doctors and philosophers of the Court, is admirably rendered in detail. Apart from the intrinsic interest of the tales themselves, the books are well worth careful reading for the enormous amount of Oriental lore which they contain, and for the minute insight into everyday Eastern customs which they afford. While nothing has been admitted which would shock the fastidious reader, nothing more than was absolutely necessary to fit the book for domestic reading has manifestly been omitted.

---

### COUNTY GENTLEMAN, *March 19th*, 1887.

The third volume of Lady Burton's sumptuous edition of the "Arabian Nights" has followed close upon the heels of the second. But, though no time has been lost in placing the public in possession of further portions of a work which may justly be described as a golden treasury of imagination and fancy, the present volume bears no marks of haste or inadequate preparation. Of the precious ore which was placed in the crucible, nothing but the fine gold has come out, and this, thanks to the faithful labours of Lady Burton and her able coadjutor, has now passed fresh from an authentic mint into the intellectual currency of British domestic life. Volume 3 consists of no less than 83 tales, which bring down the marvellous sequence of stories invented in self-defence by "the liberator of her sex" to the 557th night. Of these tales, while many of the less familiar are full of beauty and suggestiveness, the last, relating the wonderful adventures of Sindbad the Seaman will be welcomed as an old and much-esteemed friend. The old friend, too, though he does not come to us with exactly a new face, offers to our charmed recognition a face much brightened and beautified, and decked with the goodly raiment of Sir Richard Burton's inimitable translation. Many of the tales are very short, but some of the shortest are really the most delightful. Take, for example, the one recording the generous dealing of Yahya, son of Khalid, with a convicted forger, and the one referring to the Caliph Al-Maamun and the Strange Scholar. The directness and forceful simplicity of these brief narratives, which would merit a high place in any collection of succinct apologues of the virtues, as well as the almost Christianity of their teaching, cannot fail to impress any discerning reader. The note on page 58 to the first of these tales is one of similar commentaries throwing light upon Eastern customs and institutions. At the same time it marks the continuity of Oriental political ideas.

---

### ARMY AND NAVY GAZETTE, *March 27th*, 1887.

*Lady Burton's edition of her husband's Arabian Nights, translated literally from the Arabic. Prepared for household reading by Justin Huntly McCarthy, M.P. Vol. iii. (Waterlow and Sons.)*—This volume, bringing us down to the 557th night, and to the fifth voyage of Sindbad the Seaman, includes a large number of stories quite new to the reader, some of them brimful of humour, and others most interesting from many points of view, from which it would be easy to quote endless readable items. Harun al-Rashid, Al-Maamun, Isaac of Mosul, and Ja'afar the Barmecide figure here very often ; but more amusement is to be derived from the doings of lesser people, as, for example, the sharp-witted vagabonds who generally escape the chastisement they deserve by some ingenious trick, such as the Oriental mind delights in. The story of Al-Maamun and the Pyramids of Egypt (omitted by Lane) illustrates the mediæval Arabic view of those monuments—viz., that they were rich treasure-houses, which it was desirable to plunder if possible ; and there are other tales dealing with crusading times, and with the relations of Christians and Moslems. One great charm of these stories is their endless variety, which prevents them from ever becoming monotonous, and Sir Richard Burton's English has a quaint and sometimes quite archaic cast which accords well with his subject. As we said, in speaking of the earlier volumes, this is by far the best translation of the "Nights" for general reading, and we are sure, in its present handsome form, it will find a place on most library shelves.

---

CHRISTIAN UNION, *April*, 1887.

*The Arabian Nights. Translation by R. F. Burton. London: Waterlow and Sons.*—In sending forth the present edition of her husband's literal translation of this most remarkable work, Lady Burton is deserving of the highest praise of the women of England, to whom it is dedicated. The work is at once superb in its execution, and worthy the honour done by its dedication. This is the first and most complete literal translation of the "Arabian Nights," and ought on that account to be most interesting and fascinating. Those who are at all conversant with the old productions of this work will readily discover the distinctive difference and characteristic features of Sir Richard F. Burton's translation. That it excels in originality, style, and graphicness all other editions of the Arabian Nights, no one who has read the work will hesitate to accept. Regard it in whatever aspect we will, it is unique in its production, and will henceforth take the precedence of all other translations. We congratulate Lady Burton on the beautiful issue of the present edition of the work.

---

SPORTING TIMES, *April 2nd*, 1887.

The third volume of Lady Burton's drawing-room and school-girls' edition of the "Arabian Nights" is in keeping with the previous volumes published. We do not know how many volumes there are to be, but we hope not many more, or our stock of adjectives of praise will run out.

---

MORNING ADVERTISER, *April 8th*, 1887.

*Lady Burton's edition of her husband's Arabian Nights, translated literally from the Arabic. Vol. iii. (Waterlow and Sons).*—The third volume of this most fascinating collection of tales in the whole range of literature has just been issued. In this portion of the work Shahrazad or Sheherazade, as she is also known to the Western world, continues her charming stories until, at the approach of dawn, after the 557th night. she has "ceased to say her permitted say," breaking off, with her wonted adroitness, in the middle, or more probably near the end, of her narrative of the "Fifth Voyage of Sindbad the Seaman." As pointed out in previous notices of this admirable work, it possesses many charms which have hitherto been lost to European readers by the manner in which the tales have been presented to them in the current versions of the narratives. Although these stories, among many other collections, have been in circulation for ages through the East, they have not yet been known in

Europe for two hundred years. They were first introduced into Christendom, indeed, by means of the translation of Antoine Galland, a distinguished French Orientalist. They were, as a matter of course, everywhere hailed with delight, although, with perhaps rare exceptions, until the appearance of Lane's edition, the many translations of the tales into European languages, merely gave the narratives themselves. The numerous and ample notes and philological comparisons, which are profusely scattered through it, and which serve to convey the exact meaning of important words in the text, are not only most interesting in themselves, but are often of indispensable necessity to the grasping of the point of the story. Several examples of this will again be found in the present volume. In some places the translator is completely at variance with Lane, who appears, in the instances cited, to have missed the point of the story, from a misapprehension of the true signification of an important word. A remarkable example of the extent to which the force of the narrative is seen to depend on the skill of the translator, occurs in the story of "the Illiterate who set up as a Teacher," in which it is remarked in a foot-note, that Lane appears to have mistaken for a girdle, a word which simply means the usual brazier for the charcoal which serves for a fire, and so to have missed the whole point of the tale. In this volume will also be seen several fine examples of the rhymed prose, which form one of the great beauties of the work. The translations of the many pieces of Eastern poetry which adorn the tales, are most elegant and felicitous. They are also most unique in their character. In many instances obsolete words have been introduced with wonderfully pleasing effect, and in other Saxon words and Saxon locutions in close relation with modern German, from their immediate connexion with the text, the notes are full of learning—geographical, philological, and antiquarian—which contains an immense body of useful knowledge on the matters to which they relate.

---

COURT JOURNAL, *April 10th*, 1887.

The third volume has been produced in the same sumptuous manner as its predecessors, and will doubtless find much favour.

---

LADY'S PICTORIAL, *April 16th*, 1887.

It would be difficult to praise this valuable work too highly. Lady Burton pays the highest possible tribute to that sex to which she is a distinguished ornament by dedicating "To the Women of England" a work as remarkable for the erudition and research displayed in its copious foot-notes and addends as for the beauty of its diction and the artistic excellence of paper, type, and binding.

### WEEKLY IRISH SCIENCE, *April 23rd*, 1887.

"*The Arabian Nights.*" *Lady Burton's Edition. Vol. iii. (Waterlow and Sons.)*—It would be difficult to praise this valuable work too highly.

---

### DAILY NEWS, *April 28th*, 1887.

Lady Burton's Family Edition, as it may be called, of Sir Richard Burton's "Arabian Nights" has reached its second volume. It is an extremely valuable book for every one who wishes to know such things as may conveniently be known about Arab manners and customs. Mr. Justin Huntly McCarthy has revised the original notes, which were not always intended for the drawing-room table, and the book may now be studied even by young people who want an accurate knowledge of the celebrated stories. The present volume contains not many of our old friends, like "Aladdin" and the "Forty Thieves," but is rich in those Oriental stories of beasts, which often much resemble the romances of "Uncle Remus." The tale of the Animals and the Son of Adam, if one remembers correctly, does come, with a difference, in "Uncle Remus.' As an example of the value and interest of the notes, may be cited the remarks (p. 220) on the "lucky signs," which add to the value of horses. Mohammed disliked horses with white stockings on alternate hoofs. The tale of the "Wolf and the Fox" is again in Uncle Remus's style. It is a difficult thing to account for the migration of these stories. Even the Bushmen have a version of vestigia nulla retrorsum, and Professor Hartt was told similar fables by the Indians of the Amazon. Huet, Bishop of Avranches, knew that such stories were current among the Hurons and Iroquois, whose hero, if not exactly Brer Rabbit, is usually Brer Hare. The Swahilis, also, make an animal very like a rabbit take the best parts. Occasionally, the translation itself needs notes for some readers, who may ask what the Fox means when he sings of the Wolf that "garred me drain eisel and fell." It will interest some mythologists to know that dawn, in Persian, is called by a name meaning "wolf's tail." Prince Kamar-al-Zaman is in this volume in all his glory, compared to which, that of Solomon was mere tinsel. Probably only Orientalists can properly estimate the labour and erudition of these "Arabian Nights." Lady Burton's third volume contains, with many curious but brief stories less familiar, everybody's old friend, "Sindbad the Seaman," or the Sailor. The notes on the Diamond Valley, and the Roc, and other pleasant marvels, are very instructive. The following note is curious. We say melancholia, with the accent on the o. The Arabs say Mali Khuliya, with the accent on the penultimate, and probably, or rather certainly, the Greeks from whom we both borrowed the word did the same, as the Greek accent indicates. But how they read their own poetry, on this system, who can explain or understand?

COURT SOCIETY REVIEW, *May 4th*, 1887.

The fourth volume of "Lady Burton's edition of her husband's Arabian Nights" (Waterlow and Sons) brings us to the close of the seven hundred and sixty-first night. The adventures of Sindbad the Seaman are concluded, and there are the whole series of tales illustrating "the craft and malice of women." Lovers of good and beautiful books can never sufficiently thank Lady Burton for this ideal example of Bowdlerism.

---

BOOKSELLER, *May 5th*, 1887.

Lady Burton retains 3,000 of the original pages, but, by a deft turn of the wheel, eliminates 215 pages worth of words and sentences, which are only for the use of students and not for family reading. Her Majesty the Queen has graciouslyaccepted the first copy, and it has also been graciously accepted by her Royal Highness the Princess of Wales, her Royal Highness the Princess Beatrice of Battenberg, and her Imperial Majesty the Empress of Austria. It has (although the 2nd vol. is only just out) already had 54 reviews, and one and all say that it is the only real standard "Arabian Nights."

---

JUDY, *May 11th*, 1887.

The fourth volume of Lady Burton's splendid edition of the "Arabian Nights Entertainments" has reached me, and in all respects is as attractive as its predecessors. The work, when complete, should be eagerly sought for and awarded a place of honour on the library shelves.

---

COUNTY GENTLEMAN, *May 14th*, 1887.

Lady Burton and her coadjutor are issuing the household edition of Sir Richard Burton's able and faithful translation of the inimitable "Arabian Nights" with praiseworthy rapidity. The fourth volume, sumptuous without and fair within, thanks to the united exertions of editors, publishers, printers, and binders, is now before the public. It contains 23 principal tales, with numerous sub-narratives, and carries on Shahrazad's stupendous series of imaginative efforts from the 558th night to the 761st. The well-known and widely appreciated yarns of Sindbad the Seaman and Sindbad the Landsman are brought to a conclusion. The less familiar but most powerful and typically Oriental story, "The City of Brass" follows, and, though we are far from wishing to join the yelping pack already at Mr. Haggard's heels, readers of this colossal conception will feel inclined to agree with Solomon that "there is nothing new under the sun." The present volume is, however, more fully taken up than most of its predecessors with stories of love and intrigue, and in "Bowdlerising" these for the family library the editors have shown the nicest taste and discretion. A few, which Lane reckoned too gross for reproduction, are here presented in perfectly inoffensive guise, and Lady Burton deserves the thanks of the community for providing for their delectation in a purified and wholesome form some real literary dainties which must otherwise have been eschewed on account of their poisonous ingredients. The long series of stories on "The Craft and Malice of Women" is amongst the most amusing and ingenious.

---

ARMY AND NAVY GAZETTE. *May 14th*, 1887.

*The Arabian Nights. Lady Burton's edition. Preparea for household reading by Justin Huntly McCarthy, M.P. Vol. iv. (Waterlow and Sons.)*—The present volume of this excellent edition brings us up to the 761st "Night," and, like its predecessors, contains a number of stories quite unknown to the general reader. It concludes the history of Sindbad, giving a variant rendering, from the Calcutta edition, of the seventh voyage, and contains a large number of stories concerning the "Craft and Malice of Women," which are of the highest value as illustrations of social conditions, and it has besides, many tales to which it would be a pleasure to allude individually. When this issue of the "Nights" is complete, it will certainly be the best edition before the public for household reading. As a translation, it is unequalled in fidelity, and Sir Richard Burton's familiarity with Oriental scenes has enabled him to preserve the greater part of the quaint flavour of the original.

---

COURT JOURNAL, *May 28th*, 1887

Messrs. Waterlow and Sons have just issued the fourth volume of Lady Burton's sumptuous edition of The "Arabian Nights," prepared for household reading by Justin Huntly McCarthy, M.P. The stories are highly entertaining, and, being literally translated from the Arabic, they have a fresh and graphic character hitherto unattained in previous editions.

---

SPORTING LIFE, *August 13th*, 1887.

A dainty book to take with you to the seaside, or aboard your friend's yacht, the Albatross, or into the richly wooded or heath-clad country, is Lady Burton's edition of her husband's "Arabian Nights," whereof the fifth volume has now appeared. There will be another, and then the work, with a selection from Sir Richard Burton's remarkable notes, will be complete. The present volume contains "Ali Nur Al-din and Miriam the Girdle Cirl" (a most beautiful story which Lane omits); and "The

Man of Upper Egypt and his Frankish Wife," which also is a story that is not to be found in Lane's collection. "The Fisherman of Baghdad" is contained in the group embraced in the fifth volume, which brings the Nights up to the nine hundred and forty-fourth.

---

LIVERPOOL MERCURY, *August 24th*, 1887.

*Lady Burton's edition of her husband's Arabian Nights. Translated literally from the Arabic by Sir Richard Burton. Prepared for household reading by Justin Huntly McCarthy, M.P. Vol. v. (London: Waterlow and Sons, Limited.)*

We have already fully described this latest and most luxurious edition of the "Arabian Nights," and have spoken at large of its merits, both as a singularly faithful translation and a finished work of high literary art. It is the only rendering of the Nights which has any pretensions to literalness and completeness, and in this and all other respects is far away the best edition extant. The volume before us—the fifth—carries us on from the 762nd Night to the 944th. The next volume will complete the work.

---

ARMY AND NAVY GAZETTE, *August 27th*, 1887.

*Lady Burton's edition of her husband's "Arabian Nights." Translated literally from the Arabic. Prepared for household reading by Justin Huntly McCarthy, M.P. Vol. v. (Waterlow and Sons.)*—This fifth volume of the "Arabian Nights" lacks nothing of the interest that has attached to its predecessors. Bringing us up to the 944th Night, it includes the curious tale of the "Man of Upper Egypt and his Frankish Wife," and others omitted by Lane. One of the most characteristic of these is that of "King Jali'ad of Hind and his Wazir Shimas," which belongs to the oldest series in "The Nights," and has attached to it a number of animal and other fables, all very remarkable. Lane found the story "puerile," and it is very true that from many points of view, it is so; but as an illustration of the ways of Arabiân society, and an example of a class of stories largely circulated amongst the Oriental peoples of that date, it cannot be overlooked, and if read in the proper appreciative spirit, it is by no means devoid of amusement. The style of the translation, as we have previously remarked, has a strange archaic charm, and the unusual locutions of which Sir Richard Burton is master, harmonize admirably with his subject, while the rhythmic portions, which he has reproduced with so much skill, diversify and render still more picturesque the whole.

## COURT JOURNAL, *October 8th*, 1887.

Messrs. Waterlow and Sons, Limited, London Wall, have recently published the fifth volume of Lady Burton's revised version of her husband's edition of The "Arabian Nights." The merit of this edition of the famous Eastern stories is that the translation is literally from the Arabic. It has been revised by Justin Huntly McCarthy, M.P., and Lady Burton, and is the best collection of these fascinating tales; no more suitable edition for children and young people has ever issued from the Press.

---

## MORNING ADVERTISER, *October 12th*, 1887.

The fifth volume of this delightful work continues the tales down to the nine hundred and forty-fourth night, and it is thus brought within measurable distance of its close. Several of the stories comprised in this latter group are familiar under other forms in most parts of Europe, and there are few of them which do not embody the practical wisdom and the sound and generous moral precepts which are, as a rule, characteristic of the "Arabian Nights." Taken in conjunction with the numerous and excellent notes which the translator has supplied, this version, as we have before had occasion to observe, presents the exact sense of the original Arabic text, which the fanciful phraseology in which the narratives are expressed largely assists in realising, while lending an additional charm to the tales themselves. All who read Lady Burton's edition of the "Nights" will feel that it is only in this way that their many beauties can be adequately rendered for the Western World.

## MORNING ADVERTISER, *October 12th*, 1887.

### LITERATURE.

*Lady Burton's edition of her husband's "Arabian Nights." Translated literally from the Arabic. Vol. v. (Waterlow and Sons).*—In the fifth volume of this work are contained, among others, the stories of Hasan of Bassorah, of Khalifah the Fisherman of Baghdad, of Ali Nur Al-Din and Miriam the Girdle Girl, of the Man of Upper Egypt and his Frankish Wife, of the Ruined Man of Baghdad and his Slave-Girl, and the long series of tales, fables and allegories, in which the astrologers and other wise men variously interpret a dream which had disturbed the great King Jali'Ad of Hind, and on which he had consulted them. The volume contains also the interesting history of King Wird Khan, with his women and Wazirs. This monarch was weak and uxorious, and disregarding the sage counsels of Shimas the chief of his Wazirs, pursued a profligate and effeminate career, as the result of which great troubles arose in his realm, and an extensive conspiracy was formed to get rid of him. Acting on the suggestion of his favourite wife, he caused his Wazirs, grandees, and notables to be put to death after the fashion of Eastern despots. The weakness to which his kingdom was thus reduced tempted aggression by a neighbouring king, and it was threatened with immediate invasion, rapine, and slaughter. From this strait he was delivered by the sagacity of a boy whom he had accidentally fallen in with in the course of a stroll he made *incog.* one evening through his capital whilst pondering over his desperate position. The stories introduced in the course of the history contain the counsel offered him in the successive stages of his difficulty, through which he is at length conducted in safety and then returns to a more rational course of life. Lane omits this story as being exceedingly puerile. That judgment will hardly be supported by the reader when he now reads it. It is one of the two oldest tales in the whole series of the "Arabian Nights," as is here pointed out, and at the same time very characteristic.

---

THE DAILY POST, *Liverpool.*

This work, prepared from Sir Richard Burton's translation of the "Thousand and One Nights," aims to present to the women of England all the beauties and none of the improprieties of the original. The Burton book was confined to 1,000 copies, and was treated by some as a questionable "curio." The Lady Burton book—in the preparation of which she has been helped by Mr. Justin Huntly McCarthy—is all that the "Arabian Nights" was to us in its old guise, with the addition of many characteristic specialities of Orientalism. Lady Burton has been told by Orientalists that they have learnt more Orientalism in Sir R. Burton's pages than by long years of study. She desires to give the public "the real thing, not the drawing-room tales which have been put before them in the 'Arabian Nights' for the past one hundred and eighty years." The work on which the book is founded has been so thoroughly reviewed that it is not necessary to enlarge upon merits which have been simply reproduced here. Mr. J. H. McCarthy, M.P., who is a littérateur of great capacity, has done the selecting of passages to excise with faultless judgment. Out of 3,215 pages only 215 had to be sacrificed, and the book has all the genuineness of the unexpurgated edition. The binding is very appropriate and handsome, in white vellum, and the first volume is embellished by a striking likeness of Lady Burton.

---

MANCHESTER EXAMINER, *November 23rd,* 1887.

*Lady Burton's edition of her husband's Arabian Nights. Translated literally from the Arabic. Prepared for household reading by Justin Huntly McCarthy, M.P. Vol.* 5. (*Waterlow and Sons Limited.*) —The issue of the fifth volume of this work gives us an opportunity of again commending to the notice of our readers the most beautiful, as it is certainly the most scholarly, edition of a great and immortal classic. Sir Richard Burton is not only a distinguished Orientalist in the purely scholastic sense of the word, but he has had so much personal experience of social life in the "unchanging East" of to-day that his English version of a book like the "Arabian Nights," which is not only intensely imaginative but minutely realistic, inevitably possesses a quite unique value and interest. Sir Richard's translation is, however, so expensive as to put it out of the reach of any person but the wealthy collector; and being, moreover, a literal and complete rendering of a book produced in a time when, and in a clime where, other manners than ours prevailed, it naturally contains matter which renders it unsuitable for a place on the drawing-room table, or even on bookshelves accessible to every member of the ordinary English household. Such matter, however, is far from being an essential portion of the work, it can be eliminated without any serious loss or injury; and in the present edition it has been so eliminated by the practised and dexterous hand of Mr. J. H. McCarthy. We have, therefore, a version of one of the most wonderful works of fantasy which the world has ever seen, which preserves not only the essential spirit but the essential substance of the original, and yet contains no passage which the most rigid-minded father or mother could object to submit to the perusal of his or her children. Of the book itself we need not speak at length, for to praise the "Arabian Nights" would indeed be to perform a work of supererogation, as its marvellous stories have long been the delight of childhood and of age. Apart from its literary attractions, the present edition has everything that could be desired by the book lover. It is, indeed, an *édition de luxe.* Hand-made paper and exquisite typography contribute their charm, and if the delicate white binding has the defect of being only too easily soiled, it will be a very simple matter to provide a home-made supplementary cover for use when the volume is—to use the librarian's phrase—"in hand."

END OF VOL. VI.

WATERLOW AND SONS LIMITED, PRINTERS, LONDON WALL.

www.ingramcontent.com/pod-product-compliance
Lightning Source LLC
Chambersburg PA
CBHW031810270326
41932CB00008B/374

* 9 7 8 3 7 4 4 7 6 1 9 5 6 *